The ADVANCE OF
AMERICAN COOPERATIVE ENTERPRISE:
1920-1945

The

ADVANCE OF

**The Interstate
Printers & Publishers, Inc.**

Danville, Illinois

Joseph G. Knapp

AMERICAN

COOPERATIVE ENTERPRISE:

1920-1945

Library of Congress
catalog card number: 72-90890

To **Kelsey B. Gardner**

My Friend and Colleague

FOREWORD

When I started work on this history of cooperative enterprise in the United States seven years ago I thought that it could be covered in one volume. As I became more deeply involved in the project I concluded that it would require two volumes. However, when I became fully immersed in the preparation of the second volume the subject became so rich in experience and significance that I realized that a three-volume work was demanded. As I look back in retrospect I am convinced that this arrangement is logical.

The first volume, *The Rise of American Cooperative Enterprise*, revealed how cooperative organizations in the United States gradually took form in a distinctive way as the nation progressed from frontier conditions to a strong national economy. The second volume, *The Advance of American Cooperative Enterprise*, tells how cooperative organizations made great steps forward under the unique conditions that prevailed in the United States from 1920 to 1945. The third volume, tentatively titled, *American Cooperative Enterprise in the Modern Period*, will examine the growth and problems of cooperative organizations in the United States during the years of revolutionary change that followed World War II.

As pointed out in the Foreword to *The Rise of American Cooperative Enterprise*, it was my privilege to work closely with cooperatives of many kinds and types during the years covered by the time span of *The Advance of American Cooperative Enterprise*. It is hoped that this gives the book a degree of authenticity derived from continuing observation and study of how cooperatives adapted their structures and procedures in a rapidly changing social, economic, and political environment.

Cooperatives are institutional growths reflecting the need for attention to common-felt problems. They represent an effective form of free competitive enterprise available to those who wish to conduct some or all of their business affairs through democratically designed and managed organizations.

Cooperative enterprise has come a long way in the United States since 1920. Moreover, much of its most significant development came during the years covered by this volume—from 1920 to 1945. In this period of great change American cooperative enterprise became a national phenomenon. How it has been amplified, strengthened, and extended during the cataclysmic years since 1945 will be the subject of the third and final volume in this series.

Joseph G. Knapp

Bethesda, Maryland
January 1973

AUTHOR'S ACKNOWLEDGEMENTS

I hope that my indebtedness for the help of many friends in writing this book will be repaid in part by the value of the book itself as a contribution to cooperative history and development in the United States.

First among those whom I wish to single out for special mention is Dr. Edwin G. Nourse, my one-time Chief, who has given me sustaining encouragement and wise counsel on this as well as on my other books. My great respect for Dr. Nourse was attested by my dedication of *The Rise of American Cooperative Enterprise* to him as "Dean of Scholars in American Cooperative Enterprise."

Next, I wish to thank Kelsey B. Gardner—my friend and partner in cooperative adventures since 1934. He has read all of the chapters of this book as they were drafted, as well as the galley proofs, and I have benefited greatly from his counsel and his meticulous concern for accuracy. I have drawn heavily on his fund of knowledge derived from a life time of study and experience in the field of cooperative enterprise. He has lived this book with me, and it affords me much pleasure to dedicate this volume to him as "My Friend and Colleague."

Another whose help and interest have been invaluable is Dr. William I. Myers, formerly Dean of the College of Agriculture at Cornell University, who more than any other fashioned the Farm Credit Administration as a great cooperative institution. Dean Myers read the first 21 chapters as they were prepared, and his suggestions have made a rich contribution to the strength and accuracy of this book.

On many of the initial chapter drafts I have greatly valued the incisive comments and suggestions of Dr. Oscar B. Jesness, for many years Head of the Department of Agricultural Economics at the University of Minnesota, and one of the real pioneer students of cooperative business organizations.

I am deeply indebted for material assistance given me by Dr. Wayne D. Rasmussen, in charge of agricultural history studies in the United States Department of Agriculture, together with two members of his professional staff, Dr. Gladys Baker and Dr. Vivien Wiser. Together they have read carefully the manuscript for the first 22 chapters. They have caught many errors of fact and offered many interpretative comments for this book's improvement.

I wish also to record my sincere appreciation to the late Chris L. Christensen, first Chief of the Division of Cooperative Marketing and the first Secretary of the Federal Farm Board, for the helpful reading of the initial 12 chapters of this book in their manuscript form. Likewise, I wish to express my sincere thanks to Lyman S. Hulbert, whose name is inseparable with the legal development of cooperative enterprise, for his reading and offering suggestions on my first 12 chapters.

The following have graciously read and offered suggestions on one or more of the chapters in manuscript form:

E. R. Bowen, Chapter XVIII and part of Chapter XXIII.
Wallace J. Campbell, Chapters X, XV, XVIII, and XXIII.
Donald Cooper, Chapters XVI, XVII, and part of XXIII.
Dr. Forest F. Hill, Chapter XIV.
David E. Lilienthal, Chapter XVI.
Udo Rall, Chapters XV and XVII.
L. Carlton Salter, Chapter XVI and part of Chapter XXIII.

Many others have provided me with valued assistance on particular subjects through conversations or correspondence. Among them I wish to mention: Dr. Martin A. Abrahamsen; Darrell L. Achenbach; N. L. Allen; Erma Angevine; Gilbert T. Beaton; Henry P. Blewer; Joseph E. Blomgren; Henry W. Bradford; Harold E. Bryant; Robert J. Byrne; Glen W. Bunting; Harry Caldwell; Dr. Mollie Ray Carroll; Dr. Shelden L. Clement; Jane Click; Oscar W. Cooley; Leonard N. Conyers; Merton L. Corey; Howard A. Cowden; Russell E. Dennis; John W. Dysart; Herbert Emmerich; Raymond L. Fox; Luis L. Grandados, Jr.; Dr. Henry C. Hamilton; Robert Handschin; W. Gifford Hoag; Glen D. Hofer; William M. Holroyd; Robert W. Hudgens; I. H. Hull; Fred E. Hulse; Frank Hussey; Carl R. Hutchinson; French M. Hyre; Alex Johnson; Laurie Lehtin; Ed F. Lewis; Dr. James G. Maddox; Manly G. Mann, Jr.; Donald D. Martin; Dr. Raymond W. Miller; W. B. Milsop; Dr. Arthur E. Morgan; George D. Munger; Kenneth D. Naden; Claude R. Orchard; Florence E. Parker; Homer J. Preston; Dr. Theodore Saloutos; J. Kenneth Samuels; Robert G. Sayre; Fred A. Sexauer; Homer G. Smith; Dr. Leland Spencer; Dr. Elmer Starch; E. V. Stevenson; Joseph E. Swidler; Perry Taylor; Toik A. Tenhune; Stanley K. Thurston; Dwight D. Townsend; George C. Tucker; Jerry Voorhis; Gerald G. Williams; Leslie Woodcock; and Raymond Zimmerman. If someone has been overlooked who should be mentioned I hope that I will be forgiven.

I wish also to thank E. Leslie Webb, Jr., Reference Librarian of the TVA Technical Library, for supplying me with scarce materials relating to the early history of the TVA. Similar assistance has been given me on the early history of rural electric cooperatives by the Norris Memorial Library of the National Rural Electric Cooperative Association and by the Rural Electrification Administration. The library of The Cooperative League of the USA has also given me generous help on materials relating to consumers' cooperation.

The fact that I have drawn heavily on published material is evident by the book itself, and I have endeavored to record a small part of my appreciation in citations to published works.

I am also most grateful to many cooperative associations and friends for their interest in this book as expressed by advance orders to ensure its publication.

Furthermore, I wish to acknowledge with great appreciation my indebtedness to Russell L. Guin, Chairman of the Board of The Interstate Printers & Publishers, Inc., and his associates Paul A. Sims, Editorial and Marketing Manager, Ronald L. McDaniel, Editor, and Geraldine Wherry, Editorial Assistant. They have done everything possible to help me get out this book as I would like it. No one could have a more cooperative publishing firm.

Finally, I wish to thank my wife, Carol, for her many suggestions that have greatly improved the volume's literary quality.

Altogether the preparation of this book has been in itself a cooperative enterprise in which many gave generously of their time and help. However responsibility for the plan of the book and the conclusions must be accepted solely by the author.

OTHER BOOKS BY JOSEPH G. KNAPP

The Cooperative Marketing of Livestock

[with Edwin G. Nourse]
(1931)

The Hard Winter Wheat Pools:
An Experiment in Agricultural Marketing Integration

(1933)

E. A. Stokdyk: Architect of Cooperation

(1953)

Seeds That Grew:
A History of the Cooperative Grange League Federation Exchange

(1960)

Farmers in Business

(1963)

Great American Cooperators

[with associates]
(1967)

The Rise of American Cooperative Enterprise:
1620-1920

(1969)

TABLE OF CONTENTS

Part One. THE COOPERATIVE EXPLOSION: 1920-1932

The ADVANCE OF
AMERICAN COOPERATIVE ENTERPRISE:

1920-1945

Part One

THE COOPERATIVE EXPLOSION:
1920-1932

The year 1920 produced a veritable explosion in cooperative activity that brought a doubling of cooperative marketing business within five years. A combination of factors contributed. Most important was the severe post-World-War I depression which led to chronic agricultural distress in the face of general business recovery. The depression awakened interest in cooperative marketing as a means of restoring farm prosperity, and it gave birth to a strong demand for monopolistic commodity marketing cooperatives that could control farm product prices. The depression in agriculture also encouraged the newly formed American Farm Bureau Federation to promote cooperatives as a means of organizing agriculture on a sound business basis, and it forced government to recognize the value of self-help cooperative enterprises.

The first great burst of cooperative development gained legal standing for cooperative marketing associations with passage of the Capper-Volstead Act of 1922. By 1925 the monopoly control philosophy of cooperative commodity marketing had lost adherents; cooperative leadership was shifting to marketing efficiency as the primary objective of cooperative marketing. This counter movement brought with it two significant developments: the formation of the American Institute of Cooperation in 1925 and the passage of the Cooperative Marketing Act of 1926. Both stressed the importance of strengthening research and education in building strong and effective cooperative organizations. From then on, cooperatives began to improve their position by working together more closely on national programs. One important result was the formation of the National Cooperative Council in 1929 to better represent cooperatives in their relations with government.

During the 1920's cooperatives gained general acceptance as essential elements in the McNary-Haugen and other plans for farm relief. These efforts to provide a satisfactory farm relief solution reached a crescendo with the establishment of the Federal Farm Board in 1929, which was directed to promote effective cooperative marketing organizations as a matter of public policy. Although the Federal Farm Board was not able to stabilize agricultural prices in the face of the Great Depression, it greatly benefited agricultural cooperation by stressing the need for stronger cooperative marketing organizations and by providing financial assistance on a sound credit basis to help farmer cooperatives operate effectively.

While cooperative marketing occupied the center of the cooperative stage from 1920 to 1932, cooperative purchasing by farmers was steadily expanding on its own merits as a means of enabling farmers to reduce farm supply expenditures that were increasing with the advance of technology and power farming. By 1920 cooperation for the purchase of consumer goods had only begun to emerge as an economic and social movement. During the next dozen years under the wing of the Cooperative League, consumers' cooperation attained national stature. Other forms of cooperative enterprise made significant progress during these years. The credit union movement became rooted. The first large mutual automobile insurance organizations for farmers were organized. The first major cooperative housing project and the first significant plan for cooperative medical care came into being.

The period from 1920 to 1932 thus marked a great step forward in cooperative enterprise. Its recognition was apparent in the strong endorsements given cooperatives by the three Presidents of the United States who served in those years—Warren Harding, Calvin Coolidge, and Herbert Hoover. It was a time of cooperative experiment and growth that opened the way for constructive developments in the years to come.

The evolving character of cooperative enterprise under the conditions prevailing from 1920 to 1929 is portrayed in Chapters I to VI. The Federal Farm Board experiment during the Great Depression is then examined in Chapters VII and VIII. Chapters IX through XI deal with the progress made from 1920 through 1932 of cooperatives for purchasing farm supplies; consumers' cooperatives; and cooperatives for providing credit, irrigation, insurance, and other services. Chapter XII takes a broad look at structural and operational cooperative progress during this period, with emphasis on agricultural marketing and purchasing cooperatives, then the dominant forms of cooperative enterprise in the United States.

Chapter I

THE OPENING OF AN EPOCH: 1920

The year 1920 opened in a state of feverish postwar agricultural prosperity. Twelve months later prosperity had evaporated and farmers were confronted by the worst agricultural depression they had ever known. The events of this important year will be chronicled in this chapter.

Three significant developments were brought forth in 1920 which were to have a dominating influence on cooperative enterprise during the dozen years to follow: (1) the onset of the post-World-War I agricultural depression, (2) the emergence of the commodity cooperative marketing movement, and (3) the formation of the American Farm Bureau Federation. These three developments were to bring great changes in agriculture and a new relationship of government to agriculture. They were not unrelated. Commodity cooperative marketing was to play a significant role in the early history of the Farm Bureau Federation, and vice-versa, as the deep-seated agricultural depression influenced the character and actions of both the commodity marketing movement and the American Farm Bureau Federation. The long depressed condition of agriculture, following the severe price drop of 1920, also brought a significant response from government in the form of administrative and legislative activities and, in turn, this government activity influenced and was influenced by cooperative and Farm Bureau actions. These developments resulted in other developments, but the catalytic agents were primarily the postwar agricultural depression, the commodity marketing movement, and the arising American Farm Bureau Federation.

In this chapter we will examine the unfolding nature of these and related developments during the hinge year, 1920. No other year has been so important in shaping the character of modern cooperative enterprise in the United States.

Depression Replaces Prosperity and
the Government Response

Farmers "never had it so good" when 1920 opened. Prices stood at an all time high and the postwar boom was still going strong. As in all periods of this nature, the prosperity which prevailed seemed normal; there were but few prophets of gloom, and they were generally disregarded.[1] One who saw that the situation was perilous for agriculture was Dr. Edwin G. Nourse, then Head of the Department of Agricultural Economics at Iowa State College of Agriculture. In an article "Will Agricultural Prices Fall," in the *Journal of Political Economy* for March, 1920, he analyzed the impact of several disturbing factors: contraction of European demand, a weakening domestic market, growing foreign competition, and augmented production. He foresaw an inevitable decline in farm prices during the coming year and the probability of an epoch ahead of relatively low prices for farm products.

There were a number of events that presaged danger to farmers early in 1920. In the spring the Federal Reserve Board began to raise rediscount rates—a measure long advocated to curb inflation. In February, the Esch-Cummins Transportation Act terminated government control of the railroads as of March 11 and opened the way for higher freight rates on agricultural traffic, although the higher rates were not to become effective until late summer. The War Finance Corporation, which had helped finance agricultural exports, was discontinued on May 10, and on June 1, the Government removed its support of wheat prices. However, the response was not immediate, and there was no serious dip in agricultural prices until July. In the next few months the decline in farm prices had become marked, and by the end of the year prices of agricultural products had fallen by 40 per cent since June, the greatest decline in any one year on record.

The rapidity of the decline in farm prices during 1920 is shown by monthly index numbers as follows:[2]

January	219		July	224	(down 10)
February	221	(up 2)	August	209	(down 15)
March	221	(up 1)	September	194	(down 15)
April	230	(up 8)	October	178	(down 16)
May	235	(up 5)	November	158	(down 20)
June	234	(down 1)	December	140	(down 18)

Surprisingly, it was sometime before the seriousness of the fall in farm prices became evident. The excitement of the presidential election campaign in the autumn absorbed the attention of the public, and the full force of what was happening in agriculture was generally obscured. Little attention was paid to the problems of farmers either in the Republican or Democratic campaigns, although both parties recognized in their platforms that agricultural cooperation should be given more freedom to develop within the law. The country was determined to "get back to normalcy," and, anyway, it was believed that government could do little to correct the situation until a new administration could take office on March 4, 1921.[3]

In February, President Wilson had shifted David Houston to the Treasury, and E. T. Meredith who replaced him as Secretary of Agriculture had little time to get his bearings so that he could grapple with the oncoming agricultural depression. The American Farm Bureau Federation had set up a Washington office in the spring, but it had not gained sufficient experience to exert much influence.[4] Likewise, neither the National Grange nor the National Farmers' Union was then strong enough to give focus to the needs of the agricultural industry.

However, the farmers' plight did have one effect in the interim period before the new Republican administration took office. Hard-pressed farmers, through their congressional representatives, forced the Wilson administration in January 1921 to reinstate the War Finance Corporation to help finance farm product exports.[5] It was becoming clear that the government could not sit on the sidelines in the face of the disastrous decline in agricultural prices and its related effects.[6]

The drastic fall in farm prices was not shared by as sharp and enduring a decline in industrial prices, although by the end of 1920 the depression was quite general and unemployment had risen to 4,000,000. However, the fall in farm prices was beginning to have a serious impact on business concerns that primarily served farm people, such as farm machinery, fertilizer companies, and mail order houses.[7]

Let us now examine how the depression in agriculture fueled the incipient commodity cooperative marketing movement and the rapidly developing American Farm Bureau Federation.

The Inception of the Commodity Marketing Movement

For several years the concept of commodity cooperative marketing had been incubating in California under the watchful eye of Aaron Sapiro.[8] By 1920 he had concluded that what would work for California's specialty crops could be almost universally applied. His first opportunity to try out this theory came in the Pacific Northwest in late 1919 when he was called upon for legal advice in forming a cooperative wheat marketing organization in the state of Washington. This led in 1920 to the formation of the first state wheat pool in the United States and the idea soon spread east of the Rockies.[9]

While this development was getting under way, Sapiro sensed that a great opportunity for using his plan was shaping up in the cotton belt. For several years there had been a growing interest in cooperative cotton marketing, but it had not resulted in any coordinated achievement. With cotton prices sky high during the war, cotton growers had not been greatly concerned with the improvement of cotton marketing methods. But, many agricultural leaders in the South then foresaw that this abnormal situation could not last, and they began to develop plans for an efficient region-wide cooperative marketing system. This had led to the formation of the American Cotton Association in May 1919 under the leadership of John Scott Wannamaker and Colonel Harvey Jordan for the purpose of improving cotton production and marketing methods. On April 12, 1920, while cotton prices were still high, this organization convened a national convention in Montgomery, Alabama, to develop a plan to protect the interests of cotton growers. This meeting attracted most of the agricultural leaders of the South, including representatives of the federal and the state governments. The story of that convention has been vividly told by Robert Montgomery in his interesting book, *The Cooperative Pattern in Cotton.*[10]

In the words of Montgomery: "One of the most dramatic episodes of Southern history" occurred at this convention when Aaron Sapiro launched his famous plan for organizing the cotton growers of the South. It is of interest that Sapiro was present at the meeting "by apparent accident—a casual invitation from an assistant secretary." When Sapiro arrived in Montgomery, he discovered that he was not on the program which was to open on the morning of April 12. "On the night of the eleventh, Sapiro called the delegates who had arrived into informal session at the Gay-Teague Hotel. To this session he presented his . . . famous plan for organizing the American cotton farmers." The plan had been carefully developed for just this kind of opportunity, and the response at the night meeting insured that he would have full opportunity to present it to the convention. In fact, "by the time the convention formally assembled, Sapiro was the dominant factor."[11]

After delivering the opening address, J. S. Wannamaker, the President of the American Cotton Association, appointed a number of committees, including one on cooperative marketing. This committee immediately invited Sapiro to explain his plan in detail and it became the basis of the committee's report. At the last session of the convention, Sapiro was finally permitted to speak. "His brilliant two hour defense of his plan effectively demolished, for the time, all opposition."[12]

Sapiro's plan was positive and it was easy to grasp. He proposed that state cooperative marketing associations be set up in each cotton producing state, and that these state organizations be joined together in a National Cotton Exchange to perform overhead selling, warehousing, financing, transportation, and other needed services for the state associations. The plan contained eight elements which were to become the "8" commandments of "commodity cooperative marketing."

1. Organization of the association on a commodity basis;
2. Limitation of membership to actual growers;
3. Complete democratic control of the association by the members;
4. Control of deliveries by means of a long term, legally binding contract signed by every member;
5. Pooling of product according to grade; and basing returns to each member on the average annual price received for the pool to which he contributes;
6. Use of experts in all technical positions; and use of approved business methods at all times;
7. Orderly marketing of the product throughout the whole production period;
8. Control of a sufficient proportion of the entire crop to be a dominant factor in the market, and to make possible an economic distribution of overhead expenses.[13]

According to Montgomery, "It would be impossible to understand the sweep of the cooperative marketing movement in the South without an appreciation of the peculiar powers of this young California attorney." His portrayal of Sapiro as he swayed this convention brings Sapiro almost back to life.

Sapiro is a dynamic speaker. His ability to convince his audience of the soundness and importance of his proposals is almost incomparable. He is an able lawyer. He understands the weakness as well as the strength of his case, but is able to present the latter without having the former embarrass him. As a matter of fact, he presents just enough of the difficulties to convince the hearer of his complete candor, and not enough to damage his cause in the slightest degree.

It is not sufficient to say that some of his arguments are very weak (though never weakly put), that his economics is faulty, that his arguments by analogy are not legitimate, and his knowledge of the cotton trade is superficial. To this must be added that his knowledge of cotton marketing is sufficient to satisfy any but the experts; his analogy is so cleverly presented as to be usually accepted; his economic position is unassailable in its major redoubts; and the virility and versatility of his address is inimitable. As an economist, he is usually right, rarely entirely wrong. As a dramatic speaker he is superb. As a logician he is diabolically clever. As an evangelist he is without a peer . . . [14]

After Sapiro's presentation of the plan, the report of the committee was unanimously adopted. President Wannamaker, thereupon, appointed the committee on cooperative marketing provided for in the report, which represented "every group interested in the cotton trade and every cotton state."[15] This committee organized immediately with D. S. Murph, Specialist in Cotton Marketing, U.S.D.A., Washington D.C., as chairman, and arranged for a second meeting to be held in Memphis on May 17. Before that date, however, a definite cleavage had developed between those who followed Sapiro's line of thinking and those who favored building on the orthodox basis of small local associations—grouped about gins, warehouses, or local markets—which, in turn, would form state and national organizations. This latter group was opposed to the "iron-clad" contract and any attempt to control market price. As Montgomery said:

> The issue here was clear-cut and unavoidable. To Sapiro and his adherents the plan for autonomous locals, each independently making its own sales, and competing with every other one, was anathema. To the group led by Jordan, Duggar and Felsenthal, the creation of a huge central association with its local branches, central control of sales, and iron-clad contracts was ridiculous.[16]

After a week of discussion the committee was unable to reconcile its differences, so a sub-committee under the Chairmanship of Mr. Murph was appointed to prepare a report for submission to the American Cotton Association. While the sub-committee was at work, cotton prices fell sharply, and prompt action was deemed essential. President Wannamaker issued a call for another convention to meet in Montgomery on September 1, and the sub-committee hurriedly completed its report for the occasion. The report proposed a cooperative marketing structure to be built "from the bottom up" on county and community associations. Although the report was adopted, little came of it, for already, "Sapiro had run away with the movement. In three states active preparation had already begun for commodity organizations of the centralized type advocated by him; and during the next two years every state of the South followed them."[17]

To go back to the aftermath of the first Montgomery convention, Sapiro's arguments had convinced the 21 Oklahoma delegates led by Carl Williams, the editor of the *Oklahoma Farmer-Stockman*, that the Sapiro plan provided the only logical basis for organization and action. "They came back home so fired by the arguments of Sapiro that they set about at once to develop a cooperative marketing plan for Oklahoma growers" modelled along the lines he prescribed.[18] After a period of strenuous organization work, this resulted in the incorporation of the Oklahoma Cotton Growers' Association in early 1921.

Almost the same kind of situation was presented in Texas, and, within a few months after the Montgomery meeting, plans for a state-wide association were going forward under the auspices of the newly formed

Texas Farm Bureau Federation. In the planning and organizing campaigns in both Oklahoma and Texas, Aaron Sapiro was the prime mover.[19]

Wheat. While the cotton farmers were turning to commodity marketing, the idea gained wide publicity at the National Grain Marketing Conference sponsored by the newly formed American Farm Bureau Federation at Chicago on July 23-24, 1920. Here Aaron Sapiro again played a prominent role. According to O. M. Kile, "Sapiro fired the assembly to high enthusiasm by the story of California's success along cooperative lines."[20] Although Sapiro was not able to gain immediate acceptance for his wheat pooling plan, it was not possible—as we shall see in the next section of this chapter—for any future wheat marketing plan to ignore it.

As just noted, wheat pooling had started with Sapiro's encouragement in the Pacific Northwest, and it was at this time spreading over the mountains into Montana and the Dakotas. While the Northwest pools were getting underway, wheat growers in the major wheat producing states met at Hutchinson, Kansas, on May 6, 1920, to form the National Wheat Growers Association for the purpose of launching a wheat holding campaign to sustain prices after the expiration of the government price guarantee on June 1, 1920. With the drastic decline in wheat prices that set in soon after July, the holding program conducted in the early fall proved futile, although some 50,000 farmers had joined the association and pledged themselves to hold their wheat off the market. The disillusioned leaders of the National then turned to wheat pooling on the Sapiro contract plan as a more practical method for obtaining their goal. As we will see in the following chapter, wheat pooling was to gain significance rapidly in 1921.

Tobacco. Perhaps the most spectacular development of commodity marketing cooperation came in the tobacco belts. This was a companion development to the cotton cooperatives, for many tobacco growers also produced cotton. The immediate incentive for organization was the abrupt drop in flue-cured tobacco prices in the fall of 1920 which immediately turned tobacco growers toward commodity cooperative marketing as a means of obtaining relief. In December, Sapiro came to Raleigh, North Carolina, in connection with plans for developing a cotton marketing association. He so impressed tobacco growers who heard his views that it was then decided to hold a meeting of tobacco growers from the states of Virginia, North Carolina, and South Carolina in February 1921. At this gathering some 5,000 farmers assembled in the City

Auditorium in Raleigh, where Sapiro captured his hearers completely. Plans were made immediately for an organization of flue-cured tobacco growers in the three states. An organization committee of 26 members was appointed and almost immediately the campaign became a crusade supported by agricultural extension officials, county agents, Smith-Hughes teachers, college professors, publishers of agricultural journals, newspaper men, lawyers, bankers, and merchants. "In some cases all stores and other places of business were closed during the mass meetings of farmers . . . " It was a high pressure effort and within a few months over 60,000 contracts were signed.[21]

The impetus for organizing the Burley Tobacco Growers Cooperative Association came on December 12, 1920—long to be remembered as "black Monday"—when the tobacco markets opened with prices less than half of what they had been the year before. Growers were in despair, for the costs of producing the crop had been high, and the Burley Tobacco Association became the answer. The prime mover in setting up the association was Judge Robert W. Bingham, the highly respected publisher of the *Louisville Courier-Journal* and the *Louisville Times*.[22] At the suggestion of his friend, Bernard Baruch, he invited Aaron Sapiro to come to Louisville, Kentucky, on March 20, 1921, to confer with 50 prominent Kentuckians on what might be done to restore prosperity for the tobacco growers. After listening to Sapiro, the group was convinced of the practicality of his views and within a few days an organization committee of 73 leading citizens, representing business and agriculture, was set up to undertake a comprehensive campaign for organization.[23]

While the commodity marketing movement was gathering momentum throughout the nation in 1920, the American Farm Bureau Federation was rapidly achieving importance as a promoter of cooperative enterprise.

The Farm Bureau Goes into Action, 1920

Although the American Farm Bureau Federation had been set up in November 1919, it did not take permanent form until the ratification conference in Chicago on March 20, 1920.[24] It then represented "the most ambitious attempt ever made to organize the farmers of the country into a super-organization . . . "[25] Henry C. Wallace, editor of *Wallace's Farmer,* and a power in the emerging organization, well voiced the sentiment of farmers in his address to the ratification conference: "This federation must not degenerate into an educational and social institution. It must be made the most powerful business institution in this country."[26]

In 1920, the National Farmers Union was a significant force in only a few states, while the National Grange with some half-million members was primarily a fraternal organization. The field was wide open.

The new organization responded to this challenge and sprang into action by setting up a legislative department in Washington, D.C., together with other departments to handle organization work, publicity, marketing, and other business affairs. From the start, the Farm Bureau leaders recognized that agriculture could only be organized on business lines through the development of strong cooperative marketing and purchasing associations, and the development of such organizations, along with legislation, was given priority. At this time the Farm Bureau saw its role as that of an integrator, or catalytic agent, for uniting farmers and farm organizations on national programs for the benefit of agriculture.

The Farm Bureau's first big effort toward getting all farmers and farm organizations together on a marketing program was the Grain Marketing Conference held in Chicago on July 23-24, 1920. Invitations were extended to all farm organizations, groups, and agencies having an interest in grain marketing. Some 500 came for the meeting which was the largest and most representative gathering of this kind ever held in America. At this time the clouds of depression were gathering, and farm prices were showing weakness. This gave urgency to action.

There were many conflicting views and factions to be harmonized. One group represented the thousands of cooperative elevators spread throughout the grain belts. Few of these local associations were then effectively organized into federations for marketing purposes, although many were members of cooperative grain dealers associations. Another group was just beginning to gather strength—the state wheat pooling organizations of the Pacific Northwest—and this group was committed to the commodity marketing philosophy espoused by Aaron Sapiro.

The most dramatic event of the conference was an invited address by Sapiro who "fired the assembly to high enthusiasm by the story of California's success along cooperative lines."[27] Although he was not successful in swaying the conference to the adoption of his general plan, his speech exerted much influence on the plan that was eventually agreed to, and it also encouraged grain growers in a number of states to begin organizational work along the lines he prescribed. In his address, which was printed in pamphlet form and widely circulated by the American Farm Bureau Federation, Sapiro advocated what he called "cooperation-American style," in contrast to "cooperation—English style," which implied the Rochdale plan. He said: "The Rochdale plan is not a producer's cooperative marketing plan . . . It was originated for consumers' purposes, and it has been carried out on a group of consumers' ideas . . . It has been

wrongly applied to agricultural problems in the middle west." Thus
Sapiro challenged the supporters of the thousands of local cooperative
elevators, creameries, and livestock shipping associations formed along
Rochdale lines in the central states. The key to success, according to
Sapiro, was "organization by commodity—not by locality." He envisaged
an organization of wheat growers "fixing a price on production and
handling it in just the same way that the United States Steel Corporation
handles steel rails . . . "

> Now, what is the right way to start? What is the way that is economically
> sound: the American way and one that will absolutely stand the test of the law?
> First, I suggest the formation of a cooperative marketing association in every
> wheat producing state in the Union . . . It would have no capital stock because it
> does not need any...Every director would have to be a grain grower. They would
> be elected in districts so that every district would elect the man whom it con-
> sidered the best qualified to pool his wheat. There is a one-man, one-vote theory.
> The Cooperative law will permit no other theory . . . This organization would
> have one function only—the marketing of grain products. It will not monkey
> with another thing under the sun . . . This association would then make indi-
> vidual contracts with every grower of grains that it could reach in Illinois and in
> other states. These contracts would cover a term of years, preferably five . . .
> These contracts would provide that the individual will sell his grains to the as-
> sociation; the association will get absolute title to them and then will resell them,
> pooling them by grade—first by variety and then by variety within variety . . .
> The association has to get title to the wheat—that is the main thing.
>
> But the formation of state associations would be only a drop in the bucket . . .
> When you get 51 percent of the nine most important states tied up, you can go
> ahead and nothing can stop you. You have each one of these marketing associa-
> tions become a member of a national growers' or a national grain growers'
> association.[28]

This highly condensed statement of Sapiro's wheat marketing plan can
convey but little of the power of the speech, which was embellished with
practical illustrations to show that the plan was already working with a
high degree of success for prunes, raisins, and other commodities in
California. The moral was clear: *"Go thou, and do likewise."* Although
Sapiro made many converts, the delegates were not ready for such a
revolutionary program. After two days of discussion they voted to set up a
Committee of 17 to develop a national grain marketing plan. President
James Howard immediately announced the names of the committee
members and it set to work. The diverse and representative character of
the committee's membership is shown by their affiliations:

> J. M. Anderson: St. Paul, Minnesota, Manager of the Equity Cooperative Ex-
> change;
> C. A. Bingham: Lansing, Michigan, Secretary of the Michigan State Farm
> Bureau;
> P. E. Donnell: Waco, Missouri, President of Farmers' Grain Dealers' Associa-
> tion of Missouri;

John C. Boles: Liberal, Kansas, Member of Board of Directors of Equity-Union;

William G. Eckhardt: Chicago, Director of Grain Marketing Department of Illinois Agricultural Association;

C. V. Gregory: Editor of *Prairie Farmer* and Secretary-Treasurer of American Agricultural Editors' Association;

C. H. Gustafson: Lincoln, Nebraska, President of Nebraska State Farmers Union, and President of Farmers' Union Livestock Marketing Association;

William Hirth: Editor of *Missouri Farmer* and President of Missouri Farmers' Clubs;

C. H. Hyde: Alva, Oklahoma, Vice-President of Oklahoma Farmers' Union and in charge of State Union grain marketing activities;

Dr. E. F. Ladd: Fargo, North Dakota, President of North Dakota Agricultural College and newly elected U.S. Senator;

George Livingston: Washington, D.C., Chief of Bureau of Markets, United States Department of Agriculture;

Don Livingston: Pierre, South Dakota, Director of State Department of Markets;

H. R. Meisch: Argyle, Minnesota, President of Farmers National Grain Dealers' Association;

A. L. Middleton: Eagle Grove, Iowa, ex-President Iowa Farmers' Grain Dealers' Association;

Ralph Snyder: Oskaloosa, Kansas, President Kansas State Farm Bureau;

L. J. Tabor: Barnesville, Ohio, Master of Ohio State Grange;

Clifford Thorne: Chicago, Counsel for Farmers' National Grain Dealers' Association.

"When the Committee held its first organization meeting, Mr. Gustafson was made Chairman and Mr. Eckhardt, Treasurer. O. M. Kile and C. E. Gunnels were appointed Secretary and Assistant Secretary."[29]

During the next few months, the Committee of 17 held many conferences with prominent business and agricultural leaders, and its representatives undertook to find out how cooperation was successfully practiced in California, other states, and in Canada. After many meetings the committee finally agreed on a plan in February 1921 which provided for the organization of a national grain marketing organization to be called the United States Grain Growers, Incorporated. In Chapter III we will see that the plan proposed was an attempt to please everyone that satisfied none.

Flushed by the apparent success of the Grain Marketing Conference, the Farm Bureau turned to the other problem of most concern to midwest farmers—the marketing of livestock. The same procedure was followed as for grain, and a national livestock marketing conference was convened on October 8, 1920. While there was less dissension than in the grain marketing conference, there were two major schools of thought. One favored building forward on the thriving livestock shipping association movement. The other advocated setting up a network of terminal livestock commission associations. To some extent it was a conflict between the "bottom up" and "top down" theories of cooperation, for the local shipping associations represented the idea that local organization should come first. The other group felt that local handling arrangements could be worked out after the terminal livestock commission associations were formed. Following the precedent of the grain marketing conference, President Howard was directed by the conference to appoint a Committee of 15 to bring in a national livestock marketing plan. What was achieved in 1921 will be examined in Chapter III.

Chapter II

GOVERNMENT CONFRONTS THE
AGRICULTURAL DEPRESSION: 1921-1924

When the Harding administration took office on March 4, 1921, the agricultural depression was in full swing. Something had to be done about it.

In selecting Henry C. Wallace, as Secretary of Agriculture, President Harding recognized the need for a man in this post who could represent farmers' interests. As editor of the influential *Wallace's Farmer,* Wallace was the accepted mouthpiece of farmers in representing their needs and aspirations, and he was highly respected as one of the principal architects of the rapidly expanding American Farm Bureau Federation. Moreover, Wallace had worked hard for Harding's election. He had helped draft the agricultural plank in the Republican Party platform and had prepared material relating to farming for Harding's campaign speeches.

Wallace came to the post of Secretary with a deep interest in the economic problems of agriculture and he had no intention of being a "do nothing" Secretary of Agriculture. His first concern was to coordinate and strengthen the Department's economic services—particularly in research.[1] In this he was abetted by his old friend, Dr. Henry C. Taylor, then Chief of the Office of Farm Management and Farm Economics, who felt much the same way and had definite views on what could be accomplished based upon his experience within the department. From the very beginning, Taylor was Wallace's right hand on all agricultural economic policies.

It was essential for Wallace to establish immediately the fact that the Department of Agriculture was to take leadership on economic problems relating to agriculture, for his strong-willed cabinet colleague, Herbert Hoover, Secretary of Commerce, firmly held the opinion that all work relating to marketing and foreign trade should be the responsibility of the Department of Commerce. Hoover believed that the Department of

Agriculture should concern itself only with matters of crop production and he had strong backing for his economic views within the administration.[2]

Wallace almost immediately felt the force of Hoover's opposition when he proposed that a national conference of agricultural leaders be called to find ways of improving the desperate economic condition of farmers. Secretary Hoover, joined by Secretary of the Treasury, Andrew Mellon, saw no need for a meeting of this kind and their views prevailed. However, as we shall see later, Wallace didn't give up on this idea, and, as the agricultural situation worsened, he was able to get the President's approval for the conference.

Consolidation of Economic Work

In the meantime, Wallace undertook immediate steps to strengthen the structure of the Department. On March 10, 1921, he asked the Chiefs of the bureaus and offices to submit plans for better organization of the Department and on March 17 he followed up with a conference of the chiefs. Other conferences were held on March 18 and 20, and suggestions were obtained from land grant college officials, the agricultural press, and other interested persons. As a result of these actions, various steps were taken in the next several months to improve the administrative, scientific, and service work of the Department.

Of most concern to Wallace was the strengthening of the economic functions of the Department. On May 25 he appointed an economic council comprised of E. D. Ball, Assistant Secretary of Agriculture; W. A. Taylor, Chief of the Bureau of Plant Industry; J. R. Mohler, Chief of the Bureau of Animal Industry; L. M. Estabrook, Chief of the Bureau of Crop Estimates; and H. C. Taylor, Chief of the Office of Farm Management and Farm Economics. He directed this council to study the economic work of the Department and offer recommendations for making it more effective. After consulting with a representative group of land grant college men—consisting of T. F. Hunt, University of California; Andrew Boss, University of Minnesota; G. F. Warren, Cornell University; G. I. Christie, Purdue University; and T. F. Cooper, University of Kentucky— the Council reported on June 18, 1921, and recommended the consolidation of all economic research and service activities in a single Bureau of Agricultural Economics. This recommendation was accepted by Secretary Wallace, who took immediate steps to implement it. Although the proposed new Bureau could not be established officially until Congressional authorization was obtained, a first step was achieved on July 1,

1921, by bringing together the Bureau of Markets and the Bureau of Crop Estimates—which had been approved by Congress upon the recommendation of his predecessor, Secretary Meredith—and by making Henry C. Taylor the Chief of the newly formed Bureau of Markets and Crop Estimates. Taylor continued to direct the Office of Farm Management and Farm Economics through the designation of his Assistant Chief, G. W. Forster, as Acting Chief.[3] Thus the consolidation of economic work was largely achieved on July 1, 1921, although its full legal implementation had to wait for another year.

Resumption of Work with Cooperatives

One of Taylor's first steps as Chief of the Bureau of Markets and Crop Estimates was to strengthen the department's assistance to agricultural cooperatives, for the Bureau of Market's work with cooperatives had lost much of its momentum before the Bureau of Markets and Crop Estimates was formed on July 1, 1921. The part of its cooperative work relating to finance and insurance had been transferred to the Office of Farm Management and Farm Economics, and the men who had been engaged in the preparation of cooperative accounting systems and reviews of cooperative business practices had been absorbed in a cost of marketing unit. It was obvious to Taylor that work with cooperatives should be intensified in view of the great interest then being manifested in cooperative marketing and purchasing, and this was accomplished by setting up, within the Bureau, a Division of Cooperative Relations, under the supervision of L. S. Tenny, his Assistant Chief. This division was to have two main responsibilities. The first was to conduct research studies on cooperative marketing and purchasing. According to Andrew W. McKay—who rejoined the Bureau to work on this project—"Under the influence of H. C. Taylor, the new Bureau Chief, research on cooperative problems became the main objective of the staff."[4] The second responsibility was to continue the program of maintaining cooperation with state agencies in marketing work. While this was important, it could be handled by Tenny, along administrative lines, and it did not solely relate to work with cooperative associations.[5]

In developing this new program of cooperative work, Taylor was influenced by his experience in working with cooperatives as Head of the Department of Agricultural Economics at the University of Wisconsin.[6] Taylor had learned that research was the best guide for action, and he was convinced that the Department needed more knowledge about cooperatives before it could give them sound advice and service assistance. Furthermore, by placing emphasis on research, the program could be conducted in an experimental way to determine how it could best be developed. Moreover, to Taylor "it seemed wise at first to deal with non-controversial matters since the commodity marketing enthusiasts then wanted only one thing—help in organizing commodity marketing cooperatives."[7]

Taylor later attributed much significance to a study made by A. W. McKay in the fall of 1921 to help Vermont maple sugar producers find a suitable method of cooperative organization in that it demonstrated how the Department could be of service. This study showed how research could find a way for action, and this became a precedent for service work on other problems.[8]

One of the major projects carried on by the Division of Cooperative Relations was a nationwide survey of all cooperative marketing and purchasing associations under the direction of R. H. Elsworth.[9] This was designed to bring out all the facts regarding the growth and character of cooperative associations since little dependable statistical information was then available. At this time L. S. Hulbert began his studies of the legal problems of cooperatives which were to give much guidance to farmers on their cooperative undertakings.[10]

Following the National Agricultural Conference, described later, a study was begun of the organization and operations of the California Fruit Growers Exchange to find out the lessons from its successful experience. Problems of the emerging centralized cotton and tobacco cooperatives were also examined. All of this exploratory work provided a good foundation for the more ambitious program which was to be launched on July 1, 1922, when assistance to cooperatives became a responsibility of the newly formed Bureau of Agricultural Economics.

The "Farm Bloc" Brings Congressional Action

Congress could not ignore the seriousness of the agricultural depression while Secretary Wallace was taking steps to strengthen the economic services of the Department of Agriculture. At that time agriculture represented a much larger segment of the economy than it does today, and, as farm prices continued to fall, all industry became increasingly concerned.

In April 1921, representatives of all the important farm organizations came together in Washington, D.C., to consider what might be done to meet the problems brought on by the great drop in farm prices. This conference focussed attention on a number of problems, such as: the need for additional agricultural credit legislation; the need for relief on transportation costs; and the need for clarification of laws relating to cooperative organizations. It became clear at this gathering that the American Farm Bureau Federation, flushed with a great influx of members, was assuming political leadership for the farm groups under the deft command of Gray Silver, the head of the Farm Bureau's legislative office.[11]

Following the meeting of farm organization leaders, Silver assembled a number of Republican and Democratic Senators from the farm states and got them to pledge themselves to support legislation necessary for the welfare of agriculture. This was the genesis of the "Farm Bloc" which was to exert great political power during the next few years.[12]

The Joint Commission of Agricultural Inquiry

By late spring, the plight of agriculture had become so marked that the two houses of Congress—now unified by the Farm Bloc—set up by Concurrent Resolution on June 7, 1921, a Joint Commission of Agricultural Inquiry under the Chairmanship of Congressman Sydney Anderson of Minnesota. It was directed to:

> Investigate and report to the Congress . . . upon the following subjects: (1) the causes of the present condition of agriculture; (2) the cause of the difference between the prices of agricultural products paid to the producer and the ultimate cost to the consumer; (3) the comparative condition of industries other than agriculture; (4) the relation of prices of commodities other than agriculture; (5) the banking and financial resources and credits of the country, especially as affecting agricultural credits; (6) the marketing and transportation facilities of the country.

While the Commission was energetically at work, the Farm Bloc showed its influence by forcing Congress to defer adjournment until various agricultural measures were acted upon. In the summer months, under pressure from the Bloc, the Congress passed the Packers and Stockyards Act, the first Grain Futures Act (later declared unconstitutional), and legislation to continue and strengthen the work of the War Finance Corporation and to widen the powers of the Federal Land Banks.

In the fall of 1921, the Commission of Agricultural Inquiry submitted its findings in four important reports. One of its principal recommendations was that legislation should be enacted to strengthen the legal position of cooperative marketing associations. It also recommended legislation to provide for a system of Intermediate Credit Banks. Perhaps the main value of the Commission's reports was the emphasis they gave to the urgency of the problems confronting agriculture.[13]

The National Agricultural Conference

It was with this background of growing agricultural restlessness that President Harding, in December, 1921, gave Secretary Wallace permission to proceed with the Agricultural Conference that he had long advocated.[14] By this time the index of farm prices stood at 115 as compared with 123 in March when the Harding Administration took office and with 234 in June 1920 when the depression began. The Conference was scheduled for January 23-27, 1922, and Wallace energetically proceeded to do everything possible to make it successful. As this was to be primarily an economic conference, he placed on Dr. H. C. Taylor the major responsibility of developing the program.

The Conference, held at the Willard Hotel in Washington, D.C., brought together 336 delegates from almost every state in the Union. They represented agriculture, industry and labor; state governments; educational institutions; and the agricultural press. Of the group, 185 were listed as farmers and 18 as women. Secretary Wallace admitted to critics that it was a "hand picked" conference in that the delegates were invited to represent "the widest divergence of views."

The plan of the Conference called for several general sessions, but the main work was done by 12 well-qualified committees. Before the Conference assembled, the delegates were assigned to these committees by representatives of the Department on the basis of their interests and abilities. Chairmen and secretaries for the committees were appointed in advance. For example, G. Harold Powell, General Manager of the California Fruit Growers Exchange was named Chairman of the important Committee on Marketing with Asher Hobson of the Department as Secretary.

Upon the invitation of Secretary Wallace, Congressman Sydney Anderson, Chairman of the Joint Commission of Agricultural Inquiry, served as General Chairman for the Conference, while Dr. Taylor served as its Executive Secretary.

In opening the Conference, Secretary Wallace said: "Your problem divides itself into two parts: First, the present emergency and how best to break it; second, the consideration of future policies with a view to building here a permanent sustaining agriculture."[15]

An outstanding feature of the Conference was—in the words of Secretary Wallace—"the epoch making address" by President Harding which placed major emphasis on how farmers could meet their own problems through cooperative organization. He said:

It cannot be too strongly urged that the farmer must be ready to help himself . . . In the last analysis, legislation can do little more than give the farmer the chance to organize and help himself . . . Take cooperative marketing. American farmers are asking for, and it should be possible to afford them, ample provision of law under which they may carry on in cooperative fashion those business operations which lend themselves to that method, and which, thus handled, would bring advantage to both the farmer and his consuming public . . . But when we have done this, the farmers must become responsible for doing the rest. They must learn organization and the practical procedures of cooperation.

Chairman Sydney Anderson also stressed the importance of cooperatives. He said: "The Government must remove the obstacles which retard, if they do not prevent, combinations of farmers for the purpose of sorting, grading, and packing or processing their products . . . " Support for cooperatives was also voiced by Thomas Wilson, one of the leaders in the meat packing industry. He said:

The enormous losses and wastes due to unsystematic and unscientific marketing of farm products, including livestock, affect adversely both the producer and consumer. I believe that the time has been reached when associations of producers, under proper supervision, should systematize the orderly marketing of their products, especially so of perishable products, in order to prevent gluts, wastes, and losses which benefit no one. I think that the power to do so should be clearly sanctioned by law, and to that end I think the recent Capper-Volstead bill, authorizing associations to regulate shipments of farm products, is sound in principle, and would, if properly acted upon, do much toward solving many important economic problems now confronting industry in this country (p. 48).

One of the principal addresses was made by G. Harold Powell on the subject: "Fundamentals of Cooperative Marketing." He said: "There should be an affirmative statutory recognition that farmers have the right to organize, to do those things that are vital to the economical and orderly conduct of their business . . . The legality of a cooperative marketing agency should not be made to depend upon the mere form of its internal organization."

The Report of Committee No. 7 on the Marketing of Farm Products under the Chairmanship of Powell also strongly endorsed and recommended the cooperative marketing of farm products. The Committee urged that:

Congress promptly enact affirmative legislation which will permit farmers to act together in associations, corporate or otherwise, with or without capital stock, for purposes connected with the production, processing, preparing for market, handling, and marketing in interstate commerce such products of persons so engaged with specific statements of their rights, powers, remedies, and limitations, and which will permit such associations to have marketing agencies in common and to make such contracts and agreements as are necessary to effect such purposes.

This Committee also declared:

> Orderly marketing which represents the even distribution of the nation's farm products in response to the demands of the trade and of the consumer is basic in giving the farmer a fair price for his crops or products. The individual farmer is not competent to handle or even to influence this question . . . The fundamental requirements for orderly marketing include the organization of producers on a commodity basis in order that large dependable quantities of standardized products may be offered for sale with speculation and all unfair and dishonest practices in distribution reduced to a minimum . . . This committee, therefore strongly urges the formation of strongly organized cooperative associations of farmers, preferably on a commodity basis.

In his final remarks to the Conference, Secretary Wallace said:

> I think it will be found that you have presented the most well thought out, thoroughly constructive suggestions for the betterment of agriculture and for the sound building of national life in all the years to come. The interest of agriculture can not be separate from the national interest, because when all is said and done, if our agriculture breaks, everything breaks. We have come to that time in the history of this Nation when, either consciously or unconsciously, we shall determine policies which either make for a continuing self-sustained Nation here or mark the beginning of disintegration . . . This conference will be tremendously helpful to all of us here. It will be most helpful to our Department . . . We have known of your problems and difficulties and have been trying to help, but the closer contacts of this week will give us clearer vision, better understanding, and renewed zeal and inspiration.

Although the Conference offered many valuable recommendations of long-run importance to agriculture, such as measures to provide for better adjustment of supplies to demand, its main immediate contribution was the powerful boost it gave to legislation designed to further the progress of cooperative marketing associations and to provide for better financing of agriculture. Perhaps the most significant thing about the Conference was that it was held. It was in the words of the *Experiment Station Record* (March 1922) "the first conference of the kind ever convened in this country, bringing together representatives from the major farm organizations, state departments of agriculture, the agricultural colleges and various lines of business closely associated with agriculture." To use a term that has come into use in recent years, it was the first "Agri-business" conference.

The National Agricultural Conference dramatized the problems of agriculture and demonstrated the intent of government to assist on them. It greatly improved the image of the U.S.D.A. as a service agency for agriculture and weakened Hoover's contention that the work of the U.S.D.A. should be limited to the sphere of farm production. By affording farmers and farm organizations an opportunity to get things off their chests, it served as a safety valve and bought time for the consideration of permanent programs. It also gave timely support to the passage of the

Capper-Volstead Act and other important "Farm Bloc" legislation. The conference also made clear that farmers expected that government power should be used to help them, and that government could not ignore the distress of farmers. It is significant that the Conference gave the first public recognition to the "Equality for Agriculture" movement which was soon to assume a dominating place in farm relief proposals as the "McNary-Haugen movement."[16]

The reactions of the farm press to the Conference were generally favorable. An editorial in *Wallace's Farmer* for February 3, 1922, declared "Agricultural influence in national affairs has been tremendously strengthened by the conference . . . The program adopted is one that will have the support not only of the farmers but of almost every other element in the nation." Henry A. Wallace, who reported on the Conference in a feature article in the same issue, said: "The outstanding feature of the Conference was that the big businessmen of the nation, labor leaders and politicians had their attention riveted on farm problems as never before . . . People everywhere are now beginning to think about the fundamentals of agricultural prosperity more seriously than ever before."[17]

Passage of the Capper-Volstead Act

The National Agricultural Conference set the stage for the passage of the Capper-Volstead Cooperative Marketing Act. With the endorsement of the President of the United States and the National Agricultural Conference, legislation of this type could no longer be ignored. The House had already passed the measure so the nearly unanimous action in its favor, by the Senate, was decisive. It was a major victory for the "Farm Bloc" and for the proponents of cooperative marketing.

It is here important to understand that the signing of the Act by President Harding on February 18, 1922, culminated a struggle for liberalization of the federal anti-trust laws that started in 1919. While the Clayton Act of 1914 made clear that cooperatives formed on a non-stock basis were not in restraint of trade, it left the position of cooperatives formed on a capital stock basis subject to challenge. As a result, many of the milk marketing cooperatives were harassed by legal actions that endangered their future. Many large-scale capital stock cooperatives in California also felt themselves in jeopardy under existing law.

To meet this acute problem, the National Cooperative Milk Producers' Federation in 1919 had drafted a bill to expressly amend Section 6 of the Clayton Act so as to include capital stock associations. This bill was sponsored in the Senate by Senator Capper, a Republican from Kansas, and in the House by Congressman Hersman, a Democrat from California. The intent was to have the bill considered as a non-partisan measure.[18] The bill was strongly opposed by trade interests who charged that it was the product of "the Milk Trust"—the organized dairymen. This aroused farmers throughout the nation to give their support to the bill. Before the bill came to a vote, it was decided to rewrite it and have it reintroduced by Congressman Andrew Volstead of Minnesota, rather than by Congressman Hersman of California. The theory was that, if the Republicans gained control of Congress in the 1920 elections, they would be more interested in the bill if it were a Republican measure. The bill was passed by both houses in 1920, but they could not agree in conference.

The bill was entirely rewritten in 1921 to make it a more general statement of federal policy and it was then reintroduced by Senator Capper and Congressman Volstead. It passed the House on May 4, 1921, but it was not able to clear the Senate. It was this situation that made the support of the President and the National Agricultural Conference so important. When the bill came up for consideration in the Senate a few weeks after the Conference, it was passed after five days of debate with but one dissenting vote. The House concurred in the measure as passed by the Senate and with the approval of the President it became law on February 18, 1922. The passage of the Capper-Volstead Act marked a great step forward for cooperative marketing, and the Act has long been referred to as the Magna Carta of Cooperative Marketing. It made clear that farmers could organize cooperative marketing associations either on a non-stock or stock basis without danger of legal harassment on the form of their organization.[19]

The Drive for the Federal Intermediate
Credit Banks (1922-1923)

The depressed condition of agriculture in 1921 and 1922 convinced many farmers and farm leaders of the need for better short-term agricultural credit service. The Commission of Agricultural Inquiry gave this subject exhaustive analysis and found it a major requirement for agricultural relief. To facilitate action, the Commission proposed legislation to provide credit for terms running from six months to three years. Such legislation also was strongly endorsed by the National Agricultural Conference. Cooperative marketing organizations were especially interested in short-term credit legislation, for they needed generous supplies of such credit in financing their commodity operations.[20]

Under these circumstances the passage of satisfactory short-term farm credit legislation became a major concern of the Farm Bloc, and intensive hearings were held on proposed legislation during the summer of 1922. However, disagreement on the type of legislation desired made action impossible before March 1923 when the Intermediate Credit Act was passed. This act provided for 12 Intermediate Credit Banks to be administered by the Federal Farm Loan Board and to be operated in conjunction with the 12 Land Banks. The steps leading to the establishment of the Intermediate Credit Banks and an evaluation of their early importance will be more fully discussed in Chapter XI.[21]

The First Outlook Conference—1923

The agricultural situation in 1920 and 1921 had convinced Secretary Wallace and Dr. H. C. Taylor and others that agricultural production must be better adjusted to market demands.[22] This idea was encouraged by the Joint Commission of Agricultural Inquiry, and it received much attention in the National Agricultural Conference of January 1922. The popularity of this concept gave much support to the strengthening of the statistical work of the Bureau of Agricultural Economics in crop and livestock reporting and in economic analysis. This interest led to the first Outlook Conference held behind closed doors on April 20-21, 1923. It was then the theory of Taylor and others that if farmers knew the facts on the relationship of production to prices, they would voluntarily take steps necessary to reduce supplies of crops and livestock in excess of demand. Although the theory gave way in practice, the outlook program did have long-run benefits in educating the agricultural industry on the complex interplay of production and price. To some extent outlook work strengthened the hand of cooperative leaders who saw in cooperatives a mechanism for helping farmers make better adjustment of supplies to market demands.[23]

Expansion of Research and Service Work
for Cooperatives (1922-24)

With the formal establishment of the Bureau of Agricultural Economics on July 1, 1922, the Department gave increased attention to the growing importance of cooperative associations by setting up the Division of Agricultural Cooperation to replace the Division of Cooperative Relations. During 1921-22 the work with cooperatives had been more or less experimental. By July 1922 the Department had gained a clearer idea of how it could be of service. Lloyd S. Tenny, as Assistant Chief of the new bureau, remained in charge, but the work was now to be conducted under three projects with designated leaders: (1) Economics of Cooperation—A. W. McKay; (2) Statistics of Cooperation—R. H. Elsworth; and (3) Legal Phases of Cooperation—L. S. Hulbert. Work in all of these areas had been started in earlier years, but it was now to be broadened and intensified.[24]

Under the Economics of Cooperation project, an intensive study was undertaken of the California Fruit Growers Exchange to explain the reasons for its success. Less detailed surveys were made of other cooperatives, such as the Dark Tobacco Association, the Dairymen's League Cooperative Association, and the New England Milk Producers Association. A study was also started of factors that had caused cooperative discontinuance. In January, 1923, the Department published Bulletin 1109, *Sales Methods and Policies of a Growers National Marketing Agency* by Asher Hobson and J. Burton Chaney. This was a case study analysis of the American Cranberry Exchange and the forerunner of many case studies designed to show, by example, principles of good cooperative business organization and operation.[25] In this year the Division supported a study of agricultural cooperation in Denmark by Chris L. Christensen, which was to be published as Bulletin 1268 early in 1924. In January 1923 the Division of Agricultural Cooperation began publication of *Agricultural Cooperation,* a small magazine issued semimonthly in mimeographed form. It reported activities of farmer cooperatives and current research findings by members of the staff. Summaries of legal cases and decisions affecting cooperatives soon became a feature of this publication.[26]

Under the project, Statistics of Cooperation, a comprehensive survey was made to develop complete statistics on agricultural cooperatives. Questionnaires were first sent out to crop reporters to develop lists of farmer cooperatives. Follow-up questionnaires were then sent out to the 30,000 names obtained. If no reply was received, an effort was made to obtain information from county agents, postmasters, or others in the locality. In this way information on some 10,000 active marketing and purchasing associations was obtained. R. H. Elsworth's Department Bulletin 1302, *Development and Present Status of Farmers' Cooperative Business Organizations,* giving information from this survey, was not published until 1924, but much of the information developed was released during 1923 in *Agricultural Cooperation.* Bulletin 1302 was a landmark publication in that it provided comprehensive and up-to-date statistics on cooperative marketing and purchasing in the United States.

Under the third project, L. S. Hulbert developed information on the legal problems in organizing and operating cooperative associations. The results of this work were published as Bulletin No. 1106, *Legal Phases of Cooperative Associations*, which appeared in October 1922. This publication was of great immediate value to cooperatives, for it provided them with much needed general legal guidance. As noted, this bulletin was supplemented by reports of legal decisions in current issues of *Agricultural Cooperation*.

During 1923-24, the work of the Division of Agricultural Cooperation continued along the same general lines started in 1922-23, although increasingly the staff of the Division was called on for advisory services based on knowledge accumulated from its research activities and contacts with cooperatives. New work included studies of organization and operation of cooperative grain elevators, creameries, livestock shipping associations, fruit and vegetable associations, and the membership problems of large tobacco marketing associations. During the year a bibliography of marketing, purchasing, and credit cooperatives was prepared for publication as Miscellaneous Circular 11, *Agricultural Cooperation: A Selected and Annotated Reading List*. This bulletin did much to direct those interested in cooperative development to essential source information.

There was no general change in the program of the Division of Agricultural Cooperation until July 1924 when Chris L. Christensen was placed "In Charge." His appointment gave status to the program and recognized the growing need for practical service work to help cooperatives in the business management field.[27] Under Christensen, emphasis was placed on improvement of cooperative business methods and practices, and the program was soon broadened to include a new project: "Accounts and Business Practices." More and more advisory assistance was provided cooperatives on their organizational and operating problems. In retrospect, great credit can be given to Secretary Wallace and Dr. Taylor for the program of research, service, and education that they established in the Department of Agriculture from 1921 to 1924. It was based upon an objective analysis of facts and information made available to all interested parties without favoritism to any form of organization. While this program was not spectacular, it had great long-run significance in strengthening the business character of cooperative enterprise in America.[28]

The Genesis of McNary-Haugenism (1921-1924)

Complementary with the drive to develop strong cooperative commodity marketing associations came a growing demand for a program of governmental farm relief. The discontent of farmers in the Midwest began to show up in various legislative proposals as early as the spring of 1921, but it was not focussed until January 1922 when George N. Peek, President of the Moline Plow Company, began his campaign for "Equality for Agriculture" at the National Agricultural Conference. Peek was able to inject his ideas into a resolution of the Marketing Committee adopted by the Conference which declared:

> Agriculture is necessary to the life of the Nation; and, whereas, the prices of agricultural products are far below the cost of production, so far below that relatively they are the lowest in the history of our country; therefore, it is the sense of this committee that the Congress and the President of the United States should take such steps as will immediately reestablish *a fair exchange value* for all farm products with that of other commodities (Italics added).[29]

It was Peek's contention that the protective tariff laws worked to the disadvantage of American agriculture. He was not opposed to protection for industry, but he wanted its advantages shared with agriculture. He advocated persuasively that steps should be taken to give agriculture the same benefits that the tariff laws provided industry. He and his associate, General Hugh S. Johnson, had developed this idea in pamphlet form in December 1921 under the arresting title: *Equality for Agriculture,* and this was to become the battle cry for millions of farmers during the next several years. *Equality for Agriculture* had a strong appeal, not only to distressed farmers but also to industries dependent upon agriculture, and interest in its apparently simple formula for achieving agricultural prosperity spread rapidly in the major agricultural areas. Like Thomas Paine's tract of 1776, *Common Sense,* it was packed with cogent sentences which called for action:

> The doctrine of protection must be revised to insure agriculture a fair exchange value on the domestic market or the protective tariff must perish.
> There are only two ways to equalize price. One is Free Trade; the other is to segregate agricultural surplus from the domestic market and sell it in export. Free Trade is unthinkable. There remains only the method advocated in this brief . . .

Several years later in describing the McNary-Haugen movement—which grew out of Peek's plan—John D. Black said:

> The essential idea of the plan as presented in . . . [Equality for Agriculture] was exactly as it is now. The surplus above domestic consumption was to be sold in the export market at world prices, and the losses recouped by a "differential

loan assessment on each pound or bushel, when and as sold by the farmer." This was to be a way of "securing equality for agriculture in the benefits of the protective tariff." Mr. Peek had the idea that "the fair exchange value of the crop is reduced in exact proportion with the protection afforded industry." The other conspicuous feature of the plan then presented was the definition of "fair exchange value of any crop as one which bears the same ratio to the current general price index as a ten-year, pre-war average crop price bears to the average general price index for the same period." This was supposed to give a price for the crop equal to "cost of production plus a profit." . . . The assessment on the producers was to be made by paying them part of the price for their grain in the form of "script"; the redeemable value of which would be announced later when operating costs had been determined.[30]

Although Peek secured a foothold for his ideas at the National Agricultural Conference, he realized that strong support within the administration was needed if legislation were to be enacted that would put the plan into effect. He therefore remained in Washington, following the Conference, and persuaded Henry C. Taylor, then in charge of economic work in the Department of Agriculture, to hold several seminar sessions of his staff with Peek and Johnson.[31] Realizing that interest of officials in the Department was not enough, Peek and others pressed Secretary Wallace and also President Harding to arrange a Conference on the plan, to be attended by farm leaders, food processors, and dealers and financiers. With the encouragement of President Harding, Wallace acceded to this request and called a meeting in Washington on February 13 which was attended by Julius Barnes, President of the United States Chamber of Commerce and a close friend of Herbert Hoover, Secretary of Commerce; Otto Kahn and Rufus Dawes, financiers; Thomas Wilson, Wilson and Company; Fred Wells, Peavy Grain Company; and J. R. Howard and Gray Silver, respectively President and Washington representative of the American Farm Bureau Federation. Peek, Johnson, and Dr. Taylor were also present. Although there were no conclusive results, the Conference stimulated further interest in the plan, especially on the part of Secretary Wallace who kept it in the forefront of his mind.[32]

During 1922, interest in the "equalization fee" grew in farming areas but no attempt was made to develop it as a legislative measure. In the spring of 1923, Secretary Wallace asked Taylor: "How much wheat would have to be gotten rid of to put wheat on an import basis and make the protective tariff effective?" Taylor reported back that the statisticians of the Department found that the figure would be about 50 million bushels. In September, with no improvement in the economic position of agriculture, Secretary Wallace asked Taylor to see if he could find some means of helping to solve the farmers' problem. Wallace said:

We have done what we can as a Department of Agriculture but conditions are not improving . . . While we as Department workers should adhere to the national point of view, which we are certainly doing in striving to save agriculture from destruction, it does not follow that farmers as a class must adhere to the national point of view when other groups are not doing so. In fact, unless farmers as a class get busy and *fight* for their rights, we in the Department will not long be able to take a national point of view because the point of view of other interests will dominate us. I want you to think the matter over and see if you can suggest some means of helping to solve the farmers' price problem.

In response to this request, Taylor gave Wallace a statement on September 22, 1923, in which he said:

> If agriculture could be as well organized as the anthracite coal industry, for example, so as to limit production and bargain collectively in the sale of the product, this system would prove effective in reestablishing pre-war price ratios. Whether or not it reaches this degree of perfection, cooperative marketing is an undertaking that should be encouraged because of the increased efficiency in standardization and in the movement of products from producer to consumer. But, unless it reaches that state of development which enables it to control production and distribution of the staple products, we cannot look to cooperation for an early solution of the problem of proper price ratios . . .
>
> Another proposal . . . is the application of the principle of the protective tariff to farm products of which we produce a surplus. The means suggested is through the establishment of an agricultural export commission with broad powers, which would enable it to buy, store, or export farm products and to levy taxes on specific products to pay the cost of stabilizing the price of the particular product . . . This proposal, in order to be effective and not to develop more grief than satisfaction for the farmer, must carry with it such brakes on production as will avoid an unbalancing of the different lines of production . . .
>
> After all has been said, I believe it would be agreed that whether or not this is a method which it is desirable to apply at the present time, it is the only method thus far proposed which would quickly reestablish the pre-war ratios . . . and which looks toward giving immediate new hope and prosperity to the American Farmer."[33]

Wallace responded to this statement by suggesting to Dr. Taylor that he gather firsthand information from farmers and others to see what could be done to improve the situation. Taylor set forth immediately to the spring wheat area where he found the farmers "convinced that the need was for the reestablishing of prewar price ratios." Even before Taylor returned, Wallace had begun to act by bringing back to the department, Charles J. Brand, formerly Chief of the Bureau of Markets, to work as a consultant with Peek and Johnson in drafting a bill based on their views. This was the genesis of the so-called McNary-Haugen plan, introduced on January 16, 1924, in Congress by Senator Charles McNary, of Oregon and by Congressman Gilbert Haugen of Iowa.

Although the McNary-Haugen Bill got substantial support in the wheat states and in a few other agricultural areas, it was not immediately popular in the South, Far West and industrial states, and the American Farm Bureau Federation gave it but nominal approval. At that time the cooperative commodity marketing movement was in full swing, and its leaders saw the McNary-Haugen plan as a threat to their own program. It was not surprising that the bill failed passage in the House by a vote of 223 to 155 on June 3, 1924. Although this vote dealt the McNary-Haugen plan supporters a severe blow, the idea was far from dead.[34]

Smarting under the defeat of the McNary-Haugen Bill, Secretary Wallace saw that he could do little more to further legislation of this type until a new political administration came to power. The death of President Harding in the summer of 1923 was a serious loss to Wallace, for he could count on little support from President Coolidge who looked for counsel to Secretary of Commerce Hoover and Secretary of the Treasury Mellon. To keep the record straight, Wallace undertook, in the summer of 1924, to express his views in a book and, while this book was nearing completion, in October 1924, he was stricken by illness and died. The book, completed by his son Henry A. Wallace and Nils A. Olsen, of the Bureau of Agricultural Economics, was published in early 1925 under the title: *Our Debt and Duty to the Farmer*. It was a testament that gave encouragement to the revitalization of the McNary-Haugen movement. In it Wallace said:

> The most effective direct action the Government can take to ease agricultural conditions quickly is to devise a practical plan to remove the exportable surplus of certain commodities and permit domestic prices of farm products to rise to their pre-war ratio with the general commodity-price index. Such a policy would not prove a complete cure but would give a large measure of relief, assure continued improvement, and go far toward restoring the confidence of the farmer in the future of agriculture and the good faith of his government.[35]

While Wallace full appreciated the importance of cooperatives in the organization of agriculture, he recognized their impotence in controlling agricultural production and prices. In his chapter on "Cooperation" he said:

> People who point to cooperation as the quick way out of such economic difficulties as agriculture has gone through and still is experiencing, no doubt mean well, but they are directing farmers up an impassable road. Successful cooperative associations will help, just as reduction of operating costs, economy, and hard work help, but none of these get to the source of the trouble. If three-fourths of the farmers were members of strong cooperatives and willing to subject themselves to severe discipline in the production and marketing of their crops, they might be able to control the prices of many of their products. But, if such a state of affairs is ever brought about it will not be for many years. Nevertheless, the need for strong cooperative marketing associations cannot be over-emphasized. They are absolutely necessary to bring about the efficient and economical marketing and the standardization of crops. But they should be truly cooperative, controlled by their members, and kept free from domination by government agencies or commercial interests.[36]

Before we give attention to the later history of the McNary-Haugen movement, let us examine the strong cooperative drive of the American Farm Bureau Federation and the concurrent cooperative commodity marketing movement before its collapse. We will observe that as commodity cooperative marketing lost strength, its leaders yielded support to the McNary-Haugenites.

Chapter III

THE FARM BUREAU COOPERATIVE
MARKETING PLANS: 1921-1925

As 1921 opened, the Committee of 17 was just about ready to announce its grain marketing plan.[1] It had taken its job seriously and for several months it had been working energetically gathering information and ideas from all pertinent sources. Some of its representatives had visited the California Fruit Growers Exchange and other important cooperatives in the Far West; others had gone to Winnipeg to obtain firsthand information on the operations of the United Grain Growers, Ltd. Among the various experts who met with the committee were Julius Barnes, Head of the U.S. Grain Corporation during the period of World War I; G. Harold Powell, Manager of the California Fruit Growers Exchange; Huston Thompson, Chairman of the Federal Trade Commission; Leslie F. Gates, President of the Chicago Board of Trade; and Bernard Baruch, the well-known New York financier who had been Chairman of the War Industries Board.

The Grain Marketing Plan

Finally, on February 17, 1921, the committee agreed upon a plan. This was then informally presented by members of the committee to a series of state meetings where delegates were selected for a convention to be held at Chicago on April 6 to ratify the plan. In brief, the plan recommended the establishment of a non-stock, non-profit national association to be made up exclusively of grain growers. Each member was to pay a $10 membership fee and sign a contract to sell through the national organization for a five-year period under various options, one of which was local pooling. The members were to be organized into voting units at shipping points, and each voting unit annually was to send a delegate to a

35

convention to be held in its congressional district. In turn, delegates were to be selected by each congressional district to represent that district in a national convention. The board of directors was to be elected at this annual meeting by ballot.

In opening the conference for ratification of the plan, which provided for the establishment of the United States Grain Growers, Inc., President Howard said: "This morning, April 6, 1921, marks sun-up for American Agriculture." The report of this meeting as given in the *Prairie Farmer* of April 16, 1921, reflects the high spirits engendered.

> The Magna Carta of American agriculture has been signed . . . The climax of the meeting came Thursday night . . . Delegates from every corner of the United States . . . were on their feet shouting approval and pledging allegiance to the new plan . . . The vote was unanimous; there was not a dissenting voice to the universal pledge of support. The next day a board of directors of 21 outstanding leaders was appointed . . . An executive committee of seven was appointed to give their full time to the tremendous task . . . Early this week the United States Grain Growers, Inc., was incorporated as a non-stock, non-profit association under the laws of Delaware, and is now a going concern. The full board . . . will meet again next week. At that time plans will be perfected for a whirlwind organization campaign to cover the entire grain belt of the United States . . . The mark set this year is a million members. The new board realizes the stupendous task . . . but, the members are fired with the spirit of the crusaders . . . They are backed by the greatest wave of farm sentiment that has ever swept any farmers' movement on to success . . . A movement like this cannot fail, any more than the Revolutionary War could fail.

This optimistic forecast proved premature. It did not take into account the serious disagreement that was evident in the ratification conference. A second article in the same issue of *Prairie Farmer* reported that:

> The outstanding feature of the convention was the prolonged and hard-fought debate over the question of compulsory pooling of wheat. For 14 hours the [Convention] . . . discussed every possible angle of the important question of pooling and finally voted down the proposition. Pooling lost, but the discussion thoroughly established the pooling principle, and it really won the fight. This strenuous, though good-natured, debate over-shadowed the all-important fact that the grain marketing plan was unanimously adopted . . .

The debate had been opened when C. O. Moser, of Texas, offered an amendment to the Committee of 17 Plan, which provided for the compulsory pooling of one-third of all the wheat produced. Carl Williams, of Oklahoma, and George Jewett, of Washington State, supported the amendment, while J. W. Shorthill and Professor H. C. Filley, of Nebraska, and other strong farmers' elevator men opposed. The final vote was 38 for the pooling amendment and 61 opposed. One of the delegates remarked after the voting: "We're for harmony even if we have to fight for it."

Thus, the United States Grain Growers, Inc., was born on April 6,

1921, with much acclaim but under a shadow. Its plan of organization represented a compromise to meet the views of two opposing factions, and as the first board of directors was selected by the Committee of 17, the dissensions of the Committee were carried over into the meetings of the board.[2] Moreover, since few of the directors had direct grain marketing experience in any large way, board meetings were more concerned with internal politics than business management. From the start, C. H. Gustafson, who had stepped from the Chairmanship of the Committee of 17 into the Presidency of the United States Grain Growers, Inc., was unable to cope with the difficult organizational and business problems that soon arose.

The program undertaken represented a tremendous undertaking in that it called for a large membership to provide a volume of business essential to adequately support the marketing machinery that was planned. As the first job obviously was to sign up members, the United States Grain Growers, Inc., soon had an army of paid organizers in the field. However, farmers proved to be less enthusiastic than their leaders, and they did not see how they would benefit from membership. Although the organizers succeeded at heavy cost in getting about 50,000 members by the end of 1921, this was but a fraction of the avowed goal of a million. In fact, the cost of getting members largely absorbed the revenue from the $10 membership fee, and there was little left for financing the organization.

Under the plan of the Commitee of 17, the United States Grain Growers, Inc., was to set up sales agencies on the principal markets. In the face of the bitter opposition of the established grain trade, this proved to be impossible. The application for membership on the Chicago Board of Trade was turned down on the grounds that the Company was not "regular" in that it was designed to pay patronage refunds.[3]

By the end of 1921, it was becoming apparent that the United States Grain Growers, Inc., was bogged down, and even those who had been enthusiastic became critical. It was charged that "management has been extravagant and dilatory in bringing to fruition the actual marketing plan of the Committee of Seventeen; that nothing has been done to aid the grain grower in the actual marketing of his grain; that too much money has been spent in salaries for the officers, in renting expensive office quarters, and in ill-advised publicity efforts."[4]

The serious situation of the organization came out into the open at the first annual meeting of the company held on March 21, 1922. It then had a sizeable deficit and little to show for it. At this meeting, the "poolers were routed and defeated and not reelected to the board of directors." The management maintained that "the extravagance . . . was directly due to the incompetence of the retiring treasurer and leader of the pooling faction."[5] However, the newly constituted board was not able to improve the situation greatly, and it was soon apparent that more drastic action would be necessary if the United States Grain Growers, Inc., was to be saved. On May 13, 1922, the Presidents and Secretaries of the Midwest State Farm Bureaus appointed a committee of investigation. On June 21, this committee reported that a sales plan was nearly ready to function, but, on July 19, the officers of the company said they could go no further and requested the Midwest Committee to take over the organization and rebuild it. This committee then proceeded to reorganize the United States Grain Growers as recommended by the report of the investigation committee. On August 4, 1922, the entire board of directors resigned, one by one, and a new board was elected with E. H. Cunningham, Secretary of the Iowa Farm Bureau Federation, as President.[6]

These actions brought new hopes to those concerned with the success of the United States Grain Growers, Inc. This was reflected in an editorial in the *Prairie Farmer* of August 19, 1922, entitled "Under Way at Last."

> The old board of directors has been replaced by a board made up of the best farm leaders of the Middle West. An advisory committee of three of the leading businessmen of the country—Alexander Legge of the International Harvester Company, Frank O. Wetmore of the First National Bank of Chicago, and Bernard M. Baruch of New York City—is giving the new Board its active help. This means that the plans of the Grain Growers will be developed on a sound business basis, which is essential to the success of any farmers' marketing organization. Several months time has been lost. That is too bad, but not fatal . . . The important thing is that we are going in the right direction, under the guidance of competent leaders. Let's all give them our support.

The change came too late. By the time of the annual meeting in December, interest in the United States Grain Growers had evaporated and the Farm Bureau was moving toward promotion of commodity marketing of the Sapiro type. The Grain Growers limped along until 1924 when, as we shall see later in this chapter, it was absorbed in the Grain Marketing Company—an even more grandiose grain marketing plan.

The experience of the Farm Bureau and the United States Grain Growers taught an important lesson that had a temporary sobering effect. It demonstrated that a marketing plan must be built on the support of those to be served in accordance with good business principles. In the following words, Ralph Snyder, a member of the Committee of 17, wrote the epitaph of the United States Grain Growers, Inc.:

> We met, and met, and met. We developed some grandiose ideas. We also developed some rather bitter animosities . . . The conflict between the group who wanted to make use of the existing grain cooperatives and those who wanted to

develop an entirely new form of organization for wheat pooling developed into a battle royal every time we met . . . However, we organized the U.S.G.G. and set out to secure members. We first tried to get the interest of the existing cooperative elevators. We got their opposition. Then we tried to go over their heads, direct to members. That failed. And, that was the end of the U.S. Grain Growers. It never did market any grain.[7]

The Livestock Marketing Plan

The Farm Bureau's livestock marketing program met with more success. The Committee of 15 appointed by President Howard on January 3, 1921, included only one man who was on the Committee of 17. This was C. H. Gustafson who served as Chairman of both Committees.[8]

After several months of diligent work and six formal meetings, a plan was developed which was submitted to a ratification conference convened at Chicago on November 10, 1921, where, with strong Farm Bureau support, it was "carried with a whoop."[9]

The plan provided for the establishment of the National Livestock Producers Association to serve as an overhead agency for commission associations to be organized on the principal terminal markets not then served by such associations. Under the plan, farmers would be members of local livestock shipping associations, and provision was also made for stocker and feeder companies to work in conjunction with the terminal livestock commission associations.

In launching the plan, it was hoped that it would soon embrace the already existing Farmers Union terminal commission firms and the Central Cooperative Association, an important "independent" commission firm operating on the St. Paul market. However, it proved impossible to achieve this desired unification, and it was not long before the National Livestock Producers Association headed a system of Farm Bureau sponsored and supported commission firms. Although the plan did not satisfy everybody, it provided a step forward in livestock marketing coordination, and, in the next several years, the National and its member commission houses enjoyed a considerable measure of success.[10]

Other Marketing Plans

Although the grain and livestock cooperative marketing plans attracted most attention, significant Farm Bureau marketing programs were undertaken for fruits and vegetables, wool, cotton, and dairy products.

Fruits and vegetables. In 1921, there were many local and regional fruit and vegetable marketing cooperatives, but there was little coordination of their operations. The leaders in the Farm Bureau felt that a national fruit and vegetable marketing organization was needed. In September, 1921, a Committee of 21 was appointed to study this problem, and as a result the Federated Fruit and Vegetable Growers, Inc., was established on January 1, 1923. The Federated took over a large commercial fruit and vegetable marketing organization and operated with fair success until the economic crash of 1929.

Wool. Many of the state farm bureaus were operating wool pools in 1920 and 1921. At the request of state farm bureau secretaries, a Committee of 25 was set up in 1921 which recommended the establishment of a national wool pool. Although some progress was made in coordinating the work of the state pools, it was not found practicable to set up a national wool pool.

Cotton. There was not the same need for a national marketing conference for cotton since the state farm bureaus in the cotton states, from mid-1920 on, had taken an active interest in forming Sapiro-type state cotton marketing cooperatives. After a few state organizations of this type had been started, representatives met in Oklahoma City on April 18, 1921, and tentatively set up a national overhead organization—the American Cotton Growers Exchange. A cotton belt conference, sponsored by the American Farm Bureau Federation, held in Memphis a week later, endorsed this cooperative cotton program already underway.

Dairy products. Likewise, there was no great need for the Farm Bureau to undertake a general dairy marketing program, for the National Cooperative Milk Producers Federation was already organized and doing a good job of coordinating dairy marketing cooperatives. With the agreement of the National Cooperative Milk Producers Federation, the American Farm Bureau Federation called a conference on dairy marketing in Chicago on May 3 and 4, 1921. As a result of this meeting, a Committee of 11 was set up in cooperation with the NCMPA which recommended that the AFBF set up a division of dairy marketing to assist dairy marketing organizations.[11]

In 1922, the American Farm Bureau Federation's Department of Research employed Dr. Theodore Macklin of the University of Wisconsin to make a general study of dairy marketing problems. His findings, issued in "Plans for Marketing Dairy Products Cooperatively" (1924) reviewed the general theory of cooperative marketing as it related to dairy products and recommended a general plan for the organization of federated dairy marketing cooperatives. Macklin said: "In contrast with the extreme centralized plan, the general plan presented in this report holds to the principle of commodity cooperative sales companies." However, there was no general effort to make practical application of this plan in Farm Bureau programs.

The foregoing discussion of Farm Bureau Marketing activities in 1921 and 1922 shows how energetically the Federation endeavored to develop cooperative marketing programs for various commodities. With the exception of the grain marketing program, these measures met with a considerable degree of success. It should also be noted that cooperative purchasing of fertilizer, seed, feed, and other farm supplies was a prominent activity of many of the state farm bureaus, although cooperative purchasing was not actively promoted by the American Farm Bureau Federation.[12]

"All Out for Cooperative Marketing"

Although chastened by the lack of success of the United States Grain Growers, Inc., cooperative marketing still dominated the stage when the American Farm Bureau Federation held its Fourth Annual Meeting on December 11-14, 1922. It was then decided to go "all out for cooperative marketing." The delegates adopted the following resolution.

RESOLVED, (1) That we urge further progress toward proper marketing of farm products as co-ordinate with economic production in equalizing the present handicap of the American farmers.

(2) That the American Farm Bureau Federation shall continue to give outstanding attention to the marketing problem and continue the policy of strengthening and encouraging co-operative commodity marketing organizations.

(3) That the American Farm Bureau Federation maintain a division of cooperative marketing, to be managed and directed by capable and experienced cooperative marketing specialists.

(4) That this division shall in every possible way stimulate and promote the cooperative marketing movement in the United States and shall plan and carry out an extensive national education campaign for cooperative marketing of farm products.

(5) That the American Farm Bureau Federation, acting through this division, shall formulate the fundamental principles of true commodity cooperation as exemplified in the history and experience of successful farmers' cooperatives and give the same wide circulation.

(6) That this division shall tender its services as counselor and advisor to state and district organizations, and agencies, on questions relating to type and plans of organization, campaign methods, problems of operation and other related subjects.

(7) That this division shall endeavor to unify or coordinate all organizations, agencies and interests in behalf of a comprehensive and united program of cooperative marketing in the United States.

(8) That the Farm Bureau Federations, National, State and County, should be active in educating producers of farm and livestock products to the advantages offered by the cooperative marketing agencies that have been and shall be established, stressing the fact that the success of these agencies depends primarily upon the loyalty and patronage of the producers themselves.

The incoming President of the American Farm Bureau Federation, Oscar E. Bradfute, declared:

Service through cooperative marketing—that is the program of the Farm Bureau for the next year. Cooperative marketing is trumps. All the departments, all the officials, and all the employees of the American Farm Bureau Federation will be expected to play the trump card . . .

President Bradfute took immediate action to implement the declared policy by appointing Walton Peteet, at a salary of $12,000, to head a new Cooperative Marketing Department. Peteet was well known for his effective work in promoting the cotton cooperatives in Texas and other southern states and he was prominent as a Farm Bureau leader. Upon acceptance of this position, Peteet submitted to President Bradfute a detailed outline of his plans for the department which provided for a comprehensive program "(1) to stimulate and promote cooperative marketing of farm products, and (2) to unify and coordinate cooperative marketing agencies." On his recommendation, Aaron Sapiro was employed in April 1922 as Cooperative Marketing Counsel.[13]

Peteet immediately "launched an intensive campaign of organization." According to O. M. Kile, who was active in the Farm Bureau organization at that time: "Peteet was here, there and everywhere, addressing big conferences, making radio speeches, advising groups how to organize and how to operate. As often as not, Aaron Sapiro—that black-haired, black-eyed, fiery and intolerant young lawyer from California—also appeared on the program and made one of his electrifying speeches that literally raised his auditors from their chairs."[14]

Just at this time the efforts of Peteet were furthered by the publication, under Farm Bureau auspices, of Herman Steen's book, *Cooperative Marketing: The Golden Rule in Agriculture* (New York: Doubleday, Page and Co., 1923).[15] This book came out in the spring of 1923 as the first volume of the American Farm Bureau Federation Library. In the introduction, Samuel R. Guard, Director of the Department of Information of the AFBF, said: "The Farm Bureau has vitalized cooperative marketing in America. The American Farm Bureau Federation, therefore, has honor as well as achievement in presenting to the public—consumers and producers of the products of the farm—the first book to be published under its official seal and insignia." This readable book was a propaganda *tour de force* for the Farm Bureau. It told how cooperatives of various kinds had grown up in the United States and Canada and provided useful information on the elements of their success and failure. Steen gave great credit to Aaron Sapiro as the "chief advocate" of the "California plan" of commodity cooperative marketing, "now generally recognized as the essential basis for all successful cooperative marketing."

Although Peteet's program was generally popular, it soon aroused the enmity of Secretary John Coverdale and others in top leadership positions within the Farm Bureau who felt that it put all of the Farm Bureau's eggs into one basket. They feared that Sapiro and his followers would soon dominate the Farm Bureau, and they believed that the Farm Bureau should place more of its emphasis on organizational work and general legislative and educational programs. As a result of this opposition within the Farm Bureau toward aggressive cooperative work, Peteet found it difficult to get adequate support from President Bradfute and the Executive Committee on his plan to develop a strong national cooperative commodity marketing program for wheat—a program which he considered of primary importance. Peteet was then advocating a commodity marketing wheat program comparable to the then popular cooperative cotton program to replace the ineffective operation of the U.S. Grain Growers, Inc. He tried to develop a plan and get it accepted by the Farm Bureau so that he could work on it, but he had no success since Coverdale and others in the Farm Bureau were still supporting the United States Grain Growers plan.

To understand this situation it must be appreciated that during 1923 the problem of strengthening the Farm Bureau as an organization assumed great importance, since its membership had fallen off and its resources consequently had dwindled. To meet this problem, a Department of Relations had been set up to deal with matters of organization and finance, and a series of organization conferences had been held in the spring in different sections of the country to "sell" the Farm Bureau. The Department of Relations believed that Farm Bureau's marketing efforts should be more closely tied into the support of the Farm Bureau as an organization, and it was a matter of much concern to it that many of the cooperative associations, stimulated and largely organized by the Farm Bureau, did not recognize a responsibility for supporting the Farm Bureau once they got underway. As a solution, the Department of Relations had set up a staff committee to work out a plan for contractual relationships between county and state farm bureaus and cooperative associations. This plan was presented in the American Farm Bureau *News Letter* of June 14, 1923, with the following statement: "If we are to solve this problem, we must bring about a definite understanding between the Farm Bureau and the cooperative organizations, especially in the future development of cooperative organizations in which the Farm Bureau is the predominant organizing and developing factor . . . " Suggested forms of contract were presented under which for a "definite financial considera- tion" the state and county farm bureaus would perform prescribed services for cooperative associations.

After the presentation of the plan, the Department of Relations made a survey to get the reactions of state farm bureau secretaries. The response was apathetic, although a number of state secretaries gave general approval and indicated that they were endeavoring to establish closer relations and understanding with the cooperatives.[16]

Stymied by the hesitation of the Executive Committee to act on his program for cooperative wheat marketing, Peteet finally succeeded in getting a meeting called of the Midwest farm bureau secretaries on July 9 to consider the grain marketing situation. This group passed a resolution which demanded:

(1) That the American Farm Bureau Federation be requested through its Coop- erative Marketing Department, to formulate a national grain marketing policy, based on organization of producers by states, with long-term contracts, pooling by grades on basis of milling value, corn to be dealt with separately, and that appropriate action be taken to conduct organization campaigns in the several grain growing states in the order of their readiness to begin such work.

(2) We request the Executive Committee of the U.S. Grain Growers to cooper- ate with the American Farm Bureau Federation in carrying out the program outlined above.

(3) That pending the organization of state cooperative grain marketing or- ganizations, as above, we approve the plan of the Board of Directors of U.S. Grain Growers, Inc., to engage in grain selling on the plan submitted to us today, the same to be merged into or supplanted by the organizations contemplated in paragraph 1 at such time as the latter are ready to begin operations.[17]

The foregoing resolution was accepted by the Department of Coopera- tive Marketing as the grain marketing policy of the American Farm Bureau Federation "by the advice and counsel of President Bradfute." Peteet immediately took steps to make it effective by conferring with Judge Bingham and other national cooperative leaders.

The National Wheat Conference

During this period, interest in a national program for grain marketing, along the lines of the Midwest Farm Bureau's resolution, was heightened by the National Wheat Conference held in Chicago on June 19-20, 1923.

This Conference had been called by a group of seven state governors, two U.S. Senators, the presidents of the three national farmers' organizations, and Aaron Sapiro for the ostensible purpose of finding ways to increase the consumption of wheat and wheat products. However, many of the speakers used this occasion to advocate cooperative marketing as a general solution for the agricultural problem. For example, Governor J. A. Preus of Minnesota, in opening the conference, said: "Let me say that I unqualifiedly and unreservedly stand for the principles of cooperative marketing. I conceive it the purpose and duty of any permanent organization that may grow out of this Conference to devote its working efforts to solving this problem." President Bradfute said: "Cooperative marketing has been approved by every department of our Government . . . It is now up to the farmers to make use of our opportunities." Alexander Legge, President, International Harvester Company, said: "To my mind, the most constructive movement under way at the present time for the relief of the farmer is the development of cooperative marketing." He finished his address with this paragraph:

> Cooperative purpose and action are essential, I believe, to any improvement in the situation of the wheat grower and of agriculture in general. Unless and until our farmers can effectively cooperate among themselves, how can they expect or hope to get outside cooperation? To my mind there lies the true problem of this conference and of all meetings and movements looking to the relief of agriculture—how to harness this proud, fine spirit of individualism and set it to pulling the load of agriculture in the direction of prosperity for the entire farming industry.[18]

Perhaps the most significant result of the Conference was the stimulation that it gave ex-Governor Frank O. Lowden and his friend Judge Robert W. Bingham to create a committee for the promotion of wheat marketing cooperatives. For some time, Lowden had been flirting with the idea of giving his support to cooperative commodity marketing, and the National Wheat Conference impressed upon him the fact that important business leaders were becoming deeply concerned with the seriousness of the wheat problem and friendly to cooperative commodity marketing as a means of its solution. He was thus receptive to an invitation from Bingham to explore with him, Peteet, Sapiro, and a few others what might be done.[19]

At the first meeting of this group, on October 3, it was tentatively agreed that there was need for a national organization to promote cooperative wheat marketing, and this led to a larger meeting in Chicago, called by Judge Bingham, on October 8.[20] At this conference it was unanimously agreed that "the only permanent solution of the wheat marketing problem of American Farmers was to organize cooperative marketing associations that would control the flow of wheat to market and by proper financing and merchandising methods stabilize the price at levels which will return profit to the growers." It was also agreed that this objective could "best be obtained through cooperative marketing associations, based on plans generally similar to the cotton and tobacco cooperatives of the south and central states and wheat cooperatives of the southwest and northwest, the form of organization to consist of state associations with long-term binding contracts and a system of pooling, state associations to be coordinated into national groups for large scale orderly marketing."[21]

The Wheat Growers Advisory Committee

To achieve this general aim, the conference decided to set up a propaganda organization to be called the Wheat Growers Advisory Committee. Governor Frank O. Lowden was to serve as Chairman and Aaron Sapiro as Legal Counsel. As the plan of the Committee seemed to be "in complete accord with the wheat marketing policy of the American Farm Bureau Federation," Peteet had pledged the support of the Federation "in carrying out our joint program."[22]

However, it soon became apparent that the establishment of the Wheat Growers Advisory Committee gave John Coverdale and other Farm Bureau opponents of Peteet and Sapiro just the opening they were looking for. They alleged that President Bradfute had been slighted by not being invited to the organization conference and that this was a Sapiro-Peteet move to take the leadership of the cooperative movement away from the Farm Bureau Federation. It was also insinuated that Lowden had been enticed to give his support to the new organization as a means of furthering his political ambitions for the Presidency in 1924, and that he was also scheming to obtain the Presidency of American Farm Bureau Federation at the forthcoming annual meeting.[23]

The dissension within the Farm Bureau on the wheat marketing program did not come to a head until the Executive Committee met in Chicago on December 8, and then supporters of Peteet and Sapiro held the upper hand. By a vote of 7 to 4 the Committee "fired"—that is, voted to accept the resignation of—John W. Coverdale as Secretary on the grounds that he had "usurped executive powers, had disregarded instructions of the Committee and had obstructed cooperative marketing work."[24] The Executive Committee meeting was held the week before the annual meeting of the American Farm Bureau Federation, and it was understood that a hot battle would be fought between the Coverdale and Peteet factions in the Convention—"with the outcome doubtful." Peteet desired a vote of endorsement for the Wheat Growers Advisory Committee, and Coverdale and his supporters were just as determined to stop this action and thus bring about the removal of both Peteet and Sapiro.[25]

Slow Down on Cooperative Marketing

President Bradfute's opening address on December 10, 1923, made clear that the American Farm Bureau Federation was drawing back from its all out campaign for cooperative marketing instituted a year before and that the "organization men" were gaining ascendency. He said:

> Two things seem uppermost . . . Organization and orderly marketing by cooperatives. Last year we started out by placing unusual emphasis on cooperative marketing, and we have kept that up all year, and I want to here register the fact that each and every department of the American Farm Bureau Federation was loyal in the support of that work . . . I make this statement in the face of the iniquitous stories which have emanated from some place unknown to me . . . It was hoped that a campaign for cooperative marketing would of itself stimulate organization in the states, but frankly, the results have been rather disappointing in that particular. Experience teaches that organization should precede marketing, or at least go hand in hand with it. I am therefore, recommending that you, this coming year, stress organization of at least equal importance, if not superior to that of marketing . . . I think it is pretty well agreed as to the plans for procedure in both organization and marketing, but the question which seems to confront you directors and is being widely advertised as splitting this organization in two, is not how, but who? Who is to have the glory, and who is to reap the pecuniary profits?[26]

It is also significant that one of the major addresses given at the convention was made by Aaron Sapiro. Compared to his dramatic speech at the Grain Marketing Conference three years earlier, it was a tempered presentation which recognized that all the "problems couldn't be solved in years." He said:

> It is going to take us from five to ten years to take any of the great major commodities and actually undo all the wrong systems of the last two or three generations. But if we can take some of the primary commodities of the United States and, by the right type of organization, actually introduce intelligent marketing instead of dumping . . . it is going to be the greatest piece of permanent work that the American Farm Bureau Federation has ever laid its strength and endorsement and personnel to in its entire history.

He closed his speech by saying:

> Men, I beg of you, stand with us in this work of building citizens. Keep the American Farm Bureau Federation doing community work, doing home work, building up the whole background of rural culture, and at the same time giving its great leadership to intelligent direction, so that the farmers of the United

States, by their own effort, can create their permanent prosperity and their own high standard of living. There is the story of cooperative marketing.[27]

The main issue of the convention came to a head in a resolution favoring the endorsement of the Wheat Growers Advisory Committee. Peteet, in defending the resolution, explained how he could have started a wheat marketing movement controlled solely by the Farm Bureau, had there been a definite policy looking toward that end adopted early in the year. However, since the plan of the Wheat Growers Advisory Committee coincided with the policy later adopted by the Federation, he felt authorized to aid in its work. He denied that President Bradfute had been slighted in the organization of the Wheat Growers Advisory Committee and he made it clear that defeat of the resolution would be deemed a demand for his resignation. When a decision was cut off by a motion to refer the resolution to the newly elected executive committee, it was apparent that it was dead. Peteet immediately took the floor and resigned.[28]

Before this resolution became an issue, Coverdale had got his revenge in the election of the Executive Committee, for only one of the seven committeemen who had voted for his discharge had been reelected. It was evident from this election and the action on the resolution that the ambitious program on cooperative marketing, undertaken a year before, had been effectively killed. When the Executive Committee met, just following the annual meeting, the matter of cooperative marketing policy was left for consideration at its next meeting to be held on January 21, 1924, and John Coverdale was reemployed as Secretary and Treasurer and made Director of the Department of Organization.[29]

In reporting on the meeting for *Wallaces' Farmer,* Donald R. Murphy said: "The feud that has been smoldering for a year in the American Farm Bureau Federation blazed out in the annual meeting at Chicago last week. The fight which ended the feud in decisive fashion took most of the time and energy of the delegates. The convention decided by an overwhelming vote that the Farm Bureau does not want to be tied up with the Sapiro type of national commodity marketing."[30] The *Prairie Farmer* of December 22, 1923, also carried a full article on the convention under the title, "Coverdale Wins Control of A.F.B.F." This article was very critical of the "caucus ridden" meeting which gave John Coverdale an Executive Committee, entirely "subservient" to him, and of the negative position taken on marketing policy. "No report was made as to the condition of the two marketing children of the Federation, The U.S. Grain Growers and the National Livestock Producers Federation, and no plans were made to ensure their effectiveness." At another point the article said: "The Federation has lost its leadership in the cooperative marketing field. The program will doubtless be chiefly educational, in line with Coverdale's policy. It does not seem likely that it will do anything effective to bring back prosperity to agriculture." However, the article charitably recognized that a young organization had to go through growing pains, and it closed on this hopeful note: "If the American Farm Bureau Federation can be put into the hands of men who will put service ahead of personal ambition . . . it may yet justify the faith of the American farmer in it." This faith was to be severely tested in 1924.

When the Executive Committee met on January 24, 1924, it drew up a formal declaration of farm bureau marketing policy, which declared:

> We are opposed to building from the top downward, as a general policy . . . We regard the American Farm Bureau and, in turn, the state and county or community farm bureaus as service organizations having an equal and impartial concern for every character of farmers' association . . . Impartial service to all cooperative associations presupposes a harmonious working relationship between the department of cooperative marketing and the department of organization in the National Farm Bureau . . . and this is hereby recognized and adopted as a basic principle of procedure in the work of the national organization.

The Executive Committee also proposed to find a director of commanding leadership for the Farm Bureau's Marketing Department to "insure the carrying forward of this program to a successful conclusion." It proved to be impossible to find such a man during the coming year. The issues of the *American Farm Bureau Weekly News Letter*, in the early months of 1924, provide evidence that cooperative marketing had lost its glamor as compared with McNary-Haugenism, and that John Coverdale was calling the shots with regard to cooperative marketing.[31]

The Grain Marketing Company

In view of the avowed opposition of the Executive Committee to building cooperatives from the top down, it is of interest that the officers of the Farm Bureau were beginning at this time to give consideration to an even more spectacular grain marketing plan. Several of the major commercial grain concerns in Chicago had conceived the idea of selling their properties to a cooperative to be set up by the Farm Bureau. They professed to believe that cooperation was the promise of the future. Their proposal, worked on quietly with officials of the Farm Bureau, was announced to the public in June 1924. A new cooperative organization—The Grain Marketing Company—was to be established and controlled by member farmer stockholders. It would take over the remnants of the U.S. Grain Growers, Inc., and so would bury that embarrassing corpse. It would acquire the properties of grain concerns valued at $25,000,000 to be paid for out of earnings in the years to come.

Although this plan originated in the grain companies, it was "nurtured," according to Kile, by Gray Silver, the Washington representative of the Farm Bureau, and apparently John Coverdale worked in active collaboration with him. It is of interest that Gray Silver and John Coverdale became respectively President and Secretary-Treasurer of the Grain Marketing Company.[32]

A vigorous campaign was undertaken to obtain farmer stockholders but support was not forthcoming. Farmers had been burned by the United States Grain Growers, Inc., and they were suspicious of the high-powered way in which the Company had been formed. The report on marketing work in the Farm Bureau for 1924 provides information on how the Grain Marketing Company came into being. "In April it became apparent to the Washington office, as well as the Chicago office, that two or three of the large grain marketing organizations were ready to cooperate with the grain producers in organizing a cooperative company." The proposed program was discussed by the legislative committee in session in Washington, and the Chairman then decided to call a meeting of the marketing committee to consider the proposition. The marketing committee examined the program on May 5-6 and requested that a detailed study be made. The Secretary, John Coverdale, was requested "to devote his full time—and to use other means of making a complete investigation." A report was presented in June to the Marketing Committee and, thereafter, to the Executive Committee. The latter thereupon appointed a special grain committee of five, consisting of: O. E. Bradfute, S. H. Thompson, J. F. Reed, Frank Evans, and Murray D. Lincoln to study the program, and the Secretary was directed to give his full attention to the development of the program. This committee met from July 7 to 12 and unanimously adopted resolutions which provided for the creation of the Grain Marketing Company. After this action, the Grain Marketing Company was set up and directors and officers were selected.

On August 14, the special grain committee met again and recommended to the Executive Committee that it commend: "the services of the Grain Marketing Company to the grain producers of the country." The Executive Committee thereupon passed the following resolution: "That the Executive Committee also does hereby endorse, commend and urge the use of the facilities of the Grain Marketing Company to farmers everywhere, either through their cooperative elevators, pools, agencies, private elevators, or directly, and that they affiliate with the Grain

Marketing Company so that they may participate in the patronage dividends and thus market their grain at cost."[33]

While the Grain Marketing Company was getting started it was under bitter attack from the Wheat Growers Advisory Committee and the National Council of Farmers' Cooperative Marketing Associations, and from some of the state farm bureau organizations. John J. Lacey in his history of the Farm Bureau in Illinois reports on this matter as follows:

> The IAA [Illinois Agricultural Association] did a great piece of work in 1924 by helping to stop in its tracks a plan to create another cooperative known as the Grain Marketing Company, following the failure of U.S. Grain Growers. The plan had the backing of the American Farm Bureau Federation. In fact, Gray Silver, Washington representative of the AFBF was named president of the new company, and John Coverdale, secretary-treasurer, with full approval of the AFBF Board of Directors. The IAA, with help from the Indiana Farm Bureau and a few others, showed the plan up for what it was, namely, a scheme under which a number of old-line grain companies would unload their properties upon the new cooperative at a price far in excess of their true value. This was one of the few occasions when the IAA had to oppose the AFBF. At the time, it seemed likely that the IAA would withdraw from the national organization, but cool heads prevailed and the breach was healed.[34]

A cynical and highly personal account of the organization and subsequent collapse of the Grain Marketing Company is given by Ralph Snyder who was a member of the Board of Directors of the American Farm Bureau Federation at the time.

> This company, was, in the minds of a great many farmers, conceived in sin and born of iniquity. It was the brain child of two firms on the Chicago Board of Trade . . . [who] succeeded in seducing a few of the leaders in the American Farm Bureau Federation . . . Plans were never very definite as to detail and I must admit that there was something alluring about it . . . It was certainly, in its attractive prospectus, "Big Business." To begin with, Gray Silver . . . was made President at $25,000 per year. John Coverdale of Iowa, at the time Secretary of the American Farm Bureau Federation, was made Secretary at the same salary. In the minds of the wheat growers . . . the "reason why" was quite evident.
>
> I hope I will be pardoned for reciting an incident that took place in the American Farm Bureau Federation Board meeting at this time . . . Mr. Coverdale submitted his resignation as Secretary. "But," he explained, "I am being well paid by the grain company and will not have too much to do. I can just as well continue to do the Secretarial work here and at no cost to the Bureau. . . . " Being a rather timid soul, I said nothing until the President was about to put the question . . . I explained briefly what might happen to us in case of a "blow-up" and that in any event we could not, even as hard up for cash as we were, afford to let anyone else pay our bills. I moved to accept the resignation, and that was all. This caused a rather acrimonious debate for an hour or so. When I finally got to my feet again, I said that sooner or later we would have to have Gray Silver's resignation too. Mr. Silver immediately tendered his resignation and it was included in my motion and finally carried. The Grain Marketing Company afterwards "dissolved" and, like the mule, it has no "pride of ancestry or hope of posterity. . . ."[35]

The Farm Bureau Moves Toward the McNary-Haugen Plan

The Convention of the American Farm Bureau Federation, in December 1924, was a rather listless affair. Coolidge had been reelected President, and President Bradfute had been named as a member of the Conference body that Coolidge had set up to work out a farm relief policy as promised during the campaign. The usual obeisance was shown toward cooperative marketing in resolutions, and pledges for its support were given. Surprisingly, the convention gave no special attention to the status of the Grain Marketing Company. At this time, interest in the McNary-Haugen form of farm relief was growing among state farm bureaus, but it did not yet have full official farm bureau blessing.[36]

In the summer of 1925, the Grain Marketing Company passed quietly out of existence. Under the plan of organization, grain producers were required to pay the vendors $4,000,000 within one year as payment for the properties involved. Since only a small amount of stock was sold to farmers, this proved impossible and the properties reverted to their former owners.

Marketing work by the Farm Bureau was practically suspended from December 1923 when Peteet resigned until January 1925 when a plan was formulated to give counsel and advice to cooperative associations, under Frank Evans, as General Marketing Counsel. In taking this post, Mr. Evans indicated that he was going "to emphasize the value of common sense methods." One of his first jobs was to prepare a bulletin on the law of cooperative marketing.

The annual meeting of December 1925 represented a significant break in Farm Bureau policy, for those in favor of McNary-Haugen type legislation gained clear ascendency. President Coolidge's much publicized address to the convention over a national radio hook-up, in which he urged farmers to place their trust in cooperative marketing and turn away from the idea of obtaining Government assistance in surplus control, fell on deaf ears.

The report of the General Marketing Counsel for 1926 made clear that the work of the Farm Bureau with cooperatives was now limited to assistance of a service character. During this year, the General Marketing Counsel had assisted in drawing up the provision of the 1926 Revenue Law for exempting cooperative associations from payment of income tax, had served as advisor on various measures proposed in Congress for agricultural relief having a direct bearing on cooperatives, and had addressed many meetings and done other things to assist and encourage the sound development of cooperatives of all types.

Thus, the intense interest of the A.F.B.F. in cooperative marketing, which reached a peak in the "all out" program of 1923, was gradually transmuted into a more generalized program of support for cooperatives. During this same period the cooperative commodity movement, after a vigorous expansion, began to recede as the McNary-Haugen movement gained adherents. This development will be examined in Chapter IV.

Chapter IV

THE EXPANSION AND SUBSIDENCE OF COMMODITY MARKETING: 1921-1925

Commodity cooperative marketing—as advocated by Aaron Sapiro —was spreading like a prairie fire as the year 1921 opened.[1] State-wide cotton cooperatives were being set up in Oklahoma and Texas, and tobacco growers in the Carolinas, Virginia, and Kentucky were on the verge of organization. The wheat pool idea was already established in the Pacific Northwest, and it was gaining adherents in the Great Plains region—even while the Committee of 17 was bringing forth the United Grain Growers. Let us now examine the rapid progress of this form of cooperative marketing during 1921 and 1922.

The Propagation of Commodity Cooperative Marketing

Cotton. Following the lead of Oklahoma and Texas, two other centralized cotton cooperatives were formed in 1921: The Arizona Pima Cotton Growers and the Staple Cotton Cooperative Association, for staple cotton growers in Mississippi. All of these associations were able to start marketing operations during 1921.

It will be recalled that Sapiro's plan, as presented at the first Montgomery Conference, called for the creation of a national cotton exchange to coordinate state efforts and serve the marketing and other overhead business needs of the state associations. A national exchange as stipulated in the plan was set up on August 1, 1921, when the American Cotton Growers Exchange, with headquarters in Memphis, was formed by the Oklahoma, Texas, and Arizona associations.

With the encouragement of the newly formed American Cotton Growers Exchange, plus the vigorous promotion of Aaron Sapiro, the movement expanded eastward in 1922 with the formation of state

54

associations in North and South Carolina, Alabama, Georgia, Arkansas, and Mississippi. By December 1922, there were 11 commodity coopera- tive associations formed, and 9 of them were members of the American Cotton Growers Exchange. In the promotion of most of these associations, the leadership was given by the newly formed state farm bureau federations, but generally all farm organizations, land grant colleges, state extension services, and other state and federal agencies gave their support. It was a combined agricultural effort.[2]

Tobacco. Although the impetus to the formation of the Tobacco Growers Cooperative Association, known as the Tri-State Association, came in late 1920, it was not incorporated until February 1, 1922, for an intensive campaign for members had first to be conducted. In August 1921, during this drive, the organization began publication of a monthly magazine, the *Tri-State Tobacco Grower,* to whip up enthusiasm and provide information on cooperative marketing to support the campaign. The North Carolina Agricultural Extension Service also gave support to this effort by issuing an Extension Circular, "Cooperative Marketing of Farm Products"; its author, B. W. Kilgore, Director of Extension for North Carolina was to become one of the prominent national leaders in the commodity cooperative marketing movement. Some idea of the pressure engendered in the sign-up campaign is given by one of the participants, Carl C. Taylor, then Professor at North Carolina State College: "The campaign became a crusade almost immediately. Agricul- tural extension officials, county agents, Smith-Hughes teachers, college professors, publishers of agricultural journals, newspapermen, lawyers, bankers, and merchants were used as speakers at local, county and district meetings. In some cases, all stores and other places of business were closed during the mass meetings of farmers at county seats and elsewhere."[3]

Although the Burley Tobacco Cooperative got started after the Tri- State, it was organized faster, and it was able to market the 1921 crop. Following the meeting of 50 prominent Kentuckians in Louisville on March 20, 1921, mentioned in Chapter I, plans were made for the organization of a tobacco marketing association, and an intensive drive for members was begun on July 20. Verna Elsinger gives us a graphic account of how the campaign was conducted.

> Campaign organization reached into every county in the Burley region. A meeting of county leaders was followed by an open mass meeting at which the plan of organization was presented and campaign officers elected. These, in turn, appointed precinct officers. A house-to-house canvas in every precinct took the message directly to each grower in the district. Bankers, business men, news- paper and professional men in the territory took an active part. Stores and

offices frequently closed their doors for a day or longer at a time, while their representatives assisted in campaign activities. Addresses by the leaders, Judge Bingham, Mr. (Ralph) Barker, Mr. (James C.) Stone and Mr. Sapiro, sometimes numbered three or four a day.[4]

By November 15, some 55,000 contracts, equivalent to 85 per cent of the 1920 production had been signed, and the Burley Association was in position to handle the 1921 crop. By agreement with the warehouses, the opening of the markets was postponed to January 26, 1922, to give the association time to make necessary arrangements for properties, financing, and personnel. It was no little job to meet the deadline and make all of the necessary arrangements for this complex business operation. One of the problems was to ensure legality of the marketing contracts to be used. This was met by securing the passage, by unanimous vote, of the Bingham Cooperative Marketing Act on January 10, seven days after it had been introduced as a bill.[5] In order to finance the organization during its initial period, Judge Bingham personally pledged $1 million. His challenge was met by Kentucky bankers who subscribed $5.5 million in what was termed "The Burley Growers Liberty Loan." With plans well made, and competent management arranged for, the Burley association met with a considerable measure of success in marketing the 1921 crop during the year 1922.[6]

The apparent success of the Burley Association in central Kentucky soon encouraged the dark-fired tobacco growers of Kentucky, Tennessee, and Indiana to set up a like association. With the encouragement and active support of Judge Bingham and Aaron Sapiro, a whirlwind campaign signed up nearly 57,000 dark tobacco growers, or over two-thirds of the total, by October 28, 1922, and the Dark Tobacco Growers Association was formed on November 22, 1922. It was ready for business when the markets opened on January 1, 1923.[7]

Wheat. Wheat growers in the fall of 1920 had hoped that the Committee of 17 would develop a satisfactory wheat marketing plan, but when it became clear in early 1921 that pooling was to play but a subordinate part in the plan, the National Wheat Growers Association proceeded to promote wheat pools in Kansas, Nebraska, Colorado, and other major wheat producing states. At about this same time, the wheat pools in Oregon, Washington, Idaho, and Montana informally set up an overhead agency, the Northwest Wheat Growers, Associated, to provide themselves with central selling services. In February 1922, the leaders of the National joined forces with the leaders of the Northwest to form the American Wheat Growers, Associated. George C. Jewett, the manager of the Northwest, became Manager of the American, while W. H.

McGreevy, the National's Secretary, became its Secretary. The American was designed to coordinate the operations of all state wheat pooling associations and provide them with central selling services. However, three of the state associations formed in 1921 did not join the American —the Oklahoma and Texas pools set up their own sales agency—the Southwest Wheat Growers, Associated—while Kansas remained independent. By the end of 1922, there were nine wheat pools in operation.[8]

It is not possible here to describe all of the problems that had to be met by the commodity cooperative marketing associations, so rapidly set up in the early 1920's. Documents of organization and marketing contracts with members had to be drafted, and directors, officers, and management personnel had to be provided. Nothing of the kind had ever been attempted so rapidly and on such a large scale before, and it would have been a miracle if everything had run smoothly. Not only did markets and business procedures have to be established by an inexperienced group, but arrangements had to be made for the proper handling and accounting of the large volume of growers' business represented and for financing the commodity while it was being marketed over a period of time. Furthermore, the commodity marketing cooperatives represented an experiment in democracy as well as in business, for tens of thousands of farmers had to be educated to their responsibilities as members, while a satisfactory marketing service was being provided them. To make a long story short, the various associations for cotton, tobacco, wheat, and other commodities were able to establish themselves with a considerable measure of success within a comparatively short time.

The Heyday of Commodity Cooperative Marketing

Elated by the success of the Burley Tobacco Association's first year of operations and by the progress being made by the cotton, wheat, and other commodity marketing associations, Judge Bingham, fronting for Aaron Sapiro, and a group of like-minded cooperative leaders issued a call for a national cooperative marketing conference to be held in Washington, D.C., on December 14, 15, and 16, 1922. The primary purpose of the Conference was to form a national organization to promote the interests of the commodity cooperative marketing movement, and, prior to the Conference, an organization had been set up tentatively under the name National Council of Farmers' Cooperative Marketing Associations. As Chairman of this incipient organization, Judge Bingham had called the First National Cooperative Marketing Conference.

This meeting brought together representatives of most of the large regional cooperatives that then subscribed to the commodity marketing philosophy—cotton, tobacco, wheat, rice, peanut, dried fruit, potato, and dairy marketing associations, as well as representatives of the three national farm organizations. It was claimed that the cooperatives represented over a million farm producers and over a billion dollars worth of annual business. Conspicuously absent were representatives from the California Fruit Growers Exchange and other large federated marketing cooperatives, and the many local cooperatives, not members of federations.

The Conference signalled that "commodity marketing" had arrived. This was evidenced by a statement sent to the Conference by President Harding in which he said: "I know of no single movement that promises more help toward the present relief and permanent betterment of agricultural conditions than this one."

In his opening statement, as Temporary Chairman of the Conference, Judge Bingham indicated that in his study of cooperation he sought to find the best informed man on the subject and he had "found that man," who he then presented as the keynote speaker—"the one expert in the world on this subject, and the one man to whom the farmers' cooperatives owe the most—Mr. Aaron Sapiro." Mr. Sapiro then rose to the occasion by saying to his audience: "You are the turning point of the most important development in agriculture, and therefore in American life . . . " In his address, on the subject "The Farmer Is Cooperating" Sapiro reviewed the significant results already obtained through cooperative marketing and said: "Of the great industries, tobacco first, and cotton second, have learned to dominate their group through cooperative merchandising methods." He turned to the "key of the meeting," the need for a national organization of cooperatives that would "set up a permanent mouthpiece of their own" to deal exclusively with their problems.

The commodity marketing cooperatives then enjoyed the confidence of the United States Department of Agriculture. Secretary of Agriculture, Henry C. Wallace, in addressing the meeting said:

> We have to get our agriculture now on a sound, businesslike, profitable basis, one year with another, and the task of you gentlemen who are interested in cooperative marketing and the organization of *commodity marketing associations* is a task which may well challenge the very highest ability in the whole agricultural world, and a task which is at once a challenge and an inspiration to every man who wants to render a really effective service (Italics added).

At the conclusion of the three-day meeting, the associations, informally represented, voted unanimously to form the National Council as a permanent organization of commodity marketing associations. The Convention set up an executive committee of 15 under the Chairmanship of

Judge Bingham, to work out the "exact scope and details" for the permanent organization and to send the plan for ratification to all commodity cooperative associations. The Executive Committee was authorized to open an office and was to function until May 1, 1923, when the detailed plan of organization activities was to become effective. The Council was to "consider and handle the problems that are common to and directly affect cooperative marketing associations. It will not parallel or overlap the activities of any other farm organization."[9]

Just prior to the first National Cooperative Marketing Conference, the American Farm Bureau Federation had decided to go "all out for cooperative marketing" as recounted in Chapter III. In view of this development, which soon enlisted the energies of Aaron Sapiro, the National Council of Farmers' Cooperative Marketing Associations made no effort to start up officially, although the requisite number of cooperatives subscribed to the permanent plan of organization and meetings of the Executive Committee were held. We will later observe how the National Council took over leadership in commodity cooperative marketing in January 1924, after the American Farm Bureau Federation gave up its dominant position in this field.

During 1923, the commodity cooperative marketing cooperatives continued to expand with Farm Bureau encouragement. The cooperatives for cotton, tobacco, wheat, and many other commodities started in 1922 began operations, and many new associations were formed by other commodity groups. Progress was especially marked by the cotton and tobacco cooperatives. The membership of the cotton associations increased from 150,000 in 1922 to 220,000 in 1923, while the number of bales of cotton handled increased from 749,000 to 937,000. In 1923, the tobacco cooperatives handled 671,000,000 pounds of tobacco or 44 per cent of the total crop as compared with 546,000,000 pounds in 1922.[10] Although the wheat pools handled less grain than in 1922, the formation of the Wheat Growers' Advisory Committee, in late 1923, under the Chairmanship of Governor Frank O. Lowden, promised to invigorate the organization of grain growers.

Freed from their commitment to the Farm Bureau in December 1923, Peteet and Sapiro could now devote their full energies to the development and work of the National Council of Farmers' Cooperative Marketing Associations. The Executive Committee of the Council, which had functioned informally, thereupon made plans to get the Council into operation by placing Walton Peteet in charge, on January 1, 1924, as full-time Secretary and Executive Officer and by arranging for a second National Cooperative Marketing Conference.

Supporters of the National Council were in an optimistic mood when the Second National Conference was held in Washington, D.C., on February 7, 8, and 9, 1924, for the competence of Peteet as a cooperative organizer and promoter was widely recognized and the field for cooperative development was now wide open. This was noted by the *Prairie Farmer* of January 5, in an article entitled: "Progress in Cooperative Marketing," with the sub-title "National Council of Cooperatives to Take Leadership." This article said:

> The council has been dormant since its creation a year ago, largely to give the American Farm Bureau Federation and other Farm Organizations an opportunity to prove or disprove their leadership in the cooperative marketing field. Since the American Farm Bureau Federation disbanded its cooperative marketing department in December, there has been a strong demand from cooperative groups all over the United States for the National Council to take over the active leadership of their work.

President Coolidge gave the Council his blessing by saying in a message to the Conference: "I have many times declared my conviction that the development of a powerful cooperative movement in this country is one of the needs of this period of economic readjustment." He assured the Conference of his great interest in "the work it is organizing." Later in his message he said: "There is need for cooperative organizations among agricultural producers to help them both in selling their products for a better price and buying their requirements more cheaply."[11]

In his opening address to the Second Conference, Judge Bingham discussed the aims and plans of National Council. He said:

> The real reason behind the organization of this National Council, which had its first meeting in December 1922, was to provide an entirely different type of organization composed in the main of those technical experts, who, as representatives of cooperative marketing throughout the country, have been able to demonstrate that there is a sound, feasible, practicable method of bringing permanent relief to the greatest of all our industries.
>
> .   .   .   .
>
> What we are trying to do is to teach the farmers of this country to learn to merchandise their products, to get away from the old, fatal, and futile methods of dumping, and to apply the common, well-known, sound business methods of merchandising their crops, which are applied by every other, or every successful, business in the country. We want, too, *to clearly draw a line and make a distinction between genuine commodity cooperative marketing* and the mere forms of local co-operation, which have been of some advantage, but which cannot reach the root of this problem (Italics added).[12]

Bingham recognized a growing opposition to commodity marketing from competitive trade interests. He said: "The larger the movement grows, the more bitter, the more violent the opposition to our position is bound to be." An ominous note was struck by Governor Lowden who intimated that the Department of Agriculture was not giving commodity marketing its full support. He attributed this to subordinates in the Department rather than to Secretary Wallace. He went on to say:

> It is said that the Department is supported by the taxpayer's money and that, therefore, it cannot favor any particular method of marketing. If, however, a new system of marketing is vital to the well-being of the farmer, the Department should give that method its whole-hearted support . . . Cooperative marketing may be said rightfully to be the present policy of the Government. Congress enacted a law expressly to authorize the movement. The President . . . approves the movement. And so, despite objections by those personally interested, I can see no reason why the Department of Agriculture should not heartily approve of the principle, thus releasing the large army of county agents who would gladly assist in the great work without any neglect to their other duties.[13]

The occasion for this blast was a press release issued by the Department in connection with the publication of a report on the California Fruit Growers Exchange which was considered to show favoritism to the federated type of cooperative marketing.[14] This was the background for an address to the Conference by Secretary Wallace on the subject: "The United States Department of Agriculture and Cooperative Marketing." In this, Wallace pointed out the various ways in which the Department was giving its support to cooperative marketing. Then he said:

> From what I have said, I hope it will be clear to you that the Department believes in the cooperative marketing of farm products, desires to be helpful to the largest possible degree, giving information as to the sound organization of co-operatives, and proposes to be of all, of the largest possible service to them when organized.

He went on to say:

> There are limits beyond which the Department cannot properly pass in the field of organization of cooperative associations. The Department is primarily an institution for the conduct of scientific research and the dissemination of the knowledge thus gained. Practically all of its activities grow out of scientific research. It is conducted under the authority of certain federal laws. It is supported by the taxes levied upon all of the people. It cannot, therefore, properly take part in the work of organization of business activities, cooperative or otherwise. . . . So it is in the work of the Department with relation to cooperative enterprises. We can properly seek out and make available sound principles upon which successful cooperation depends. We can point out conditions which make for success and those which make for failure. We can present historical facts which ought to help those who are interested in the organization and conduct of cooperative enterprise to profit from the experience of similar efforts in the past, both in this country and abroad. But it is no more a part of the duty of the Department to engage in the work of organization than it is a part of the duty to go into the fields and plow, sow or reap . . .

> Frequently the criticism is made that the Department of Agriculture is not in sympathy with cooperative commodity marketing. Most of the critics very generously absolve me personally, but insist that the spirit of the Department is not sympathetic.[15]

Wallace refused to admit this charge. He maintained that the attitude of the Department was sympathetic to all forms of cooperation—"commodity or otherwise." He added: "I regard true cooperation as applied Christianity."[16]

The discussions of the Second National Cooperative Marketing Conference indicated that the problems of operation were becoming more important that those of organization. One of the important talks was on "Field Service as a Factor in Successful Cooperative Marketing," by C. O. Moser, Secretary of the American Cotton Growers Exchange. Verna Elsinger, in charge of community organization for the Burley Tobacco Growers Association, spoke on "Social and Community Service of the Burley Tobacco Growers Association." Calling for a program of more education for cooperative members, she said: "Ultimately the test of cooperation must lie in the strength and loyalty of its membership." Several talks were devoted to improving information services for members. Another important talk stressed the value of better cooperative accounting systems.

The following resolutions passed by the Conference reflected the interests of the associations represented.

> That the principal economic difficulty of farmers at this time is the lack of an efficient system of marketing their products and the remedy is a system of cooperative marketing which will enable farmers to carry on marketing processes in commodity groups in ways that will permit orderly selling or merchandising in place of the wasteful and expensive practice of dumping and blind selling.

> We believe that cooperative marketing associations should be organized by farmers and owned and controlled by them.

> That we are opposed to all forms of price fixing by Government; first, because it would be a perversion of Government authority and would ultimately bring ruin to farmers and endanger the Government; and second, because if the principle of government control of prices of farm products should be established, producers of agricultural products being, in the case of each commodity, a minority of the total population, would be compelled to accept prices fixed by a consumers' majority.

> That we endorse heartily the efforts of our executive committee to secure for the *commodity cooperative movement,* full and sympathetic support of the U.S. Department of Agriculture, the State Colleges of Agriculture and the State Bureaus of Markets, and we hereby instruct them to continue their efforts in that respect (Italics added).

> That we express our sincere appreciation of the splendid service rendered to American agriculture by Aaron Sapiro in the development and fearless cham-

pionship of *the fundamental principles of cooperative commodity marketing.*
Through his broad knowledge of law, economics and agriculture he has made a
contribution to the cause of cooperative marketing of inestimable value (Italics
added).

The final resolution reflected the acclaim that Aaron Sapiro then
enjoyed with the commodity marketing cooperatives he had been
instrumental in forming.

Following the Conference, Peteet devoted his full energies to the work
of the Council as provided for by the organization agreement developed
by the Executive Committee of 15.[17] This agreement set forth the
purposes and aims of the Council as follows:

> a—to establish contacts between cooperative marketing associations and to
> enable such associations to consider and handle common problems directly af-
> fecting them;
> b—to supply the various associations with news items about cooperative
> marketing for use in their official organs or for use in general publicity;
> c—to compile all possible information in reference to cooperative marketing,
> for use by existing cooperative groups or agricultural colleges or groups which
> may become interested;
> d—to develop national publicity by special articles or otherwise on the
> aims, purposes, methods and results of cooperative marketing;
> e—to establish contacts in Washington and elsewhere for cooperative mar-
> keting associations with the Federal Executive Department, the Department of
> Agriculture, the Department of Commerce, the Interstate Commerce Bureau,
> the Federal Trade Commission, various government bureaus and Congress on
> matters that directly affect cooperative marketing associations;
> f—to enable cooperative associations to form definite policies in reference
> to legislative matters and to put them in contact with other groups to help secure
> the passage of proper legislation by the States or Federal Congress;
> g—to furnish correct and reliable information to farmer groups throughout
> the country as to the forms of organizations and tendencies of modern coopera-
> tive marketing movements;
> h—generally, to enable cooperative marketing associations to unite for the
> purpose of expressing and furthering the fundamental aims, activities, and
> needs of this movement.[18]

Peteet was able to achieve considerable progress in all of these areas
during 1924. Help was given in the organization of new cooperatives, and
existing associations were advised on problems of law, finance, membership education, field service, management, accounting, and publicity. The
members were kept informed by monthly reports and circulars on matters
of common interest so that the Council Office became, in effect, a
coordinating center for the member associations.[19]

In Chapter III we pointed out how the formation of the Wheat
Growers Advisory Committee, in the fall of 1923, had brought about the
disruption of the cooperative program of the American Farm Bureau
Federation. The work started by the Committee under Governor Lowden

was actively supported by the Council in early 1924. An able speaker, with a magnificent voice and commanding presence, Lowden covered the grain producing regions preaching the gospel of commodity marketing. Although the Committee did effective work in helping to organize the Indiana Wheat Pool and in helping to consolidate wheat pooling efforts in Kansas, it did not meet the full expectations of Lowden who came to realize that cooperative marketing could not be effectively promoted from the outside by high pressure methods. By early summer, funds for financing the work of the Committee ran low, and, in view of the coming national elections and excellent crop prospects that made farmers less receptive to cooperative action, it was decided to disband the Committee. As we will see later, this experience eventually made Lowden receptive to George Peek's view that the surplus problem could only be handled by cooperatives with government assistance, but he did not immediately give his support to the McNary-Haugen plan.

The commodity cooperative marketing movement reached the peak of its development in 1924. Most of the major commodity cooperative marketing associations appeared to be making substantial gains and several new ones were formed. In his annual report for 1924 as Secretary, Peteet said:

> The year just closed has been a settling down and testing out period for many new cooperative associations . . . and a fighting time for cooperatives everywhere . . . On the whole, the cooperative movement is in better shape than it has ever been. Many of the more important associations have passed beyond the experimental state and are now recognized as legitimate and permanent parts of the commercial system . . .[20]

He maintained that many scattered and isolated cooperatives were being welded or fused "into a homogeneous movement with a common spirit and unified aims and purposes."

The general progress of commodity cooperative marketing and of the National Council was likewise expressed in Judge Bingham's opening address to the Third National Cooperative Marketing Conference, held in Washington, D.C., January 5, 6, 7, 8, 1925. He said:

> The growth of commodity organizations in these last three or four years has been simply extraordinary, widening out over the whole country from Texas to Maine, from the West to the East, involving the great essential crops. This Council today has more than 600,000 grower-members. It is today, the largest farmers' organization in the United States, much the largest. It is an organization not in conflict in any way with any other farmers' organization, but one devoted directly and specifically to the business of merchandising the products of the farm. It has been kept entirely free from any sort of political aspect . . . [21]

At this time American cooperative leaders were being thrilled and inspired by the remarkable achievements of the Canadian Wheat pools which had been built during 1923 and 1924 with the assistance of Aaron Sapiro. They were in the limelight as a great demonstration of what could be done with all hands on the wheel. Sapiro was very proud of this demonstration of commodity marketing which had followed his formula to the letter. During the Conference he said: "In Canada they have sewed up over fifty per cent of the wheat acreage . . . under five year contracts, a thing that was scoffed at in the United States when it was first suggested and was declared to be impossible . . . So, if Canada has done that, we can do that, and we will do it if the groups here determine that it shall be done, and will begin to guide the American Farmer to that end."[22]

However, not all was as calm as appeared on the surface. Difficulties had arisen in the operation of several of the larger associations, and there was evidence that to some extent the movement was going on the defensive. The period of promotion had given way to the necessity of proving the efficiency of theory in practice, and the weaknesses of excessive promotional activity were beginning to show up. This situation had been evident in the activities of Secretary Peteet during the year, in endeavoring to strengthen organizational and financial structures, to improve field work and publicity techniques and management and membership education.

Of great concern to the Council during the year had been the beginning of an organized campaign of opposition to cooperative marketing led by the "grain trade" and other vested business interests. Most serious was the attack on Aaron Sapiro—and thus on cooperative marketing—then being waged by Henry Ford's weekly magazine, the *Dearborn Independent*. The position of the Council on this attack was reflected in Peteet's comments in his annual report:

> The most spectacular, as well as the vilest attack of the year upon cooperative marketing was that made by Henry Ford's paper, the *Dearborn Independent*. For utter villainy, that series of articles is without a parallel in the history of American journalism. Under a thin disguise of an attack upon Aaron Sapiro, a malignant assault has been made upon the fundamental principles and honest practices of cooperative marketing associations and a vast number of lies, insinuations and innuendos have been put in printed form for convenient and widespread circulation by the enemies of the movement. Aaron Sapiro has been made to suffer vicariously not only for his race and religion, but for the cooperative marketing movement. The value of his services to the movement may be measured by the malignity of these attacks upon him . . .

While the National Council of Farmers' Cooperative Marketing Associations had carried on a vigorous publicity program to counter the charges made against Sapiro and the cooperative movement, it was admitted by Peteet that much harm had been done. He said: "This attack has temporarily hurt the cooperative movement by creating doubt and suspicion in the minds of some who were not in position to know of its utter falsity and of the malice and intrigue which prompted it. It has also forged a weapon in the form of printed matter, which will for a long time be used by the enemies of cooperatives whenever and wherever membership campaigns are conducted." As foretold by Peteet, this malicious attack was to impair Sapiro's usefulness and have an unfortunate effect on public support for cooperatives, for unsupported insinuations, widely disseminated, can create myths that cannot be answered by facts before they have done much harm.[23]

In view of the allegations made against Sapiro and other prominent cooperative leaders in the current articles of the Dearborn Independent, it was encouraging to have talks at the Conference by President Coolidge; Secretary of Commerce, Herbert Hoover; and Secretary of Agriculture, Albert Gore—in which they affirmed their faith in the cooperative movement. President Coolidge in his address said:

> There has been too much tendency to surround cooperative organization and processes with mystery. It has ben announced solemnly and sepulchrally from the hollow depths of self-constituted oracles, that Americans are not the sort of people who possess the genius for cooperation. We have been assured that they are too individualistic, too loath to yield any part of their independence and initiative. People who indulge this kind of nonsense invariably assume that cooperation is a new and comparatively untried formula. Their whole treatment of it proves that they have not caught the idea ... They have overlooked the fact that all human society is a vast system of cooperation and cooperations. From its simplest to its most complex manifestations, there is nothing to it but cooperation. It began with the discovery that two people could together roll a heavier stone or move a bigger log, than could be done by one alone ... The truth is, and it cannot be too often or earnestly emphasized, that cooperation is the earliest of man's social discoveries, the one that has served him beyond all others in making material progress . . . There could be no civilization without cooperation. To charge that any particular people lacks in capacity for cooperation is to charge that it has not been civilized. To allege that against the American people is to deny all of the obvious facts about our country. . . .[24]
>
> To precisely such men and women as you who are gathered here, we must turn for the kind of agricultural leadership the country needs. We want combination preached as a principle, not a panacea. It will not perform miracles. It will not accomplish the impossible. But it is a sound, tried, demonstrated principle that must be introduced [as] the basis of agricultural establishment. It demands that the individual shall surrender some part of his complete independence for his own and for the general good . . . The cooperative association which establishes grades and standards, encourages the good and eliminates the poor varieties, increases the efficiency of production, provides a unified product adapted to its market, organizes its distribution, creates confidence in its products and its methods—that kind of an association is doing the best that cooperation can do . . .
>
> As a last word, let me assure you again of the profound sympathy which your Government feels for all your efforts, and its eager purpose to help in every practical way the achievement of the ends you are seeking.[25]

When the Council was meeting in January 1925, there was much interest in the forthcoming report of President Coolidge's Agricultural Conference. Many cooperatives represented in the Council feared that some of the recommendations of the Conference would prove more harmful than helpful. While they were very much opposed to any type of McNary-Haugen legislation, they were just as much opposed to legislation that would make cooperatives in any way subservient to the federal government. Sapiro voiced the anxieties of the Council in this regard in an address on "State and Federal Legislation Relating to Cooperative Marketing." He said:

> . . . The Williams bill is the bill that is being pushed with most cleverness and most skill. The Williams bill is the one which is supposed to be very close to the hearts of certain men on the Agricultural Committee. The Williams bill is the one about which the gossip has spread that it is to be reported out and be recommended to Congress.[26]

Sapiro criticized the Williams Bill on several counts: that it would group speculators with cooperatives, that it would endanger benefits enjoyed under the Capper-Volstead Act, that it would jeopardize farmer-control of cooperatives, and that it would encourage waste of government money. He summarized his comments on the bill by saying: "I am against the Williams Bill because I tell you it involves illegal arrangements. I further tell you that it is another one of the attempts to have the United States Government dominate the marketing of farm crops instead of leaving the marketing of farm crops to the groups of farmers themselves, who can do it better than the Government."[27]

As we will see in Chapter VI, the opposition of the National Council of Farmers' Cooperative Marketing Associations and other strong cooperatives largely defeated the "Williams Bill" recommendations of the Agricultural Conference. This was a high water mark in achievement for the National Council of Farmers' Cooperative Marketing Associations which was then at its full power.

The Disintegration of the Commodity Marketing Movement

During 1925, the problems of the commodity marketing cooperatives grew in intensity, and members became restive as payments were delayed until their crops were sold. Iron-clad marketing agreements were of little avail when there was a widespread opposition to their enforcement. The Dark Tobacco Growers' Cooperative Association was the first to show weakness when its directors passed a resolution in October 1925 stating that no legal action would be taken against a member selling his crop outside the association. At this time it was becoming clear that the Burley and Tri-State Associations could not go on without drastic reorganization. Moreover, several of the cotton, wheat, and other commodity-type marketing cooperatives were also having serious management and membership problems.

Under Peteet's leadership the National Council intensified educational and other efforts to improve conditions. It was then believed that most of the problems represented growing pains that would be alleviated as the cooperatives learned how to deal with them and increased in organizational and marketing efficiency.

When the National Council held its Fourth Cooperative Marketing Conference on January 12, 13, 14, 15, 1926, the perilous condition of the major tobacco cooperatives was not generally known but in the inner circles of the Council it was a factor that contributed to the malaise of the meeting, for the tobacco associations until then had been the dominant examples of successful commodity cooperative marketing.

The seriousness of the situation was not evidenced in the annual report of Peteet as Council Secretary. He said: "The year just closed has been a period of expansion of service of cooperatives rather than of expansion in number and membership. The organization of new cooperatives has gone steadily on and many associations have increased their membership, but considered as a whole, growth has been in the direction of efficiency and integration of services rather than of size." However, it soon became evident in the meeting that a serious rift was developing within the leadership of the National Council. One faction, largely represented by the cotton and grain cooperatives, was becoming convinced that some kind of surplus control legislation of the McNary-Haugen type was needed to supplement cooperative efforts if prices of farm commodities were to be stabilized and raised. This line of thinking was unacceptable to Sapiro and Bingham who held steadfast to the belief that commodity cooperative marketing, if properly developed, could best serve the farmers' interests.

It was significant that even Governor Lowden, stout friend of commodity cooperative marketing, admitted that "it will be many years . . . before the cooperatives of the staple farm products are sufficiently organized to take care of this present problem of surplus . . . " He then made this suggestion:

> Suppose we had a federal farm board. Suppose that board should find that the producers of any farm commodity were sufficiently organized as to be really representative of all the producers of that commodity. Suppose that when it had ascertained this fact it should authorize such organized producers to take care of the surplus, either storing it to so meet a possible future domestic need

or exporting it upon the best terms available, the expenses and losses incurred for storage or export to be borne proportionately by all the producers of that particular commodity. Such a board could function successfully, in my opinion only if it operated through and in hearty sympathy with cooperative commodity associations. We could expect to prevent ruinous over-production only through such associations. It is vital to any plan, therefore, that it should be so formed as to strengthen and not to weaken the cooperative movement.[28]

This suggestion was simply the McNary-Haugen plan revised so that it would operate through and with the assistance of cooperatives. Governor Lowden did not spring this idea on the spur of the moment. During the preceding months he had been increasingly impressed with the arguments of George Peek, and a number of cooperatives were veering in this direction.[29] Even Walton Peteet had become convinced that this was the right approach.[30]

Lowden's talk gave great support to those who were veering toward the McNary-Haugen camp. The address of Judge Bingham went further. It infuriated them and alienated them from the Council. Bingham said:

The most important thing that has happened in cooperative marketing during the past year has not happened inside of the cooperative marketing movement itself. It has been the unreserved recognition of cooperative marketing by the President of the United States and the Secretary of Agriculture . . . The President has courageously and effectively announced his approval and advocacy of cooperative marketing. *The leader of the cooperative movement in this country now sits in the White House;* and we who have dreamed and hoped for this day— we must now follow that leader (Italics added).[31]

In his talk, Sapiro endeavored to mollify the group by endorsing fully the Jardine Bill that would set up a Division of Cooperative Marketing, while opposing legislation of the McNary-Haugen type. He concluded with this paragraph:

Men and women, my conclusion is this: get behind the Jardine bill as the one piece of legislation of this session. Don't ignore the surplus problem. Recognize it and respect it, but let's find what is within ourselves to solve that problem before leaning on Government . . . I hope we will put through the legislation that will let the Department of Agriculture help us on cooperative marketing. I hope we may solve the surplus question, but I hope we will solve it in our way and not in the way of politicians.[32]

The resolutions adopted by the Convention could not ignore the surplus problem. Provision was made for a special committee to consider the problems arising out of the surplus. The report of this committee was to be submitted to member associations for a referendum vote at the earliest possible date, and the final decision of such vote was to be the expressed policy of the National Council for the ensuing year. This vote was never taken, for the Council was in a state of dissolution following the Conference.

The main troubles of the Council lay beneath the surface. Sapiro had gradually antagonized many of the other cooperative leaders by his arbitrary methods, and it was charged that he was largely running the Council.[33] Moreover, a serious conflict had developed between Sapiro and Bingham and Peteet, in which Sapiro and Bingham charged Peteet with giving aid and comfort to the McNary-Haugen group.[34] A meeting of the executive committee held during the convention disclosed the deep-seated discontent of some of the member organizations. Some were highly critical of Bingham's statement that "the leader of the cooperative movement in this country now sits in the White House." As Coolidge was little respected by cooperatives favorable to McNary-Haugen legislation, this had fired their bitterness.

Although the National Council continued to function for several months after the Fourth National Conference, its usefulness had largely been destroyed by the dissention in its ranks. Peteet and his close associate, Robin Hood, endeavored to reorganize the Council so that it would be more representative of all agricultural cooperatives, but the residue of bitterness from the Fourth Conference made revival impossible, and the Council passed out of existence in the early fall.

An important factor that contributed to the disintegration of the National Council was the collapse during the spring of the three major tobacco cooperatives who were its mainstays. Their discontinuance was primarily due to their inability to maintain market control through membership contracts although many other factors contributed.[35]

Sapiro, himself, admitted the failure of the commodity marketing movement in an address at the meetings of the American Institute of Cooperation held on the St. Paul campus of the University of Minnesota in the summer of 1926. He said:

" . . . I do not know of a single year in which cooperatives have had to face such black calamities as they have in this year. In the first place, there has been a very general collapse of interest in cooperative marketing." He attributed the obvious paralysis of cooperative growth, which had been marked by the recent failure of the large tobacco and potato cooperatives, to a deflection of the farmer's interest into political channels and the lack of a real educational program that would teach farmers the full meaning of cooperation. On this he said: "You cannot succeed unless you do real educational work among the farmers, and you cannot do it unless you yourselves carry it in your hearts . . . When we have instilled into the minds and hearts of the American farmer the great idea of cooperative marketing as a part of cooperative living, I believe then that cooperation will be here to stay, and we will then have achieved the great end at which we are all aiming."[36]

With the dissolution of the National Council of Farmers' Cooperative Marketing Associations, the commodity marketing movement ceased to be significant. This does not mean that all of the so-called commodity cooperatives failed. In fact, many improved their business and membership procedures and continued into the present. What is meant is that the driving force of the commodity marketing idea as set forth by Sapiro was henceforth muted, although it came back into attention during Farm Board Days and it frequently reappears in modified form as a solution for agricultural ills. However, from 1926 on, the term "commodity cooperative marketing" ceased to have the market control meaning that Sapiro and his associates gave it, and the somewhat different term "centralized cooperative association" has largely taken its place.[37]

One very significant legacy of the National Council was the *Cooperative Marketing Journal* which evolved out of the experience of Robin Hood and Walton Peteet who came to see the need for a journal of this kind to solidify and strengthen the cooperative marketing movement. It was a private venture largely carried on by Robin Hood, for Peteet was incapacitated by illness soon after the publication was launched in late 1926. The *Journal* was the link between the old Council—The National Council of Farmers' Cooperative Marketing Associations—and the new Council—The National Cooperative Council—(now the National Council of Farmer Cooperatives), which was formed in 1929, and of which Robin Hood became the general secretary in 1930. The important role of the *Journal* in helping integrate the Cooperative marketing movement during the interim period before the new council was formed will be examined in Chapter VI.

Before we turn to an examination of the contemporary developments of cooperation—apart from the commodity marketing movement—during the years from 1920 to 1928, it should be emphasized that with all of its shortcomings the commodity cooperative marketing movement as led by Sapiro was not so much a failure as a great experiment. It had a clarifying influence on cooperative marketing theory and practice in the United States and in foreign countries and from it came many contributions of significant value to future cooperative growth.[38]

Chapter V

THE MAINLINE COOPERATIVE MOVEMENT: 1921-1928

When Aaron Sapiro brought his commodity cooperative marketing plan over the mountains, in 1920, to the great central agricultural region, a vigorous cooperative expansion was already under way. For example, the Minnesota Cooperative Creameries Association, later to be named the Land O' Lakes Creameries, Inc., was in the process of formation through the federation of local creamery associations, and a number of other federations for various commodities were being established. These large organizations were evolving from local associations along natural cooperative lines. Imbued with the object of market control, Sapiro had little use for the local-federated approach, and he proposed scrapping it so that existing cooperative structures would be largely superseded or merged into strong centralized organizations.

The "Ground up" Versus the "Top down" Philosophy

There was immediate resistance to Sapiro's dramatic ideas. This was evident in the plan developed following the Montgomery, Alabama, Cotton Conference in 1920, which proposed building a cotton marketing program for the South from the ground up, using the existing cotton cooperatives as building blocks. But, as we have seen, this plan—regardless of its merits—was swept away by the enthusiasms generated by Sapiro for the plan he espoused. On the contrary, the local and federated grain cooperatives of the Midwest resisted Sapiro's ideas in the formulation of the plan of the Committee of 17, which provided for a grain marketing structure—the United States Grain Growers, Inc.—based largely upon extension and development of existing organizations.

Those opposed to Sapiro's views patterned their thinking largely on the experience of the California Fruit Growers Exchange which had demonstrated its success over a long period of years. They turned for leadership to G. Harold Powell, the highly competent and articulate General Manager of the Exchange who favored the "ground up" philosophy for building strong cooperative organizations.[1] While the contest between the two forms of cooperative organization was gathering force, Powell died of a heart attack on February 18, 1922. However, there were others in sympathy with Powell's philosophy who increasingly made their position clear. Prominent among them was Dr. Edwin G. Nourse, who had been making a number of careful studies of grain and livestock cooperatives as Head of the Department of Agricultural Economics of Iowa State College. He had been one of the group sent by the Iowa Farm Bureau to California in 1920 to determine whether California's experience could be utilized by the Committee of 17. He came back convinced that the best form of organization for grain marketing could be developed on the foundation of local cooperatives, federated together for central selling and other overhead services. When Nourse became Director of the Agricultural Division of the Institute of Economics (now The Brookings Institution) in Washington, D.C., in late 1922, he was in even better position to assume leadership of the counter-Sapiro point of view.

The disagreement between the exponents of "commodity type" marketing cooperatives and of those set up along more orthodox cooperative lines led to a long drawn-out conflict before the champions of the two forms of organization composed their differences and began to pull together. The group represented by Powell and Nourse was often characterized as the "ground up" evolutionary school of cooperative development in contrast to the Sapiro led "top down" high-pressure school. In reality, the first group can better be characterized as the "mainline" school, for it represented the major development of agricultural cooperatives up to that time, while the group led by Sapiro represented a challenge to supersede it. The main line school was democratic, eclectic, and pragmatic in nature and was willing to absorb ideas that might be helpful. On the other hand, the commodity cooperative marketing school, especially in its early days, was autocratic, dogmatic, and didactic and was inclined to maintain operations according to formula.

Thus, during the period when the commodity cooperative marketing idea was spreading rapidly, it did not fully capture or supplant the advocacy of cooperation built from the ground up that constituted the mainline of cooperative development. There were many convinced cooperators who were not swept along by the persuasiveness of Aaron Sapiro, although they recognized his great promotional abilities.[2]

The Counter-attack on "Sapiroism"

In view of its importance to the history of cooperative thought in the United States, it is essential that we understand the nature of the counter-attack made by Nourse and others on the philosophy that was being injected into the cooperative movement by Sapiro. Nourse first gave national expression to his views in an article in the April 1922 issue of the *Journal of Farm Economics,* entitled "The Outlook for Cooperative Marketing." At the beginning he made clear that he had great faith in the future of cooperation, by saying:

> Cooperation is a form of business organization which has emerged in the slow evolution of economic institutions to meet the needs of the complex life of today. It is destined, I believe, to play a part as large and as brilliant as that of the old-line corporation and the "trust" so called . . . I am bound to feel, therefore, that the outlook for cooperative marketing presents a broad and inspiring view (p. 80).

Nourse saw two conflicting goals struggling for supremacy in co-operative marketing.

> Baldly stated, these two goals . . . are, on the one hand, centralized market control and, on the other, decentralized business organization for the more efficient standardization, assembly and market distribution of farm products. Obviously, these two ideals are not antithetical nor even mutually exclusive . . . To waste no words . . . I shall state it as my conviction that the outlook for cooperative marketing after the first of these patterns is extremely bad . . . It would be extremely unfortunate if the interest in and enthusiasm for coopera-tive marketing which is being manifested at the present time were to be largely dissipated in attempts to do the impossible at the terminal market, whilst the necessary work of organizing the producing territory solidly and effectively was neglected. But it appears that just that mistake is being made today by several prominent agencies which have been entrusted with the leadership of the farmers' marketing movement . . . (p. 81).

He also said:

> It is noteworthy that no project of large-scale cooperative marketing is launched without great stress being laid on the allegation that it is "built from the ground up." In a number of outstanding cases, however, this appears upon examination to be mere lip service to a worthy idea whose real meaning has unfortunately been missed (p. 82).

Furthermore he warned:

> One particularly unfortunate result of the present over-promoted phase of cooperative marketing development is that great numbers of people who nat-urally cannot be expected to be accurately informed . . . will leap to the con-clusion that the cooperative principle has been discredited by the collapse of some of these too ambitious schemes (p. 83).

Nourse followed up his attack with a scholarly article in the *American Economic Review* of December 1922 entitled "Economic Philosophy of Cooperation," which has become a classic in cooperative literature. In this article, which stressed the evolutionary character of cooperation, his criticism of the Sapiro school of cooperation was even more blunt. Here he referred to "the new cooperative cult in America which cries down the Rochdale principles and exalts the new 'cooperation American style,' along lines of big business bargaining efficiency and ruthlessness. It is producer cooperation, legalistic in philosophy, monopolistic in spirit and zealous for control of the market."

At a meeting of the National Association of State Marketing Officials in December 1923, Nourse carried his intellectual assault further in an address on "Some Fundamentals of Cooperative Marketing." He said:

> There is a strong tendency in much of the recent expansive movement in American cooperation to centralize power and to cause the authority of the central agency to touch the individual member directly and to this end his obligations, contractual or otherwise, run direct to this governing head . . . We shall, I think, save ourselves much personal friction if we now, while it is yet early, turn away from such autocratic types of organization which are being foisted upon the fundamentally democratic cooperative movement, and let the genius of our people for local autonomy, representative government and federation, express itself naturally and constructively in the building of our large-scale cooperative organizations.

He continued:

> Those who urge centralization and direct overhead control are impatient for immediate results and are optimistic as to the goals that can be reached if only unlimited power be put in the hands of those who stand at the head and front of a marketing organization. They are preaching a gospel of force and are simply dazzled by the apparent success of such tactics in the case of great business corporations and the more aggressive of the labor unions.

This led Nourse to state "baldly" as a fundamental, that "Cooperative organization wisely handled can accomplish great and permanent gains in the way of net price for the grower; but it does this not by power to coerce the market so much as by skill in meeting the market."[3]

Another who was highly skeptical of Sapiro's promises and techniques was Dr. Henry C. Taylor, Chief of the new Bureau of Agricultural Economics, informally set up in July 1921 and formally established a year later. Taylor had come to the United States Department of Agriculture in 1919 with a rich background of experience in cooperative development in Wisconsin and he was not one to be swayed by popular psychology.[4] It is here significant that the incoming Secretary of Agriculture in 1921, Henry C. Wallace, leaned heavily upon him for advice on all matters relating to agricultural economics. During his first year as Secretary, Wallace was disposed to favor Sapiro's plan for centralized commodity marketing organizations until Taylor tempered his thinking by espousing democratic organizations from the "ground up" as contrasted with the "autocratic" institutions espoused by Sapiro. The occasion followed a conversation between Sir Horace Plunkett and Secretary Wallace, where the two were "quite out of harmony" on "the merits of centralized cooperatives." Taylor felt constrained to give Wallace his frank views in a personal memorandum in which he said:

> It takes more personal courage for a man who possesses the power of leadership to devote himself to the use of democratic methods and the building of democratic institutions than it does to proceed by autocratic methods. The former involves the education of the masses to wise conscious action. The latter involves gaining control of the masses and directing them in accordance with the leader's plan. The former means education from the top down and control of action from the bottom up. The latter means control from the top down and less attention to education. The end in view may sometimes be attained more quickly by autocratic methods, but the results are much less permanent and the resulting civilization is entirely different.
>
> These two methods of approach have been made to the problem of agricultural organization. Sir Horace Plunkett is the outstanding leader of the very large group of workers throughout the world who believe in taking the time to educate the people, and help the people build for themselves the agricultural organization which they require to improve their living conditions . . .
>
> Recently, however, a strong movement has been led in this country, by Aaron Sapiro, who uses autocratic methods. The central feature is the contract which is intended to give absolute control of the marketing of the commodity organized, to the officials of a highly centralized organization. In this system, the farmers do not organize themselves . . . They are organized, or rather their commodity is organized, by a group of expert organizers. The education of the farmers consists largely of inducing them to sign the contract. This done, the central organization does the rest . . .
>
> The emergencies following World War I . . . may have justified the speeding up of agricultural organization by autocratic methods, but if the results are to be permanent the work must be democratized.[5]

Supported by the moderating influence of Taylor and backed up by Wallace, the Division of Agricultural Cooperation in the Bureau of Agricultural Economics did not get on the bandwagon for all out promotion of "commodity cooperative marketing." This was apparent in Wallace's statement at the First National Cooperative Marketing Conference held in Washington, D.C., in December, 1922, which set forth what the government could and could not do to aid the cooperative movement. He made it clear that the Department of Agriculture was a "department of service" to help farmers on their marketing problems through all types of cooperative organization. The cooperative studies of the newly organized Division of Agricultural Cooperation in the Bureau of Agricultural Economics represented this position, for they included case studies of the California Fruit Growers Exchange and a study of cooperation in Denmark which emphasized the advantages of democratic cooperatives built from the ground up, as well as case studies of centralized commodity organizations which showed both the strengths and weaknesses of such organizations.

During the early twenties, the subject of centralized vs. federated cooperative organizations was a matter of great concern in Minnesota, as in other states. This led Dr. John D. Black and Dr. H. Bruce Price, of the University of Minnesota, to make a valuable analysis of the relative advantages of cooperatives of both types in an influential study, *Cooperative Central Marketing Organization.*[6] Black later admitted that this bulletin was written to counter Sapiroism, but it never mentioned Sapiro by name, and it gave credit to certain advantages of both centralized and federated types of cooperative organization. The following statement from this bulletin reflects its character.

> It is the practice to say that there are two distinct types of cooperative organizations operating in the central market, namely, the "federated" type, and the "commodity" or "centralized" type. The term "centralized" is the better term for the latter type. Cooperative marketing, except in a few instances, such as the handling of fuel and feed and occasionally livestock, by grain elevators, or the handling of eggs by creameries, always has been by commodities. The use of the term "commodity" for the centralized type of organization suggests that this is a distinct feature of this type of organization, which is contrary to the facts. The two types of organizations do, however, differ somewhat in this respect, as will be explained. The essential difference between the two types of organizations is that the centralized organizations believe that it is absolutely necessary that all, or a large part of any one crop or commodity, shall be under the control of one organization, so that the movement of the crop to market can be absolutely regulated, and the price at which the crop is sold can be arranged by bargaining between this organization, acting as a unit, and the buyers; whereas, in the federated organization, control more largely resides in the local cooperative unit, the central organization often merely acting as a selling agent for the locals, and ordinarily making little or no effort at collective bargaining. The difference between the two is therefore in the degree of centralization and control . . . [7]

Later on in the bulletin there is this statement:

> The judgement of the authors is that in the future we shall have intermediate types of organizations representing various degrees between the extreme federated type—like the California Fruit Growers' Exchange—and the extreme centralized type—like the California Sun-Maid Raisin Growers before it was reorganized. No type will be accepted as "standard" even for one commodity.[8]

Professor O. B. Jesness also helped bridge the ideological gap between the advocates of centralized and federated organizations by emphasizing the business side of cooperative marketing in his book *The Cooperative Marketing of Farm Products,* published in 1923. Jesness was well qualified for this task. From 1915 to 1920, he had served as a cooperative specialist in the Bureau of Markets of the United States Department of Agriculture, and in this position he had helped bring into being many of the major cooperatives of the country. As Professor of Markets and Rural Finance in the College of Agriculture at the University of Kentucky, he was also intimately informed on the operations of the Burley Tobacco Growers and other commodity marketing cooperatives in that state.

In his book, Jesness did not support or oppose any type of cooperative organization. He simply dealt with them as business institutions and reported their experience. He made clear that he did not believe that farmers' marketing organizations would evolve into powerful monopolies detrimental to consumers, for he did not see how they could possibly effect control of production. In a final chapter, Jesness dealt with the "future of cooperative marketing." Here, he did not anticipate cooperative developments that would satisfy either those who believed that cooperatives would bring a new era into agriculture or those who looked forward to their ignominious collapse. He thought that in the future they would occupy "a middle ground." He was, however, positive in his belief that "cooperative marketing organizations must be built from the ground up" whether on the centralized or federated pattern. He thought that there was a "grave danger that an extensive superstructure was being erected on a foundation that will lack permanence." However, he saw much substantial progress being made, and he finished his book with these words:

> Future years will witness a continued growth in numbers of marketing organizations at local points and in the establishment of central organizations for areas having similar problems. Progress will be made in the development of organization plans. Farmers are thinking and talking cooperative marketing in such a way that they are rapidly gaining clear conceptions of the essentials and possibilities of cooperative marketing. Educational institutions and agencies are aiding by their investigations and courses of instruction in the field of cooperative marketing. Men are becoming trained in the business management of cooperative marketing associations, and this means much for the future development because poor management has been a frequent weakness in the past. Much progress can still be made in increasing the efficiency of existing associations. Weaker organizations include many which are doomed to fail. Those which continue operations will learn and grow stronger by experience. There is so much of value in cooperative marketing on an effective basis that the future prospects are indeed very bright for cooperative associations formed to render specific services in the marketing of farm products.[9]

Dr. Henry E. Erdman, Professor of Agricultural Economics at the University of California, also helped stabilize cooperative thinking in the mid-twenties. At the annual meeting of the American Farm Economic Association in December 1923, he presented a paper, "The Commodity Cooperative Association—Its Strength and Weakness." Among the weaknesses he listed overemphasis on price, eagerness to attempt new and untried methods, a tendency toward extravagance and inefficiency, too rapid growth, difficulties in meeting competition, membership problems, and overdependence on contracts. On the other hand, he gave commodity cooperative marketing organizations credit for the following strengths—singleness of purpose, opportunity for development of experts, risks born by the commodity, ability to bargain, influence on quality, ability to develop markets, and better management. He summed up by saying that "the greater weight is on the elements of strength," and he predicted "the commodity type of organization probably is here to stay."[10]

Erdman followed up with a circular on the "Possibilities and Limitations of Cooperative Marketing" that made clear from his long experience as a student of cooperatives in California and the Midwest what cooperatives could and could not be expected to do. He maintained that "Cooperative associations cannot arbitrarily 'fix' prices; Cooperative organizations cannot 'eliminate the middleman'; Cooperative marketing cannot cut costs greatly."[11] Dr. Henry C. Taylor later said: "It took courage to make those statements in the middle 1920's. Certain agitators of that day who led farmers to believe that cooperatives would wield a large influence on prices were far more popular with the farmers than the agricultural economist who tried to tell them the whole truth."[12]

The foregoing references indicate that the cooperative movement of the early 1920's was not entirely dominated by Sapiro's philosophy, although much credit can be given him for injecting a new vitality into the thinking and procedures of cooperative development. He raised horizons and challenged assumptions, and this brought forth an intellectual response of great future importance which eventually gave to the cooperatives the advantages of hybrid vigor.

As will be pointed out in the next section, the coming of the American Institute of Cooperation provided a forum for the harmonizing of divergent cooperative views. Moreover, the conversion of many of the commodity marketing leaders to McNary-Haugenism to attain their objectives helped subordinate the "market control" concept of Sapiro to the "adjustment to market" concept of Nourse. However, this basic disagreement on cooperative objects and procedures was to continue down the years, and it persists even today in a transmuted way.

Birth and Early Contributions of the American Institute of Cooperation

Although there was much enthusiasm for agricultural cooperation in the early 1920's, there was also much disagreement among cooperative leaders on the way it should be organized and practiced. As we have observed in Chapter I, a schism had soon developed between proponents of "top down" commodity cooperative marketing and advocates of Rochdale cooperation "from the ground up" through local and federated associations. Charles W. Holman, Secretary of the National Cooperative Milk Producers Federation, believed that this situation was causing unnecessary confusion and endangering the sound development of cooperative enterprise. He believed that the time was ripe for reviving in a more comprehensive way the educational work which had been carried on by the National Conference on Marketing and Farm Credits, 1913-1916, of which he had been Secretary. When he presented this idea to a group of cooperative dairy marketing leaders in the summer of 1923, it appealed strongly to Richard Pattee, Manager of the New England Milk Producers Association, and he joined with Holman in promoting the conception. Referring back to the genesis of the American Institute of Cooperation, two years later, Pattee said: "The thought was brought out that in some way the country ought to be apprised of the extent, the purpose and the significance of the cooperative idea, the cooperative method of business practice, the system of cooperation which was seemingly crystallizing into a movement . . . What was it? What did it mean? What was it seeking to do and how did it operate?"[13]

While cooperative leaders agreed that something should be done, there was little agreement on "how this thing could be done." Holman suggested a program fashioned along the lines of the Institute of Politics then being conducted at Williamstown, Massachusetts, "whereby the leaders in the various local and regional units might be brought together for a study of their individual problems and the general fundamental problems that underlie all of these problems."[14]

This approach was tentatively accepted; and to start the ball rolling, Mr. Pattee presented it at the annual meeting of the National Cooperative Milk Producers Federation held at Pittsburgh in November 1923. The Federation adopted a resolution which endorsed the proposal "for a voluntary, non-resoluting, educational body dealing with cooperation." It was envisaged that "such a body should hold educational conferences, conduct undergraduate and graduate classes, confer academic credits and otherwise do educational work on agricultural cooperation."[15] A committee set up by the Federation then proceeded to bring the proposal to the attention of cooperative and agricultural leaders. "In every case there seemed to be an instant response to the suggestion that something of this sort be done . . . The question then was how to bring it about?"[16] These conversations led to a general meeting of various farm and cooperative organizations in Washington, D.C., on February 11, 1924, where it was unanimously agreed that the proposed program should be undertaken— "which in itself at that period, was no small accomplishment in cooperation."[17] Significantly, Secretary of Agriculture, Henry C. Wallace, who was present promised the full-hearted cooperation of the Department.[18]

Following this meeting, committees were set up to deal with the various problems of organization, and these committees, in turn, reported back to a second conference which voted to proceed with the establishment of an organization, with Mr. Pattee to serve as Chairman and Mr. Holman as Secretary of the Organization Committee. Two subsequent conferences were held—in Cleveland and Chicago—which resulted in the incorporation of the American Institute of Cooperation in January 1925, as an educational institution under the laws of the District of Columbia.[19]

The plan of organization provided that any cooperative organization could become a member and be represented in an assembly of members, which would select a board of trustees that would, in turn, elect officers and carry on the affairs of the Institute. There was no provision made for membership fees, dues, or assessments, and participating organizations assumed no financial responsibilities. It was understood, however, that voluntary contributions would be welcomed from general farm and cooperative organizations, individuals, and other interested parties.

One of the problems of the organizers had been to obtain financial backing to ensure success. On this problem Charles W. Holman, Henry C. Taylor, and Edwin G. Nourse, who had already agreed to serve as Chairman of the Institute's program committee, went to New York City in the fall of 1924 to confer with Beardsley Ruml of the Laura Spellman Rockefeller Fund. Ruml was attracted by the idea of an educational organization of this type but he did not like the name "International Institute of Cooperation" then being used by the Institute's promoters. He suggested that American Institute of Cooperation would be a simpler and more effective name and this name was accepted. Thereupon, Ruml agreed that the Laura Spellman Fund would match dollar for dollar contributions made by others up to $12,500 for the first two years, and $15,000 for the next three years.[20]

From the outset the organizers recognized that the success of the new organization would depend upon its ability to develop a program of vital interest. It was deemed essential that the Chairman of the Program Committee be a man of recognized standing in the educational world, with a broad interest in agricultural and other forms of cooperation, and good working relations with land grant colleges and universities, officials of the U.S. Department of Agriculture, and leaders in the general farm and

cooperative organizations. Fortunately, a man with the qualifications
deemed essential was available in the person of Dr. Edwin G. Nourse,
who was then well known as a leader and writer in the field of
cooperation. Moreover, as Director of the Agricultural Division of the
Institute of Economics (now The Brookings Institution), he was located
in Washington, D.C., where he could work closely with Holman, who was
the agreed upon Secretary of the new organization, and with officials of
the U.S. Department of Agriculture and other government agencies.[21]

Nourse entered enthusiastically into the work of building the program
for the first summer session of the Institute, for he was convinced of the
"sincerity of desire for constructive effort." He hoped that the first annual
Institute meetings would "express a small, coherent, sound, and tenable
philosophy of cooperation" and also introduce "an organizing factor into
agriculture itself."[22] In developing the program, Nourse conferred and
corresponded with representatives of the U.S.D.A. and with college, farm,
and cooperative officials and leaders.

The American Institute of Cooperation made its bow to the world in
the spring of 1925 in an attractively printed brochure which carried program information for the forthcoming summer session to be held at the
University of Pennsylvania at Philadelphia. Its opening statement declared: "In offering to the public the first summer session of the American
Institute of Cooperation, the trustees are attacking the solution of a
problem that has an important bearing upon the economic and social
development of the North American continent. For the first time in the
United States, the history, principles and practices of the cooperative
movement will be treated intensively by a distinguished group of
authorities." The general objects of the Institute were presented as
follows:

> 1. To collect and make available a body of knowledge concerning the co-
> operative movement in America and other lands.
> 2. To serve as a means of clarifying thought as to what the cooperative
> movement really is and of bringing about more harmony and unity of action
> among organizations directly or indirectly connected with cooperation.
> 3. To serve as a means of training and developing leaders and workers in
> the cooperative movement.
> 4. To serve as a means of assisting educational institutions throughout this
> country to improve their teaching courses in cooperation, and investigational
> work in cooperation.
> 5. To focus the spirit of the cooperative movement as a means of community
> and national development.

The brochure stated that the Institute had enjoyed the full support of
Henry C. Wallace, the late Secretary of Agriculture, and endorsements
were quoted from his successor, William M. Jardine; Herbert Hoover,

Secretary of Commerce; and Frank O. Lowden, former Governor of Illinois.

The program outlined for the Institute meetings provided for a consideration of general topics during each of the four weeks of the Institute and for direct discussion of the problems of various kinds of cooperatives. The broad coverage of the program is indicated by the general topics listed for study over a four-week period.

FIRST WEEK—Economic Principles and Legal Structure of Cooperation, including, (a) history of cooperation; (b) ideals of the movement; (c) development of types; (d) possibilities and limitations; (e) status of state and federal legislation.

SECOND WEEK—Organization and Membership Problems: (a) preliminary market surveys; (b) forms of organization; (c) organization finance; (d) patronage costs; (e) education work with members; (f) the cooperative and the community.

THIRD WEEK—Operating Methods and Management Problems: (a) source of personnel; (b) business practices; (c) auditing and accounting; (d) marketing finance; (e) warehousing; (f) grading and standardization; (g) methods of pooling.

FOURTH WEEK—Sales Policies and Price Problems: (a) orderly marketing; (b) selling plans for various commodities; (c) development of markets; (d) price objectives of cooperatives; (e) selling problems; (f) credits and collections; (g) effect of today's prices on tomorrow's production.

The ambitions of the American Institute of Cooperation were far-reaching. They were well expressed in a boxed statement on the back cover of the brochure.

A new era begins in the history of American Cooperation. The formative period is closed. The movement is now recognized as a permanent force in our economic and social life. The cooperative principle and the cooperative form of organization have achieved recognition as the most vital forces in the sphere of agriculture; they have become noticeable factors among urban consumers. The next step will be the development of trained man-power to hold what has been accomplished and to carry forward the successful operation of the idea in its many forms . . .

The first summer meetings of the Institute brought together some 400 persons from 36 states and 6 foreign countries, although many did not attend all four weeks of the meetings. The participants on the programs included most of the national leaders in agricultural cooperation with the exception of Aaron Sapiro—who was listed as an attendant. Among the 100 or more who gave papers or led discussions were such prominent persons as H. E. Babcock, John D. Black, M. L. Corey, Chris L. Christensen, A. U. Chaney, Earnest Downie, Frank Evans, Henry E. Erdman, C. R. Fay (Canada), Secretary Jardine, O. B. Jesness, I. W. Heaps, B. W. Kilgore, Frank O. Lowden, Benson Y. Landis, Forest

Ketner, C. O. Moser, John D. Miller, E. G. Nourse, A. R. Rule, L. J. Tabor, J. W. Shorthill, Herman Steen, Henry C. Taylor, Lloyd S. Tenny, M. W. Thatcher, C. W. Warburton, and L. D. H. Weld. The program provided for full discussions on all subjects considered, and the entire proceedings were faithfully recorded by court reporters.

One of the highlights of the first session was the attempt made in a conference on the tests of cooperation to determine the full meaning of the word "cooperation."[23] In his opening remarks as Chairman of this meeting, E. G. Nourse said: "We should not call an enterprise cooperative unless it does bear the earmarks of something distinctly different, that distinctly different thing being that it is putting together their [the members'] units of the business." One of the participants, O. B. Jesness, saw little advantage in trying to define cooperation. He said: "My philosophy . . . runs this way. The cooperative marketing organization is purely—and I want to emphasize the word purely—a business organization." He went on however to indicate that an organization could be called a cooperative only if it was organized to carry on the farmers' business and for the purpose of benefiting the farmers in that business. In the discussion Pattee said that he wanted to find out "just what we have got to do to be entitled to be considered a cooperative. I am wondering if thought along this line has gone far enough to enable us to set up a definition that is fixed and standard and that can be applied with exactness . . . It seems to me that there is a tendency on the part of the people to misunderstand the purpose and intent of the cooperative movement . . . The public should know the real purpose and intent of this thing." At another point he said: "It is highly important that the public understand the true meaning of cooperation, in order that its enemies may not, by ways with which they are familiar and expert in the use of, attach to it, in the public mind the stigma we attach to Socialism . . . " Although the group did not arrive at a consensus as to the meaning of cooperation, it did stimulate much thought of a beneficial nature.[24]

The first meetings of the American Institute of Cooperation included many talks by persons prominent in commodity marketing cooperatives, but there was no sweeping address extolling the philosophy of commodity cooperative marketing while denigrating other cooperative marketing efforts. The wave of enthusiasm for this idea had passed, and commodity cooperative marketing was finding its place as a part of the mainline cooperative movement—characterized by eclecticism and vigorous experimentation. The emphasis was now turning from grandiose conceptions of market control to methods of achieving cooperative efficiency and better services for the members and the public, and to the meaning and significance of the cooperative form of business enterprise. While the sessions brought out the diversity of cooperative forms of organization, they also indicated how potentially strong cooperatives were becoming as a group.

Although primary attention was given to cooperative marketing because of its overwhelming importance to farmers, other forms of cooperation were not ignored. Richard Pattee, in his opening address on the "Purposes of the American Institute of Cooperation" said: "It is not the purpose of this Institute to limit itself to cooperative effort in the agricultural or commodity distributive field. In future programs it is hoped and expected to consider in greater detail the application of the cooperative principle to other business enterprises.[25]

In the session devoted to cooperative supply buying, H. E. Babcock, General Manager of the Cooperative Grange League Federation Exchange, and John D. Zink, General Manager of the Eastern States Farmers Exchange, made it clear that this form of cooperative enterprise was rapidly coming into prominence.

Although the first annual Institute served primarily as a clearing house in the field of cooperative thought and practice, it also served as an educational training center for present and future cooperative leaders. A number of courses in cooperative organization and operation were offered with the assistance of such well-known professors as John D. Black, H. E. Erdman, and C. R. Fay. The students were required to attend the general sessions, and seminar type classes were held each afternoon. Many of the students were county agents, vocational teachers, college teachers, and instructors. This program met with their approval, for at the end of the term they submitted a resolution thanking the Institute officials for holding the Institute and recommending that it "be made an annual event."[26]

The holding of the first annual meeting of the American Institute of Cooperation was also a public relations achievement of considerable importance. Held at a prominent American university, conducted with dignity, and with broad support from the agricultural and business community, it brought great respect to cooperatives—the full presentations at the sessions and the open discussions showed that the movement had nothing to hide. Holman, as Secretary, recognized the importance of publicity, and he saw to it that the meetings had good press coverage.

One of the far-reaching decisions made by the Trustees of the Institute was to publish the proceedings. It was wisely appreciated that such valuable information would be lost if it was not made available promptly in permanent form. In this way the Institute provided textbook information and valuable reference material on current cooperative problems and methods for many interested persons who could not attend the sessions. The proceedings were published in two volumes under the title *American Cooperation* and were priced at $35 for the set. The price dropped the following year to $20, and after a few years to regular book prices. Thus was started a practice which continues to the present. The proceedings of the successive Institutes provide the greatest fund of information on agricultural cooperation available for any country in the world. For this accomplishment, great credit can be given to Charles W. Holman for his insistence that the proceedings be published promptly after each Institute and for seeing to it that this work was well done.

The first Institute was recognized immediately as an outstanding success. It helped harmonize the thinking of cooperative leaders and broadened their goals and objectives. As Secretary Jardine was to say at the Institute sessions the following year: "It did much to give the cooperative movement unity and cohesion." It also contributed a great deal to the development of professional attitudes and standards among cooperative workers. It stimulated research on cooperative organization and procedures. Furthermore, it emphasized the basic importance of adequate employee and membership education.

Dr. Nourse expressed his satisfaction with the results of the first session of the Institute at the meeting of the National Association of Marketing Officials held in November 1925. Speaking on the subject "Recent Trend of Cooperation Among Cooperatives," he noted a "strong get-together movement among cooperatives" as evidenced by the recent Institute of Cooperation meetings. He said: "I think the American Institute of Cooperation accomplished a very substantial amount of progress with reference to the cooperative movement. It came in just at this time when there was questioning, when a great many people thought it might be possible to go forward, and yet did not see how. It came at a very opportune time."[27]

The first Institute also ushered in an "era of good feeling" among cooperative organizations in the form of more teamwork. This was evidenced immediately in the unanimity expressed by the cooperatives in getting behind the bill which was to result in the setting up of the Division of Cooperative Marketing in the United States Department of Agriculture the following year. It also was expressed in the full support of cooperative leaders, given to the work of a committee set up shortly after the Institute meetings by the National Education Association, to develop a textbook on cooperation for use in the high schools of the country.[28]

The success of the first Institute meetings ensured that this program would go on, and plans were immediately made for an Institute to be held the following summer at the University of Minnesota. This started the practice of holding the annual sessions of the Institute in cooperation with a recognized university. This practice, which has continued to the present, later caused Charles W. Holman to characterize the Institute as "literally a college on wheels."[29]

The Institute sessions at the University of Minnesota gave special consideration to the problems of the Midwest, and emphasis was placed on training and education. A number of three-day short courses were also given for managers and directors of livestock shipping associations, cooperative creameries, and farmers' elevators. In addition, 12 one-hour academic short courses were offered jointly with the University of Minnesota for which academic credit was given. The subjects taught and those who assisted show the variety and quality of the instruction.

Price Analysis and Policies—Dr. Holbrook Working, Dr. Warren Waite
Cooperative Marketing Organization—Dr. John D. Black, Albert G. Black
Cooperative Marketing of Livestock—Dr. Paul L. Miller, Dr. Waite
Membership Control Problems—Dr. O. B. Jesness
Cooperative Accounting—Frank Robotka, Budd A. Holt, George M. Peterson
Cooperative Sales Promotion—Dr. Theodore Macklin
Cooperative Administration—Paul L. Miller and Cooperative Managers
Cooperative Marketing of Grain—Dr. H. Bruce Price, George M. Peterson
Cooperative Marketing of Dairy Products—Dr. J. T. Horner, Dr. H. Q. Ross, T. G. Stitts
The Economic and Legal Foundations of Cooperation—Dr. E. G. Nourse
History and Progress of Cooperation—Dr. Hector McPherson, Dr. H. Bruce Price
Seminar on Cooperative Problems—Professors just listed.

Many years later, Orion Ulrey, who was one of the students at the Minnesota Institute, recalled the deep impression that this education program made upon him. He writes: "The discussions about cooperatives and the rural economy at meals and during the evenings, left deep impressions on the students who were searching for ideas on 'improved systems.' "[30]

Since 1926, the American Institute of Cooperation has continued to play a constructive role in the American Cooperative development. Similar institutes were to be held at Northwestern University (1927), University of California (1928), and Louisiana State University (1929). Since then, Institutes have been hosted by many more of the leading universities of the United States.

Clarification of the Income Tax Exemption

Another factor which brought cooperatives closer together was their common interest in federal income tax exemption. Prior to 1926, federal income tax laws were somewhat ambiguous on the income tax status of agricultural cooperatives.[31]

This situation, under pressure from the cooperatives, was clarified by Section 231 of the Revenue Act of 1926 which contained the following provision:

> Farmers', fruit growers', or like associations organized and operated on a co-operative basis (a) for the purpose of marketing the products of members or other producers, and turning back to them the proceeds of sales, less the necessary marketing expenses, on the basis of either the quantity or the value of the products furnished by them, or (b) for the purpose of purchasing supplies and equipment for the use of members or other persons, and turning over such supplies and equipment to them at actual cost, plus necessary expenses. Exemption shall not be denied any such association because it has capital stock, if the dividend rate of such stock is fixed at not to exceed the legal rate of interest in the State of incorporation or 8 per centum per annum, whichever is greater, on the value of the consideration for which the stock was issued, and if substantially all such stock (other than non-voting preferred stock, the owners of which are not entitled or permitted to participate, directly or indirectly, in the profits of the association, upon dissolution or otherwise, beyond the fixed dividends) is owned by producers who market their products or purchase their supplies and equipment through the association, nor shall exemption be denied any such association because there is accumulated and maintained by it a reserve required by State law or a reasonable reserve for any necessary purpose. Such an association may market the products of nonmembers in an amount the value of which does not exceed the value of the products marketed for members, and may purchase supplies and equipment for nonmembers in an amount the value of which does not exceed the value of the supplies and equipment purchased for members, provided the value of the purchases made for persons who are neither members nor producers does not exceed 15 per centum of the value of all its purchases.[32]

No significant change in the 1926 law was made until 1951.[33]

One of the contributions of the income tax exemption for cooperatives as expressed in the Revenue Act of 1926 was its establishment of acceptable standards of cooperative performance.[34] It gave guidelines which helped keep cooperatives on the straight and narrow path. Although they received exemption, it was carefully prescribed and the benefits served as a strong incentive to obtain cooperative adherence to sound principles. The exemption was in keeping with the other legislative acts of the period which recognized the public policy benefits of agricultural cooperation.

The Cooperative Marketing Act of 1926 and Its Impact

Another major step in the advancement of an eclectic and pragmatic philosophy of cooperative enterprise came with the passage of the

Cooperative Marketing Act of 1926. As we have already noted, the establishment of the American Institute of Cooperation in 1925 paved the way for this important cooperative legislation. The meetings and discussions at the first Institute had created a comradeship among cooperative leaders and a greater understanding of their mutual problems. From the Institute's deliberations had come an appreciation of the importance of research and educational assistance for cooperatives that could best be provided by government. The constructive work then being done by the Division of Agricultural Cooperation also had an opportunity to make itself evident in the Institute discussions, and there was a natural desire to have this program broadened and strengthened as a means of meeting the rapidly growing technical problems of cooperative organization and operation.

Dr. William Jardine had come to the post of Secretary of Agriculture in March 1925 as an educator with a firm belief in agricultural cooperatives. He saw cooperation as a means whereby farmers could solve many of their own serious economic problems. As he became better acquainted with what the Department had done and was doing to help cooperatives, he looked with favor on legislation that would enable the Department to be more helpful. It is significant that Jardine, prior to taking the position of Secretary, had been a member of the President's Agricultural Conference which had proposed that work to assist cooperatives could best be done by an independent farm board. Jardine had supported this view in the hearings on the proposal but after the bill was killed he came to see, as Secretary of Agriculture, that the Department could do much of what was necessary if given more financial assistance.

The bill which became the Cooperative Marketing Act was prepared by Jardine's staff in the fall of 1925 after it had become evident through conferences with cooperative leaders that they would welcome and support such action. At the hearings on the bill, which soon became known in cooperative circles as the "Jardine Bill," Jardine presented a letter addressed to him by 33 leaders of cooperative associations who were his advisors in drafting the bill. This letter contained these paragraphs.

> The undersigned, representing farmers' cooperative marketing organizations, have been called into conference by you to consider ways and means for extending the services of the Department of Agriculture to cooperative marketing. After careful and earnest consideration of many measures and proposals, we are of the opinion that this can best be done at this time by establishing a division of cooperative marketing in your department and equipping it with the means to give information, counsel and guidance to farmers on cooperative marketing in harmony with its traditional policy of service without domination . . .

Such a division wisely administered will be of great service to the cooperative marketing movement and the public welfare. It will be able to render to
cooperatives the kind of aid most needed by them without in any way impairing
their own initiative and responsibility.

Two points in these paragraphs are of special significance. First,
cooperative marketing was emphasized to the exclusion of cooperative
purchasing. The term "cooperative marketing" had gained wide popular
acceptance and was considered more agreeable to Congress. As McKay
has reported: "A few wanted the name, Division of Agricultural Cooperation, retained. The majority pointed out that antagonism of the competitive trade to farmer marketing cooperatives was subsiding, while the
prejudice against purchasing associations still was intense. By way of
compromise . . . [it was agreed to broaden the term "cooperative
marketing"] to include 'processing, warehousing, manufacturing, storage,
the cooperative purchasing of farm supplies, credit, financing, insurance,
and other cooperative activities.' "[35] Secondly, the statement made it
clear that the cooperatives desired "services without domination" and
were anxious to preserve "their own initiative and responsibility." This
attitude reflected the concern that cooperatives had expressed the year
before when the Agricultural Conference approved a bill which provided
for auditing and issuing of licenses to approved cooperatives and which
was defeated with strong cooperative opposition.

Although at this time there was disagreement among farm and
cooperative leaders on how far the government should go in farm relief
legislation of the McNary-Haugen type, there was practically unanimous
approval for an act designed to help strengthen cooperatives as business
organizations. Even those more interested in legislation of the McNary-
Haugen form saw no harm in strengthening cooperatives, for they might
help in the administration of the McNary-Haugen proposal, if, and when,
enacted. On the other hand, those opposed to McNary-Haugen legislation
saw in the Jardine Bill a way of strengthening cooperatives so that they
could bring necessary relief to agriculture and thus weaken the pressure
for direct government assistance. Thus, Aaron Sapiro, speaking at the 4th
National Cooperative Marketing Conference in January 1926, said:

This bill was really drawn by Secretary Jardine . . . after conferences with
practically all the important cooperative leaders of this country. He had them
come in separately and in droves. He really made an effort to find out what the
cooperatives wanted. Here was his conclusion: that they wanted administrative
support, but that he did not have in Government, enough men to do it or enough
facilities . . . I unreservedly recommend, and I think every man here agrees with
me, that we put ourselves behind the Jardine bill and see that it is passed . . . We
have never before had anything like this kind of support from the United
States Government. [36]

Charles W. Holman appeared in the Hearings supporting the bill as a representative of the National Board of Farm Organizations and of the National Milk Producers' Federation. He said:

> We wish to see a permanent policy established in the Department, so that irrespective of the wishes, or, let us say, the desires of succeeding Secretaries, this work can go on for the benefit of that part of the agricultural public who wish to market their products in a cooperative way, and to use the cooperative principle in other forms of business. By having it put into the basic law and appropriations made directly for it, it will be very difficult to disband a cooperative division again.[37]

Although this bill had the full support of the Administration, it was not enacted until a number of other farm relief proposals failed of support. In fact, many in Congress accepted the "Jardine Bill" as a compromise and palliative of little real significance. It became law as the Cooperative Marketing Act on July 2, 1926.

The Cooperative Marketing Act had one basic objective—to strengthen the assistance then being provided farmers through their cooperatives by the establishment of a Division of Cooperative Marketing in the United States Department of Agriculture which would function under certain guidelines as set forth in the Act. The Division was directed to "render service to associations of producers of agricultural products, and federations and subsidiaries thereof, engaged in the cooperative marketing of agricultural products, including processing, warehousing, manufacturing, storage, the cooperative purchasing of farm supplies, credit, financing, insurance, and other cooperative activities." The Act thus made clear that the term "cooperative marketing" was to be broadly interpreted to include cooperative purchasing of farm supplies and other forms of agricultural cooperation. It should also be noted that services were to be limited to "associations of producers of agricultural products." The Division of Cooperative Marketing was authorized:

> 1. To acquire, analyze, and disseminate economic, statistical, and historical information regarding the progress, organization, and business methods of cooperative associations in the United States and foreign countries.
> 2. To conduct studies of the economic, legal, financial, social and other phases of cooperation, and publish the results thereof. Such studies shall include the analyses of the organization, operation, financial, and merchandising problems of cooperative associations.
> 3. To make surveys and analysis if deemed advisable of the accounts and business practices of representative cooperative associations upon their request; to report to the association so surveyed the results thereof; and with the consent of the association so surveyed to publish summaries of the results of such surveys, together with similar facts, for the guidance of cooperative associations and for the purpose of assisting cooperative associations in developing methods of business and market analyses.

4. To confer and advise with committees or groups of producers, if deemed advisable, that may be desirous of forming a cooperative association and to make an economic survey and analysis of the facts surrounding the production and marketing of the agricultural product or products which the association, if formed, would handle or market.

5. To acquire from all available sources, information concerning crop prospects, supply, demand, current receipts, exports, imports, and prices of the agricultural products handled or marketed by cooperative associations, and to employ qualified commodity marketing specialists to summarize and analyze this information and disseminate the same among cooperative associations and others.

6. To promote the knowledge of cooperative principles and practices and to cooperate in promoting such knowledge, with educational and marketing agencies, cooperative associations and others.

7. To make such special studies, in the United States and foreign countries, and to acquire and disseminate such information findings as may be useful in the development and practice of cooperation (44 Stat:802).

Another important section of the Act (Section 5) "cleared up a certain twilight zone of joint action among cooperatives.[38] It provided that:

Persons engaged, as original producers of agricultural products, such as farmers, planters, ranchmen, dairymen, nut or fruit growers, acting together in associations, corporate or otherwise, in collectively processing, preparing for market, handling, and marketing in interstate and/or foreign commerce such products of persons so engaged, may acquire, exchange, interpret, and disseminate past, present, and prospective crop, market, statistical, economic, and other similar information by direct exchange between such persons, and/or such associations or federations thereof, and/or by and through a common agent created or selected by them.

The Cooperative Marketing Act also authorized the Secretary of Agriculture to call in advisors to counsel with him on specific problems of cooperative marketing of farm products or on any other cooperative activity. This provision has been utilized several times since 1926.

The Cooperative Marketing Act carried authorization for an appropriation of $225,000 which represented a sizeable increase over the funds then being spent for the work of the Division of Agricultural Cooperation. This permitted a strengthening of staff and a much more comprehensive program of work.

Upon passage of the Act on July 2, 1926, Secretary Jardine transferred the staff of the Division of Agricultural Cooperation to the new Division, and named as Chief, Chris L. Christensen, who was then in charge of the Department's work with cooperatives.

Although the establishment of the Division of Cooperative Marketing has been mistakingly considered of little real significance by those not intimately concerned with the development of agricultural cooperation,[39] there are few pieces of legislation that have proven of greater long-run significance to agriculture. The Cooperative Marketing Act was so wisely drawn that it has never been necessary to amend it, although the work that it provided for has been administered by several agencies of government under different political party administrations. Like the Capper-Volstead Act, it has served as a guarantee of the government's interest in helping farmers meet their own problems through cooperative effort.

Probably the major contribution of the new act was the emphasis it placed on research in cooperative organizational and operational problems. It made available to farmers, through their cooperatives, research capabilities that would otherwise have been unattainable.

With a larger budget the new Division of Cooperative Marketing was in a position to broaden the research and educational program already underway in the Department, and a number of well-qualified men were added to the staff. Among them were several who were to become nationally known as cooperative leaders: Kelsey B. Gardner, C. G. Randell, Hutzel Metzgar, John J. Scanlan, John F. Booth, W. J. Kuhrt, J. W. Jones, B. B. Derrick, and H. M. Bain. In accordance with the general guidance of the new Act, the staff was organized into the following commodity and functional units: Dairy Products; Grain, Cotton, and Tobacco; Livestock and Wool; Poultry; Fruits and Vegetables; Business Methods; Legal Problems; Membership Relations; Education; and History and Statistics.

The emphasis of the new Division was placed on improving cooperative business efficiency through research and related service and advisory work. Studies of three main types were undertaken: (1) studies of groups of cooperatives handling specific commodities; (2) case studies of significant associations, and (3) special studies of pertinent cooperative problems.

In the first category may be grouped studies of terminal livestock commission agencies, cotton ginning associations, local cooperative elevators, state cotton marketing cooperatives, milk marketing associations, fruit and vegetable cooperatives and a study of cooperative oil buying associations in Minnesota—a new form of cooperative enterprise. These were historical, descriptive, statistical, and economic studies and were designed to determine the best methods of organization and operation for such cooperative associations.

In the case studies, a detailed critical analysis was made of a single organization—its membership relations, pooling and accounting methods and management policies—and examination was made of the external economic factors which affected its operations. Studies of this type included an analysis of the Poultry Producers of Central California and an examination of the organization and operations of the Producers

Livestock Commission Association of East St. Louis, Illinois. In making these in depth studies of particular associations, general standards of business efficiency were sought that could be applied to like organizations.

Among the special studies undertaken by the Division during its first year, the following were representative: a study of the experience of the Canadian wheat pools to obtain lessons that might be useful for grain growers in the United States; a study of the benefits obtainable from the operation of a joint sales agency by the California Fruit Growers' Exchange and the California Fruit Exchange; and an economic analysis of the prune industry of the Pacific Northwest with special reference to cooperative operations. Other special studies were made of membership relations programs, management, accounting, financing and legal problems—such as the use of subsidiary corporations—and business policies and methods. Altogether there were studies made of many kinds to fit specified needs. The Division made available the results of its work in printed bulletins and circulars, and in mimeographed publications. These reflected the deep interest and professional competence of the staff.

The Act creating the Division of Cooperative Marketing gave its staff authority "to promote the knowledge of cooperative principles and practices and to cooperate in providing such knowledge with educational and marketing agencies, cooperative associations and others." During the first year, the Division participated in the conduct of several cooperative marketing short-course schools which were generally held at an agricultural college under the auspices of state extension services.

The work of the Division was effectively kept before the public by Christensen and his staff. It was vigorously supported by Secretary Jardine who said in his annual report for 1927: "I believe the time will come when farmers cooperative institutions will be as permanently established as our great organizations of industry, transportation, and labor . . . They are now 'infant industries.' It has long been our concern to encourage the growth of industry."

The program undertaken in 1926-27 was amplified in ensuing years.[40] It became the practice for cooperatives to call on the Division for advice on problems relating to organization and operation. Although research was the basis for the Division's work, research findings through service work were increasingly brought to the attention of cooperatives by publications, addresses, and advisory and educational activities. In his report on the work of the Division for 1928-1929, Christensen said:

> Demand for service by cooperatives emphasizes the importance of the research of the Division. The need for the collection and analysis of data

regarding the organization and operation of cooperatives becomes more apparent as the functions and responsibilities of the associations increase. The service of the Division becomes increasingly valuable as its fund of facts becomes greater. Approximately 60 percent of the work carried on by the Division at present may be classed as research, and it is highly desirable that this ratio should be maintained.

It is not easy to assess the value of the work of the Division of Cooperative Marketing but it unquestionably helped raise the standards of cooperative performance. Writing in 1929, Dr. John D. Black said: "What marketing principally needs is better integration. Cooperative marketing is contributing considerably in this direction. The new Division of Cooperative Marketing is very effectively assisting development in this field. Its work should be expanded . . ."[41]

Steps Toward Establishment of a New National Cooperative Council

The get-together spirit engendered by the American Institute of Cooperation and the collapse of the National Council of Farmers' Cooperative Marketing Associations also opened the way for the establishment of a more broadly based representative body of cooperative organizations.

It will be recalled that, following the Fourth National Cooperative Marketing Conference in January 1926, Walton Peteet, who had broken with Sapiro, and Robin Hood, who had been Director of Information for the original Council, undertook to determine how the Council might be reformed on a basis acceptable to the many large cooperative marketing associations that did not subscribe to the philosophy of commodity cooperative marketing as espoused by Sapiro. Their probings disclosed that most of these associations demanded three things of a national cooperative organization: "(1) recognition that there is no 'one particular brand of cooperation'; (2) a governing board composed exclusively of persons connected with cooperatives in an executive or directional capacity; (3) by-laws and operating plans that would insure equitable representation of both large and small associations of varying types."[42] To encourage and facilitate the formation of a new Council that would meet these requirements, Hood undertook to prepare a proposed set of by-laws for a "National Council of Farmers' Cooperatives." These were published in the first issue of *The Cooperative Marketing Journal* in December 1926.[43]

In *The Cooperative Marketing Journal* for March, Hood followed up by reporting on a survey made during January to determine the possible interest of leading cooperatives in the formation of a new council. The questions and the responses are of interest.

1. Should there be a national federation of cooperatives?

   The response was generally favorable. One Cooperative manager frankly held that no reorganization should be attempted "until the tyrannical and dictatorial leadership of the old council can be eliminated."

2. Should it include all types and sizes of cooperative associations, or should it be restricted to large commodity type cooperatives?

   The preponderance of opinion favored breaking down all distinctions between the large commodity cooperatives and the rest.

3. Should it maintain an office in Washington, D.C.?

   The great majority answered "yes" without qualifications.

4. What should be the chief purpose?

   "Legislative representation" was considered the most important, followed by "consideration of common problems" and "exchange of information."

5. Who should be responsible for carrying out these purposes?

   The great majority favored having a governing board and special committees with an executive secretary only to carry out detail. As Hood commented: "Generally, it may be concluded from the answers that cooperative leaders are inclined toward decentralized control and administration."

6. What are the chief dangers to be avoided?

   The gravest problem noted was "danger of control falling into the hands of a few," followed by "disruption from participating in partisan legislative issues."

7. What suggestions can you offer to guard against these dangers?

   Most of the answers suggested various measures for securing "democratic control."

Hood summarized the results of the survey by saying:

It will be seen that a new national council cannot hope for success unless it is formed upon the basis of a policy directly the reverse of the policy of the old one. The sense of the replies is that the thing primarily demanded is democratic control, in contrast to the autocratic control charged against the defunct organization, and blamed for its failure.

It was Hood's hope that a convention of cooperative leaders could soon be held to establish a new council, but nothing along this line occurred until the need became apparent to the major cooperatives. Then the preliminary work done by Hood rapidly bore fruit.

The reopening of the question came at the meetings of the American Institute of Cooperation, held at the University of California in Berkeley during 1928. At this gathering a session of the program was directed to the subject: "Cooperation Between Commodity Groups." At this session the opening address was made by Charles W. Holman, Secretary of the

American Institute of Cooperation and also Secretary of the powerful National Cooperative Milk Producers' Federation. Speaking on the subject, "National Unity for Cooperatives," Holman said: "Today's session of the Institute will deal with the question of better coordination of agricultural cooperatives for the solution of their national problems. It is to be hoped that, before this day's session is over . . . we may find the basis of coordinated action."

Holman then described the significant achievements of the National Cooperative Milk Producers' Federation in representing the legislative and other interests of the dairy cooperatives since its formation in 1916 and the progress made by other cooperative groups in achieving coordination. He saw the need for some plan by which all cooperatives could better work together, and he asked for action of a "constructive character." Strong support for this plea came from C. O. Moser, General Manager of the American Cotton Growers Exchange and one of the active leaders in the old National Council of Farmers' Cooperative Marketing Associations. Speaking on the subject "How Commodity Groups Can Best Effect Further Coordination," Moser pointed out that a national organization of commodity associations could properly and effectively engage "in activities relating to organization policy, operating methods, public good will, legislation, and self-defense." On the latter point he said: "As far back as history goes, the one compelling and eventually controlling cause for cooperation is self-defense." He then said: "The recent pronouncement of the Agricultural Trades Association, organized in Chicago during the past few months, is not only a challenge but a threat to the American cooperative marketing movement dealing in farm commodities." Moser held that this organization, comprised of strong well-financed middlemen agencies who considered themselves ordained to be "farmer masters," virtually denied "the right of the farmers to organize effectively for self-protection and for the purpose of injecting into their business the same principles which have made industry so successful and profitable." He continued: "It is reported that they propose to assemble a large fund for the purpose of destroying the cooperatives . . . " He said that to counter such concerted opposition, "a stronger cementing together" of the cooperatives was needed so that they could take protective measures.[44]

In the discussion following the presentation of papers, it was agreed that Holman would name a representative committee to devise "some kind of plan . . . to decide just what we want to do on this national organization." The committee, so authorized, under the Chairmanship of C. O. Moser, held meetings during the ensuing year and developed a plan for the organization of a National Cooperative Council. This was

ratified at a specially called meeting held at the time of the meetings
of the American Institute of Cooperation at the Louisiana State University in Baton Rouge during July 1929.

The National Cooperative Council—which in 1940 adopted its present
name the National Council of Farmer Cooperatives—thus was set up on a
very modest basis, "largely as a conference body and contact agency,"
with Mr. Charles Holman as Secretary, just as the Federal Farm Board
was assuming its responsibilities.[45]

Summary

We have seen in this chapter how agricultural cooperation grew in
scope and significance with the encouragement of government from 1920
to 1929. Although part of this growth came from the stimulation given by
the commodity marketing movement, more of it came from the strengthening of the already existing mainline cooperative movement as a
counter response to the commodity marketing movement. The formation
of the American Institute of Cooperation, the passage of the Cooperative
Marketing Act of 1926, and the establishment of the National Cooperative
Council were primarily manifestations of the growing power of the mainline cooperative movement. Although these developments opened the
way for the Agricultural Marketing Act of 1929, which provided for the
Federal Farm Board, this act—as will be shown in the next chapter—came
more as a direct result of pressure for farm relief engendered by the
McNary-Haugen movement.

Chapter VI

THE COOPERATIVES AND THE
McNARY-HAUGEN MOVEMENT: 1924-1928

George Peek was by nature a fighter, and the defeat of the first McNary-Haugen Bill in June 1924 only strengthened his determination to achieve victory.[1] Immediately after the vote he declared that he was going to continue the fight, and, with his supporters, he soon set up an aggressive propaganda organization, the American Council of Agriculture, "to secure the enactment by Congress of such legislation embodying the principles of the McNary-Haugen Bill as shall be necessary to secure for agriculture equality with labor and industry." The Executive Committee of the American Council included officers of most of the major farm organizations. As the "father of the movement," Peek was elected President.

As 1924 was an election year, the American Council of Agriculture worked energetically to get support for McNary-Haugen principles from the three presidential candidates. John W. Davis, the Democratic candidate, promised, if elected, to call a special session of Congress to consider the needs of agriculture. The Progressive candidate, Senator Robert LaFollette, gave his full support to legislation of the McNary-Haugen type; President Coolidge, the Republican candidate, was equivocal.[2] However, late in the campaign he recognized the insistent demand of farmers for relief by promising to appoint a well-qualified conference group to investigate agricultural conditions and recommend legislation to the Congress.

The death of President Harding in the summer of 1923 had been a hard blow to the advocates of the McNary-Haugen idea, for he had given Secretary Wallace considerable support on agricultural matters. President Coolidge from the beginning of his administration had looked to Herbert Hoover for advice on economic and agricultural problems, and Hoover was strongly opposed to the McNary-Haugen plan of farm relief. The death of Secretary Wallace, on October 25, 1924, was an even more significant loss to friends of the McNary-Haugen plan, for it placed Secretary Hoover in a strategic position to influence agricultural policies during the interim period while Albert Gore of West Virginia was serving as Secretary of Agriculture. The sweeping victory of Coolidge in November by the largest plurality in Republican history piled more gloom on the McNary-Haugen plan advocates.[3]

The interest of Secretary Wallace in the McNary-Haugen Bill had been matched by Secretary Hoover's dislike of it. In cooperative marketing, Hoover saw a method of agricultural organization that could be used to make legislation of the McNary-Haugen type unnecessary.[4] In early 1924, Hoover had become interested in a bill introduced in Congress by Congressman Arthur B. Williams of Michigan which called for a "Federal Cooperative Marketing system" to be administered by a federal board and commodity advisory councils.[5] The federal board was to provide for registration and auditing of cooperatives and for "a financial check-up very similar to what is now exercised by the Comptroller of the Currency in dealing with the Banks."[6] According to Mr. Williams, copies of his bill were submitted to Secretary Hoover who "in the course of two or three weeks sent for me and said that I had approached the subject in the right way, and he had some suggestions which he desired to make with reference to the bill."[7] Congressman Williams then incorporated Hoover's suggestions in a new bill introduced on April 14, 1924. Under the second bill, the Secretary of Commerce, as well as the Secretary of Agriculture, would be members of the federal board, and there would be five members appointed by the President. This bill provided for "cooperative clearing houses" to coordinate operations of marketing cooperatives and commercial shippers and "regulated terminal marketing associations," and for a fund of 7½ million dollars for administering the Act. Part of this was to be used as a "revolving fund to cooperatives to help them increase membership."

With the defeat of the McNary-Haugen Bill in June, Secretary Hoover began to actively promote—in speeches to business groups and in business publications—the ideas in the Williams Bill, as an antidote to McNary-Haugenism. His views were fully presented in an article under the title "Cooperative Marketing" in the *Manufacturers' News*, published in the fall of 1924. This article is of much interest in view of the influence that Hoover then had on President Coolidge. The first sentences read as follows: "I wish to state at the outset my faith that the future of our marketing of agricultural products lies in the larger development of the cooperative principle. I believe that the time has come when we must take strong and definite steps in its further development." In Hoover's opinion "the whole problem of improved marketing" lay in the "elimination of waste." After listing several types of waste he said: "Cooperative marketing has been developing for many years, and any study of it will show that it has succeeded just so far as it has eliminated some of those wastes . . . If we can get an organization going which will eliminate all the wastes, or any large part of them, we shall have brought about a revolution in our distribution system." Later in this article Hoover said:

> I am no believer in governmental compulsion as a method of attempting to build up any kind of government activity . . . I believe, therefore, that we must devise machinery for the development of organization, the joining of which would be purely voluntary and the advantages of membership in which would be such as to swiftly secure within their ranks the preponderating marketing of particular commodities, and would set in action the forces for the elimination of waste . . .
>
> Six months ago, after prolonged investigations by the Department of Commerce, I made certain proposals in this direction which were later incorporated . . . into the Capper-Williams Bill . . . The plan I offered at that time was somewhat as follows: First, that we should create a Federal marketing board, this board to be comprised of certain Cabinet officers, a majority of its members, however, to be ultimately chosen by the cooperatives which joined the plan and a minority from certain terminal marketing associations to be organized under the general plan . . . I proposed that this board should have the following function: That the board should provide a staff of men skilled in the organization and administration of cooperatives who could give skilled advice on needs and methods. That the board should have authority to establish standards of cooperation with producers and the Department of Agriculture; to cooperate with that Department in amplifying inspection and certification to the end that all interstate goods could be shipped on standards certified to by the Federal authority. That it should cooperate in the distribution of such market information as will lessen the chaos in shipments. That it should cooperate with the Department of Commerce in export questions . . .
>
> In order that we should create larger confidence among the farmers in the cooperative idea and in the administration of cooperatives, I proposed that *the board should be authorized to grant Federal charters to cooperatives* in certain minimum conditions. These conditions are in addition to requirements of State laws that the cooperatives would adhere to . . . , *that they would submit to periodic inspection* and report on their accounts and financial methods . . . The Board should be authorized to approve the formation of clearing houses for joint action in control of shipments . . . and *I would authorize the cooperatives to take private shippers* into these clearing houses if cooperatives so wished . . . The Board should be authorized to give *charters to associations of distributors,* including representatives of cooperatives, in our different terminal markets . . . (Italics added).[8]

These statements reflected Hoover's penchant for system and order and they were no doubt well-intentioned. However, Hoover never could quite understand how farmers' minds worked, for he assumed that he knew best what was good for them. While Hoover's views were naturally attractive to industrial and commercial leaders who favored docile and tractable cooperatives, they had little appeal to farmer members of cooperatives and cooperative officials who had no desire to be regulated. All they desired was the consideration accorded to other forms of business.

Had it not been for the sweeping victory of President Coolidge at the polls and the death of Secretary Wallace—the champion of farmers— Hoover's proposals, as incorporated in the Williams Bill, would have gained little support. However, the reelection of Coolidge gave Hoover just the opportunity he desired to get his views accepted by means of the "Agricultural Conference," that President Coolidge had promised to set up after the election. This body was appointed by President Coolidge on November 7, 1924. It was obvious to well-qualified observers that the members were hand-picked politically for their conservative views. As Murray Benedict later wrote: "It was a group not likely to come out with radical proposals that would be embarrassing to Coolidge."[9]

Governor Robert D. Carey of Wyoming was named Chairman of the Agricultural Conference. Other members were: O. E. Bradfute, President of the American Farm Bureau Federation; Charles W. Barrett, President of the National Farmers Union; Louis J. Tabor, Master of the Grange; Ralph P. Merritt, President of Sun-Maid Raisin Growers; R. W. Thatcher, Director of the New York Experiment Station; W. C. Coffey, Dean of the Minnesota College of Agriculture; and Fred H. Bixby, President of the American Livestock Association. Shortly after the initial appointments, William M. Jardine, President of Kansas State College of Agriculture, and soon to take office as Secretary of Agriculture, was added to the Conference. It should be observed that only Mr. Merritt was associated in a prominent way with cooperative marketing operations, and that he was a close personal friend of Secretary Hoover.

The Agricultural Conference held its initial meeting with President Coolidge on November 17 and continued its deliberations over the next two months. During this period, it received testimony from many individuals and organizations but no public record was made of the views expressed. However, the statement that Secretary Hoover gave to the Conference was made available in a press release of the Department of Commerce, January 20, 1925. In this he said: "Government assistance can be rendered to cooperative marketing and should be rendered in far more forcible and constructive ways than hitherto."

In late January, the Conference reported its recommendations on agricultural legislation. This report was apparently just what President Coolidge wanted, for he immediately transmitted the report to Congress with the recommendation that it "be embraced in suitable legislation at the earliest possible date." The Conference Report sidestepped the McNary-Haugen issue by saying that the American farmer should be given the "full benefit of the American market" through the application of the protective tariff system. "Any form of legislation or plan that tends toward a stimulation of production of any particular product for export will result in even further ill balance to our agriculture. There must, therefore, be established a balanced American agriculture by which production is kept in step with domestic markets and with only such foreign markets as may be profitable."

The Conference report set up six general principles "to be applied upon voluntary action by commodity marketing organizations, producers, and distributors." The key sentences are here given:

1. For the purpose of promoting equitable and advantageous distribution and disposition of their products, cooperative marketing associations or any of them may pool their products, exchange crop and market information, and make and carry out orderly production and marketing programs; and for such purposes, producers and distributors of such product may cooperate with such associations.

2. Groups of producers desiring to organize cooperative organizations should be given opportunity for application to the Government to make a survey of the distributing problems involving any commodity . . .

3. Commodity marketing organizations upon application to the proper Federal agency, and purely as a voluntary act, may apply to be Federally registered upon demonstration of the soundness of financial standing of the organization and an agreement to submit their books to Federal inspection for audit semi-annually . . .

4. The establishment of grades and standards for various agricultural products of the country is essential . . .

5. Upon application to the Federal agency distributors at terminal markets may create Federally registered exchanges or associations, the members of which shall operate under rules and regulations formulated by them and approved by the Federal authority creating the charter . . .

6. Upon application to the Federal agency by an agricultural industry through its cooperative organization, the Federal agency should consider and advise upon the problems confronting the industry in any phases of production, financing or marketing . . .

In addition to the preceding principles applicable to all cooperatives, the following principle was recommended for perishable products.

Cooperative marketing organizations, upon application to Federal authority, may have the right to create clearing houses, for the purpose of eliminating the over supply or under-supply in various consuming markets without interference with the restraint of trade laws . . .

These so-called principles implied a degree of government supervision and control that had heretofore been absent in the relations of government and cooperatives, and it was recognized that some new form of "administrative authority" would be required to administer the principles set forth. On this the conference report said:

> . . . For the proper development of cooperative marketing organizations, it is quite apparent that there is need for a central unit which would make available to producers all facilities now in existence and those which might be brought about relating to the different phases of cooperative marketing. Such a unit would act as a coordinating agency, and producers' organizations would get in touch with it directly for any help or assistance they might legitimately seek.
>
> [Therefore] . . . there should be instituted a separate board, as is now the case in industry and banking. This board would be able to use all the facilities of all Government departments and interlock all the problems of agriculture, both those of production with those of distribution.

The proposed board was to "arise from the commodity organizations themselves by nomination to the President." In the words of the report:

> There should be created a Federal cooperative marketing board of five members, two members to be the Secretary of Agriculture and the Secretary of Commerce, and three others, including a chairman to be appointed by the President, to be nominated by the Federally registered cooperative marketing organizations, upon the expiration of the terms of the three members first appointed by the President. The salaries of the three appointed members should be $12,000 a year. They would serve terms of one, two and three years respectively, with succeeding members to serve terms of six years each. For the purposes of establishing the board and of carrying on its first year of operation, the sum of $500,000 should be appropriated.

The report of the Conference was received with little enthusiasm from the cooperatives. In fact, they were practically unanimous in condemning it as an attempt to bureaucratize the cooperative movement.[10]

Immediately following the report, Congressman Williams—who kept in close touch with members of the Conference—again adjusted his thinking and introduced his bill in revised form to make it acceptable to the Conference. It was understood that his fifth bill accurately followed its recommendations. Upon receipt of the Conference report, the House Agricultural Committee held extensive hearings on the Williams Bill and related legislative proposals. The main spokesmen for the cooperatives were Aaron Sapiro, who represented the National Council of Farmers' Cooperative Marketing Associations, and Charles W. Holman, who represented the National Board of Farm Organizations, which included the influential National Milk Producers' Federation, and other cooperatives and farm organizations.

Sapiro vigorously opposed the provisions of the Williams Bill as being dangerous to the aspirations of cooperatives, and, in fact, he saw no need for cooperative legislation of any character.[11] The cooperatives and organizations represented by Holman were equally vigorous in opposing the Williams Bill but they favored "a mild type of Government assistance without registration or regulations." As an alternative to the Williams Bill, Holman and his associates had helped draft the Dickinson Bill which provided for a Federal Marketing Board of four with the Secretary of Agriculture as an ex-officio member. The board would operate with an appropriation of $500,000 and would work closely with and supplement the work of the Department of Agriculture. Holman said: "We produced this Dickinson Bill as something which would help and not harm . . . There are important objections to practically any other bill that we have had an opportunity to read."

In the examination of Holman in the Hearings, there was this interchange:

> Congressman Voight, of Wisconsin: "I have looked over your bill, and I cannot find a single thing in it where the cooperative is put under compulsion by any Government agency."
> Mr. Holman: "If there were, we would oppose it."
> Congressman Voight: "Your theory is that whatever is done by a Government Agency should be simply by way of encouragement features?"
> Mr. Holman: "Yes sir, encouragement, and it might go a little further in the way of giving some direct help."[12]

After prolonged discussion, the House Committee found the Williams Bill unacceptable, and undertook to draft its own measure—the Haugen Bill—to incorporate the views of the Agricultural Conference. However, after a "severe fight in the House" the Dickinson Bill was substituted for the Committee measure. Although the Dickinson Bill passed with a substantial margin in the House, it failed of support in the Senate.

On March 6, 1925, *Wallace's Farmer* carried an article "Congress Kills Fake Farm Relief," which explained how Congress dealt with the Williams, Haugen, and Dickinson Bills. The sub-title was "House Gives Final Blow to Hooverization of Cooperative Marketing." The leading paragraph said:

> The Williams Bill, which embodied Secretary Hoover's ideas on cooperative marketing, really was beaten in committee some time ago, when the house agricultural committee threw it out and wrote its own bill. The Hoover ideas, however, got a final blow to the solar plexus last week when the house decided that even the committee bill had a scent of the Secretary of Commerce about it and substituted for it the measure proposed by Representative Dickinson of Iowa. The test vote showed 203 for the Dickinson bill to 175 against it.

The article then explained:

> This action . . . has more significance than may at first appear. It really marked the final defeat . . . of a long matured and well laid plan to cripple cooperative marketing, transfer marketing work from the Department of Agriculture to the Department of Commerce, and divert farm attention from the export bill. This is a negative victory, but it is a real one. Few people realize

just how vigorous and well prepared has been the campaign for this three-fold purpose and how nearly it succeeded.

According to Professor John D. Black, the recommendations of the Conference were rejected summarily by the Congress in view of the strong opposition of the cooperative front. Writing in 1928 he said:

> When the Capper-Haugen cooperative marketing bill, embodying the Agricultural Conference's idea on this subject, was introduced in February 1925, it was attacked and defeated by the agricultural bloc, on the ground that it took cooperative marketing out of the Department of Agriculture, where it belonged, and put it where the Department of Commerce could get hold of it, and in addition, set up rather rigorous governmental machinery for its control . . . The cooperatives back in 1925 were carrying their syndicalism almost to the point of complete non-intervention. Friendly assistance, such as they were getting from the Department of Agriculture, they welcomed; but not the kind of supervision that certain mercantilistically minded members of the Agricultural Conference deemed highly necessary for them . . . [13]

The defeat of the Administration's plan for cooperative marketing legislation ensured that McNary-Haugenism would again take the center of the political stage when the new Congress convened in the fall. However, the debate over the proposals of the Conference was to have a significant effect on future cooperative legislation. It popularized the idea of a Federal Farm Board with broad powers to assist cooperatives, and it also gave emphasis to the value of the research and advisory work with cooperatives carried on in the Department of Agriculture. Thus it paved the way for the Cooperative Marketing Act of 1926, as well as for the Agricultural Marketing Act of 1929.

Although unsuccessful in its major proposals for cooperative legislation, the Conference can be given credit for other measures of substantial value to cooperatives. The Purnell Act (approved February 24, 1925), passed with the support of the Conference, provided for funds that enabled the state experiment stations to expand studies in marketing and cooperation. The exemption of agricultural cooperatives from Federal Income Tax, under certain conditions, was also given effective support by the Conference.[14]

In a way, President Coolidge precipitated the drive for a more dynamic McNary-Haugen movement that was to hold the center of the political stage for the next four years. In addressing the American Farm Bureau Federation at its annual meeting in Chicago in December 1925, Coolidge made clear his distaste for the McNary-Haugen approach to farm relief. Instead he urged farmers to place their faith in cooperative marketing. He said:

> Various suggestions of artificial relief have been made . . . One of the methods by which that has been sought, though put forward chiefly as an emer-

gency measure as I understand from its proponents, was to have corporations
organized through which the Government would directly or indirectly fix prices
or engage in buying and selling farm produce. This would be a dangerous
undertaking, and as the emergency is not so acute, it seems at present to have
lost much of its support . . . I propose actively and energetically to assist the
farmers to promote their welfare through cooperative marketing.

According to a well-informed observer: "His words fell on the audience like a wet blanket. As the presidential party left the room, the
applause was notably slight and the atmosphere chilly and barely re-
spectful."[15] Furthermore, the speech backfired, instead of helping Oscar
Bradfute, the incumbent President of the Farm Bureau, gain re-election,
it assured his defeat by Sam Thompson, President of the Illinois
Agricultural Association, and a forceful advocate of McNary-
Haugenism.[16]

Although no significant farm relief legislation was passed in 1925, farm
support for the McNary-Haugen idea continued to grow, and the
opposition of cooperative marketing organizations began to subside. By
mid-year, Governor Frank O. Lowden had become convinced that
cooperative marketing organizations could not by themselves handle the
surplus problem, and he evidenced his interest in the McNary-Haugen
plan. Lowden had tremendous influence as a farm leader, and his
endorsement would have great weight.[17]

A number of significant developments put the McNary-Haugen
movement in high gear in January 1926. On January 4 the Dickinson
Bill—designed to manage the surplus through use of the cooperatives—
was introduced.[18] When the National Council of Farmers' Cooperative
Marketing Associations held its annual conference in Washington, D.C.,
on January 12-15, it was disclosed that Lowden and other outstanding
cooperative leaders were no longer opposed to the McNary-Haugen type
of legislation. Shortly afterwards, on January 28, a conference of farm
leaders at Des Moines, Iowa, set up the "Executive Committee of 22" to
work for McNary-Haugen principles. During the next three years, this
group was to be a driving force for passage of McNary-Haugen
legislation.[19] However, all attempts failed to get McNary-Haugen legislation passed in 1926. The only significant agricultural measure passed that
year was the Cooperative Marketing Act, which was non-controversial
with regard to McNary-Haugenism, and which had the blessing of
Secretary Jardine and the great majority of cooperative organizations.

By 1927, the McNary-Haugen forces had succeeded in obtaining
almost full support of American agriculture—except for areas not concerned with the great staple crops, such as New England, California, and
Florida—and a revised McNary-Haugen Bill, designed to satisfy the

marketing cooperatives was passed by both houses of Congress, only to be vetoed on February 2 by President Coolidge, with a biting message drafted by Hoover and Secretary of the Treasury, Andrew Mellon, which charged the bill with being "price fixing" in character, an insinuation almost as insulting to its proponents as would be the accusation that they favored breaking the Seventh Commandment.

Under the continuing leadership of George Peek, the McNary-Haugen forces—backed by the American Farm Bureau and strong cooperative support—attempted to meet the objections of the 1927 veto message in a revised McNary-Haugen Bill introduced in both houses in the spring of 1928. This measure passed both houses but again it could not override the veto of President Coolidge. His veto message of May 25, 1928, was even more caustic in its condemnation of the measure than that of the year before. It appeared that the McNary-Haugen plan was dead at last, but George Peek refused to surrender. When Chester Davis said to Peek, in the spring of 1928: "George, this is the last heat I trot. We can't dump surpluses over the sort of tariff walls they're rearing over the water now." Peek curtly replied: "The hell we can't."[20]

This was the situation as the country turned to the presidential election of 1928. If Hoover were elected there would be little chance of legislation of the McNary-Haugen type. The only hope was to support Governor Al Smith but this proved futile for Hoover had strong support from the industrial states and from those who opposed Smith's views on prohibition, religion, and other issues. The election was decisive—but the efforts of the McNary-Haugenites were not all in vain, for they forced Hoover to promise farm relief legislation embodying many of their views, and the Agricultural Marketing Act of 1929 was the result. During the Farm Board interlude, 1929-32, the McNary-Haugen fires were banked, but as we shall see in Chapter XIII, they were to erupt in modified form in the Agricultural Adjustment Act of 1933.

In retrospect, the debate over McNary-Haugenism did much to condition the nation for later government programs to aid agriculture. Indirectly, McNary-Haugenism also greatly influenced the development of agricultural cooperation, for it is doubtful whether the Coolidge administration would have given its all-out support to cooperatives and cooperative legislation during the four years from 1925 to 1928 without this prod. The Agricultural Marketing Act of 1929 also went a long way to gain the support of those in the McNary-Haugen camp who demanded positive action by government in aid of farmers.[21]

Chapter VII

THE COMING OF THE FEDERAL FARM BOARD:
1924-1929

With the election of Herbert Hoover as President in November 1928, the stage was set for the establishment of a Federal Farm Board. The idea had been a prominent feature of most of the farm relief proposals during the preceding four years.

The Farm Board Idea Emerges

The germ of the plan was embodied in the Williams Bill that Hoover helped draft in the spring of 1924.[1] The idea had been accepted by the President's Agricultural Conference in 1925 and was made a part of the Haugen Bill drafted to put the Conference's ideas into effect. Even the cooperative counter proposals embodied in the Dickinson Bill of February 1925 accepted the idea of a Federal Farm Board. However, the farm board as envisaged in these early measures was not to be empowered to carry on price stabilization operations. We have noted in Chapter VI how the McNary-Haugen Bills of 1927 and 1928 recognized the need of an administrative agency of a federal farm board type to work in conjunction with cooperative marketing organizations, and how the Coolidge Administration had responded to the pressure of the McNary-Haugen forces by accentuating its support for cooperative marketing. The Cooperative Marketing Act of 1926 had proved popular but this act simply provided for the strengthening of cooperative marketing and purchasing associations through the amplification of research, service, and educational programs in the Department of Agriculture. It did not make the cooperatives instruments of public policy for raising prices through the administration of surpluses of agricultural products.

109

Although Secretary Jardine had sponsored the Cooperative Marketing Act of 1926 he was convinced that a Federal Farm Board—as recommended by the Agricultural Conference in January 1925—might prove helpful in better management of agricultural surpluses. Moreover, he recognized that a bill providing for a farm board clothed with broad powers would provide the Administration with a positive alternative plan to the McNary-Haugen and Export Debenture plans then being strongly advocated in Congress. The proponents of the McNary-Haugen and Export debenture plans were then wooing the cooperatives by promising that they would have an important role in their administration.

Secretary Jardine's views on how a farm board could function were first introduced into Congress in January 1927 as the Curtis-Crisp Bill. This bill provided for a "Federal Farm Board" which was to promote orderly marketing and make advances to cooperative associations to enable them to buy and withhold from the market any non-perishable product, whenever there was proved to exist a surplus of it "above world requirements," and when this surplus threatened to "depress the price of such commodity below the cost of production with a reasonable profit to the efficient producer thereof," and a revolving fund of $250,000,000 was to be provided to carry out these provisions."[2]

In an article in the *Farm Journal,* August 15, 1927, Jardine modified his views to provide for "commodity stabilization corporations operated by the farmers themselves or by their marketing organizations under the general guidance of a Federal Farm Board." Jardine explained his plan more fully in the *Oklahoma Stockman and Farmer* of November 1, 1927.

> There should be a Farm Board, consisting of able men who understand agriculture and are sympathetic toward its problems . . . This board would be a recognition of a public responsibility toward agriculture, in encouraging sound business methods in agriculture and in minimizing price fluctuations due to unpreventable surpluses and shortages. This board would be backed by two main supports: First, a more adequate statistical service . . . Second, a revolving fund from which the board could make advances to commodity organizations.
>
> The activities of this board, in addition to enhancing the growth of sound organizations in every practical way, would fall under two main heads: First, to aid in minimizing price fluctuations due to unpreventable surpluses, second, to help in adjusting production to market demand.
>
> There would be established for each major commodity a stabilization corporation, with a nominal capital stock owned by properly organized commodity cooperatives. When an exceptional season resulted in a crop surplus, the stabilization corporation, under the general guidance of the Farm Board, would take part of that surplus off the market to prevent the price from dropping to an abnormally low level.[3]

Big Business Lends a Hand

During this same period the seriousness of the agricultural situation was not being ignored by American business leaders. In 1925, the National Industrial Conference Board made a general study of the agricultural problem in the United States "to clarify the problem as a whole so as to contribute to a better and more general understanding of it, not only by American industry but by the general public, and so to provide a common basis for such sound policies as may assure the country a prosperous agriculture as a part of a prosperous economy."

The report giving the results of the study was published in April 1926 under the title: *The Agricultural Problem in the United States.* It was prepared by Dr. Virgil Jordan and the research staff of the Conference Board, with the cooperation of its Advisory Committee on Agriculture which included such prominent figures as Alexander Legge, President, International Harvester Company; Frank O. Lowden; John R. Mitchell, Chairman, Federal Reserve Bank of Minneapolis; S. H. Thompson, President, American Farm Bureau Federation; and Owen D. Young, Chairman, General Electric Company. The foreword to the report declared:

> The position of American Agriculture is of vital concern to all the people of the United States, not only for today but for the future as well . . . The development of sound, farsighted national policies in respect to agriculture is, therefore, one of the most important problems before the country today. Our agriculture is now going through a crucial transition in its character and in its relationship to our national life. The success or failure of this readjustment will be of the greatest significance for our future.

The report was well received as a fair analysis of the serious problems confronting agriculture. It did not offer remedies but it did suggest an approach to their solution in its "Summary and Conclusions."

> It would seem proper and desirable in the national interest for leading representatives of American industry, commerce, transportation and finance in conjunction with leaders of agriculture, to study jointly and sympathetically on the basis of the Conference Board's report, the agricultural situation and its causes, to appraise its consequences and to present to the consideration of the public their mature judgement of its possibilities and desirable avenues of remedy and readjustment. In this way it is possible that . . . there may be developed a sound and far-sighted national policy embracing and justly balancing all the interests involved (p. 150).

As a result of this suggestion, a "Business Men's Commission on Agriculture" was soon set up jointly by the National Industrial Conference Board and the Chamber of Commerce of the United States "to study the conditions of agriculture in the United States and to suggest measures for its improvement." The Commission consisted of 10 executives of industrial, railway, and banking corporations under the Chairmanship of Charles Nagel, a former Secretary of Commerce. Professor Frank D. Graham of Princeton University was employed as economic advisor. The Commission undertook its assignment in a very responsible and sympathetic way, for it admittedly had "no ulterior purpose to serve, political or economic." Hearings were held in a number of cities from December 20, 1926, to April 20, 1927, and some 170 witnesses were heard.

The report of the Commission, published in book form in November 1927 under the title *The Condition of Agriculture in the United States and Measures for Its Improvement* was widely acclaimed as a constructive document, and it had great influence in widening the public's understanding of the agricultural problem. The Commission found early in its investigation that: "For a situation at once so comprehensive and complicated there is no one panacea . . . Unquestionably there is an answer, but that answer should not be sought in the vague and extravagant promises of this or that slogan. On the contrary, it must be found in the adoption of a comprehensive agricultural policy, the success of which will depend upon the generous and intelligent cooperation of private initiative and state and Federal agencies" (pp. 5-6). The Commission was opposed to a policy of letting things drift. It declared: "*Laissez faire* is of the past and the practical question is how far shall we be driven in the other direction" (p. 11).

In its examination of "measures for agricultural improvement" the Commission placed much emphasis on what farmers could do for themselves through cooperative action. The report said: "The success of farmers in meeting their own difficulties depends in the main upon their organized cooperative effort" (p. 195). The Commission not only recognized the important role of well-managed cooperatives for marketing improvement but also saw that cooperation could contribute to more efficient agricultural production. The report maintained that:

> Cooperation should start with the purchase of goods needed in agricultural production. Fertilizer, seed, feed, machinery, feeder cattle, feeder lambs, and many other commodities can often be bought cooperatively better than through the private trade. The cooperative method concentrates the buying power of many farmers into a single channel and makes possible considerable savings through wholesale buying and shipment in carload lots. It also tends to eliminate unnecessary services, such as advertising, storage, and credit extension (p. 197).

Although the Commission favored the expansion and strengthening of cooperative marketing associations, it did not recommend their use for stabilizing farm income—the problem which was then demanding most urgent attention. For effective stabilization of the agricultural industry the Commission proposed:

> 1. There should be established a Federal Farm Board consisting of a small number of men appointed by the President and paid by the government, to aid in the stabilization of prices and production in agriculture by advising farmers and farm organizations fully and promptly regarding the planning of production and the marketing of crops . . . This Board should be assisted in its work by a number of advisory committees . . . Through the appointment of its members and through its advisory committees this Board should be made as directly responsible to farmers and farmers' organizations as possible.
>
> 2. With the advice and assistance of the Federal Farm Board, effort should be made to establish stabilization corporations to engage in the buying and selling of farm products for the purpose of stabilizing price. Such corporations should be established through the cooperation of farm organizations, of private business organizations directly interested in the processing and merchandising of farm products . . . and of the government acting through the Federal Farm Board. The capital necessary for the establishment of these corporations should be supplied partly by the farmers' cooperatives, partly by other private business interests, and partly by the Federal government. . . . (pp. 181-182).

This proposal in the words of Dr. Edwin G. Nourse was "Novel, not to say startling."[4] The conception of Federal Farm Board with broad discretionary powers was favorably received in business circles and by many careful students of the agricultural problem. Among those who highly commended the Commission on its report was Joseph S. Davis, Director of the Food Research Institute of Stanford University. In a Round-Table on "An American Agricultural Policy" held at the Institute of Politics (Williamstown, Massachusetts) in August 1927, he said:

> The recent admirable report of the Business Men's Commission on Agriculture affords quite the most reliable, well-rounded, convincing discussion of the agricultural problem that has yet appeared. . . . The next step in our agricultural policy, I believe, should be to set up an agency competent to take steps, and charged with gradually working out, not in the closet but in practice, a solution that defies all efforts to reach it in advance of experience. A Federal Farm Board, if wisely chosen and properly constituted, might well perform such a service, provided it were given adequate powers and not saddled with impossible duties. It should not be expected to administer a fully developed plan laid down by Congress . . . [5]

By 1928, it was quite clear that the Coolidge administration looked with favor on stabilization corporations and a Federal Farm Board. In the Report of the Secretary of Agriculture for 1928, the administration's position was expressed as follows:

> The surplus problem is of national importance not only to agriculture but to the nation as a whole. It is therefore proper to make the solution of it in some measure a governmental responsibility. This need not involve going further than the Government has gone in aid of other economic interests, although legislation dealing with the agricultural surplus necessarily must be

sufficiently different from other legislation to meet the peculiarities of the problem. No law dealing with the problem would be entirely adequate at first . . . Changes in a surplus control program probably would be necessary in the light of experience. As an initial step, it should suffice to create a Federal Farm Board with adequate authority to finance the handling of surpluses through central stabilization corporations, for which purpose a revolving fund should be provided. Advisory committees responsive to the farmers should be created to assist the Board. In this way, the surplus problem would, I am convinced, be brought nearer to a solution.[6]

The Growth of the Clearing House Idea

While Hoover's Farm Board idea was gaining adherents there was a marked expansion of interest in his conception of cooperative clearing houses comprised of cooperatives and private shippers as a means of achieving better coordination in marketing. In 1924, when Hoover first espoused clearing houses in the Williams Bill and while he was making his recommendations to the President's Agricultural Conference in 1925, there was a recurrence of interest in such organizations especially in California where the idea had been endemic for some 30 years.[7] In the next few years as the problem of surplus control became more pressing a number of clearing house plans were developed for specialized California crops with varying degrees of success, and similar organizations arose in other states. One of the most ambitious undertakings of this type was the formation of the Florida Citrus Growers Clearing House Association in June 1928 with the advisory assistance of the Division of Cooperative Marketing. This organization grew out of a suggestion made by Secretary of Agriculture Jardine, "that a clearing house of growers," be set up in a conference held with representatives of the Florida Citrus Exchange and other groups in the Florida citrus industry. After many meetings and much organizational work a plan for a clearing house was devised and taken to growers in an intensive drive conducted by Merton L. Corey. Although full cooperation was not obtained from shippers the organization continued to function with moderate success until it was discontinued in November 1933, following the enactment of the Agricultural Adjustment Act which provided for marketing agreements and licenses.[8]

Interest in clearing house associations reached a peak at the meetings of the American Institute of Cooperation held at the University of California in Berkeley during July and August of 1928. Although several cooperative leaders spoke favorably on the basis of their limited experience with clearing house plans, there was much opposition to the clearing house idea from others who felt that it represented a step backward. For illustration, Dr. Milton Nelson, Professor of Economics, Oregon State College, said:

The clearing house plan, as generally understood involves something like this, that the cooperatives will combine with the independent distributors in one organization with the understanding that those distributors will make a contract with the independent growers. The independent growers agree not to ship through distributors who are not in the organization and not to have anything to do with the cooperatives. From that time on, in other words, the cooperatives stand still and the independent growers commit themselves to the distributors. . . . That means that the cooperative movement stands still during the operation of the clearing house plan.[9]

It was the well balanced view of Chris L. Christensen, Chief of the Division of Cooperative Marketing, that

. . . a clearing house attacks the problem from the top down. There is not the close tie-up with growers and specific control of marketing functions that exists in a cooperative marketing association. I confess, it is difficult for me to see how overproduction can be regulated or kept in check by a clearing house organization, while there are possibilities of extending some degree of control through a genuine marketing association.[10]

Dr. Edwin G. Nourse saw in the clearing house movement "a revival of the 'commodity marketing' theory which was so vigorously exploited in this country a few years ago." He did not believe that the clearing house as "a market distribution device" touched "the larger problem of productive organization which is the heart of the farmers problem."[11]

In the following chapter we will see how the clearing house idea was incorporated into the Agricultural Marketing Act of 1929 and the extent of its use by the Federal Farm Board during the Great Depression.

The Federal Farm Board Becomes a Fact

In the presidential campaign of 1928, the Republican Party platform said this on the agricultural problem:

We promise every assistance in the reorganization of the marketing system on sounder and more economical lines and, where diversification is needed, Government financial assistance during the period of transition . . . The Republican party pledges itself to the enactment of legislation creating a Federal Farm Board clothed with the necessary powers to promote the establishment of a farm marketing system of farmer owned and controlled stabilization corporations or associations to prevent and control surpluses through orderly distribution . . . We favor, without putting the Government into business, the establishment of a Federal System of organization for cooperatives and orderly marketing of farm products. . . . [12]

While Hoover recognized the seriousness of agriculture's plight, he did not spell out his farm board plan until he spoke at St. Louis on November 2, the Friday before election day. He then said:

We propose to create a Federal Farm Board composed of men of understanding and sympathy for the problems of agriculture; we propose this board should have power to determine the facts, the causes, the remedies which should be applied to each and every one of the multitude of problems which we mass under the general term "the agricultural problem."

This program further provides that the board shall have a broad authority to act and be authorized to assist in the further development of cooperative marketing; that it shall assist in the development of clearing houses for agricultural products, . . . and in the solution of other problems as they arise. But in particular the board is to be built up with initial advances of capital from the Government, farmer-owned and farmer-controlled stabilization corporations which will protect the farmer from depressions and the demoralization of summer and periodic surpluses. . . .

This is an entirely different method of approach to solution from that of a general formula; it is flexible and adaptable. . . . It is a direct business proposition. It marks our desire for establishment of farmers' stability and at the same time maintains his independence and individuality. . . . It puts the Government in its real relation to the citizen—that of cooperation. . . . I would consider it the greatest honor I could have if it should become my privilege to aid in finally solving this the most difficult of economic problems presented to our people, and the one in which by inheritance and through long contact I have my deepest interest.[13]

According to an editorial in *Wallace's Farmer* on November 16, immediately after the election, the speech was a great success. "He delivered a splendid message that night, much more forceful in character than any other statement he made during the campaign. *This speech was undoubtedly the turning point in the farm vote."*

The editorial went on to say: "It is unquestionably true that many thousand farm folk in Iowa and the middle west construed Mr. Hoover's statement as a promise to deal adequately with the exportable surplus. We believe that it can be fairly said that Mr. Hoover owes the large vote he received in the agricultural states to this very thing . . . " On the basis of this understanding of Mr. Hoover's program, the editor then said: "We pledge him our support. . . . Equality of agriculture is the paramount task of Mr. Hoover's administration and the promises made in the campaign must be redeemed. . . . All will wish him well in the great task ahead of him.[14]

Hoover's victory at the polls, ensured that the time for the Federal Farm Board idea had come. However, there was not great jubilation in farm circles. The American Farm Bureau Federation passively waited for the Federal Farm Board "to take form and reserved comment."[15]

The organ of the agricultural cooperatives, *The Cooperative Marketing Journal*, January 1929, simply said:

The conclusiveness of the ballot which elected Herbert Hoover President of the United States, spells the doom of the twice-vetoed McNary-Haugen Bill. The Equalization fee, as a feature of farm relief, is therefore as dead as the dodo bird—at least until other plans have been tried and found wanting. The present moment, therefore, is an ideal time for farm cooperatives to take inventory and initiate new legislative policies.

In his first message to Congress upon taking office President Hoover called for a special session of Congress primarily to enact his Federal Farm Board plan. He deemed necessary "creation of a great instrumentality clothed with sufficient authority and resources" to "transfer the agricultural question from the field of politics into the realm of economics . . . " In April, bills incorporating Hoover's views were introduced in both houses of Congress and further hearings were held.

The immediate response was muted, perhaps best expressed by O. M. Kile: "A stony silence was noted in farm organization circles."[16] *Wallace's Farmer* held that the plan provided "a chance to develop some capable large scale cooperatives" and that "it should be given a fair and honest trial. If it turns out to be ineffective in a year or so, perhaps there may be less objection to letting the farm organizations try out remedies in which they have confidence . . . "[17] Herman Steen said: "Washington is startled with the broad powers proposed to be granted to the new farm board. In many respects it is the most far-reaching bill presented to Congress since the Federal Reserve Act was written in 1913 or the original Interstate Commerce Law was drafted in 1886. In fact, the farm board bill is parallel to some extent to these measures."[18]

With regard to the emphasis given to cooperatives Steen said:

> What this means, in plain English, is that the Government will put up the money to organize and perfect the cooperatives, to acquire the property necessary to carry on the business, to store and market the product, to set up the stabilization corporations . . . The emphasis is put on cooperative organizations all the way through . . . The bill may be summarized by saying that it is the handsomest offer that any government has ever made to the cooperative associations. It grants them tremendous privileges, gives them far-reaching opportunities, places great funds and power at their disposal. There is no precedent in American history for this offer.

Although Steen thought the President would get his way in the Republican-dominated Congress, he foresaw that the bill would have bitter opposition. "Oddly enough," he said, "the cooperative leaders are also rather opposed to the bill." He gave two reasons: "(1) the fear that the government will have too much power over them, and (2) they don't want the clearing-house idea." In summary Steen said: "It must be borne in mind that this [bill] would not offer any great amount of immediate help to the farmer. It's too big . . . It is a long-time program and the speed with which it is put under way depends more than anything else upon the development and support by the farmers themselves of organizations that can handle the surplus."

President Hoover did not get his bill passed without a struggle in Congress from supporters of the export debenture plan. Moreover, there was a surprising lack of enthusiasm displayed by the cooperative marketing associations. They seemed more interested in obtaining legislation that would provide more liberal credit for cooperatives, and they were apprehensive that under the proposed legislation cooperatives might be given impossible tasks and be subjected to too much government interference and control.

The views of the principal agricultural cooperatives on the proposed Federal Farm Board were presented in the Senate Hearings on Farm Relief Legislation on March 28, 1929, by Charles W. Holman, Secretary of the National Cooperative Milk Producers' Federation. While representing the strongly organized dairy cooperatives he also presented a statement in behalf of a group which called itself the National Committee on Cooperation and which included in its membership most of the major agricultural cooperatives. In his testimony Holman called for:

> A definite expansion of the present national policy of encouraging cooperatives through the cooperative marketing devices of the Department of Agriculture. That Department is doing marvelous work in assisting the cooperatives to consolidate where needed, to reorganize when needed, to improve the efficiency of operation. I think that we all recognize that the program of developing cooperation is one that can not be done over night. The movement is only 10 years old, and perhaps it can be said to have barely gotten beyond the local stage.

Holman also urged the extension of rural cooperative credit facilities but he was opposed to placing them under the proposed Federal Farm Board. He said:

> Our people think the question of trade credit facilities, so far as they apply to the routine operations of the cooperatives, should not be placed under a Federal farm board whose major duties would be to care for the strategy of marketing surplus. There are two entirely different jobs. We know that if the minds of the board would be on the question of marketing the entire product of the industry, they would not have the time and would not necessarily be qualified to take care of the day-to-day routine needs of our association, which we believe is very important.[19]

In the statement that Holman presented on behalf of the National Committee on Cooperation, prepared following a conference in Washington, D.C., on March 21 and 22, the following specific views were presented on surplus control legislation:

> The entire conference was in complete agreement . . . that no plan for surplus control of any commodity could be permanently effective, or even avoid disastrous consequences, unless provisions were made . . . to effectively control overproduction. Members of the conference were also agreed that no

stabilization corporation should be created unless there is overwhelming evidence that a substantial majority of the cooperatives dealing in a commodity are desirous of having them created. Members of the conference were also agreed that if stabilization corporations are created there should be a separate corporation for each important commodity and these corporations should be subsidiaries of the cooperative commodity organizations dealing in that commodity and should be under their control and management. It was also the consensus of the cooperatives that the establishment of stabilization corporations independent of the cooperatives would be detrimental to cooperative organizations and would therefore be contrary to the avowed policy of the Nation as expressed by leaders of the Administration and both Houses of Congress.[20]

On June 15, 1929, the Administration's measure was finally enacted by substantial majorities of both houses of Congress as the Agricultural Marketing Act. This represented a great personal triumph for President Hoover, in that he was "himself responsible—for conception of the idea, nurturing of the policy, influencing the drafting of bills, and the promotion of legislation based upon that policy."[21]

While to general observers the Act appeared to be the answer to cooperative prayers, the mood of cooperative leaders was to wait and see how the new legislation would be administered. Of great concern to them was the possible membership of the Federal Farm Board. President Hoover had promised that he would appoint the best qualified men for membership, but cooperative leaders were skeptical. They had to be shown.

In the next chapter we will see how the Federal Farm Board plan worked out in practice under the conditions of the Great Depression.

Chapter VIII

THE FEDERAL FARM BOARD EXPERIMENT: 1929-1932

Although the Agricultural Marketing Act brought together a number of ideas that had been before the public for some time, it was, in itself, an innovation in public policy with regard to agriculture. For the first time it gave the government an active hand in the administration of agricultural affairs. It was the first major government agricultural action program, and it marked a break with the *laissez-faire* or *assisted laissez-faire* programs that had prevailed up to 1929. The Agricultural Marketing Act also culminated a series of Acts favorable to the cooperative form of business enterprise. The Capper Volstead Act of 1922 had assured legality for cooperative marketing associations. The Cooperative Marketing Act of 1926 had given them encouragement and effective help through government research, service, and educational assistance. Now, the Agricultural Marketing Act of 1929 went a step further and provided them with powers and financial assistance to help stabilize the agricultural industry.

Provisions of the Agricultural Marketing Act

The official description of the Agricultural Marketing Act (approved June 15, 1929) read as follows: "An Act to establish a Federal Farm Board to promote the effective merchandising of agricultural commodities in interstate and foreign commerce, and to place agriculture on a basis of economic equality with other industries."

Section I of the Act declared it to be the policy of Congress:

. . . to promote the effective merchandising of agricultural commodities in interstate and foreign commerce, so that the industry of agriculture will be placed on a basis of economic equality with other industries, and to that end to protect, control, and stabilize the currents of interstate and foreign commerce in the marketing of agricultural commodities and their food products—

(1) by minimizing speculation;

(2) by preventing inefficient and wasteful methods of distribution;

(3) *by encouraging the organization of producers into effective associations or corporations under their own control for greater unity of effort in marketing and by promoting the establishment and financing of a farm marketing system of producer-owned and producer-controlled cooperative associations and other agencies* (Italics added);

(4) by aiding in preventing and controlling surpluses in any agricultural commodity, through orderly production and distribution, so as to maintain advantageous domestic markets and prevent such surpluses from causing undue and excessive fluctuations or depressions in prices for the commodity.

The Federal Farm Board created by the Act was to consist of nine members, eight to be appointed by the President, with the Secretary of Agriculture to serve as *ex-officio* member. The Act also provided for the setting up of Advisory Commodity Committees from cooperative associations representative of designated commodities.

Of much significance were the special powers vested in the Board. Paragraphs (1) and (2) of Section 5 are of special interest. This section declared: "The Board is authorized and directed—

(1) *to promote education in the principles and practices of cooperative marketing of agricultural commodities and food products thereof;*

(2) *to encourage the organization, improvement in methods, and development of effective cooperative associations* (Italics added);

(3) to keep advised from any available sources and make reports as to crop prices, experiences, prospects, supply and demand, at home and abroad;

(4) to investigate conditions of overproduction of agricultural commodities and to advise as to the prevention of such overproduction;

(5) to make investigations and reports and publish the same, including investigations and reports upon the following: Land utilization for agricultural purposes; reduction of the acreage of unprofitable marginal lands in cultivation; methods of expanding markets at home and abroad for agricultural commodities and food products thereof; methods of developing by-products of and new uses for agricultural commodities; and transportation conditions and their effect upon the marketing of agricultural commodities.[1]

Section 6 provided for a revolving fund of $500,000,000 to be administered by the Board. The Board was authorized to make loans to cooperative associations for (1) effective merchandizing of agricultural products; (2) construction or acquisition of physical marketing facilities; (3) formation of clearing house associations; (4) extending membership of the cooperative associations; and (5) making higher advances to growers than could be provided through other credit agencies.

Of particular importance was Section 9 which provided for setting up stabilization corporations for the purpose of controlling any surpluses that might arise. Loans could be made to these corporations from the revolving fund. If earnings of such a corporation were inadequate to repay the loan, the loss would be absorbed out of the revolving fund.

The way in which clearing houses were to be assisted was set forth in Section 10 as follows:

> Upon application of any cooperative association handling an agricultural commodity or of producers of an agricultural commodity, the board is authorized . . . to assist in forming producer-controlled clearing house associations . . . The board may provide for the registration, and for the termination of any clearing house association . . . Independent dealers in, and handlers, distributors, and processors of the commodity, as well as cooperative associations handling the commodity, shall be eligible for membership in the clearing house association . . . [2]

Under the Act the President was authorized to transfer to the jurisdiction and control of the Board the whole or any part of "any office, bureau, service, division, commission, or board in the Executive branch of the Government engaged in scientific or extension work, or the furnishing of services, with respect to the marketing of agricultural commodities." This provision made possible the bodily transfer of the Division of Cooperative Marketing from the Department of Agriculture to the jurisdiction of the Federal Farm Board.

The Farm Board Gets Under Way

President Hoover lost no time in appointing the members of the Federal Farm Board, as he was aware that the success of the Farm Board experiment would depend upon the competence of the men who constituted its membership. He named as Chairman his friend and well-known industrial leader, Alexander Legge, the President of the International Harvester Company. Hoover recognized that he needed for this post a man of assured executive capacity who would be sympathetic to the objectives of the Agricultural Marketing Act.[3] The other members were appointed after a study of hundreds of nominations submitted mostly by farm leaders, such as officials of farm organizations and cooperative marketing associations, editors of agricultural publications, and Presidents and Deans of agricultural colleges. Selections were made to represent geographical sections of the United States and principal agricultural products.[4]

Within one month after the Agricultural Marketing Act became law the membership of the Board—except for a person to represent the small grain interests—was complete, and Hoover could start the Board out on its official life with a meeting at the White House on July 15. President

Hoover made clear his high aspirations for the Board's success by saying to the group: "If we are to succeed, it will be by strengthening the foundations and the initiative which we already have in farm organizations, and building steadily upon them with the constant thought that we are building not for the present only but for the next decade."

At this first meeting the Board elected James C. Stone as Vice-Chairman, and appointed as Secretary, Chris L. Christensen, then Chief of the Division of Cooperative Marketing of the United States Department of Agriculture.

The Board lost no time in getting under way. Steps were immediately taken to organize the grain producers, and, on July 26 and 27, the Federal Farm Board called together representatives of the principal grain cooperatives and launched plans for the formation of a nation-wide grain marketing cooperative—the Farmers National Grain Corporation.

Soon afterwards (July 29-August 8), the American Institute of Cooperation held its 5th annual session at Louisiana State University at Baton Rouge. What the Board would do and how it would do it was of dominating interest, and Chairman Legge and other members of the Board availed themselves of this opportunity to present their views to the cooperative leaders of the nation.

If there had been any doubt as to Legge's belief in the cooperative method of organization and operation and his friendship for the objectives of cooperatives, his address, which was nationally broadcast by radio, dispelled it. He made clear that the Federal Farm Board was committed to the development of strong cooperative marketing organizations. He said: "The major policy of the Board will be the expansion and strengthening of the cooperative movement." Some of the views he expressed are here quoted:

> The Federal Farm Board, aside from its chairman, is composed of men of long cooperative experience. All of its members, including the chairman, are in complete sympathy with the cooperative movement.
> The Board believes that it can be of great assistance to American farmers by encouraging the development of large-scale, central cooperative organizations.
> The Board has reached the conclusion that its first operations can be most useful, and more safely carried on, if it undertakes to further the activities of established agencies in the cooperative field.
> There are many people who think that the Board's activities should be directed to the arbitrary raising of the price level for agricultural products. The Board cannot raise prices arbitrarily . . . What the Board hopes to do is to assist farmers to become better able to compete with other groups in the markets of the nation and the world.
> Farmers' cooperative associations are more than mere distributing agencies . . . Effective coordination of production with demand must be brought about through the cooperatives.[5]

At this time the nation was living in the so-called "New Era" and economic conditions—except for agriculture—seemed prosperous. Few then foresaw the imminent stock market crash and the dramatic drop in commodity prices that would follow.[6] Under these circumstances Legge saw no immediate necessity for forming stabilization corporations as provided for in the Agricultural Marketing Act. In fact, he said: "It seems to me that it may well happen that cooperatives now in existence or improved organizations growing out of existing cooperative organizations, may prove to be all that is needed to carry out the idea of stabilization corporations."

Legge finished his talk by saying, "The improvement of agricultural conditions must be based on self-help. The Board can contribute largely and will contribute to such improvement. In the long run, however, the Board will render the greatest service to agriculture and to the Nation by helping the farmer to help himself."

Legge's forthrightness and friendliness, plus his apparent common sense, made a very favorable impression. In reporting on the sessions of the Institute, Robin Hood, the editor of *The Cooperative Marketing Journal*, said:

> Alexander H. Legge, Chairman of the Farm Board, entered the cooperative picture at a disadvantage. As the Institute opened, there were plenty of expressions of dissatisfaction with the appointment of any manufacturer as Chairman of the Board . . . But a bad beginning meant no hardship to Legge. Within a half day of his arrival, he had displayed a grasp of fundamental cooperative concepts and an understanding of the internal problems of specific cooperatives that can only be credited to a deep student after long study. He soon demonstrated an appreciation of agricultural welfare that earned him a hearty welcome to the inner doors.[7]

Back in Washington the Board considered the organization of wheat growers into a national organization of first importance, for the wheat market was showing signs of weakness. To carry on business during the period of heavy grain movement, while the national organization was being set up, the Board announced its willingness to make supplemental commodity loans to enable existing wheat marketing associations to advance more to their members than could otherwise be done. The Farmers National Grain Corporation, incorporated under Delaware law on October 29, as a Capper-Volstead cooperative, brought together wheat cooperatives of all types in one organization—regional federations and pooling associations. While the wheat program was getting underway, plans were being made for somewhat similar national cooperatives for other commodities.[8]

The Farm Board was able to get started fast because it could draw on the vast fund of information on agricultural cooperatives already assembled by the Division of Cooperative Marketing. One of the Board's first acts was to request the President to transfer the Division to its jurisdiction, and this was done by Executive Order 5200 on October 1, 1929. This gave the board a group of talented and highly qualified employees who personally knew most of the important cooperative leaders throughout the nation from work with the organizations they represented. These men were in a position to assist in the formulation of organization plans and in the execution of Board policies. As the Division of Cooperative Marketing was already set up along commodity lines, the specialists for individual commodity groups soon were working closely with the members of the Board who had direct responsibility for developing programs related to the same commodities.[9]

From the beginning, the Farm Board planned to center its loan assistance to cooperatives—insofar as possible—through the proposed national organizations, which would, in turn, funnel the funds borrowed to meet the needs of member associations. Until this program could be shaped up, the Board made loans to the regional and other organizations that would later become members of the national organizations.[10]

Wheat was the test case for Farm Board policy. Even before the Farmers National Grain Corporation could be set up there was an ominous drop in grain prices. The Board endeavored to meet this problem by making loans to the regional grain marketing associations so that they could hold wheat for an expected upward trend in the market. After the Farmers National Grain Corporation was in operation, such loans were made through it. This action of the Board, in attempting to hold up wheat prices, was applauded by farmers and farm organizations but the established grain trade immediately charged that the Farm Board had interfered with the forces of the market and had put the government into business.[11] In discussing the "Policy and Program" of the Federal Farm Board at the annual meeting of the American Farm Economic Association, on December 27, 1929, Legge said:

> While wide discretionary power is given to the Board in carrying out policies, the charter was pretty fairly written and clearly defined in the Act— the attack on the problem to be along the line of cooperative, collective action on the part of the agricultural producers of the country. That term "cooperative" is written in almost every paragraph of the bill. Clearly, it indicated that the intention was that the problem should be approached in that way and that has been the line of approach on which the Board is working.

Legge also said: "You will notice that we are trying to centralize the scattered efforts that have heretofore been going on along cooperative lines." In the discussion following his talk, Legge indicated that the central cooperative "will control, under one sales management, a sufficient percentage of the commodity to have some reasonable influence on making the market, which under the old system never did and never could, exist." This was an echo of Sapiro's views on what could be accomplished through strong cooperative commodity marketing organizations.[12]

At this same meeting Dr. Joseph S. Davis, who, in December, had been appointed Chief Economist of the Federal Farm Board, spoke on "Some Possibilities and Problems of the Federal Farm Board." Davis expressed the hope that the Board would dissipate, in part, "the fog of discontent and bafflement" that had permeated agricultural affairs. He thought that there was a reasonable possibility that, under the guidance of the Federal Farm Board and with a measure of control through its lending policies, there would be a "more general observance of tried principles." He conceived of the task before the Board as being "a gigantic one" and he hoped that too much would not be immediately expected. He held that "the problem of to restrain or regulate production is one of the most important that the Board will have to face." In the discussion which followed the presentations of Legge and Davis, the attitude on the whole was friendly—the Board should be given a chance.

Even before the end of 1929, there were indications that the United States Chamber of Commerce was not happy with the Board's energetic promotion of cooperative marketing, backed up with loans to cooperative associations. In January, the Chamber declared: "The Chamber advocates cooperative marketing and measures in support of it insofar as they are not discriminatory against other business enterprise . . . " This led Legge to dryly remark: "They want the Farm Board to hang its clothes on a hickory limb but not go near the water."[13]

Fighting the Oncoming Depression

As the economic depression increased in intensity in early 1930, the falling prices of wheat and other agricultural commodities gave the Farm Board increasing concern. Farm groups demanded that the Board do something to hold prices up by establishing stabilization corporations as provided for under the Act. In February, the Board concluded that the situation justified this action and the Grain Stabilization Corporation was authorized.[14]

This action was applauded by the farm press. Such publications as the *Country Gentleman* and the *Progressive Farmer* took the position that the operations of the Board were constructive in character. However, the United States Chamber of Commerce became increasingly critical as the Farm Board took positive steps to meet the farm crisis.

The conflict of the Board and the Chamber broke out into the open at the annual meeting of the Chamber on April 30. At this meeting Chairman Legge defended the Board's policies and actions while the attack on the whole concept of the Agricultural Marketing Act was presented by Daniel A. Millett, an investment banker and stockman from Denver, Colorado. Legge, in his address, pointed out that the United States Chamber of Commerce had actively promoted the legislation which resulted in the Agricultural Marketing Act. He called attention to the referendum of the Chamber, submitted to its members while the legislation was being drafted, which committed the Chamber to the creation of a Federal Farm Board and support of the principles of cooperative marketing. The vote had been 2,816 for and 117 against. It seemed strange to Legge that many in the Chamber were "now branding as socialistic or anarchistic" the Agricultural Marketing Act. Legge said "There was much more involved when the stabilization operation was undertaken than merely the price of wheat. The whole farm commodities market was threatened."

Millett said: "The Agricultural Marketing Act is part and parcel of what is to me the fantastic dream, world-wide, of stabilization, with or without governmental agency, so that every producer in every line will be assured a profit through control of production, and without the discipline of the economic law of supply and demand, working through price, which eliminates the marginal producer." He also said, "This Act does not *yet* give the Farm Board dictatorship over production, though that body is advising the unsound policy of reduction, but when it comes to the second factor in control—marketing—the aspect is more serious, for it gives the Board, through its controlled subsidiaries, what may become monopolistic control over American markets for agricultural products." Millett held that the Agricultural Marketing Act should be repealed.

In the discussion that followed the presentations of Legge and Millett, several speakers—mostly representing agricultural business interests—supported Millett, while the Farm Board was defended by John Brandt, President of Land O'Lakes Creameries; Alfred H. Stone, Vice-President of the Staple Cotton Association of Mississippi; and Louis Tabor, Master of the National Grange. One of those who vigorously upheld the Act was Congressman Franklin W. Fort who had been a member of the House Committee that framed the Act. He said: "I am here to stand by what we did."

Following the discussion the Chamber passed a resolution which reaffirmed the referendum vote of the membership "in supporting the principle that the producers of agricultural commodities should have the benefits which cooperative marketing of their products along sound economic lines can confer . . . and in advocating a Federal Farm Board to assist agricultural producers and their organizations in solving the problems peculiar to agriculture." However, the resolution also declared: "We . . . express our continued opposition to the use of Government funds in providing capital for the operation of agricultural cooperatives, and for the buying and selling of commodities for the purpose of attempted stabilization." It went on to propose that the Agricultural Marketing Act be amended to "repeal the authority of the Federal Farm Board for such a purpose."[15]

The attack of the U.S. Chamber of Commerce was just what the Federal Farm Board needed to solidify farm and cooperative forces behind it. *The Cooperative Marketing Journal* said: "For one great favor, cooperatives may thank the Chamber of Commerce from the bottom of their hearts. The Chamber's position has unified agriculture as no issue in many, many years. The Chamber's adverse attitude is the best thing that could have happened to the Farm Board and the Cooperative movement." The *Journal* also carried an article by Senator Arthur Capper who pointed out that "the cooperative marketing plan of the Agricultural Marketing Act was not the farm relief plan of the farm organizations . . . It was the plan recommended by the Nagel Commission [Business Men's Commission on Agriculture] approved in principle by the Chamber of Commerce in its nationwide referendum on the subject." He said: "The Chamber of Commerce . . . now has denounced its own plan as 'socialistic,' 'revolutionary' and 'putting the Government into business.' " In another article Dr. B. H. Hibbard of the University of Wisconsin called the resolution of the Chamber of Commerce condemning the Farm Board "an intolerable impertinence."[16]

During the spring of 1930, the Grain Stabilization Corporation undertook to support the market by buying cash wheat and May futures with the result that it gained control of approximately one-half of the visible wheat supply. As prices declined with the coming of the new crop, the Board took steps to hold prices in line by increasing the holdings of the Grain Stabilization Corporation. The situation in cotton was somewhat similar. Loans to the American Cotton Association enabled the cotton cooperatives to maintain prices during 1929-1930, but in June 1930 it was found necessary to set up a Cotton Stabilization Corporation. Thus, by the end of its first year the Farm Board was deeply involved in stabilization operations for both wheat and cotton.

In the spring of 1930 the Federal Farm Board gave its support to an industry-wide program for stabilizing the demoralized California grape market. This resulted in the formation of the California Grape Control Board in the early summer to perform stabilization operations by buying surplus production. The Control Board also operated a clearing house to effect more orderly marketing with limited results. In 1932 the Federal Farm Board abandoned the California Grape Control Board, and it was then superseded by a growers' prorate plan.[17]

While wheat and cotton price stabilization problems consumed a great deal of the Board's attention during the first year, all kinds of cooperatives were assisted through guidance and loans. The extent and character of this important assistance is too often overlooked in discussions of the Farm Board's experience because of the more dramatic character of the stabilization operations. Throughout its career, the Farm Board effectively carried on an incessant campaign to build and strengthen cooperative marketing organizations. In this work, the Board enjoyed the cooperation of the federal and state agricultural extension services, the vocational agricultural teachers, and the general cooperative and general farm organizations.

The *First Annual Report of the Federal Farm Board,* issued later in the fall, provided a detailed account of the operations of the Board during its first year. According to the report, the major activities of the Board had been "centered in the up-building of cooperative marketing associations," since "such organizations, well managed and properly financed, will enable farmers to control their industry both as to production and marketing." Much of the report was devoted to the progress and problems of the national cooperative organizations formed with the Board's encouragement and support. The problems of control and prevention of agricultural surpluses had been found to be "vast and complex," and the conclusion had been reached that "measures for prevention of surpluses, through control of excessive production, were absolutely essential to stabilizing farm prices and income.[18] It was held that "cooperative associations and stabilization corporations, supplemented by other de- vices, may prove able to deal with temporary or occasional surpluses" but "none of these, nor all together, nor any Government agency can protect farmers from the consequences of repeated or continuous production in excess of market requirements.[19]

When the Agricultural Marketing Act was passed it was believed that encouragement would be given to the formation of clearing house associations as provided for in Section 10 of the Act. However, in its *First Annual Report* the Federal Farm Board aid: "The board has deemed it wise to defer the exercise of these provisions (for clearing houses) until such time as its program for the establishment of the system of producer-owned associations handling each commodity has been developed to a point where the necessity for this other type of marketing agency is more clearly indicated" (p. 51). There was no further reference to clearing house associations in later reports of the board.

The progress made by the Federal Farm Board during its first year was reviewed at the meetings of the American Institute of Cooperation held at Ohio State University in August 1930. By this time the Federal Farm Board was well established. Now, attention was directed to how it was working.

The principal talk, presenting the views of the Board, was made by its Vice-Chairman, James A. Stone. He explained what the Board did in its first year and why it was done. He held that the price situation forced the Federal Farm Board into stabilization operations, first for wheat and then for cotton. He said: "The Farm Board, using the authority and means at its command, did nothing more for the agricultural commodities market than bankers and businessmen did to meet the emergency in the securities market crash . . . Although the Stabilization Corporation may lose some money in the wheat it has bought, no one can say that its loss will be one-fiftieth as much as the losses would have been to the entire country if a complete collapse of farm commodity prices had occurred."[20]

A more measured expression of Board policy was given by Dr. Joseph S. Davis, Chief Economist of the Board. Speaking on the subject, "What the Country Expects of the Cooperative," he said: "The country has never looked to business corporations, as now it looks to the cooperatives, as prime agencies for attaining a high and difficult objective of national policy." He held that cooperatives were not appropriate agencies to carry on major stabilization operations, and he viewed the stabilization corporations authorized by the Agricultural Marketing Act as experiments. He said: "The true objective of such operations is not price-pegging or price-fixing; it is rather a cushioning of extreme price declines, and particularly the prevention of a degree of decline unwarranted by fundamental conditions of supply and demand; it necessarily implies subsequent moderation of extreme fluctuations upward as well."

At these meetings there were talks by top officials of the Farmers National Grain Corporation and by many others on various aspects of Farm Board policy and operations. No one could complain that the Farm Board experiment was not being carried on in full daylight.

The Second Year

The problem of the Federal Farm Board increased in scope and intensity during its second year. The Great Depression had now become worldwide, and prices of agricultural staples continued their downward trend. The average price per bushel of wheat received by farmers which had amounted to $1.11 on October 15, 1929, had fallen to 88¢ per bushel by June 15, 1930, but in the next 12 months it was to fall to 52¢ per bushel, (June 15, 1931). The average price per pound of cotton received by farmers was 17.57¢ on October 15, 1929, but it had decreased to 14.02¢ by June 15, 1930. During the next 12 months it fell off to 7.69¢ by June 15, 1931.[21]

The Board attempted to halt the fall in prices through operations of the Grain and Cotton Stabilization Corporations, but with no permanent success. The experience of these stabilization efforts can be briefly summarized.[22]

On June 30, 1930, the holdings of the Grain Stabilization Corporation amounted to 65,545,201 bushels of wheat. In November 1930, a sharp break in world wheat prices convinced the Board "that an emergency existed which could be met only by increased stabilization purchases." In the ensuing four months, the holdings were continuously increased until they exceeded 250 million bushels on March 31, 1931. Wheat prices during this time continued to fall, although the stabilization operations cushioned the fall by holding domestic prices somewhat above world prices.

The Cotton Stabilization Corporation was not incorporated until June 5, 1930. It immediately acquired the unsold stocks of cotton held by member associations of the American Cotton Growers Association, amounting to 1,241,509 bales. This enabled the cotton cooperatives, with loans from the Farm Board, to gradually increase their own holdings until they reached about 2 million bales in January 1931. On June 30, 1931, the cotton financed by the Board, held either by the cooperative associations or the Stabilization Corporation, amounted to nearly 3.5 million bales. The Federal Farm Board maintained that these stabilization purchases were justified by the abnormal market situation, but, with the continuing decline in wheat and cotton prices, doubt increased as to the wisdom of the action.[23]

As agricultural conditions worsened, the gloom of farmers increased. In Iowa, the Farm Holiday Movement urged drastic remedies, and support was again voiced for the equalization fee and export debenture plan as a means of raising farm prices. From the beginning, the Federal

Farm Board had been a political issue, and, in the Congressional elections of 1930, it came under vigorous attack. It is not surprising, in view of the prevailing hard times, that the Republicans lost control of the House and strength in the Senate. During this period, the critics of the Farm Board became more vocal, and more and more people became convinced that the Farm Board was responsible for their troubles. Under these circumstances, it became increasingly difficult for the Farm Board to get a fair hearing.

With the failure of the Federal Farm Board to turn back the tide of depression, criticism of the Board grew in intensity. By 1931, the depression, which had been at first largely confined to the United States, had spread throughout the world, and this, in turn, made recovery difficult as markets were closed and foreign investments lost. The times demanded a scapegoat, and the Hoover Administration was held largely responsible by many for the desperate condition of the country. Commercial interests, opposed to cooperative competition, charged that the Federal Farm Board was socialistic and unfair to private business.[24]

While much of the criticism of the Farm Board simply reflected the despondency felt throughout the nation over the government's inability to do the impossible and bring prompt relief from the deepening depression, a larger part of it was the result of a well-organized propaganda campaign supported by trading interests opposed to farmers' marketing cooperatives. Many persons became confused and hardly knew what to think.[25]

This situation greatly concerned cooperative leaders who believed that the public was being poisoned against cooperatives, and they found it almost impossible to get a fair hearing for their views. One who endeavored to meet the "relentless attacks" through reasoned analysis was John D. Miller, the highly respected General Counsel of the Dairymen's League Cooperative Association.[26] During 1931 he wrote a series of articles for the *Dairymen's League News* which were reprinted in a pamphlet, "The Federal Farm Board and Its Critics." Excerpts from this document well reflect the frustration that farmers and their cooperative leaders felt at that time:

> We hold no brief for the Agricultural Marketing Act and so far as we know, none of the leading cooperative marketing associations of the country had any part in writing it . . . With the enactment of the bill into law, cooperative marketing associations were called upon to make momentous decisions. Should they help or refuse to help the Farm Board in its administration of the law? The most of them deferred decision until the personnel and policies of the Farm Board had been announced.
>
> If Government loans to farmers' cooperative marketing associations are

socialistic and are attempts to loot the Federal Treasury, why not the loans the Government makes to ship owners?

There has been so much misrepresentation and there is now such wide-spread misunderstanding of the difficulties confronting the Farm Board in its operation of the stabilization corporations, that the splendid work that has been and is now being done by the Board in assisting farmers to establish better marketing agencies is obscured and mainly forgotten.

If farmers in ever-increasing numbers will join cooperative marketing associations and assist in the building of large organizations, they will bring nearer and still nearer the day when they themselves, through these associa-tions, can solve the vexatious agricultural problem upon the solution of which depends the future of American agriculture . . . Farmers will make a stupendous and costly error if they expect the Farm Board to do this work alone. All that the Board can do is to help farmers help themselves.

A very helpful appraisal of the problems encountered by the Farm Board in administering the Agricultural Marketing Act was presented by Joseph S. Davis, Chief Economist of the Farm Board, in an article entitled "The Case for the Agricultural Marketing Act" in *The Annals of the American Academy of Political and Social Science* for May 1931. He presented his views "not as a lawyer's brief but as an economist's interpretation, *a case for* an Act which is properly the subject of wide public interest and great controversy" (p. 1).

Davis opened his article by saying: "I regard the Agricultural Marketing Act as a major departure in our national agricultural policy, designed to pave the way for working out solutions of important problems that concern not only farmers but the Nation at large." He indicated that the Agricultural Marketing Act represented certain ideas that the country was ready to have tested—a Federal Farm Board, independent of the United States Department of Agriculture; the fostering of a special type of business organization, farmers' cooperative marketing associations; stabilization corporations for control of agricul-tural surpluses. Holding that "there has been an unfortunate tendency in many quarters to expect the impossible of the Act and the Board," he said:

> In the nature of the case, no swift and striking transformation of the agricultural situation for the better could rightly be expected from this or any other measure. Under the conditions that have obtained in the past eighteen months—a world-wide economic crisis developing into a general agricultural and industrial depression—no measure, no agency, old or new, has proved adequate to prevent disasters or even to mitigate them in impressive degree. Such positive contributions as have been made have appeared to be submerged in the tide (p. 3).

Davis gave the Board credit for its efforts. "The Board frankly took the position that action, even at great risk, was preferable to inaction; that neither the situation nor the Act nor public opinion warranted delays or inaction until success at every step could be assured" (p. 4). On the cooperative marketing features of the Act he said:

> The theory of the Act is that the development of a farmer-controlled farm marketing system will yield to agriculture advantages which organization has brought to industry; that this will facilitate economies in distribution; more orderly marketing, and better adaptation and adjustment of production to requirements of processors and of the market as a whole. There were substantial grounds for believing this theory to be sound; but it must remain a theory until proved correct or incorrect.
>
> Our traditional system of marketing farm products, after all is said about its perfection, must fairly be regarded as falling far short of perfection from the standpoint of either farmer or consumer. There are numerous ways in which, at least in many lines, there is large room for improvement which cooperatives seem potentially capable of effecting. *While I am not disposed to overrate these potentialities, I consider that they are on the whole more far-reaching than has yet been realized by farmers and cooperative leaders themselves* (Italics added).

Davis defended the promotion of cooperatives through loans and educational assistance by saying: "The policy of Congress in this respect may be likened to the protection given under our tariff policy to infant industries—continued for many years, in fact after maturity had been or should have been attained . . . " He believed that the cooperative marketing features of the Act merited testing over a period of several years to definitely answer the question of their feasible contributions to the solution of the agricultural problem.

As to the surplus control efforts of the Board, Davis believed that these had to be made, even though the experience had led to "certain important and sobering conclusions." He made the important point that the results of the experience "in determining what can and what cannot be undertaken to advantage may well be worth considerable cost to the public treasury and to private business. What is essential is that the policy and the procedures, and in due time the Act itself, should be modified in the light of the experience fairly appraised, rather than that policies proved undesirable should be continued. The Agricultural Marketing Act permits and presumably contemplated just this" (pp. 7-8).

The Board lost two of its effective leaders in the spring of 1931. First, Chairman Alexander Legge resigned, and, shortly afterward, Charles C. Teague left the Board. Both men had stayed longer than they had initially planned so their resignations were not unexpected. Yet, their going marked a change in the vigor of the Board, for Legge could forcefully speak the language of big business—and make big business like it—while Teague was an experienced cooperator and confidant of President Hoover.[27] With the resignation of Legge, Vice-Chairman James C. Stone took command as Chairman, and Sam Thompson, President of the

American Farm Bureau Federation, was named to fill the vacancy left by Legge. Mr. Thompson's appointment was well received in agricultural circles, for he had been an active advocate of the McNary-Haugen plan. It was believed that he would be able to work from within to bring about an amendment of the Agricultural Act that would make it more satisfactory to farmers.

When the American Institute of Cooperation met at Kansas State College of Agriculture, Manhattan, in June 1931, friendly but careful students of cooperative enterprise were becoming concerned over the Board's big business philosophy and high pressure tactics. For example, Nourse, in evaluating the livestock marketing work of the Farm Board, had this to say after calling attention to three "conspicuous merits of the Federal Farm Board's programs," namely:

(1) The value of a comprehensive plan of organization;
(2) The possibilities of more economical and effective distribution of live- stock by the full development of direct selling methods; and
(3) The bringing of adequate financing at reasonable rates within the reach of the industry.

"The efforts of the Federal Farm Board in the field of livestock marketing are very much of a piece with their efforts in other fields, notably grain and cotton. They reflect an exaggerated fear of the evil effects of compe- tition between marketing agencies and an exaggerated hope of what could be accomplished through the suspension of competitive selling by the several units of the system." He concluded his statement by saying: "At the present time I fear we are witnessing an effort to make speed by short cuts of the industrial big business type and by compromising cooperative principles. The next few years will create a demand upon all of us for a careful analytical and educational campaign."[28]

A somewhat similar view was expressed by O. B. Jesness in his evaluation of the grain program of the Federal Farm Board. He said: "If the Farmers National Grain Cooperative is to be the sales outlet for grain growers generally, it will have to obtain the support of a consider- able portion of the business which up to the present time has not become aligned with the program . . . We must not stress too much the matter of volume of business. A national sales outlet needs sufficient volume to permit of economic operation. The problem of efficient and economical service should receive much more consideration than that of mere size."[29] Earlier in his article Jesness pointed out that he viewed the stabilization features of the Agricultural Marketing Act as "window dressing." He considered it "primarily a measure placing Government support more squarely behind farmers' cooperatives and aiding in (their) develop- ment."[30]

Murray R. Benedict in evaluating the Board's wool program, emphasized that: "We are not here to laud cooperation but to study it." In his analysis he said: "It is time we dropped the off-hand assumption that one marketing agency is the ideal to be sought, and looked at the problem frankly to see if this or some other arrangement is likely to be most efficient and workable."[31]

In the *Second Annual Report of the Federal Farm Board* for the year ending June 30, 1931, the Board claimed that its stabilization operations had given farmers and business organizations a "breathing spell," but it was evident that this phase of the Board's operations was coming to a close. By June 30, 1931, the Board's revolving fund of $500,000,000 was largely committed either in loans to cooperatives or in advances to the stabilization corporations. As of June 30, 1931, the loans outstanding for wheat and cotton stabilization amounted to $235,102,644, while total loans outstanding to marketing cooperatives were $109,499,255. Without replenishment by new funds—and Congress was in no mood to grant them—the Board could do little until the revolving funds could be rebuilt through payment of loans or sale of products impounded by the stabilization corporations. The Board thus found itself in the weak position of a lame duck Congress, for its power to exert influence was largely spent. The Board noted in its report that it had reached a new stage in its stabilization operations. "The first test of the stabilization features of the act is not yet completed. The initial phase, making stabilization purchases, has been finished; but the second phase, selling stabilization stocks, is just beginning" (p. 72-73).[32] However, the Board did not recommend changes in the Agricultural Marketing Act. It held "that the wiser course would be to wait until the various provisions of the Act have been tested over a longer period and in more favorable economic circumstances." This luxury was not to be forthcoming—for economic conditions were to worsen in the next two years.

In its report the Board emphasized the significant progress being made in cooperative marketing. "The most important activities of the Board during the year were in helping cooperative marketing associations . . . Out of the trying experiences of the year, important lessons have been learned and definite improvement has been made in cooperative organization and management."

The Third Year

With the cessation of stabilization corporation operations, except for the disposal of stocks acquired, the Federal Farm Board could get on with one of its primary missions—the development of strong and efficient cooperative marketing associations, or as the Board phrased it in its Second Annual Report, "to develop a national program of improved marketing and production adjustment for the permanent betterment of American agriculture."

In the first two years of its operations, the Board had been largely concerned with the formation of national and regional cooperative marketing associations and with the operations of the wheat and cotton stabilization corporations. Now, the Board could devote its major attention to improving the efficiency of central cooperative organizations that had been set up. By this time the Board had established its working procedures and had developed a seasoned staff of well-qualified workers. It was in a position to render effective advisory and lending services to cooperative marketing associations throughout the nation. Although its loan activity during 1931-1932 declined appreciably from the preceding year, it still amounted to $101,103,169, mostly in the form of loans to nation-wide central associations who were already borrowers.

The criticism of the policies and procedures of the Board in working with cooperatives—which found expression at the American Institute of Cooperation meetings at Manhattan, Kansas—continued during the year. A statement of the Oregon Cooperative Council released on October 16, 1931, voiced the complaints of many cooperative leaders who were not unsympathetic to the Board's efforts. The Council, while favoring large-scale organization, held that cooperatives "should be built from the bottom up and not from the top down." It believed that the Board had carried national centralization too far, and it did not favor "such rapid organization and promotional methods as those used in establishing Government sponsored national organizations." The Council was also critical of the way in which the Division of Cooperative Marketing was operating under the Board. It recommended transfer out from under Farm Board control "unless the Farm Board can render the kinds and types of ['unbiased and understanding'] service previously rendered by the Division of Cooperative Marketing."[33]

In reviewing its operations for the year ending June 30, 1932, in its *Third Annual Report* issued in the late fall of 1932, the Farm Board said: "The condition of farmers was desperate; it is difficult to imagine how much worse it might have been had not the Board been in a position to throw practically the full weight of its resources to the aid and support of the system of 'producer-owned and producer-controlled cooperative associations' which it had helped to build in conformance with the Agricultural Marketing Act" (p. 5).

During the year the Board's Division of Cooperative Marketing had worked energetically to help cooperatives meet their problems through advisory assistance. The Board said:

> During a period in which nearly every other field of business enterprise has been strewn with bankruptcies, cooperative associations have increased in membership, volume of business and quality of service rendered, both to producers and consumers. In spite of the substantial progress which has been made, the cooperative movement is still in the beginning steps of its development. Further investigation and organization are urgently needed in many fields. The full possibilities of cooperatives have not yet been explored and developed (p. 2).

The Board now considered its stabilization operations closed.

> Experience with stabilization thus demonstrates that no measure for improving the price of farm products other than in encouraging the demand of consumers can be effective over a period of years unless it provides a more definite control of production than has been achieved so far. In a few limited and specialized lines, cooperative associations have made progress toward such control. For the great staple products, however, the problem still remains for future solution (p. 62).

The Final Year

The Farm Board opened its fourth and final year on July 1, 1932, in a seriously weakened condition. Most of the revolving fund was tied up, and new loans to cooperatives could be made only as outstanding loans were repaid. Moreover, pressure on government to reduce expenditures was forcing the Board to drastically cut its operating budget and greatly reduce its professional staff.[34] This impaired morale and the effectiveness of its work.

When the American Institute of Cooperation met at the University of New Hampshire, in Durham in August 1932, there was little sign of the depression's abatement.[35] The mood of the country and of the cooperative leaders was sober. People were searching for hope, and solutions were not apparent. The American Institute of Cooperation meetings provided a forum where those concerned with cooperatives and the agricultural crisis could pool their views in frank and open discussion. By now the Farm Board had lost much of its popularity, for its power to be of help through financial action was largely spent. But cooperative leaders were still sympathetic to its earnest efforts to be helpful. It was a time of appraisal, of searching for new approaches. If the Federal Farm Board was not the answer, what was?

One of the key speakers was Carl Williams, the "cotton" member of the Farm Board. He defended the work of the Board and asserted that cooperatives had made great progress with the Board's assistance under extremely difficult conditions. He pointed out that the number of cooperatives and their volume of business had increased in spite of the declining price level, and he maintained that cooperatives were being unfairly attacked by organized business interests. While he admitted that the Agricultural Marketing Act was not perfect, he asked: "Do you want it stopped?" He called on farmers to defend "your law" and do "your part" in making it effective.

While sympathetic to the good intentions of the Federal Farm Board, Dr. E. G. Nourse, on the basis of his studies of cooperative enterprise, believed that the time had come to question the basic premises on which the Federal Farm Board had been operating. Speaking on the subject, "Cooperative Stimulation and Farm Board Policy," Nourse said: "I believe that the first phase of the Federal Farm Board's career can most aptly be described by the label 'neo-Sapiroism.'" He pointed out that the "first personnel of the Board [its membership] would have made a very creditable faculty in a Sapiro College of Cooperatives." He asserted that the Board had "exaggerated the potential benefits of centralized and consolidated action" and he criticized the lending policies designed to build nation-wide "monopolistic" commodity cooperative organizations as being a "perennial recrudescence" of Sapiroism.

These were fighting words to Carl Williams who made a spirited defense of the Board's philosophy and policies. In turn, he accused Nourse of having a mental attitude based upon his own "perennial recrudescence of opposition to Sapiroism." In responding to this riposte, Nourse said:

> You will recall that at the Patee memorial service, when Mr. Holman referred to the great leaders in cooperation, I took the liberty of saying that Mr. Sapiro was probably the most striking, dramatic and dynamic personality that we have had in the movement. I added that he made definite contributions from the legal side and from the personal leadership or evangelism side. I am sorry that we have not capitalized that leadership. I called attention, also, to the fact that he had brought cooperation into the field of large-scale financing at a time when the bankers were not ready to accept it. So much for Mr. Sapiro in person. When I was talking here about Sapiroism, I was talking about a particular attitude toward an economic process.

This spirited exchange of views was not marred by personal bitterness. Mr. Williams in a rejoiner said: "We are each seeking the truth. We are each, I think, eager to seize it as we find it . . . This discussion is helpful to me in that I get, in such a clarified and intelligent presentation, other angles of the problem which the Board faces."

Nourse was not alone in his criticisms of the Board. Dr. W. E. Grimes of Kansas State Agricultural College subjected the grain marketing program of the Federal Farm Board to vigorous analysis. He said, with reference to the Farmers National Grain Corporation: "If one accepts the theory that all cooperative agencies handling grain in the United States should be coordinated in a unified system, then there can be little criticism of the general plan as outlined . . . It is not the plan that seems most subject to criticism but the apparent methods of putting it into operation." Moreover, Grimes held that the Farm Board had made little progress in securing more orderly production of grain, and he was of the opinion that a national cooperative agency could not accomplish this result. He declared: "The problem of production control must be accomplished through other means than Cooperative Marketing agencies."

These views of Nourse and Grimes were those of friends rather than enemies. They reflected a general loss of confidence in the ability of the Board to accomplish the objectives it had set for itself under the terms of the Agricultural Marketing Act. In his report on this meeting in *The Cooperative Marketing Journal* under the title, "They Didn't Mince Words at Durham," Robin Hood, the editor, said:

> The Federal Farm Board's stimulation of national agencies for the sale of cooperative products was subjected to piercing examination at the American Institute of Cooperation. Market changes, cooperative financing, and a long list of problems faced by various commodity groups were also given penetrating examination . . . One fundamental issue overshadowed all others: Is national centralization of cooperative control going too far, or should greater effort be made to develop strong, autonomous, local and regional organizations federated into national groups with restricted powers? Williams and Nourse met so squarely on the issue that press correspondents described the discussions in terms of attack and defense of federal activities in behalf of cooperative associations. Cooperative leaders, however, viewed the debate as a constructive and friendly effort to arrive at an understanding of what the Government is doing and why.[36]

The Farm Board was now on the defensive, and during the election campaign of 1932 it became known as "The Republican Farm Board."[37] Even President Hoover found little to say in its defense in the election campaign, and it was generally admitted in agricultural circles that the Farm Board plan of price stabilization had been tried and found inadequate. New measures were being called for to bring production under control through governmental power. It was time for a change.

With the sweeping Democratic victory in the national elections, which gave control of both the House and Senate to the Roosevelt administration, it was apparent that the days of the Farm Board were numbered to March 4, when the new administration would take office.

Up until December 7, 1932, the Federal Farm Board had made no recommendations on legislation to improve the Agricultural Marketing

Act.[38] On that date in a special report, the Board offered three recommendations, as follows:

1. Modify the stabilization section of the Agricultural Marketing Act so as to provide some means of elevating the returns to farmers from the production of exportable farm products, in such a way as, (a) to pay the costs, if any, on a continuous and self-sustaining basis, and (b) to provide an effective system for regulating acreage or quantities sold, or both. This would provide a means of working toward *income elevation* as an alternative to the mere *price* stabilization for which the Act now provides. The Board does not recommend the specific form such legislation should take, but states these essential conditions it should cover.

2. Define the powers of the Board with respect to loans to cooperatives so that it would be definitely authorized to make loans to cooperative associations engaged in purchasing equipment and material for farm production.

3. Place the Board's cooperative financing operations and service to co-operatives on an adequate basis by restoring to the revolving fund sufficient funds, in addition to the present value of the moneys already on loan to cooperatives, to restore the Board's ability to properly finance the development of farmers' cooperative associations with funds for cooperative use definitely ear-marked and set apart from portions of the revolving fund subject to other demand; and by authorizing the Board to compromise claims against debtor associations where necessary in its judgement to carry out the policy laid down in Section 1.[39]

Although these recommendations had merit, there was no disposition in the "lame duck" session of Congress to amend the Agricultural Marketing Act before the new Administration took office. As a matter of fact, there was more disposition to repeal the Act, but this was strongly resisted by the cooperatives united in the National Cooperative Council who, in their annual meeting held January 25 and 26, 1933, at Washington, D.C., demanded preservation of the Agricultural Marketing Act and the Federal Farm Board.[40]

In February, President-elect Roosevelt indicated that he was appointing Henry Morgenthau, Jr., to the Chairmanship of the Federal Farm Board with plans to merge all federal farm credit agencies. To make way for this reorganization, James C. Stone resigned as Chairman of the Board, effective March 4. The Federal Farm Board experiment had come to an end. In a sweeping presidential order, effective May 26, the Board was abolished and the authorized position of Chairman of the Farm Board was changed in name to Governor of the Farm Credit Administration.[41]

Lessons Learned from the Farm Board Experiment

When we look back on the Farm Board experiment, several facts become clear.

1. The Farm Board was not the "dismal failure" so often portrayed. It

never had an opportunity to function under normal conditions, and its stabilization efforts can be given some credit for softening the blow of the Great Depression on farmers. Most careful students of the Farm Board experience hold that with less abnormal conditions the Federal Farm Board might have attained more of its objectives and gained greater recognition for its constructive accomplishment. The Farm Board did not have the power or financial resources necessary to reflate the entire economy. As Murray Benedict has remarked:

> It must be conceded that some such experiment had to be tried, either in this form or that of the McNary-Haugen plan, the export debenture plan or something similar. Farmers, political leaders and the public were not yet thinking in terms of the far more aggressive and costly measures undertaken in the next Administration . . . The Farm Board approach may be looked upon as a stage in the evolution of the programs that were to come later.[42]

2. The Farm Board program of encouraging the development of strong and efficient cooperatives backed up by government loans led to the formation and operation of many strong cooperatives that survived the depression. As one keen observer later said:

> The experience of the Farm Board demonstrated that cooperatives could not be made a major component of American business overnight. The Farm Board's effort . . . accomplished a great deal for the cooperative movement. In the course of its creation and operations, it brought together cooperative and other agricultural leaders from all over the country, which resulted in an emphasis that gave the cooperative movement nationwide recognition and encouragement to go forward. . . . [43]

3. The Farm Board's emphasis on concentration and integration of operations, sound business and financial structures and good management, and the development of effective loan policies and practices for making loans to cooperatives was to serve as a useful foundation for the operations of the Banks for Cooperatives when the Farm Credit Administration was set up in 1933. In fact, the most significant innovation of the Farm Board consisted largely in its loan program for marketing cooperatives which provided them with access to needed capital at a time when many sources of credit had literally "dried up." Without this important assistance numerous associations would not have been able to survive the financial pressures of the depression.

4. Under the Agricultural Marketing Act, the Federal Farm Board was ordained to work as an independent agency—apart from the United States Department of Agriculture. This enabled the Board to concentrate its efforts on an aggressive program of promoting cooperative marketing associations—but, in doing so, it placed undue emphasis on the formation and operation of large national and regional organizations set up from the

top down. The Board was confronted by emergency conditions, and it came to operate more by formula than in response to a study of the needs of actual situations. Prior to 1929, the Division of Cooperative Marketing in the Bureau of Agricultural Economics based its recommendations on current research studies of cooperative organizations and problems. After the Board took over the work of the Division, it became a service agency for implementing the Board's policies. Fortunately, it could draw on the research "fat" that had been accumulated, but it lacked the vital guidance that could come from continuing research.[44] Thus the program of the Farm Board lost a certain degree of flexibility and responsiveness that reduced support from many who were friendly to its basic objectives. Also, the Agricultural Marketing Act placed all of its emphasis on cooperative marketing. As a result of this restriction, the Board could not give adequate attention and financial support to the growing interest of farmers in cooperative purchasing associations.

5. One of the difficulties of the Farm Board came from its centralization, in Washington, D.C., of lending and other functions. This overemphasized the relationship of cooperatives to national government and national politics. When the general functions of the Farm Board were assumed by the Farm Credit Administration in 1933, it was possible to decentralize the lending operations through the 12 Banks for Cooperatives, so as to achieve great flexibility in working with local groups. This made possible more local involvement in the development of cooperative enterprises.

6. Although the Federal Farm Board made little direct use of clearing house associations as a means of coordinating marketing by cooperatives and other handlers, Section 10 of the Agricultural Marketing Act gave such organizations federal government approval and thus some encouragement. The limited use of the clearing house plan in the stabilization operations of the California Grape Control Board sponsored by the Board demonstrated the weakness of such plans even with governmental support and substantial financial assistance. This experience helped to open the way for prorate plans enforced by the state of California which, in turn, led to the marketing agreement and licensing provisions to be incorporated in the Agricultural Adjustment Act of 1933.

7. The Federal Farm Board experiment demonstrated the dangers of forceful development of cooperatives by government fiat under which "the Government put itself in the role of promoter, guide, and banker."[45]

After the enthusiasm of the first year or so was spent, it became apparent that cooperative enterprise thrived best from internal strength free from external bureaucratic controls. The Board's experience made clear the need for sound cooperatives with full membership understanding of their possibilities and limitations in the face of existing circumstances.

Chapter IX

PURCHASING COOPERATIVES CATCH HOLD:
1920-1932

Cooperative purchasing of farm supplies expanded even more rapidly than cooperative marketing of farm products in the years from 1920 to 1932. According to government statistics, the amount of cooperative purchasing increased from $58 million in 1921 to about $215 million in 1930-1931.[1] This growth was due to several factors, of which the following were of most importance: (1) the pressure to reduce expenditures for farm supplies during a period of general agricultural distress; (2) the rapid spread of power farming which greatly increased cash expenditures for petroleum products; (3) the extension of cooperative know-how among farmers, and; (4) the emergence of some very imaginative and capable business leaders. These factors will be evident as this chapter unfolds.

By 1920 there was only one well established large-scale cooperative purchasing association—the Fruit Growers Supply Company—and it functioned as an adjunct of the California Fruit Growers' Exchange.[2] However, two large regional purchasing cooperatives were getting well started in the Northeastern states—the Eastern States Farmers' Exchange and the Cooperative Grange League Federation Exchange (the GLF). In the Midwest, the Farmers' Union State Exchange of Nebraska was then flourishing. By 1932, the Eastern States Farmers' Exchange and the GLF had become strong organizations, each operating over several states, while the Farmers' Union State Exchange, after a period of internal readjustment, was again beginning to grow. By this time, many other strong, large-scale purchasing associations were well established in all sections of the country except for the deep South.[3]

In this chapter we will examine the progress of cooperative purchasing as it developed during this period, and we will direct special attention to the rise of major purchasing cooperatives.

The Eastern Regional Purchasing Associations

Cooperative purchasing of feed, seed, and fertilizer and other supplies had become popular with farmers in the Northeastern states before 1920.[4] In general, this area was forced to import feed supplies from the grain producing states. In the years from 1920 to 1932, three great purchasing associations developed which demonstrated what could be accomplished by farmers working together. These organizations were formed on a centralized basis with individual farmers as direct members.

The Eastern States Farmers' Exchange

The Eastern States Farmers' Exchange, with headquarters at Springfield, Mass., had begun to establish itself by 1920.[5] But, it had not been able to resolve its many problems. Although its volume of business had expanded to $1,612,000 in 1920, a loss of $20,000 had been suffered with the severe drop in farm prices. This loss was financed by friends of the organization until it could be recouped from later savings. At this time the Exchange was putting its faith in the development of county and local cooperative exchanges, and it was under pressure to provide marketing and consumer services.[6]

Evolution of a centralized organization. In 1920 there was a general belief among New England agricultural leaders that the Eastern States Farmers' Exchange should be reorganized as a federation to serve county exchanges. Professor Alexander Cance of the Massachusetts Agricultural College was the leading proponent of this view. He maintained that this was the only way to build large-scale organizations "from the ground up." When the Exchange held its annual meeting in February 1920, it was apparent that the organization was moving in this direction for the membership in attendance was comprised largely of representatives of county and local exchanges.

Soon afterwards, the idea of transferring control to the county exchanges was given further encouragement when Howard Selby, the General Manager, proposed to the Executive Committee that a subsidiary stock corporation be formed to own and operate feed mills and warehouses. He believed that the county exchanges could largely supply the necessary capital for financing this subsidiary. In the light of this recommendation, the Executive Committee established a special committee for the formation of an "Eastern States Supply Company." When the plan of organization was presented at a meeting of county and local exchange representatives in June 1920, one group favored the complete reorganization of the Exchange to make it a federation of capital stock county exchanges, while a second group preferred to modify the Exchange form of organization by setting up the "Eastern States Supply Company" as a subsidiary corporation. While this problem was being considered, the by-laws were revised at the Exchange's annual meeting in January 1921, giving dominant control to the county exchanges.

This action was looked upon with satisfaction by the *New England Homestead* (April 30, 1921), which reported that "the dirt farmers had assumed control of the Exchange." A further step toward making the Exchange more responsive to those served was taken at the annual meeting in January 1922, when it was voted that the Board of Directors composed of 25 persons should mainly "represent farmers cooperative associations, with no less than two such representatives from any one state."

However, the movement toward reorganization was eventually halted by the inability of the county exchanges to function effectively during the depressed conditions of 1922. It increasingly became clear that they could not adequately finance themselves, not to speak of financing a central organization. On the other hand, while the county exchanges were having difficulty in surviving, informal buying groups were prospering and giving increasing support to the Eastern States Farmers' Exchange. After 1922, support for reorganization of the Exchange as a federation "died a natural death" with its membership being increasingly represented by the local buying groups. Likewise, little more was heard of the "Eastern States Supply Company," for the Exchange was finding that during the hard times of that period it could operate successfully as a brokerage agency. In view of the lower prices that prevailed in 1921, as compared with the preceding year, the volume of business of $1,567,000 showed little decline and no deficit was incurred.

The problem of what to do in the way of marketing was also settled by the adverse economic conditions of 1921. While group purchasing operations, which required no facility and little labor cost, flourished, it was difficult to develop an acceptable plan for marketing diverse crops on a territorial basis.[7] After months of experimentation, subsidized by the Eastern States Agricultural and Industrial League, the Executive Committee of the Exchange decided that it would no longer attempt to develop a marketing program.

While this debate over reorganization and marketing was going on, the Exchange was strengthening its feed, fertilizer, and seed operations. Feed was handled on a brokerage basis, with the Exchange arranging for feed supplies from New York and New England mills. Fertilizer was handled on a pooled basis with farmers placing orders through local representatives or county and local exchanges with the Eastern States arranging for sources of supply. The experience of the Exchange in pooling fertilizer orders was significant in that it demonstrated the usefulness of this technique. During 1921, 5,395 tons of fertilizer were purchased through two seasonal pools as compared with 2,892 tons in 1920 before the pools were used. The success of the fertilizer pools did much to condition the way for the adoption of a comprehensive pool plan for feed the following year.[8]

The feed pools. The 1922 feed pool grew out of a conference of feeding authorities called by the directors of the Eastern States Farmers' Exchange to determine a set of rations that would best serve the needs of New England milk producers. Among those present was Professor E. S. Savage of Cornell University, the leading advocate of "open formula" feeds. As a result of this conference, three open formula dairy rations were formulated, and shortly afterward the directors arranged with the American Milling Company of Peoria, Illinois, for a supply of feed to be manufactured in accordance with the recommendations of the conference.[9] Distribution of the feed purchased was to be effected through the creation of a gigantic feed pool that would blanket the Exchange's operating territory which now included Delaware.

Under the pool plan, farmers signed contracts under which they agreed to pay cash upon delivery, the pool price to be based on the actual cost of ingredients plus storage charges before delivery. Those entering the pool also signed non-interest bearing promissory notes that could be used as collateral by the Exchange in financing the whole operation through a group of New England banks. This was a large operation involving 30,000 tons of feed with a value of $1.25 million.[10]

The feed pool was an "epochal event," and it greatly enhanced the reputation of the Eastern States Farmers' Exchange. Largely as a result, business volume in 1922 rose to $2,021,000, or 28 per cent above 1921.[11] Of more importance, the feed pool stabilized the structure of the Eastern States Farmers' Exchange, as it brought thousands of farmers not hitherto served into the orbit of the Exchange. The pool recognized them as participants in the ambitions of the Exchange's purchasing program and gave farmer representatives, who obtained orders and arranged for delivery at the car, an opportunity to demonstrate how effective they could be as local agents for the Exchange.

Until this time, membership in the Eastern States Farmers' Exchange had little real meaning. From now on, membership would be composed of individual farmers regardless of how they obtained local service, and representation on the Board of Directors would be largely in their hands.

Significantly the by-laws were amended in August 1923 to define members as "all farmers who shall purchase from or through the Eastern States Farmers' Exchange . . . "

The success of the 1922 feed pool insured that a larger feed pooling effort would be carried on in 1923, and, again, feed for the pool was obtained from the American Milling Company. This year the feed was bought in cooperation with the GLF and a number of other regional cooperatives who worked together under a joint purchasing arrangement. By this time, the Exchange had developed a system of several hundred local representatives who received a commission for obtaining orders, arranging for distribution off the car, and for collecting payment.

Under the agreement with the American Milling Company for feed to meet the needs of the greatly expanded 1923 feed pool, it was necessary for the Exchange to make a deposit of $450,000 in trust as a security to guarantee the faithful performance of its contract. To obtain this large sum, the Eastern States Farmers' Exchange arranged to pledge as collateral the farmers' notes of $10 per ton which accompanied their purchasing agreements. To facilitate this operation the Eastern States Agricultural Corporation was formed on August 23, 1923. Through the medium of this credit corporation, the Exchange was able to rediscount farmers' notes with the Federal Intermediate Credit Bank of Springfield, which loaned 50¢ on each $1 of collateral. This started a relationship with the Springfield bank which was to continue for many years.

The 1923 feed pool was even more successful than that of the year before, and, largely as a result, the business volume of the Exchange mounted to $4,652,000 and substantial savings were realized. In a reorganization that had taken place earlier in the year, provision was made for the return of savings to members in proportion to their purchases, after a surplus fund of $100,000 was accumulated. In 1924 the services of the Exchange were extended to Pennsylvania and Maryland at the request of farm groups in those states.

The purchase of the big mill. The feed pool plan was continued in much the same way in 1924, and the fertilizer and seed departments also thrived. Business volume for the year reached $5,527,000. At this juncture, the Exchange took another progressive step forward by acquiring a large feed mill to supply its total feed requirements. To understand this situation it is necessary to realize that almost from the beginning the Eastern States Farmers' Exchange had looked forward to the time when it could have its own feed mill. Experience under the pool plan in obtaining feed manufactured by the American Milling Company made the Exchange directors aware of the danger of becoming dependent upon a single commercial source of supply. Moreover, the feed pool operations of

1922, 1923, and 1924 demonstrated the advantages that would accrue from mill ownership through providing for better control over the quality of feed produced and through providing added savings from plant operations as volume increased. In the light of this situation, the directors began to search for a mill that would meet the requirements of the members.

In the spring of 1925, a small committee composed of two directors— Horace Moses and Edward W. Hazen, both wealthy businessmen and farmers—found just what the directors were looking for, The Cloverleaf Mill of the Arcady Farms Milling Company, one of the largest feed mills east of Chicago. It was located in Buffalo, a strategic place to distribute quickly by rail to all parts of the Exchange's territory, and it could be obtained for $300,000. Moses and Hazen closed the deal by personally buying the mill on the spot, for they feared that the price would be raised if it became known that the Exchange was considering purchase. To finance the acquisition, an Eastern States Milling Corporation was set up with common stock held only by the Eastern States Farmers' Exchange, and with preferred stock that could be used to raise capital. Moses and Hazen, thereupon, each invested $100,000 in the preferred stock, and, in addition, Moses took a mortgage of $100,000, which provided the $300,000 necessary to meet the cost of the purchase. The mill proved so successful that the preferred stock was retired by 1928, and by 1932 the mill was free of debt. The purchase of the mill had a very profound effect on the Eastern States Farmers' Exchange. It gave the organization a new enthusiasm and marked the beginning of a real quality program.

Another significant development occurred in 1925 when the Eastern States began the publication monthly of the *Eastern States Cooperator*. This membership magazine was designed to help farmers make the best use of the Exchange in their farming operations, and it did much to weld the organization together by providing information on the Exchange's program, services, and methods.

With the acquisition of the feed mill, Eastern States was in position for vigorous growth. Its business volume rose to $5,979,965 in 1925; to $6,279,810 in 1926; to $7,722,900 in 1927; and reached $12 million in 1930 when volume was cut back by the Great Depression. In 1926 the by-laws were amended to provide for election of directors on a district basis for three-year terms, with one-third to be elected annually. The form of organization and system of operations was at last settled.

Now that the Exchange could directly control the ingredients used in feed manufacture and the formulas used, the quality program took on a new significance. This facilitated research in feeds and feeding to better meet the needs of members.[12] Quality seed distribution had been given much attention following the establishment of a seed department in 1923. In 1928 the Eastern States erected a seed warehouse at the Buffalo feed plant to improve its seed service, and in the early 1930's the Exchange acquired its own seed trial grounds at Springfield. The fertilizer program kept pace with the feed program. In 1926 the Exchange introduced double strength fertilizer on an open formula basis. To ensure better quality, the Exchange undertook the operation of its own fertilizer mixing plant at Boston in 1931, and another plant was soon opened at Wilmington, Delaware, to better serve the Exchange's southern territory. A laboratory for soil testing work was established at Springfield in 1933. During the years from 1921 to 1931, the growth in fertilizer tonnage grew from 5,518 tons to 14,343 tons, or almost threefold, while in terms of plant nutrients the growth was almost fourfold. By 1932, no fertilizer handling agency in the nation was so actively promoting high-analysis fertilizer.

In the fall of 1932, the Exchange opened its first area warehouse to supplement the service provided by its local representatives. By the end of 1932 there were four, and by 1964 when the Exchange merged with the GLF to form Agway, Inc., the number had grown to 127.[13]

By the end of 1932, the Eastern States Farmers' Exchange was in position to move forward when the depression lifted. Feed shipments were being handled at low cost by 475 local representatives, fertilizer shipments by 374 local representatives, and seed by 527 local representatives. Its membership totalled 42,000. At this time no organization, cooperative or otherwise, was more conscious of the value of quality in farm production supplies. Its slogan "Value in Use" implied that no product would be handled that was not designed to be of maximum value to the member purchaser.

The Cooperative Grange League Federation Exchange (the GLF)

The GLF opened for business on June 28, 1920, but for two years it floundered until H. E. ("Ed") Babcock was drafted to serve as General Manager.[14] Babcock was an unusual man who pragmatically built the organization without a model. He had not only great leadership capacity; he also had shrewd common sense and a gift for communicating his ideas both in written and spoken form. He had one fixed goal: the improvement of agricultural conditions for the members of the GLF, and he never deviated from it.[15]

From the start the GLF had endeavored to operate its own feed mill without great success. In the fall of 1922, the problem of feed production was largely turned over to the American Milling Company of Peoria,

Illinois, and the GLF centered its attention on building a feed distribution system through the use of a pooling plan, somewhat similar to that used by the Eastern States Farmers' Exchange. At this time the operating territory of the GLF was widened to include New Jersey and the northern tier of counties in Pennsylvania so as to embrace the entire "New York Milk Shed."

Finding that local cooperatives could not be built rapidly enough to serve the needs of farmers, Babcock and his associates turned to local feed dealers and enlisted them in providing service on a franchise basis. In this way a network of local cooperatives and local distributors—later called "agent buyers"—was built up. This was a unique partnership arrangement which took into account the customary relations in the territory served.

The GLF was formed to provide farmers with supplies of dependable quality at a reasonable cost. "Seeds That Grow," "No Filler Fertilizer," and "Open Formula Feeds" were battle cries from the start. "More Milk and a Better Cow Left" was one of the most effective slogans promoted by Babcock. These programs paid off in farmer support, for farmers soon came to trust their own organization in meeting its commitments.

The low price policy. During its formative years under the management of Babcock, the GLF put its emphasis on building volume through a low-price policy. All savings after payment of dividends on capital stock were used to build necessary facilities. Babcock took the position that payment of patronage refunds could wait until the organization was in an impregnable financial position. Farmers supported him in this program. They appreciated the benefits that the GLF was bringing them in the form of lower prices for supplies of good quality, and they were quick to accept Babcock's challenge that the GLF was building for future generations rather than for the day.

By June 30, 1925, the GLF was forging ahead with a wholesale volume of business for the preceding year of $6,635,364. This was a three-fold increase in the three years since Babcock was placed in command. In this year the GLF opened an experimental retail store at Ithaca, N.Y. Its success led to the promotion of a system of retail stores operated on a chain store basis. By June 30, 1932, there were 91 stores of this type.

After 1925 the GLF was to enjoy phenomenal growth. By 1929-1930 the wholesale volume reached $29,239,098, and on June 30, 1930, the total assets amounted to $5,521,834, with $3,347,126 representing the investment of members. In less than 10 years the GLF had become the largest cooperative purchasing association in the United States and it was nationally known as the pace-setter in this field.

As the GLF feed program expanded, it became increasingly apparent that the GLF could no longer be dependent upon the American Milling Company for its feed requirements, even on a joint manufacturing basis. With a volume of feed business of 300,000 tons annually, it seemed prudent to construct a large feed mill at Buffalo, New York, to meet the needs of its members, and the arrangement with the American Milling Company was terminated on January 1, 1931. This was a wise action, for it provided economies from manufacturing and transportation and gave a better control over the quality of feeds produced. Although its volume of business fell off greatly during the depression years and savings almost evaporated, the GLF continued to strengthen its capacity for service so that it was in position to resume rapid expansion when the Great Depression eased in 1933-1934.[16]

The Virginia Seed Service

The forerunner of the present Southern States Cooperative, Inc.—the Virginia Seed Service—got its start in 1921 when a group of farmers organized the Virginia Crop Improvement Association with W. G. Wysor, Extension Agronomist of Virginia Polytechnic Institute, as Secretary.[17] By 1922, more than 500 members of the association were producing certified seed in considerable quantities, but they could not market it through the established seed trade even though there were many farmers who desired clover and alfalfa seed of known origin to produce a satisfactory crop. In April 1923, some 150 farmers, mostly members of the Virginia Crop Improvement Association met in Richmond to deal with this problem, and the result was the organization of a cooperative association, named the Virginia Seed Service. W. G. Wysor, the primary organizer, was on the initial Board of Directors, and, when the board held its first meeting, he was made General Manager. Thereupon, he resigned both as a director and as extension agronomist at V.P.I. and gave his full attention to the work of building the organization.

The VSS opened for business in Richmond on July 1, 1923, with a paid-in capital of $11,000. It weathered the early contempt of commercial seed handlers and slowly began to grow. It applied a business principle that had much appeal with farmers—operation *for the user of the business* rather than *for the owner of the business.* The volume of seed handled the first year was $105,000, and the net saving was $390. The second year volume reached $190,000, and savings increased to $1,600.

One of the first problems was to develop a method of distribution since the regular dealers would not handle VSS seeds. Although the few local cooperatives in the state were willing to stock VSS seed for their members, a wider system of distribution was necessary. Before such a system could be developed, business was done by mail order, but in a few months a "pooler" system of distribution was begun. A pooler was a farmer who, for a small commission, would assemble seed orders from his neighbors, and then deliver the seed to them. Within two years there were over 300 farmers in all parts of Virginia performing this "pooler" service. In all pooled shipments the order of each patron was bagged separately.

The results obtained from VSS seed pleased farmers and the volume of business nearly doubled in 1926, the third year. Satisfaction with the seed service caused farmers also to turn to VSS for help on their feed buying problem. At that time mixed feed prices were unreasonably high, and the quality of feed was often unsatisfactory. The Board of Directors pondered this problem and, in 1925, set up a feed department. The first supplies of feed were obtained from the GLF on a cost of service basis.

On feed, the VSS adopted the GLF's open-formula policy which was like the public specifications policy already in use for seed. In 1926, the Board of Directors moved on to fertilizer on an open-formula basis. For many years it was difficult for VSS to obtain fertilizer supplies of satisfactory quality for distribution, but in time (1936), this problem was mastered through the acquisition of its own fertilizer plant at Baltimore.

As the line of services increased from seed to feed and then to fertilizer, the "pooler" system of distribution largely changed to a system of distribution through local dealers who agreed to handle VSS supplies on agreed upon terms. As more local purchasing cooperatives were formed, they also became distributors of VSS supplies. In 1928, the VSS set up its first "affiliated local cooperative" to render retail service, and, by 1932, there were several of these retail stores in operation.

The progress during the first five years was slow, but during that time the confidence of farmers in VSS steadily grew and volume expanded, although the net operating savings for the entire five years amounted to only $21,000. Rather than distribute it as patronage refunds, it was plowed into the business as reserves. In the sixth operating year that ended June 30, 1929, net savings amounted to more than $18,000 on a total volume of business of $618,742, and a patronage refund was made.[18]

With the organization established, the VSS was reincorporated in 1930 under the Virginia Cooperative Marketing Act, which had been amended to authorize the incorporation of cooperative purchasing associations. The authorized capital was set at $500,000 with the par value of preferred stock fixed at $100 per share and the common stock valued at $5 per share. By this time the number of patrons had grown to about 35,000.

In the summer of 1930, disaster struck the region served by the VSS in the form of a drought, but the ability of the organization to cope with this problem for the benefit of all farmers placed the VSS in a strong position to go forward. At the request of a Drouth Relief Committee, appointed by Governor Pollard of Virginia, the VSS set up a hay purchasing agency through which farmers could pool their purchases of desperately needed hay for carrying their livestock through the winter. For many weeks hay orders from Virginia and adjoining states averaged more than 100 carloads per day. Within three months 3,000 cars of hay were obtained and shipped from the Platte River Valley of Nebraska to meet the emergency.

The volume of business grew rapidly after 1929, even in the face of the Great Depression, as shown by the following figures. For fiscal years ending June 30, volume was $2,524,000 for 1930; $4,194,000 for 1931; and $2,315,000 for 1932.[19] Net savings for these years averaged but $22,000 annually, but in none of these years were losses suffered. By 1933 the VSS was in position to grow rapidly and extend its operations into nearby states. In that year VSS changed its name to Southern States Cooperative, Inc.[20]

The State Farm Bureau Purchasing Associations

The formation of the American Farm Bureau Federation in 1920 and the rise of strong state farm bureau federations gave a great impetus to cooperative purchasing. After considerable experimentation, several important state purchasing cooperatives were established. Among the most significant were those found in Indiana, Ohio, and Michigan. These organizations first handled feed, fertilizer, and farm supplies, but, as power farming increased, they also began to handle petroleum products. By 1932, most of these associations were either organized as federations of county farm bureau associations or were moving toward the federated form of organization.

The Indiana Farm Bureau Cooperative Association

The Indiana Federation of Farmers' Associations, the forerunner of the Indiana Farm Bureau Federation was organized in March 1919. As the harvest season approached, the officers of the Federation found that binder twine prices were going to range from 21¢ to 28¢ per pound. They found one company that would sell at 20½¢ and advertised this to members. This brought all prices down to meet the competition and showed the power of organized farmers. In 1920, the Federation attempted to get a discount on fertilizer but found that all suppliers had a gentlemen's agreement to sell at a fixed price. The same was true for farm machinery.[21]

The demand from farmers for help on their buying problems was so insistent that the Federation joined with the Indiana Grain Dealers Association and the Indiana State Grange in December 1920 in a co-partnership, the Federated Marketing Service, which was designed to serve as a brokerage agency. It was to gather the orders of local groups and elevators and to combine their purchasing power to get maximum discounts for fertilizer, seed, feed, coal, and similar supplies that could be handled in bulk. The Service was to operate through county and local committees that would assemble the orders and arrange for some method of distribution after the supplies arrived. The expenses of the Service were to be shared by the co-partners until the Service could become self-supporting.

During 1921, the Federated Marketing Service did a volume of business of about $200,000 in fertilizers, coal, and twine and made modest savings, but dissension developed and the partnership was dissolved in March 1922, leaving the Federated Marketing Service under the control of the Farm Bureau and the Grange. With the withdrawal of the Grain Dealers Association, cooperative elevators could no longer be used for distribution, and so the Federated Marketing Service selected a representative for each county to solicit orders and forward them to the Service. At this time the pricing policy was changed from "cost plus" to sale at prevailing market prices with savings prorated back in patronage refunds. The Federated Marketing Service expanded its operations in 1922, but the co-partnership arrangement still was not satisfactory. In early 1923, the Federation took over the Grange interest and assumed complete control under the name, the Indiana Farm Bureau Purchasing Department, Inc.

Fertilizer operations. In this year the Purchasing Department found itself almost completely boycotted by the established manufacturers of fertilizer. Then occurred a development which the cooperative leaders termed "providential," for it came almost as if in answer to a prayer. Just at that time the Tennessee Copper and Chemical Corporation found itself with a supply of sulphuric acid that could best be used in the manufacture of fertilizer. Thus "the company had to have an outlet for its sulphuric acid at the exact time when the Farm Bureau, boycotted by the industry, was searching for a source of fertilizer. An agreement was quickly worked out whereby the Company would build and operate a fertilizer manufacturing plant, the distribution to be handled by the Farm Bureau."[22]

This arrangement, which was extended to include the cooperative operations of the Ohio and Michigan Farm Bureau Federations, proved very profitable to the three cooperatives, and it made unnecessary the shopping around every season for a source of fertilizer. It enabled the Indiana Farm Bureau Purchasing Department, in 1923, to pay a patronage refund to farmers of almost 8 per cent. This program was continued on a year to year basis until 1931 when a "participating contract" was negotiated under which "all profits and losses of the manufacturing operation were to be divided on a fifty-fifty basis between the manufacturer and the distributing cooperatives."[23]

With fertilizer operations on a sound basis, the Purchasing Department could devote more attention to the strengthening of its programs for other supplies. In 1924, an ambitious program was undertaken to distribute feed through a pool arrangement patterned on the Eastern States Farmers' Exchange and GLF pools. The results were satisfactory in the fall of 1924, but, in 1925, a drop in prices proved disastrous and resulted in a substantial loss.

In 1924, the Purchasing Department began to set up its own warehouses as centers for serving farmers. These were located at strategic points to serve farmers throughout the state and were under the complete control of the Purchasing Department. By the end of 1925, there were 10 "chain store" branches of this type.

The volume of business done for the year 1925 shows the supplies handled at that time.

Fertilizer	25,018 tons	$789,416
Feeds	13,760 tons	571,040
Coal	37,600 tons	225,640
Seeds	11,521 bushels	176,991
Lubricating oil	328,538 gallons	197,123
Binder twine	797,300 pounds	103,649

There was much dissatisfaction with the way in which the Purchasing Department was operating. Even though patronage refunds on fertilizer were paid during this year, a deficit of $12,000 had been incurred. According to Paul Turner: "The purchasing department had proven itself a failure as a business institution. It had accumulated no capital; it had provided no reserves; its distribution system had failed to operate successfully; its control had been centralized so that those who were supposedly its beneficiaries had no part in its management; a partisan attitude had kept its program from spreading out to include all farmers."[24] It was felt that something had to be done to get the Department on a better business basis, and the Board of Directors responded to this sentiment at its meeting in February 1926, by bringing in I. H. Hull[25] as General Manager, with instructions to close the warehouses and work out a plan of reorganization with James K. Mason and Lewis Taylor.

Adoption of Rochdale principles. During the spring, Hull, Mason, and Taylor in laboring on the problems of the Purchasing Department "stumbled upon" the Rochdale principles which gave them the answer they were seeking. They, thereupon, recommended a federated system of county cooperatives that would be owned and controlled by those who used them, with all savings being returned to patrons in proportion to purchases. They proposed that the new system should be open to all farmers, whether or not members of the Indiana Farm Bureau Federation.[26] In accordance with these recommendations, the Board of Directors decided, on July 3, 1926, to reorganize the business and reincorporate the Department. In effect, it became from that time the Indiana Farm Bureau Cooperative Association, although this name was not legally adopted until 1930.[27] The new plan complied in general with the Rochdale principles of organization in that the common stock was to be held only by county cooperative associations, and the Indiana Farm Bureau Federation ceased to control the organization. In 1929 Hull said: "It is the exact Rochdale plan, as nearly as we can adapt it to our conditions . . . We refund earnings to everybody. We will develop a plan of making them all stockholders."[28] The reorganization marked a significant turning point in the history of cooperative purchasing in Indiana. From then on, the program and direction was clear-cut, and progress was to be rapid and continuing.

Building the county units. When the Purchasing Department was reorganized on February 1, 1927, it was designed to serve member county farm bureau purchasing associations but none were in existence. The first efforts, therefore, had to be concentrated on the organization of efficient county farm bureau cooperative associations set up on a common basis. One of the most difficult problems was to sell stock to finance the new associations since farm conditions were depressed and farmers were hesitant to invest in the proposed county associations. In the words of Harvey Hull: "The proposal to build similar local cooperatives in each county and tie them together with common ownership of a state wholesale buying unit seemed to many to be too huge an undertaking to be practical. After trying in a few counties, we weren't even able to sell $10,000 worth of stock for operating capital." This problem was met by developing "a limited liability bond on which a farmer could sign an agreement to underwrite part of a bank loan to his co-op. Many farmers were willing to sign the bond, limiting the individual liability to $100 or $200." Although such loans generally were condemned by many bankers, in most counties bankers were found who would make the loan when 100 or more farmers had signed the security. This program worked out well, and no bank lost money on loans secured by the bonds. Moreover, the plan gave "an extra psychological incentive to help support the program."[29] Most of the initial capital for county warehouses was obtained in this way, although in later years a few of the county associations obtained initial capital by the sale of common stock with a par value of $5 and preferred stock with a par value of $25. As the county cooperatives got into operation, they built up capital by retaining savings in reserves and by issuing patronage refunds in the form of common and preferred stock. By the end of 1927 there were 29 county units in operation. During 1928 the number increased to 55, and by 1932 the number had reached 82.

The Indiana Farm Bureau Cooperative Association (then the Purchasing Department) got its initial operating capital by retaining a substantial part of its savings in the form of reserves, while distributing the balance to the member units in the form of cash patronage refunds. Largely in this way it acquired a net worth of $115,000 by the end of 1929. The main concern of the organization was then to build a strong network of member associations. The return of substantial patronage refunds in cash helped bind the member associations to their central organization.[30]

Inception of petroleum services. As shown by the volume of business in 1925, the bill for petroleum products in Indiana had become an important farm operating expense. An irritating problem was the poor performance of lubricating oils which shortened the life of tractors and other farm machinery. After several years of effort to obtain a satisfactory source of lubricating oil, the association, in 1929, decided to set up its own laboratory and blending plant for lubricating oils and greases. This operation proved so satisfactory that in nine months savings equalled the $20,000 invested in the plant. Realizing that a larger volume would further reduce costs, the Association invited the Farm Bureau Services of Michigan and the Ohio Farm Bureau Service Company to become partners in this operation in 1930. As a result the Farm Bureau Oil Company was formed, and, under an arrangement worked out in 1931, each of the partner organizations agreed to contribute capital in proportion to use. At first Indiana's share was to be 70 per cent; Ohio's, 18 per cent; and Michigan's, 12 per cent; the proportion was to change as usage determined. The Farm Bureau Oil Company was successful from the start, and in 1936 it was reorganized under the name United Cooperatives, Inc., to broaden its operations and serve other regional purchasing cooperatives.

In March 1928, the Montgomery County Farm Bureau Cooperative Association set up a bulk plant and began distributing gasoline and other petroleum products by means of tank wagons. The operation proved so successful that it paid for the facilities that were used three times during the first year. In 1929, the Indiana Farm Bureau Cooperative Association hired V. L. Everson, the man who had built the petroleum program in Montgomery County, to head up a new petroleum department. He soon began to help other county organizations set up bulk plants, with much of the construction work being done voluntarily by the local farmers as a community effort.[31] Nine county associations started bulk plant operations in 1929 and from then on progress was rapid. Twenty-three more were organized in 1930; 22 in 1931; and 7 in 1932. Thus, by 1933, the majority of the 82 county associations had bulk plants.

Ohio Farm Bureau Service Company

The early development of cooperative purchasing in Ohio was comparable to that in Indiana. In December 1920, the Ohio Farm Bureau Federation joined with the cooperative elevator association and the state Grange to set up the Farmers Commercial Service Company. This organization at first operated with considerable success as a brokerage agency in supplying farmers—through local elevators and buying groups—with fertilizer, feed, and other farm supplies, but the three partner organizations found it difficult to work together. This condition led Murray Lincoln, the Secretary of the Ohio Farm Bureau Federation, to say: "Let's do it ourselves."[32] The Ohio Farm Bureau then bought the others out and set up the Ohio Farm Bureau Service Company, on January 9, 1923, with all of the stock held by the Farm Bureau directors. In 1923 the Farmers Commercial Service Company did a business of $1,582,890, mostly in fertilizer and feed. Under the newly formed Ohio Farm Bureau Service Company, business increased to $3,160,000 in 1924 and to $4,500,000 in 1925.

On September 8, 1925, the Ohio Farm Bureau Federation set up the Ohio Farm Bureau Corporation, with Murray Lincoln as General Manager to serve as a management and financing service for its marketing and purchasing program. All of the capital stock of the Ohio Farm Bureau Corporation was held by the Ohio Farm Bureau Federation. In the next few years the Ohio Farm Bureau Service Company began to promote the chain store method of farm supply distribution through stores managed from a central office. By 1928, there were 6 stores of this type, and this number increased to 15 in 1929, and to 30 in 1932.[33] The volume of business of the Service Company reached $5,744,188 in 1929, but it declined to $4,327,191 in 1930.

During the depression, the locally controlled county cooperatives in Indiana made progress while the business of the centrally directed stores in Ohio continued to decline. In late 1933, it was decided to replace the Ohio Service Company by a new "completely decentralized" organization modelled on Indiana experience—the (Ohio) Farm Bureau Cooperative Association. Perry Green, President of the Ohio Farm Bureau Federation at that time, later said: "This program would eliminate any question of cooperative democratic control, which criticism had arisen previously. Then, too, this form of organization was supposed to free it from the restrictions of the National Recovery Act—'Blue Eagle' set up."[34]

Michigan Farm Bureau Services, Inc.

Cooperative purchasing activities were started by the Michigan State Farm Bureau Federation at the time of its organization in 1920. After several years of trial and error, a purchasing department gradually evolved which did a business—largely through car door purchasing groups and agents—of $3,700,000 in 1929, mostly in fertilizer, feed, seed, and other farm supplies. In this year the purchasing department was incorporated as Farm Bureau Services, Inc., with common stock held by the Michigan Farm Bureau and preferred stock sold to Farm Bureau members, local cooperatives, and others. Service was rendered through local cooperatives, dealer representatives, and a few local branches similar to those used in Ohio. In 1931, a joint plan of selecting directors was introduced—five from the Michigan Farm Bureau and four from the member cooperatives. By 1932, the organization was beginning to provide a wholesale service on petroleum products.[35]

Other State Farm Bureau Purchasing Organizations

Several other state Farm Bureaus promoted cooperative purchasing of fertilizer, feeds, seeds, and other supplies in the 1920's, mostly through state purchasing departments which distributed through car door purchasing associations or local cooperatives. In 1930, significant operations of this type were being carried on in West Virginia, Maryland, Alabama, Louisiana, and Mississippi.[36]

The First Petroleum Purchasing Federations

The rapid upswing of power farming in the Midwest states brought a great increase in petroleum consumption for use in tractors, trucks, and farm automobiles. In 1920 the use of petroleum products on United States farms was less than 1 billion gallons. By 1930, it was over 2.2 billion gallons.[37] The four principal organizations that sprang up to serve farmers needs for petroleum were: the Minnesota Oil Federation (now Midland Cooperatives); the Illinois Farm Supply Company (now FS Services); the Farmers' Union Central Exchange; and the Union Oil Company (now Farmland Industries).

The Midland Cooperative Oil Association

The first local petroleum cooperative purchasing association in the United States—the Cottonwood Oil Company—was organized by farmers near Cottonwood, Minnesota, on July 7, 1921, to get gasoline at lower prices.[38] Its immediate success soon led to the formation of other oil cooperatives in nearby communities. By December 1926, there were 40 associations of this type operating in Minnesota. One of these associations was the Freeborn County Cooperative Oil Company, set up in 1924 at Albert Lea, Minnesota. The main promoter was E. G. Cort, the county agent, who saw the need for cooperation among the rising oil cooperatives.[39] As a result of his driving efforts, the Minnesota Oil Federation was formed at Mankato, Minnesota, on November 13, 1925. Its primary purpose was to share information on prices, operating methods, and quality of products and to defend the right of cooperatives to distribute petroleum products. On September 8, 1926, this organization gave way to the Minnesota Cooperative Oil Company which was incorporated to pool petroleum purchases. E. G. Cort was hired as Manager, and office space was rented. Business was handled on a brokerage basis, with shipments being made from refineries to the bulk plants of the local oil cooperatives. It was set up as a non-stock, non-profit membership cooperative, and savings were accumulated through issuance of certificates of indebtedness or in the form of reserves. The association grew steadily as new oil cooperatives were formed. The 25 member associations in 1927 increased to 40 in 1929 when the name Midland Cooperative Oil Association was adopted to recognize the fact that membership was spreading to Wisconsin. The name was changed to Midland Cooperative Wholesale in 1934. By the end of 1932 there were 92 member associations. Midland's volume of business then amounted to $883,736, and savings to $26,906. Total assets by this time had reached $132,700.[40]

Illinois Farm Supply Company

Prior to 1925, the Illinois Agricultural Association—the state farm bureau organization in Illinois—did not become actively interested in cooperative purchasing, although some of the county farm bureaus jointly purchased serums and limestone with considerable success. However, starting in 1923, several of the county farm bureaus formed cooperative oil companies patterned on Minnesota experience. In view of the growing interest in the county farm bureaus in cooperative purchasing, the Illinois Agricultural Association in 1925 appointed an investigating committee to determine the desirability of establishing a state-wide purchasing service. The report, made in the fall of 1925, recommended a wholesale purchasing service for feeds, seeds, and similar supplies, but no special attention was given to service on petroleum products. Before action was taken on this report, the representatives of counties having cooperative oil associations met and requested the I.A.A. to make a detailed study of such associations. In view of the pressing interest in the formation of county oil associations, consideration was first given to determining the proper form of organization for such associations, and a plan, including model articles of incorporation and by-laws, was worked up and presented to the counties. Under this plan the Marshall-Putnam Oil Company was incorporated in April 1926, and by November there were four more companies formed, making a total of nine farm bureau oil associations in the state. Upon their request, the Illinois Farm Supply Company was chartered in April 1927. Under the plan developed, the Company was owned by the county service companies through issuance of common and preferred stock, but an issue of "B" stock gave the I.A.A. power to control the policies of the organization. This arrangement, worked out by Donald Kirkpatrick, attorney for the I.A.A., "was devised to maintain forever" the status of the Illinois Farm Supply Company as a Farm Bureau affiliate.[41]

The Illinois Farm Supply Company met with immediate success under the forceful management of Lloyd R. Marchant. "During its first six months of business, Farm Supply sold more than a million gallons of fuel and its total business amounted to $155,907." The number of member companies grew rapidly from 20, with a volume of business of $677,818 in 1928; to 51, with a volume of $1,852,572 in 1932. Savings expanded from $16,300 in 1928 to $103,788 in 1932, and at the end of 1932 the company had a net worth of $248,690.[42]

Farmers' Union Central Exchange

In 1927, the Farmers' Union Terminal Association, with M. W.

Thatcher,[43] as General Manager, took over the assets and the business of the Equity Cooperative Exchange and established headquarters in St. Paul, Minnesota, to serve as the grain marketing agency for Farmers Union members in Minnesota, Wisconsin, North Dakota, and Montana. This organization set up the Farmers' Union Exchange in 1927 as a subsidiary to handle cooperative purchasing operations. Through the Exchange a large business was done in purchasing twine, and operations were then extended to lubricating oil, coal, salt, and other farm supplies. The success of the program in lubricating oil led to a demand for a broader petroleum service. As a result, the Exchange, in 1928, assisted in the formation of a number of cooperative oil associations in North Dakota, and by the spring of 1929 there were 20 "affiliated" cooperatives of this type. As the number of such associations increased in other states served by the Exchange, a stronger form of central purchasing organization was called for, and the Farmers' Union Central Exchange was incorporated (January 15, 1931), as a wholesale purchasing federation for local Farmers Union buying cooperatives under their ownership and control. In 1931 the Farmers' Union Central Exchange had 91 member associations and did a volume of wholesale business of $906,272. In 1932—in the face of the depression—the number of members increased to 156, and the volume of business rose to $1,678,346. It then had total assets of $167,663. Although the F.U.C.E. was formed to provide a general purchasing service, over 95 per cent of its early business was in gasoline and other petroleum products.[44]

The Union Oil Company (Cooperative)

Howard A. Cowden was well known in farm circles when he was forced by organizational rivalries in 1927 to leave the Missouri Farmers' Association where he had long served as Secretary. Aware that petroleum products were becoming increasingly essential to farmers, he set up the Cowden Oil Company at Columbia, Missouri, in January 1928, to supply petroleum products to bulk plants springing up in Missouri. The Cowden Oil Company was little more than a commission agent between the large supplier and the retail outlet. By the end of the year Cowden was beginning to think in terms of a chain of Midwest petroleum cooperatives supplied by a wholesale association, so he moved his headquarters to Kansas City, Missouri, where he dissolved the Cowden Oil Company and, with a few close friends, incorporated on February 16, 1929, the Union Oil Company (Cooperative).[45] The charter of the Union Oil Company gave it great latitude, including authority to own and operate a refinery. The organization was capitalized at $100,000 with 4,000 shares of stock with a par value of $25. Control was placed in a six-man Board of Directors selected by the incorporators. Cowden, one of the six directors, was immediately elected by the Board as President, and appointed General Manager.

Building the Union Oil Company (Cooperative). In this position Cowden undertook an aggressive advertising and promotional campaign. He wrote and distributed leaflets, talked at farm meetings, and visited local and regional cooperatives in the area to obtain their support. He was a natural organizer and promoter with a high sense of idealism, and he had vision to see that the time was right for a great expansion in the cooperative purchasing of petroleum products throughout the agricultural regions of the United States. He envisaged an organization that would not be bounded by state lines. While there were state petroleum associations operating in Minnesota, Illinois, and other states, the field was wide open in Iowa, Missouri, Kansas, Oklahoma, Nebraska, Colorado, and other Western states. He realized that it would be desirable to get the cooperation of the general farm organizations of this area by providing an efficient wholesale purchasing service before they organized such associations for themselves.

On February 13, 1929, just as the Union Oil Company was taking shape, Cowden outlined his ambitions in a radio talk over Station W.O.S. of Columbia, Missouri. In his talk, addressed to "everyone interested in saving money on gasoline and oil," Cowden pointed out that the Union Oil Company (Cooperative) "had been organized for the sole purpose of combining local efforts and resources and establishing throughout the United States, standardized grades of gasoline, kerosene, and motor oils for cooperatives; for cooperative buying and cooperative advertising, and merchandising." He maintained that the Union Oil Company "seeks to promote the new day spirit of cooperation in business," and that its goal was "to serve cooperatives from coast to coast." He then said: "Thus is unfolded one of the most interesting and quite likely one of the most significant developments in the history of cooperative purchasing." He predicted that the slogan, "Our Profits Are Your Dividends" would soon become nationally known, and he foresaw an almost unlimited future. "It is the plan of the Union Oil Company," he declared, "to, at the earliest possible moment, own a cooperative refinery."[46]

Significantly, Cowden did not allow himself to get involved in the controversial farm relief politics of the times, for he feared that any statement of position might alienate support from the program he was endeavoring to get underway. His commitment was to cooperation.[47]

As support began to come from cooperatives and farm organizations, property for plant and offices was bought in North Kansas City, Missouri, on May 13, 1929, and soon afterwards a small compounding plant was constructed. This plant, the first oil cooperative compounding plant in the United States, although not finished until August, began compounding oil on July 22. This move into oil compounding was dictated by the large savings that could be made on this operation.

Reaching out. While Cowden was energetically working to gain support for the Union Oil Company, he found a national forum for his views at the meetings of the American Institute of Cooperation, held at Louisiana State University in Baton Rouge, Louisiana, in July 1929. In discussing the subject: "Cooperative Oil Stations," he spoke of the 400 cooperative oil companies in operation and said: "From the very beginning cooperative oil companies have been uniformly successful. We do not know of a failure." He also said: "The members of the Union Oil Company are gradually developing a national chain of cooperative oil companies . . . We now own and operate the only cooperative oil compounding plant in the United States . . . As soon as the volume will justify it, we hope to contract for the output of a refinery or to finance a refinery on a cooperative basis."[48] While Cowden, at this time, was operating on a shoestring, he had unbounded confidence in the success of the organization he headed.

By the end of 1929, the Union Oil Company was a going concern. There were now 22 member cooperative associations signed up on contracts that required that they buy all of their petroleum products from the Company. Sales for the year reached $309,891, and savings of $4,945 were made, of which $3,049 was distributed to member companies in patronage refunds. Cowden was anxious to make good on the slogan he had coined: "Our Profits Are Your Dividends."

Most of the Union Oil Company's initial capital for operations came from the sale of $3,000 in stock to the original six member associations. Additional capital was built up through sales of stock to other cooperatives as they became affiliated with the Company or through the accumulation of reserves. By the end of the first year the ownership interest of the member cooperatives amounted to $23,954.

In 1930, the number of member associations rose to 70, mostly in Missouri and Kansas, and the volume of business expanded to $894,437, and the savings to $26,103. Cowden in his annual report as President for this year expressed great optimism. He said: "We anticipate an increase in our volume in 1931 over the past year of at least 100%." Cowden measured the significance of the Union Oil Company in the savings provided by its member cooperatives to individual consumers. He saw the Company as a means to an end. He said: "We estimate the aggregate profit of our member companies for the past year at $504,000. In other words, they are returning to their members in dividends more than one-half million dollars." Cowden felt that the record proved "that our companies are well-managed and that we are rendering a service satisfactory to our membership, which is in excess of 100,000 consumers." Cowden concluded his talk with this statement: "The National Chain is gradually lengthening. May the time come when it will be an endless chain—long enough and strong enough to bind together the producers and consumers of petroleum products throughout the country."[49]

In January 1931, the Union Oil Company was reincorporated under Kansas law to make it a fully Rochdale type cooperative organization. At this time provision was made for electing directors on a district basis in proportion to the amount of business done in each of six state districts. Under this arrangement Missouri was given four directors; Kansas, four; Colorado, two; Nebraska, South Dakota and North Dakota, each, one. This allocation of directors showed how the organization had begun to spread.

Business volume for 1930 of $981,490, an increase over the preceding year of only 11 per cent, reflected the low prices brought about by the depression. This is shown by the fact that physical volumes of business made much greater gains. Sales of refined fuels increased from 1,196 to 1,766 in carloads or by 48 per cent; sales of lubricating oil in gallons increased from 319,584 to 510,881, or about 60 per cent; and sales of grease in pounds increased from 189,981 to 378,268, or by 100 per cent. The number of member associations had grown by 37 to 107, and net savings nearly doubled to $45,900.

In the face of the worst year of the depression—1932—the number of member associations increased to 132, and the volume of business rose by 36 per cent to $1,433,041. Moreover, the oil compounding and grease plant now furnished over $100,000 of the supplies sold. Although savings, as a result of the stiff competitive pressure of the hard times, declined to $26,103, the net worth of the company at the end of the year stood at $125,000. The organization was geared for rapid expansion with the improvement of economic conditions.[50]

Cooperative Purchasing by Marketing Cooperatives

Many marketing cooperatives were engaged in sideline purchasing activities in 1920.[51] This kind of business increased rapidly during the next dozen years. By 1932 there were 1,645 "cooperative purchasing associations" but many of these were also engaged in cooperative marketing. There were also over 8,000 "cooperative marketing associations," and 40 per cent of these were also engaged in purchasing activities. Associations were classified as "marketing" or "purchasing" cooperatives if more than 50 per cent of their business was in marketing or purchasing.[52]

By 1930 several of the large marketing cooperatives were doing substantial volumes of business through supply departments. The Land O' Lakes Creameries of Minneapolis, for example, reported in 1930 a purchasing volume of $2,148,742, mostly in creamery supplies. The large poultry and egg cooperatives on the West Coast also had large feed departments. Of these, the Washington Egg and Poultry Association did a feed and supply business in 1930 of $7,897,969, while the Poultry Producers' of Central California in 1930 did a business in feed and supplies of $5,131,738. Moreover, the Fruit Growers' Supply Company—the purchasing arm of the California Fruit Growers' Exchange—did a supply business of $9,513,846 in 1930.[53]

Summary

In this chapter we have watched cooperative purchasing come into national importance during the years from 1920 to 1932. Several of the organizations, whose beginnings have been portrayed, are today recognized among the major enterprises in the nation.[54] Their progress will be described as this book unfolds.

Chapter X

THE NURTURING OF CONSUMERS' COOPERATION: 1920-1932

While agricultural cooperation was going through a period of exuberant growth during the Republican administrations of Harding, Coolidge, and Hoover, consumers' cooperation was slowly gathering internal strength.

Consumers' cooperation had become a recognizable entity by 1920—following the organization of the Cooperative League in 1916. With the infusion of faith[1] and funds, supplied by the President of the League, Dr. James Peter Warbasse, which made the organization strong enough to carry on an effective propaganda campaign, the League had established itself as the national center for consumers' cooperation.[2]

While the Cooperative League had gained ascendency by 1920, it still represented many factions and conflicting philosophies. The great need —which was fully understood by Warbasse—was to develop unity.

The League's 1920 Congress

The Proceedings of the Second American Cooperative Convention held at Cincinnati, Ohio, November 11-14, 1920, under the auspices of the Cooperative League of America, reflected the turbulent period which consumers' cooperatives had been passing through during the preceding two years. Since the first convention, held at Springfield, Illinois, in November 1918, enthusiasm for consumers' cooperation had been generated by the abnormal boom conditions that followed the war, and there were many problems to be resolved. In his opening address as President of the League, Warbasse said: "Two eventful years have passed into history . . . During these two years societies have multiplied and the movement has assumed proportions never before seen in this country . . . While the interest in cooperatives has grown, much of that growth has been far from sound."[3] He then went on to give his ideas on what the Congress should endeavor to accomplish:

(1) The first need . . . is for national unity in the Cooperative movement . . . Besides a national organization there should be a State or District League in every State, which should have local autonomy . . .

(2) Standardization of cooperation in the United States is another essential . . . The requirements for true cooperation should be specifically agreed upon and defined. And in order that the true societies may be known to the public, a designating word and a symbol or seal should be copyrighted and made available for the use only of such societies.

(3) A standardized system of accounting should be adopted . . .

(4) Education must be the foundation upon which our movement is built . . . Two forms of education should be carried on. The education of the general membership of societies in order that they shall be cooperators is the first essential. But this must be supplemented with the even more imperative education of experts who are trained to administer the affairs of our societies and serve the people as teachers and guides . . .

(5) The problem of buying commodities for our societies can be solved only by applying to societies the same principles which we advocate for individuals. Wherever there are several neighbor societies, they should unite for joint buying. Out of such union should grow wholesale societies . . .

(6) . . . A model state law should be drafted, accepted by this convention, and its introduction in the statutes of every state planned.

Dr. Warbasse then said:

I am in position to inform the delegates here assembled that all of these questions have been given long and thoughtful consideration, and that measures have been worked out for applying them. None of this program has been left to chance. We are going forward with a well-defined plan, conscious of the ultimate power of Cooperation to win its way. I tell you, my fellow cooperators, this is an historic gathering. Future generations will so proclaim it.[4]

The Call to the 1920 Conference had invited all consumer cooperative societies that met general Rochdale standards to send representatives on the basis of one delegate for every 200 members. Labor unions, educational bodies and similar organizations were encouraged to send fraternal delegates without the right to vote. Thus it was a convention of representatives of Rochdale-type consumer cooperative societies, rather than a general meeting of cooperatives and cooperative well-wishers. In the Call, delegates were requested to come prepared to vote on two general questions: "(1) Are you in favor of state or sectional leagues? (2) Are you in favor of district wholesales, as the basis for the ultimate development of a national wholesale association?"

While the convention took affirmative action on both of these questions, bitter dissent was expressed by representatives of the National Cooperative Association and the Pacific Cooperative League who did not subscribe to what they considered Warbasse's doctrinaire Rochdale views and resented what they deemed his "autocratic" methods. Warbasse made clear his position by saying:

> A great responsibility rests upon the organization which I represent. Until the Cooperative League of America was formed, there was no central body in this country to which people could turn for standardized information on cooperation . . . This country has been the land of cooperative mistakes . . . The National Cooperative Association [Wholesale] and the Pacific Cooperative League are following the method of frenzied finance . . . The Cooperative League is in duty bound . . . to advise [cooperatives] not to affiliate with the Pacific League or the National Cooperative Association so long as they remain under their present management and continue with their present methods.

The Convention upheld the actions of Warbasse in a resolution which declared:

> Resolved, that this convention go on record as fully endorsing the action of the Cooperative League of America and its officers calling the attention of cooperative societies and individual cooperators to the vicious methods and mismanagement of affairs as practiced by the present officers and employees of the National Cooperative [Wholesale] Association and the National Consumers Cooperative Association (p. 61).[5]

The convention then voted to unseat the delegates of these two organizations. Although the delegate of the Pacific Cooperative League was not unseated, he was to a large extent unfrocked.

Although the most dramatic aspect of the Convention was the battle for supremacy unsuccessfully waged against Warbasse, the Convention was marked by a number of constructive actions which placed emphasis on the improvement of cooperative business efficiency and the promotion of educational procedures. Of most importance was the adoption of a permanent constitution which met the demand for national unity—considered by Warbasse to be the matter of paramount importance. By this action the League put itself in position to move forward.[6]

The expressed object of the League as given in the Constitution was as follows: "to promote the cause of cooperation . . . to form a union of all consumers' cooperative societies in the United States of America . . . " The immediate purposes of the League, which stated the ongoing program to be undertaken, were spelled out as follows:

> To unite in its organization the consumers' cooperative societies of the United States of America.
> To assist and encourage the organization of District Cooperative Leagues;
> To carry on the work of teaching the facts, principles and methods of Cooperation;
> To carry on education for the training of technical cooperative advisers and of administrators of cooperative enterprises;
> To conduct schools for these purposes;
> To provide lecturers and teachers of cooperation;

To give aid in organizing cooperative enterprises in every field, thus helping the people by means of cooperative societies to secure the best possible access to the things they need by taking into their own hands the administration of their economic and social affairs;

To give technical, legal, commercial and general advice on all subjects pertaining to the practice of Cooperation;

To collect, compile, edit and publish information on Cooperation and allied subjects;

To provide arbiters in matters of dispute or difference arising between cooperative societies, between individual members of cooperative societies and between societies and individuals;

To do all things necessary or expedient for the accomplishment of all objects specified in its constitution;

To acquire property, to receive and hold funds, legacies, bequests, and loans in furtherance of its work; and

To assemble a National Congress of delegates of its constituent cooperative Societies, annually, biennially, or at such times as seem best for the interest of the Cooperative Movement.

Before 1920 the League was largely a self-contained organization. The original board of directors was comprised of Warbasse and his fellow organizers.[7] Later directors were in effect co-opted to represent cooperatives and labor, educational, church, or other interests. The 1920 Constitution gave the League a definite democratic structure.[8] It provided for government through a general meeting or "Congress" of delegates from the constituent societies. Business affairs were to be administered through a Board of 15 Directors with 10 alternates. The Directors were to elect from their number a President, a Vice-President, a General Secretary, and a Treasurer, and only the Secretary and the Treasurer were to be paid salaries fixed by the Board.

The report of the Secretary for the year ending November 1, 1920, showed the wide variety of activities then being carried on by the League. In response to requests, the League had sent out 170,287 pieces of literature and 1,257 books. The League had received and answered 13,960 letters asking for information and help from individuals and societies starting stores. Circular letters—13,500—on the routine work of the movement were sent out; card catalogues were being kept up to date covering all cooperative enterprises in the United States. One hundred five meetings were addressed by speakers supplied by the League. A news service was being sent out each month to 81 papers of the Labor Press. Thirty-nine special articles written by the League's staff had been published in labor papers and magazines of general interest. Fifty thousand copies of Cooperation, the League's magazine, had been distributed. According to the Secretary's report, the membership of the League then consisted of 290 societies, representing 91,000 families, and 916 individual members, not having the voting privilege.

The League was far from self-supporting in carrying on this vigorous program. The Treasurer's report for the year ending November 1, 1920, showed total receipts of $19,090.57. Of this, only $716.40 came from membership dues, while subscriptions to *Cooperation*, sale of literature and books, contributions to the education fund, etc., amounted to $6,924.17. The balance of $11,450 came from "loans," which largely represented personal contributions made by Dr. and Mrs. Warbasse, which were never repaid. The League was now housed in its own building made possible as a gift from Warbasse, although the dedication ceremony was not held until May 13, 1922.[9]

The strongest single organization in the Cooperative League in 1920 was the Cooperative Central Exchange of Superior, Wisconsin. By then the cooperatives largely comprised of first and second generation Finns, located in the northern parts of Wisconsin, Minnesota, and Michigan, had built the Cooperative Central Exchange as a strong wholesale federation which continued to flourish throughout the decade. In 1920 its sales volume was $409,391; by 1930 volume had increased to $1,767,760. Other important supporters of the League in its formative years were a few strong local cooperatives largely comprised of Finns or of other nationality groups, located in New England or in the Middle Atlantic states.

It is significant that two cooperatives formed in 1920 were destined to play a role of increasing significance in the League during the coming decade. The first was Consumer Cooperative Services, which was started as a cooperative cafeteria by Mary Arnold in 1919.[10] In a short time other cafeterias and other services were added until within a few years Consumer Cooperative Services was doing a business of several million dollars annually and serving thousands of members. The second organization formed in 1920, the Franklin Cooperative Creamery Association, grew out of a strike of milk drivers in Minneapolis. This organization was designed to serve consumers and thus it was termed a consumers' cooperative, although in time it took on "more and more the aspect of a workers' productive association." Its members consisted of milk drivers and consumers who bought shares at $100 per share. In the middle 1920's it had over 5,000 shareholders and did a volume of business of about $5 million which made it the largest cooperative then in the League. At first it paid patronage refunds, but, after 1924, it adopted a policy of giving benefits in the form of better service and quality and in making contributions for social and public purposes. Its manager, Harold L. Norby, until his death in 1931, was one of the main supporters of the League.[11]

In accordance with a decision made at the 1920 Congress, a prize had been offered in *Cooperation* for a symbol that would serve to identify the League and its work. Although some 100 submissions were made, none were deemed satisfactory by the Executive Board. Dr. Warbasse then developed the now internationally known twin-pines in a circle symbol. It was adopted by the League at the 1922 Congress and then was copyrighted as the League's trademark. This may seem but of minor importance in the history of an institution, but it was to play an important role in gaining recognition for the League.[12]

As the postwar business boom gave way to depression in late 1920, interest in consumer cooperatives subsided, and many of the jerry-built cooperative structures collapsed. The League now saw its immediate job as one of building networks of strong cooperatives, joined together in state or district leagues as provided for by the 1920 Congress. It was then believed that much of the work of organization and education could best be performed by state or district Leagues, leaving to the Cooperative League functions that could best be handled nationally. The first organization of the district type was set up in Ohio in November 1920, while another was formed in Missouri the following month. Two more district leagues were started in 1921 in New York and New Jersey, and two more in 1922, one at Cleveland, Ohio, and the Northern States Cooperative League with headquarters at Superior, Wisconsin. It moved its headquarters to Minneapolis in 1925. However, only the last organized league was in effective operation in October 1922 when the League held its Third Congress at Chicago.

Gathering Strength

At the Chicago Congress a general spirit of harmony prevailed. Gone were the bitter dissensions that had consumed so much attention during the Second Congress. The Third Congress marked a new stage in the League's development, for it was a representative gathering in that only delegates from societies which were members of the League had the right to vote. The mood of the Congress reflected the seriousness of the prevailing depression. In his report, the Secretary said: "The present hard times and unemployment have retarded the forming of new societies. During the war new groups were started every week . . . They did not survive. Now societies are built more carefully with more attention to education. They are surviving. Slowly but surely the League is gathering into its organization the substantial [consumer] cooperative societies in the country."

During the preceding two years the League had carried on a

prodigious campaign of propaganda and education. During these years, according to the Secretary, the League had sent out 177,360 pieces of literature and 1,696 books. It had published two monthly magazines, averaging 12,000 copies per month. It had published a number of practical bulletins such as "Model Form for Setting Up Store Reports," "How to Give Credit," "Do Not Destroy the Store," "Membership Drives," "The Manager and Your Store," "Are Your Employees Cooperators?," "Accounting Methods," and "Do Not Overbuy." It had revised and brought up to date a number of its pamphlets, including "The Story of Cooperation," "Cooperative Education," and "The British Cooperative Movement," while issuing several new pamphlets, such as "How to Start a District League" and "Suggestions to Store Managers." The League had built up a news service for 150 papers of the Labor Press. It had received and answered 6,879 letters asking for advice and information and had sent out 20,000 circular letters. It had furnished speakers for 273 meetings and had supplied 124 special articles for magazines and newspapers. It had also provided legal advice on incorporation, charters, taxation, and litigation and had investigated and lodged formal complaints on fake cooperatives with authorities in several states.

This extensive program was largely financed by Dr. Warbasse and other well-wishers of the League. According to the Report of the Treasurer for the period from November 1, 1920, to September 30, 1922, income totalled $39,466. Of this, $30,889 was accounted for by "contributions"; the balance came from dues from individuals, $480; dues from societies, $641; and sales of literature, subscriptions to *Cooperation,* or for payment for services rendered.

In the deliberations of the 1922 Congress, a plan was submitted for increasing dues so as to make the League more self-supporting. Although dues were then but $1 per society or individual member, Warbasse opposed this plan on the grounds that the first objective should be to get all the societies into the League so that "we shall then have a league of societies. The value of the League should steadily impress itself upon the member societies, and in the course of time there should be no question but that they would adequately finance the League" (*Proceedings,* p. 129). Warbasse's views, plus his willingness to assume the burden of financing, prevailed, and it was many years before the League became self-supporting.

Much of the attention in the Third Congress was devoted to education. Dr. Warbasse in his opening address as President declared:

> In all parts of the country are societies, affiliated with the Cooperative League which have sturdily weathered the storm of economic depression and are moving

on toward greater success . . . Sound cooperative methods, education, coupled
with efficiency, have spelled success. The Cooperative Movement in the U.S. has
come to a critical point. The interest in cooperation is everywhere aroused . . .
Shall [cooperatives] grope blindly? or Shall they have instruction and guidance
that make for success? The failure of a cooperative society is unnecessary.

Warbasse maintained that the country should be divided into districts,
and he advocated that a vigorous program of training and education be
conducted by carefully selected district advisors. The recently formed
Northern States Cooperative League was now finding the way.

One of the highlights of the Third Congress was a report of the
Committee on Education presented by V. S. Allanne, then Director of
Education for the Cooperative Central Exchange. This report proposed a
constructive and practical program which provided the pattern for the
League's educational efforts in the next several years. Another significant
report was that of the Committee on Promotion of Cooperation by Trade
Unions, comprised of representatives from 13 trade unions. It recommended that every large trade union and central body should have a
committee on cooperation and that every state federation of labor have
such a committee. The Congress also featured a comprehensive review of
agricultural cooperation by W. C. Landson, national organizer of the
National Farmers' Union and a director of the League, in the form of a
report of a committee on agricultural cooperation. Other committees
reported on District Leagues, Credit Unions, accounting, credit trading,
store management, cooperative housing, cooperative bakeries, cooperative
restaurants, cooperative laundries, and cooperative coal distribution. All
of these reports were favorably received, and they provided a good basis
for the ongoing work of the League.

All in all the Congress was a very constructive gathering. There was
general agreement on goals, and emphasis was placed on achieving them.
A spirit of harmony now replaced the acrimony that had marked the 1920
Congress. Prior to the meeting of the Congress, the Board of Directors
had incorporated the League under its present name: The Cooperative
League of the United States of America.

The Third Congress gave a lift to the spirits of the League leaders,
and Warbasse declared in an editorial in *Cooperation,* December 1922:
"The Cooperative Movement in the United States is going forward
quietly and without ostentation. The future was never so bright."

As the new year opened, the League announced a lecture course on
the cooperative movement to be given at the new school of Social
Research. Other educational activities were going well. Under the
leadership of V. S. Allane, the newly formed Northern States Cooperative
League was beginning to demonstrate what could be accomplished by a

well-designed educational program. Another significant event in 1923 was the publication of the first comprehensive statistical study of consumers' cooperatives: *Consumers' Cooperative Societies in the United States in 1920,* by Florence E. Parker, which was issued as Bulletin 313 of the Bureau of Labor Statistics, U.S. Department of Labor. This bulletin gave consumers' cooperation official standing and also helped popularize the term "consumers' cooperation" in the United States.[13]

The year 1923 was also marked by the publication of Warbasse's *Cooperative Democracy.* Although there were other books available on consumers' cooperation, Warbasse did not consider them satisfactory texts for use in educational and promotional development. As he was experienced as a writer he proceeded to supply the need. The result was a book which was to serve during the next decade as the bible for consumers' cooperation in the United States. *Cooperative Democracy* presented a philosophy of consumers' cooperation that drew heavily on the "illuminating discussions of this subject" by Leonard S. Woolf, Sidney and Beatrice Webb, Percy Redfern, Henry W. Wolff, Emerson P. Harris, and Albert Sonnichsen. All of these writers had stressed "the primacy of the consumer" and saw in consumers' cooperation the ultimate form of economic organization.[14]

A few sentences from *Cooperative Democracy* will convey its Messianic message.

> In the Cooperative Movement the ultimate tendency is toward the creation of a new social structure that shall be capable of supplanting both profit-making industry and the compulsory political state by the cooperative organization of society (pp. 10-11).
>
> The primary hypothesis of Cooperation is that the consumers are everybody, and that all of the machinery of industry and the organization of society should be for them; for when this supremacy of interest is brought to pass, it will be found that the consumers have become producers and that the interests of producer and consumer are one (p. 11).
>
> In this book, by Cooperative Democracy will be understood the organization of the social fabric upon a cooperative basis (p. 12).
>
> As the development of Cooperative Democracy proceeds in its orderly way, meeting new needs, performing larger and larger functions, the transference of the control of industry from the hands of the many goes on without social disturbance . . . Although its end is the very end which economic revolutionists seek, its method is free from violence and cataclysm. It is the peaceful revolution in action (p. 13).

At this time, when *Cooperative Democracy* was being published, there was widespread sympathy in the United States for the Russian experiment in communism. This was especially strong among the Finnish cooperative leaders who were strong supporters of the Cooperative League. Warbasse recognized this delicate situation, but he made his own position clear by saying: "There can be no such thing as state-controlled and administered cooperation. It is an impossibility" (p. 149). He also said: "Communism may succeed in Russia; Cooperation may succeed; but not both at the same time" (p. 151).[15]

The problem of how to deal with communism was to give concern to the Cooperative League for the next several years. To understand this situation one must realize that many of the Finns who settled in the United States after 1900 brought with them a strong socialist philosophy, which led to the formation of the Finnish Socialist Federation at Hibbing, Minnesota, in 1906. Many of the early cooperatives started by the Finns in the upper lake region of Minnesota, Wisconsin and Michigan and in Massachusetts were closely allied to Finnish socialist clubs. With the Bolshevik revolution in Russia a split occurred among socialists in the United States with one faction declaring for communism. This group had gained a substantial following in the Finnish cooperatives by 1920.[16]

The American Communist Party formed in 1921 was not strong in numbers but it was able to penetrate several labor unions comprised largely of immigrant groups and, in a few instances, was able to gain temporary control over them. Its policy in the early 1920's was to work within the labor movement and to gain control from within. This led to an unsuccessful attempt to capture the Farmer-Labor party in 1924. In 1929, this policy of attempting to gain control of labor organizations and other institutions through internal activities was to be reversed. American communist leaders were then called to Russia and ordered to adopt a new policy known as "The Third Period," under which labor and socialist leaders were denounced as more dangerous enemies than the fascists. Communist philosophy under "The Third Period" held that reform as espoused by labor and socialist leaders was worthless and even harmful. Later in this chapter we will see how these shifts in communist thinking were reflected in changes of policy toward consumer cooperatives.[17]

Warbasse opened the year 1924 by saying in the January issue of *Cooperation*: "Many countries have built a cooperative movement first, and then a cooperative culture. In the United States we are building a culture upon which to build a movement." There was much point in this statement. During the early twenties the League was fashioning a philosophy of consumers' cooperation and gaining support for it in the intellectual community through a vigorous campaign of publicity and education. Dr. Warbasse knew many of the liberal leaders of the country, and he was able to gain their interest and good will for the work of the League. Among his wide circle of friends at this time were Jane Addams, Roger Babson, John Graham Brooks, John Dewey, Paul Douglas, James

Ford, Florence Kelley, Franklin Giddings, John Haynes Holmes, Horace Kallen, Harry Laidler, Walter Lippman, Frederic C. Howe, and Ordway Tead.

The Fourth Congress of the Cooperative League held in New York City in November 1924 was a working conference. Dr. Warbasse characterized it in *Cooperation,* in December 1924, as follows: "Every one of our four congresses has been a milestone. Before the days of the League the feeble attempts at cooperation were mostly scattered and unrelated. Now, the practical problems of cooperation are being jointly solved."

The League at this time was busily promoting the formation of District Leagues and stressing training and educational activities. There were now 333 affiliated societies, but income from membership dues from individuals and societies for the year ending September 30, 1924, amounted to only $1,005, while expenditures amounted to over $22,000. Income from publications and services totalled $8,494, and the balance of $12,513 was supplied by Dr. Warbasse and associates through trust fund donations and loans.

The problem of the relationship of communism to cooperation began to receive increasing attention in cooperative ranks during 1924, and it became a matter of controversy in the 1924 Congress. At this time the center of communist strength in the United States was in the Finnish and other immigrant groups, and the greatest economic strength of the cooperatives in the League came from these same groups.[18] Warbasse and the League had to tread lightly in discussing the Russian experiment in communism for fear of alienating the Central Cooperative Exchange and other important member societies.

To see for himself how cooperatives were faring in the Soviet Union, Warbasse had visited cooperatives in Russia in August 1924, prior to the Congress of the International Cooperative Alliance[19] held in Ghent, Belgium. Upon his return he reported his impressions of Russian cooperatives in *Cooperation* for February and March 1925. It was his tempered view that "The student of Russian problems gets the impression that the cooperative movement of Russia is that country's most hopeful system of organization." However, this trip opened his eyes to the true character of communism, and from then on he was less inclined to accept communist propaganda. In fact, he was soon consistently opposing communism in all its forms as being inimical to true cooperation. Years later in commenting on this experience, Warbasse said: "I went to Russia with a mind unprejudiced and hopefully optimistic . . . After I came back and had time to think it over. I became disillusioned as to its possibilities."[20]

During 1925 and 1926, *Cooperation* carried a series of feature articles entitled: "Why Cooperation Is Not Enough." These were written by well-known representatives of various philosophies. One of the articles in this series was by the well-known American communist, Earl L. Browder, who presented the viewpoint then held by American communists toward consumers' cooperation in the following paragraph:

> The cooperative movement can be used to the advantage of the workers in their struggle provided it is organized and led on the basis of the fundamental class struggle . . . All revolutionary workers should join the workers in the cooperative movement, engage earnestly in its work and energetically advance the following program: (1) The cooperative must always consider itself an organization of the working class in its struggle against capitalism; (2) Draw the cooperative into close contact and united actions with the trade unions; (3) The cooperatives cannot be neutral in the political struggle, but must always support the working class political struggle against the bourgeoisie; (4) The cooperatives should assist in mobilizing the masses in direct struggle for control of markets, prices, etc. . . . (6) The cooperatives must continuously renew their controlling bodies *from the ranks* of the workers in the shops and factories.

Browder summed up by saying: "It is the task of revolutionary workers to enter earnestly into the cooperative movement with this program always before them as the guide to their practical activities.[21]

Browder's article and other articles in this series were unfavorably received by many staunch supporters of the League. L. S. Herron, a Director of the League, representing the (Nebraska) Farmers' Union State Exchange, was highly critical of this series of articles for giving ammunition to opponents of American cooperatives. In a letter to the editor, Herron wondered "whether cooperation would be advanced by furnishing space to some persons to tell what they don't know about cooperatives." He considered it a "waste of valuable space."[22]

The problem of communism was to take the center of the stage when the Fifth Congress of the Cooperative League was held in Minneapolis, November 1926. At this Congress, a faction sympathetic to communism, led by the delegation from the Central Cooperative Exchange, almost succeeded in getting a resolution adopted which would have abrogated the well-known principle of political neutrality espoused by the Rochdale cooperators. A brief unsigned item in *Cooperation*, after the Congress (January 1927), entitled "When Is a Cooperative Congress Not a Congress?," reflected the seriousness of the situation that had been developing. It was pointed out that about half of the time of the recent Congress had been spent on resolutions of a "semi-cooperative character —such as proclaiming that the cooperative movement is a workers movement. This is a waste of valuable time that should have been used constructively."

Aside from this political issue, the Fifth Congress of the League dealt with the current organizational and operational problems of cooperatives. A national mood of complacency had set in with the growth of business prosperity, and it was becoming more difficult to attract new members into consumers' cooperatives. In fact, the number of cooperatives had ceased to increase, and many cooperatives were finding it hard to continue. However, Warbasse and the League leadership were undaunted. In reviewing the Congress in the January 1927 issue of *Cooperation,* Warbasse said: "Since 1922 we have been slowly recovering some of the lost ground . . . We have seen more cooperative societies in the United States than we have today, but never have we seen them so well united, such good education work done, so many local publications, such strong district federations." He was steadfast in his faith that consumers' cooperation would overcome all obstacles. [23]

One very constructive development during the past two years had been the polarization of League strength in three strong district cooperative leagues which were steadily gaining adherents. Of these, the Northern States Cooperative League, with headquarters now in Minneapolis, was the most important, but the Central States Cooperative League, with headquarters in Bloomington, Illinois, and the Eastern States Cooperative League, headquartered with the Cooperative League in New York City, were also attaining strength. Other district leagues had not succeeded in establishing themselves.

To supplement the educational work of the League it was decided early in 1927 to set up a correspondence school under the direction of Colston E. Warne, Professor at the University of Pittsburgh. For several years this school provided an important service in leadership training.

During this period the League was working hard to attract support from the farm supply purchasing movement which was beginning to grow rapidly. In an article in *Cooperation* for September 1927, Dr. Warbasse argued that a farm supply cooperative was a consumers' cooperative. He said: "The farmers' cooperatively organized society that buys for the members is a cooperative consumers' society."

At this time the League had two directors representing farmers' cooperative buying federations. One was L. S. Herron of the Farmers' Union State Exchange, although the Exchange did not become a member of the League until 1929. The other was Albert S. Goss of the Grange Cooperative Wholesale, Seattle, Washington. Many leaders of farmers' cooperative purchasing associations were unwilling to accept Warbasse's philosophy—as expressed in his book, *Cooperative Democracy*—that cooperative marketing could not be considered true cooperation because its objective was economic gain for farmers. At that time farmers were generally favorable to cooperative marketing.

Another form of consumers' cooperation was beginning to be of importance in 1927—cooperative housing.[24] The first significant cooperative housing development was sponsored by the Amalgamated Clothing Workers Union of New York City under its President, Sidney Hillman, and it began operations on November 1, 1927, as the Amalgamated Housing Cooperative. It was set up to take advantage of a New York State Law passed in 1926 designed to encourage low-rental housing by providing certain tax advantages. Abraham E. Kazan was the manager of this enterprise, and he showed great abilities and leadership qualities in getting the project under way and established. Its basic plan was simple. The member residents were called upon to invest $500 per room in the Amalgamated Housing Corporation for the apartments they would occupy and then to pay a monthly rental to cover carrying charges on the amount borrowed to finance the enterprise. From the very beginning the following basic principles for organization and administration have been in effect:

(1) Membership would be open to all without any restrictions to race, creed or color;

(2) Irrespective of the amount of his investment, each stockholder would have one vote in the affairs of the corporation;

(3) Speculation was prohibited on the sale of the members' equity stock;

(4) Membership was not to be confined to people from any one industry;

(5) The greatest possible flexibility was permitted for the joining and withdrawal of members;

(6) The individual cooperator was made cognizant of the fact that he was not the owner of his apartment, but more importantly, he, collectively with all the others, was the owner of the entire cooperative;

(7) Perpetual leases were banned; instead, short-period leases were used;

(8) No dividends were to be declared on the stock and refunds were to be made on the basis of the total amount paid in carrying charges during the fiscal period;

(9) The sponsoring Union always emphasized that it was not the owner and did not exert any influence on the cooperatives. Its interest was the general solvency of the development;

(10) There would be a program of continuous education.

The Amalgamated Housing Cooperative plan worked so well that it has long served as a model for other enterprises of this type throughout the United States.[25]

The Communist Threat

The growing rift with communism increased during 1927 and 1928. In an article on "Soviet Cooperatives and the International Cooperative

Alliance" in *Cooperation* for February 1928, Dr. Warbasse said: "The last three congresses of the Alliance admitted the Russian communists, who took more and more of the time of each congress to talk communism to the exclusion of cooperation." He then quoted the leading article of an ICA bulletin which said:

> Step by step, the Soviet cooperatives have been slowly increasing their attitudes of aggression towards, and irreconcilability with, all that exists outside their own regime. Never before have the leaders of the Soviet cooperatives stood forth as they did at Stockholm, stripped of all pretenses of supporting the aims of the ICA —except so far as they could be interpreted in terms of communism, the United Front, and dictatorship of the Proletariat.

Warbasse concluded his article by saying: "This position of the International Alliance is similar to that of the United States."

This opposition was anathema to those members of the League who could see no wrong in communism, and a decision had to be made. Was the principle of political neutrality to be upheld, or was it to be discarded? At this juncture, in March 1928, two strong member societies in the League—the Franklin Cooperative Creamery of Minneapolis, and the Consumer Cooperative Services of New York City—forced the issue by requesting that a referendum be sent out to all the societies affiliated with the League to ascertain their wishes. The resolution to be voted on read as follows:

> Resolved that in the interest of harmony and unity, The Cooperative League hereby, directs, by action of its constituent societies, the exclusion from discussion at its Congresses of these two fields of divisive, controversial opinion.
>
> 1. Communist, Socialist, and other political or economic theories.
>
> 2. The attitude cooperators, and the Cooperative Movement should take toward such political or economic programs and movements.
>
> And be it Further Resolved that the Board of Directors be authorized and instructed to apply this resolution and to define what constitutes such divisive or controversial discussion.

This resolution was first sent to the 16 Directors of the League for an expression of their views. Twelve of the 16 favored the resolution, while 4 were opposed.[26]

While the resolution was being considered by member societies, Cedric Long, Secretary of the League, had an important article in the June issue of *Cooperation* entitled: "How May Disruptive Controversies in the League Be Avoided?" After discussing the principle of cooperative neutrality as developed by the Rochdale pioneers, Long pointed out how political controversy had been growing until there were "red" cooperatives, "white" cooperatives, etc. He termed the resolution being sent out as a referendum—an attempt to put a stop to this growing tendency toward sectionalism or party-ism within the League. He said: "It is an effort to prevent now, while there is still time, an open break which would give us in America two consumers' cooperative Federations." It was obvious that the League was confronted by a "clear and present danger."

In the vote on the resolution, the membership of the League gave overwhelming support to the principle of political neutrality. The results—208 *for* and 42 *against*—were reported at the Sixth Congress of the League held at Waukegan, Illinois, in October 1928. This Congress was historic, for the communist faction almost succeeded in passing an amendment to a resolution that would have called for the election of the Committee on Committees from the floor. The amendment was defeated with 32 votes in favor and 35 opposed. The amendment would have passed if several members of the Cooperative Central Exchange delegation had not abstained from voting for fear that this would result in a split of the League.[27]

This incident, which could have disrupted the League, was later described as follows by Warbasse:

> At the Congress of the League in Waukegan, Illinois, in 1928, the communists were still a threat, but had been partially subdued. Their influence was enough to mess up the real cooperative character of discussions, and to require considerable political intrigue to thwart their designs. At this Congress, the capture of The League seemed imminent. They had the votes. I left the chair to the Vice-President and spoke on the floor. Then a few brief words in private with the pro-communist cooperative leader (Eskel Ronn) made it clear to him that a communist victory would mean a split of The League into two hostile cooperative leagues in the United States. When the vote was taken, the communists and their fellow travelers, who constituted the majority, abstained from voting, and The Cooperative League remained intact.[28]

Although the League survived the 1928 Congress, the issue was far from settled. The battle for supremacy was now to rage in a struggle to gain control of the Cooperative Central Exchange, then the strongest center of consumers' cooperation in the United States. This struggle was so significant to the future life of the Cooperative League that it is here described in some detail.

Following the Waukegan Congress, a "democratic revolution" began to loosen the grip of the strong communist element on the Cooperative Central Exchange. The change of thinking was no doubt greatly encouraged by the educational program incessantly carried on by V. S. Allane, the well-liked and highly respected Executive Secretary of the Northern States Cooperative League.[29] In the Fourth Yearbook of the Northern States Cooperative League, issued in 1928, Allane said:

> On one hand we have those cooperators who urge that our movement must be considered a part of the labor movement and that it should in its activities, assume the class-struggle attitude. On the other hand, there are those coopera- tors—and the undersigned is in sympathy with them—who do not believe in the vision of tying our movement too closely with any political movement . . . we must strive to build our movement on the broadest possible basis and not let it become divided by any class or party lines . . .

According to Eric Kendall, who was a witness to this period in the history of the Cooperative Central Exchange, "Allane's fellow Finnish- Americans up north read, and believed, as testified to by the successful anti-communist house-cleaning that broke out one year later."[30]

However, it was the arbitrary actions of the Communist party leaders themselves that freed the Exchange from communist control.[31] To understand this situation it is necessary to realize that in early 1929 the Commintern (Communist International) decreed that the world had now entered "The Third Period of Post-war Capitalism" or the period of "Final Collapse of Capitalism." This meant that the "immediate order of the day must be the revolutionary struggle for the conquest of power and the establishment of the dictatorship of the proletariat in all capitalist countries." The American Communist party was now ordered to change its program and tactics from working within existing mass organizations of workers and farmers, such as trade unions and cooperatives, to one of working only through organizations that would submit themselves to the leadership of the Communist Party.

Since there were many supporters of the Communist Party in the Finnish-dominated cooperatives, the Communist Party "short-sightedly but naturally enough" calculated that control of the Cooperative Central Exchange would bring control of the "cooperative stores all along the line." The representatives of the party could not understand that the Cooperative Central Exchange was not built "like a chain store outfit" where control was vested in the top—but was controlled by the local associations that owned it. As many of the leaders and department heads of the Cooperative Central Exchange, and the majority of the Board of Directors, in the spring of 1929, were members of the Communist Party, it was believed by the party leaders that it would be "an easy coup" to gain control of the organization for the service of the party.

The first demands upon the Directors and responsible executives of the Cooperative Central Exchange were simply feelers. The party asked for a "loan" of $5,000, which the Board refused to grant. Then the party insisted upon a contribution of $1,000 for its "Trade Union Unity League" convention at Cleveland, Ohio. The Board granted $250 and sent its own fraternal delegate to observe the proceedings. After these preliminary skirmishes, a representative of the Communist Party made clear to the Board what was really wanted. "He coolly set forth the request that the Cooperative Central Exchange must be made to finance the Communist Party at a rate of at least one per cent of its total sales." He also suggested that these contributions be hidden from the membership since they would naturally object. He thought that this "one per cent drag," which it was hoped would yield around $20,000 annually, could be "very easily arranged" by paying fictitious fees to a dummy lawyer in New York City.

Even though party members then constituted a substantial majority of the Board of Directors, the Board as a whole and the executives of the Exchange refused to submit to this demand. When the party leaders saw that such direct methods would not work unless key leaders of the Exchange were removed, they began a campaign to get rid of Eskel Ronn, the Manager; H. V. Nurmi, the head of the Auditing Department; and George Hallonen, the Director of the Educational Department. The first goal was to obtain the dismissal of Hallonen as a disciplinary measure, and, on October 30, 1929, the party leaders officially presented their demand for Hallonen's removal and the appointment of a man "acceptable to the Party" in his place. In its refusal to comply, the Board stated that "The Cooperative Central Exchange is not controlled by any outside group or organization; that all the questions of principles, control, and authority of its directors are laid down by the annual meetings of the delegates of its affiliated societies . . . "[32]

Unable to force out Hallonen and "clean out at least half of the entire staff of executives and other employees," the party leaders decided to carry on a campaign to create "a general uprising of the masses" against the leadership of the Exchange so as to force subordination before the annual meeting to be held in April 1930. The demands of the party became increasingly evident as expressed by editorials in *Tyomies*, the Finnish Language publication then controlled by the Communist Party. It was demanded: (1) that the Cooperative Central Exchange and its affiliated stores must be transformed into Auxiliaries of the Communist Party; (2) that the established program of the Central Exchange must be scrapped in favor of a more revolutionary program in line with the "Third Period" outlined by the communists; (3) that the cooperative movement must no longer observe the principle of impartiality and non-partisanship towards all other labor organizations, and must now declare itself openly opposed to all such organizations as the American Federation of Labor, its affiliated unions, the I.W.W., the Farmer-Labor Party, the Socialist Party, etc.; and (4) that the cooperative movement must support only the Communist Party and whatever "revolutionary" unions or movements it chooses to create.

The confusion that resulted from the campaign to discredit the management of the Cooperative Central Exchange finally forced its Board of Directors to make known its position to the membership. A comprehensive statement was prepared setting forth the official policy and principles of the Exchange which "repudiated the proposed efforts to transform the organization into an auxiliary of any outside group." As *Tyomies* refused to publish the statement, the Board sent it out to affiliated societies in mimeographed form. Since *Tyomies* had refused to publish the statement, it was set up for printing in the November 1929 issue of the *Cooperative Pyramid Builder*, the Exchange's own publication. When the party functionaries found out this intent they made a desperate effort to keep it out of the mails by confiscating and burning about 1,500 copies of the *Builder*. However, a great part of the edition was saved and sent out to the subscribers.

This act brought on open warfare. Obstinate employees and directors were expelled from the Communist Party in quick order, or they dropped out themselves. On the other side, as the annual membership meetings of the local affiliated societies came around, the members of the overwhelming majority of the societies declared themselves in support of the Cooperative Central Exchange. Moreover, the annual meeting of the Cooperative Central Exchange, April 21, 22, 23, 1930, gave almost total support to the Board of Directors and repudiated the "spurious cooperative program" and attacks of the communist delegates. Less than a fifth of the votes were at any time cast for the "leftists" on any question of principles at issue. Moreover, to make its position clear, the annual meeting removed from the Board three members who had capitulated to the party.

The annual meeting did not dispose finally of the communist problem. Seeing that they could not obtain control of the Cooperative Central Exchange, the communist leaders adopted a policy of "rule or ruin" and endeavored to "wipe out" not only the Cooperative Central Exchange but every loyal cooperative store as well. However, this "cracking policy," as it was called, failed utterly, as affiliated stores rallied to the support of the Exchange.

This dramatic effort of the Communist Party to gain control of the Cooperative Central Exchange, here presented in brief, gives the background for the situation when the Cooperative League held its Seventh Congress at Superior, Wisconsin. During the first day of the Congress the communists insisted that they be given time to present "greetings." Dr.

Warbasse granted the request, and Karl Reeve, the communist district organizer from Minneapolis, then proceeded to "heap abuse and invectives" upon the heads of the "Warbassians." When Reeve finished his speech, Warbasse smilingly remarked: "The Congress has listened to the greetings from the representative of the Communist Party. We may console ourselves that we were not attacked, because if these were greetings, what would an attack have been?" Eskel Ronn, the manager of the Exchange, then attempted to answer certain accusations made by Reeve in his speech . . . Reeve's followers . . . began to heckle Ronn, calling him such names as "traitor" and "renegade." This provoked Ronn to exclaim: "We have listened to you; now, you will have to listen to us or get out." At that moment Reeve gave a sign to his followers and they stamped out of the hall. One of the "secessionists" who left with Reeve was Matti Tenhunen, who had been president of the Cooperative Central Exchange from 1918 through 1927. After his action the delegates to the convention declared his place on the Board vacant, and, ironically, George Hallonen, who the communists had attempted to purge, then replaced Tenhunen as Director.[33]

The attempts of the communists to gain control of the Cooperative Central Exchange and the Cooperative League was no matter of minor importance. If the communists had achieved their ends it would have destroyed the League and impaired confidence in the cooperative movement as a democratic force. As Warbasse said many years later in referring to this period: "This unhappy experience with communism cannot be looked upon lightly. It was a real threat, and in several countries has meant destruction."[34]

New Problems

Little real progress was made by consumers' cooperatives in the years from 1926 to 1929 while the communist problem was causing internal dissension among their leaders. Well-established cooperatives continued to grow but few new consumers' cooperatives were established. Except for agriculture, this was a time of euphoric general prosperity, and people generally were smugly satisfied with things as they were.[35] Moreover, the rapid growth of chain stores was changing the retail environment and removing opportunities for cooperative development through a general improvement in retail efficiency.[36]

This concern with chain store competition increased interest in cooperative wholesaling, especially in view of the success of the Cooperative Central Exchange which demonstrated what could be accomplished.

In 1929, the Eastern States established the Eastern States Cooperative Wholesale. Although the Central States Cooperative League manifested an interest in having a separate wholesale as early as 1931, it was not able to establish one until 1936.

The main new consumer cooperative development during these years was the formation of housing associations in the New York City area, as previously described. Prior to 1929 there was no significant progress in the field of cooperative medical care.[37] In that year, Dr. Michael M. Shalid conceived the idea of organizing a cooperative hospital in Elk City, Oklahoma, to serve the medical and hospital needs of farm families in the surrounding area. Although confronted by many obstacles, Dr. Shalid obtained the necessary support in the community and established the Farmers Union Cooperative Hospital on a sound professional and financial basis. This pioneer effort paved the way for the more extensive developments in this field which started in the middle 1930's.[38]

Of potential importance was the growth of farmers' oil buying associations which were gradually coming into the orbit of the consumers' cooperative movement through their relationship with the Northern States Cooperative League.[39]

The Cooperative League had much to be thankful for when the Seventh Congress was held at Superior, Wisconsin, in October 1930. It had survived the difficulties of the early postwar years, and it had largely achieved its original aim of becoming the national unifying center for consumers' cooperation. It had carried on a prodigious educational program and had gradually built up a network of cooperative societies joined together in three virile district leagues. It had gained financial strength and was started on the road to economic self-support. It had the general respect of a small but important segment of the public, and it was successfully purging itself of any taint of communist influence. The Congress of 1930 reflected this spirit of achievement. As V. S. Allane said in an editorial in *Cooperation* following the meeting: "It was a good Congress all through, undoubtedly the most constructive the League has ever had. Not one of these 'big' congresses with several hundred delegates in attendance, but a Congress at which every delegate seemed to be really interested in the serious work of trying to build a solid consumers cooperative movement . . . " He concluded by saying: "There is no doubt that the Seventh Cooperative Congress will take a conspicuous place in the annals of the consumers cooperative movement   in the United States."

The highlight of the Congress was the presentation of a report entitled "Plans and Program of the League for the Next Two Years" by Executive

Secretary, Cedric Long. He saw one of the great needs to be more income through various income producing activities. To attain this objective, he said: "Of utmost importance, we must eliminate the last vestige of friction which still remains because of political controversy within the League, slowing up all our work, impairing our efficiency in countless ways." He saw the need of strengthening and extending the auditing work done by the three district leagues, the development of a well-organized insurance department, the extension of wholesaling in all organized territories; and the employment of more competent field men working out of the national or district offices. He urged expansion into new services, especially "the development of oil distribution, gold mine for any wide awake society which wants to make money." He continued: "We are beginning to reach the place where our movement has real financial stability, where it is attaining some measure of philosophical unity. . . . We shall very soon have to follow out the logic of this development and do a little modest trumpeting of our convictions and our purposes to the non-cooperative world of American men, women and children."

However, he warned, progress in terms of growth was not enough.

> Both the national and the district league offices fail utterly in their task if they emphasize only the material side of the movement, the enlargement of membership rolls and the extension of trade. They must unceasingly point out the spiritual, the social significance of consumers cooperation as one of the chief avenues of approach to a new social and economic order . . .

The problem of the relationship of cooperation to government was opened up by Dr. Warbasse in an article in *Cooperation* (January 1931). It was his view that "Cooperatives must expect to be abolished whenever socialism comes in." He said: "In all countries cooperatives are learning that no kind of politics can mix with cooperation." He was of the opinion that the British consumers' cooperative movement had made a mistake in tying up too closely with the British Labor Party. Colston E. Warne, one of the directors of the League and the director of the League's cooperative correspondence courses, found himself in "strong disagreement." In *Cooperation* (March 1931) he said: "Probably the persistence of (political) neutrality in America can be best laid to political stupidity which has characterized our populace."

Several months later the argument was resumed. In an article in *Cooperation* (January 1932) entitled "The Cooperative Movement and Politics," Warne maintained that "A persistent fallacy has too long dominated cooperative thinking in the United States. It is the feeling that the cooperative movement should maintain an attitude of aloofness from politics." Warbasse answered in a rejoinder in the same issue of *Cooperation*.

He said: "The idea of introducing controversial matter into a cooperative society in order to stimulate thinking is naive. Experience has taught me differently. What cooperation *needs* is more friends . . . Cooperation thrives best by avoiding the muddle of politics." In view of this exchange of views, it is of interest that the League was to become more politically active with the coming of the New Deal.

In October 1931 the League suffered a severe blow with the untimely death of its very effective Executive Secretary, Cedric Long, who had served in this post since 1924. A man of high principles and great ability, Long had done much to build respect for the League through his administrative and diplomatic activities. By serving as editor of *Cooperation,* he had enabled Warbasse to carry on more general activities. Under him the post of Executive Secretary had come to be a position of influence in the work of the League.[40] With the loss of Long, the burden of maintaining the League again fell fully on Warbasse, who resumed editorship of *Cooperation,* until Oscar Cooley, a trained journalist, came in as Executive Secretary, and editor of *Cooperation* in February 1932.

In October 1932, just before the national election, the League held its Eighth Congress in New York City. It was not an impressive occasion, for the long period of economic depression had tempered the enthusiasm of cooperative advocates. However, there were some notes of optimism. The Farmers' Union State Exchange and the Midland Cooperative Oil Company had widened the base for the League by coming in as members. Moreover, Miss Mary Arnold, the indefatigable Treasurer, could report that the League was progressing from "partial to full support."[41]

In November 1932, a meeting was held in Chicago that was destined to bring new life into the League. At that time representatives of the large farmers' purchasing associations came together to develop plans for a national purchasing federation. The resulting organization, National Cooperatives, Inc., organized in 1933, was to join hands with the Cooperative League and give the League the broader base and economic sinews that it needed to develop a program of national importance. This development will be discussed in Chapter XVIII.

Chapter XI

COOPERATIVE PROGRESS IN CREDIT
AND INSURANCE: 1920-1932

During the years from 1920 to 1932, great strides forward were made by cooperative credit and insurance organizations which opened the way for more spectacular developments with the coming of the new Deal.

Expansion of the Cooperative Farm Credit System

With the constitutionality of the Federal Farm Loan Act of 1916 established by the Supreme Court in 1921, the cooperative system of long-term credit provided by Federal Land Banks and national farm loan associations was in position to grow. Progress was steady if not spectacular.[1] The plan provided for the eventual ownership of the Federal Land Banks by the national farm loan associations, and this goal was nearly reached by 1931 when the severe depression made necessary a fresh infusion of government capital.[2]

It will be recalled that the passage of the Federal Farm Loan Act of 1916 did not satisfy those who desired action on short-term credit. This sentiment, which never died down entirely, gained new strength during 1920 after the government discontinued the War Finance Corporation, the agency that had helped finance agricultural exports during the war and early postwar period. Farmers then demanded that the War Finance Corporation be reinstated to help finance farm exports, and their pressure was so strong that this was done over the veto of President Wilson in January 1921. Although this action was more a token of discontent than a measure to bring permanent credit relief to agriculture, it marked a significant step toward a federal program to provide short-term credit. To the emerging commodity marketing cooperatives, the reinstatement of the War Finance Corporation was of the utmost importance, for it provided a mechanism through which they could obtain operating capital that might otherwise have been unavailable to them. "Early in July, [1921] the Corporation agreed to advance $5 million to the Staple Cotton Cooperative Association to enable it to finance the holding of 100,000 bales of cotton until they could be exported in an orderly manner. Later in the year the Corporation made advances to other cooperative marketing associations . . . for the same purpose."[3]

As the agricultural situation worsened, it became apparent that additional farm credit machinery was needed. In setting up the Joint Commission of Agricultural Inquiry in the late spring of 1921, Congress specifically directed it to report "upon the banking and financial resources and credits of the country, especially as affecting agricultural credits." In order to provide relief until this Commission could make its report and until permanent legislation could be enacted, Congress, on August 24, 1921, amended the War Finance Corporation Act to empower the Corporation to make advances to "any bank, banker, or trust company in the United States, or to any cooperative association of producers in the United States . . ."[4]

It is doubtful whether the commodity cooperatives for cotton, tobacco, and other farm products would have expanded so rapidly in 1921 and 1922 had it not been for the sympathetic assistance given them by the War Finance Corporation. As Baird and Benner later said: "The experience of the War Finance Corporation . . . " showed that "safe methods of financing the orderly marketing of agricultural products could be devised . . . In its work with the cooperative marketing associations, it guaranteed them credit at a time when these newly created marketing agencies were finding it difficult to secure funds."[5]

The passage of the Agricultural Credits Act of 1923, signed by President Harding on March 4, 1923, marked a second great step forward in providing for the present cooperative farm credit system. It set up 12 Federal Intermediate Credit Banks owned and operated by the government. These banks, located in the same cities as the 12 Federal Land Banks served identical districts. Moreover, the Federal Farm Loan Board was given supervision over the Intermediate Credit Banks. The main purpose of the Intermediate Credit Banks was to provide a system for rediscounting agricultural paper for loans from six months to three years. Loans were to be made direct to cooperative marketing associations, secured by warehouse receipts for storable products. Agricultural paper from commercial banks, agricultural credit corporations, and livestock loan companies was to be rediscounted.[6]

The Intermediate Credit Banks thus continued the type of assistance to cooperative marketing associations that had been provided by the War Finance Corporation.[7] In 1926 loans to such associations reached nearly $103 million. Under the encouragement of the program of the Federal Farm Board to promote producers' marketing cooperatives, such loans rose to $145 million in 1931.

Although the direct loans from the Intermediate Credit Banks were of primary importance to the marketing cooperatives at this time, it was also significant that the Agricultural Credits Act of 1923 enabled cooperative marketing associations to provide production credit through credit corporations. In fact, the real beginnings of the production credit system that was set up by law in 1933 largely grew out of production credit experience with such credit corporations.[8]

Many of these credit corporations were set up in order to maintain deliveries of members' crops to the marketing associations, for, if the members had obtained their production financing from trade sources, they would have been forced as a rule to market their products where the creditors directed. As Baird and Benner have said:

> Cooperative marketing associations entered the field of production credit in part for the purpose of reducing production costs for their members . . . If members can borrow from agricultural credit corporations which rediscount producers notes with the Intermediate Credit Banks, the cooperative can operate its supply business on a cash basis. The primary reason for cooperatives venturing into the field of production credit was to promote cooperative marketing. Very early the state-wide cotton and tobacco associations realized that their members dependency upon credit institutions indifferent or unfriendly to the cooperative movement prevented deliveries.

Cooperatives felt that they had

> . . . to fight fire with fire. It was in this mood that many agricultural credit corporations were formed in the first few years. Since the crop mortgage system prevailed throughout most of the cotton and tobacco areas, all cooperatives faced this problem of securing deliveries. As a result they either encouraged the formation of credit corporations friendly to cooperative marketing or organized their own credit subsidiaries.[9]

Credit corporations were most commonly set up by the cotton marketing cooperatives, although some were formed by livestock and other types of marketing associations.[10]

The establishment of the Federal Farm Board in 1929 expanded the significance of the Federal Intermediate Credit Banks in serving cooperatives. In making loans to marketing cooperatives, the Board required that they first borrow any funds available from other agencies. Thus to get Farm Board money, it was necessary to first obtain, if possible, funds from the Intermediate Credit Banks. Moreover, the Federal Farm Board encouraged cooperative marketing associations to set up subsidiary financing corporations by providing funds that could be used for capitalizing such institutions.[11]

The Federal Farm Board carried lending assistance to cooperative marketing associations several steps further. Up to 1929, financial assistance from the Intermediate Credit Banks was limited to loans made on the security of commodities covered by warehouse receipts or to rediscounting paper of their subsidiary agricultural credit corporations. The Agricultural Marketing Act authorized the Federal Farm Board to make loans to help in the effective merchandising of agricultural commodities; in construction or purchase of marketing facilities; in enlarging membership of existing cooperative marketing associations; and to make higher advances to association members than could be made with other types of financing. The Federal Farm Board thus greatly extended the scope of lending services hitherto available from the Intermediate Credit Banks.

The experience during the Great Depression demonstrated the value and need of soundly organized credit corporations to serve farmers and stockmen.[12] In 1932 the Secretary of Agriculture was authorized by Congress to make loans "for the purpose of assisting in the formation of local credit corporations or of enlarging the resources of credit organizations already in existence, and a $10 million revolving fund was provided for this purpose." In the same year the Reconstruction Finance Corporation was authorized to create in any of the 12 Federal Land Bank districts a regional credit corporation with a paid-up capital of not less than $3,000,000 to be subscribed for by the Reconstruction Finance Corporation.[13] These and other emergency measures helped many farmers to survive the most difficult year in our agricultural history.

As the year 1932 drew to a close, it was apparent that the incoming Roosevelt Administration was planning comprehensive changes in governmental machinery to help farmers meet their financial problems. There was a general feeling that much had been learned from the experience of the Federal Land Banks, the Intermediate Credit Banks, and the Federal Farm Board that should be utilized in providing the agricultural industry with a comprehensive and better coordinated farm credit system. In Chapter XIV we will see how this sentiment culminated in the passage of the Farm Credit Act of 1933 which set up the Farm Credit Administration.

The Campaign for Credit Unions

By 1920 credit unions had obtained a toehold in the United States.[14] In the next dozen years they were to gain national recognition. There were but 190 credit unions in the United States in 1921 with a total membership of 72,000 and total assets of $10,000,000. By 1930, there were 1,300 credit unions with a total membership of 300,000 and total assets of nearly $50,000,000.[15]

This rapid expansion came about largely through the interest and financial support of one man, Edward A. Filene, who in 1921 set up and financed the Credit Union National Extension Bureau to promote this form of cooperative financial institution.[16] Filene realized that the success of the Credit Union National Extension Bureau would depend upon the character and capacity of the person selected to manage it, and in Roy M. Bergengren he found a man with the legal, business, and leadership qualities needed.[17] Together they set up this agency and agreed upon four objectives. According to Bergengren:

> We agreed on the first day that the Bureau had four objectives, and these objectives have never been changed or amended. Our first objective was to make it possible, by adequate legislation, to organize credit unions anywhere in the United States . . . Second, we appreciated the need for a vast experimentation with the credit union plan, its complete Americanization . . . This second objective involved the organization of individual credit unions until the plan had been popularized and methods of credit union mass production had evolved. The third objective looked forward to permanent, self-sustaining state leagues of credit unions which would, in each state, take over the local direction of credit union development. Finally, it was our purpose, from the beginning to organize the Credit Union National Association as a national union of credit unions . . . and turn over to the Association when organized, the permanent direction of the cooperative credit movement in the United States . . .[18]

The immediate need was to get state laws enacted that would make possible credit union development, and this was made the Bureau's first order of business. In 1921 there were only 4 states with effective credit union laws; by 1932 the number had passed 30.

One of Bergengren's early efforts toward achieving the Bureau's objectives was the preparation of a book that would explain what credit unions were and how they could be of service. The book, *Cooperative Banking—A Credit Union Book*, published in 1923, was to serve as the bible for credit union development until 1931 when it was superseded by a second volume, *Credit Union—A Cooperative Banking Book*. The change of order in the titles reflected the great progress made by credit unions in seven years.

Bergengren's first book provides a description of the extent of credit union progress in the various states and thus gives us a bench mark of growth as of 1922. At that time the leading states in credit union activity were Massachusetts and New York, and the only other state with an active credit union movement was North Carolina—where the interest was primarily rural. Bergengren admitted that the credit union movement was "in its infancy" (p. 242). In his second volume, seven years later, he characterized the first book as a "sort of pioneer's guide" or as an "explorer's map."

It had become evident to Bergengren by 1923 that the great opportunity for credit union expansion was among urban workers: "The credit union almost certain of success is that organized among the employees of a well-established industrial unit" (p. 129). He was impressed, however, by the promise of the rural credit union movement then being vigorously promoted in North Carolina as a means of helping farmers on their short-term production credit problems. To him North Carolina was a laboratory where the idea was being tested so that it might be more widely applied (pp. 191-223). He then believed that the movement in North Carolina had largely passed through the experimental stage, and he was hopeful that its plan would soon spread to rural areas in other states. Perhaps this would have occurred had it not been for the severe agricultural depression of the early 1920's which forced farmers to demand government action on their production credit problems. With the setting up of the Intermediate Credit Banks in 1923, the steam was taken out of the North Carolina movement, and it never recovered its earlier vitality.

Bergengren in 1923 was greatly encouraged by the altruistic attitude toward credit unions then being expressed by such public-spirited industrial leaders as Henry S. Dennison who had fostered one of the early credit unions in his manufacturing concern, the Dennison Manufacturing Company of Framingham, Massachusetts. Bergengren hoped that the recent appointment of Dennison as "Director of Personnel" for the United States Post Office Department would soon result in the encouragement of credit unions among postal workers.[19] The first postal credit union was established at Brockton, Massachusetts, before the book could be printed. By 1932, there were 240 credit unions operating in post offices in 32 states. Bergengren saw much hope in such enlightened business leadership.

> The newer type of industrial leader approaches his industry as it should be approached in a democracy. He sees that the permanency of any system of government depends on the average happiness of the people who live within its jurisdiction. Such a man is interested in profit-sharing, in group insurance, in employee's mutual benefit associations, in rest-rooms, in credit unions and in the thousand and one things which make for harmonious relationships between capital and labor (p. 335).

Although not unsympathetic to the emerging consumers' cooperative movement of that time, Bergengren did not become closely associated with it, for he was single-mindedly concerned with the setting up of credit unions for people who needed and desired them, and in this he was supported by Filene. He saw the danger of embroiling the credit union movement in ideological disputes that might weaken its appeal to industrial leaders or government officials, whose support was essential. In fact, Bergengren welcomed interest from any quarter—government, industry, labor, churches, universities, cooperatives—that might help in the general extension of credit unions. If consumers' cooperatives would set up credit unions, this was to be encouraged, but he showed them no favors compared to others. He was concerned with only one thing, cooperative credit, and he would not allow himself to get involved in any extraneous issues. He considered it important to form credit cooperatives to help people meet their financial problems even if they were little interested in the wider application of the cooperative idea. It is doubtful whether credit unions would have become a mass movement in the 1920's unless Bergengren and Filene had adopted this pragmatic philosophy of getting support wherever it might be available.

In 1924 the National Credit Union Extension Bureau began publication of a monthly magazine, *The Bridge,* to provide timely information on credit union problems of organization and operation. Under Bergengren's editorship, *The Bridge* greatly stimulated the growth of credit unions and helped combine them into a national credit union movement. Largely as a result of Bergengren's energetic efforts and effective publicity work, the number of credit unions rose to 419 in 1925 or more than double the number in 1921.[20] In the next five years they again more than doubled.

It is significant that the credit union movement came into prominence just about the time that business organizations were beginning to give attention to employee problems as a factor related to business efficiency through the establishment of personnel departments.[21] Many industrial concerns saw in credit unions a means of reducing labor turnover and otherwise increasing the contentment and output of their workers. A breakthrough of much significance came with the acceptance of the value of credit unions by the management of Armour and Company.

How this strategically important support was gained is of considerable interest because of the immediate impact it had on credit union expansion, and because the leader in this program, Claude Orchard, later played an important role in the advancement of federally incorporated credit unions (see Chapter XIV). For many years Orchard, as a minor official of Armour and Company at Omaha, Nebraska, had been sympathetic to the financial problems of the workers in the plant, many of whom were foreign-born. He saw how they were victimized by saloon keepers who cashed their pay checks and by the depredations of loan sharks who loaned them money to meet emergencies at high interest rates, and he did what he could to be of help to them. In 1929 he became interested in the possible contribution that a credit union could make to this problem and gained permission to give the idea a trial. Armour officials were so pleased by the early results achieved at Omaha that they decided to encourage the formation of credit unions in all major Armour plants. Orchard was assigned the job of explaining the credit union plan to Armour employees with the cooperation of Tom Doig of the National Credit Union Extension Bureau. Moreover, Armour and Company encouraged representatives of other companies to attend the meetings where the credit union idea was expounded so that the benefits of this work were shared with other concerns. This enlightened program helped spread the credit union idea. Within five years there were over 100 credit unions serving employees of Armour and Company, and similar credit unions were serving employees of Swift and Company and other meat packing plants.[22]

The progress made by the credit union movement by 1930 when Bergengren completed his second book was phenomenal. He indicated that "The credit union pioneer has become a settler." The second book reflected the changed character of the credit union movement, for it placed emphasis on credit union problems, credit union mechanics, and credit union practice, administration and accomplishments.

In his second book Bergengren asked the question: "What are the possibilities of rapid national expansion of cooperative credit in the next few decades?" He answered that in view of the progress registered in the past seven years there was "no real limit to credit union expansion." He went on: "*Somehow . . . everyone in need of credit union services and capable of self-help can be reached; not only that—they will be reached.*"[23] Bergengren felt that one could have faith in the broad national application of the credit union plan for:

> We know that the credit union of fifty members works as well as the credit union of five thousand members. We have demonstrated again and again that, within the average group may be found folks who can develop in capacity for the successful management of financial business which in many cases, reach major proportions. Here we have made a profound and very cheering discovery . . . We have had to do with very large employee groups—350,000 in the postal service, for example—and understand that they may be reached by chain development . . . We have seen the plan successfully applied to sixteen thousand employee members of the credit unions with the New England Telephone and Telegraph Company and to city employees, state employees, federal employees, to national and racial groups; to fraternal orders and American Legion posts; to large and small labor bodies, to community neighborhood and social groups.[24]

Bergengren's experience had taught him that any

> Cooperative business . . . must in order to survive and to prove itself in
> service operate with every modern device which makes for successful business
> . . . The personnel of a cooperative society must equal in skill and training the
> most skilled managers of competing private businesses . . . [F]rom it must be
> divorced, whenever the need exists, any collateral political considerations which
> seek to encumber cooperatives with this party label or that in order to promote,
> not the cooperative enterprise in question, but the particular political "ism"
> which seeks to make capital out of the cooperative plan.[25]

According to Richard Y. Giles: "In ten years Bergengren had a credit union movement that was unique in the world, just as American mass-production economy was unique . . . Some of the credit for Bergengren's success must be laid to the fact that credit unions are simple things which fill an obvious need, but a great deal of his success is due to the fact that both Filene and Bergengren had a keen sense of the immediate necessity."[26]

The first rural credit unions set up in North Carolina had been formed independently of other cooperatives and they had not generally proven successful. A more promising development of rural credit unions came in 1930 under the leadership of Harvey Hull, General Manager of the Indiana Farm Bureau Cooperative Association. Hull believed that credit unions could help meet one of the serious problems of its member county farm supply distributing associations by providing members with a supplementary source of credit. Two credit unions were formed as auxiliaries of county associations in 1931 and two more in 1932 with favorable results, and the program soon spread to many more of the county associations.[27]

Critics of Bergengren held that his methods, subsidized by Filene, promoted "hot house" growth. Bergengren frankly admitted "that much that has been accomplished has resulted from operating under high pressure to rapidly build a strong foundation for substantial growth."[28] He and Filene were only concerned with one immediate objective: Building the credit union movement so strong that it could grow from internal democratic strength. From the very beginning they gave their full support to the organization of state credit union leagues as the foundation for a credit union national association.

The first credit union league was organized by Bergengren and Filene in Massachusetts in 1921 prior to the establishment of the National Credit Union Extension Bureau. Before that time credit unions in Massachusetts and other states had been largely promoted by public-spirited men like Filene. From then on the credit union movement became self-generating, and, as the number of credit unions increased, similar state leagues were formed in other states. By 1932 there were more than a dozen state credit union leagues in operation. How such credit union leagues were joined together in 1934, to form a national organization—The Credit Union National Association—will be described in Chapter XXI.[29]

New Developments in Mutual Insurance

One of the oldest forms of American cooperative enterprise, the Farmers' Mutual Fire Insurance Company, was well established in 1920.[30] During the next dozen years such companies intensified their operations, and new mutual companies arose to meet rural insurance needs resulting from the growing use of automobiles and power machinery.

Changes in farmers' mutual fire insurance companies. The total number of farmers' mutual fire insurance companies continued to be about 2,000 during the period from 1920 to 1932, for new organizations formed were largely offset by dissolutions which generally represented consolidations of smaller mutuals. On the other hand, the volume of property insured by these companies continued to show a steady but marked increase—from about $8 billion in 1920, to over $10 billion in 1932. By 1932 there were also over 50 specialized windstorm insurance mutuals, providing property protection of over $2 billion and about 40 specialized hail insurance mutuals.

One of the significant trends in the field of farm mutual insurance was an increasing emphasis upon effective inter-company cooperation, largely provided and achieved through state associations of farm mutuals with the encouragement of the National Association of Mutual Insurance Companies that had been established in 1895. This did much to break down company individualism and brought about steady improvement and standardization in forms and practices. There was also a shift from post-loss to advance-assessments with an increased emphasis upon reserves or safety funds. Reinsurance services also expanded, either through companies designed to furnish this service or through reinsurance arrangements made between two or more of the mutuals.[31] More attention was also directed to loss prevention practices, especially periodic inspection of risks, rating of property to reward good construction and maintenance, support to rural fire protection organizations, and education for prevention of fire hazards. Taking all of these constructive developments into consideration, the farm mutuals greatly improved their position by 1932,[32] although they were severely handicapped by the Great Depression.[33]

The first mutual automobile insurance companies. The most spectacular development in mutual insurance during the 1920's was the arrival and rapid expansion of mutual automobile insurance. The pioneer in this new activity was George J. Mecherle, a farmer from Merna, Illinois.[34] Realizing the great need of farmers for automobile insurance and seeing the possibilities of using the principles that had been developed by the mutual fire insurance companies to provide farmers with mutual automobile insurance, Mecherle, in 1921, began promoting the idea of a "different kind of insurance company" to provide farmers with automobile insurance at low cost. He first expounded his ideas at the state convention of the Illinois State Association of Mutual Insurance Companies at Streator, Illinois, in February 1922, where he pointed out that since the farm mutual insurance companies "did not sell automobile insurance, their agents could add to their income by taking on the line that he proposed to offer." The delegates approved of Mecherle's idea and gave it their unanimous endorsement. With this encouragement, Mecherle then proceeded to perfect his plan and get it approved by the state authorities. On June 7, 1922, his brain child, the State Farm Mutual Automobile Insurance Company, was officially launched. Its first policies provided coverage for liability and property damage, fire and theft, and collision with movable objects.

There was little that was original in the State Farm plan but it combined several novel features. While other insurance companies collected premiums annually, State Farm adopted a semi-annual payment plan, which was, in effect, an application of the installment credit idea. This arrangement had the advantage of reducing the first cost and spreading the payment, and this was attractive to hard-pressed farmers. While other insurance companies then required their agents to obtain renewals of premiums, State Farm took over this work and relieved the local agents of this burden. Moreover, by issuing all policies through the State Farm office, the local agents were freed of this unproductive clerical work. State Farm's most unusual feature was its life membership fee. Any person who joined State Farm did so for life, or at least as long as he remained a good risk. The membership fee was not a premium. It was, instead, an "admission and inspection" fee and it was not returnable. At first, State Farm operated on a returnable dividend plan but this was soon replaced by a net premium plan under which the charges were fixed in advance on the basis of calculated costs. All of these features resulted in a package of advantages that made possible the charging of lower rates, and this gave a great inducement in building membership.[35]

The growth of State Farm was phenomenal. During its first half year—1922—it enrolled 1,327 members and made an income of $22,000. By 1927, income had reached $1,568,000 and its policies numbered 370,045.

State Farm was launched at an auspicious time. The automobile was rapidly coming into farm use, and Illinois farmers were becoming well organized in county farm bureaus affiliated with the Illinois Agricultural Association. As a farmer himself, Mecherle saw the advantage of building a close relationship with the highly popular county farm bureaus. In his address to the Illinois State Association of Mutual Insurance Companies, he had said: "No application will be accepted from any but members of Farm Bureaus, members of Farm Mutuals . . . or those eligible to membership in such organizations."[36]

In 1924, the Illinois Agricultural Association endeavored to persuade Mecherle that State Farm should become a part of the I.A.A., but Mecherle preferred to maintain his freedom of action. As a counteroffer he proposed that farm bureau advisors become agents for State Farm. This arrangement was accepted and was continued until 1927 when the I.A.A. decided to set up its own mutual insurance company along lines very similar to those of State Farm.[37]

A highly significant development came in 1924 which was to inaugurate expansion of State Farm outside of Illinois. After careful study of the insurance needs of its members, the Indiana Farm Bureau Federation invited State Farm to provide service in Indiana under an arrangement whereby the Federation would be its state agent. The "invasion" of Indiana was at first opposed by conservative members of State Farm's board of directors who felt that "the time had not yet come to expand beyond the borders of Illinois."[38]

The Indiana program, begun in April 1925, worked so well that it soon led to similar arrangements with other state farm bureau federations. Later in the year, the program spread to South Dakota, and then, in 1926, it moved on to Missouri, Minnesota, and Michigan. In 1927, Colorado, Iowa, Kansas, Kentucky, and Nebraska joined the parade, to be followed the next year by California, Mississippi, Montana, Nevada, Texas, Utah, and Washington. In 1929 and 1930, Arizona, Idaho, New Mexico, West Virginia, Wyoming, North Carolina, Oklahoma, Oregon, and Virginia became State Farm states.[39] By 1932 State Farm thus was operating in over two dozen states under the sponsorship of State Farm Bureau Federations.

The contracts between State Farm and the state farm bureau federations were mutually satisfactory. They enabled the farm bureaus to offer low cost insurance desired by members and provided them with a source of much needed revenue to support their general programs. They also greatly benefited State Farm by rapidly giving it widespread publicity and a large volume of business which reduced its costs, which, in turn, facilitated further expansion.

The Ohio Farm Bureau Federation would have entered into an agency agreement with State Farm had the Ohio Insurance Department permitted. The Ohio Federation, in 1925, invited Mecherle to set up the program in Ohio, and he would have done so but the State Insurance Commissioner would not issue a license. Murray D. Lincoln, Secretary of the Ohio Farm Bureau Federation, then set up a committee to develop a plan for "its own company" which was unanimously approved by the Federation's directors. Formed to a large extent on the model of State Farm, the Farm Bureau Mutual Automobile Insurance Company was incorporated on December 17, 1925. State Farm helped set up the Ohio Company and, for this assistance, received a percentage of every coverage written during the first year.[40] The Ohio Company made one early decision that was to prove of much significance in the years to come. It was decided to not restrict service to Farm Bureau members or farmers.[41]

The success of the Farm Bureau Mutual Automobile Insurance Company (which in 1955 became Nationwide Insurance Companies) was immediate. By December 1926, it had developed assets of $114,000, and within two years it was invited by state farm bureau federations or similar organizations to provide service in Vermont, Delaware, West Virginia, and North Carolina. In 1929 service was likewise extended to Pennsylvania and Virginia. By 1933 the company had 105,301 policies in force and its total admitted assets amounted to $3,130,657.[42]

We have already mentioned the fact that the powerful Illinois Agricultural Association endeavored to gain control of State Farm in 1924. Since this couldn't be achieved, the I.A.A. decided to set up its own automobile insurance company, which began operations in April 1927 as the Illinois Agricultural Mutual Insurance Company. By the end of the first year this company had received 7,200 applications for policies—"a sensational record."[43]

The plan of the Illinois Agricultural Mutual Insurance Company was quite similar to that of State Farm but its policies were more tailor-made for farm people. It was one of the first mutual insurance companies to include a non-owner provision which was based on the theory that hired men or neighbors driving the owner's car should be covered. The original policy limited protection on collisions to movable objects. This was changed soon to afford protection in case of collision with stationary objects.[44]

In 1929 the Illinois Agricultural Mutual Insurance Company began to write employer's liability policies. By the end of 1932, when the company was less than seven years old, 36,249 applications for automobile insurance policies had been received, together with 1,966 policies for employer's liability policies. The company had then built up a surplus of $475,000.

A third state farm-bureau-sponsored automobile insurance organization was set up in New Hampshire in 1928 to write insurance for farm bureau members. It was formed as the Farm Bureau Automobile Mutual Insurance Company, but a few years later, when it began writing fire insurance and allied lines, it adopted the name Farm Bureau Mutual Insurance Company. From its beginning it has provided insurance at reasonable cost to members, and it now also operates in Maine and Vermont.

The experience of the Ohio, Illinois, and New Hampshire farm-bureau-sponsored companies was significant in that it pointed the way for other state farm bureau federations to break away from State Farm and set up their own mutual automobile insurance companies.[45] We will deal with this development in Chapter XXI.

Many of the early farm mutual fire insurance companies had been formed as affiliates of Grange organizations. With this heritage of experience, it was natural for members of the Grange to demand their own mutual company for automobile insurance. In 1923, the National Grange Mutual Liability Company was set up at Keene, New Hampshire, to provide automobile coverage. This organization, limited to members of the Grange, proved successful from the start, and it has continued to prosper to the present day.[46]

Up to 1920, the mutual insurance companies of farmers were largely local in character and their operations were confined to fire or other farm risks. During the next twelve years, many of these local companies federated together to increase their effectiveness, and state and national mutual insurance companies were formed by farmers to obtain automobile insurance protection. In later chapters, we will see how some of these companies came to extend their coverage to life or other forms of insurance.

Summary

In this chapter we have recorded the significant development from 1920 to 1932 of cooperative credit and insurance organizations. Their progress helped broaden the conception of cooperative enterprise.

Chapter XII

COOPERATIVE DEVELOPMENT IN
RETROSPECT: 1920-1932

In preceding chapters we have examined the political, economic, and social conditions affecting the development of American cooperative enterprise from 1920 to 1932. In this chapter we will consider the impact that these factors had on the character of agricultural cooperation—the cooperative segment, then most highly developed.[1]

The most important change that these environmental factors brought about was the growth in number and power of large-scale cooperatives. Although small cooperatives continued to be important in the local sphere, the emphasis came to be directed toward the organization and management of area-wide organizations. While local cooperatives could perform certain functions well, the need was recognized for services from larger organizations—whether federated or centralized in form. As John D. Black and H. Bruce Price pointed out, there were at least 16 problems that local cooperatives acting alone could not solve satisfactorily: control of quality; standardizing production; adjusting production to consumption; stabilizing production; controlling consumption to fit production; controlling the flow to market; distribution of product; inspection; claims; selling; financing; bargaining and price policy; elimination of competitive wastes; improving business practices; utilization of by-products; and research.[2] The same general forces that were bringing big business organizations into the limelight were also bringing about an enlargement of cooperative organizations and operations.[3]

The need for large-scale cooperative organizations was already accepted by 1920, and the California Fruit Growers' Exchange and other large California cooperatives were showing the way. The process of federation of local creameries to form the state-wide organization that later became the Land O'Lakes Creameries, Inc., was well started, and the grain elevators, livestock shipping associations, and other types of local cooperatives were thinking in terms of central sales agencies. Milk bargaining and marketing associations, coextensive with the market, were also rapidly rising in various parts of the country, as were area-wide purchasing cooperatives.

While federation of local cooperatives was considered by most students of cooperative enterprise as the preferred way to build large-scale cooperatives, there were many who had begun to look with favor on the building of large centralized organizations which would provide whatever local service facilities might be necessary.

Large-Scale Cooperatives to the Fore

It was at this time that Aaron Sapiro brought the philosophy of large-scale commodity marketing to the attention of the farming public. This had a profound effect on the character of cooperative enterprise up to the time of the New Deal. Although promising much more than could be delivered, the commodity marketing movement resulted in the formation of scores of large centralized cooperatives throughout the nation within a period of three years. While many of these failed after a few years of struggle, some learned from experience and survived as effective cooperative enterprises. Looking back on the wave of organizational fervor that led to the formation of the commodity marketing cooperatives for cotton, wheat, tobacco, and other crops, one must give credit to Sapiro for his propaganda *tour de force*. The times were ripe for a cooperative evangelist, and he supplied the spark of leadership, plus the legal guidance, that was necessary to bring these organizations into being, and get them started on their way.

Many farmers felt that big organizations were needed to meet the crisis in farm prices and that such organizations could not be built fast enough by the process of federation. There was logic in Sapiro's assumption that only centralized commodity marketing cooperatives could be formed soon enough to count, and he struck while farmers were so desperate that they were willing to try a new idea. Farmers were constrained to think in terms of big organizations that would undertake things that had seemed impossible, and this gave a natural impulse to the formation of cooperative organizations from the top down. The man needed to galvanize the farmers into action was at hand. Without Sapiro's Messianic leadership it is doubted whether the commodity marketing movement would have got off the ground and emerged as a strong force.

When one considers how much was attempted in such a short time, one must be charitable on the degree of accomplishment. Nothing of this sort had been attempted on such a broad scale before. To make Sapiro's dreams come true it was necessary to build from scratch an entirely new system for marketing the staple agricultural products—with members and officials little experienced or trained for such work. Management had to be provided; accounting systems and records set up; adequate finances secured; sales facilities and contracts arranged; and members kept enthusiastic until demonstrated results could be obtained. It was a Herculean task, and the fact that it succeeded in many instances was a tribute to the great need that the commodity marketing movement endeavored to meet and to the capability and dedication of its leaders.

In the beginning it was naively believed that all that was necessary was to get the bulk of producers of a given commodity to sign up their crops for delivery to the association. Emphasis was placed on the membership campaign, and the problems of operation were left for later attention. As a result, after a period of euphoria, disillusionment rapidly set in. However, in expiation of the promoters, it must be admitted that these organizations could not have obtained their large sign-ups and got started on the basis of measured promises at the same time. The situation required a gamble on the ability of the organizations to meet expectations, once they were set up.[4]

It must be kept in mind that the commodity marketing cooperatives that sprang up under the mesmerizing influence of Sapiro were designed to achieve monopoly control over the supply of a commodity. Robert Montgomery, in describing the beginnings of the Texas Farm Bureau Cotton Association wrote: "Under the spell of the dramatic and ardent Sapiro, many confidently expected the new organization to sweep aside the old order, and to give the embattled farmer power to dominate the market and fix his own prices. That this could be done was rarely questioned." However, when it became evident that this couldn't be done, the commodity marketing cooperatives began to accept more limited objectives. Confronted by practical day-to-day problems, the energies of the organizers had to be devoted to getting the business into operation and then in seeing to it that it survived. In the light of the facts of life much of the automatic philosophy of cooperative commodity marketing had to be jettisoned.[5]

As the impossibility of achieving mastery over the supply became apparent, the cotton and other commodity marketing cooperatives began to stress the importance of business operating efficiency, and the emphasis on market domination was played down. As the control idea lost its strength, it became the practice to use the term "centralized cooperative" or "large-scale marketing cooperative" as being more descriptive than the term "commodity marketing cooperative" for large organizations with individual farmer members. This was especially true after changes were made to liberalize the "iron clad" contracts to give members freedom to withdraw, if not satisfied, and to provide various options in the way their crops were to be pooled and marketed.[6]

It is significant that O. B. Jesness, who was a close observer of the cooperative commodity marketing movement as it developed in Kentucky,[7] ignored the term "cooperative commodity marketing" in his book *Cooperative Marketing of Farm Products*, published in mid-1923, although he described fully the centralized form of large-scale marketing cooperatives. John D. Black and H. Bruce Price gave the term "commodity cooperative marketing" the *coup de grâce* in their influential bulletin, "Cooperative Central Marketing Organization," published in 1924. They said:

> It is the practice to say there are two distinct types of cooperative organizations operating in the central market, namely the "federated" type, and the "commodity" or "centralized" type. The term centralized is the better term for the latter type. The use of the term "commodity" for the centralized type of organization suggests that this is a distinct feature of this type of organization, which is contrary to the facts . . . The sense in which the term "commodity" applies to the centralized type of organization is in the sense of "all of one commodity marketed as a unit" but the term itself does not suggest this meaning and it is not ordinarily so understood.[8]

As we observed in Chapter IV the leaders of the two forms of large-scale cooperative organization closed ranks with the establishment of the American Institute of Cooperation in 1925. By then it was recognized that both the federated and centralized forms of organization had distinctive merits and had much to contribute to cooperative development. Pragmatic results became more important than organizational orthodoxy. It was found that their objectives were more similar than opposite and that, in fact, the competition of the two types of organization imparted vigor and variety to cooperative development.

The Emergence of Membership Relations Work

The importance of working closely with members was recognized by the California Fruit Growers' Exchange as early as 1913 when it set up a field service department to help improve the quality of citrus fruit marketed. However, the concept of membership relations work did not become popular until the early 1920's when such work with members was actively promoted by the cotton, tobacco, and other commodity market-

ing cooperatives. Practically all of them established field service departments in setting up their plans for operation, and the activities of these
departments widened as the importance of working more closely with
members became apparent. At first their main work was to carry on the
campaigns for membership and get marketing contracts signed. After the
organizational work was completed, it was found that there was need for
field men to represent the associations in contacts with members,
especially in obtaining delivery of commodities under the marketing
contracts. It gradually became clear that field service departments could
perform a highly constructive role by building up membership support
through various kinds of service and educational programs.

The Texas Farm Bureau Cotton Association was one of the first of the
marketing cooperatives to recognize the value of broadening the conception of field service work, and its experience influenced the character of
field service work in the other cotton marketing cooperatives. A further
advance in the administration of field service work came with a meeting
of field service directors of 12 state member associations in the American
Cotton Growers' Exchange held in December 1925 when a standard field
service plan was developed for use of all member associations.[9]

As work with members became increasingly important in the large-
scale centralized cooperatives, it became popular to refer to it as
"membership relations work" . . . The term "public relations work" was
already common to describe the work done to gain the good will of the
public, and it seemed logical to use the term membership relations work
for activities designed to strengthen the tie between members and their
cooperative associations.[10] This term caught hold rapidly after it was
used in Kentucky to describe the Community Relations program carried
on by Verna Elsinger for the Burley Tobacco Growers Association.[11]
Impressed by the need for giving this new activity more careful study
Chris L. Christensen, in charge of the Division of Agricultural Cooperation of U.S.D.A., employed J. W. Jones, who had been working with Miss
Elsinger while on the staff of the University of Kentucky, to make an
analysis of the membership relations problems of the tobacco and cotton
cooperatives. His report, *Membership Relations of Cooperative Associations (Cotton and Tobacco)*, published in 1927 as U.S.D.A. Circular 407,
soon gained national recognition for the importance of membership
relations work for all kinds of cooperatives. Jones made clear that a
cooperative organization "must give its members the facts and encourage
sound thinking regarding the underlying principles of cooperation and
marketing . . . This is the real work of the field service department of an
association . . . Like all true educational agencies, field service must seek

to give complete facts and to develop sound principles" (p. 28). The term "membership relations" met a deep need for an expression that would designate the necessity of maintaining close rapport between members and their cooperative associations, and, after the publication of Jones's circular, his conception of membership relations work found a permanent place in American cooperative development.

Probably nothing did more to popularize the importance of membership relations work than the troubles of the big tobacco cooperatives in 1926. As a business operation, the Burley Tobacco Growers Association had been a great success. Just before the organization "folded" it was lauded by Judge Robert W. Bingham as "the outstanding success in the United States among the large scale organizations."[12] It was well organized and well financed, and its general manager, James C. Stone, who later became Chairman of the Federal Farm Board, was nationally respected for his competence. During its four years of existence it had greatly improved the economic condition of all burley growers. Why then did it collapse? The answer, enigmatically, was that its very success brought on its failure. As it improved tobacco prices not only for members but for all growers, more and more members were tempted to sell outside the association so as to get the full price for their crop at the time of delivery. Eventually the loyal members refused to support the "outsiders," and the association was forced to discontinue operations.

Verna Elsinger attributed the association's failure to an overemphasis on "immediate price returns, rather than on the association's greater achievement in the development of a stable and equitable marketing system." Although the Community Relations Department made a valiant attempt to educate members so that they would fully support their organization, this program was never given strong backing by the directors, and some even opposed it. Looking back on this experience, Miss Elsinger said: "Undoubtedly, a thorough plan of membership contact, a large and far-reaching program extending into every corner of the Burley's territory, developing friendly membership relations, membership understanding and responsibility would have gone far toward writing a different final chapter in the history of the Association.[13]

Much the same situation caused the failure of the Tri-State Tobacco Association. During its three years of operation it had remedied many of the defects in its original form of organization and methods of operation, but by late 1925 it suffered from anemia in the form of weak membership support, and a disgruntled group was able to throw it into receivership. Too little effort had been given to the necessity of teaching members that it was their own organization and that they were largely responsible for its success.[14]

Membership relations work was also furthered by the changed attitude toward publicity that came with the "commodity marketing movement." Campaigns for membership could not be carried on without providing farmers with information on the aims, methods, and achievements of the associations, and almost every association of the commodity type soon found it desirable to have its own membership magazine or house organ to maintain the interest of its members. The idea soon spread to associations of the federated type, for they likewise needed to tell their story as a means of maintaining the support of their member associations and related farmers. Through publications of this type many farmers came to have a better understanding of the operation of their cooperatives and of their importance in American agriculture. From the hard knocks of experience, cooperatives came to understand the force of J. W. Jones's succinct statement that "an association must meet its responsibilities both in business administration and membership administration if it is to succeed."

Improvement of Legal Standing

Prior to 1920, the legal position of cooperative associations had been fairly well established by state laws that provided for incorporation of cooperative associations. However, the Clayton Act of 1914 left obscure the question of whether cooperatives formed with capital stock—or even non-stock associations—were subject to prosecution under anti-trust laws. This problem was of great concern to all cooperatives, for it restricted the development of cooperative enterprise. The Capper Volstead Act of 1922 decisively settled this problem by authorizing the formation of cooperative associations "with or without capital stock."

The centralized cooperative associations which employed membership contracts were much concerned as to the enforceability of such contracts. Sapiro recognized this problem and promoted the passage of state laws that would protect the ability of centralized associations to control the deliveries of their members. The model law of this type was the Bingham Cooperative Marketing Act of Kentucky passed in January 1922. The constitutionality of this act was established by the Supreme Court in 1927. In referring to this legislation John Hanna, a respected legal scholar, called Aaron Sapiro "one of the few men of this generation whose individual activities have genuinely altered the world in which he found himself. The statute law of cooperative marketing and the contractual law of the relations of members to cooperative associations are to a great extent the products of his intelligence and enthusiasm."[15]

The legal status of cooperative associations was further strengthened by the Cooperative Marketing Act of 1926 which directed the federal government to encourage such associations through research and service activities. The Agricultural Marketing Act of 1929 carried recognition of cooperative marketing associations further by declaring their formation to be public policy. Moreover, during this period, agricultural cooperatives which complied with certain regulations based essentially on their being organized and operated in accordance with accepted cooperative principles and objectives were granted exemption from federal income taxes.

The significance of legal problems to cooperatives through the period from 1920 to 1932 was evidenced by many articles in law review journals and by various books and bulletins dealing with this subject. Of particular importance was L. S. Hulbert's U.S.D.A. Bulletin 1106, "Legal Phases of Agricultural Cooperation," published in 1923. This bulletin, with subsequent revisions, provided a handbook on legal problems for cooperative managers and for lawyers, legislators, government officials, and others who had occasion to deal with such organizations. It did much to improve legal knowledge about cooperatives. A major contribution to public understanding of the cooperative form of business organization also was made by E. G. Nourse's scholarly book, *The Legal Status of Agricultural Cooperation* (1927). This book examined the legal evolution of the cooperative form of business enterprise in the light of its economic and social objectives. Nourse concluded: "It is well that cooperation, even of the forceful modern pattern, has been accepted as a going institution of present-day business." Another important and useful book in the legal field was John Hanna's *Law of Cooperative Marketing Associations* (1931) which provided information on federal and state statutes and legal decisions. Hanna saw cooperative corporations as a potential asset of great importance in agriculture.

Thus, during the years from 1920 to 1932, the legality of the cooperative form of organization in agriculture was established and further clarified by cooperative literature. After 1932 it could no longer be claimed that there were serious legal impediments to the formation and operation of cooperative associations.

Management Development

In no area was progress greater from 1920 to 1932 than in the improvement of management both in local and large scale cooperatives.

By 1920 it had become evident that cooperative marketing, or cooperative purchasing, was a business undertaking which required management by skilled men—not a political or fraternal matter. The great mortality of cooperatives not well managed had taught farmers that there was a fundamental difference between operating a farm and managing a cooperative business. They had found out that more was needed in a manager than horse trading ability and being a good fellow.

Yet, it was hard for farmers to comprehend that they could not obtain good managers without paying salaries that would attract them. It took time—and many disastrous results—for most farmers to realize that a competent well-paid manager could produce benefits that would be unobtainable from an incompetent manager, even if his services could be obtained at less salary cost. By 1932 this lesson was becoming well learned, and, by then, many cooperative managers were as well paid as managers in comparable business firms. Much of the improvement in management during this period came from the emphasis that was placed on its importance. As knowledge of the qualifications of good managers spread, their employment became the rule rather than the exception.

As cooperative organizations grew in size and complexity, the need for professionally trained managers and for other technical personnel became more evident. One of Sapiro's principal contributions in the early 1920's was his insistence on professional competence in the organizations he promoted. One of the key provisions of his 1920 plan for cotton marketing associations held that: "A cooperative marketing plan must concentrate the marketing and other problems through expert specialists. These experts must be sought wherever they can be found to take charge of statistics, finance, organization, sales, warehousing, transportation, etc. When once the association is organized, it must be conducted from the standpoint of sheer efficiency."[16] As a result of such emphasis, and of the demonstrated value of good management by cooperatives of all types, the quality of management in cooperatives steadily improved.[17]

Most of the early managers had to train themselves on the job, for there were then no management training schools. As cooperatives grew in size, they were able to train understudies for various positions and to build a larger supply of men with managerial experience and capabilities.

It should be observed here that management in a cooperative is comprised of two elements: (1) the board of directors, which is responsible for the general conduct of the business, including the hiring and firing of the chief executive, the general manager; and (2) the general manager who is the executive officer who is charged with the responsibility of conducting the business. It is implicit in the foregoing discussion that there was a great improvement in the operation of boards of directors during this period. Greater care was given by members to the selection of board members who could give guidance and counsel to the general manager in operating the business. By 1932 many cooperatives could boast that their boards of directors were equal in competence to those of any competing business.[18]

Strengthening of Financial Management

The problem of financing cooperatives became more difficult when cooperatives undertook extensive warehousing and processing operations. Under the orderly marketing plans of the commodity marketing cooperatives it was necessary to borrow large amounts to finance the storage and movement of the crop. Fortunately, this problem could be met, at first, largely by loans from the War Finance Corporation and, later, from the Federal Intermediate Credit Banks.

During the early 1920's many cooperatives found it desirable to set up subsidiary corporations to attain various advantages in financing.[19] Such subsidiary corporations, with the common stock held by the cooperative, could draw capital from private investors and operate much more flexibly than the parent association.[20]

Even before 1920, the revolving fund method of financing had demonstrated its value as a means of adjusting the financial burdens of members in accordance with their use of an association. This method of financing was given wide publicity when it was adopted by the Dairymen's League in 1919, and during the 1920's several other cooperatives experimented with the plan and found it workable. This set the stage for widespread acceptance of the plan in the 1930's.[21]

As cooperatives grew in size and scope, financial management became of ever increasing importance, and budgeting came into use as a means of planning and controlling expenditures. By 1932 most large cooperatives were as skilled in financing operations as other large corporate firms.

Better Business Practices

There was a steady improvement in cooperative business procedures from 1920 to 1932. Much progress had been made in accounting and record keeping before 1920, but the standards were still low at that time except for a few large cooperatives. Auditing was usually done by a committee of board members, and external audits by certified accountants were the exception rather than the rule.

The coming of the large-scale commodity marketing cooperatives brought about a rapid change, for their success required a high degree of business efficiency. The complex programs undertaken by these organizations could not be handled without well-designed accounting forms and records. This fact was fully appreciated by the American Cotton Growers' Exchange, which, in 1922, set up a standard system of records and accounts for its member state cotton marketing associations.

As early as 1918, the Farmers' Union of Kansas had established an auditing association to make audits for local cooperatives. Its services gradually expanded, and by 1925 it was making nearly 500 audits for local cooperatives in Kansas and nearby states. The Illinois Agricultural Association set up an auditing service in 1925 to serve Illinois cooperatives that proved immediately popular. At about this time, the Wisconsin Department of Markets also developed an effective auditing service for Wisconsin associations. The importance of auditing was stressed at the *American Institute of Cooperation* meetings in 1925, where George R. Wicker, director of the Department of Cooperative Accounting, Illinois Agricultural Association, gave a talk on "The External Audit as a Guide to Management."[22]

Few cooperatives issued comprehensive annual reports in 1920. Most associations were small and a brief oral report presented at the annual meeting sufficed. It was generally believed then that the less said about business operations the better so that no secrets would be given away to competitors. One of the few cooperatives that held that members should be kept fully informed was the California Fruit Growers' Exchange which had begun issuing printed annual reports as early as 1912. The great expansion of large centralized and federated associations after 1920 did much to spread the idea that full business reports were essential, for, as cooperatives grew in size, it became apparent that members could not be well-informed, loyal members without published information. By 1932 most cooperatives, both large and small, were issuing rather complete annual reports.

During the 1920's cooperatives discovered the importance of issuing informative financial statements. In 1925 A. V. Swarthout of U.S.D.A.'s Division of Agricultural Cooperation said: "An increasing number of cooperatives are coming to appreciate the moral value of issuing complete financial statements." He urged simplification of presentation and avoidance of technical jargon to make them more understandable to members. He also emphasized that well-prepared financial statements would help build public good will in that cooperatives were still on trial and needed to develop the confidence of the public.[23]

Another factor that caused an improvement in accounting and financial reports was the growing relationship of cooperatives with banks, business firms, and government agencies. It was important that cooperatives maintain business record systems and provide information that would be respected in the business as well as the agricultural community. Office management also received more attention as cooperatives became more conscious of its value.

Processing and Manufacturing Beginnings

Few marketing cooperatives in 1920, except cooperative creameries and cheese factories and dried fruit associations in California, were engaged in processing operations. Marketing was largely a matter of assembling farm products for sale and finding a market for them. A few fruit marketing associations were seeking an outlet for cull fruit through canning, and the California Fruit Growers' Exchange was experimenting in by-product manufacturing operations. The cooperative livestock packing plants, organized by unscrupulous promoters, had largely run their course and were now mostly out of business.[24]

A major development in cooperative processing came with the establishment of the Dairymen's League Cooperative Association in 1921 which found it desirable to operate country milk plants. In 1926 there were 175 plants of this type, besides a central plant in New York City. In the beginning the Land O' Lakes Creameries was primarily a sales agency for cooperative creameries, although some of them gradually became engaged in the manufacture of milk powder. Processing operations were most widely developed in California—where the Sun-Maid Raisin Growers operated the largest dried fruit processing plant in the world. The by-product operations of the California Fruit Growers' Exchange also continued to expand in the 1920's. With such important exceptions, the manufacturing operations of marketing cooperatives were of only minor importance during the period under review.

The situation was different in cooperative purchasing. The Fruit Growers Supply Company began its box manufacturing operations as early as 1907.[25] When the GLF was formed in 1920, an avowed purpose was to own a feed plant, and it soon acquired one. After gaining experience with this operation and from a partnership arrangement with a large milling concern, the GLF built its own large feed mill in Buffalo in 1930. In 1925 the Eastern States Farmers' Exchange became convinced that it controlled sufficient volume to undertake feed manufacturing operations, and a large mill was acquired in Buffalo and then operated with great success. The experience of these cooperatives in manufacturing feed soon led them into fertilizer and other manufacturing operations and demonstrated that manufacturing could be effectively carried on by cooperatives. Moreover, the cooperatives handling petroleum products soon became involved in oil compounding.

As late as 1932 it was the "conventional wisdom" among cooperatives that processing and manufacturing of most agricultural products and farm supplies could best be done by large industrial establishments. For example, it was assumed that cooperatives could not compete in meat processing and distribution with the great meat packers. As one student of cooperative enterprise said: "While there are no inherent reasons why American farmers cannot succeed in processing meat, their prospect of success is, to say the least, remote."[26] It was also assumed that cooperative purchasing associations could not undertake a complex manufacturing operation, such as the making of farm machinery which was then under the control of large industrial firms. However, as the cooperatives gained strength and professional competence, their horizons rose and there was less tendency to say that something was impossible.[27]

Research Encourages Progress

Research, as a means of finding ways to improve cooperative organization and operation, was already well established by 1920 through the studies made by G. Harold Powell, B. H. Hibbard, Henry C. Taylor, and others. Such work was intensified as cooperatives grew in importance after 1920. It was given strong encouragement by H. C. Taylor in 1922 who made research on cooperative problems an important activity of the Bureau of Agricultural Economics.

Of particular value were the case studies of the California Fruit Growers' Exchange and the Tri-State Tobacco Association and similar organizations that examined the causes of success or failure of particular cooperatives, and the studies of problems in operation of groups of like cooperatives. The significance of such work was given greater recognition by the Purnell Act of 1925 and by the Cooperative Marketing Act of 1926. The importance of research related to cooperatives was also heavily stressed by many of the participants in the early sessions of the American Institute of Cooperation. For example, the 1926 meetings directed attention to the need for more research conducted by cooperatives themselves.

The necessity of research on cooperative problems was recognized in 1932 when a study of research needs in this field was undertaken by the

Social Science Research Council under the general direction of John D. Black. The results of this study were published under the title *Research in Agricultural Cooperation—Scope and Method*. Some 80 different research projects were outlined under two categories: (1) Cooperation in General, and (2) Cooperation by Forms of Activity. In the first category, projects were grouped under five headings: cooperative structure; cooperative procedure; economic and other social bases of cooperation; legal basis of cooperative organization and procedure; and public relations. In the second category, projects were grouped as follows: cooperative selling; cooperative buying; cooperative production; cooperative credit and insurance; and "in the field of public utilities." This latter group included projects relating to electricity, telephone service, and motor transportation. The broad coverage of projects proposed by this monograph shows how well research had become established by 1932 as a means of strengthening cooperative enterprise.[28]

Although this report highlighted many unsolved questions concerning cooperatives that needed further research analysis, its significance here is that it showed how much worthwhile research work had been performed in this field up to this point. The fact that an entire bulletin was devoted to this subject by a scientific society in 1932 shows the vitality of the interest then current in the cooperative form of organization and in ways in which it might be strengthened.

The Expansion of Cooperative Knowledge

There was a revolutionary increase in cooperative knowledge in the years from 1920 to 1932. At the beginning of this period there were few books providing information on cooperative principles and practices, and none of them were both comprehensive and up-to-date in character. The best book dealing with agricultural cooperation was still that of G. Harold Powell, *Cooperation in Agriculture*, published in 1913. The more recent books, one by Emerson P. Harris, *Cooperation: The Hope of the Consumer* (1918), and the other by Albert Sonichsen, *Consumers' Cooperation* (1919), dealt primarily with urban consumers' cooperation.

The intense interest generated in cooperation, both rural and urban, after 1920 was soon manifested in the publication of a number of useful books as well as in the issuance of various bulletins and articles by government and educational institutions. Among the books published during the decade, the following were most influential:

O. B. Jesness, *Cooperative Marketing of Farm Products* (1923)
Roy F. Bergengren, *Cooperative Banking—A Credit Union Book* (1923)

Peter Warbasse, *Cooperative Democracy* (1923)
Herman Steen, *Cooperative Marketing: The Golden Rule in Agriculture* (1923)
Victor N. Valgren, *Farmers' Mutual Fire Insurance in the United States* (1924)
Elliot Mears and Matthew Tobriner, *Principles and Practices of Cooperative Marketing* (1926)
Edwin G. Nourse, *Legal Status of Agricultural Cooperation* (1927)
Federal Trade Commission, *Report on Cooperative Marketing* (1928)
A. W. McKay and C. H. Lane, *Practical Cooperative Marketing* (1928)
Robert Montgomery, *The Cooperative Pattern in Cotton* (1929)
Newell H. Comish, *Cooperative Marketing of Agricultural Products* (1929)

Some idea of the proliferation of literature concerning cooperatives in the early 1920's is given by Chastina Gardner's bibliography of cooperative literature issued by the U.S.D.A in 1927. This annotated bibliography listed an abundant quantity of books and other source materials, many of which had been recently printed. Miss Gardner also listed nearly 100 cooperative magazines and house organs that were then being published in the United States.[29]

During the 1920's, cooperation was much before the public eye with newspapers, magazines, and farm journals pouring out information on the subject. Cooperative problems and developments were then being discussed in the meetings of the American Farm Economics Association, the National Association of State Marketing Officials, and in other professional organizations. The flow of cooperative literature was increased by the publications of the Cooperative League of the U.S.A., the National Council of Cooperative Marketing Associations, and, after 1925, by the comprehensive annual volumes of the American Institute of Cooperation. In 1927 publication was also begun of *The Cooperative Marketing Journal* which became the mouthpiece of agricultural cooperation after the National Cooperative Council was established in 1929.

The national interest in cooperative business was further encouraged by the passage of the Agricultural Marketing Act of 1929 which made support of cooperative marketing a public policy. From 1929 to 1932, no subject was more widely discussed in agricultural circles than agricultural cooperation.

Only a few land grant colleges provided instruction in agricultural cooperation in 1920, but by the end of the decade the subject was generally included in the curricula of such institutions of this type. Moreover, the subject was then being taught in short courses sponsored by the federal and state agricultural extension services and in high schools by the departments of vocational agricultural education.

Thus, during the period from 1920 to 1932, cooperative enterprise came to be well known and generally well respected by the American people.[30]

Gains in Public Recognition

Great progress was made during the years from 1920 to 1932 in gaining public recognition for the cooperative form of business. This was evidenced by the support given cooperative organizations by Presidents Harding, Coolidge, and Hoover and by many other prominent persons. Cooperatives also enjoyed widespread support from the farm and public press. The self-help principle embodied in cooperatives met with a deep response as long as these organizations applied it in a practical manner. Americans have always respected success, and, as long as cooperatives grew and promised success, they could count on public support.

There was also a great amount of goodwill expressed by business and industrial leaders for the work of cooperatives during this period. The seriousness of the agricultural problem made them sympathetic to the attempts of farmers to meet their own economic problems through joint action. In no like period have cooperatives enjoyed so much general goodwill.

Advertising by cooperatives also improved their public image through associating them with high quality products. The pioneer cooperative trade marks, "Sunkist," "Sun-Maid," and "Diamond," were joined by "Land O' Lakes," "Nulaid," and "Dairy Lea," and many others which brought recognition to the cooperative form of agricultural business.

Statistical Progress of Farmers' Cooperatives—1920-1932

The memberships in some 9,000 cooperative marketing and purchasing associations totaled about 1 million in 1920.[31] These associations, together, did a volume of business of nearly $1 billion. By 1925-1926, the number of memberships had increased to 2.7 million and the number of associations had expanded to nearly 11,000. The volume of business of these cooperatives then amounted to $2.4 billion. In the face of the collapse of the large tobacco cooperatives and other hastily built commodity marketing cooperatives, there was no great increase in volume of business during the next few years. By 1928 the number of cooperatives had increased to nearly 12,000 and the number of memberships to 3 million.[32] With the general decline of agricultural prices during the Great Depression, the volume of business of marketing and purchasing cooperatives in 1932 fell to about $2 billion. This was not a bad record in view of the fact that from 1929 to 1932 farm prices fell more than 50 per cent, while prices of goods and services farmers had to buy declined 32 per cent. The cooperative decline in volume would have been much greater had it not been for the encouragement and financial assistance given cooperatives by the Federal Farm Board. There was no great change in the number of such cooperatives at this time, and the number of memberships continued at about 3 million.[33]

Thus, in general terms, the number of farmer marketing and purchasing cooperatives increased from 9,000 in 1920 to 12,000 in 1932, or by 33 per cent, while the number of memberships increased from 1 to 3 million, or by 200 per cent, and the dollar volume of business rose from $1 billion to $2 billion, or by 100 per cent. Although this showing is impressive, it does not reflect fully the growth in cooperative business volume because of the declining level of prices. Allowing for the greater purchasing power of the dollar in 1932, the actual growth in units of commodities sold or of supplies purchased more than tripled from 1920 to 1932.[34] This is supported by available information on the increases in physical volumes of agricultural products marketed or supplies purchased cooperatively during this period.[35] Under any system of measurement, cooperative marketing and purchasing had gained a substantial place in the agricultural industry by 1932.

Although some of the increase in business volume came from the expansion or enlargement of the local cooperatives, much of it came from the development and rapid expansion of large scale cooperatives. In 1920 only a score or more of the associations could be described as "large scale." By 1932 there were at least 200 of such associations and of these more than one-half were centralized in form. In 1920 large-scale cooperatives did perhaps one-fifth of the total volume of business. By 1932 they represented more than one-third of it.

Chapters X and XI have described how consumer cooperatives, credit unions, and insurance mutuals substantially increased in business significance during this period. However, the real center of cooperative strength in 1932 still remained in agriculture.

Economic Benefits

Although many associations returned savings to members in the form of patronage refunds during the 1920's, no attempt was made to estimate the extent of patronage refund payments before 1936. In that year, 4,000 associations reported total patronage refund payments of $25,380,000. In addition, these associations reported retained savings of $13,306,000, giving a total of reported savings of nearly $40 million. On the basis of records for individual associations for the years from 1920 to 1932, it can be conservatively estimated that savings for these 12 years, either returned to farmers in the form of patronage refunds or in amounts added to farmers' equities in their cooperatives, averaged at least $20 million per year, and thus amounted in the aggregate to well over $200 million.

Moreover, these figures do not reflect the savings in the form of higher prices which members received for their products or lower prices which were paid by members for farm supplies. In addition, it should be observed that many marketing cooperatives which operated on a pooling basis returned to members all proceeds after costs were deducted and did not use the patronage refund method to return savings. Thus savings were reflected in higher prices received for products sold and do not appear in any summary figures of savings effected by means of cooperatives.

Moreover, it should be pointed out that the economic benefits from cooperative operations were not limited to members. By injecting competition into the market, all farmers benefited in higher prices received for farm products and in lower prices paid for farm supplies. While it is not possible here to estimate the amount of this benefit, margins taken on farm products or on supplies sold often fell appreciably after cooperatives began operations in a community.

Growth in Financial Strength

Even though cooperative marketing and purchasing associations had become established by 1920, they then did not represent much financial power except in California. Many of the early cooperatives required little capital for facilities, as grain elevators, creameries, or cheese factories could be erected at nominal cost, and livestock shipping associations could operate with practically no expense for facilities. On the basis of limited information, it is believed that the total assets of the 9,000 associations in 1920 did not exceed $75 million and that the investments of farmers in these associations did not amount to more than $50 million.

With the coming of large-scale cooperatives requiring extensive warehousing, processing, and other facilities, capital costs increased. For example, by 1932 Land O' Lakes Creameries had accumulated total assets of over $5 million, and, of this, net worth or farmers' ownership exceeded $1 million. By 1932 the Dairymen's League Cooperative Association had developed total assets of $17 million for its widespread local and central plant operations, and, of this amount, member equities represented in the form of certificates of equity amounted to $14,500,000. The total assets of the GLF reached $5 million by 1932, and the investment interest of members then amounted to $4 million. In view of such expansions in assets and net worth with the growing intensification of operations, it can be estimated that the total assets of cooperative marketing and purchasing associations rose to $450 million by 1932, while net worth, or ownership equities of farmers reached $250 million.[36]

Summary

Cooperatives grew rapidly from 1920 to 1932 because they performed services needed by farmers at reasonable cost. These organizations injected a new competitive force into the agricultural industry that gave farmers the benefits of grading, standardization, and better sales and purchasing services. By setting up large-scale cooperative organizations and operating them effectively, farmers also brought big business methods into the marketing of farm products and into the purchasing of farm supplies. Like the chain stores that flourished in the same period, marketing and purchasing cooperatives developed rapidly because they were more efficient than the economic system they superseded.

There was a significant improvement in the business performance of cooperatives during these 12 years. Of particular importance was the qualitative strengthening of the membership constituency. Farmers became much better informed on organization, management, and operation of cooperative business enterprises. They came to have a better understanding of what cooperatives could or could not do. They came to realize that they could develop bargaining power both in marketing and purchasing, although experience soon taught them that cooperatives could not achieve dominant monopoly power. One might say that their economic literacy was greatly raised. During this period, farmers lost much of their business inferiority complex, for they came to see that they could operate big as well as little businesses for their own benefit. This gave them trust in their organizations, but it did not weaken their vigilance to ensure that their interests would be respected.

Part Two

THE NEW DEAL IMPETUS:
1933-1940

Improvements in organization structure and operating practices in cooperative enterprises between 1920 and 1932 set the stage for many developments and experiments that were to be unlocked by the New Deal administrations of President Franklin D. Roosevelt. In 1933 cooperatives were already a strong national movement, with widespread support in agriculture and in educational institutions. They were in position and ready to build as opportunities were opened to them.

The New Deal was a response to a crisis, so intense that it called for deep-seated measures and long-applied effort. The concept of cooperation was endemic, for the New Deal represented a national effort to work together for national goals. Government had been used before to achieve economic and social ends but never in so comprehensive a way. This period was marked by experimentation and innovation. There was a willingness to try out new things and new institutions to regain prosperity for the nation.

Government agencies brought forth by the New Deal had a profound effect on cooperative enterprise. The Agricultural Adjustment Administration relieved marketing cooperatives of the major responsibility for production control and reemphasized the importance of marketing efficiency. The Farm Credit Administration broadened and strengthened credit services for agricultural cooperatives and gave encouragement to the use of cooperative business organizations. The Tennessee Valley Authority demonstrated the feasibility of cooperative rural electrification, thus opening the way for a national system of rural electric cooperatives financed through the Rural Electrification Administration. Moreover, the TVA helped build the foundations for the development of regional and national fertilizer cooperatives. Likewise, the Resettlement Administration and its successor agency, the Farm Security Administration, made use of cooperatives for rural rehabilitation and gave stimulation to the cooperative idea.

Altogether the New Deal period was a time of ferment. Many new ideas relating to cooperatives were tried. Some worked, others foundered. The New Deal brought changes also in the nature of American life. Cooperatives, like other business organizations, had to act by new rules, reflecting an increased relationship between government and business. The New Deal also brought the consumer to the forefront, and agencies for the protection of consumers began to arise. It was a time when consumer cooperatives were buoyed up by enthusiasm and great hopes. Cooperation was touted as "the Middle Way," the alternative to Communism or Fascism. Broadly speaking, it was a period of significant advance in the acceptance of the cooperative form of business organization.

In this group of chapters we will examine the progress of cooperatives under New Deal conditions from 1933 through 1940. Separate chapters are devoted to cooperative developments connected with the Agricultural Adjustment Administration, the Farm Credit Administration, the Tennessee Valley Authority, the Rural Electrification Administration, and the Farm Security Administration and its antecedent agencies. After examining the relationship of cooperatives to these governmental programs we will describe and evaluate the progress of important kinds of cooperatives in these years: marketing cooperatives; farm supply purchasing cooperatives; consumer cooperatives; and service-furnishing cooperatives for credit, insurance, health, housing, and other purposes.

Chapter XIII

THE TRIPLE A AND COOPERATIVE MARKETING: 1933-1940

The experience of the Federal Farm Board demonstrated that direct government intervention was needed to control agricultural production so as to raise farm prices. In his 1932 electoral campaign, Franklin D. Roosevelt made it clear that he would support Congressional action to achieve this end. Between his election and inauguration his representatives—Henry Morgenthau, Jr., and Rexford G. Tugwell—held continuing conferences with representatives of the general farm organizations to work out plans for satisfactory farm legislation. It was not possible to develop bills that could be enacted by the lame duck Congress, but many troublesome questions were settled before the new Congress convened on March 5, 1933.[1]

Upon taking office, President Roosevelt set the wheels in motion for a farm bill that would help meet the crisis in agriculture.[2] Following conferences with farm leaders, a bill was hurriedly drafted within the Department of Agriculture, and on March 16 it was sent to Congress with a "very persuasive" letter from the President in which he said:

> Deep study and the joint counsel of many points of view have produced a measure which offers great promise of good results. I tell you frankly that it is a new and untrod path, but I tell you with equal frankness that an unprecedented condition calls for the trial of a new means to rescue agriculture. If a fair administrative trial of it is made and it does not produce the hoped-for results, I shall be the first to acknowledge it and advise you.[3]

While Congress was working on the proposed farm bill, emergency action was required to meet the serious financial distress of farmers. How significant progress toward solving this problem was made through setting up the Farm Credit Administration will be described in the next chapter.

On May 12, after careful consideration and amendment, the Agricultural Adjustment Act of 1933 was passed as Part I of a three-part Agricultural Act which was designed to help bring about national economic recovery. Under it, for the first time, the power of the federal government was called upon to achieve ends that could not be obtained by farmers through their own organizations, even with the financial assistance of the government.

The Agricultural Adjustment Act declared it to be the policy of Congress "to establish and maintain such balance between the production and consumption of agricultural commodities, and such marketing conditions therefor, as will re-establish prices to farmers at a level that will give agricultural commodities a purchasing power with respect to articles that farmers buy, equivalent to the purchasing power of agricultural commodities in the base period" (1909-1914). To achieve this end, the Secretary of Agriculture was empowered: (1) to reduce acreage or production for market, or both, of any "basic" commodity (wheat, corn, cotton, hogs, rice, tobacco, and milk) through voluntary agreements with producers, or by other methods, such as rental or benefit payments; (2) to enter into marketing agreements with processors, associations of producers, and others for the purpose of controlling the prices paid to producers and the margins allowed to handlers and dealers, and (3) to issue licenses permitting processors, associations of processors, and others to engage in the handling of any agricultural product for the purpose of eliminating unfair practices or charges.

As the principal means of financing the rental and benefit payment programs the Secretary was given authority to levy processing taxes on farm products up to the amount of "the difference between the current average farm price for the commodity and the fair exchange value of the commodity."[4]

The Marketing Agreement and Licensing Provisions

Of special interest to cooperatives were the marketing agreement and licensing provisions of the Act. They represented a compromise between those who favored strong production control measures and those who advocated achieving higher farm prices through marketing procedures as called for by the McNary-Haugen plan. Thus, through these provisions, the Agricultural Adjustment Act partially incorporated the McNary-Haugen idea that was largely dormant during the Federal Farm Board period.[5] As Murray Benedict has observed, the marketing agreement and licensing provisions were incorporated "at a relatively late stage in the drafting of the bill'" and "as first proposed the marketing agreement technique was intended as an alternative or possibly a supplement to production control."[6]

It was originally intended that the use of marketing agreements would be limited to the designated basic crops. However, representatives of the California Farm Bureau Federation saw the desirability of getting the benefits of the Act for growers of California specialty crops, and, with the support of the American Farm Bureau Federation, the marketing agreement and licensing provisions were made applicable to all crops.[7]

As pointed out in Chapter VII, producers of California fruit and vegetable specialty crops had long been plagued by the problem of excessive production and uncorrelated marketing. This had caused their representatives to experiment with the formation of cooperative clearing houses which, in turn, had led to a demand for state measures that would help adjust supplies to market requirements. By 1933 it had become clear that governmental power was a requisite for any effective marketing control plan and this had led to the [California] Agricultural Prorate Act passed on June 5, 1933. Thus the California Prorate Act, near passage when the Agricultural Adjustment Act was being drafted, served somewhat as a model for the marketing agreement and licensing provisions of the Agricultural Adjustment Act.[8]

The licensing provisions of the Agricultural Adjustment Act, although not directly a part of the marketing agreement provisions, gave strength to the marketing agreement provisions and "at first officials of the AAA regarded this power as an adjunct to the marketing-agreement power, to be used to compel recalcitrant firms to comply with an agreement that had already been concluded."[9] As will be noted later in this chapter, difficulties in using the licensing power were to lead to the replacement of licenses by Secretary's Orders through amendments of the Act in August 1935.

The AAA Gets Underway

The administration of the AAA was placed in the Department of Agriculture, and Secretary Wallace immediately made it clear that he would assume full responsibility for its execution. He proceeded promptly to reorganize and strengthen the Department to enable it to effectively carry out the provisions of the Act. This was a formidable task, for it called for an "action" program of a new and novel character and for the assembling of men competent to get such a program underway. As Administrator of the new Agency, Wallace appointed George Peek, and as Co-administrator, Charles Brand—both men who had been strong advocates of McNary-Haugen type legislation.

The AAA lost no time in getting started. A program for reduction of cotton production was immediately devised, since this crop was already planted when the Act was passed. If anything was to be done to curtail the current crop, drastic steps were imperative. The cotton plan was designed to persuade farmers to plow up a portion of the acreage planted in cotton in return for benefit payments. The object was to reduce the acreage in cotton so as to bring about a decrease in production of 3 million bales. This plan was announced by Secretary Wallace on June 19, and the sign-up goal was reached on July 19. As the AAA had as yet no field organization, the problem of getting acreage signed up was assigned to the Agricultural Extension Service. Altogether some 22,000 persons— including county agents and other extension personnel—worked together on this campaign.

The cotton plow-up campaign proved that the AAA meant business, and this had a pronounced psychological effect on all farmers. A somewhat similar program for wheat was planned, but, because of the worst drought in living memories that had set in during the spring, it was not necessary to engage in crop destruction. Instead, a plan was announced on June 18 under which farmers would receive payments in 1933, 1934, and 1935 for agreeing to reduce wheat production for 1934 and 1935. The objective was to bring cash to wheat farmers so as to enable them to carry on despite their heavy losses from the drought.

While these production control programs were proceeding, attention was also being centered on using the marketing agreement and licensing provisions of the Act both for basic and non-basic crops. On the day the Act was passed, a proposed milk marketing agreement for the Chicago milk shed was submitted, and, soon afterwards, similar agreements were proposed for fruits, vegetables, and nuts.

The cotton sign-up campaign had just been completed when the American Institute of Cooperation, meeting at Raleigh, North Carolina, July 24-29, focussed attention on the Agricultural Adjustment Administration. This gathering provided a forum for presenting the plans and current programs of the AAA and for voicing the concern of marketing cooperatives on how they would be affected. It should be realized here that while the AAA was becoming established, there was much fear among cooperative marketing leaders that cooperative marketing would be shunted off to a side line and rendered impotent by the new federal program. Would there be a need for strong cooperative marketing enterprises if the Government took over the responsibility for production control, a problem that the cooperatives had been unable to master?[10]

The 1933 Sessions of the American
Institute of Cooperation

The spirit of the A.I.C. meeting was one of hopefulness. Confidence was already developing in the aggressive measures being undertaken by the AAA to control production so as to raise prices, and there was a widespread interest among cooperatives on how they could make use of the marketing agreement provisions of the new act. The address of the new Secretary of Agriculture, Henry A. Wallace, set the stage for the gathering. Speaking on the subject "Cooperation and the Program of the Administration," he said:

> I suppose the topic of most intense interest at this annual meeting is the effect that the Agricultural Adjustment Act may have upon the cooperative movement . . . If your interest lies in the progress of the cooperative ideal, then you have a right to feel tremendously encouraged. As practical men, you are also interested in the new machinery set-up to further that ideal, and you may be wondering whether the new machinery is likely to supplant the old machinery, or supplement it. As a matter of fact, I think the new machinery may do a little of both.[11]

Secretary Wallace, in reviewing the futile efforts of cooperatives to control production, said: "The experiments have been hazardous to the cooperative movement. The centralizing power of the Federal Government, it seems to me, offers a far greater prospect for success."[12] He then said: "The whole program of this Administration and the course of the cooperative movement, are very closely related. There is every reason for the healthiest sort of cooperation between us."[13]

It was in this spirit of tolerance and good will that Dr. Edwin G. Nourse examined "The Cooperative Marketing Movement Under the 'New Deal.' " Nourse said: "The point of view from which I want to approach this thing is: "What new things have been brought into the life of the cooperative movement?" He then pointed out that a new philosophy of government relationship to cooperatives was in the making. He interpreted it as follows:

> Under the Agricultural Marketing Act of 1929, cooperative organization was definitely adopted by the Government as the device through which agricultural rehabilitation was to be effected, and the Government put itself in the role of promoter, guide and banker to cooperatives. The cooperative movement was officially sponsored and to a considerable degree controlled along bureaucratic lines. The present administration seems clearly to have renounced the role of promoter and to have withdrawn quite completely from the role of school-master, both in its instructional and its disciplinary aspects. The attitude in a word seems to be: "We shall be happy to deal with the cooperatives on the same terms as others. Cooperative organization is primarily your concern, not ours. Make your associations as large and as strong as you like under the coop-

erative laws and we shall deal with them as fully and effectively as we can. They are incidental to a larger scheme for enhancing agricultural prices and stabilizing the agricultural industry."

Nourse welcomed this shift in government policy away from paternalism as being more "in conformity with the old doctrine of self-help." He did not think that the cooperatives would necessarily suffer by the government's taking over the responsibility for production adjustment. In fact, he thought it conceivable "that the cooperative movement would be stimulated rather than superseded by the Government's participation in active adjustment efforts." He also thought that "the marketing agreement phase of the AAA's program would give widened opportunities for cooperative marketing associations."[14]

Chester C. Davis, then Director of the Production Division of the AAA, supported the views of Dr. Nourse. He said: "The expanding role which is beginning to unfold for cooperatives in the working out of this new legislation is evidence of their larger potential usefulness to the farmer. As a matter of fact, the Agricultural Adjustment Act will probably do the cooperative movement more good than an act directly fostering cooperative marketing would have done." He also said:

> As newly conceived, the task of the cooperative movement loses nothing in appeal or magnitude. The movement is not cast for a subordinate role in the rehabilitation of agriculture. It is simply cast for a different one than some of us had imagined, a task in which the odds will not be stacked against it by unregulated production. With controlled production, the worst pitfalls will be gone from the path of the cooperative movement. It will not have to think continually about supporting prices in overstocked markets. It will be free to get on with its own proper job.[15]

Several other key officials of the AAA reiterated the views of Wallace and Davis. For example, Clyde L. King, Chief of the AAA's Dairy section, pointed out that organizations of dairymen were essential to the success of the AAA programs, while Jesse Tapp, Chief of AAA's Special Crop section, indicated that the Administration considered it highly desirable to work with cooperatives in the formulation of proposed marketing agreements.

It should be realized that the parts of the Agricultural Marketing Act of 1929 which made cooperative marketing a national policy were not repealed. In fact, the parts of the Agricultural Marketing Act relating to loans to cooperatives were then being placed on a stronger basis through the establishment of the Banks for Cooperatives in the newly formed Farm Credit Administration. The important work of the Banks for Cooperatives in strengthening cooperatives will be discussed in the following chapter.

The Program Expands

During August, while cotton acreage was being plowed up, the wheat reduction campaign was launched, although the sign-up was not completed until later in the fall. The first milk marketing agreement became effective for the Chicago market on August 1, but this program developed slowly because of legal and technical questions and because of disagreements within the AAA's administrative staff on how the marketing agreements program should be developed.[16] The 15 initial marketing agreements, signed by the end of the year, were supplemented by licenses to make them effective for all producers and handlers. The AAA had more initial success with marketing agreements for special crops where farmers were already well organized through cooperative marketing associations. The first agreement of this type (for California cling peaches) was approved on August 17, 1933, and it proved immediately beneficial. Other agreements soon followed for almonds, citrus, and other specialty crops.[17]

The hog reduction campaign. One of the problems that gave the AAA great concern was the anticipated heavy production of pork. Outlook reports in the summer indicated that the large number of swine coming to market would have a serious impact on prices. To meet this problem, a program of slaughtering small pigs and brood sows was devised under which the producers would be paid benefit payments and the meat produced would be distributed for relief needs. This program completed during the fall was bitterly assailed as "inhumane," but from an economic standpoint, it met a difficult emergency situation. In their appraisal of early AAA experience, Nourse, Davis, and Black said of this action:

> Slaughter and plow-ups may be likened to the acts of the forest ranger who builds a "back-fire"; the shipmaster who jettisons valuable cargo when storm threatens to sink his craft, or the fire marshal who dynamites stores and homes to confine a fire within the narrowest possible limits of destruction. Our analysis leads us to the conclusion that at the time at which they were applied and within the limits to which they were held, these measures were constructive in the sense of protecting against worse ills.[18]

The tobacco program. The most successful of the 1933 AAA programs arose from an emergency situation. When the flue-cured tobacco markets in North Carolina opened on August 29 with unreasonably low prices, the Governor of the State—J. C. B. Ehringhaus—declared a marketing holiday and closed the markets until a program could be developed to relieve the situation. The solution to this problem was a marketing agreement entered into between the federal government and the large tobacco companies, under which the latter agreed to pay higher prices for tobacco on the understanding that a production control program would ensure reduced production the following year. This worked extremely well as an emergency measure and set a precedent for similar marketing agreements for burley and other types of tobacco.[19]

The beginnings of the Commodity Credit Corporation. Although not specifically a part of the Agricultural Adjustment Act, government action designed to effectuate the Triple A programs for cotton and corn was to have a profound influence on the AAA's future. To help farmers hold their crops until prices could improve under the cotton and corn reduction programs, the Commodity Credit Corporation was set up by Executive Order (October 17, 1933) as a government financing agency. Under the initial program, provision was made for loans of 10¢ per pound on warehoused cotton of ⅞-inch staple or better. If the borrower did not choose to pay off the loan, the CCC would take the collateral and cancel the loan. Similar "non-recourse" loans were made on corn without risk to the borrower. In effect, the plan established a price floor for the commodity and thus reinstated stabilization activities somewhat similar to those provided by the Federal Farm Board. In general, this program gave satisfaction, for it was begun when farm prices were beginning to move upward; whereas the Farm Board stabilization operations had been undertaken when prices were starting to decline rapidly. As we will see later in this chapter, the CCC became the vehicle for carrying out Secretary Wallace's "ever normal granary" plan which introduced price support as a part of the government's agricultural program.[20]

The Triple A at the End of 1933

Although internal conflict was rife in the AAA until December 15 when Chester H. Davis replaced George Peek as Administrator, much had been accomplished. The wheat, cotton, corn, hogs, tobacco, and rice production control programs were working well, and some progress had been made in using the marketing agreement and licensing feature of the Agricultural Adjustment Act. The spirit of gloom that had pervaded 1932 was at last lifted. Farm income from marketings was up from $4,682 million in 1932 to $5,278 million in 1933, and the latter figure was increased to $5,409 million by government payments of $131 million.[21] Although the increase was not spectacular it gave hope to farmers and more confidence to the business community. It is not surprising that President Roosevelt, Secretary Wallace, and other advocates of the new farm program were in a jubilant mood as the AAA entered 1934 with a new Administrator in charge.[22]

Cooperatives and the Dairy Marketing Problem

No problem gave the AAA more difficulty than the formulation of a satisfactory program for the dairy industry. In December, Clyde L. King, who had favored the use of the existing milk producers cooperatives as the foundation for milk marketing agreements and licenses, became so dissatisfied with the way the program was being hamstrung that he resigned as head of the AAA's Dairy Section. This was part of a larger controversy between those who favored the marketing agreement rather than the production control approach in the effectuation of AAA policies, which led to the resignation of George Peek as Administrator and his replacement by Chester C. Davis, a strong advocate of both production control and cooperative marketing.[23]

In January, the long-pending differences over the dairy policies of the AAA broke out in "verbal hostilities" between the Secretary of Agriculture and the dairy cooperatives. The dispute which grew out of resentment on the part of the dairy cooperatives toward the indecisiveness of the AAA in drawing up and enforcing dairy marketing agreements and licenses was well reported by Robin Hood, Secretary of the National Cooperative Council, in an article entitled: "Has the Milk Plan Turned Sour?" According to Hood:

> The controversy began smouldering last summer, shortly after the AAA established its dairy division. The Government admittedly moved very slowly and indecisively in drawing up dairy marketing agreements and licenses. In December the controversy reached newspaper headline stages when Secretary Wallace termed these instruments futile unless bound up with production curtailment. George Peek, AAA Administrator, as well as Clyde L. King, dairy administrator, and a score of other officials resigned or sought transfers because they believed the Secretary's attitude was preventing expeditious development of sound programs. In a number of public statements, the Secretary charged that producers of dairy products were not receiving adequate benefits because representatives of the dairy industry were "reluctant to face the facts and to consider any effective production control program." Such statements struck fire . . .
> Lack of enforcement of agreements and licenses has been a subject to arouse cooperative criticism and near-vituperation for many months . . . When the Chicago dairymen lost patience and decided to "go it alone" they called for termination of their AAA agreement and license. Wallace accommodated them, and when a wave of dissatisfaction with non-enforcement came from various other agreement areas, the Secretary terminated all milk agreements.[24]

The conflict between the dairymen and the Secretary of Agriculture was not resolved for many months. With the termination of the marketing agreements, licenses were reinstated and in time strengthened, but this did not satisfy the dairy cooperatives. At its annual meeting in Washington D.C., March 21-24, the National Cooperative Milk Producers' Federation demanded use of the old dairy marketing agreements and supporting licenses in markets where desired by a majority of the industry, and passed a resolution which declared:

> We believe that the only permanent and satisfactory solution of the agricultural problems of this country lies in the encouragement and development of the cooperative movement. It has been our experience that the AAA rather than helping our cooperatives is weakening and destroying them by public and private attacks and innuendoes cast upon the integrity of our leaders which is the age-old method used by distributors of farm products to destroy the faith of the farmers in their cooperatives and by a disposition to give more consideration to chiseling non-cooperating minorities than is given to our cooperatives.

The resolution then continued:

> We demand a new deal for our cooperatives under the AAA and the establishment of a policy in the administration designed to strengthen and develop our cooperative associations in accordance with the published statements of President Roosevelt, the declared policy of the Congress of the United States as enunciated in the Capper-Volstead Act, the Cooperative Marketing Act of 1926, the Agricultural Marketing Act, and the Farm Credit Act and in accordance with the declared policy of the several states who have continually provided legislation for the formation, encouragement and development of the cooperative movement.[25]

The meeting also severely criticized the recently proposed dairy production control plan of the AAA and presented instead one which was considered more practical. When the dairy adjustment program of the AAA did not receive the general approval of farmers, it was withdrawn on April 23.

As an outgrowth of the strong position taken by the National Cooperative Milk Producers' Federation, a bill was introduced in Congress which would require that the Secretary respect the desires of local groups in the formulation of federal licenses to cover fluid milk areas. While action on this bill was pending, the AAA continued to issue milk licenses, and violations of the licenses continued to "pour in" from the various markets. In an attempt to work out a settlement that would result in a modification of the AAA's policy along the lines requested by the representatives of the dairy farmers, a number of conferences were held between Congressional leaders and the Administration. The meetings disclosed that the Administration was now willing to compromise on its position. This was the situation when the American Institute of Cooperation met in Madison, Wisconsin, in mid-July of 1934.[26] Before we examine developments at this important gathering, reference should be made to measures that had been enacted to make production control mandatory for cotton and tobacco producers.

The Move Toward Compulsory Cooperation

Although the voluntary production control programs had worked quite well for cotton and tobacco in 1933, there was a widespread demand among participating producers that the program should be made mandatory on those who did not sign the crop control contracts. This demand resulted in the Bankhead Cotton Control Act of April 21, 1934, which provided that the restrictions on cotton production would apply to all cotton producers by imposing heavy taxes on the ginning of cotton and the issuance of tax exemption certificates to cooperating farmers. The intention was to force growers into the volunary contract system. The Kerr-Smith Tobacco Control Act of June 28, 1934, provided a somewhat similar method for controlling tobacco production. The rationale of these acts was that without such restrictive measures the effectiveness of the programs would be impaired and the benefits would go largely to non-participants who were not limited in plantings. In the words of Murray R. Benedict, "The principle involved was similar to the union shop provision in labor contracts. There, every worker must join a union if he wishes to work. Here, every grower had to come into the program if he wished to sell without paying a prohibitive tax."[27] These programs were to be binding for 1934 but they were to be extended to subsequent years only if approved by substantial referendum votes.[28] The Bankhead and Kerr-Smith Acts were significant in that they made participation in the cotton and tobacco programs compulsory. Secretary Wallace justified the measures by calling them instruments for achieving "social discipline," but they aroused much concern among those who feared government domination over the agricultural industry.

The 1934 Sessions of the American
Institute of Cooperation

When the American Institute of Cooperation met at Madison, Wisconsin, in July, the AAA's honeymoon period was over, and cooperative leaders were in a critical mood. The dairy marketing license program was not working well, and the establishment of mandatory production controls for cotton and tobacco under the Bankhead and Kerr-Smith control acts made many fearful that they would usher in widespread regimentation of farmers. The mood of the gathering was caught by Charles W. Holman, Secretary of the American Institute of Cooperation and, also, Secretary of the powerful National Cooperative Milk Producers' Federation. In his opening talk Holman declared that the main problem before the Institute was "What will be the effect upon cooperative institutions of the so-called 'New Deal' type of legislation advanced with 'New Dealer' interpretations?" Holman asked several basic questions worth quoting:

> Will the cooperatives change as to function, as a result of the New Deal?
> Will the future bring about a more complete partnership between government and its people as represented by the cooperative agencies, or will we have a picture of the New America, operated from Washington by long and sinuous lines of social controls, functioning upon the locality under bureaucratic domination?
> Will we have self-help, voluntary cooperation, trudging down the road, stumbling and getting up, and trudging on again, or will we have compulsory cooperation?
> Will we have government operating plants in competition with our cooperatives and private industry, or will we have a continuance of the competitive regime?
> Will we have some of our commodities translated into public utilities?
> Will we have in some instances governmental recognition of the quasi public service character in the cooperatives by the granting to them of monopolies, or will we have governmental recognition in communities of minorities to the extent that such minority agencies would contribute further to chaos and competition if the hand of the government were lifted?[29]

One of the keynote addresses was given by Dr. Glen Frank, President of the University of Wisconsin, who spoke on the subject: "Democracy at the Cross Roads." He declared:

> The farmers of the United States must choose between a sweeping regimentation of agriculture from Washington and a sweeping reorganization of the total agricultural forces of the nation in cooperative units, nationally coordinated that can think with expert leadership, speak with power and act with authority. They cannot have both. The permanent adoption of regimentation means the prompt death of the cooperative movement.[30]

Other speakers reflected a similar concern. Professor B. H. Hibbard, of the University of Wisconsin, saw a drift toward compulsion in the New Deal production control program. Professor O. B. Jesness, of the University of Minnesota, was apprehensive that cooperative marketing was being pushed into the background because of the time and attention that the adjustment plans required. Chris L. Christensen, Dean of the College of Agriculture at the University of Wisconsin, asked this question: "Can the administration put forward and carry out so far-reaching a program as this one without the wholehearted participation of agriculture through its organized cooperatives?"

Speaking on the subject: "The Farmer, the Cooperative and the Government," Dr. Nourse was less critical of the AAA program as it was evolving. He was concerned with the question of what cooperatives could do with the government undertaking to "maintain the farmers in a position of stabilized prosperity." While he agreed that the AAA had to a large extent superseded cooperative effort in the field "of price determining activity," he was not a defeatist on the role that cooperatives could play, especially under the marketing agreement features of the act. While admitting that the present period was a difficult one for cooperatives, he concluded:

> Is the result to be that the farmer will decide that the government is the only agency to which to look for economic salvation, allow his cooperative to fall into decay, and thus cut himself off from the steady, though less spectacular benefits which they are capable of rendering for him? For some years cooperative promoters and officials were prone to promise too much. Now those chickens have come home to roost. The farmer must be re-educated as to the true field of service which cooperative associations are designed to perform and as to how their services are complemented by the functions of government and not superseded.[31]

Nourse made his views doubly clear by saying in the discussion following his talk: "I say that whatever is to be done in raising *basic* prices will have to be done by an agency as powerful as that of government. Cooperatives clearly cannot accomplish that result. But once you get whatever can be accomplished through control of production, if anything can be accomplished, then the cooperatives' distinct task as such remains what it has been."[32]

The program of the AAA was vigorously defended by Administration leaders. H. R. Tolley (Assistant Administrator of the AAA), speaking on "The Place of Cooperatives in the Agricultural Adjustment Program," said:

> The Agricultural Adjustment Administration has been criticized by some cooperative leaders as antagonistic to cooperatives . . . If by "antagonistic" they mean endeavoring to undermine the cooperative movement among farmers or to develop programs which work to the disadvantage of farmers who are members of cooperatives they are dead wrong.

He concluded by saying:

> . . . I wish to make it absolutely clear that the essence of agricultural adjustment is cooperation among farmers in the production and marketing of their products.[33]

Mordecai Ezekiel (Economic Advisor to the Secretary of Agriculture) examined "The Cooperative Approach to Production Control." He declared that "this year's experience with the Bankhead Cotton Act and the Kerr-Smith Tobacco Act will give farmers an excellent opportunity to determine whether they wish to 'regiment' themselves in this way." It was his view that "cooperative adjustment of production, whether it be through entirely voluntary means or whether it involves the choice of measures by the overwhelming majority to insure that a small minority shall go along with them, is merely extending to one more important field of human activity the basic principle of American Democracy."[34]

The sessions of the Institute were helpful in that they showed clearly that the views of the cooperatives could not be ignored in the conduct of the AAA. It was highly significant that Secretary Wallace in his talk appealed to the cooperatives for support by saying: "The farmers of America must, in self-defense, hold on to and improve the machinery provided by the Agricultural Adjustment Act. That line will not hold, however, unless the 12,000 cooperative marketing associations of the United States wish it to. The Adjustment Act is your baby as much as ours. And if there are ways in which our plans can be shaped so as to increase your incentive, we want to know about them."[35]

"Toward a Balanced Abundance"

Other than in dairy marketing the Triple A program went well during 1934. Amendments to the AAA Act widened the definition of basic crops, and drought conditions—even worse than 1933—helped keep agricultural production under control. Farm prices improved and cash income from farm marketings rose to $6,273 million, or almost a billion more than the preceding year. In addition, farmers received $447 million in benefit payments.

In his annual report for 1934—the opening section of which was entitled "Toward a Balanced Abundance"—Secretary Wallace expressed satisfaction with results from the AAA "after two seasons of trial." He saw the end of the period of "emergency adjustments" and "of drastic reductions in the farm output" coming into view, and he looked ahead to "production adjustment" which implied "producing different quantities in the proper amounts and proportions." He welcomed "cooperative action as prescribed in the Agricultural Adjustment Act" as the means for achieving a better balanced abundance for agriculture, and he repelled the term "regimentation" as not applicable to the AAA program. He asserted that this term implied "compulsion from above, whereas the farm adjustments in which we are engaged depend essentially upon the choice of the participating farmers." He then said: "Strictly, the adjustment of farm production under Federal guidance, involves not regimentation but social discipline." Wallace held that "the farm program looks toward an economic democracy thoroughly in harmony with our political democracy," and he saw in the county control associations "effective instruments in economic self-government."[36]

The Dairy Cooperatives Achieve Recognition

The frank give and take discussions at the Madison American Institute of Cooperation meetings did much to clear the air for a more constructive solution of cooperative-AAA relationships, and the National Cooperative Council, which met during the Institute, took advantage of the occasion to negotiate a better understanding between the cooooperatives and the AAA.[37] In the months that followed, it became clear that the government was showing more consideration for the views of the marketing cooperatives in attempting to strengthen its procedures under the licensing provisions of the Agricultural Adjustment Act. Although progress was made, it was apparent by the end of the year that most of the licenses were unenforceable, that amendment of the act was essential, and that little could be accomplished without the full collaboration of the cooperatives concerned.[38]

"In order to clarify the situation once and for all," the National Cooperative Council, at its annual meeting in January 1935, "drew up a detailed statement of its position and of the administrative attitude that it thought was incumbent upon AAA authorities. This memorandum was presented in person to the officials concerned and discussed with great thoroughness and entire good nature. Agreement was reached as to courses of action which would effect equality of treatment in fact as well as in spirit."[39] The Council's statement in the form of a resolution recommended that the Agricultural Adjustment Act be amended by insertion of the following paragraph:

> [The Secretary of Agriculture] in administering this act shall endeavor to effectuate the policy of Congress of encouraging the organization of producers into effective cooperative business associations or organizations under their own control, for greater unity of effort in marketing and to promote the establishment and operation of a farm marketing system of producer-owned and producer-controlled cooperative associations . . .

Another resolution called for the amendment of the AAA Act so as to require the Secretary of Agriculture to recognize the action of a cooperative association of producers as being representative of its membership.[40]

Shortly after this meeting Administrator Davis said in submitting to Congress amendments for the Agricultural Adjustment Act: "The Agricultural Adjustment Administration intends, and believes it to be the intent of Congress, that the functioning of the Act shall, whenever possible, accord recognition and encouragement to producer-owned and producer-controlled cooperative marketing associations." When the amendments were finally approved in August 1935 they provided that the Secretary would "accord such recognition and encouragement to producer-owned and producer-controlled cooperative associations as will be in harmony with the policy toward cooperative associations set forth in existing acts of Congress . . . " The amendments also provided that "the approval or disapproval by any cooperative association of producers" would be considered "the approval or disapproval of the producers who are members of, stockholders in, or under contract with, such cooperative association of producers."[41]

Marketing Agreements Issue Settled

The amendments of August 24, 1935, substituted Secretary's Orders with or without related agreements in place of agreements and licenses.[42] This represented a "distinctive change" in the authority delegated to the AAA by Congress. Under the amendments Congress spelled out the precise powers of market regulation which it intended to delegate to the Secretary of Agriculture and specified that any action taken under these powers should take the form of an official act of the Secretary of Agriculture instead of authorizing local supervisory bodies to promulgate such actions or orders. Both the marketing agreements and orders provided for under the act required approval of the agricultural producers concerned. The change from reliance on licensing to Secretary's Orders was of great administrative importance. Under the licenses there was much legal ambiguity and the only method of enforcement was termination of licenses, while under the Secretary's Orders, the Secretary of Agriculture could impose fines or take other corrective action to regulate marketing conditions. The cooperatives were well pleased with their improved position under the amendments, and, from then on, they did everything they could to make the new system work. Since the Secretary's Orders were not imposed without approval from a substantial majority of producers, they became, in effect, marketing agreements supported by the power of government.[43]

As Francis Wilcox pointed out it was of special significance that the 1935 amendments "gave producers and their cooperative marketing organizations a more definite place in the development and operation of these programs. The law now required the Secretary of Agriculture to determine whether producers favored the issuance of an order, and no order could go into effect unless two-thirds of the producers by number or volume of the commodity produced in the area concerned favored the order.[44]

With recognition gained on the marketing agreements issue, co-operative marketing leaders became less critical of the Agricultural Adjustment Administration, and, from 1935 on, they accepted the AAA programs as one of the facts of life. It had become "the Government program." By this time, with the financial and technical support of the Farm Credit Administration, marketing cooperatives were regaining confidence in their own strength as marketing organizations, and their interest shifted to their own operating problems as cooperative institutions. This new attitude was reflected in the lessened attention given to Triple A programs in the annual sessions of the American Institute of Cooperation after 1935.

From Conservation to Permanent Adjustment

Two major features of the AAA program—the power to levy process-ing taxes and the power to enter into acreage reduction contracts with farmers—were abruptly terminated by the Hoosac Mills Supreme Court decision on January 6, 1936. In view of this decision Congress promptly repealed the Bankhead and Kerr-Smith Crop Control Acts. The New Deal Administration met this staggering blow by developing an alternative way to control crop production under the guise of a soil conservation program, and, on February 29, 1936, the Soil Conservation and Domestic Allotment Act of 1936 was passed by Congress.[45] It did not give the same degree of control as that provided for under the Agricultural Adjustment Act of 1933 but the economic position of farmers had improved, and it was thought that the measure would serve until a stronger act could be passed.[46]   Several factors—recurrence of normal weather, an increase in crop surpluses, and a decline in farm prices—focussed attention in 1937 on the failure of the conservation program to bring about crop reduction as a by-product of better land utilization. This led to the passage in February 1938 of the Agricultural Adjustment Act of 1938. The new Act—hailed by Secretary Wallace as "a new charter of economic freedom for farmers"—attempted to combine in one permanent program the best features of other programs and to insure that they would not be ruled outside the powers of Congress by the Supreme Court. However, the marketing agreement provisions of the Agricultural Adjustment Act of 1933 (which had not been invalidated by the Supreme Court's decision) were not included in the new Act, for they had already been reaffirmed and strengthened in a separate Agricultural Marketing Agreement Act of 1937.[47]

The most important new feature of the Agricultural Adjustment Act of

1938 was provision for marketing quotas with penalties on excess marketing of various crops. Thus marketing control was substituted for direct production control. The new legislation also included Secretary Wallace's "ever-normal granary plan of balanced abundance" by providing for the greater use of the Commodity Credit Corporation in financing surplus products until needed.[48]

Although the Agricultural Adjustment Act marked a new and permanent stage in government intervention in agriculture, it did not become fully operative until the 1939-1940 marketing year, and soon afterwards the war in Europe began to reduce the clamor for production control. By April 1941, farmers were being urged to increase production of certain crops, and, by 1943, the second year after our entry into World War II, marketing quotas became inoperative.

The "Complementary Relationship" of 1939

In addressing the American Institute of Cooperation held at the University of Chicago in August 1939, Secretary Wallace spoke on "The Cooperative Movement and the American Way." He maintained that "year by year cooperative action becomes more necessary to the maintenance of the American way of life." He saw the principles of cooperation working not only in cooperative marketing and purchasing associations but also in the county associations and committees of the Agricultural Adjustment Administration, and in many other programs of the Department of Agriculture. He held that the adjustment and conservation programs had brought to the support of the work of cooperatives handling basic products the power which they had formerly lacked, "the power to bring about some adjustment of the total supply available to the market." "Thus," he said, "the programs under the Agricultural Adjustment Act of 1938 freed the hands of the co-ops dealing in the affected commodities to deal with the problems which they can effectively deal with—those of rendering marketing services at minimum costs." He continued: "In the same way, the marketing agreement and order programs and the surplus removal programs . . . have made it possible for cooperatives to join in effective efforts to regulate the volume of products going to market." Thus Secretary Wallace saw a "complementary relationship between cooperative marketing associations and cooperative governmental programs of adjusting production and regulating the flow of products to market . . . "[49]

These views of Secretary Wallace were well received in 1939 by cooperative marketing leaders, for by then agreement had been reached with the government on many points of friction, and it was apparent that cooperative marketing was not being adversely affected by the operations of the Agricultural Adjustment Administration. In fact, it was generally accepted that the AAA deserved credit for bringing about a substantial degree of agricultural recovery that had given cooperative marketing associations a better opportunity to serve the business needs of farmers.

Experience had also demonstrated that organized producers were the backlog for successful operation of marketing agreements and Secretary's Orders. It had been found that the most successful marketing agreement programs were those operating in industries where strong producer cooperatives had been built. Such programs supplemented the efforts of cooperatives and made cooperation more effective.[50]

Although some regretted that "cooperative marketing" had lost its prominent place in the public's eye to the more dramatic new government program, its economic importance had not declined. In fact, by 1940 cooperative marketing organizations were generally handling larger volumes of commodities and were operating with greater effectiveness and efficiency as marketing institutions than in any prior period. While much of this progress could be attributed to the operations of the AAA and related programs of the Department of Agriculture, which enabled marketing cooperatives to concentrate attention on performing an efficient marketing service, a larger measure of it was due to the assistance rendered cooperatives through the Farm Credit Administration—as will be made clear by the next chapter.

Chapter XIV

BUILDING THE COOPERATIVE
FARM CREDIT SYSTEM: 1933-1940

The antecedents of the Farm Credit Administration go far back in the history of American agriculture. Of particular importance was the creation of the Federal Land Banks in 1916 to meet the long-term mortgage credit needs of farmers.[1] In 1923 the government entered the field of short-term credit with the establishment of the intermediate credit banks, and in 1929 credit was provided for cooperative marketing associations through the Federal Farm Board.[2] Experience during the Great Depression indicated the need for a stronger and better coordinated system of government credit agencies for agriculture, and this led to the creation in 1933 of the Farm Credit Administration to embrace, expand, and improve the programs already in existence.

The catalytic agent that brought about this new development was the near breakdown of agriculture in 1932 and the election of Franklin D. Roosevelt as President. It was apparent that agricultural credit reform was an imperative need, and, by the time of his inauguration on March 4, 1933, plans were made for the consolidation of all federal programs for agricultural credit. Steps were promptly taken to put them into effect. To understand the setting for this situation it is necessary to go back to the closing months of 1932.

Following the election in early November, President-elect Roosevelt put Henry Morgenthau, Jr.,—his agricultural advisor—to work on the job of developing a program to meet the acute financial problems of agriculture, while at the same time work was going forward on a program to raise agricultural prices through production control measures.[3] Morgenthau called on Cornell University for help. Dr. William I. Myers, Professor of Finance and Marketing, was given a leave of absence for three months so that he could devote his full time to the problem. Myers was already well informed on the operations of the Federal Land Banks, the intermediate credit banks, the Federal Farm Board, and the other financial institutions serving agriculture, and he had definite ideas on what might be done.

Following initial conferences with Morgenthau in November, Myers went with Morgenthau to Washington, D.C., on December 3, 1932, to confer with agricultural leaders on the farm programs then being considered. At this meeting Myers outlined the farm credit program on which he had been working. On December 10, Myers and Morgenthau presented this plan to Roosevelt who gave it to reporters as part of the farm program of the new administration. This program provided for three actions: (1) combining all federal farm lending agencies in one organization; (2) refinancing farm mortgages and other debts to meet the acute distress in agriculture; and (3) providing a permanent system of long- and short-term credit for farmers and their cooperatives. [4]

On December 12-14 Morgenthau and Myers met with representatives of the national farm organizations to consider the recommendations of a committee on farm credit set up by these organizations. This committee proposed that the Federal Land Banks would be used to refinance farm mortgages, that the joint stock banks would be liquidated, and that the regional agricultural corporations and the intermediate credit banks be transferred to the Federal Farm Board. The continuation of the Federal Farm Board was not acceptable to Morgenthau, who, representing Roosevelt, made it clear that the Farm Board was too great a political liability to be continued, although its constructive credit function for cooperatives should be retained. [5] Work on the general problem of agricultural relief did not permit a full consideration of the agricultural credit problem at this conference. However, a committee to work on the credit question was appointed, and a program of legislation was to be agreed upon early in 1933. [6]

On December 22, 23, and 24, at a meeting with Congressional agricultural leaders and representatives of the Conference of National Farm Organizations, Myers presented the credit program which had been generally approved by Governor Roosevelt. It was presented in two parts: (1) emergency plans to meet the crisis, and (2) long-time plans to provide a sound credit system for agriculture on a business basis. In effect, Myers provided a working blueprint for the development of the Farm Credit Administration and its policies.

To meet the emergency problem he suggested:

(1) that there should be set up debt conciliation committees in every county;
(2) that the Federal Government establish an emergency loan fund to make

small loans on second mortgages or other security to facilitate settlements with minor creditors of good farmers;

(3) that the federal land banks should pursue an aggressive but sound policy in making new mortgage loans. To enable the federal land banks to make new loans, it was recommended that funds should be provided by the purchase of stock in the land banks by the United States or by the purchase of land bank bonds by the United States Treasury;

(4) that the Federal land banks defer payment by farmers of principal and/or interest where necessary for any period up to four or five years;

(5) that the charters of the joint stock land banks be cancelled and that these banks be taken over by the Federal Farm Loan Board under some arrangement for their liquidation. Myers said: "This is the best way to handle a bad situation at a reasonable cost."

(6) that the safety of land bank bonds be increased by increasing the amount of their capital through the purchase of non-voting stock by the U.S. Government. Myers held that this would bring about a decrease in the rate of interest on land bank bonds.

To provide a sound long-time credit system for agriculture on a business basis, he suggested:

(1) that all federal agencies concerned with agricultural credit be consolidated in one system under a Federal Agricultural Credit Board of about 15 members appointed by the President. This board would determine policies. Responsibility for carrying out the policies of the Board would be placed in the hands of responsible executives.

(2) that the control and operation of all Federal agricultural credit institutions be decentralized on a regional basis so as to give responsibility and authority to regional boards of directors;

(3) that the Intermediate Credit Act be amended so as to make all of the credit facilities of the intermediate credit banks available to all sound cooperative purchasing and marketing cooperatives;

(4) that the federal land banks be allowed to eliminate or increase the maximum margin allowed of one per cent so as to provide for meeting costs of service. Myers also proposed that the subscriptions of the U.S. Treasury to non-voting stock of the federal land banks be increased by two hundred to five hundred million dollars;

(5) that there be established a third division of the agricultural credit system to make long-term loans to sound cooperative marketing and/or purchasing and/or credit associations. Service would be provided through "federal cooperative facilities banks" which would be parallel to the federal land banks and the federal intermediate credit banks. They would be twelve in number with the same offices and territories as the federal land banks. These new institutions would take over the long-term financing of cooperatives recently carried on by the Federal Farm Board. The cooperative facilities banks were to be operated on a cooperative basis with each borrowing association taking stock in the banks to amount of 5% of the loan obtained. The regional boards of directors of these banks should be at least in part elected by their cooperative borrowers. These banks were to be capitalized by using the remainder of the revolving fund of the Federal Farm Board for investment in their capital stock. These banks were to make loans either directly to individual local cooperatives or through regional or national cooperative associations of such locals.[7]

These suggestions, which were to be generally embodied in the set-up of the Farm Credit Administration, were approved in principle by the conference. Myers' suggestions served the following strategically important purposes:

> 1. They directed attention to both emergency and long term problems, insuring that the long-term program would get proper attention.
> 2. They provided a practical way of meeting the emergency problem.
> 3. They emphasized the necessity of consolidating all federal lending services in one agency of Government.
> 4. They helped gain acceptance for the demise of the Federal Farm Board by providing for the continuation of its lending services through special banks to serve cooperative needs on a sound basis.
> 5. They recognized the necessity of broadening provisions for production credit and the reorganization of the intermediate credit program.
> 6. They recognized the importance of making the credit institutions to be set up cooperative in character and of operating them on a decentralized basis.
> 7. They stressed the importance of operating the credit agencies on a sound business basis.

During January and February 1933, Myers worked as the Administration's representative with the committee set up by the general farm organizations and with representatives of Congress on successive revisions of the farm credit plan. Although no alteration was made in its basic objectives, many desirable changes were made in the structure of the contemplated individual credit agencies. For example, in place of the proposed "federal facilities cooperative banks," provision was made for banks for cooperatives that would provide long- and short-term credit for marketing and purchasing cooperatives. Although Myers' plan did not provide for production credit corporations, he was deeply interested in finding a better way of serving the farmer's need for better production credit service. From this interest evolved the development of plans for production credit corporations and local production credit associations.[8] The suggestion of a Federal Farm Credit Board to supervise the completed farm credit system was found impracticable because of the necessity for prompt and effective executive action in the emergency. It is of interest that a board of the type recommended was eventually set up in 1953.[9]

The First Hundred Days

"When President Roosevelt took office on March 5, 1933," Myers has written:

> We were ready for action. Henry Morgenthau was appointed chairman of the Federal Farm Board with the responsibility of carrying out the administra-

tion of the farm credit program and I was given a leave of absence by Cornell to assist in this project. The first step was the issuance by the President of an Executive Order [6084] on March 27 which became legally effective on May 27. This order created the Farm Credit Administration from the basic structure of the Federal Farm Board and transferred to it supervision of all federal agencies concerned with farm credit: the federal land banks, the federal intermediate credit banks, the regional agricultural credit corporations and the emergency crop and seed loans of the United States Department of Agriculture.[10]

In transmitting this Executive Order to Congress the President declared:

> This Executive Order consolidates in one agency—the Farm Credit Administration—the functions of all present Federal organizations which deal primarily with agricultural credit . . . The functions of the Federal Farm Board with regard to further stabilization operations are abolished by the order. A better coordination of the agencies involved in our agricultural credit system will produce a more uniform program for agricultural credits and will result in substantial economies . . .

> Important as are the foregoing, of *greater and controlling importance* is the maintenance of the long standing policy of the Federal Government to *maintain and strengthen a sound and permanent system of cooperative agricultural credit,* subject to Federal supervision and operated on the basis of providing the maximum of security to present and prospective investors in bonds and debentures resting on farm mortgages or other agricultural securities—all for the purpose of meeting the credit needs of agriculture at minimum cost (Emphasis added).

While Morgenthau was largely occupied in getting the new Farm Credit Administration staffed and under way, Myers worked with the lawyers on the task of translating "the specific points [of the program he had been developing with farm organization and cooperative officials and congressional agricultural leaders] into legal language to be included in bills for consideration by Congress, and then in explaining and defending these bills to the committees having jurisdiction in both Senate and House."[11] In the words of Myers:

> The Emergency Farm Mortgage Act was introduced in Congress on April 4 and was signed by the President on May 13. This law enabled the Federal Land Banks to begin the enormous task of refinancing debts of farmers threatened with foreclosure. As soon as this bill was passed, I began work with the lawyers on the third major point of the credit program, the completion of a permanent system of long and short term credit for farmers and cooperatives . . . To accomplish this objective we prepared the Farm Credit Act of 1933 which was passed by Congress on June 16, 1933.

Myers has summed up this accomplishment by saying: "Within 100 days of March 4, the Farm Credit Administration was created, it obtained essential legislation and was ready to operate . . . These new programs were begun at the bottom of the greatest depression in our history and there was no way to go but up."[12]

Meeting the emergency credit problem. Before attention could be given to the development of plans for the Farm Credit Administration, Congress had to act on the demoralized farm mortgage situation to avoid the bankruptcy of much of American agriculture. To meet this problem, the Emergency Farm Mortgage Act of 1933 was enacted on May 12, 1933. This act authorized the Federal Land Banks to issue $2 billion in farm loan bonds on which only the interest was to be guaranteed by the federal government "for the purpose of making new loans, or for purchasing mortgages or exchanging bonds for mortgages."[13] Provision was made for the purchase, reduction, and refinancing of farm mortgages; extension of Land Bank loans; reduction of interest on Land Bank loans, both old and new, to 4½ per cent; and the deferment of principal on these loans for a period of five years. The Act also introduced a new device to meet the acute problem caused by statutory limitation of Land Bank loans to 50 per cent of value and to first mortgages by authorizing Land Bank Commissioner loans, which could be made by the Land Bank Commissioner or his representatives. These so-called "rescue" loans to the amount of $200 million were to be used for the purpose of making loans on the security of first or second mortgages up to 75 per cent of the "normal value" of the farm property involved, or 25 per cent above the loan limitation of the Land Banks. The concept of "normal value" first used in this act permitted the Federal Land Bank Commissioner to appraise land in terms of its expected value when times were not abnormal, and thus enabled such loans to be made at higher amounts than at the depressed values that then prevailed. These and other provisions of the Act gave the Federal Land Banks a new lease on life.[14]

The significance of this Act soon became evident. As Benedict has said:

> As a means of meeting the most pressing agricultural emergency of the time, this was one of the most practical and important steps that could be taken. It contemplated refinancing, through land bank loans, thousands of farm mortgages that were being called by private lenders. The amount of private credit available to agriculture was being contracted at an unprecedented rate. Hence, the injection of government-sponsored credit was the only practical way to ease the situation, and save to their owners such farms as could qualify for loans from the land banks.[15]

To administer this important program, Albert S. Goss was named Land Bank Commissioner on July 1, 1933. Goss was highly respected in agricultural and cooperative circles, and he was experienced in the problems of Land Bank operation through his active participation in the work of a national farm loan association and membership on the Land Bank Board of Spokane. As a representative of the National Grange he had worked closely with Myers in developing the Emergency Farm Mortgage Act, and he had been a champion of the "normal value" concept for land appraisals included in the Act. He believed in cooperatives of all kinds and with quiet determination had a great drive to achieve results.

While the Emergency Farm Mortgage Act was being enacted, the Farm Credit Administration under Governor Morgenthau continued programs already in effect. With the passage of the Act it was soon possible to begin the refinancing of farm mortgages by a tremendous expansion of appraisers and employees of the Land Banks to handle the deluge of applications that followed.

The Farm Credit Administration takes form. With the enactment of the Emergency Farm Mortgage Act, Congress could turn to the completion of plans for the Farm Credit Administration. With the full support of organized agriculture, Congress passed the Farm Credit Act of 1933 which was approved by President Roosevelt on June 16, 1933. This Act gave the Farm Credit Administration a permanent legal structure. It "cleared away some obsolete and unworkable phases of earlier credit legislation, and, for the first time, provided a balanced, practical, and comprehensive system of federally sponsored agricultural credit agencies."[16]

Under the Act the Farm Credit Administration would have four principal divisions; 12 Federal Land Banks under a Land Bank Commissioner (instead of under the Federal Farm Loan Board which was abolished); 12 intermediate credit banks, under an Intermediate Credit Commissioner; 12 production credit corporations, under a Production Credit Commissioner; and 12 district banks for cooperatives, plus 1 central bank for cooperatives, under a Cooperative Bank Commissioner. The Governor of the Farm Credit Administration appointed by the President was to be in charge of the whole system.

The Federal Land Banks were already in operation with small but experienced staffs which could be expanded when the Farm Credit Act was passed. So were the intermediate credit banks, but they were administered by the Federal Land Banks, so had few separate officers. The banks for cooperatives and the production credit corporations were entirely new agencies which had to be organized and staffed before they could begin operations. All of these banks were to operate in the same cities and for the same territories under common boards of directors.

Little change was necessary in the procedures of the Federal Land

Banks except that from now on they would operate under Federal Land Bank presidents responsible to the Governor of the Farm Credit Administration rather than under the Federal Farm Loan Board which was abolished by the Act. The intermediate credit banks would operate under presidents whereas formerly they had operated as subsidiaries of the Land Banks. From now on the intermediate credit banks were to function largely as banks of rediscount for the production credit associations to be set up and supervised by the production credit corporations as provided for under the Act.

Of special interest from a cooperative standpoint were the plans made for the new credit institutions which were designed to serve cooperative associations—the 12 district banks for cooperatives and the Central Bank for Cooperatives. By setting up separate banks for cooperatives, the concern of cooperative leaders that cooperatives not be given a back seat was recognized. The decentralization of the district banks overcame one of the major weaknesses of the Federal Farm Board which had centralized operations in Washington and primarily served large regional and national cooperatives.

The 12 district banks for cooperatives and the Central Bank were to continue the loan services to cooperative marketing associations which had formerly been provided by the Federal Farm Board. They were also empowered to make business operating loans to cooperative purchasing associations—a new development that recognized the growing importance of cooperative purchasing operations. Borrowers from these banks were required to buy voting stock in them equal to 5 per cent of their borrowings. The object was to eventually retire the government stock and make the banks for cooperatives cooperatively owned and controlled institutions. The Central Bank for Cooperatives was designed to be a central bank for the district banks for cooperatives and perform other functions. The activities of the Central Bank would supplement rather than duplicate the services of the district banks and give flexibility to their operations. The Central Bank would make loans directly to the large regional and national cooperatives, by participating with the district banks in such loans, and by making loans direct to the district banks. Thus, the Central or thirteenth Bank was designed to give the system the means of financing large cooperatives whose credit requirements were too great to be handled with the financial resources available to any of the individual banks. The Central Bank also provided a mechanism for servicing loans formerly made by the Federal Farm Board until the district banks were in position to undertake at least part of this service.[17] To finance the banks for cooperatives, the Governor of the Farm Credit

Administration was empowered to purchase Class B stock on behalf of the government with funds that had been made available from the Revolving Fund of the Federal Farm Board.

The 12 production credit corporations were designed to organize, finance, and supervise the local production credit associations which were to make production credit loans to farmers.. These associations, modelled on the national farm loans associations, were to be cooperative in form of organization and to be controlled by their own boards of directors. Borrowers were to buy common stock in them to the extent of 5 per cent of their borrowings which could be deducted from the face of the loans. To provide initial capital for their organization, the Governor of the Farm Credit Administration was authorized to invest in each of the production credit corporations from funds made available by the Reconstruction Finance Corporation. The production credit corporations, in turn, were to provide capital for the individual production credit associations in return for a stockholding interest.

The four regional units to operate in each Federal Land Bank district were to be under the control of the Land Bank Board for the district but this board was to be revamped by the election of one director to represent borrowers from the district banks for cooperatives, one to represent the borrowers from the production credit associations, and one to represent the borrowers from the Federal Land Banks. There were to be four other directors appointed by the Governor of the Farm Credit Administration. While the major control was vested in the Governor, the importance of each of the separate units directly serving farmers or their associations was recognized. Moreover, the Farm Credit Act of 1933 provided that there was to be only one board of directors for each district to serve as the board for each of the separate banking units.

The Farm Credit Administration Gets Under Way

The Farm Credit Administration was in the early stage of organization when the American Institute of Cooperation met at North Carolina State College in Raleigh, North Carolina, during the week of July 24-29, 1933. Three of the four commissioners who were to be in charge of its four banking divisions had been appointed, but the Central Bank for Cooperatives, the 12 regional banks for cooperatives, and the 12 production credit corporations were not yet organized. Although the Land Bank system was already functioning, its operations were to be greatly expanded by the heavy pressures for land mortgage relief. Likewise, the intermediate credit banks were to undergo significant changes in operation under the Farm Credit Act of 1933.

Thus, the Farm Credit system was only in skeleton form when the American Institute of Cooperation convened its meeting, although the legislation providing for its organization and operation was in effect. Great interest was shown in how the new system would work and in how it would serve the needs of farmers and their cooperatives.

There was no equivocation in the views presented to this meeting by Henry Morgenthau, Jr., Governor of the Farm Credit Administration. He said: "We intend to assist cooperative enterprise and to promote cooperation." He pointed out that each of the four divisions of the Farm Credit Administration was designed to encourage the cooperative principle in its relations with farmers. He declared:

> The Cooperative Bank Division will carry on the function of assistance to cooperative marketing organizations conferred on the Federal Farm Board by the Agricultural Marketing Act, but in a way which we believe will be found more business-like and more likely in the end to promote the sound growth of the cooperative movement . . . The new laws were not written by foes of the cooperative movement but by its friends, and I can assure you that during this administration they will be administered by its friends.

Morgenthau saw the Farm Credit Act resulting in "another great step forward for the cooperative movement . . . We have taken it off a centralized and temporary basis and foreseen permanency for it." He concluded by saying: "I believe in cooperation, both as a way of advancement and as a necessity for the American farmer."[18]

Of particular interest to the cooperative leaders at this gathering was an address by Frank W. Peck, the newly appointed Cooperative Bank Commissioner, since the loan services previously provided by the Federal Farm Board were now under his supervision. Peck made it clear that the Farm Credit Administration, in all of its relations with cooperatives, would be sympathetic, fair, and helpful, but that it intended to be firm and insistent upon sound business financing in the belief that it could best serve the permanent development of agriculture with this point of view. He allayed the fear of many that the new administration might scrap the functions of the old Division of Cooperative Marketing, but he was not then in position to indicate how the work provided for under the Cooperative Marketing Act of 1926 might be continued. The discussion following Mr. Peck's talk made it obvious that this matter was of great concern to cooperatives, and this expressed interest was helpful to the preservation of this activity while the program of the banks for cooperatives was taking form.[19]

Clearing the Deck for Activity

Although the Farm Credit Act of 1933 had set forth the general plans for the Farm Credit Administration, there were many problems left for the determination of the Governor and his staff that had to be decided by administrative rulings. Of particular importance was the question of how the regional units were to be organized. The temper of the times called for immediate action, and this favored the centering of authority in each district in one man. In the words of C. R. Arnold, who was deeply interested in this problem at the time as a key official in the production credit program, "It would have been possible to have had one man as president of all 4 district units and this man as general agent reporting to the Governor in Washington, with just necessary routine clearance through the district boards of directors. With 4 directors to be appointed by the Governor, this could have definitely centralized controls over all activities and personnel. On the other hand, under the law, it would have been possible to set up 4 distinct and separate corporations or banks with practically no coordination among them."[20]

Although Governor Morgenthau at first favored the centralized approach, the men who were directly responsible for getting the banks organized and established—Myers, Goss, and Peck—realized that it would be unfortunate if too much power were centralized in Washington, and they advocated that separate officers should be in charge of each of the four banking programs to be set up so as to give them a considerable degree of independence. A compromise was reached resulting in four separate and distinct district organizations, each with its own officers and employees, with a general agent serving as coordinator and performing prescribed duties for the Governor. Common services such as legal, personnel, and information were to be administered through the general agent's office.

In each Farm Credit district there was to be a single board of directors for the four banking institutions, known as "the Council of the FCA for the District," and an advisory committee composed of the presidents of the four lending institutions. The work in each district was to be coordinated through a general agent, nominated by the Governor of the FCA and appointed by the District Council. According to the first Annual Report of the Farm Credit Administration, the form of organization was "designed to provide a coordinated cooperative system to meet the entire range of credit needs for agriculture on a permanent basis."

This compromise between extreme centralization and extreme decentralization put each unit on its own feet and helped it develop strength. It promoted administrative efficiency while it gave status to the new credit agencies being organized. Many years later F. F. Hill, a later Governor of the Farm Credit Administration, maintained that in the hectic period of 1933 when the "overriding" emergency problem of the FCA was to refinance mortgage indebtedness, proper attention would not have been given to the development of the production credit corporations and banks for cooperatives if they had not been independently organized and staffed.[21]

To meet the many problems of organization and administration of the new agency, the headquarters staff under the direction of the Governor was steadily expanded. It soon included not only the Commissioners of the four banking institutions and their assistants but also personal assistants to the Governor with assigned responsibilities and a number of special staffs to deal with general services needed by all parts of the Farm Credit Administration. By the end of 1933 the Farm Credit Administration headquarters staff numbered several hundred, including economists, farm management specialists, statisticians, accountants, appraisers, examiners, lawyers, and specialists in personnel, information, and in cooperative organization and operation. It was well equipped to coordinate the operations of the district offices and to provide services needed for the system as a whole. The total number of persons employed in the whole farm credit system then exceeded 10,000.

Governor Morgenthau from the very beginning had emphasized the importance of staffing the Farm Credit Administration and its district agencies with the best qualified persons available, regardless of political considerations, and of paying them well. As his biographer has written: "The task of the Farm Credit Administration was so complex, the sums of money it handled so large, that Morgenthau needed an honest, efficient and resourceful staff. To obtain one, he had to battle for generous salaries and for freedom from political interference in making his selections . . . He refused to pay what he called 'cut rate' salaries and won his point."[22]

Governor Morgenthau resigned in November 1933 when he became Under Secretary and then Secretary of the Treasury. W. I. Myers, who had served as his deputy, was then appointed as Governor. This made possible a continuity of program, for Myers had worked closely with Morgenthau during the formative period of the Farm Credit Administration and was well informed on all of its problems. In fact, even before he became Governor, he was actively in charge, for Morgenthau was required to devote much of his time to helping the President on monetary and other problems.

Revamping the Land Bank system. The Land Banks were already going concerns when the Farm Credit Administration was established. Their methods were generally established and their small staffs were experienced in making farm loans although they were generally in a weak financial condition because of high delinquency of borrowers. They needed an infusion of capital funds for loans and an increased sense of mission, and these were imparted to them by Albert Goss, backed up by Governor Morgenthau and President Roosevelt. Armed with the powers given by the Emergency Farm Mortgage Act and the Farm Credit Act of 1933, Goss proceeded to revitalize the Federal Land Bank system. With abundant capital made possible by the Emergency Farm Mortgage Act, the Land Banks were in position to rapidly expand their operations. However, they required enlarged staffs and improved organizational efficiency to meet the enormous load of new business.[23]

One of the most pressing problems was the need to improve the operations of the national farm loan associations through which Land Bank loans were made to farmers. Most of the associations were then moribund—severely weakened financially by the Great Depression—and few were in a healthy condition. Little attention could be immediately given to this problem, for the urgent need was to provide service. The system had to be utilized regardless of its weaknesses. However, with greatly expanded loan operations, their operating revenues could be rapidly expanded, thus enabling them to gradually improve management and services.

Goss lost no time in getting the Land Bank emergency program into action, and with an infusion of capital the Land Banks soon began to expand their lendings. "By heroic efforts the total of mortgage loans increased from month to month to over $98 million in December."[24]

One of the major problems during this emergency period was to replace existing indebtedness of farmers with lower interest bearing obligations made possible by the Land Bank Commissioner loans. In many cases this involved a scaling down of indebtedness to an amount that could be repaid under normal conditions. In this, Goss invited the support of state governors and in many cases voluntary debt adjustment committees were formed. Governor Morgenthau and President Roosevelt also issued statements calling for such voluntary support.

During this period the staffs of the Land Banks had to be greatly increased to expedite the handling of this rapidly expanded volume of applications. A large amount of training work was necessary, especially for newly appointed land bank employees and secretary-treasurers of the national farm loan associations. In order to handle the enormous increase in loan applications, a large staff of appraisers was required, and before they could be of use they had to be given a minimum amount of training. When the Emergency Farm Mortgage Act was passed, the number of appraisers had dwindled to about 200. By the end of 1933, seven months later, the number had grown to 5,000.

By the end of December, the Land Bank system had gotten well organized for action, and with an infusion of more government capital it was in position to greatly expand its operations in 1934. How this was done will be told later in this chapter.

Organizing the production credit system. The problem of organizing the production credit system for action in time for financing the 1934 spring crop appeared to be an almost insurmountable job. Production credit corporations had to be organized and staffed for each of the Land Bank districts, and, in addition, production credit associations to serve farmers directly had to be set up and made ready for business operations. To head up this program, Sterling M. Garwood was appointed Production Credit Commissioner on September 19, 1933. Garwood had done an outstanding job in organizing local production credit associations in Arkansas during 1932, and he was recognized as the ideal person for this position.[25]

First, attention had to be given to the creation of the production credit corporations which were, in turn, designed to organize, finance, and supervise the local production credit associations. The first production credit corporation was organized at St. Louis on August 9, 1933, and the twelfth on December 19, 1933, at Louisville.

There were many questions to be settled before the local production credit associations could be formed. How large a territory should they serve? Should they be organized to serve single groups of farmers—such as fruit growers, or cotton producers, etc.? Should separate associations be set up for Negro farmers? How should secretary-treasurers be selected?

Some of these problems were not fully answered when the first production credit association was formed at Champaign, Illinois, on September 12, 1933, and a number of the early associations had to be re-formed. However, gradually certain principles were established: that production credit associations would serve all farmers for the areas where they were formed; that they would cover areas large enough to support an effective service rather than be formed like the Land Bank associations for relatively small areas; and that they would have a considerable amount of autonomy in selecting secretary-treasurers who would carry on their business operations. Eventually, with the formation of an association at Rifle, Colorado, on March 20, 1934, the job was completed, and farmers in all agricultural counties of the United States and Puerto Rico were included in the territory of some 600 production credit corporations.[26]

Starting the banks for cooperatives. Like the production credit corporations, the banks for cooperatives had to be built from scratch. Each bank had to have a president and other qualified officers. Teams of workers under the direction of Frank Peck, Cooperative Bank Commissioner, completed this task in December 1933 with the organization of the St. Louis Bank for Cooperatives. This work was carried on so that the production credit corporations and banks for cooperatives were established in each district at the same time. Thus, when the production credit corporation and the bank for cooperatives were set up to serve a Federal Land Bank District, organization of all four banking services was completed for the district since the Land Bank and intermediate banks were already in existence. In each case a district-wide meeting was held to inform farmers and farm leaders of the credit services that were available in the new organization.[27]

The Central Bank for Cooperatives—designed to supplement the services of the district bank for cooperatives—was organized in Washington, D.C., on September 12, 1933. Provision was made for a board of seven directors, appointed by the Governor of the Farm Credit Administration, with the Cooperative Bank Commissioner as Chairman and executive officer, under a plan which would later give borrowing cooperatives a voice in selecting directors. It was necessary to get this bank into operation immediately after organization in order to handle outstanding loans made through the Federal Farm Board.[28]

To finance the system, the Farm Credit Administration, on behalf of the government, initially invested $50 million in the capital stock of the Central Bank for Cooperatives and $5 million for capital stock in each district bank.

The FCA at the end of 1933. By the end of 1933, the Farm Credit Administration had made a good start. It was beginning to bring relief in the mortgage credit field, and the production credit corporations and banks for cooperatives were open for business. The first annual report issued in early January 1934 modestly said: "The organization of the Farm Credit Administration and the volume of business handled by it during the first 7 months of its existence represent considerable achievements in view of the difficult agricultural situation in which the new institution commenced to function."

Governor Myers could look back with considerable satisfaction on the progress made by the FCA when he addressed the annual meeting of the

American Farm Economic Association in late December 1933. He likened his situation to that of a coach with a new system of plays, with a team made up mostly of sophomores. He emphasized the point that the Farm Credit Administration was "not, generally speaking, lending government money," in that its funds were obtained largely from private investors. He also called attention to the fact that part of the work of the Farm Credit Administration was temporary—the emergency farm mortgage refinancing —while the other part represented "an endeavor to develop a permanent workable credit system for agriculture—a cooperative system based on business like methods."[29]

Developments During 1934

With emergency financing problems holding the spotlight, 1933 had been a year of creation for the Farm Credit Administration. The year in which emphasis could be placed on the development of a complete unified system of permanent credit institutions to serve farmers and their cooperatives was to be 1934.

The Federal Farm Mortgage Corporation Act of 1934. Although the Federal Land Banks had done a Herculean job in 1933 in helping many hard-pressed farmers survive the depression, the problem was so enormous that something more was needed to enable the banks to cope with the heavy demands made upon them. The Federal Farm Mortgage Corporation Act of January 31, 1934, was passed to relieve this serious situation. It created a Federal Farm Mortgage Corporation with the Governor of the Farm Credit Administration as Chairman of its Board of Directors.[30] This Corporation was provided with a capital of $200 million, and it was empowered to issue up to $2 billion in bonds fully guaranteed as to principal and interest by the federal government. The Federal Farm Mortgage Corporation was authorized (1) to make loan funds available to Federal Land Banks by purchasing their bonds and (2) to make loans to farmers on second mortgage security and, in certain cases, on first mortgages. It thus made a market for Federal Land Bank bonds which enabled the Federal Land Banks to increase their loans on first mortgages. It also permitted the Land Bank Commissioner to substantially increase Commissioner loans on second mortgages. The Federal Farm Mortgage Corporation fully met expectations.[31] In summing up its experience, Murray Benedict said:

> The Federal Farm Mortgage Corporation was one of the most appropriate and effective emergency measures of the farm program of the 1930's. Earlier action of similar character would have saved many farms and avoided much

hardship. When the Corporation was set up, it brought quick and vital financial relief to many thousands of farmers, and to their creditors as well. It was so designed as to supplement and strengthen the established long-term farm credit agencies rather than to replace them, compete with them or continue in operation after the emergency was over.[32]

Inauguration of production credit service. In 1934 the production credit associations got off to a good start in view of the fact that they had little experience to build on.[33] They found a heavy demand for their services as soon as their doors opened, for often "there was no other place to go" for production credit, since previously existing sources of agricultural credit had dried up because of the depression. By the close of the year, 288,000 applications for loans had been received and nearly 93,000 loans had been closed. Moreover, 5,029 loans had been taken over from regional agricultural credit corporations which were liquidated as soon as the production credit associations were in position to handle this business.

Many lessons were learned during 1934, particularly the things that farmers desired in the way of production credit service. One of the main problems was to reduce "red tape" so as to make funds available without delay, and training schools were conducted for officers of production credit associations to help them meet technical problems. It was necessary to find out how farmers could best be served so they could get funds for crop production purposes as and when they were needed. Standards had to be set up so that borrowed funds would be used productively and repaid. It was found that much would need to be done to improve methods and operations but much progress was made in finding out how this could be done.[34]

It is of particular interest that during this year the production credit system "was embarking on the wide use of a generally new concept of lending related directly to a farmer's cash flow. Heretofore in large measure production loans to farmers were made based on a percentage —and often a low percentage—of the value of chattels or other property on a 90-day or 6-month basis with the property often taken if the loan was not repaid at maturity." Under the cash flow concept the production credit associations were given the job of determining "how much money a farmer would need, and when, and the times at which he would have cash returns from sale of crops and livestock to repay the loans."[35] The budget loan plan developed in 1935 grew naturally from the cash flow concept. Under the budget loan plan funds were provided the farmer as needed, thus assuring him of adequate credit to complete his production operations. It also reduced his interest cost to the minimum because interest was charged only for the time the money was actually in use. This method of lending was popularized in the system as "the Farm Management Approach."[36]

Getting the district banks for cooperatives underway. There were many problems to be solved in getting the new district banks for cooperatives into operation, for their methods represented a significant change from the procedures followed by the Federal Farm Board. The requirement that each cooperative buy stock in proportion to its borrowings seemed unnecessary to many cooperatives who were more concerned with obtaining credit at low cost than in sharing in the ownership of the banks. However, with gifted leadership from Governor Myers, Commissioner Peck, and the presidents of the district banks for cooperatives, initial problems were overcome and the banks began to provide service on a financially sound basis to an increasing number of cooperatives.[37]

In the beginning the staffs of the district banks had to learn on the job as there were few precedents to follow.[38] However, as experience was gained by one bank it was shared with the others, so that by the end of 1934 all were operating with a fair degree of efficiency. From the start the officials of the district banks looked upon the banks as more than lending institutions. They realized that the success of the banks depended upon a clientele of efficiently organized and operated cooperatives, and they endeavored to do everything possible to strengthen the cooperatives served.[39]

During 1933, loans of the newly formed district banks had totalled less than $1 million. By the end of 1934, their total advances to cooperatives from time of organization amounted to nearly $20 million, while the advances of the Central Bank for Cooperatives for the same period reached nearly $48 million. It was becoming apparent by the end of 1934 that the loan volume of the district banks would soon exceed that of the Central Bank.

Reestablishment of the cooperative research and service program. Of great interest to farmer cooperatives was restoration of the research, service, and educational assistance for cooperatives which was provided for under the Cooperative Marketing Act of 1926. This program had been submerged under the Federal Farm Board, and the cooperatives feared that it would be subordinated in the operations of the new Farm Credit Administration. There was reason for this concern. In the hectic period of 1933, the provision of emergency credit services held the spotlight, while research and advisory services for cooperatives were relegated to a minor role. When the Farm Credit Administration was created as an independent agency, the Division of Cooperative Marketing disappeared as a separate entity, and its staff was attached to the newly organized Cooperative Division as the Cooperative Bank Service. Several of its members were assigned to assist in the organization of the banks for cooperatives while others worked on studies deemed important at the time. It was then the view of some officials of the Farm Credit Administration that the research and service staff inherited from the Federal Farm Board should be decentralized with at least one member being attached to each of the district banks for cooperatives.

As we observed earlier in this chapter, the concern of the cooperatives for the preservation of this function, as provided for by the Cooperative Marketing Act of 1926, was expressed at the meetings of the American Institute of Cooperation held in July 1933, when assurances were given by Frank Peck, the newly appointed Cooperative Bank Commissioner, that this program would be continued in an effective way. However, in the stress of getting the banks for cooperatives organized in the fall of 1933, little attention could be devoted to the resurrection of this program.

When the National Cooperative Council held its annual meeting in January 1934, it took a firm position in requesting the Farm Credit Administration to establish a separate unit for research, service, and education, to be under the direction of a deputy cooperative commissioner. One of its resolutions read as follows:

> Therefore, be it resolved: That we earnestly recommend that the Farm Credit Administration establish in the Cooperative Division a separate unit charged with the duties of conducting . . . education investigations, service and research work under the direction of a deputy commissioner to the end that responsibility for such work may be definitely fixed.[40]

This request was favorably received by the Farm Credit Administration, and, in April, Commissioner Frank Peck announced that "a research section" for "studying the problems of cooperative marketing and purchasing associations" and a "service and educational section" had been set up within the Cooperative Division "to make research findings directly available" to such associations. Although this action did not go as far as the National Cooperative Council had requested, it did recognize the importance of this type of work. However, two months later, the plan to establish two sections was abandoned, and Henry M. Bain, who had been vice president and general manager of the Central Bank for Cooperatives since its establishment, was placed in charge of a coordinated section for cooperative research, service, and education. With this decision a revival of such work was got underway.

The response to its request gave the National Cooperative Council much satisfaction. On October 2, 1934, the Secretary of the Council said:

> The Farm Credit Administration has fulfilled every wish with respect to research and service work in cooperative buying and selling; the appropriate section has been established; it is separate from the credit activities; it is headed by a man exclusively responsible for it; adequate funds have been allocated; and unless Congress or the Budget Bureau demur, its appropriation for the next fiscal year will be equal to that of the Division of Cooperative Marketing when absorbed into the Farm Board in 1929.[41]

Another significant development in 1935 was the inauguration of a new Farm Credit Administration publication by its Office of Information, to provide current information to cooperatives—the *News for Farmer Cooperatives*. It was designed primarily to afford an outlet for the research studies and educational work of the research and service subdivision but it was not an exclusive organ of this subdivision.

In 1937 the research and service program was given increased recognition by making it the Research and Service Subdivision of the Cooperative Division. In 1939 the importance of the work of the subdivision was further recognized by the reorganization of the subdivision so that it became the Cooperative Research and Service Division.[42] This name was retained until 1953 when the Division was returned to the Department of Agriculture to become the Farmer Cooperative Service.[43]

Inauguration of the federal credit union program. The work of the Farm Credit Administration was expanded on June 26, 1934, by the passage of the Federal Credit Union Act which authorized the organization of federal credit unions under charters issued by the Governor of the Farm Credit Administration, who was also made responsible for approving their by-laws and prescribing regulations for their operations. How this program came to be administered by the Farm Credit Administration has been explained by W. I. Myers, then Governor of the Farm Credit Administration, as follows:

> In the spring of 1934, the Credit Union National Extension Bureau, under the leadership of Roy F. Bergengren, was endeavoring to get passage of a Federal Credit Union Law. A serious problem was to find a suitable home for the agency that would supervise the operation of the law . . . Someone got the idea that it might be supervised by the FCA and they called me by phone to ask me if I would accept it. I was reasonably familiar with operation of credit unions and since the credit unions were cooperative credit institutions and needed a home, I agreed to accept it . . . Herbert Emmerich was very helpful in setting up the administrative organization and we already had an excellent examination division to audit PCA's and farm loan associations and we followed the same general rules in the examination of local credit unions.[44]

Myers looks back on this experience with much satisfaction. "I have always felt that our venture into this field was worthwhile since it did not injure our farm credit operations or handicap them in any way. I am glad we helped out with the Federal credit union program at a critical time in its early history."[45] The late Herbert Emmerich, who, as Myers' administrative assistant, took over much of the burden of organizing and supervising this program was of the opinion that "the real credit for Farm Credit espousing a program—the only one not agricultural—goes to the breadth of view of Governor Myers, who knew that the FCA had the cooperative understanding to make it a success. When he agreed to accept the responsibility, Morgenthau and the White House really got behind it."[46]

Upon the recommendation of Bergengren and other credit union leaders, Claude Orchard, who was well known for his effective work in organizing credit unions for Armour and Company, was obtained to direct the new program. The first federal credit union was chartered October 1, 1934, and by the close of the year, 78 applications for charters had been obtained in 22 states. During the next few years this program expanded rapidly, and by the end of 1940 there were 4,210 federal credit unions in existence.[47] Further discussion of the work of the Farm Credit Administration with federal credit unions will be deferred to Chapter XXI.

Progress in administrative management. With emergency problems less pressing, the Farm Credit Administration in 1934 could devote attention to the building of an efficient, permanent, operating organization, and great progress was made in improving its operating efficiency. The Farm Credit Administration became recognized as one of the best-managed agencies of the federal government, noteworthy for the high morale of its employees. By the end of 1934, its work in personnel administration was recognized by other government agencies as outstanding, and it was being used as a model for other government personnel programs.[48] During 1934 a planning section was set up in the Administrative Division to facilitate the development of efficient organization and procedures, both in Washington, D.C., and in the field. This proved useful in handling problems relating to facilities, office space, housing, and equipment.

Strengthening the Cooperative Farm Credit System, 1935-1937

During 1933 and 1934 the energies of the Farm Credit Administration had been largely absorbed in meeting the refinancing crisis and in getting the new cooperative credit institutions into operation. By January 1935 the crisis was over, and attention could be directed to the problem of improving the permanent cooperative features of the Farm Credit system. Although refinancing operations continued to be important, they were significantly reduced as compared with the previous year. Whereas loans made by the Federal Land Banks and by the Land Bank Commissioner had totalled $1,283,000,000 in 1934, they subsided to only $445 million in 1935. The better situation was also marked by a return of insurance companies, banks, and other private lenders to the farm mortgage loan field, and by the first public offering of Federal Farm Loan bank bonds since 1930.

The improved situation was reflected in the first sentence of the Farm Credit Administration's annual report for 1935 which declared: "Having largely completed the emergency jobs . . . [the Farm Credit Administration] . . . was principally concerned during 1935 with its permanent work—that of supervising the group of banks, corporations and local associations which comprise a permanent system of agricultural credit designed to operate on a cooperative plan."

Experience during the first two years had shown the need for additional legislation to strengthen the program of the banks for cooperatives. Under the Farm Credit Act of 1935, approved June 3, 1935, it became possible for the banks for cooperatives to provide a more complete credit service to farmer cooperative business associations. Authority was given for extending loan service to cooperatives performing business services—such as for insurance or irrigation—and the banks were also authorized to make physical facility loans to cooperative purchasing associations. This act also enabled the banks for cooperatives to make loans to cooperatives on the security of commodities and rediscount them with the intermediate credit banks. As a result of these changes, the banks for cooperatives could make all types of loans to every eligible farmer cooperative.

When the banks for cooperatives were first set up, the major amount of business was done by the Central Bank for Cooperatives. As the district banks developed experience, they were able to service more of the cooperatives in their operating territories, and by 1936 the combined business of the 12 district banks exceeded that of the Central Bank. In 1935 the total advances of the 12 district banks increased to $40 million while the advances of the Central Bank declined to $29 million. This trend was encouraged by the Farm Credit Act of 1935 which gave the district banks opportunity to participate in some of the large loans of the Central Bank. By the end of 1935 it had become the practice of the district banks for cooperatives to hold annual meetings of stockholders where mutual problems of the cooperative association borrowers and the banks could be resolved.

By this time the research and service program for cooperatives was getting back to the philosophy, methods, and standards of the Division of Cooperative Marketing prior to its absorption by the Federal Farm Board. This work was carried on in close cooperation with the banks for cooperatives, but it was also available to any farmer cooperative association. In many cases, such work acquainted non-borrowing cooperatives with the financial and other services available from the banks for cooperatives.

With the operations of the banks for cooperatives well established, Frank Peck felt that he could resign as Cooperative Bank Commissioner at the end of 1935 to resume his position as Director of Agricultural Extension at the University of Minnesota. He had been the ideal man to get this program underway. The man who replaced him, Samuel D. Sanders, then general manager of the Washington Egg and Poultry Association of Seattle, was admirably equipped by experience and temperament to expand and intensify the progress made under Peck. He expressed his viewpoint at his first meeting with the presidents of the banks for cooperatives: "I believe I am safe in saying that more cooperatives have failed for the lack of a thorough understanding that a cooperative organization is a business institution and should be regarded as such, than for any other reason." Sanders was a firm believer in the revolving fund method of cooperative financing and under his leadership this method of financing by marketing cooperatives was to be greatly expanded.[49]

By January 1936 much progress had been made in coordinating the work of the four credit units in each district but it was evident that much remained to be done in developing a closer working relationship between local production credit associations and national farm loan associations. The objective, as expressed in the 1935 annual report of the Farm Credit Administration, was "that a farmer anywhere in the United States may be able to go to one office within convenient driving distance for both mortgage loans and production loans from his own cooperative system."[50] By December 31, 1935, progress toward this goal included the establishment of 78 "experimental set-ups" under which the boards of directors of the production credit associations and national farm loan associations located in the same community arranged to use the same secretary-treasurer and to work out an equitable allocation of expenses.

Another basic problem in 1935 was to begin the rehabilitation of the national farm loan associations. The need for such work had been recognized when the Farm Credit Administration was created but little could be done until pressure for refinancing assistance began to subside. Early in 1935 a program for developing group management was initiated, and by the end of the year there were 248 "group management set-ups," involving 766 national farm loan associations. Under this program several small national farm loan associations made use of the same secretary-treasurer. This was a step toward an eventual reduction in the number of local farm loan associations, and it permitted more economical and efficient local service.

The first year of operation of the production credit associations had indicated the need for much improvement in their operating methods. To simplify procedures, reduce length of time to close loans, and achieve all around greater efficiency, a general study was made in 1935 which resulted in changes that greatly improved performance. In this year the production credit system gave special attention to the holding of annual stockholder's meetings of production credit associations as well as group meetings of their boards of directors. The purpose of the annual meetings was to inform members on the operations and financial condition of their associations and acquaint potential borrowers with production credit association service. During January and February 1935 such meetings were attended by more than 60,000 persons.[51]

In 1936 the volume of loans made by the production credit associations to 234,651 farmers reached $288 million. The system was taking hold.

Higher farm income in 1936 eased the burden on the Farm Credit Administration and enabled it to get on with the job of developing a permanent agricultural credit system. In his fourth Annual Report for the year 1936, Governor Myers said: "[The] first three years were devoted to salvaging and building; 1936 was a year of consolidation." He also said: "For the first time since the Farm Credit Administration began to function, it was free to pursue the primary long-view purpose for which it was designed."[52]

During 1936 the Federal Land Banks were able to concentrate attention on the strengthening of the national farm loan associations. Much progress was made in group management, thus achieving economies while providing farmers with better loan service. Significant advances were also made in transferring greater responsibility from the land banks to the national farm loan associations for the effective servicing of outstanding loans, so as to bring the whole farm loan system closer to the borrowers. Funds were made available in the form of a definite schedule of allowances to compensate for services performed by the farm loan associations that had previously been provided by the land banks. This enabled the associations to employ more competent secretary-treasurers and provide better facilities for service. A significant new development in the Land Banks in 1936 was the establishment of a membership relations division in the Land Bank Commissioner's office to promote interest in the Land Bank program and devise methods of making membership control in the national farm loan associations more effective.

It was quite clear during 1936 that the national farm loan associations were gradually becoming a group of strong, well-managed cooperative associations. This was emphasized in a talk by Albert S. Goss, Land Bank Commissioner, at the 1936 American Institute of Cooperation in June at the University of Illinois. Goss maintained that the national farm loan associations were complying with all the standards of good cooperation and that they should be considered part of the family of cooperatives.[53]

In his fifth and last report as Governor issued for the year 1937, W. I. Myers was proud to say: "Almost a million farmers are—directly or through their cooperatives—participating stockholders in a nation-wide farm credit cooperative." He pointed out that "nothing of greater significance has occurred in the history of the Farm Credit Administration's operations than the passage by Congress of the Farm Credit Act of 1937, which assures the permanency of the fundamental cooperative ideas underlying them."[54] One provision of the new Act put the national farm loan associations on a one-man, one-vote basis, whereas previously voting was by shares up to a maximum of 20. The new Act also approved the grouping of neighboring national farm loan associations under a common board of directors.

The 1937 Act also gave member borrowers a greater responsibility in the selection of directors for the federal land bank districts which became under the Act, "farm credit districts." The new law provided for the election of one director respectively by national farm loan associations, production credit associations, and borrowing cooperatives of the banks for cooperatives. While the Governor of the Farm Credit Administration was to retain appointive power over three directors, the seventh was to be chosen by the Governor from three nominees of national farm loan associations in the district. The annual report hailed this as "a further step toward placing increased responsibility with the borrowers."

During 1937, further emphasis was placed on the decentralization of operations in the land bank system. The allowance plan, begun in 1934 to help strengthen national farm loan associations, was expanded to include many more associations. By December 31, 1937, all but one district had allowance plans in effect, and 3,886 associations, or 86 per cent, were functioning under such plans. Moreover, the national farm loan associations had continued to steadily set up joint offices with a single competent management for two or more associations. By the year's end there were 828 joint offices serving 3,064 associations. These joint management set-ups usually led to consolidations of the associations under one management, thus reducing the number of ineffective associations. By December 31, 1937, the land bank commissioner had approved 149 consolidations involving 411 national farm loan associations, and 97 tentative approvals affecting 344 associations were pending.

In the years from 1935 to 1937, the Farm Credit Administration was carrying on an enlightening information program. Circulars and bulletins were abundantly issued to explain how the national farm loan associations, production credit associations, and banks for cooperatives performed their functions. Many of these publications were designed to help increase employee efficiency, but many were issued to keep farmers and the general public informed on how the Farm Credit Administration was carrying on its work and serving agricultural needs. Moreover, in cooperation with the Office of Information of the Farm Credit Administration, the district offices of information were issuing magazines and pamphlets to provide information for those served in the district and for public officials and educational leaders. This active information program provided much educational information of value to those in the system and did much to gain support for the Farm Credit Administration from the general public.

During these years the agencies of the Farm Credit Administration were engaged in a constant and systematic effort to improve procedures and efficiency through management training and other education programs. The attendance at stockholder meetings of all of the lending agencies steadily increased, and, in addition, many conferences were held for Farm Credit employees and borrowers from Farm Credit Administration agencies.

The Subsidy Question, 1936-1937

In 1937 the Farm Credit Administration was steadily becoming more cooperative in character. Its leaders looked forward to the time when ownership and control of the system could be held by farmers or farmer cooperatives. Of growing concern was the subsidization of interest on land bank loans which had been started in 1933 at 4½ per cent as a recovery measure and later reduced to 3½ per cent. This low rate was popular with farmers, for agriculture was still in a distressed condition. However, it was recognized by Governor Myers and by Land Bank Commissioner Goss that the perpetuation of the subsidy would endanger the long-run objective of establishing the Farm Credit Administration as an independent cooperative business institution.

Goss outlined this problem in an address to the American Institute of Cooperation at the University of Illinois in June 1936. He said:

> To me [the problem of government subsidy] is the greatest fundamental problem which farmers must face and decide. The question is whether we want to develop a cooperative credit system owned and controlled by its members, or whether we want a governmentally supported and governmentally controlled credit system. Under the cooperative plan, if we operate on sound principles, we can have constant access to the money markets of the nation and can command credit rates practically as low as the government itself . . . Under the governmentally supported system, farm credit will be subject to the whims of changing Congresses. Political pressures of many lending interests must be met with political power on the part of the farmer if rates are to be kept low. This of course suggests the constant possibility of political interference with the danger of preference and the injection of unsound credit principles.[55]

Governor Myers was in full accord with Goss on the danger of the subsidy and he "fought valiantly against the clamor being made to have it renewed."[56] In addressing the American Farm Economic Association in late December 1936, he said: "While courage is required for the elimination of any subsidy, the time has come for facing the fact that these direct Government subsidies must be tapered off if the goal of a business credit system for agriculture is to be attained."[57]

However, the general farm organizations favored the subsidy until farm prosperity could be assured, and it was extended in 1937 for another two years. This did not deter Myers from pressing his view that the continuance of the subsidy would endanger the permanent independence of the Farm Credit Administration. In an address to the American Institute of Cooperation at Iowa State College in the summer of 1937, he said:

> The desire for low rates, possible only through continued subsidies, is in my judgment the greatest single peril to the existence of a cooperative credit system in this country. . . . We might be able in this country to have either a permanent subsidy or a cooperative system. In my judgment we cannot have both and very soon we are going to have to choose. . . . Ownership and control go together and a desire that these institutions continue to preserve the farm point of view calls for more than the elimination of subsidies. It calls for a program looking forward in an orderly manner to the ultimate repayment of Government capital.[58]

This forthright statement was well received by many cooperative and farm leaders, but it irritated many representatives of farmers in hard-pressed farm areas and certain officials in the United States Department of Agriculture who were more interested in catering to the immediate demands of farmers than to the development of a permanent cooperative credit institution. It posed a question that had not been resolved when Governor Myers resigned in September 1938 to resume his work with Cornell University. His successor, Forest F. Hill, who had served as Deputy Governor since 1934, was in full agreement with Myers and vigorously endeavored to sustain his views.

The Takeover by the Department of Agriculture

The Farm Credit Administration was enjoying enviable support in early 1939 from farmers, farm cooperatives, and farm organizations for the job it had done in helping farmers get back on their feet. It had the goodwill of the National Cooperative Council and the major cooperatives of the country. The American Farm Bureau Federation, at its annual meeting in December 1938, had declared: "Farmers are appreciating more and more that the credit facilities of the Farm Credit Administration are being built for their own industry and justify a continuing and increasing support as well as a greater participation on their part in the direction and management of these credit agencies.[55]

Just when things were going well, a cloud appeared. For several years there had been a national sentiment growing up for the reorganization of governmental agencies which had proliferated under the New Deal. In 1937 this sentiment had blossomed in a report of the President's Committee on Administrative Management, under the Chairmanship of Louis Brownlow, which proposed a reduction in the number of agencies reporting directly to the President.[60] Although a reorganization bill designed to give the President authority to consolidate and rearrange agencies was defeated in 1938, largely because of the animosity aroused by the Supreme Court reorganization fight, Roosevelt was able to get Congressional approval in early 1939 for a modified reorganization act that gave him power to reorganize agencies if not disapproved by Congress within 60 days. This matter did not greatly concern Farm Credit Administration officials before April 25, 1939, when they were surprised by the announcement of a presidential reorganization plan that transferred the Farm Credit Administration to the United States Department of Agriculture.[61]

To understand this situation it is necessary to realize that the Agricultural Adjustment Act of 1938 had greatly strengthened the Department's powers, and that the general reorganization of the Department in October 1938 had coordinated the Secretary's control over the agencies within the Department. It was Secretary Wallace's view, shared by his close associates, that complete control over all agencies of government working with farmers was essential to their better administration.[62] In 1936, the Department had obtained control over the Resettlement Administration, which became the Farm Security Administration in 1937, and the other major agricultural agencies then not in the Department of Agriculture's system were the Farm Credit Administration, the Commodity Credit Corporation, and the Rural Electrification Administration.

There was no great opposition to the transfer of the Commodity Credit Corporation to the Department, for it was already under its control. Likewise the transfer of the Rural Electrification Administration was not seriously opposed, although the REA Administrator, John Carmody, chose to resign at the time (see Chapter XVII). The proposed transfer of the Farm Credit Administration, however, aroused fear among its officials and supporters that this would increase political pressures on Farm Credit Administration policies and procedures, which had been singularly free from political interference up to this time. From its establishment, the Farm Credit Administration had maintained that its primary responsibility lay in the efficient performance of credit services for farmers and their cooperatives, and it had resisted pressures to use its credit machinery to enforce compliance with Agricultural Adjustment Administration programs.[63]

It should be borne in mind that in early 1939 Wallace was showing a marked interest in the presidential nomination for 1940, for it was not then believed that Roosevelt would seek a third term.[64] Since the 1936 election, Paul H. Appleby, Assistant to Secretary Wallace, had been actively promoting his chief for the presidency in 1940. Appleby was a man of no little ability, and he had built up a strong machine in the administrative structure of the Department of Agriculture. He was widely recognized as Wallace's *alter ego*, who accomplished ends that Wallace wanted to see accomplished. *The Kiplinger Letter*, of January 23, 1937, called attention to Appleby's growing influence and raised the question of "whether the Secretary of Agriculture is Wallace or Appleby."[65] It is significant that most of the reorganizations and significant personnel changes in the Department since 1935 had been largely engineered by Appleby, and many gave him credit for achieving a high degree of administrative efficiency in the Department. His views had, moreover, greatly impressed Louis Brownlow and his Committee on Administrative Management and officials of the Bureau of the Budget.[66] Appleby's "overriding concern" was admittedly "to put the Secretary in a position where he could be responsible for his Department, thus enabling the President to be responsible for this segment of the executive branch, and upholding the responsibility of Congress."[67] In this ambition he had Wallace's complete confidence and handled many things for him, such as contacts with Senators, Congressmen, and other government officials, while he maintained a close control of programs within the Department.[68]

Wallace wanted to obtain control of the Farm Credit Administration himself but he hesitated to ask for it. In reply to a request for recommendations for changes under Reorganization Plan I, Wallace wrote to Harold D. Smith, Director of the Bureau of the Budget, on April 20, 1939, only five days before the announcement of the transfer of the FCA to the U.S.D.A., as follows: "In view of my strong feeling that we must not at this time awaken hostility on the Hill, or among groups throughout the country, I am holding my recommendations involving transfer to this Department to a minimum. I am not suggesting, for example, that the Farm Credit Administration, the Rural Electrification Administration or the agricultural activities of the TVA be transferred to Agriculture."[69] However, within the next few days the decision was made, probably with the advice of Brownlow, Gulick and the other advisers of the President on matters of administrative management. What role Appleby played in bringing about this decision is not known, but in view of his known views and actions it seems reasonable to assume that he was instrumental in achieving it.

The intense opposition of cooperative and general farm organizations to the proposed transfer came somewhat as a surprise to President Roosevelt who had tacitly understood that this action would not involve any significant change in the administrative operations of the Farm Credit Administration. He had seen it as a logical move toward better governmental administration in line with the recommendations of the Brownlow Committee, and apparently he thought that the move would be more nominal than functional. At this time Wallace stood high with the President, for he was attracted by Wallace's liberal views, and he needed the important political support that Wallace was giving him. Moreover, he greatly admired the way Wallace was administering the Department of Agriculture.[70]

To allay the anxiety of those who were made apprehensive by the announcement of the transfer, Secretary Wallace issued a public statement on May 22, 1939, which was approved by the President. It gave assurance that the Farm Credit Administration would not "become an integral part of the Department of Agriculture." While its Governor would, in the future, report to the Secretary of Agriculture, but "for carrying out the many federal statutes which form the basis for the several types of farm credit, for information and execution of operating policies, for control of fiscal, personnel, legal, informational, and related affairs . . . the Farm Credit Administration will be an autonomous Federal Agency as heretofore.[71]

This statement was followed on June 3, 1939, by a Secretary's memorandum, also approved by the President, which delegated to the Governor of the Farm Credit Administration all the powers over the Farm Credit Administration conferred upon the Secretary by the President's Reorganization Plan I, except for the provision that the Governor would report to the Secretary of Agriculture henceforth, and a further provision that the Secretary retained authority to modify or rescind the provisions of the memorandum at any time.[72]

For the time being, opposition to the transfer was quieted, and the Farm Credit Administration proceeded to operate with little change. To facilitate the transfer, Wallace, on May 4, 1939, appointed Paul Appleby his liaison representative to make all necessary arrangements. Appleby, who had been the major advocate of the transfer, was not happy with the way in which the proposed transfer had been softened by the Secretary's statement and memorandum, although he recognized that they were politically expedient, and he watched for an opportunity to strengthen the powers of the Department over the Farm Credit Administration. Even before the transfer became officially effective on July 1, he had confidentially dispatched two trusted agents into the St. Paul Farm Credit District, where there was reported disgruntlement on the tight-fisted operations of the Federal Land Banks, to obtain information that would force a reexamination of the Department's relationships with the Farm Credit Administration. Frank Hook, a Democratic Congressman from Michigan, and a member of the House Committee on Agriculture, had complained that constituents were writing that the Farm Credit Administration was "militantly Republican," and he had requested the latest information on whether the Farm Credit Administration "will or will not become an integral part of the Department of Agriculture under the Reorganization bill." Appleby pointed out to Hook, in a letter dated July 1, 1939, that a press release had been issued

> . . . that makes a clear distinction between the Farm Credit Administration and the other agencies in the Department of Agriculture. In the case of all other agencies, there is common departmental scrutiny through units of the Secretary's office . . . Through review and scrutiny conducted by these units, work in the various agencies is continually coordinated with considerable detail, and

there flows to the Secretary varying types of information about activities conducted in the various bureaus, so that the Secretary becomes equipped both with controls and with information which enable him to live up to the responsibility with which he is charged.

Appleby then pointed out that the Farm Credit Administration was to be free of such control.

Since the usual departmental scrutinies and reviews are not to apply in the case of the Farm Credit Administration, the relationship between that Administration and the Department is simply one of personal contact between the Governor of the Farm Credit Administration and the Secretary, and there is possible only the broadest sort of authority in the Secretary.

However, Appleby made it clear that this was not necessarily the final word. He went on to say:

It is extremely difficult . . . to accept an administrative responsibility unless we have the usual controls that are necessary in a big organization. Nevertheless, I am right now sending out into the Minnesota area two men in whom we have special confidence to make a thoroughgoing study of the situation. This study can be the basis for discussion and negotiations, at least, with the Farm Credit Administration. I have an idea it will be two or three months before the study is in such shape as to warrant the consultations with the Farm Credit Administration, however.[73]

It was not long before the "two men in which we have special confidence" found that conditions in the economically distressed Northwestern states called for a considerable degree of Departmental surveillance in the affairs of the Farm Credit Administration. They alleged that the Farm Credit Administration was taking a hard line in foreclosing farms.

About the time that the Department was ready to use the information obtained "as a basis for discussion and negotiations" with the Farm Credit Administration, the hands of the Secretary were freed by a ruling of the Comptroller General on September 26, 1939, which held that the Secretary did not have legal authority to make such a sweeping divestment of authority to the Governor of the Farm Credit Administration as had been made in his memorandum of June 3, 1939.

For a few months following the transfer of the Farm Credit Administration to the Department, there had been little change in the operations of the Farm Credit Administration, except that appointments over a certain salary range were required to be approved by the Secretary. However, in October, based on the "revelations" of the study of disgruntled farmers made by the Department's confidential agents and the abrogation of the hands-off policy by the ruling of the Comptroller General, the Department began to exert pressure for changes in the administration of the Farm Credit Administration. When Governor Hill resisted this pressure, he was charged with being non-cooperative, and at the end of October his resignation was requested by Secretary Wallace. Hill, however, stood his ground and refused to resign unless requested to do so by the President, since he had been appointed by him. He also let representatives of the cooperatives and farm organizations know of the pressure being placed upon him for his resignation.

While this situation was coming to a boil, the Executive Committee of the National Cooperative Council, on December 8, 1939, passed a resolution which affirmed its past support of the Farm Credit Administration and which urged that "the independent status of the Farm Credit Administration be restored at as early a date as possible." By this time it was widely known that Secretary Wallace was determined to make the Farm Credit Administration an integral part of the U.S.D.A. by appointing his own man as Governor. This imminent action was vigorously opposed by officials of the Grange, AFB, and National Cooperative Council, who made their concern known to the President. In response to a telegram sent to him by John D. Miller, President of the National Cooperative Council, President Roosevelt replied as follows:

> I have your telegram of December 13, 1939, in which you express concern respecting the welfare of the Farm Credit Administration should it become an integral part of the Department of Agriculture. I am convinced that your fears are unfounded. The purpose of the Farm Credit Administration is to assist in providing farmers and farm cooperative associations with credit upon the most favorable terms possible, consistent with sound lending practices. The achievement of such objectives will be gained in greater degree if the activities of the Farm Credit Administration are coordinated with other activities designed to improve the economic position of farmers. To the extent that such benefits accrue, the greater coordination of all agricultural activities will be welcomed by farmers who are now borrowers, or who may hereafter have occasion to use the facilities of the Farm Credit System.[74]

Although this letter was somewhat nebulous, it made obvious that Governor Hill's resignation would be welcomed, and on December 20, Hill resigned, saying:

> I do not believe it possible to maintain such a [cooperative credit] system on a sound basis if it becomes an integral part of a Department of Government responsible for the administration of programs which provide for millions of dollars in direct benefit payments and grants to farmers annually; for the making of commodity loans, frequently at or above current market levels; and for the extension of credit . . . to assist in the financial rehabilitation [of farmers] who cannot meet the credit standards which must be maintained by self-supporting credit institutions, whether cooperative or private . . .[75]

The President, thereupon, appointed Dr. Albert G. Black, one of Secretary Wallace's close associates, as Acting Governor.[76] It was clear

that Wallace was determined to dovetail the work of the FCA into the
U.S.D.A.

The Threat to Cooperative Independence

The Farm Credit issue dominated the annual meeting of the National
Council of Farmer Cooperatives held in early January 1940.[77] In his
presidential address to the annual meeting of the National Council of
Farmer Cooperatives, Judge Miller reviewed the developments that had
come to a head with the appointment of Governor Black.[78] Although he
accepted several statements of the President, Secretary Wallace, and
Governor Black that "the sound credit policy heretofore followed by
Farm Credit Administration will be adhered to," he went on to say "We
should recognize, however, that Administrations, Secretaries of Agriculture and Governors of Farm Credit Administration come and go, and no
one can now give assurance that after January 1, 1941, such sound policies
will be adhered to." He pointed out that it was in view of this uncertainty
that the Executive Committee of the Council had adopted the resolution
which urged that the independent status of Farm Credit Administration
be restored at as early a date as possible. He then continued:

> In creating the several credit agencies that are now units of Farm Credit Ad-
> ministration, Congress recognized that to be successful as an agency to supply
> the sound, long-time credit needs of farmers and farmers' cooperatives, it was
> necessary for Farm Credit Administration to adopt and follow sound lending
> policies . . . [designed to serve] not only present but also future farmers . . .
> Farm Credit Administration has been and is more than a Governmental depart-
> ment. It is an agency through which the Federal Government, farmers and
> farmers' cooperatives have engaged in a joint financial enterprise, each becom-
> ing part owners of the voting capital stock of several credit agencies that are
> units of Farm Credit Administration.

He maintained that it was a violation of ethics to change the status of
the Farm Credit Administration and "transfer its control to others." He
went on to say:

> In enacting the several statutes creating these agencies, the Federal Government
> invited farmers and farmers' cooperatives to become joint owners with the
> Government, with the hope that in due time farmers and farmers' cooperatives
> could become the entire owners of the agencies, thus removing them entirely
> from the federal budget. That farmers and farmers' cooperatives desire to be-
> come in due time the owners of these agencies is shown by the fact that they
> have now invested in the voting capital stock of these several agencies the sum
> of 130 million dollars; and justice now requires that the status or control of the
> agencies should not be changed without their consent.

Judge Miller recognized the danger in the Department of Agriculture of departmental politics, and he said: "Farm Credit Administration, now partly owned by farmers, should not be imperiled by continuing to be one of the many agencies in such department."

The official resolutions of the Council passed at its annual meeting expressed regret on the change of policy which had terminated the independent status of the Farm Credit Administration, and the Council requested that Congress restore at an early date the independent status so long accorded to the Farm Credit Administration. After pledging loyal support to the current officials of the FCA, the resolution urged that the general policies of the Farm Credit Administration "be continued as in the past, with progressive increases in the cooperative nature of its structure."[79]

Following its annual meeting, the Council, in cooperation with the National Grange and the American Farm Bureau Federation, began work on a bill which was designed to re-establish the independence of the Farm Credit Administration. This bill was introduced in the Senate by Senator Guy Gillette of Iowa on March 4, 1940, with Harry Truman as one of the co-sponsors. It would have placed the Farm Credit Administration under the supervision of a Board of five, appointed for 10-year terms by the President. Although this bill was not reported out of the Committee, it helped solidify opposition to measures that threatened to weaken the Farm Credit Administration's cooperative structure.

The Wheeler-Jones Bill. Before the Gillette Bill could be considered in the Senate, the apprehensions of those who thought that the Department's control of the Farm Credit Administration would impair its cooperative character were confirmed when Senator Burton K. Wheeler and Congressman Marvin A. Jones introduced identical bills on March 4, 1940 (Senate Bill 3509 and H.R. 8748, 76th Congress, 3rd Session), which were designed to drastically change the Federal Land Bank system. It was well understood that these bills represented the views of Governor Black and Secretary Wallace. The preambles to the bills do not fully disclose their intent or significance. They simply stated that they were designed to accomplish the following results:

> To reduce permanently the interest rates on Federal land bank and Land Bank Commissioner loans; to relieve Federal land bank borrowers of stock liability; to place the Federal land banks on a self-supporting basis; to refund and guarantee the bonds of such banks; to increase the functions and responsibilities of national farm-loan associations and county committees of farmers; to provide for the adjustment and refinancing of farm-mortgage debts; to limit the institution of foreclosure proceedings and the taking of deficiency judgements; and for other purposes.

Under the proposed bills, the rate of interest payable on Land Bank loans was to be fixed at 3 per cent (later changed to 3½ per cent), and all farm-loan bonds were to be "fully and unconditionally guaranteed, both as to interest and principal, by the United States." Most important from a cooperative standpoint was the provision for doing away with the capital stock structure of the national farm loan associations which had been established by the Federal Farm Loan Act of 1916. The farmers' investments in these associations which then totalled $108 million were to be refunded to them, and, in turn, the national farm loan associations would cease to hold a like amount of investment in the Federal Land Banks. It is of interest that as of December 31, 1939, the national farm loan associations and borrowers with direct loans held 47 per cent of the capital in the Federal Land Banks. The national farm loan associations were to be reorganized as membership organizations with members paying a $10 membership fee. The bill was so nebulous—if not ambiguous —with regard to how these associations would be formed and operated that it was not clear whether or not borrowing farmers would be required to pay the membership fee.

In addition to the national farm loan associations, there were to be county debt adjustment associations patterned somewhat on county Agricultural Adjustment Administration committees. Although this Act ostensibly related only to the Federal Land Bank system, its passage would have weakened the linchpin of the whole Farm Credit Administration's cooperative structure. It is hard to see how the production credit associations or the banks for cooperatives could have long continued on a common stock membership basis when their sister organizations were operating as non-stock membership organizations.

As might have been expected these bills met with a storm of protest from cooperative leaders, for the idea of doing away with the ownership interest of farmers in the national farm loan associations was to them almost sacrilege. By this time, Albert Goss, Land Bank Commissioner, felt compelled to resign, for he was unalterably opposed to the Wheeler-Jones Bill.[80] Within a short time he was the active leader of the forces opposed to the Wheeler-Jones Bill and the champion of the effort to restore the independence of the Farm Credit Administration.[81]

To build support for, and counter opposition to, the provisions of the Wheeler-Jones Bill, Governor Black early in April directed the presidents of the Federal Land Banks to process and mail out under frank to all of the 600,000 borrowers from the Land Banks Secretary Wallace's views on the desirability of the changes proposed by the Wheeler-Jones Bill. Wallace's two-page single-spaced statement was presented as a memorandum to A. G. Black, Governor, Farm Credit Administration. In it

Wallace said: "I was astounded to learn that more than half of the local national farm loan associations in the United States are insolvent and that only 40% of them are sufficiently solvent to be able to accept applications and sell their stock to members." This statement was highly misleading in that it did not take account of the great progress which had been made by the Land Banks under the Farm Credit Administration in grouping associations so that farmers could be more efficiently served. However, it served his purpose of undermining confidence in the national farm loan associations. Wallace asked Black these questions: "Does this not raise the issue as to whether the stock which farmers have had to purchase in order to obtain loans has not carried a liability much larger than it should have borne? Also, I wonder if the borrowers have always been informed of the exact financial position of the association before they purchased stock?"

The memorandum made clear that Wallace favored paying off at par all stock now owned by borrowers, whether or not the stock was impaired, and making loans in the future without requiring farmers to purchase stock. Wallace also conveyed the idea that government guarantees of Federal Land Bank bonds would enable them to "sell at sufficiently low rates of interest to give the farmers permanently the same low emergency rates they are now receiving or even perhaps lower" without costing the government any subsidy. Wallace concluded with this sentence. "Since the Farm Credit Administration is now a part of the United States Department of Agriculture and not an independent agency or under a Loan Board, I personally am particularly impressed with the need for improving the farm mortgage situation along these lines and not limiting our thinking to the existing system and procedures."[82]

The memorandum proved to be a dud in that the great majority of the 1,600 replies were critical of Wallace's views. Moreover, it had an adverse effect on Senators and Congressmen, and it helped strengthen opposition to the Wheeler-Jones Bill. Undaunted, Wallace carried his campaign against those who were unfavorable to his proposed changes in the Land Bank system to the country by means of a large mass meeting held at St. Paul, Minnesota, on April 27. This meeting was attended by some 20,000 of his supporters, of whom many came long distances on Triple A expense accounts.[83]

In his address, Wallace pulled out all the stops in assailing those who disputed his views. Naming them as "enemies of agriculture," he belittled the charges that he was in favor of cheap money and the emasculation of the cooperative features of the Land Bank system. He claimed that the "enemies of agriculture" had seized a new opportunity to attack the farm program when the Farm Credit Administration was transferred to the

Department "by Congress and the President." He maintained that "many farmers looked upon the transfer as a chance to make the farm credit program a vitally important part of the national farm program." Wallace identified the "enemies" as "the same financial, journalistic and political interests which always gang up against anything which really will help the farmers." No mention was made of the fact that such important farm groups as the American Farm Bureau Federation, the National Grange, and the National Council of Farmer Cooperatives were leading the attack against his proposals, although he admitted that "some even of our friends have been deceived by the false picture which the enemies of the farm program have been spreading over the country."

Wallace then proceeded to nail down the "falsities" of those who opposed his position. He declared that after the Farm Credit Administration came to the Department of Agriculture he had found the farm mortgage situation "worse than was generally realized." He disavowed that the Land Bank system was being wrecked by the Department; that the Department would make the Land Banks into "soft credit" or "loose credit" institutions; that it would impair the value of Land Bank bonds; or destroy the "so-called 'farmer-owned' credit system." However, his disavowals did little to change the minds of those who had labored to create a cooperative credit system. They couldn't agree with his declaration: "Under the present system I don't think it will ever be possible to make cooperation in the farm loan associations a really living thing."

Wallace's address, given over a national broadcasting network, created a furor among American Farm Bureau leaders who were already disturbed by the political machine that Wallace was building up through the county and township AAA production control committees. They saw this as an attempt to go further in the same direction, and it marked the end of the support that the Farm Bureau gave to the Department under Secretary Wallace.[84]

On April 22, 1940, in response to a request from Senator Robert Wagner of the Committee on Banking and Currency, Secretary Wallace expressed his views on the Gillette Bill, which called for the reestablishment of the Farm Credit Administration on an independent basis. After examining the provisions of the bill he called attention to President Roosevelt's statement in his message transmitting Reorganization Plan I to the Congress, in which he said: "Since 1916 the Congress has established from time to time agencies for providing loans, directly or indirectly, for the stimulation and stabilization of agriculture, and such agencies should in my opinion be grouped with the other agricultural activities of the Government . . . " Then Wallace said: "While new within the Department of Agriculture, and under the general direction and supervision of the Secretary of Agriculture, the status of the Farm Credit Administration and the Federal Farm Mortgage Corporation as individual establishments has not been changed otherwise." No reference was made to the rather comprehensive changes he was endeavoring to bring about.

On June 7, 1940, Secretary Wallace reiterated his views on the need of a drastic change in the Federal Land Bank system in a statement before the Senate Committee on Banking and Currency, which was then examining the Wheeler Bill. Wallace gave particular attention to "the contention that certain provisions in the bill would do away with the cooperative feature of the system." On this he said:

> These so-called cooperative features are the provisions which require a farmer to buy stock in a local association equal to five percent of his loan. In my opinion, . . . this requirement of stock ownership has failed to make the farm credit system cooperative. And, after twenty-five years of experience with the present method, there is no reason to burden ourselves any longer with the illusion that the stock purchase requirement ever is likely to result in an effective cooperative farm credit system.

Later he said:

> It seems indisputable that requiring farmers to buy stock in local associations is not the way to get effective farmer cooperation in the farm credit system. I want to make it clear that I favor preserving and extending *genuine* cooperative principles in the farm credit system, but I want to make it equally clear that I do not favor keeping in that system methods which . . . defeat the effective operation of cooperative principles.

Turning to the provision in the bill for making the farm loan associations into membership organizations, he said:

> This proposal would not hamper the farmers' participation in the work of the system. They would still be members of local associations and would run the associations' affairs. Stock ownership is not essential to the right of association members to elect association directors and manage association activities.[85]

However, Wallace's testimony was unavailing, for the Wheeler Bill was not reported out of the Committee.

"What Is to Be the Future of the FCA?"

The farm credit controversy was still boiling when the American Institute of Cooperation met at Michigan State College in July. Speaking on the subject: "What Is to Be the Future of the Farm Credit Administration and Its Policies?," Albert Goss said that the real question was "Shall the Farm Credit Administration be operated as an independent cooperative institution or shall it become a direct Government lending agency under political control?" He continued: "The issue is clearly drawn and cannot be obscured by calling a political bureau a cooperative." Goss vigorously defended the past policies of the Farm Credit Administration and made clear his views:

> I believe it is a serious mistake to place a supervisory agency under an operating Department. Immediately the Department wants to run the agencies they are supposed to supervise. We need nothing more than the experience of the past 12 months to prove this point. Although there was a very clear and definite agreement before the President's order transferring the Farm Credit Administration to the Department took effect, that the Farm Credit Administration would continue in an independent operating status, almost from the start the agreement was ignored. For example, the appointment of any employee anywhere in the system, above certain salary ranges, had to be approved by the Secretary, and studies were started leading up to the Wheeler-Jones bill which [would take] away practically all autonomy and authority from the farm loan associations and the land banks and concentrate most unusual powers in the hands of the Government. The cooperative features would be completely eliminated by this bill and the system changed into a direct Government lending agency.[86]

Goss saw no alternative to the existent situation except legislative action to place the Farm Credit Administration under an independent Board, and, during the next few years, he was to give his major attention to the defeat of legislation that threatened the independence of the Farm Credit Administration and to the enactment of legislation that would restore its independent status.

Former Governor Myers also spoke vigorously in opposition to the provisions of the Wheeler-Jones Bill on the same assigned subject. After calling attention to his basic beliefs with regard to agriculture and cooperation, he called for careful consideration of any action that would drastically change the Farm Credit Administration. He maintained that:

> If the Land Banks are changed to a non-capital set-up with financial strength derived from a government guarantee of bonds, the result would be the substitution of government credit for cooperative credit . . . The control of any business, cooperative or private, goes with ownership . . . Regardless of the provisions of any proposed bill, the substitution of government-guaranteed bonds for member capital in the Land Banks would end the hope for any effective farmer control.[87]

Myers held that under centralized government control, "characteristic of existing government credit agencies and action programs, the Federal Land Banks and the farm loan associations would become mere branch offices with no real power to adjust lending policies to meet local conditions." To him "the change to centralized control would involve the loss of the greatest factor of strength in the present land bank system— regional and local operation and responsibility."[88] Like Goss, Governor Myers saw no alternative except the re-establishment of the Farm Credit Administration as an independent agency of government under a small bipartisan board.

Kenneth W. Hones, representing the National Farmers' Union on the same program, strongly differed with the views of Goss and Myers. He maintained that the best reason for the transfer of the Farm Credit Administration to the Department of Agriculture was: *"That is where it belongs."* He asserted that "Farm Credit is to agriculture as the finance department of any manufacturing company or business corporation is to the whole unit." He declared: "Farm credit belongs to agriculture and not to the bankers, insurance companies, and coupon clippers . . . This is the first time in our history that the Farm Credit Administration has been shaken loose from high finance and put into the hands of our friends, and we are going to keep it if you know anything about farmers."[89]

Hones belittled the claim that the national farm loan associations were cooperatives. "Where is there any cooperative feature? All officers are just rubber stamps. What does an ordinary farmer care about its being fully cooperative as long as he is given a fighting chance to save his home." As to the charge that the change would make the FCA more political, he scoffed: "Political! Well, it always was political and always will be. Our bill changes nothing in that respect."[90]

By August it was clear that no basic change was to be made in Farm Credit Administration legislation during 1940. Farm prices now were moving upward as a result of the European war, and the cost of farm credit was becoming of less concern to farmers. Moreover, on September 4 Wallace resigned as Secretary to actively campaign as the vice-presidential nominee, and his successor, Claude Wickard, was not inclined to carry on a fight for a lost cause. When the 1940 report of the Farm Credit Administration was submitted by Governor Black, it was clear that few basic changes had been made in the methods of the Farm Credit Administration, or that any were in the offing. The challenge to the cooperative character of the Farm Credit Administration had been met, and its future seemed secure. In a later volume we will see how the Farm Credit Administration was eventually restored to independent status in 1953 after a long campaign which got its impetus from the attempt in 1940 to change its cooperative structure.

The FCA at the End of 1940

In the face of the challenge from the transfer to the Department of Agriculture, the Farm Credit Administration had established itself by the end of 1940, and its cooperative structure seemed secure. The national farm loan associations, production credit associations, and banks for cooperatives were all functioning well and the system itself enjoyed a high degree of public and agricultural support. This was reflected in the *Eighth Annual Report of the Farm Credit Administration* issued early in 1941, which declared:

> The job of the credit institutions operating under the supervision of the Farm Credit Administration is to provide a dependable source of credit where responsible farmers and ranchers, and their cooperative associations, can obtain the credit they need on terms suited to their individual requirements at interest rates as low as sound business practice will permit. However, in addition to the farmers who use the credit units operating under the supervision of the Farm Credit Administration, hundreds of thousands of farmers not operating from these institutions benefit indirectly because other credit organizations tend to follow the lead of these institutions in improving the terms on which they make loans to farmers and in lowering interest rates (p. 1).

Summary

In this chapter we have shown how the Farm Credit Administration knitted together existing and new federal farm credit programs into an efficient cooperative lending agency for American agriculture. With capable administrative guidance and high standards of performance the Farm Credit Administration helped American farmers and their cooperative organizations weather the Great Depression and get back on their feet. By 1939 the Farm Credit Administration had become so highly respected by farm and cooperative organizations for the efficiency of its operations as a service agency for American agriculture that it was able to withstand heavy political pressure designed to reduce its essential independence.[91]

Chapter XV

COOPERATIVES FOR RELIEF: 1933-1940

In the preceding chapters we have been dealing with the effect of the
New Deal on what may be called orthodox cooperatives, or those which
gained acceptance as economic institutions on their own merits. These
cooperatives were formed by individuals and groups to meet economic
needs, and they developed as part of the prevailing free competitive
private enterprise system. In this chapter we will examine cooperatives
generally sponsored by government to achieve certain social and economic goals designed to reform much of the character of our national life.

It should be realized that the New Deal released a great charge of
social energy following a long period of repression brought on by the
depression. As Paul Conkin has expressed this: "The depression that
began in 1929 was a powerful catalyst in the modern American reaction
against the idea of individualism and against the well-established
institutions which gave that idea reality."[1] The philosophy of this new
spirit was voiced in a verse written many years before by Rexford G.
Tugwell as a sophomore at the University of Pennsylvania:

> I am sick of a nation's stenches,
> I am sick of propertied czars . . .
> I shall roll up my sleeves—
> Make America over.[2]

Tugwell still held these views when he became one of Franklin D.
Roosevelt's "Brain Trust" in 1932, and more than any other he was to give
expression and direction to the attempt within the New Deal to make
America over. When the Roosevelt administration took office on March 4,
1933, there was a widespread belief that social and economic change was
imperative. This attitude made possible the greatest period of institutional
experimentation this nation had ever known, and with it came a great
surge of interest in the cooperative form of business enterprise.

Much of this development was a reaction against an economic system that was held largely responsible for the nation's plight. It was not so much an extension of the existing cooperative movement as a new growth, based on the earlier communal philosophy of Robert Owen that cooperative institutions could change the character of man. Thus, it was a reversion to an earlier stage of cooperative development in America, buttressed by a belief that planning and social engineering could accomplish what had hitherto proved impossible. Much of this development was also an effort to alleviate suffering. Cooperatives responded to a deep human need for help on the pressing problems of personal survival by bringing people together for their mutual aid. During this period, cooperatives were as much concerned with temporary as with permanent ends.

It is of interest that the first manifestation of New Deal interest in cooperatives came as response to the needs of the self-help cooperative movement.

The Self-help Cooperative Movement

In the depth of the Great Depression, desperate unemployed workers began to join together to find ways to survive by exchanging goods and services. This was not something without precedent. In the hard times of the 1890's the same phenomena produced the same result in the formation of barter cooperatives, and such organizations had been formed by the followers of Robert Owen a century before. The first significant self-help cooperatives were formed in Seattle and Salt Lake City in the summer of 1931.[3] Almost immediately similar organizations sprang up in California and other states so that by early 1932 the movement was well lodged in most parts of the nation. By early 1933, several hundred self-help organizations were serving some half-million persons through some system of barter.[4]

When the Federal Emergency Relief Act was passed on May 12, 1933, the self-help cooperatives could not be ignored, and a modest provision was made for using them to provide assistance to those in need. Under this Act the Administrator was empowered to make grants "to aid in assisting cooperatives and self-help associations for the barter of goods and services." Soon afterwards a Division of Self-help Cooperatives was set up in the Federal Emergency Relief Administration to assist such associations by means of technical aid. With grants provided through the state relief administrations and with provision for advisory assistance, the self-help associations were able to improve their methods and extend their services. After the establishment of the Division of Subsistence Homesteads in the Department of Interior on August 23, 1933, an agreement was worked out between M. L. Wilson, Director of the Division of Subsistence Homesteads, and Jacob Baker, Assistant Administrator of the FERA, by which the Division of Self-help Cooperatives would also assist in the organization of cooperative activities for the subsistence homesteads projects. This arrangement was to prove very helpful in the development of cooperatives at the homestead projects.

The expansion of self-help associations was temporarily arrested by the massive Civil Works Administration relief program which was in effect from November 1933 to March 1934, as this diminished interest in self-help activities. When this program was terminated, interest in self-help cooperatives revived with a new administrative regulation which authorized small grants to permit these cooperatives to produce articles needed by their members. One well-informed observer, Joanna C. Colcord, called this "a momentous decision" in that it provided federal help to enable the unemployed "to create their own subsistence . . . " She went on to say: "A new relief era opens, and the cooperative self-help associations, as partners in the new plan, may hope to have their effectiveness vastly increased."[5] Supported by this broadened authority, the Division of Self-help Cooperatives greatly strengthened its program. Information was provided to enable self-help cooperatives to improve their methods. Management assistance was rendered, and an accounting manual was prepared to help them meet their bookkeeping problems.

During the next two years a great variety of self-help activities were assisted by FERA grants and by technical assistance from the Division of Self-help Cooperatives. Among them were:

> Dairying, butchering, poultry and rabbit raising, plumbing, fishing and fish processing, flour milling, logging and sawmilling, carpentry, house wrecking, graphic art work, dentistry, printing, bakeries, broom making, mattress and quilt making, furniture making and upholstery, crate making, coal mining, auto repairing, laundering, locksmithing, handicrafts such as weaving, wood carving and copperwork, making of soap and cosmetics, of cider, maple syrup, pickles, jams, shoe repairing, radio repairing, operating of barber shop, beauty shop, cafeteria, wood yard, garage, laundry, etc.[6]

It is not possible here to fully describe the self-help cooperative movement during the early New Deal years, but it was of no little importance. From 1933 to 1935, highly significant self-help cooperative organizations flourished in the areas around Los Angeles, San Francisco, Seattle, Salt Lake City, Denver, Minneapolis, Richmond, and in many localities throughout the nation—generally with the goodwill and encouragement of state and local civic bodies. These organizations can be given credit for enabling many people to come through the depression largely on their own combined efforts.[7]

A movement of this kind naturally attracted the interest of political, leaders, and, in California, where the self-help movement reached its highest development,[8] Upton Sinclair endeavored to take over the self-help cooperatives as part of his "EPIC" crusade to "end poverty in California," by espousing "production for use" by the state government. Although the California self-help cooperatives survived this campaign, it impaired their public acceptance.[9]

Although the self-help cooperative movement has now receded into the dimly lighted past, it was not a failure in terms of its commitment to help unemployed persons meet desperate depression conditions. Like many other New Deal experiments, it served the abnormal needs of the times and helped many people keep their self-respect during this period of national distress. Moreover, it had this permanent significance—it taught many thousands of persons some of the principles of cooperative enterprise, especially the importance of management. Many who became active leaders in the development of successful cooperatives in later days cut their cooperative eyeteeth as members or sponsors of self-help cooperatives. One of the most influential was Jerry Voorhis, later the President of the Cooperative League of the U.S.A.[10]

With a slight improvement in economic conditions and with a more comprehensive program of work relief under the Works Progress Administration, it became evident in 1935 that the self-help movement had largely run its course. Although the Division of Self-help Cooperatives continued to function into 1937, the number of self-help cooperatives gradually declined. However, there were still 140 associations of this type as late as January 1, 1939, and a number continued to function until economic conditions improved with the coming of World War II.[11]

The self-help cooperative movement was a spontaneous development which was given federal and state support. Now, let us turn to government relief programs that made use of cooperatives as a means of accomplishing their objectives, and evaluate this experience in the light of cooperative accomplishments.

The Subsistence Homesteads Experiment[12]

With the coming of the New Deal it was apparent that the subsistence homestead farm colony idea would be tried out in some form. For several years proposals of this type had been promoted by Elwood Mead, the leading authority on irrigation; Milburn L. Wilson, a well-known Montana agricultural economist; and a number of others.

After World War I, Mead had succeeded in getting state support for two experimental colonies in California which had not survived the postwar depression. He had interested many people in his projects, including Senator John H. Bankhead and his brother, Congressman William B. Bankhead, both of Alabama. In brief, Mead proposed a new kind of planned community land settlement based upon governmental, financial, and technical support. Under his scheme each "colonist" was to be carefully selected, and each would have an acreage for farming and a plot for subsistence gardening. The farm operations and related marketing and business activities were to be directed by trained agriculturists and to be carried on, to a large extent, cooperatively. The homes were to be grouped into communities of 50 to 100 colonists.[13]

Wilson's interest in the possibilities of subsistence homestead colonies combined with self-help cooperative activities grew out of his deep interest in better land use during the middle-twenties.[14] He was seeking a way through which farmers in the dry land sections of Montana and other arid states could successfully operate farm enterprises. Supported by the interest of Dr. Henry C. Taylor, Chief of the Bureau of Agricultural Economics, and of Henry C. Wallace, Secretary of Agriculture, Wilson in 1924 succeeded in getting underway, with the financial support of the Laura Spellman Rockefeller Fund, what became known as the Fairway Farms Project in Montana. The farms in the experiment were to be operated in a "fair way," and hence the name. Wilson's object was to determine the conditions under which large-scale farming could be profitably carried on with centralized management under the arid conditions of the Great Plains. A number of farms were purchased and operated under Wilson's supervision with the research cooperation of the Montana State Agricultural Experiment Station. Although drought and depression forced the closing of the experiment in 1928, it demonstrated that the plan was basically sound, and this experience was to have a profound influence on later land use programs of the New Deal. Far from discouraged, Wilson waited for a favorable opportunity to undertake a more comprehensive trial of his ideas.

As the depression deepened after 1929, Wilson became more than ever convinced of the merit of planned agricultural settlements along the lines of the Mormon villages of the West. In a talk to members of the American Society of Agricultural Engineering in 1932, he said:

> The most significant thing in American life today is the typical Mormon village . . . The blocks are not cut into lots. Each occupant, instead of living on a lot, lives on a town block of a little more than two acres. If industry could decentralize into, let us say, such widespread villages of not more than a hundred thousand population with the factory in the center and the people living in Mormon village style, one- and two-acre suburban blocks for fifteen

or twenty miles around, then we would bring back to industry security for the workers, and the opportunity for constructive use of leisure time . . . All these things are made possible because of the machine age, rural electrification, the Model A instead of the Model T, mass production, housing, etc. . . . As economists, we recognize no limits to the sweep of science . . . But we are coming more and more to think that the ultimate ends and objectives of life are to be found in philosophical, religious, esthetic, and ethical values.[15]

The back-to-the-farm movement of the depression years also impressed many of the need for a restructuring of rural life, and several prominent persons became ardent promoters of some kind of planned colony development. Among them were Bernarr Macfadden, the well-known physical culturist and publisher of *Liberty* magazine; Ralph Borsodi, author of *This Ugly Civilization* and exponent of better urban living conditions; and Hugh MacRae, wealthy engineer and businessman, who had already undertaken experiments in rural colonization in eastern North Carolina. Business leaders such as Henry Ford and J. C. Penney also looked favorably on the farm colony idea. Thus interest in subsistence homesteads was strong when Franklin D. Roosevelt took office in March 1933, and Roosevelt himself was intrigued by their possibilities. It is not surprising that almost immediately bills were introduced in the Senate and in the House by the Bankhead brothers to provide for federal financial assistance for subsistence homesteads. When they failed to gain support, administration forces, under the leadership of Senator Bankhead, gained a foothold by attaching a rider to the National Industrial Recovery Act passed in May. This apparently innocuous amendment, which went through Congress with little attention, paved the way for "one of the most interesting social experiments in American History."[16] This amendment, which became known as Section 208, read as follows:

> To provide for aiding in the redistribution of the overbalance of population in industrial centers $25,000,000 is hereby made available to the President, to be used by him through such agencies as he may establish and under such regulations as he may make, for making loans for and otherwise aiding in the purchase of subsistence homesteads. The moneys collected as repayment of said loans shall constitute a revolving fund to be administered as directed by the President for the purposes of this section.

Section 208 made no mention of planned colonies. It simply gave the President a blank check to work something out. Roosevelt thereupon delegated responsibility for administration to Secretary of Interior, Harold Ickes, by Executive Order 6200 (June 21, 1933), who, in turn, sought advice and guidance from various persons on how to get the program set up and underway.[17]

It was decided to develop the program under a separate division, headed by a Director, and, upon the recommendation of President

Roosevelt, Secretary Ickes appointed Wilson to this post and gave him a free hand to employ staff and get the program started. By August 23, the Division of Subsistence Homesteads under Wilson began to function with an initial staff that included Carl C. Taylor and Bruce Melvin, rural sociologists; Ernest Wiecking and W. A. Hartman, agricultural economists; Clarence Pickett of the Friends Service Committee; and Roy F. Hendrickson, a newspaperman from the Midwest.[18]

To assist Wilson on the new program its well-wishers set up a nonofficial national advisory committee which held its first meeting in September upon the call of Henry I. Harriman, President of the United States Chamber of Commerce. Among those present were Senator John H. Bankhead, who served as Chairman; Secretary Ickes; Rexford G. Tugwell; Bernarr Macfadden, the publisher; Hayden B. Harris, a prominent Chicago banker; Edward O'Neal, President of the American Farm Bureau Federation; L. J. Taber, Master of the National Grange; Philip V. Carden, Director of the Utah Agricultural Experiment Station; John D. Black, Harvard University Agricultural Economist; Louis Brownlow, Specialist in Public Administration; Ralph E. Flanders, a Vermont industrialist later to become Senator for Vermont; and William Green, President of the American Federation of Labor.[19]

From the beginning Wilson saw the program as experimental in character, and he welcomed projects of diverse types, although his deepest interest was in what he called "the community or Utah idea." Under this concept he envisaged "a new village life with handicrafts, community activities, closer relationships, and cooperative enterprises." He had great faith in the cooperative way of doing business, and, soon after he became Director of the Division of Subsistence Homesteads, he said: "Cooperation will be the basis of our future society if we are to maintain our individual freedom and not bow to the force of a dictator. *I believe that the subsistence homesteads community can well serve as a cradle for a new growth of the cooperative attitude*" (Italics added).[20]

The first loan for a homestead project was made in October to one promoted by Ralph Borsodi at Columbus, Ohio. Another, the Arthurdale Community Project, for stranded coal miners at Reedsville, West Virginia, soon followed. This project soon attracted national attention because of the great interest taken in it by Mrs. Eleanor Roosevelt.[21]

In November the Division of Subsistence Homesteads issued an information circular to explain the purposes and policies of the program. Stressing the experimental and demonstrational character of the program, a proposed typical community was delineated. It would contain from 25 to 100 families living on individual homesteads of from 1 to 5 acres to accommodate an orchard, vegetable garden, poultry, a pig, and, in some cases, a cow. Eventual ownership was promised. The community sites were to be approved by agricultural experts, and the homestead development was to be in accordance with approved planning and architectural and engineering practices. Houses were to be of moderate cost but in conformity with standards of convenience, durability, attractiveness, and sanitation, and essential utilities were to be provided. Funds were to be lent by a Federal Subsistence Corporation to local corporations set up for each homestead community.[22]

It had been apparent from the beginning that the business operations envisaged for the subsistence homesteads program could not be carried on directly by the Division of Subsistence Homesteads. Obviously, some form of government-owned corporation would be needed that could freely perform for the Division such functions as acquiring, holding, and disposing of title to land, buildings, and personal property on a community basis; entering into contracts; and bringing suit to enforce contracts.[23] In response to this need, the legal staff of the Division devised a plan for a Federal Government Corporation, with separate subsidiary corporations for each project. On December 2, Secretary Ickes set up the Federal Subsistence Homesteads Corporation under Delaware law, and on December 12, subsidiary local corporations were set up at several homestead projects. The Federal Corporation was simply to be the arm of the Division which could perform all of the planning, supervision, and administrative work required. The parent corporation would have complete control over the local subsidiary corporations which were to be the "operating vehicles" for each project. The local corporations, which would borrow the money needed, construct the communities, and issue purchase contracts to the homesteaders, were to be the foundation of Wilson's administrative organization.[24]

By the end of December four types of subsistence homestead projects were being developed. In a paper on "The Place of Subsistence Homesteads in Our Economy," presented at the annual meeting of the American Farm Economics Association in late December, Wilson outlined them as follows:

> First, Stranded industrial groups . . . Attempts will be made to give these homesteaders opportunity for part-time wage employment and to develop the rural-urban village type of community life.
>
> Second, Industrial decentralization and subsistence homestead communities. This involves moving out of a population center an industry and surrounding it by subsistence homesteads. A search is being made for private industries willing to cooperate in such experiments.
>
> Third, Workingmen's garden homes at the periphery of present centers of

employment which means building homes on plots of land of from one to five acres reasonably convenient to existing industry.

Fourth, Stranded agricultural population. Assisting families who are now on sub-marginal land to shift to communities on better land . . .[25]

In this paper Wilson also said: "The present subsistence homesteads movement . . . is not a sporadic outburst . . . The setting-up of a Division of Subsistence Homesteads in our Federal Government marks a national recognition of what agricultural economists in the past have called part-time farming, and city planners have called garden cities or garden suburbs . . . " (p. 75). He also warned: "The subsistence homestead community should not be over-sold as a panacea nor a Utopia . . . It should be approached by what Rex Tugwell called, several years ago, an experimental technique . . . " (p. 83).

At about this same time, a subsistence homestead was officially defined by the Division of Subsistence Homesteads as follows:

> A subsistence homestead denotes a house and out buildings located upon a plot of land on which can be grown a large portion of the foodstuffs required by the homestead family. It signifies production for home consumption and not for commercial sale. In that it provides for subsistence alone, it carries with it the corollary that cash income must be drawn from some outside source. The central motive of the subsistence homesteads program, therefore, is to demonstrate the economic value of a livelihood which combines part-time work and part-time gardening or farming.

Finding it difficult to attract the interest of industries in providing employment for the homesteaders, Wilson gradually found it desirable to place more emphasis upon "cooperative and community developments."

Even with all of the problems of getting the program started, the Division at the end of six months had approved more than 30 projects and the Federal Subsistence Homesteads Corporation had authorized loans of around $10 million to the local subsistence homesteads corporations. At this time the program was dealt a heavy blow by a ruling of the Comptroller General.

It had been assumed upon legal advice that the local corporations would not have to conform to the complicated accounting procedures required of regular government agencies. However, on March 15, a decision of the Comptroller General "required the same accounting procedures from the local corporations as from government agencies." This nullified one of the primary purposes of the corporate device and made it necessary for Wilson to place complete control over the local projects in the Federal Subsistence Homesteads Corporation, although it was possible to continue the local corporations as informal advisory bodies.[26] From the beginning Secretary Ickes had not liked the decentral-

ized administrative approaches of the Division of Subsistence Homesteads, which to Wilson were essential. When Ickes, on May 12, issued an
order that abolished all control by the local corporations so as to
"completely federalize" the program, Wilson felt compelled to resign, and
he returned to the Department of Agriculture as Assistant Secretary,
taking with him many of his close associates. With Wilson's resignation,
Ickes made Charles Pynchon, Director, but he soon became highly critical
of his administration of the program.[27]

Cooperative development under M. L. Wilson. During Wilson's 10-
month tenure he had accomplished much. Experimental colonies of
various types were either in operation or in the planning stage, and many
lessons had been learned that were later utilized in the program of the
Resettlement and Farm Security Administrations. Of particular interest to
this study was the encouragement given by Wilson to the cooperative
form of business enterprise. His views on cooperatives were reflected in
an article by his close associate, Roy Hendrickson, who was in charge of
informational activities for the Division. This article made clear that the
subsistence homesteads communities themselves were looked upon as
cooperative experiments and that to the extent possible the affairs of the
communities were to be carried on cooperatively. Hendrickson said:
"Application of the principle of self-help is the rule in the establishment
of subsistence homesteads." He pointed out that "the principle of self-help
is the outstanding characteristic," and he expressed the hope that "self-
help will have a place where it may thrive and grow in every community
established with the aid of funds available to the Division." Much of
Hendrickson's article was devoted to a description of how the subsistence
homestead community at Crossville, Tennessee, was being established
along cooperative lines. In concluding his article Hendrickson said:
"Establishing subsistence homesteads, building houses, requires group
enthusiasm, but much more too. It is a mature undertaking which calls for
the most careful planning, for patience, and for a sustained capacity to
cooperate . . ."[28]

Wilson, like others in the Division, was concerned with the cooperative over-enthusiasm that was a characteristic of early New Deal days.
The dangers of this euphoria were expressed by Dr. William E. Zeuck,
Specialist in Cooperation for the Division of Subsistence Homesteads, as
follows:

> Those who promote secular cooperative communities have been persons
> who combine in themselves social idealism and economic romanticism . . . As a
> result the plans of organization of cooperative communities are usually ideal
> plans for ideal people rather than practical plans for real people . . . Those

who wish to form cooperative communities should keep everlastingly in mind that the human materials they have to work with are persons who have been formed, molded, or conditioned from birth in a competitive, dog-eat-dog, everybody-for-himself and devil-take-the hindmost world . . . The transition from competitive behavior patterns to cooperative behavior is a hard, long, and harrowing transition . . .

Dr. Zeuck thought it doubtful that the transition to effective cooperative behavior could be achieved on a voluntary, democratic basis, and he urged delegation of a large measure of arbitrary power to able managers, although he was aware that he would be "damned" for this view by those to whom "democracy is a dogma." Although this was "strong medicine" for many of the Utopian theorists who advocated subsistence homesteads and cooperatives, generally for others rather than for themselves, it reflected a real problem. Few cooperatives on the subsistence homesteads projects survived for long without forceful and able management and sound membership training in sound cooperative procedures.[29]

While the subsistence homesteads program was getting underway a somewhat similar program was evolving in connection with the rural relief operations of the Federal Emergency Relief Administration. This program was to prove highly significant.

The FERA Farm Colonies

Under the Federal Emergency Relief Act, funds were made available to state governments to help the unemployed. In Texas the state relief administrator, Colonel Lawrence Westbrook, conceived the idea of using relief funds to set up planned colonies which could give employment to rural people and help them develop a satisfactory village community life.[30] Westbrook had been active in farm cooperative organizations, and he favored the widest possible use of cooperatives in the communities to be set up.

Under his plan there would be farms operated cooperatively, and each family would have its own 3-acre subsistence plot. Handicraft and processing industries were to be operated cooperatively. Plans for a community at Woodlake, Texas, were completed in January, and the construction of the homestead homes was soon begun by those who would occupy them. This project was to be a model for most of the later Federal Emergency Relief Administration communities. According to Conkin, "it had some of the characteristics of a European village with its outlying fields or of a Russian co-operative farm, with its individual subsistence plots and its collectively operated fields."[31]

Impressed by Westbrook's conception, energy, and leadership abilities, Harry L. Hopkins, Administrator of FERA, brought him to Washington, D.C., in the early spring of 1934 and gave him a free hand to promote his ideas nationally as Director of a newly formed Rural Rehabilitation and Stranded Populations Division. This gave Westbrook a limited opportunity to promote his colonization ideas in a number of states with the Woodlake community as a model. The FERA communities differed from the communities set up by the Division of Subsistence Homesteads in that they were developed primarily for farm people who were relief clients. Their most notable feature was the combination of village subsistence plots with large cooperative farms. Moreover, under the Federal Emergency Relief Act, Westbrook could develop decentralized local corporations to carry on the business work of each community, while Wilson was prohibited from using this kind of program for his subsistence homesteads communities. Further, Westbrook could center attention on forming communities suitable for agricultural conditions, while Wilson had to accommodate the divergent views of often competing interests. The FERA communities did not really represent a new idea, for they simply focussed efforts on the improvement of one form of homestead plan already being experimented with under Wilson.[32]

The FERA program developed rapidly. By summer the Woodlake community was completed and in operation. By January 1935, two more communities were largely completed and a dozen more were being planned.[33] In May 1935 when the FERA rural community program was taken over by the newly formed Resettlement Administration, there were plans for 25 rural industrial communities, although only a few had then been totally completed.

Forward with the Resettlement Administration

The community type projects started by the Subsistence Homesteads Division and the Federal Emergency Relief Administration were to be given a dose of adrenalin by Rexford G. Tugwell, as Administrator of a new agency—the Resettlement Administration. Under it, experimental programs using cooperative institutions were to reach their highest point in the New Deal.[34]

By the spring of 1935, Secretary Ickes wanted to free himself from the headaches of the subsistence homesteads program. At the same time the rural rehabilitation work of the FERA was being phased into the Federal Work Relief program of the new Works Projects Administration. What was to be done with the unfinished community programs? About the only important government officials deeply concerned with their success were Tugwell, who saw in them both a challenge and an opportunity, and President Roosevelt and Secretary Wallace, who concurred in their potential usefulness.[35] When the Resettlement Administration was set up by Presidential Executive Order on April 8, 1935, it was to be an independent agency that would bring together all complementary programs relating to land use, rural relief, and rehabilitation. According to Tugwell: "The idea for this agency was my own, and I was made its Administrator. President Roosevelt was, however, immediately interested because it touched matters he cared about a greal deal . . . It had logic because it brought together agencies complementary to each other . . ."[36]

Tugwell's appointment as Administrator was logical in that he was already Under Secretary of the Department of Agriculture. In this new position he would be able to give continuity to the land use work of the Department being transferred to the Resettlement Administration and would be able to tap resources of the Department. With the inherited agencies, Tugwell began with a sizeable responsibility, for operations were already being carried on actively in all parts of the nation.[37]

Tugwell came to his new post with great confidence and enthusiasm, for he believed that, through planning, a better society could be developed. In the words of Conkin, "Tugwell desired an organic society, with a unity of purpose, with a cooperative and collective economy, and with a purposeful, functioning government . . . Tugwell did not expect ideality to be just around the corner. He knew that planning implied a revolution, with new attitudes, new disciplines, revised legal structures, unaccustomed limitations on freedom, and an end of completely private business."[38]

It soon became apparent that the farm community ideas started by the Division of Subsistence Homesteads were to be prosecuted vigorously in the new agency and that many new additional experimental projects of this general type were to be undertaken. To effectuate these programs a Resettlement Division was set up under Dr. Carl C. Taylor, who had served as Wilson's right hand man in the Division of Subsistence Homesteads. The new community projects had one common characteristic—emphasis on agricultural operations. While some of the projects taken over had provided for operation of farms, the new projects made farm operations a major activity.

Cooperation in the rural communities. Cooperation was to be the keynote of the rural communities under the Resettlement Administration.

The attitude of Tugwell toward cooperatives has been well stated by Conkin:

> Tugwell believed that cooperatives could teach the fallacy of individualism and competition. He declared that cooperation was the easiest, most natural thing in the world. In the earliest days of the Resettlement Administration he secured the authority to make loans to cooperative associations as part of the rehabilitation program. Most of these loans, contrary to past government lending policies, went to producers' cooperatives, including many of the community projects. Tugwell deplored the almost entire emphasis in the past on consumers' cooperatives, declaring that, if the government credit agencies were "socially minded," producer cooperatives might arise. Tugwell advocated cooperation as a practical need and not as a religious crusade, as it almost had been under the Rochdale movement. He refused to subscribe to the dogmatic views of existing cooperative movements and rejoiced at being able to use government funds to break "large cracks in orthodoxy." Only on one point did the Resettlement Administration force conformity to orthodox cooperative theology. It required that all its cooperatives include in their by-laws a provision that each member should have only one vote.[39]

The community projects soon became laboratories for cooperative experimentation. "As soon as a community was completed," Conkin points out, "it usually went through a period of rapid cooperative organization, with an unbelievably large number of cooperative activities carried on at some projects. Many cooperative associations carried on ten or twelve different programs." Among the services, facilities, and activities organized on cooperative lines in the various communities were the following:

> . . . farms, pasture, dairies, wood lots, greenhouses, rock quarries, poultry enterprises, hog breeding, cattle breeding, lime crushing, canneries, barbershops, cobble shops, feed grinding, gristmills, handicraft industries, orchards, vineyards, factories, tearooms, inns, restaurants, hospitals, potato-drying houses, garages, filling stations, medical associations, blacksmith shops, warehouses, cane mills, farm equipment, cotton gins, coal mines, seed houses, hatcheries, sawmills, freezing plants, and even a burial association.[40]

Cooperatives for production. Prohibited from subsidizing private industries in the projects by rulings of the Comptroller General, the only alternative was establishment of cooperative industries as a means of bringing employment to the economically stranded communities. As Conkin has expressed this: "Although cooperation was desired as a substitute for individual enterprise, in many projects cooperative enterprises became almost entirely a matter of economic necessity rather than of ideological desirability."[41] The first major loan for this purpose, amounting to $550,000, was made for a cooperative at Cumberland Homesteads, Tennessee, in December 1936, to provide for the establishment of a sorghum plant, a cannery, and the operation of a coal mine. Similar loans were made to cooperatives operating in connection with the projects at Tygart Valley, Red House, and Arthurdale in West Virginia, and at Westmoreland, Pennsylvania. However, none of these loans provided for industrial enterprises which could give basic employment to the settlers. It was not until June 1937 that legal clearance was obtained so that loans could be made to cooperative associations for significant industrial purposes. The responsibility for getting such enterprises into effective operation was soon to be assumed by the Farm Security Administration, as will be discussed in the next section of this chapter.

The cooperative farms. Of all the rural community experiments, none attracted so much attention or opposition as the all-cooperative farms. The first, largest, and best known was started at Casa Grande, Arizona, in September 1936. This project was not planned as a cooperative farm, but those concerned gradually became convinced that more income could be derived from operating the property as one big farm. As Edward C. Banfield has said in his classic case study of the Casa Grande cooperative farm project: "The process by which the 80 forty-acre farms became a 5,000 acre cooperative was gradual and, as it seems in retrospect, ineluctable."[42] Banfield explains the origin of the cooperative farm projects in terms of economic determinism. While he admits that "there were some in government who had the itch to create a real, live Utopia," he maintains that "the values that were really decisive were of a much more practical kind: the cooperative farm was evolved as an expedient way of helping people who were destitute." He went on to say: "Tugwell had the projects on his hands . . . The only hope of making them work, it seemed to him, was to enlarge their land base sufficiently to give the settler an opportunity to produce for sale as well as for use. For this purpose group operation of the land seemed to him to be a 'sheer necessity' and it was for this reason, rather than because of any theoretical or ideological interest in cooperation or the cooperative movement that the cooperative form of organization was adopted."[43] How this and the other cooperative farms turned out will be examined in connection with the operations of the Farm Security Administration.

Greenbelt towns. Tugwell was not only interested in improving rural life but he also saw the need for suburban communities for displaced rural people. Many years later he plaintively recalled his disillusioning experience in trying to establish "greenbelt" towns.

> We had hoped to construct a good many of these projects. They were to be places where those who were being displaced from small-scale farming could go. They would show how good planning and decent building could supplant the crowded neighborhoods and jerry-built houses being offered by real estate speculators. We would surround each community with a green belt, and we

would provide the necessary community facilities for each group of homes. We came under such savage attack immediately that our plans for 60 projects had to be abandoned, and we were limited to three. These three were never really finished, and they were presently disposed of to speculators, too.[44]

The cooperative activites of the greenbelt towns—which are now being recognized as valuable "new town" experiments ahead of their time—will be explored later in this chapter.

Cooperatives for rural rehabilitation. The FERA had already begun a program of helping destitute farmers through loans and grants from its Rural Rehabilitation Division. This often involved giving aid to farmers through various kinds of cooperatives. Under the Resettlement Administration this program—broadened to include low-income farmers—steadily assumed greater importance. By January 1, 1937, when the Resettlement Administration was taken into the Department of Agriculture, it had become the most important part of its program.

The hallmark of the rural rehabilitation program under the Resettlement Administration was "supervised credit." This term came to imply that the employees of the Resettlement Administration would prescribe and supervise the use of credit to help borrowers farm more efficiently.[45] It soon became the practice under this program to make loans to enable low-income farmers to purchase cooperatively a purebred sire, tractor, combine, or other equipment which they could not afford to own individually. Cooperative purchasing and marketing associations were also encouraged by loans and grants.

Of particular interest in the rural rehabilitation program were the group medical care services. These were first organized on an experimental basis with government assistance in the form of loans, grants, and expert advice. This program was justified on the grounds that poor health and physical disability were contributing factors to economic failure. In January 1936, the Resettlement Administration set up a Public Health Section, headed by a medical officer to formulate and develop a broad program of public health care. "During the first year of experimental development, borrowers in eight counties were helped to organize medical care associations. Through these associations, borrowers could obtain medical care at a cost they could afford, prepaying annual fees into a pooled fund. Membership was voluntary and the members had free choice of physicians."[46] This pioneer program, which has been widely acclaimed as a great step forward in rural medical care, will be given more detailed attention as it was developed under the Farm Security Administration.

Under Tugwell the Resettlement Administration became a major government agency in Washington with some 13,000 employees. On the whole, a commendable job of administration was done but Tugwell was under continuous attack as a "whipping boy" for the New Deal. By the summer of 1936 it was apparent to him that the work of the Resettlement Administration was being handicapped by his connection with it. He became convinced that if the program were under the wing of the Department of Agriculture it would not come under so much attack, and he began to urge Wallace to accept it for the Department. Wallace held back, for he was not sure that the type of program represented by the Resettlement Administration should properly be in the Department. However, in November, after Wallace had been named Chairman of a Special Commitee on Farm Tenancy set up by President Roosevelt, on the recommendation of Tugwell with instructions to submit by February 1 "a long term program for action to alleviate the short-comings of our farm tenancy system," he was persuaded by Tugwell to examine for himself what the Resettlement Administration was doing in the South. This trip had a profound effect on Wallace, for up to then he had little conception of the seriousness of the rural poverty program, nor of how well the Resettlement Administration was working on it.[47] Almost immediately after this trip Wallace took steps to bring the Resettlement Administration into the Department, and on December 31, 1936, Tugwell resigned, and his deputy, Will W. Alexander, took over as Administrator.[48]

The Resettlement Administration under the U.S.D.A. There was little change in the program of the Resettlement Administration following its transference to the Department, although work was soon centered on the completion of construction on community projects already underway. In February the Special Committee on Farm Tenancy made its report. This highly significant document recognized the value of much of the work being done by the Resettlement Administration but its principal recommendation was the inauguration of a tenant purchase program under which the government would buy land to be sold to disadvantaged farm families under long-term contracts at low interest rates.[49] The Bankhead-Jones Farm Tenant Act, designed to improve the farm tenancy situation along the lines recommended by the Special Committee, became law on July 22, 1937.

This new development gave Wallace an opportunity to reorganize the Resettlement Administration so as to provide for administration of the tenant purchase program under a more apt name, the Farm Security Administration,[50] and, on September 1, 1937, the Resettlement Administration became the Farm Security Administration. The community projects and the rural rehabilitation programs were continued although the land use program was retransferred to the Bureau of Agricultural Economics in the Department of Agriculture. The main new work to be undertaken had to do with the implementation of the Bankhead-Jones Act. No basic change was made in administration—with Will Alexander continuing in charge as Administrator.

The new Farm Security Administration thus brought together all programs for disadvantaged farmers and was a more functionally cohesive and better coordinated body than the old Resettlement Administration.

Cooperative Intensification Under the FSA

The Farm Security Administration did not turn its back on cooperatives. In fact, it intensified and amplified its work with them, both in the farm and urban communities and in its rural rehabilitation program. Let us look at each separately.

The community projects. When the FSA took over from the Resettlement Administration there were 38 community-type projects with construction completed, while there were 84 with construction uncompleted. There were then 4,444 families in residence. During the next two years most of the uncompleted projects were to be finished, increasing the total population to over 1,000 but no new projects were to be started.[51] By 1939 the main job with the communities had become one of financing and management. As Paul Conkin has said: "Although the community program was in an eclipse, heading toward completion rather than expansion, the all important task of managing the completed communities had only well begun."[52]

In general the community projects under the FSA made use of cooperatives along the lines already developed by the Resettlement Administration, and a great deal of effort was expended by FSA employees in a generally unsuccessful attempt to create effective cooperatives. Although an endeavor was made to get them operating on their own feet as responsible organizations, it was not possible to avoid a high degree of paternalism. In many communities the members looked upon the FSA officials as the bosses and accepted their direction as a matter of course and necessity rather than from inner conviction. There was little new experimentation with cooperatives by FSA. Past methods were continued but not radically changed.

Although Tugwell and his followers attributed the final collapse of the planned communities to a hostile local and national environment, the real cause of their decline was economic. They were unable to establish themselves as going concerns—even with heavy subsidization and a plethora of advisory and technical assistance. Primarily their failure was due to the artificiality of the communities which depended upon subsidy for survival. In general, they suffered from a lack of confidence in the future of the communities, a continuous turnover of settlers, and from frequent changes in FSA supervisory personnel and policies, as well as from the general weaknesses that caused cooperative failure: lack of a stake in the success of the enterprise; bureaucratic procedures; lack of membership education; over-expectations due to over-promising; poor management or over-management; inexperience in cooperative procedures, etc.[53]

The foregoing comments apply especially to the general types of cooperatives—cooperative stores, marketing and purchasing associations, etc.—that were common to most of the communities. Two general types of resettlement project cooperatives deserve special mention: (1) the cooperatives set up for industrial production and (2) the cooperative farming communities.

The industrial cooperatives. As just noted, the Resettlement Administration was just getting underway a program of financing cooperative industrial plants when it turned over the reins to the Farm Security Administration. Among the industrial plants constructed under this program was a tractor assembly plant at Arthurdale, West Virginia, which was managed by an organization set up by a group of four regional purchasing associations under the name, American Cooperatives, Inc.[54] Other plants of this type were a wood dimension mill at Tygart Valley; a pants factory at Westmoreland; and five hosiery mills at Cumberland Homesteads, Tygart Valley Homesteads, Penderlea Homesteads in North Carolina, and Bankhead Farms and Skyline Farms in Alabama. In all of these cases the loans were made to cooperative associations for buildings, equipment, and working capital. Except at Arthurdale, the cooperatives worked out managerial agreements with private industrial concerns for plant operation. However, since the FSA was the financing agent it was in reality the major party to such arrangements.

During the next few years the FSA worked hard with its cooperative representatives to get these industrial properties into profitable operation, but without success. The causes for failure were many: lack of initial planning, weak management, extravagance, inexperienced personnel, poor plant location, etc. The most that could be said for this experience was that it temporarily afforded "a degree of economic security" for the occupants of the projects.[55]

The cooperative farms. In general, the farms in the communities were operated as individual farms but, in some cases, farming was carried on cooperatively. In three instances the entire community was operated as a cooperative farm. In view of the widespread and adverse publicity given to these rather unique experiments in cooperative organization and procedure, it is essential that we examine them in some detail.

It will be recalled that the idea of the cooperative farm evolved under Tugwell in the days of the Resettlement Administration. The first and largest project of this kind at Casa Grande, Arizona, was just getting underway when it was taken over by the Farm Security Administration. During the next several years it went through a stormy existence which has been dramatically described in *Government Project* by Edward C. Banfield.[56] Technically, the Casa Grande farm was organized as a cooperative by settlers recruited for the project, who became the members. Banfield has well described how this was done. "In June 1937, when the preliminary farm plan was complete and ready to be sent to Washington, four farm laborers were hastily recruited, and with a Resettlement Official to serve temporarily as Secretary-Treasurer, Casa Grande Valley Farms was incorporated under the laws of Arizona."

This was necessary since the cooperative had to have a legal existence before it could receive an operating loan or even apply for one. After incorporation "the incorporators passed a motion accepting a set of by-laws prepared by the FSA and elected themselves as members, then empowered their treasurer to obtain a Resettlement loan of $173,288. By this legal play-acting the cooperative was brought into existence and enabled to engage in the production and marketing of agricultural produce . . . "[57]

The entire farming operation was carried on as one big farm under a superintendent supplied by the Farm Security Administration—although he was ostensibly the employee of the cooperative. The members were paid wages, with the understanding that net income after payment of all costs would be returned to them on the basis of their respective work contributions. Although the project survived for several years with heavy infusions of government capital and a great amount of governmental assistance provided by economists and home economists, agronomists, accountants, cooperative specialists, personnel workers, psychologists, and social workers, it never succeeded in becoming an organization strong enough to stand on its own feet. After examining the evidence, Banfield concluded that constructive and gifted "leadership was decisively lacking at Casa Grande." He expressed the interesting thought that "if Casa Grande had been called a 'Government poor farm' instead of a 'cooperative' the situation would have developed in such a way as to greatly reduce its inherent stress. The word 'cooperative' introduced a whole complex of freedoms and accompanying uncertainties . . ." He concluded his analysis by saying: "We should make use of existing institutions and organizational forms wherever possible and should expect to make progress by changing these old structures rather than by inventing new ones." This was in accord with the view of many experienced workers in the field of cooperative enterprise, that progress can only be made by the use of knowledge developed from past experience.

The unhappy experience of the Casa Grande Cooperative Farm was largely duplicated by the ones at Lake Dick, Arkansas, and the one at Terrelbonne, Louisiana.[58]

The cooperatives in the greenbelt cities. It will be recalled that three garden city type projects known as greenbelt towns were also established by the Resettlement Administration. The cooperative experience at these towns can be well mentioned here. All of the three greenbelt cities—completed by the Farm Security Administration—provided for retail shopping centers. As the cities were being constructed, the Consumer Distribution Corporation (founded with a grant from Edward A. Filene in 1936 to further consumers' cooperation) leased the commercial centers and had stores ready for operation when the residents arrived. "The externally financed cooperative service was to operate the stores only until the citizens could establish their own consumers' cooperative." In 1940 the local cooperative at Greenbelt, Maryland, was independently organized, and it became a nucleus for what has become the largest concentrated development of consumers' cooperation in the nation. In retrospect, this arrangement which enabled the citizens to work out their own cooperative destiny appears to have been wise.[59]

Although the FSA continued to sponsor and assist cooperatives in connection with the community projects, few came up to expectations. By 1941 even FSA officials had lost confidence in them. Robert Hudgens, Assistant Administrator of the FSA, made no reference to this type of cooperative in his talk on FSA cooperative programs at the American Institute of Cooperation in January 1942.[60] By this time the whole community project idea was in disarray, and it had become of minor importance in the total program of the FSA. This is evidenced by a book prepared by the FSA for training personnel in 1941—*Toward Farm Security*—for there was no reference to communities. In 1942 the critical appraisal of the subsistence homesteads projects by Lord and Johnstone found that they had generally failed to live up to hopes. The whole flavor of this study was negative. It was really a report on a disappointing experiment, and there were few general suggestions for its resurrection.[61]

Cooperatives in the rural rehabilitation program. Although cooperatives played generally a declining role in the community projects, as the latter came under political attack they became more and more important in the FSA's rural rehabilitation program. Here a variety of cooperative programs were carried on, which may be grouped into four categories: (1) informal group cooperative activities; (2) cooperatives for economic services, such as marketing and purchasing associations; (3) medical care associations; and (4) land leasing cooperatives.[62]

Informal group cooperatives. The encouragement of farmers to work together in informal groups began during the early days of the Resettlement Administration after "a substantial caseload of standard borrowers had been built up," making it practical for the rural rehabilitation program to encourage group action among low-income farmers.

The objective was to correct a main weakness of the small family-farm operator by getting several of them to join together in purchasing necessary farm machinery or purebred livestock that none of them could afford to buy individually. According to James Maddox, "the group service enterprises were nothing more than informal, unincorporated groups of two or more farmers who entered into an agreement to use jointly, farm machinery, purebred sires, trucks, or similar capital items and who made arrangements to acquire and operate such facilities by pooling their resources." As Maddox has pointed out, the sharing of the use of heavy farm equipment was an old custom among farmers, and joint ownership as well as joint use of such items as threshing machines had been a common practice in many areas for decades.

The Farm Security Administration encouraged two general types of group-service enterprise: (1) "master borrower" and (2) "joint ownership." Under the first, there was individual ownership and joint use. A loan would be made to an individual who would purchase the needed capital goods and then make them available to other farmers on agreed upon terms. In the second type, there was joint ownership and joint use. Under this plan, loans were made of equal amounts to the participants so that they each could buy an equal share in the facility. For example, a group of 10 farmers might desire to purchase a purebred sire costing $300. A contribution of $30 would be needed from each participant, and individual loans of $30 would be made to those requiring financial aid. The participants would choose a manager and work out service fees and other necessary arrangements.

This program grew rapidly. From its start in 1935, under the Resettlement Administration, to June 30, 1939, there were 5,079 group services developed. The number grew by 4,857 in fiscal year 1939; by 4,835, the following year; and by 6,795, in fiscal year 1941. A special survey made as of June 30, 1942, indicated that of the 17,015 group services then active, slightly over half were of the master-borrower type, and that well over 90 per cent were designed for the purchase of machinery or sire service.[63] As of this date there were 191,517 farmers participating in such services, and of these only 70,886, or 37 per cent, were borrowers from the Farm Security Administration. These group service arrangements were then operating in every state with the greatest concentration in Utah, where Mormon farmers had long worked together.

On the whole, this program of group services was highly successful. In addressing the American Institute of Cooperation at Atlanta, Georgia, in January 1942, Robert ("Pete") Hudgens, Assistant Administrator of the Farm Security Administration, pointed out that the group services had proved to many farmers that "group action makes possible achievements which are beyond reach of the man who works alone."[64]

Cooperatives for economic services. Wherever possible the Farm Security Administration promoted the utilization of cooperatives to serve those who received FSA rehabilitation loans. It did this by four different methods: (1) by means of direct loans and grants to cooperatives who served FSA farmers; (2) by making loans to individual farmers to permit them to purchase a membership equity in an association that would serve their needs; (3) by using a combination of (1) and (2), i.e. by making a direct loan to an association, plus loans to individual farmers to purchase stock in an association; and (4) by making what were called service loans. Here a part of the individual rehabilitation loans were pooled into an association account for the purchase of goods or services. For example, small amounts from each individual's loan were combined, and a joint purchase was made for supplies or services which were then allocated to each borrower.

Through these various methods some 2,000 cooperative associations had been financed in connection with the rehabilitation loan program up to the beginning of World War I. Of these, the most common type was the local purchasing and marketing association, for there was a "specially designed" effort on the part of FSA to encourage all "standard borrowers" to buy their supplies through such cooperatives. These were generally organized on a county-wide basis. Next in importance were cooperative grain elevators. Many loans were made to help such associations which had been hard hit by drought and depression. Of special importance was a program worked out in collaboration with two large regional grain marketing cooperatives—the Farmers' Union Grain Terminal Association, St. Paul, and the West Central Grain Company of Omaha—under which loans, grants, and technical assistance were given to groups of FSA clients to help them restore to operation 177 local grain cooperatives. This was one of FSA's most successful achievements in helping cooperatives, and it was warmly appreciated by the two regional cooperatives and their member associations.[65] Other cooperatives were assisted in the marketing of fruits and vegetables and other products, and cooperatives were formed to provide veterinary, water supply, and other essential service. The veterinary services, patterned on the health associations to be described later, were of much importance, particularly in areas where such services were difficult to obtain and otherwise expensive. Another group service of great value in certain areas provided insurance on workstock. Here a group of farmers paid fees to provide for such service on a group insurance basis.

In most areas the cooperatives were set up as local or county associations. In only a few southern states—Mississippi, Alabama, Louisiana, and Arkansas—were overhead federations set up. These were fairly satisfactory but never developed great strength.

In making loans to cooperatives certain criteria were followed: (1) Control had to rest in the membership on the basis of one vote for each member. (2) Proxy voting was not permitted. (3) Local associations were required to follow a policy of selling goods and services only for cash. (4) There was no restriction on admission. However, membership was usually confined to rehabilitation members. (5) Savings were paid to members in the form of patronage refunds. (6) No loans were made to an association if it could obtain loan service from a Bank for Cooperatives or other lending agency.

Medical care associations. We have already indicated how cooperative medical care services originated under the program of the Resettlement Administration. This program was to be carried much further by the Farm Security Administration. As Maddox has pointed out: "Attention was centered upon devising techniques by which families . . . could be assured of a minimum amount of the kind of medical services available within the local areas where they lived and worked . . . The method of approach was to organize families into local groups for the purpose of pooling funds and entering into agreements with members of the medical profession so as to be assured of certain medical services . . . The promotion, financing and supervision of these groups was the single most important aspect of the health program. It was in effect, an experiment in voluntary health insurance among low-income farm families."[66]

According to Maddox "the really significant feature of the group approach was that the payment for medical services was put on a planned and organized basis." Services varied but "in connection with every medical care unit there was an annual prepayment of a uniform, base fee on the part of each member-family, and an agreement on the part of the participating members of the medical profession to render specified services at rates agreed upon in advance."

Most of the medical care units were set up on a county basis. There were two common forms of group health organization: (1) the trusteeship and (2) the health association. In the first, there was no definite organization of FSA borrowers as members. They simply signed participation agreements in what was a governmentally operated program. Of more importance from a cooperative standpoint were the health associations which were ordinarily informal, unincorporated cooperatives. These had boards of directors and officers chosen by the members, and the members often assumed important management responsibilities. The funds of the associations, arising from the annual membership fees, were administered either by a treasurer or by a trustee approved by the board of directors. The medical care associations were, in effect, "a specialized type of farmer cooperative" in that they were similar to local purchasing and marketing associations in form of organization. The program was carried forward by the FSA through a headquarters staff of laymen, physicians, and dentists under the direction of the Chief Medical Officer, but the responsibility for promulgating the development among FSA borrowers fell on the operating divisions and, particularly, on the regional, state, district, and county FSA personnel.

In time, certain principles of operation were developed: (1) borrowers were not to be compelled to participate in order to receive FSA loans; (2) family participation fees were to be paid in advance on an annual basis with all families paying the same base amount for agreed upon services; (3) each participating family was to be free to choose any physician or dentist signed up on the program; and (4) monthly or quarterly bills, submitted to the associations for medical services rendered to members, were to be reviewed by a local committee of members, before being submitted to the treasurer for payment.

It early became evident that the goodwill and cooperation of the organized medical profession was essential for the success of the program. This led to the adoption of a basic policy that FSA employees would not attempt to organize medical care groups in a state until an agreement could be reached with the State Medical Association. This policy was deemed essential for two reasons. First, it gained the cooperation of local physicians and dentists, and, second, it protected the program from criticism within the medical profession. With the endorsement of the State Medical Association, local cooperation was then obtained by explaining the program to the local physicians and dentists who would be involved. Generally, they were willing to participate after they understood how the plan would work to assure them of prompt payment for their services. Significantly, over two-thirds of the practicing physicians and dentists participated in the areas where medical groups were organized.[67]

The program grew rapidly. In 1937 there were but 142 counties in the program. By 1939 the number had grown to 402, and by 1941 it reached 888. In this year there were 103,679 families participating in the program in practically all of the states.

There is no question but that the medical care program of the Farm Security Administration was a significant accomplishment in bringing better health care to American rural communities. It did much to popularize the idea of group health cooperatives and prepaid medical service. Unfortunately, this program lapsed with the collapse of the cooperative programs of the Farm Security Administration during the war years and it was never re-established.

The land leasing associations. The report of the President's Special Committee on Farm Tenancy recognized the possibility of improving tenure conditions by the use of cooperative land leasing associations. The first use of this idea was made during the winter of 1938-1939 when T. Roy Reid, then Director of the Farm Security Administration, Region VI (Arkansas, Louisiana, and Mississippi), undertook to make loans to cooperative associations of tenants and sharecroppers so that they could lease entire plantations on which they resided. This plan was tried out successfully by 17 associations with 827 member families. Fourteen more associations were started in 1940, giving a total membership of 1,699 families, of whom 949 were Negro and 750 white. From then on they were an important part of the FSA's rural rehabilitation program.

This program arose because the FSA's general program of aiding individual farm tenant borrowers by helping them to obtain good leases from their landlords was not applicable to the plantations of the South. Where the plantation was the important operating unit it was usually under the close direction of the owner or a manager, and it often had among its enterprises a cotton gin or commissary, as well as pasture and feed crop land, all of which were operated as integral parts of the total plantation. Under this form of agriculture, there was a heavy concentration of low-income farmers "shackled to the plantation system, with its stultifying social institutions and caste-like relations between the operator and the tenants, sharecroppers, and laborers." It was to meet the needs and problems of the plantation areas that the land-leasing association approach to the tenure problem was invented.[68]

Land leasing associations were cooperatives which leased land, usually plantations, from private owners and subleased individual tracts to their members. The land leasing associations sometimes operated cotton gins, commissaries, grist mills, tractors, and large-scale farming equipment. Thus, in effect, the cooperative took over the job of the plantation operator. "On the one hand, they were the exclusive stockholders of a cooperatively-owned corporation which leased privately owned land for sub-lease to its stockholders, and which also often operated other enterprises supplementary to its main function of leasing and sub-leasing land. On the other hand, they were the tenants, sharecroppers or laborers of the corporation they owned."

The land leasing associations were largely organized and operated by FSA employees. The personnel of the FSA assumed the task of finding owners who were willing to lease their plantations as a total unit, and the charter and by-laws of the cooperatives were usually drawn in the FSA regional office. Members consisted of the tenants, croppers, and laborers on the plantation who subscribed $1 each for a share of non-par stock and elected a board of directors. Individual leases to members were drawn for periods of 5 to 10 years. The loan agreement between each association and the FSA provided that the manager and bookkeeper would be FSA employees or, if employed by the association, would be under the direction of the FSA. Thus for all practical purposes the staff were FSA employees, even if the salaries of some of them were often paid by the association. As members could know relatively little about the organization of which they were members until well after it was launched, one of the important functions of the manager was development of an understanding among the members of their interests and responsibilities. As a consequence, it was often the second or third year before the members began to participate effectively. During this time, however, there were regular monthly meetings of the boards of directors in which management policies were reviewed and problems discussed.

While the land leasing associations were admittedly government controlled and operated, no other method could have functioned so effectively in meeting the tenancy problem on the plantations. Without the guarantee of the government the plantation owners would not have cooperated. Moreover, the members realized that the FSA could not loan them funds without taking steps to ensure that the plan would work. The government thus became a guardian for the associations until such time as they might develop managerial capacity to operate independently. From a pragmatic point of view the cooperative method worked and gave satisfaction both to the landlords who leased their lands to the associations and to the tenant families who became members. We will never know how the program might have developed over a period of years had it not been terminated in 1943 by governmental restrictions placed on the FSA's cooperative activities. However, James Maddox who was administratively close to this program considers that the leasing association "was quite an acceptable and promising new institution . . . One of the tragedies of the experiment was that its life was cut short before any comprehensive and detailed studies were made of the operations of the associations, and the relation of the member-families to their cooperatives . . . The available evidence indicates that the families thus served made as good, if not better, progress than the borrowers in areas of scattered farms . . ."[69]

What Was Learned

In the early days of the New Deal, men like Rex Tugwell, M. L. Wilson, Harry Hopkins, H. A. Wallace, and Franklin D. Roosevelt looked upon their efforts to create new institutions to meet the great economic and social stress that then prevailed as experimental in character, and this is the best way to evaluate them. Many new ideas were tried, and some panned out, while others were disastrous failures.

In these experiments much faith was placed in cooperatives, and many novel cooperative concepts were used. Taking a broad view, the record does not throw any discredit on the cooperative form of enterprise. Their success should be measured in terms of the difficulties that were confronted rather than in the framework of more normal conditions. While cooperative approaches did not succeed in accomplishing the impossible, they did help meet many of the problems of a sick society.

If there was any one thing that the cooperatives set up for relief purposes proved, it was that there are no short cuts to cooperative success. It was found that such organizations cannot be devised almost spontaneously by government fiat and then be expected to succeed. They can grow only out of the experience of people in using them, not by forced measures. The experience of most of the relief-type cooperatives generally confirmed the principles that cooperatives must be able to meet an economic need and that those who are served must have an interest and a voice in their management. For example, it is significant that the local cooperatives, developed in connection with the rural rehabilitation program of the Farm Security Administration, proved to be the most successful. Here, there were definite groups of cooperators who could be organized for their own welfare. On the other hand, the ambitious attempts to arbitrarily create cooperative farms even with large amounts of government funds were dismal failures.

It is questioned whether it is proper to consider the "cooperative farms" set up by the Resettlement Administration and the Farm Security Administration as true cooperatives. They were not formed by farmers who joined together to operate farms in common. Rather, they were organized and operated by government officials on a so-called cooperative pattern because the term "cooperative" seemed to have wide appeal, and a cooperative legal structure could be made use of for the ends sought. Thus, they were cooperative in name only. Those who joined the projects came into a nominal cooperative framework but they came as tenants or laborers, generally without land, capital, or skills to contribute. They were more like government farms, and this idea was voiced by Banfield who used the term *Government Project* as the title for his book on the Casa Grande cooperative farm project.

One of the things that is apparent in reviewing the experience of the cooperatives formed for relief purposes was the fact that most of those, who were, or became, involved, were amateurs in cooperative effort. They came into this field with great enthusiasm and high idealism but with little knowledge of how cooperatives work. If there had been more acceptance and study of tested cooperative principles, much more could have been accomplished.

Was there any useful residue from this experience? Indeed there was. Many of the mistakes made by these cooperatives have not been repeated in subsequent years, although there are many who still optimistically ignore the failures of the past. Moreover, many lessons from this period have been put to use in government programs designed to help develop cooperatives in under-developed countries or in disadvantaged areas of this country. It should also be noted that through their work and contacts with cooperatives set up for relief purposes, many glimpsed the possibilities of such organizations when soundly set up and properly managed. In the years since the New Deal we have had stronger cooperatives arising from the ashes of this experience.

Chapter XVI

COOPERATIVES IN THE TVA: 1934-1940

The establishment of the Tennessee Valley Authority by Act of Congress on May 18, 1933, was destined to have a considerable effect on the development of cooperative enterprise in the United States. Under the TVA Act, the Government for the first time embarked on a significant experiment in regional economic and social planning. The measure enabled cooperative forms of organization to play a role of vital significance in accomplishing the overall objectives of the TVA, as this chapter will make clear.

The TVA Act climaxed a development that began late in 1917 when President Wilson, under the National Defense Act of 1916, "designated Muscle Shoals as the site for nitrate plant development, and authorized the construction of a gigantic dam there to supply power for the plants."[1] Two nitrate plants were constructed at a total cost of $82 million but neither of the plants was completed in time to meet World War I needs. After a test run in 1919, Plant No. 2 was maintained on a standby status. The dam included in the project, later named the Wilson Dam, was not completed until September 1925. Its completed cost was $47 million.

In the early postwar period no agreement could be reached on what to do with this property. One group comprised largely of agricultural organizations strongly favored government operation of the nitrate plants for fertilizer production and research. Another group which represented industrial interests was adamantly opposed to this idea and urged disposal of the plants to private industry.[2]

In March 1921 the government invited proposals from private concerns for acquisition of the nitrate plants but received no offers. When the government then advertised for bids on the property, Henry Ford responded with his famous offer in which he agreed to pay $5 million for the two nitrate plants for use in the production of nitrogen and other fertilizer mixtures at a profit not to exceed 8 per cent. He also agreed to complete the Wilson Dam for the government at cost in return for a lease of the dams and power plant for a period of 100 years. This offer was received with favor from farmers in the South and Midwest who felt that it would provide them with cheap fertilizer. However, it met with much resistance from power and fertilizer interests, and from those who believed that the government should not turn over this great natural resource to any private concern. Although the Ford proposal finally got a House majority in March 1924, it was defeated in the Senate, largely due to the efforts of Senator George W. Norris, Chairman of the Senate Committee on Agriculture and Forestry. He believed that it would be indefensible to turn over the Muscle Shoals properties to a private firm.

Norris then intensified his campaign for government operation of the Muscle Shoals properties and facilities.[3] Twice he succeeded in getting both houses of Congress to agree on a bill, in 1928 and 1931, but the bills were vetoed by Presidents Coolidge and Hoover as incursions of government into the field of private enterprise. In the course of this long controversy, the Muscle Shoals issue increasingly became a contest between private and public power advocates, although Norris and his supporters maintained that government operation of Muscle Shoals would provide for "the unified development of the Tennessee River." This broad concept covered flood control, conservation of natural resources, cheapening of fertilizer costs, encouragement of rural electrification, and similar objectives.

The collapse of the Samuel Insull holding company empire in the spring of 1932 and the disarray of the private utility companies which followed strengthened public support for Norris's views on Muscle Shoals legislation. During the presidential campaign later in the year it was clear that Roosevelt was favorable to legislation of this type.

The TVA Idea

It was Franklin D. Roosevelt who lifted the thinking with regard to the disposition of Muscle Shoals into the realm of a great economic and social experiment. After visiting the Tennessee Valley area with Senator George Norris, in January 1933, before he took office, the President-elect saw what could be accomplished and gave the vision of Norris a new dimension. Following this trip someone asked Norris, "Is he really with you?" Norris replied with satisfaction: "He is more than with me, because he plans to go even farther than I did."[4]

In one of his first messages to Congress after he took office, on April 10, 1933, President Roosevelt called for the creation of the Tennessee

Valley Authority—"A corporation clothed with the power of government but possessed of the flexibility and initiative of private enterprise. It should be charged with the development of the natural resources of the Tennessee Valley drainage basin and its adjacent territory for the general social and economic welfare of the nation."

Three days later Roosevelt called in Dr. Arthur E. Morgan, President of Antioch College and a nationally known engineer, to determine whether he had the drive, capacity, outlook, and imagination to give leadership to the about-to-be-established Tennessee Valley Authority. He found in Morgan "an engineer with a social conscience"—just the man he desired—and within an hour he had asked him to serve as Chairman of the Board of Directors for the TVA when formed. From then on Morgan helped with plans for the new agency and assisted in the drafting of the nearly completed TVA bill.[5]

In outlining his views on how the proposed TVA could raise the social and economic well-being in the Tennessee Valley, Roosevelt asked Morgan:

> Is it possible, especially down in this region, where people never have had adequate incomes, is it possible for us to develop small industries, where people can produce what they use, and where they can use what they produce, and where, without dislocating the industry of America, we can absorb a lot of this unemployment, and give the population a sound footing on which it can live, possibly with restricted standards, but still live soundly and in a self-supporting way until we can work our way into a new economy.[6]

From the time of this first meeting with Roosevelt, Dr. Morgan "saw the TVA primarily as a grand experiment in regional development. To him the key concept was to be social and economic planning not only for the Tennessee Valley but for the nation, and the TVA was to go wherever this concern might lead it, and serve as a laboratory for building a new social and economic order."[7] The TVA was to be not primarily "a dam-building job, a fertilizer job or power-transmission job . . . " It was to be an experiment in social reconstruction: "the improvement of . . . total well-being, in physical, social and economic conditions . . . "[8] The TVA was to be Arthur Morgan's "trumpet call for a reawakening of the American spirit, not that aberration known as rugged individualism where selfish traits seemed to foster survival, but the spirit of cooperation, of experimentation, of pragmatism, the antithesis of 'enlightened selfishness.' " Morgan has been well compared with Woodrow Wilson, in that he was a man "committed totally to an ideal. He wanted the best for the Valley, but like a good old fashioned parent, he expected as a matter of course to guide the growing child."[9]

While the TVA legislation was taking shape, Morgan helped get the

TVA into motion by making preliminary studies of properties, arranging for an initial staff of engineers and other essential personnel, and by working out arrangements for cooperation with federal agencies having an interest or activities in the Tennessee Valley states. With the consent of Roosevelt he also conducted a search for two other directors suitable for the TVA. On the basis of his investigations, he recommended the appointments of both Dr. Harcourt A. Morgan and David E. Lilienthal. Both were the obvious men for selection.[10]

Under the terms of the Tennessee Valley Authority Act (48 Stat. 58), passed by Congress on May 18, Herman Pritchett has pointed out:

> A corporation was created which was directed to take over the Muscle Shoals properties, to utilize the nitrate plants in a commercial or experimental fertilizer program, and to dispose of the surplus power generated at Wilson Dam over the Corporation's own transmission lines. These two provisions were largely lifted from previous bills. But, in order to give effect to the expanded role which the President had indicated the Authority should assume, two new provisions were added, first, the corporation was authorized to construct dams, powerhouses, and navigation projects on the Tennessee River and its tributaries. Second, two "planning" sections were included to furnish the basis for a program of regional planning and development: they authorized the President to make surveys of and general plans for the Tennessee basin which might be useful in guiding and controlling its development through the expenditure of public funds or the guidance of public authority, with the general aim or "fostering an orderly and proper physical, economic, and social development" of the area.

Pritchett went on to say that there was little congressional interest in or comprehension of these new powers given the authority. "From the statutory point of view, the Tennessee Valley Authority was merely the Muscle Shoals Corporation of previous years, with some additional ill-defined powers and functions."[11]

The TVA Directors

With the passage of the Act, Roosevelt made known his selection of Dr. Arthur E. Morgan as Chairman of the Board of Directors, and shortly afterwards the appointments of Dr. Harcourt A. Morgan and David E. Lilienthal were announced. In view of the influence these men had on cooperative development within the TVA, it is important to know something of their backgrounds and interests.

Arthur E. Morgan, born at St. Cloud, Minnesota, was 55 years of age in 1933. He was then President of Antioch College and also President of the Dayton Morgan Engineering Company. His career was the saga of a man who had raised himself by his own bootstraps. As a youth with poor health he had worked on farms, cut cordwood, dug coal, and gathered much experience in Colorado and other places. With only a few weeks of college training, he followed his father into the field of surveying and at the age of 22 started out on his own. From then on he rapidly established himself as a leading engineer in the growing field of land reclamation.

When the Miami Conservancy (Ohio) was set up following the great flood at Dayton, Ohio, in 1913, Morgan was named Chief Engineer. His outstanding work on this project gave him a national and international reputation. This experience was important, for it demonstrated his ability to direct a major undertaking such as that envisaged for the Tennessee Valley Authority. Moreover, the methods and arrangements employed in dam construction for the Ohio Conservancy District could be applied in the construction of the TVA dams.

Morgan's humanitarian instincts gave him a deep interest in education and social reform. This had led to his becoming President of Antioch College in Yellow Springs, Ohio, in 1920. Here he inaugurated a novel experiment in college education through an arrangement made with business and industrial firms so that students could alternate periods of work in the classroom with periods of employment in business and industry. While President of Antioch, Morgan had continued direction of the Dayton Morgan Engineering Company which gave him close association with industrial affairs. Through his speeches and "Antioch Notes" he was broadly known as an advanced thinker when Roosevelt asked him to become Chairman of the nascent Tennessee Valley Authority.[12]

Harcourt A. Morgan, the second to be appointed Director of the TVA, was a Canadian by birth and no relation to Arthur E. Morgan. Following graduation from the Ontario Agricultural College in 1889, he became, at the age of 22, Professor of Entomology and Entomologist for the Agricultural Experiment Station, Louisiana State University. In 1893 he was made Head of the Department of Zoology and Entomology in the university. During the next few years as a state and federal employee he gained a national reputation in the campaign for tick eradication and control of the boll weevil, and in 1905 he was appointed Director of the Tennessee Agricultural Experiment Station. His exceptional work in that position led to his appointment as Dean of the College of Agriculture at the University of Tennessee in 1913.

From this post he was named President of the University of Tennessee in 1919. During his long career at the University, Morgan, more than any other, helped build it into a modern educational institution. By 1933 he had become widely known throughout the South and nation for his agricultural and educational leadership. Significantly, in 1913, he was a member of the American Commission to Study Rural Credit and Cooperation in Europe, and in 1927 he served as President of the Association of Land Grant Colleges and Universities. His broad interests had made him a strong advocate of the decentralization of industry and the better balancing of agricultural and industrial development.

Dr. H. A. Morgan's appointment gave recognition to the South where the TVA was to operate, and none doubted his high qualifications—personally, professionally, or politically. As Mougan Peters, his biographer later reported: "He made the TVA safe for Tennessee and Tennessee safe for TVA." No one had a better grasp of what the TVA could mean to the Tennessee Valley area and the nation. In fact, he had been plugging for its objectives for many years, and, to a great extent, he had influenced the conception of the TVA as a broad attack on the social and economic problems of the area.[13] While others in the South had been advocates of Henry Ford's plan to acquire the Muscle Shoals plant to provide cheap fertilizer for the South, he had opposed the program on the grounds that this property should be developed as a public resource. One acute observer, James Rorty, in later assessing Morgan's contributions to the TVA in an article for *Commonwealth*, in 1948, referred to Morgan as an "ecologist-statesman." He went on to say: "there are indeed very few practitioners of Morgan's science in America or in the world, human ecology being a new and difficult discipline. Morgan spent most of his adult years in preparing himself for it."[14]

David E. Lilienthal was only 34 when he became the third director of TVA. Following his graduation from DePauw University in Indiana—where he had made something of a reputation for himself as a leader and speaker, as attested by his election as president of the student body—he had entered the Harvard Law School. Here he soon attracted the interest and friendship of Felix Frankfurter, the Dean of the school. Following graduation he worked for the law firm of Donald Richberg in Chicago, but after a few years he struck out on his own as a lawyer in public utility matters.

In 1931, Governor Phillip La Follotte appointed him to the Wisconsin Public Utilities Commission where his abilities as an advocate of the public interest soon attracted national attention. He was highly recommended for appointment to the TVA Board by Frankfurter, Justice Brandeis, and Donald Richberg, as a man who was not only exceptionally well qualified and ambitious but one "with the right point of view." President Roosevelt in considering potential members for the Board of Directors with Senator George Norris, in the early spring of 1933, is reported to have said: "If we could get Lilienthal it would be a ten strike."[15]

Both Harcourt A. Morgan and David E. Lilienthal were men of high character with strong convictions and great leadership capacities. No one could expect them to rubber stamp the views of the Chairman, although they were in substantial agreement with him on the importance of the TVA as an agency for economic and social progress. They soon developed a close affinity for each other, almost the relationshp of father and son.[16] Both were practical idealists with a strong Jeffersonian bias toward decentralized government who believed that government should respond to the needs and wishes of people rather than control them in any paternalistic way. Although appreciative of Dr. Arthur Morgan's recognized abilities as an engineer, they could not fully accept his somewhat authoritarian conception of economic and social planning.

The TVA Gets Under Way

The TVA Board of Directors held its first meeting on June 16, 1933, at the Willard Hotel in Washington, D.C. Dr. Arthur Morgan was already at work on TVA problems, and the Board gave him temporary authority to act as General Manager. Moreover, President Roosevelt had named him Chief Engineer for the Authority on June 7. Thus, at the outset, Chairman Morgan was the dominant figure in getting the TVA into action, and his thinking on social and economic matters permeated the organization during its initial months.

While Arthur Morgan proceeded to make plans for the construction of Norris Dam, authorized by the Board of Directors at its first meeting, Dr. Harcourt Morgan and Lilienthal were forced to take time to get their personal affairs settled. It was late July before they were able to devote full time to TVA matters. In the intervening seven weeks, Chairman Morgan was in effect the TVA. He made decisions with regard to the construction of Norris Dam, answered correspondence, selected personnel, dealt with other government agencies, and did anything that he thought was necessary.

During this interval, Chairman Morgan took a great interest in the subsistence farm program. Secretary Harold Ickes reports how he found Dr. Morgan on July 12, 1933, "presenting a complete plan to the President, including the personnel" for a subsistence farming division.[17]

When H. A. Morgan and Lilienthal reported back for active service they were little prepared for the "expansive program" envisaged by the Chairman in a memorandum dated July 30. He proposed "a total integrated and planned development of all power sites on the Tennessee River system; a plant for making Portland cement and dry ice at Muscle Shoals; a sweeping forestry program; steady development of a general socio-economic plan for the Authority; and the development of cooperative distribution of the products of local industry." To H. A. Morgan and Lilienthal, many of the proposals seemed "impracticable" and "highly visionary" and they decided that "Morgan's authority and catholic interests must be limited."[18] They, therefore, prepared a counter-memorandum of August 3, under which each director would be given primary responsibility for certain phases of the TVA's program. In essence, each director was to act in two capacities—"as one of the three members of a policy forming board, and as the administrative head of one segment of the total TVA program."[19]

Confronted by majority opposition, Chairman Morgan accepted this proposal which allocated responsibilities in the following way: He would be responsible for the general engineering program; the educational and training program (except for agriculture); land use and regional planning and subsistence homesteads; matters relating to social and economic organization and planning; forestry, soil erosion, and Civilian Conservation Corps relationships; and matters concerning raw materials for fertilizer. Chairman Morgan was to share with Harcourt Morgan responsibility for industry and encouragement of cooperatives. He was also given the special task, as Chairman, of "integration of the parts of the program into a unified whole, including the administration of the general functions, such as accounting." Under the plan, Harcourt A. Morgan became responsible for supervision of all matters relating to agriculture, including rural life planning and rural organizational industries; the entire chemical engineering program, involving not only fertilizer research and production but also research and development in the manufacturing of cement and dry ice; and public relations in east Tennessee and adjoining areas. David Lilienthal's responsibilities would include all matters pertaining to the power program, supervision of the legal department, the land acquisition program, and the economics of transportation.[20]

This three-fold allocation of responsibilities among the directors had a direct effect on the development of cooperatives within the TVA system. It soon became evident that Chairman Arthur Morgan was primarily interested in the broad social aspects of cooperatives, while Harcourt Morgan and David Lilienthal were more interested in them as business mechanisms to carry out agricultural and electric power responsibilities. The personalities and approaches of the three directors are apparent in the way the cooperative programs of the TVA developed during its formative years.

Cooperatives for Social and Economic Improvement

To Chairman Morgan, the key to a new social and economic order was cooperative organization. In a National Broadcasting Company radio address, on August 15, 1933, he called for "the encouragement of cooperatives and the rejuvenation of small businesses."[21] Morgan had a vision of how the Tennessee Valley region might be developed to serve as an example of what could be done by people working together with the help of their government. However, while he had a strong bias in favor of cooperative organizations, his actual experience with their operations was limited. He idealized them in terms of how he thought they should work, or could be made to work, and, like Robert Owen a century earlier, he visualized cooperative communities where people of mutual goodwill would live and work together happily. The subsistence homestead idea which was then enjoying widespread support greatly appealed to him, and he hoped to employ the idea to the extent possible in the Tennessee Valley region.

Speaking at the University of Tennessee on November 9, 1933, Morgan reflected on the possibility of a region setting up its own local economy. Letting his imagination go, he launched into a description of such an economy. First, he would create a cooperative system. He would have "a central purchasing organization, a central sales organization, and a central distributing organization." He even went so far as to say: "I think I'd have that cooperative organization have its own tokens of credit—a sort of local money" under which each person producing for home consumption would be paid at least in part in the money of the cooperative.[22] This speech, given extemporaneously but taken down by a stenographer, was later to be used against Morgan as evidence of his wild schemes.[23] However, when this talk was made, barter methods were widespread because of the breakdown of the monetary system, and many ideas were abroad in the land that later were to seem fantastic. In fact, in the winter of 1933, Morgan had introduced a barter scheme at Antioch College under which college professors were paid half in cash and half in scrip.[24] In fairness, Morgan's statements should be looked upon more as an expression of his outlook and vision than as a definite program. He was endeavoring to get people to think about their problems and ways of solving them.

The construction of the dam at Norris gave Chairman Morgan an opportunity to try out his cooperative ideas. It should be realized that the most urgent job facing the newly organized TVA was to start the dam building job, and all recognized that Arthur Morgan was the ideal person to direct this project. With the consent of the other directors to build the dam, which Morgan soon named the Norris Dam, he brought in a staff of engineers and took over the initial work already started by the Army Corps of Engineers. Following the precedent of his Miami Conservancy experience, he made plans for a camp to house the work force.[25] Morgan proposed not an ordinary workers camp, but one that would continue as a town after the work of dam construction was completed, and the other directors rather reluctantly went along with his plans. The construction of Norris, the name given to the new town, was begun in the early fall with plans developed by a landscape architect. The houses were built on a well-planned, low-cost basis with plots for subsistence farming and many were completely electrified.[26]

The development of the town of Norris gave Arthur Morgan an opportunity to try out his ideas. He conceived of it as a model community in which most of the activities would be done cooperatively. Norris was also planned to be a cooperative training center for employee improvement throughout the TVA system. Many TVA officials took residence there as it was only 20 miles from Knoxville—the headquarters for the TVA. One year later (October 1934) in an address to the Technical Club of Madison, Wisconsin, Arthur Morgan reported on the cooperative progress made:

> The employees [living in Norris] have a cooperative bank, cooperative laundry, cooperative shoe repair and clothes pressing service, and will soon have a cooperative dairy, a cooperative store, a cooperative chicken raising plant, and other cooperative efforts. Training in cooperative management will prepare them for leadership in a great cooperative movement to get those millions of mountain people, now so largely unemployed and rusting away, to produce the things they need for themselves.[27]

Although this was a somewhat glowing account of actual accomplishments, it reflected the sanguine cooperative thinking of Arthur Morgan at this time. In fact, the cooperatives formed or planned for Norris were not able to establish themselves, and within a few years Norris became known as a "company town," largely managed by and for TVA employees.[28]

Enthusiasm for cooperatives was the "in thing" in the TVA during 1934 and 1935, and it attracted much national attention. After describing TVA cooperative plans and activities underway, an unsigned article, "Cooperation in the Tennessee Valley," in the March-April 1934 issue of *The Cooperative Marketing Journal* concluded: "Altogether the program is one which cooperators should watch with interest." Many employees, especially in the TVA's industry division, were then imbued with the belief that a new economy based on the principles of cooperation was being forged in the Tennessee Valley.[29] During this period cooperatives were assisted through studies made by the Industry Division[30] and by technical assistance provided through the Tennessee Valley Associated Cooperatives, an organization which will be presently described.

TVA's interest in cooperatives during 1935 was reflected by two articles in *Consumers' Cooperation*, written by Dr. James P. Warbasse, the President of the Cooperative League, and Dr. Arthur Morgan's friend, after visits that he made to the Tennessee Valley as a consultant for the TVA. Dr. Warbasse was greatly impressed with the cooperatives then being developed at Norris and other points and the cooperative progress being made under the Tennessee Valley Associated Cooperatives. He found a "consumer consciousness" slowly "penetrating" the Tennessee Valley which "may spread throughout the country," and he reported that the TVA was "hastening the organization of all forms of consumers cooperation."[31]

In view of the importance of the Tennessee Valley Associated Cooperatives in the first phase of TVA's support of cooperatives, it is here discussed in some detail.

The Tennessee Valley Associated Cooperatives, Inc.

Although the TVA had no direct authority to promote cooperative organizations, it did have a mandate to improve the social and economic conditions in the Tennnessee Valley. Recognizing that cooperative organizations could assist in the realization of this objective, the TVA, under Chairman Morgan's leadership, proceeded to obtain a grant of funds from the Federal Emergency Relief Administration for use of a cooperative promotional and financing organization, the Tennessee Valley Associated Cooperatives, Inc., which was incorporated on January 25, 1934, under the laws of Tennessee.[32] The TVAC, Inc., was authorized by its Articles of Incorporation "to promote, organize, establish, manage, finance, coordinate and assist in any way in the development of cooperative enterprises in the Tennessee Valley."

While the TVAC, Inc., was not part of the TVA it was closely related in that the three directors of the TVA were its incorporating directors, with Arthur Morgan as Chairman. The capital stock of TVAC, Inc., consisted of 100 shares of common no-par value, which were subscribed for by the TVA directors in behalf of the United States. The Administrator of TVAC, Inc., was Arthur Jackson, a friend of A. E. Morgan. He and his assistants and their expenses were paid by the TVA and charged to "regional development." Such administrative expenses, during the three years this arrangement continued, amounted to about $90,000 per annum.[33] As Pritchett has pointed out "the relationship of the TVAC to the TVA was rather anomalous. The fiction of a distinction between the two agencies was maintained" so that the TVAC "was in the happy position of having no administrative expenses."[34] To finance its operations, the TVAC received on March 12, 1934, an outright grant of $300,000 from the Federal Emergency Relief Administration, through the Governor of Tennessee. No funds were ever advanced outright to the TVAC, Inc., through Congressional appropriations for the TVA.

The affairs of the TVAC were managed by the Administrator, pursuant to directives of the Board of Directors.[35] Any loans made by it were to be authorized by the directors, and any repayments of loans were to be used to make new loans so that its funds would be revolved. Terms were to be based upon projected needs, and interest rates were to be at a minimum. Because the program was "more or less a relief" measure, the amount of the loans was determined more by the needs of the borrowing cooperatives than by appraisals of their soundness. To qualify for loans, cooperatives had to be set up under the cooperative laws of the state in which they were located, and officers and members were required to be producers. Loans had to be justified on the grounds that they would relieve distress among farmers. To facilitate this program, the TVA entered into an agreement with TVAC, Inc., to provide certain services of an advisory character. Under the arrangement, the Authority would receive data and other information based upon the experience gained from the cooperatives.

One of the earliest efforts of the TVAC, Inc., carried on during the spring and summer of 1934, was to help organize, with the cooperation of the state extension services, four cooperative cannery associations in western North Carolina and eastern Tennessee. Many of those who were expected to benefit from the program were on relief and had no funds to assist in financing these enterprises. After the cooperatives were formed, they were granted financial assistance by TVAC, Inc. The 500 mountain farmers who became cannery members generally had little or no experience with cooperatives and had little or no knowledge of producing commodities for canning. They were unfamiliar with grading standards and inspection methods. Although the prospects were not favorable from the standpoint of producing conditions, the cooperatives did at least succeed in establishing themselves.

After the first year, the cannery cooperatives and the TVAC, Inc., agreed that it would be desirable to organize a regional cooperative of the federated type to perform marketing and other services. This resulted in the formation of the Land O' the Sky Mutual Association, on March 15

1935, with headquarters at Waynesville, N.C. This regional cooperative entered into a contract with TVA on July 1, 1935, for studies, demonstrations, and experiments relating to the problems of agricultural cooperative organization and operation; the production and preparation of farm products for market; and the development of improved systems of purchasing, merchandising, and accounting. Under the contract then developed between Land O' the Sky and its member associations, all produce was to be graded according to U.S.D.A. standards and was to be marketed either fresh or processed. Separate grower contracts were used for products to be sold fresh and those to be canned. The commodities handled included blackberries, huckleberries, beans, turnip greens, spinach, beets, tomatoes, okra, and rhubarb. On the whole, the Land O' the Sky Mutual Association was well managed and conscientiously administered. Failure to catch hold immediately was due more to the unfavorable location of the canneries and the independent characteristics of the mountaineer members than to lack of finance or poor management. During World War II this association was to operate quite successfully.

In 1935, TVAC, Inc., also helped set up a cooperative milling company at Newport, Tennessee, and a dairy cooperative at Brasstown, North Carolina, both of which survived for a number of years. In addition to its support of the canneries and other marketing cooperatives, the TVAC also promoted a number of craft cooperatives. Of most importance was the Southern Highlanders, Inc., of Norris, Tennessee, which was formed in May 1935 to aid and assist handicraft producers in techniques of production and in improved methods of merchandising their products. Its general objective was to contribute to the general improvement of the economic and social status of persons engaged in the production of handicraft products in the southern Appalachian region. To promote this venture, TVAC, Inc., purchased preferred stock and agreed to provide advisory assistance. On July 1, 1935, Southern Highlanders also contracted with TVA for the conduct of a joint program of study, experimentation, and demonstrations. In November 1935, a sales outlet was obtained in Rockefeller Center, New York City, which insured successful operations.

By 1936 it had become clear that the cooperatives sponsored by the TVAC were of minor importance compared with those growing out of the TVA's electricity and fertilizer programs. In this year, J. Ed Campbell, an employee of the TVA, replaced Arthur Jackson as Administrator of TVAC, and after study of its operations Campbell recommended that the TVA disassociate itself from the TVAC and undertake a more general research and education program for agricultural cooperatives.[36] In 1937, with a general reorganization of the TVA, the relationship with the TVAC was discontinued and TVA shifted its interests to a more general cooperative development program. Soon afterwards H. A. Morgan and David Lilienthal resigned as board members of TVAC, although Arthur Morgan, who was no longer a director of the TVA, continued for several years as a member of the TVAC board.[37] With the withdrawal of TVA from the TVAC John E. Barr, the manager of the Land O' Sky Mutual Association, became the TVAC administrator.[38]

Let us now examine how cooperatives arose and flourished in connection with the TVA's electricity program.

The Development of Electric Cooperatives

In the early days of the TVA the overriding problem was the development of a policy for the distribution of electricity to be generated at the dams and power plants to be operated by the TVA. Section 10 of the TVA act stipulated that the TVA would give preference in the sale of power "to states, counties, municipalities and cooperative organizations of citizens or farmers not organized or doing business for profit, but primarily for the purpose of supplying electricity to its own citizens or members." The act (48 stat. 64) provided further, "That the board is hereby authorized and directed to make studies, experiments, and determinations to promote the wider or better use of electric power for agricultural and domestic use, and for small or local industries, and it may cooperate with State governments, or their subdivisions or agencies, with educational and research institutions, and with cooperatives or other organizations, in the application of electric power to the fuller and better balanced development of the resources of the region."

In light of these instructions, the directors of TVA lost little time in developing a power policy which was announced on August 25, 1933. It contained the following provisions:

(3) The interest of the public in the widest use of power is superior to any private interest.
(5) The right of a community to own and operate its own electric plant is undeniable. This is one of the measures which the people may properly take to protect themselves against unreasonable rates.
(9) Every effort will be made by the Authority to avoid the construction of duplicate facilities, or wasteful competitive practices. Accordingly, where existing lines of privately owned utilities are required to accomplish the Authorities objectives, . . . a genuine effort will be made to purchase such facilities from the private utilities on an equitable basis.[39]

In accordance with this policy declaration, Lilienthal proceeded to negotiate arrangements with the Commonwealth and Southern Corporation, the Alabama Power Company, and the Mississippi Power Company for the acquisition of their power transmission systems being operated in Tennessee Valley states. While these arrangements for the control of power were being negotiated, in the fall of 1933 Lilienthal also gave his attention to the problems of retail power distribution to farmers and other consumers. He was particularly aware of the intent of Congress, as expressed in the authorization given by section 10 of the TVA Act: "to promote and encourage the fullest possible use of electric light and power on farms." Before coming to the TVA, Lilienthal had become conscious of the farmers' difficulties in getting electric service. On this matter he has said:

> When I was a Commissioner on the Public Service Commission of Wisconsin (1931-1933); even in that rich farming state there was hardly a farm with electricity. As a Commissioner I found there was nothing we could do to change that practice, as the utilities insisted that there was "no market," and that the cost of rural lines and service made rural electricity impossible. If that were true in affluent Dane County, Wisconsin, for example, what chance would farmers in poorish Northern Mississippi have? It was with that frustration in my innards that in 1933 I went on to TVA and its electricity program.[40]

The TVA gave Lilienthal an opportunity to correct this situation and being a pragmatist he believed in using anything that would work. The problem was to determine how electricity could best be distributed to farmers and consumers. It soon became obvious to him that the cooperative form of organization might well meet this need. Moreover, at this time, Lilienthal was being greatly impressed by the "grass-roots" thinking of Dr. Harcourt A. Morgan, who held that people would respond to and support programs in their interest when given an opportunity to participate in their development.[41]

Formation of Alcorn County Electric Power Association. While Lilienthal and his staff were examining this problem, an opportunity to try out the cooperative approach arose at Corinth, the county seat of Alcorn County, Mississippi, which was then being supplied with power by the Mississippi Power Company. With the expiration of its contract for power from the Wilson Dam, TVA would become the wholesale source of power for the Corinth distributing system, then owned by the Mississippi Power Company. It would then be possible to set up a cooperative association to acquire the Corinth system which was then confining its service largely to the city of Corinth.

It was evident to Lilienthal that the cost of distributing facilities at Corinth could be repaid by a cooperative organization using TVA power in a very few years, "so profitable was the electricity business if properly run." Moreover, he realized that "if the city were to include the farmers of the entire county, the operation would still be profitable and viable—though repayment of the debt for the city part of the plant would be somewhat slower. By combining city and county in a single cooperative, here might be one answer to the economic and business problem of providing electricity to all (or virtually all) farmers of that typical southern county."[42]

There was then in Corinth, a favorable community sentiment for working with the TVA in developing an organization of this type; so with this situation in mind, Lilienthal, assisted by Joseph E. Swidler[43] of the TVA's legal staff, worked out general plans for a cooperative association that would serve the needs of both rural and urban consumers of Alcorn County. Lilienthal presented the plan to a meeting of businessmen and farmers in the back of a furniture store in Corinth, on December 6, 1933.

This meeting became a landmark in the history of rural electrification, for The Alcorn County Electric Power Association which grew out of it was to serve as the pathfinder for other TVA electric cooperatives and for the rural electric cooperatives later sponsored by the Rural Electrification Administration.[44] Although the charter of this association was granted on January 17, 1934, the organization could not begin to function until June 1, 1934, when the TVA could take legal possession of the distributing system of the Mississippi Power Company that then served the city of Corinth. In the interim period, plans were perfected for the organization, by-laws were written, and a power contract was developed by TVA attorneys stipulating procedures to be followed. During this interval, the association built up its membership and arranged for management so that it would be ready to go when power from TVA became available.

While the Alcorn association was taking shape, Lilienthal was also giving attention to the establishment of another organization that was to play an instrumental role in the success of Alcorn County Electric Power Association and other associations of this type. Before continuing with the story of how the TVA electrical cooperatives were developed, this important organization and its work will be briefly described.

The electric home and farm authority. From the beginning Lilienthal realized that cheap power produced and distributed by TVA would not in itself be enough to make a success of TVA's electric power program. There were too many other factors holding back consumption of power which was the end sought if the operation were to be efficient. For one thing, the cost of electrical appliances was generally prohibitive. To meet this problem, TVA electrical engineers were set to work to develop low cost equipment that could be standardized and sold at much lower prices.

While this would be of great value, there was another difficult problem. Many consumers were not in position to buy appliances during the depressed conditions that then prevailed without more generous credit terms from retail suppliers. Appreciating this problem, Lilienthal conceived the idea of a government financing agency that would enable appliance dealers to rediscount at low interest cost the notes of customers given for appliance purchases. The genesis of this organization, which became the Electric Home and Farm Authority, has been set forth by Lilienthal as follows:

> I spawned this enterprise as a response to my initial negotiations with Wendell Wilkie (President of Commonwealth and Southern Corporation), contrary to the press hullaballoo, in the outset of TVA's relations with the utilities. I was looking for a basis of agreement at the time the first properties were sold to TVA in the agreement he and I reached in early January 1934. "Load building" was one area of agreement; EHFA was my version of how to make this a reality. EHFA did in fact break the atmosphere among credit companies and utilities that "there is no market for major appliances" in the Tennessee Valley.[45]

The Electric Home and Farm Authority (or "Little Eva" to Lilienthal) was an ingenious corporate device to adapt the methods of installment buying to the needs of electricity.[46] It was created by an Executive Order 6514 of President Roosevelt on December 19, 1933, with "the powers and functions of a mortgage-loan company and with provision for a capitalization of $1 million. Following the Order, the EHFA, Inc., was incorporated under the laws of Delaware on January 17, 1934, with headquarters at Chattanooga. In the beginning, the services of EHFA were to be confined to the area served by the TVA and were to be made available to public and private utility companies, cooperative electric associations, and merchants handling electrical appliances.[47] The three directors of the TVA were to be the three directors of the EHFA, with Lilienthal as President.

Aware of the potential importance of EHFA to the total success of TVA's power program, Lilienthal personally recruited as Manager, George D. Munger, a man who had gained national recognition for his work in promoting the use of electricity with a public utility company in New York State. With information developed by TVA electrical engineers, Munger proceeded to negotiate agreements with appliance manufacturers to produce according to EHFA specifications an electric range, a refrigerator, and a water heater which would retail at prices far below normal levels.[48] The EHFA then entered into agreements with the distributors of TVA power—cooperatives, municipals, and the large private power companies—in the area under which they would purchase conditional sales contracts—covering approved appliances by approved dealers—which were, in turn, to be purchased by EHFA. The electric users were to be billed for their appliance purchases on their monthly bills for electricity.

When the EHFA program was put into effect in May 1934, appliance financing plans in the area and throughout the South were highly inadequate. At that time according to Munger: "Private finance companies charged exorbitant rates, offered short periods of time over which an appliance could be financed, and were very restrictive in the dealers whom they would service. Most farmers and residents in small towns could not get the benefits of any organized financing plan, and they had to pay cash or get a loan from the local bank." He then went on to say: "EHFA met this situation by offering financing costs which were greatly reduced over those normally in effect (its interest rate was 6% on receding balances); by sharply increasing the period over which payments could be spread; and by being more liberal in the selection of dealers whose paper could be purchased. Thus the service was made available to all users of electricity."[49]

The operation of the EHFA proved to be almost a spontaneous success, as evidenced by a spectacular expansion in appliance sales and increased consumer use of electricity throughout the Valley states. Thus when the Alcorn Electric Power Company began operations on June 1, 1934, it had available the effective services of the EHFA to help it get off to a good start.

Alcorn County shows the way. The Alcorn County Electric Power Association began active distribution of power on June 1, 1934. On that date the TVA acquired from the Mississippi Power Company the distribution system serving Corinth, and the TVA, in turn, sold this property to the newly formed association. The purchase price was $115,000, payable to the TVA from revenues of the association.

The association was set up as a non-profit organization conducted for the benefit of its members.[50] Each member was limited to one vote in the affairs of the association, regardless of stock owned or purchases made, and votes could not be cast by proxy. Capital contributed in the form of membership fees or otherwise was to be paid interest only and would not otherwise participate in the savings. Membership was open to all persons, firms, municipalities, associations, etc., having property to be served electrically. The membership fee was set at $100, which could be paid in full at the time of application with a reduction of 20 per cent, or members could make a down payment of $10 or some other sum and make small monthly payments until the membership fee was fully paid.

The association was authorized to engage in the buying and selling of electrical equipment, and in the wiring of houses, farms, etc., although in the beginning the association limited its activity to the distribution of electrical energy. Appliance sales were handled by local dealers who cooperated closely with the association in the maintenance of displays and in other promotional activities. An arrangement was made for dealers approved by the Electric Home and Farm Authority to sell appliances financed by that agency with the association acting for the Authority in collecting and forwarding the monthly amortised payments.

Government of the association was placed in a board of five "managers" (directors), who, in turn, appointed a superintendent to carry on the day-to-day operations. The Board was selected for three-year terms, with some to be elected each year, at the annual meeting of members. In view of the fact that the TVA provided all of the financing, it protected its investment by entering into a 20-year contract with the association under which it provided wholesale power. Under the contract the association also agreed to TVA approval of retail rates, and the latter was given access to association books at all times. The TVA prescribed the accounting records and was to provide required accounting and technical services. The Authority also was to have approval of all employed personnel. Thus the association was devised to be closely related and responsible to the TVA.

Joseph Swidler, who supervised the preparation of the original documents of organization and power contracts for the Alcorn County and like TVA early associations, said that there was little experience to draw on in drafting the organization documents for the Alcorn Association, although available information on the few small electric cooperatives then in existence was examined. He writes: "The Alcorn County cooperative was organized under a general Mississippi law which had been on the books for some time . . . *The key document was not so much the law or the charter as the power contract with TVA, which specified rate levels, rate adjustment procedures, and the disposition of the proceeds from operations.* It is noteworthy that none of the cooperatives in the Tennessee Valley area were organized on Rochdale principles; that is, they did not charge prevailing rates, and were not required to set up ownership accounts for the individual members or to pay patronage dividends. They were organized rather on the basis of using all of their resources to keep rates as low as possible. I believe this feature has had a favorable effect on their growth and stability" (Italics added).[51]

L. Carlton Salter, a close observer of the early progress made by these associations, holds that the sentence just italicized needs further emphasis "because here is the key to both cooperative and municipal successful operations. All income over costs was required to be plowed back into the business to improve service or lower rates charged for electricity. No revenue receipts could be diverted to any other use."[52]

The program got off to a good start in that it took over an existing commercial distribution system with 1,599 customers of whom a large number were initial members. By the end of the first six months, the number of customers had grown to 1,627 and the great majority of these held memberships. It is significant that residential consumption jumped from 49 kilowatt-hours per customer in May, the last month of private company service, to 83 kilowatt-hours at the end of the seventh month of operation by the Association. Total residential revenue increased by 13 per cent. In the first six months the domestic load was increased by the addition of 211 refrigerators, 90 ranges, and 32 water heaters. Due to the increased consumption, the average rate per kilowatt-hour to residential customers was reduced during this period from 3.1 to 2.6 cents. At the end of the first year, gross revenue from operations amounted to $79,000, and, after deducting cost of power, distribution, taxes, depreciation, and interest, there remained a balance of $26,750, or 35 per cent of the gross income which became available for retirement of debt, new construction, or other required need.

When the Association began operations the number of farmers served was less than 100. The number steadily increased until by 1960 all of the 3,883 farms in the county were electrified. In May 1939 the Association made its last payment to the TVA on the original long-term debt. From then on membership fees were gradually reduced to $10 by 1943, with earlier members being repaid the balance from larger amounts that they had paid. As of June 30, 1966, the total value of assets of the Alcorn Association was $3,595,277, and the combined ownership interest of members in the form of retained savings amounted to $3,305,149.[53]

From its beginning, Lilienthal took an active interest in the development of the Alcorn County Electric Power Association, for he was aware that its success was essential to the success of the TVA power program. He took great pleasure in explaining the Alcorn County plan to President Roosevelt when he visited the area in November 1934, and it is probable that this influenced the President in his plans for a national rural electrification program. In an entry in his *Journal* for October 5, 1935, Lilienthal said:

> There is somehow a magic about TVA kilowatts . . . We have really stirred public imagination about electricity . . . To have electricity apparently opens up

a new world for people and to have the form of organization whereby electricity is brought to them through the beginning of cooperative activity in which they participate is really an accomplishment. That is what is actually going on. These county-wide cooperative associations [of which the Alcorn County Association was the prize example] are teaching great lessons about the relation between town and country . . . This vigorous fighting attitude for the principle of cooperation has implications far beyond electricity.[54]

It was not long after the Alcorn County Association was started that another was formed, and from then on the number steadily increased until there were 28 in 1939. These associations found it desirable to also set up a cooperative billing service to serve TVA cooperatives and municipal utilities in 1937, under the name Central Service Association. Savings over costs were returned to the member associations or municipals.[55]

The electric cooperatives served by the Tennessee Valley Authority have over the years demonstrated the soundness of Lilienthal's conception that electric cooperatives could well serve both urban and rural consumers. Joseph Swidler, who has watched their progress from the beginning, writes:

The fifty [electric] cooperatives served by TVA are among the largest and most successful in the country. A primary reason is the pattern established by the Alcorn County cooperative of combining urban and rural loads . . . which made it possible in the case of later acquisitions of public utility properties to turn over to cooperatives the service responsibilities in many communities of substantial size but yet not large enough to operate their own municipal systems on an economic basis, or to take responsibility for serving the countryside. These cooperatives, therefore, have profited from the growth of the towns they serve instead of being required to yield territory as the towns grew, which is the situation for the cooperatives which serve around the periphery of the larger cities having their own municipal systems.[56]

Cooperative Aspects of the Fertilizer Program

Under the Tennessee Valley Authority Act of 1933, the TVA was given broad authority in the area of fertilizer production and experimentation. The Act empowered the TVA "to manufacture and sell fixed nitrogen, fertilizer, and fertilizer ingredients at Muscle Shoals by the employment of existing facilities, by modernizing existing plants, or by any other process or processes that in its judgment shall appear wise and profitable for the fixation of atmospheric nitrogen or the cheapening of the production of fertilizer." Moreover under the Act, the TVA was authorized "to arrange with farmers and farm organizations for large-scale practical use of the new forms of fertilizers under conditions permitting an accurate measure of the economic return they produce." The Board of

TVA could also "cooperate with National, State, district, or county experimental stations or demonstration farms, with farmers, landowners, and associations of farmers or landowners, for the use of new forms of fertilizer or fertilizer practices during the initial or experimental period of their introduction, and for promoting the prevention of soil erosion by the use of fertilizers or otherwise."[57]

Dr. Harcourt Morgan, who had responsibility for agricultural development on the Board of Directors, was in complete accord with these directives. As a long-time student of agriculture in the region, he recognized that its well-being, as well as that of the United States, depended upon the more abundant use of fertilizer, especially phosphate. Morgan did not believe that the TVA should produce and promote nitrogen which was contributing to the bad agricultural practices of the region. In his opinion, a fertilizer material was needed that would help in the control of soil erosion, prevention of floods, and in increasing the productivity of valley farms. He believed that concentrated phosphates promised the best solution.

In the light of his recommendations, the Board left idle the ammonium nitrate producing capacity of the Muscle Shoals plant and turned, instead, to an experimental program with phosphatic fertilizers. The TVA had several complementary purposes in view: production of more highly concentrated forms of phosphatic fertilizer than were then available; reduction of costs for producing it through improved processes and equipment; securing of a base load for the Wilson Dam power plant by using electric furnaces in its production; and the utilization of the product in a general program of soil improvement education for the conservation of the Valley's resources.[58]

While plans were being made for revamping facilities at nitrate plant No. 2 to produce superphosphate of high concentration, TVA arranged for the production of high-concentrate phosphatic fertilizer in a semi-works-scale laboratory for its experimental use by the state agricultural experiment stations in the Valley states. By May 1934 this pilot plant operation went into production so that some 20 tons of experimental phosphate products were produced by June 30—the end of TVA's first operating year. The results of the agronomic test-pot trials soon revealed that "the new phosphates compared very favorably in their effects on soil and crop with the standard materials."[59]

Following this experimental work, the TVA proceeded to build a commercial size electric furnace in nitrate plant No. 2. Operation of this furnace resulted in the production of triple superphosphate in October 1934, and, by June 30, 1935, the end of TVA's second year, some 19,210 tons had been produced. This was a landmark in production of phosphatic fertilizer by the electric furnace method. With a supply of triple superphosphate available, it was possible to begin the testing of the fertilizer under actual field conditions in the spring and summer of 1935.[60]

The test demonstration program. For field testing the new phosphatic fertilizer, an ingenious plan was worked out in line with the long established demonstration procedures of the Extension Service that Seaman A. Knapp had introduced early in the century for fighting the boll weevil.[61] The plan provided for the designation of certain farms as "test demonstration" farms under cooperative arrangements which would be supervised by the agricultural extension forces of the Tennessee Valley states. Under the plan the TVA would supply the phosphatic fertilizer to be used on the land for soil conserving crops. In return, the demonstration farmer would agree to map and inventory his farm, adopt an intensive five-year farm management program, keep records of his results, and pay the freight cost on fertilizer used. According to Pritchett: "Each test demonstration farm became in a sense a community enterprise, for the selection of the farm was made by the farmers of the area under the leadership of the county agricultural agent . . . and the neighboring farmers visited the test farm and watched results."[62] Under this plan, 984 test demonstration farms were established in the Tennessee Valley states by June 30, 1935, and a total of 1,986 tons of triple superphosphate were distributed through 95 "soil conservation associations."[63]

The immediate popularity of the program caused the TVA to say in its Second Annual Report: "Although the program . . . with respect to fertilizer and its use is being conducted within the Tennessee Valley, it has distinct national implications. There is a phosphate deficiency in most soils of the United States, and concentration of phosphatic plant foods will make transportation sufficiently cheap so that practically all regions may be reached." Within a few years the demonstration program was extended in modified form to a large number of states outside of the Valley.[64]

While the TVA was getting its plant into production, the supply of concentrated phosphatic fertilizer for test farm experimentation was limited, and the program was restricted to individual farms. At the end of TVA's second year (June 30, 1935), supplies of triple superphosphate were ample to permit an expansion of the program. It was evident that area-wide demonstrations were feasible, with entire areas or small watersheds designated for demonstration purposes. Then all farmers in an area could follow the same general plan. This would permit more extensive programs of crop readjustments to conserve water, to control erosion, to help build soil fertility, and to promote better farm management. From this time on, the test demonstration program was largely carried on through area-wide associations. As favorable results from this program began to show up in better production records for the demonstration farms, other farmers were influenced by their example. Many of them joined together to buy fertilizer or other farm supplies. This experience soon led to more general community cooperation. Farmers working together for soil improvement began to buy threshers, grading equipment, blooded bulls, and other things which none of them could afford individually. In the words of R. L. Duffus "a kind of contagion of better farming began to catch hold."[65] Thus the cooperative technique came to be used by the TVA in developing its fertilizer program. Dr. H. A. Morgan did not start out with the idea of forming orthodox farmer cooperatives. Rather he stressed the general idea of people and institutions working together to meet a general need. However, as this program advanced, it took on more and more cooperative characteristics and provided a seed bed for other cooperative developments which later were to result in more formal cooperative organizations.

TVA Recognizes "Cooperative Power"

The support given to the fertilizer and electric cooperative programs made clear that the people of the Valley must participate in the development, control, and operation of the programs designed to serve them. By 1936, it was becoming understood that TVA's assistance to cooperatives could not be imposed from above but must be in response to the needs and desires of the people involved. There was arising an appreciation of "cooperative power" resulting from people working together with the technical assistance of the TVA. As R. L. Duffus has said: "The Valley people . . . saw how men working together . . . could do a magnificent thing . . . In the sweep of things beyond the routine of construction the key was cooperation. There was little that TVA did alone."[66]

The replacement of Arthur Jackson, a well-meaning idealist, by J. Ed Campbell, "a hard headed" TVA employee, as Administrator of TVAC reflected the new emphasis. It was Campbell's job to take stock of TVAC's work and determine what TVA should be doing to further practical cooperative advancement. On the basis of his findings, it was decided in 1937 to sever relations with TVAC and set up a "Cooperative

Research and Experiment Division" within the TVA to help strengthen farmer cooperatives.

L. Carlton Salter, a man well-trained and experienced in the field of agricultural cooperation, reported as Chief of the new division on January 1, 1938.[67] Salter immediately acquainted himself with the cooperatives already operating in the Valley and the nature of their problems. Thus he found out what work was being done with cooperatives in the region by the state colleges and extension workers, Banks for Cooperatives, and the state governments. One of his first undertakings was a study of the experience and methods of the 15 cooperative electric associations then served by TVA for the purpose of offering recommendations for their improvement. This study, completed in November 1938, proved exceedingly useful.[68] Salter early realized that general information should be assembled on farm cooperatives in the Valley states. This resulted in several reports prepared jointly by the Authority and the State Experiment Stations.[69]

The value of Salter's work with cooperatives was reflected in a better relationship of the existing cooperatives with the TVA. They came to see that the TVA was interested in working with them, not in dominating them. As Salter has said "We instilled the concept that TVA's interest in cooperatives was not possessive or dictatorial—a belief that had grown up under a prior regime."[70] His work also helped TVA officials understand the importance of the cooperatives operating in the Valley states and gave them training in the principles and methods of sound cooperative development. In 1940, this program was well established in the TVA, and, as will be seen in later chapters, it had an important bearing on TVA work with cooperatives during the war and postwar years.

Summary

In the TVA, cooperatives soon became means to ends for the accomplishment of specific objectives. None of the three first Directors were concerned with the promotion of cooperatives because of any special knowledge or interest in such organizations, but each in his own way found them essential to his aims within the framework of the Tennessee Valley Authority. The contribution of Arthur Morgan was primarily Utopian, that of Harcourt Morgan and David Lilienthal mostly pragmatic.[71] Thus the TVA became a laboratory and testing ground for the application of cooperative principles to the development of natural resources for the general social and economic welfare of the nation.

Chapter XVII

RURAL ELECTRIFICATION VIA
COOPERATIVES: 1934-1940

Rural electrification did not come as a bolt from the blue with the establishment of the Rural Electrification Administration in 1935 through an Executive Order by President Franklin D. Roosevelt.[1] Rather, it was an idea whose time had come. President Roosevelt was responding to a long felt demand from farmers and farm organizations for help in obtaining rural electric service.

Steps Toward Rural Electrification, 1900-1935

It took a third of a century for rural electrification to evolve into a practical program. The highlights of this development can be briefly told. Shortly after the turn of the century, farmers began to get some benefits of electricity through small home generators. Although inadequate and expensive to operate, they aroused a desire for better and cheaper service.

By 1910 the electric power companies were becoming aware of the potentialities of the farm market for electricity and a nation-wide survey was undertaken by the commercial section of the National Electric Light Association to determine the profitability of providing central station service to rural areas. The report from this study disclosed that the number of bona fide farmers using electricity was almost too small to report. It advised the industry to wake up and go after rural business, but it warned that farmers must "be served on the same basis of rates as applies in adjacent towns and cities." Although this report brought the problem of rural electrification to national attention, it did not have a great effect, for rates charged were generally so exorbitant that only a few prosperous farmers living near towns or cities could obtain or afford service.[2]

Beginnings. Confronted by this situation, farmers in a few areas began to set up electric non-profit cooperatives to obtain power from city plants. In 1914, a group of farmers at Granite Falls, Minnesota, decided to act for themselves by setting up what was known as the Stony Run System to provide themselves with electric service. It was a simple affair, following the precedent of the mutual telephone companies. The farmers built their own lines and obtained power from the municipally owned plant. A few more associations of this type arose in various parts of the country during the next few years but such "snake-line" systems were of minor importance until the close of World War I.[3]

After the war the number of cooperative associations increased. In 1919, several were organized in the area surrounding Webster City, Iowa, with power supplied from the city's plant.[4] In 1920 a non-profit farmers' mutual company in southern Idaho built 265 miles of lines after getting a favorable power rate from a Bureau of Reclamation hydro plant. "Here for the first time," to quote Clyde Ellis, "a cooperative organization was purchasing relatively cheap hydroelectric power from the Federal Government, and in turn reselling it to members at a reasonable rate."[5]

Another significant cooperative development of this kind attracted wide attention in the early 1920's. Unable to get economical service otherwise, farmers in the vicinity of Tacoma, Washington, built a number of power lines and bought their power from the city plant. The Granges of Washington State backed this project and succeeded in establishing the right to organize public utility districts for developing and distributing power.[6] By 1923 some 31 voluntary farmer cooperatives had been incorporated in nine states, and, although relatively unimportant as a part of the total rural picture, they represented "prophetic clouds on the utility horizon."[7]

The interest of farmers in rural electrification was increased by the controversy over what was to be done with the Muscle Shoals development after the war. As a war measure the government had spent millions of dollars on an electric power dam and nitrate plant at Muscle Shoals, Alabama. Henry Ford and others had attempted to obtain this property at little cost, but Senator George Norris had urged that the property be utilized to provide cheap electric power for farmers. The American Farm Bureau Federation had struggled to have the facilities used for fertilizer production. Although nothing was done immediately on this matter, it made farmers conscious of the possible benefits of public power.[8]

The CREA. Conscious of the growing interest of farmers in obtaining electricity, the American Farm Bureau Federation in 1922 began working with the private power industry to determine how electric power might be brought "more abundantly" to American farms. This led, in 1933, to the setting up of the Committee on the Relation of Electricity to Agriculture, which soon became known as the CREA. This organization was closely allied to the American Farm Bureau Federation which furnished office space and clerical assistance to the Committee's full time director, whose salary and expenses were borne by the National Electric Light Association.[9] The general objectives of the CREA were (1) to develop "various methods by which electrical energy can be profitably utilized on the farm . . . and (2) to develop "facts regarding the transmission lines and electrical equipment needed to furnish the farmer electric service comparable in quality with that already supplied in the industrial field."[10]

During the next decade the CREA carried on a comprehensive research and education program with agricultural engineering departments of the land grant colleges and others designed to promote the use of electricity on farms, and much effective work was done.[11] However, the CREA was not set up to deal with the economic problems of how to reduce costs of electricity so that farmers could afford it. Morris L. Cooke, the first Administrator of the Rural Electrification Administration, later referred to CREA as "an organization designed to continue the talk and at all costs to keep rural electrification in commercial hands." He continued: "However, the shadow of the 'Great Forester was looming o'er the land.' "[12] Cooke was referring to the influence of Gifford Pinchot, governor of Pennsylvania (1923-26), the first chief of the Forest Service and long a strong advocate of public power.

The Giant Power Survey, 1925-1927. Gifford Pinchot did not believe that rural electrification was unobtainable. When he took office in 1923 he was committed to bringing electric power to Pennsylvania farmers, and he was soon working with the State Grange on the problem. On the basis of his explorations, he secured legislative authorization for a survey of the Giant Power Industry in Pennsylvania to examine among other matters "the generation and distribution of electrical energy such as will secure for the industries, railroads, farmers and homes an abundant and cheap supply of electric current . . . " Pinchot, in instituting the survey, foresaw the widespread use of electricity on the farm. He said: "From the power field perhaps more than from any other quarter we can expect in the near future the most substantial aid in raising the standards of living, in eliminating the physical drudgery of life, and in winning the age-old struggle against poverty . . . Our first concern must be with the small user . . . particularly the farmer . . . "[13]

To direct this survey Pinchot obtained Morris L. Cooke, a mechanical engineer, who, while Director of Public Works for Philadelphia, had successfully fought the organized power industry in the famous Philadelphia rate case.[14] In undertaking this work, Cooke attributed great importance to the subject of rural electrification, and, of the 500 pages in the Giant Power Report, some 150 were devoted to rural electrification. One valuable feature was a study of the density of farms made by Perry Taylor. He measured the country roads in Pennsylvania and divided this mileage by the number of farms. His findings proved to Cooke that rural electrification was not far off.[15]

Probably the most important thing about the Giant Power Survey was that it made Cooke determined to help bring electricity to farmers. It gave him the concept of area coverage, for the study made it obvious that if all farmers of an area were provided service from a central power plant the cost per farmer for such service could be greatly reduced. The Giant Power Survey also gained national attention for the problem of rural electrification. As Cooke later said: "Before the organization of the Giant Power Survey, practically all references to rural electrification had been casual or limited to a high cost service."[16]

The New York State Power Authority, 1931-1933. During the 1920's, the private power companies were riding high, and nothing apparently could be done to change their course. With the Great Depression, the situation changed. The disclosures following the collapse of the jerry-built Samuel Insull empire in 1932 made the public conscious of the greediness of the private electric power industry, and opened the eyes of many as to its organic weaknesses.[17] This brought about a greater interest in public power and set the stage for the creation of the Tennessee Valley Authority in 1933.

One deeply interested in the possibilities of public power during the 1920's was Franklin D. Roosevelt. He had become attracted to the problem of rural electrification as early as 1924 while convalescing at Warm Springs, Georgia. At that time he determined to do whatever he could to bring cheap electric power to farms.[18]

Roosevelt had later followed the efforts of Pinchot and Norris to gain acceptance for public power, and he was in general agreement with their views. When he became Governor of New York State in 1929, he immediately showed his interest in the power problem by obtaining from a "reluctant legislature" authority to create a Public Service Survey Commission, and, upon the recommendation of this Commission, the Legislature in early 1931 set up the New York State Power Authority "to take whatever steps might be necessary to deliver cheap power to consumers."[19]

Significantly, Roosevelt appointed Morris L. Cooke as one of the members of the newly constituted Power Authority. At this time Roosevelt was intensely interested in the possibilities of getting cheap power from the St. Lawrence River not only for New York industries but for farmers as well. This involved making a distribution cost study, a duty which was given to Cooke, who found from his investigation that "widespread rural electrification was generally feasible."[20]

Rural Electrification Gains Public Support, 1933-1935

When Roosevelt became President in 1933, he was already committed to the control of electric power in the Tennessee Valley, and one of the first Acts of his Administration provided for the Tennessee Valley Authority, which had as one of its objectives the extension of electrical power to Tennessee Valley farmers. The establishment of the TVA represented a tremendous step forward in the progress of rural electrification as pointed out in the preceding chapter. As Clyde Ellis has well said: "TVA was the incubator of the Federally promoted and financed rural electrification program."[21]

While the TVA was getting under way in the summer of 1933, Secretary Harold Ickes set up the Mississippi Valley Committee in the Works Progress Administration, to study the natural resources of the Mississippi Valley. Morris L. Cooke was named Chairman, and he made rural electrification a matter of primary concern.[22] In reporting to Ickes on the progress of this committee in January 1934, Cooke proposed that a joint committee be set up comprised of representatives of the private power industry and the government to develop a coordinated plan for rural electrification. Ickes contemptuously turned down the suggestion but agreed to the idea if it were carried on wholly as a governmental undertaking.[23] Following this lead, Cooke lost no time in preparing a hard hitting report which he called "National Plan for the Advancement of Rural Electrification Under Federal Leadership and Control, with State and Local Cooperation and as a Wholly Public Enterprise."

The Cooke Report. Cooke submitted his report to Ickes in two copies on February 13, 1934. Ickes immediately passed one copy on to President Roosevelt, who later referred it to Harry Hopkins, then in charge of relief activities, and to Daniel C. Roper, Secretary of Commerce. All were favorably impressed, causing Cooke to say later: "It may be said that the reception accorded this report made certain that the Federal Government would see that rural electrification was made an essential feature of our economy."[24] The report was tersely written, and, on the cover, to gain attention, were inscribed these words: "This report can be read in 12 minutes." Believing in showmanship, Cooke dressed up the report with a "bizarre black-and-white striped cover [which] kept it circulating among those in high place and so out of the wastebasket."[25] As this report is one of the seminal documents in the development of rural electrification, it is presented here in some detail. Cooke himself later said: "I would consider the argument in this report . . . the detonating force which started rural electrification."[26]

To introduce the report, Cooke quoted several statements of President Roosevelt. The first read as follows: "Electricity . . . can become the willing servant of the family in countless ways. It can relieve the drudgery of the housewife and lift the great burden off the shoulders of the hard-working farmers."

The opening section of this persuasive document was devoted to the question: "Why Is Rural Electrification Important?" On this Cooke said:

> Agriculture is a major problem. We must evolve toward the status of a dig-nified and self-sustaining sector of our social life. So agriculture demands all the *pertinent* production and comfort facilities now available to industry . . . Emergence from depression compels a program of public works—i.e., of collec-tive assistance to works having public service character . . . Those should be favored which (1) contribute to social life, (2) require united investment beyond interest and capacity of private industry. Rural Electrification inher-ently meets these specifications and technically demands large scale development instead of endless piece-meal extensions. The reflex influence of widespread rural electrification on industry providing electric power and light would be enormous. This development would probably afford the beginnings of real control of the electrical industry.

The next section of the report dealt with the question: "What Is the Task?" Primarily, the task was to bring electric service to over 5,000,000 farms. "Unless the Federal Government, assisted in particular instances by state and local agencies, assumes an active leadership and complete control, only a negligible part of this task can be accomplished . . . Hence no private company is likely to create a new center of power production, simply in order to serve a rural area."

The report then pointed out: "Existing Rural Service Constitutes the Fringe of the Present System." Cooke asserted that there was no real reason why only 10 per cent of the nation's farms were electrified since "the essential elements of a rural electric system are simple and easily manipulated. Distribution involves only poles, wires, transformers and meters. Even the generating units now obtainable require a minimum of attention and are all but fool proof."

"The advantages of rural electrification" were then examined. It was maintained that "both for the farmer and his wife the introduction of electricity goes a long way toward the elimination of drudgery. The electric refrigerator will effect a considerable change in diet—more fresh vegetables, and less salt and cured meats. The inside bathroom, made possible by automatic electric pumping, brings to the farm one of the major comforts of urban life. Electricity will be a strong lever in keeping the boys and girls on the farm—in encouraging reading and other social and cultural activities . . . "

On the question. "How [to] Make the Start?" the report said:

> Having recognized the advantages of rural electric service and reached the conclusion that only under Governmental leadership and control is any considerable electrification of "dirt farms" possible, the obvious obligation is to get it done . . . An allotment of $100,000,000 annually to build independent self-liquidating rural projects would exert a mighty influence in various directions . . . *This proposal does not involve competition with private interests . . . This plan calls for entering territory not now occupied or not likely to be occupied to any considerable extent by private interests . . .*

As to "Source of Power for Rural Service," this could be either through existing private or public generating or transmission systems or through creation of an independent source of power. To soften opposition it was declared that "perhaps when first getting under way the preference would be given in connecting up with existing lines where fair prices for current can be assured. Independent sources of power might well be kept in the background." But, in any case, it was held that "electric current . . . can be made available to the rural population at a figure considerable below what is charged for it on existing rural lines . . . "

Emphasis was placed on the fact that "Large Use [is] the Key to Low Rates." It was maintained that real rural electrification implies large average use of current, "for, without large use, rates cannot be made low enough to effect the coveted social advantages."

> The electrical industry, because it secures over 60 percent of its revenue from small consumers, is all but stymied by its high-rate low use situation. In planning for national rural electrification, we must do everything to encourage the largest possible average use. Large average use, especially in the initial stages, seemingly requires a planning and investment beyond the capacity of a private company to initiate. Perhaps only the power and force of the Government can master the initial problem.

On the matter of "Rates," it was pointed out that only recently it had been proven that most of the wide variation in rates had little relation to cost. A simple schedule of rates was suggested that would be practicable, that would cut the average existing rural rate in half.

Technical information was provided on such problems as "distance between farms," "financing of lines," and costs that would be incurred. It was believed that it might be "wise temporarily to utilize emergency legislation and funds to get this work started." However, "there would appear to be no legal objection to organizing the work upon a permanent basis." It was suggested that "a system of banks established expressly for the purpose could be set up, similar to existing Acts for the extension of agricultural credits, such as the Federal Land Bank Act of 1916. If it is desirable to operate by direct loans without the use of a special banking system, authority is found in the appropriating power of Congress under the so-called 'General Welfare' clause of the Constitution."

Attention was also directed to the "State Legislative Situation." Here it was recognized that laws in some states would act as a practical bar to rural electrification along the lines proposed. "Even here, however, the plan might be put into effect through farmers' mutuals operating without profit." However, "a part of the plan would be to set up uniform state legislation and have the farmer-folk within the several states press for its adoption . . . "

The concluding section of the report was entitled: "The Answer—A Rural Electrification Agency." This section of the report is given in full.

> It is proposed to set up in the Department of the Interior—a section, manned by socially minded electrical engineers, who, having standardized rural electrification equipment, will cooperate with groups within the several states in planning appropriate developments. In many instances, no Federal financing will be required. Where such schemes are self-liquidating, financing in whole or in part may be provided. The possible bearing of proposed municipal power developments on rural electrification might properly influence allotments during the life of P.W.A. In fact, the proposed Rural Electrification Section should take an active hand in planning the rural use of current from such developments as Grand Coulee, Ft. Peck, Bonneville, Boulder Dam, Tygart Dam, etc. Cooperation with the Electric Home and Farm Authority would be an important function of the Rural Electrification Section.

This report culminated the studies of Cooke and his associates which had been carried on over a period of some 20 years to find a way to bring about widespread rural electrification.[27] It was, in effect, a strategy paper for top Administration officials, and it had but limited circulation. More important in public influence were the comments on rural electrification in the reports of the Mississippi Valley Committee and of the National Resources Board.[28]

The report of the Mississippi Valley Committee of October 1, 1934, showed "shockingly small amounts of rural electrification in the several watersheds constituting the Mississippi Valley."[29] The Committee summarized its recommendations in one paragraph.

Having recognized the advantages of rural electric service and reached the
conclusion that only under government leadership and control is any considerable electrification of "dirt farms" possible, we face the obvious obligation of
getting it done . . . An allotment of $100,000,000 annually to build independent,
self liquidating rural projects would exert a mighty influence in various
directions.[30]

The National Resources Board in December 1934 also advocated
strong action to achieve rural electrification. The Board said: "It seems
necessary for the Government to stimulate the extension of this service in
many areas."[31]

It is also significant that the Federal Emergency Relief Administration
directed attention to the possibilities of rural electrification as a means of
reducing unemployment. As a supplement to the Farm Housing Survey of
the Civil Works Administration in 1934, a National Survey of Rural
Electrification was made "to obtain information on the present availabili-
ty of electric service to farmers, its use, and the possibilities of extending
service to other farms." It clearly indicated "vast opportunities for
expanding rural electric service."[32]

Although many problems were yet to be resolved, the idea of a rural
electrification agency of some type was beginning to take shape. The deck
was now cleared for action. With the "Go Ahead" signal from President
Roosevelt and Secretary Ickes, a small group, under Cooke, continued
their studies of rural electrification while a way was sought to get the
program started. It is of interest that while Cooke and his associates were
developing plans for a national program of rural electrification, the
Tennessee Valley Authority was undertaking to extend rural electrification throughout the Tennessee River Valley through use of the cooperative form of organization. This development, described in the preceding
chapter, was to have a galvanizing effect.

Indiana begins cooperative electric program, 1934-1935. While sentiment was forming for government aid to encourage rural electrification,
cooperative leaders were not waiting for government action. Harvey Hull,
the General Manager of the Indiana Farm Bureau Cooperative Association and one of the most innovative cooperative leaders in the United
States, had long had an interest in rural electrification. His own farm had
been electrified since 1922, and he realized how important electric power
could be to Indiana agriculture if it could be obtained at reasonable
rates.[33] Hull's eyes were opened in the summer of 1934 when he saw for
himself the progress made by Danish and Swedish farmers in rural
electrification through cooperative organization. He said to himself, and
to others, "If they can do it, so can we," and he began to figure how the
job could be done.

His first step was to take his entire board of directors to Knoxville, Tennessee, to consult with the officials of the TVA to determine whether power produced by the TVA could be made available for Indiana farmers, and to obtain information on the TVA's experience in helping develop a cooperative electric association in Alcorn County, Mississippi. While the officials of the TVA informed Hull and his delegation that they could not count on TVA as a direct source of power, they suggested that the Indiana group proceed to organize county-wide rural electric associations along the lines of the association in Alcorn County, with power obtained through arrangements with municipal power plants, if possible.

Upon their return home, Hull and his directors went into action. Their first step was to direct the association's attorney to draw up plans for a state-wide organization—The Indiana Rural Electric Association—which would promote the organization of county-wide electric cooperative associations and provide them with legal, financial, and other overhead services. The attorney was also directed to draft a state law for the consideration of the state legislature that would ensure the legal status of such organizations when formed. The state law—The Indiana Rural Electric Membership Corporation Act—after a stiff fight in both Houses of the Legislature, was signed by Governor Paul V. McNutt on March 9, 1935, two months before the REA was set up by President Roosevelt as an emergency measure. The Indiana State-wide Rural Electric Cooperative, Inc., was immediately incorporated under this law with the directors of the Indiana Farm Bureau Cooperative Association serving also as its directors.

With the way legally cleared, the Indiana Farm Bureau Cooperative Association with the Indiana Rural Electric Cooperative began to organize a rural electric cooperative association in Boone County as a model for similar associations to be formed throughout the state. The directors of the IFBCA authorized loans to the IREC to get this job done, and invested $87,000 in development work for which it was later reimbursed by the REA. The Ohio Farm Bureau Cooperative Association followed with great interest the Indiana experience and soon moved in the same direction to set up a state-wide Rural Electric Cooperative. While Indiana and Ohio cooperatives were getting set for action, the REA came into being, giving them great encouragement.

Groundswell develops for rural electrification. By 1934 an upsurge for rural electrification was developing. This was evidenced by the interest in the subject then being given by the American Farm Bureau Federation and the National Grange. At its annual convention in November, the National Grange called for a government program "that will deliver power to the people." A month later the AFBF, at its annual convention, passed a resolution which declared: "We recommend that electrification of agriculture should be extended into every possible section of the country . . . that ways and means be provided through the Farm Credit Administration for financing at low interest rates cooperative electric light and power associations."

While there was arising within the government a general fund of information and a sentiment favorable to government assistance to get the rural electrification job done, there was some question on how to proceed. The Administration did not feel that support from organized agriculture was then sufficiently strong to warrant an attempt in Congress to set up a federal agency to promote rural electrification. It seemed more sensible to take a more indirect route through assisting rural electrification as a means of providing relief for the unemployed. There was some pressure to do this within the Federal Emergency Relief Administration. Seeing that the time was ripe for action along this line, President Roosevelt, in his annual message to Congress on January 4, 1935, included rural electrification among desirable emergency relief projects as a means of relieving unemployment and improving the nation's welfare. At this time the problem of unemployment was acute, and relief expenditures for "pump priming" to reestablish prosperity were popular. It was politically possible to start rural electrification as a relief measure. Any rural electrification benefits that might be derived were considered more or less incidental.

The advantages of this approach appealed to the American Farm Bureau Federation. Edward O'Neal, President of the AFBF, was then representing agriculture on an advisory committee appointed by the President to make recommendations to him of worthy relief projects. On February 28, 1935, O'Neal presented the recommendations of the Committee to the President. They included a $150 million item for rural electrification. The Ohio Farm Bureau Federation gave support to this idea by approving a resolution adopted by 300 officials of Farm Bureau units in Ohio's 88 counties which directed President Perry Green and other executives of the organization to outline a system of establishing cooperative utility companies in rural areas throughout the state and, if possible, to seek part of the $5 billion appropriation proposal for relief to aid in the construction of power plants.

REA is set up. In line with these views, the Emergency Relief Appropriation Act of April 8, 1935, made available $100 million for rural electrification. This opened the way for Roosevelt to create by Executive Order No. 7037 the Rural Electrification Administration on May 11, 1935.

He immediately named Morris L. Cooke, Administrator. The new agency was frankly designed to serve only an emergency purpose, and it was not designed to last more than a year. The Order was brief and instructions given by it were general. The Administrator was authorized "to initiate, formulate, administer, and supervise a program of approved projects with respect to the generation, transmission and distribution of electric energy in rural areas." The wide discretion given the Administration by this authorization made it difficult to know how to start. One fact was clear, it would be necessary to comply with the restrictions that governed all relief expenditures.

In selecting Morris L. Cooke to be Administrator of the REA, President Roosevelt made no mistake, for Cooke was the ideal man for this post. He was not only committed to the idea of rural electrification but he was uniquely qualified for the task of setting up the new agency and getting it into operation. As a leader in the scientific management field, he knew the importance of building on a sound foundation so as to make every step count, and he proceeded to make haste slowly—but deliberately. "When Cooke took over," as one of his colleagues later said: "there were no designs on the trestle board, so to speak. An abstract idea, not too well defined was placed in his hands—a mere seed which he was to plant, cultivate, nurture and control."[34]

The REA Gets Underway

However, the establishment of the REA didn't come as a surprise. For several months a small group of government officials had been meeting with Cooke to consider problems that might arise. In one of the meetings it was proposed that a study be made of rural cooperative electric experience so that information would be available should it be found desirable to work closely with cooperatives. The job of making this study was assumed by Jacob Baker, Assistant Administrator of the Federal Emergency Relief Administration, who assigned it to Udo Rall, Director of the Division of Self-Help Cooperatives in the FERA. The importance of Rall's report will be considered later in this chapter.

The way in which the REA got started has been well told by H. S. Person:

> The day after Executive Order No. 7037 was signed, the Administrator, a man of vigorous and direct action, opened an office in a suite of rooms loaned by courtesy of Secretary Harold L. Ickes in the basement of the old Interior Building. His first responsibility was to assemble a nucleus staff of engineers, attorneys, accountants, and other professional people . . . Within a week a small staff had been assembled, more permanent quarters leased, and shortly

after the middle of May REA moved to the building at 2000 Massachusetts Avenue, at one time occupied as a residence by James G. Blaine. Here the staff concentrated on its problems and discovered that "how to get started" was really a problem.[35]

One of the immediate questions that had to be considered was how the REA could function under the restrictions of the Emergency Relief Appropriation Act which required, among other things, that at least 25 per cent of funds should be spent directly for labor and that 90 per cent of labor should be procured from relief rolls. It was soon found that the REA could not develop a technical program that required the employment of skilled labor with such restrictions and that the REA could best carry out its objectives as a lending agency. This problem could not be settled until August 7 when President Roosevelt issued a regulation that freed REA from many of the requirements of the relief act. According to Person, this regulation "set the permanent pattern—that of a lending agency . . . This was the first and probably the most far reaching fundamental policy decision in the history of REA. It established promotion of rural electrification as an orderly lending program on an interest bearing, self-liquidating basis."[36]

While this frustrating problem was being resolved, Cooke and his staff had the problem of launching the program. Believing that the quickest way for getting into action lay through working with the private utility industry, Cooke convened a meeting of industry leaders in Washington, D.C., on May 20, where he presented to them the program as he envisaged it, and asked for their cooperation. This meeting was attended by most of the important private power companies. No conclusions were reached but it was agreed that the representatives of the power industry would make a comprehensive study to determine how they might best work with the REA.

The private power industry proposal. The report on this study was made in the form of a letter to Cooke two months later, dated July 24, 1935.[37] On the surface it appeared to be all that he could ask for. It suggested "a program for 1935-1936 amounting to $239,249,000, to serve and equip a total of 351,000 rural prospects, of which number 247,000 are farms . . . " The letter then set forth two premises on which this program could be attained:

   a. That the utilities consider the immediate urge for rural electrification is a social rather than an economic problem, and undertake to "carry" the increased rural business outlined in this memorandum over the necessary long development period;
   b. That the Federal Government extend credit to the new customers on a basis that will permit them to purchase the necessary equipment to use electric

energy to the extent that will make the building of new lines possible, and advance funds to the privately owned utilities to cover the cost of rural lines and service facilities.

Another provision of the letter stated the industry's attitude: "The problem of the farmer is not one of rates, but of financing and purchase of appliances."

The letter went on to propose that:

a. One hundred million dollars is to be made available to the electric industry for extending the facilities for electric service in rural districts;

b. Through the REA and/or other Federal agencies, the prospective rural customers on present lines and new lines will be financed for any service extensions to be provided by the customer, for the wiring of premises and for the purchases of appliances and appurtenances; and

c. The REA and other Federal agencies in cooperation with the electric industry will conduct a national educational campaign on the advantages of electric service to rural inhabitants.

The letter maintained that the "privately-owned utilities can absorb the full $100 million available under the Work Relief Appropriation for construction of additional rural facilities" and that "the program can be started as soon as funds are available and pursued as rapidly as the prospects are sold on the Government's financing plan." It was suggested that the financing plan provide for "money to be furnished to the utilities at specially low interest rates on long term payment."

It is apparent from these statements that the private utility industry was then confident that its proposals would be accepted, for it believed that its cooperation was indispensable to the REA. This is evident from the following statements given in the letter: "Our committee has been instrumental in submitting to you several formal applications from power companies for approval of certain line extensions contingent upon the advancing of funds by the government, upon terms and conditions to be agreed upon. . . . We understand that discussion of definite terms and conditions will be involved in your early consideration of these applications . . . Our committee has set up an organization of trained technicians, thoroughly familiar with all phases of rural electrification, to cooperate at all times with REA . . . "

However, the final paragraphs of the letter struck a discordant and somewhat smug note which could not be ignored by the REA Administrator.

The problem of actively promoting rural electrification has received serious consideration of utility companies for many years . . . *As a result, there are very few farms requiring electricity for major farm operations that are not now served. Additional rural customers must largely be those who use elctricity for household purposes,* and where the total use should bear a fair relationship to the cost of extending and furnishing the service (Italics added).

The inherent difficulties in the economics of the problem have been discussed at length with you and your staff during the past nine months. It seems unnecessary to lengthen this communication by repetition of such difficulties or restatement of the financial risks already assumed by companies generally in such development work.

We believe that the Rural Electrification Administration can provide new ways and means for performing an outstanding job of rural electrification during the coming year. It is in this belief that our committee herewith submits its definite suggestions to you and tenders its further pledge of active cooperation.

Cooke lost no time in replying to the industry's letter. Although desirous of the industry's cooperation, he could not accept the industry's plan without qualifications. His letter in reply of July 31, 1935, showed his independence.

It is gratifying to note that your estimate of the expenditures which can economically be made for rural distribution lines is fully as large as the Congressional estimate of the funds initially required for rural electrification. Indeed, the carrying out of your plans in entirety would make it necessary for the Government materially to expand its program of rural electrification. This would be necessary because we have many sound projects pending, submitted individually and in substantial part by public bodies and farm cooperatives, for which funds must and will be provided. More projects of this kind are shaping up. I feel confident, however, that our program can be enlarged sufficiently to take care of all the projects you contemplate, as and when they are put into more concrete form.

. . . While we recognize the widely differing rate systems to which you refer, we cannot agree from this that "the problem of the farmers is not one of rates." *On the contrary we hold rate simplifications and even rate reductions over large areas to be the heart of the problems of electrifying rural America.* Naturally, in weighing the relative desirability of loans it will be necessary for REA to consider carefully existing and proposed rate structures with reference to developing the large use essential to the success of our program . . . (Italics added).

We are now organized and authorized to receive requests for loans for rural line construction from public and private agencies. May we invite your further good offices in advising those sections of the industry with which you are now in touch that our routines have been established and the maximum activity is now our desire.

In a press release of July 31 the REA referred to the exchange of letters as reflecting a working accord "as to the social desirability and economic feasibility of the expenditure of one hundred million dollars for the construction of electric distribution lines in rural areas, not now having power and light services." At this time Cooke still hoped that the program of the REA could be largely achieved with the goodwill and cooperation of the private power industry. It soon became clear that such goodwill and cooperation was not to be forthcoming, but instead there would be strong opposition to REA activities. To understand this situation it should be realized that just at this time the private power industry was being aroused by the battle over the Wheeler-Rayburn bill which was designed to control the electric industry holding companies. This bill, termed the "death sentence" bill by the private power interests, antagonized many of those who had been looking with favor on the plans of the REA to promote rural electrification.[38]

The meeting with farm and cooperative leaders. While Cooke was angling for the support of the private power industry, he could not overlook the agricultural interest in rural electrification. He therefore called a meeting of farm organization and cooperative leaders in Washington, D.C., for June 7, 1935. The response was enthusiastic with about 100 in attendance.

Cooke used this occasion to explain how the REA proposed to operate and indicated that applications for loans from cooperatives would be welcomed. One of the features of the meeting was a talk by Joseph Swidler, Chief Engineer of the TVA, who explained how the Alcorn County Cooperative in Mississippi had been set up in June 1934 with TVA assistance and how it had operated successfully during its first year. This was practically a model for the cooperatives later to be formed with the assistance of the REA.

On the whole, the meeting was quite encouraging, for it assured cooperation from the farm organizations and cooperatives who went home to make plans for participation in the program. However, even with this expression of interest and support, Cooke was not confident that the cooperatives could be developed fast enough to be of great effect in accomplishing the goals of the proposed emergency program. He still believed that it would have to be carried out largely through the organized power industry which was already staffed and equipped to quickly undertake a large-scale effort. While welcoming cooperative participation, he put his faith in the industry while awaiting their report.[39]

It is not surprising that Cooke—who was then unaware of the great potential strength of cooperatives—hesitated to give them his full confidence. When REA was set up there were only a handful of small embryonic cooperative electric associations in existence, and most of these were getting power from private power companies, or municipal or reclamation service plants. Although the State Farm Bureau cooperative organizations in Indiana and Ohio were laying plans for comprehensive state-wide rural electric programs, these were largely in the planning stage, and Cooke had little knowledge of the capacity of these and like organizations to quickly mount a strong program.

This lack of faith in what the cooperatives could do during the formative period of REA is indicated by the recollections of early meetings with Cooke while he was trying to determine which way to turn. Murray Lincoln, who at the time was Secretary of the Ohio Farm Bureau Federation, recalls how he went down to Washington to meet Cooke when the REA was set up.

> I told him that we of the Farm Bureau wanted to avail ourselves of the benefit of this program and set up our own utility plants. "What do you know about the utility business?," Mr. Cooke asked. "Not a thing," I admitted cheerfully . . . Mr. Cooke suppressed a smile and said indulgently, as one might explain something to a child: "Well now, we expect about 90 percent of the rural electrification to be done by the presently existing utilities and about 10 percent by public utilities and cooperatives. As you may know, it is a highly technical job and I doubt whether your people are equipped to handle it." I said: "I'll turn those figures around on you if you'll let us try it." Mr. Cooke's demeanor changed. "Young man, you're crazy." "Okay," I replied, "But just give us the opportunity." Mr. Cooke struggled a little and then sighed. "Well, I suppose I must because the law states that I must. But I'll be frank. I don't have much hope for you."[40]

Harvey Hull, then manager of the Indiana Farm Bureau Cooperative Association, also recalls how he went to Cooke's office when the REA was established and explained that the Indiana Farm Bureau Cooperative Association was already at work developing a state-wide system of rural electrification cooperatives.

> When I left he shook my hand and said: "This meeting is the answer to a prayer!" Those were his exact words. He seemed to have gotten a picture of a workable plan and program. A month later I had a letter from Cooke asking me to come to his office. When I got there his attitude was completely changed. He said: "It's foolish for farmers to think they can build and finance and operate rural electric systems when trained and wealthy power companies can't do it." He had talked to leaders of the power companies and was completely unsold on our Indiana plan. I tried to persuade him but didn't succeed.
> Cooke's cold water was just the challenge Hull needed. He want on to say: "We went ahead in Indiana and built the program, but *don't, don't* give any credit to Cooke," though I guess he did soften some after the cooperatives began to prove they could to the job . . . I never saw Cooke but the two times. While he *did* not and never *would* have started the co-op program, I do think that probably his fear and caution caused more careful planning which resulted in fewer difficulties and failures later on.[41]

The negative response of the organized power industry made Cooke more responsive to the cooperatives, although he continued to keep the door open to the private power companies and hoped for a change in their attitude. However, few applications came in from them for loans.

From a cooperative standpoint a highly significant document in mimeographed form was distributed but not discussed at the Conference with farm organizations and cooperatives on June 7, 1935. It was a report entitled: "A Study of Cooperative Consumer Associations for Rural

Electrification," prepared by Udo Rall, Chief of the Division of Self-Help Cooperatives of the Federal Emergency Relief Administration. This report came at an opportune time, "in light of the completely amorphous state of the [REA] program . . ."[42]

Rall's study brought together available information on cooperative experience in rural electrification to help determine "the feasibility of consumer associations for the distribution of electricity." It offered recommendations "toward a Federal policy that would result in lasting benefits to potential rural consumers of electric energy at small ultimate cost to the Federal Government."[43] This report was very timely, for it presented a rationale for the utilization of cooperatives in the REA program. Because of its importance—especially in educating members of the REA staff on the way in which cooperatives function—it is here quoted in some detail.[44]

The Rall Report. In introducing the body of the report, Rall listed five points for general consideration. "(1) Private power companies are organized for profit and as a rule do not care to extend their lines to sparsely populated areas promising only small returns on investments . . . (2) Public ownership of rural lines by cities or counties is often not possible or feasible because municipalities object to inclusion of rural areas in a power district and because the areas in need of electrification are often not contained within county lines . . . (3) The logical consideration for rural populations unable to obtain electricity at fair rates from private or public power distribution agencies is, therefore, a plan of organization of the potential beneficiaries themselves . . . (4) Past attempts along this line have often ended in failure due sometimes to poor organization, but more often to insufficient capitalization to permit the proper construction and maintenance of needed facilities . . . (5) The feasibility of cooperative distribution of electricity in rural areas has been demonstrated here and abroad . . . "

After briefly examining the experience of several of the unsuccessful attempts to establish rural electrification cooperatives, attention was devoted to those that were in operation in four states. Although the record of those in three states—Idaho, Washington, Minnesota—was not impressive, it was significant that several had survived for many years. They represented a laboratory in which experience had been gained. The other association described in the report—the Alcorn County Electric Power Association in Mississippi—had been in operation for less than a year, but it represented the most promising development of this kind to date. This association had been formed with the encouragement and guidance of the TVA, and it was becoming well established. The for-

mation and early experience of this association has been described in
the preceding chapter.

Rall summarized his report by saying: "The organization of electric
consumer associations is generally discouraged by private power companies. This fact in itself is an admission of their potential feasibility . . ."
While recognizing the difficulties involved in the formation and operation
of such associations, Rall declared: "Nevertheless, it is evident from
the information submitted in this memorandum that electric consumers
associations offer a practical solution to the rural electrification problem,
in many instances even the only favorable solution . . . " On the basis of
his analysis, Rall offered a number of recommendations for consideration
in connection with a federal rural electrification program.

> 1. A comprehensive survey of needed lines and their construction cost in any
> state shall preceed any earmarking of funds for that state.
> 2. After funds have been earmarked, the Federal Administration shall reach
> agreement with the state and its governmental subdivisions regarding those
> lines whose ownership and operation are to be vested in such public bodies.
> The remaining proposed lines shall be grouped according to feasibility, regard-
> less of county boundaries, and the prospective consumers in each group area
> shall be canvassed as to their desire to own and operate such lines. [This
> recommendation reflected the thinking of the FERA in its work with state gov-
> ernments on relief problems. It should be noted that there was then no pattern
> for Rall to follow.]
> 3. Any such group of prospective consumers, before formal organization,
> shall elect three or more representatives who, with the assistance and advice of
> the Federal Administration, shall investigate the best possible source of obtain-
> ing power, whether through generation or through purchase from a public or
> private power producer . . . If reasonable rates cannot be assured by voluntary
> commitment of the power producer, nor by a ruling of the State Power Com-
> mission, the Federal Administration shall consider the erection of a generating
> plant to be purchased by the consumer association.
> 4. Only when the problem of power supply has been satisfactorily met . . .
> shall the formal organization of the [consumer association] be encouraged and
> assisted by the Federal Administration . . .
> 5. The proposed organizational set-up and the by-laws shall be reviewed by
> the legal staff of the Federal Administration and shall be subject to approval by
> the latter . . .
> 6. The Federal Administration shall construct the network of trunk, primary
> and secondary lines, and of connections with properties, furnishing all materials
> including also transformers and meters. Where necessary, it shall also construct
> the generating plants. It shall, as far as feasible, employ association members
> in construction, and purchase material, such as poles and crossarms, from asso-
> ciation members . . .
> 7. The Federal Administration shall make a contract with the association
> for the sale of the finished line or lines to the latter on an amortised basis . . .

These recommendations had the merit of being positive, and they
recognized that the job of rural electrification could best be done through
cooperative organizations with the financial and technical assistance of

the federal government. In many respects, the ultimate procedures of the REA drew on these recommendations.

Cooperatives take the stage. The foot dragging of the organized power industry made Cooke more responsive to the cooperatives, although he continued to keep the door open to the private power companies, and he hoped for a change in their attitude.[45]

While the private power companies held back, the farm organizations and cooperatives enthusiastically welcomed the opportunity of getting federal assistance to develop rural electrification. The response in Ohio, as recounted by Perry Green, long-time President of the Ohio Farm Bureau Federation, was representative of what was occurring in other states. He writes:

> The most spectacular of all the cooperative efforts of the [Ohio] Farm Bureau was that of the Cooperative Rural Electrification associations . . . With the coming of the Rural Electrification Administration, no efforts were overlooked in taking full advantage of all it had to offer. Meetings were held by the County Farm Bureaus to promote the signing up of members in their respective rural areas. No other cooperative effort had met with such immediate and energetic response. The prevailing high rates and the exorbitant charges made for providing such service to the rural areas by the operating power companies had aroused the farmers to the point where they were willing to avail themselves of any means which opportunity then made available.[46]

When "the first allocation for projects from relief funds of $2,351,355 was made on September 9, 1935, one was to a state rural electrification authority, two to power districts, five to county electric cooperatives of which two operated under state-wide cooperatives, one to a municipal plant, and one to a private corporation which was in effect a cooperative."[47] These borrowers were scattered among a half dozen states in the Midwest and Southwest.

The interest of cooperatives in providing service made Cooke aware that he needed someone on his staff who understood cooperative problems and could work with them. In July 1935 he found in Boyd Fisher, an industrial management engineer, just the man that he needed, and Fisher performed a valuable function in the next few months in working with cooperatives and in explaining how cooperatives operated to the staff of the REA.[48]

During this period, Cooke lost no time in getting the REA in shape to handle applications for projects. One of his first actions was to announce a "new viewpoint" which would govern REA in its relationships. This policy statement "brought together the points of advance reached by the most progressive operating companies." He followed up with a general statement in July on how the REA would operate. "Only loans not grants, were contemplated; loans would be made only for self-liquidating projects; the program as a whole would include electric wiring and installations as well as line extensions; and all groups 'willing to undertake to supply farmers' whose financial and operating proposal proved satisfactory" would be served.[49]

One of the first problems in rural electrification was to provide a method of financing the consumer purchase of electrical equipment and appliances so as to increase the use of electricity and make service more economical. The TVA had demonstrated that this could be done through the Electric Home and Farm Authority, described in the preceding chapter. To make this program available nationally, the EHFA was reincorporated in the summer of 1935 with Cooke as Chairman of the Board of Directors.

In the beginning a minimum of organization structure was necessary for REA. Almost spontaneously a legal department developed to handle the many legal questions arising, and an engineering department was soon created to handle technical matters. Gradually management, finance, personnel, and other departments came into being as the need for them arose.[50] It took about six months for the REA to get tooled up to operate effectively. From then on progress was pronounced. The line of direction was now clear, and the structure was set up to provide essential services.

The way in which the cooperatives gained importance in the REA program came as something of a surprise to the REA staff which had been somewhat skeptical of the ability of cooperatives to develop effective projects. As one of them later said: "Suddenly it was realized that the commercial power companies were not, in fact, going to be willing to do the job. Meanwhile, the idea of cooperatives was gaining great importance and the picture was entirely reversed. Private utilities were receding into the background as far as REA loans were concerned, and many new cooperatives were springing up."[51]

By boycotting the REA, the private utilities changed the character of the organization. If they had cooperated with it they would probably have made it into a lending agency largely subservient to their interests. By opposing it, they caused it to become a major competitor in the field of rural electrification.

By December 1935, Cooke had come to realize that the cooperatives had taken over the REA program in default of the willingness of the private power industry to participate and that they would have to be their mainstay. He later said: "Before December . . . it became apparent that the industry was not going to use even a substantial portion of the funds available for rural electrification, and farm organizations of a cooperative character forged to the front as the principle borrowers under the REA program."[52]

This situation brought a reversal of attitudes within the REA, and confidence in the idea of carrying on the program through cooperatives began to develop. From then on, the staff of the REA no longer resisted the cooperative idea but helped make it work. This resulted in a significant change in the character of the REA. If the industry had cooperated, the REA would no doubt have become primarily a government lending agency, something like the Reconstruction Finance Corporation. But its obduracy forced the REA to assume broader functions of an entreprenurial nature. How this process cumulatively developed and how it changed the character of REA has been well told by Frederick William Muller.

> Had REA been able to make its loans to systems already established, there is no reason to believe that its functions, organization, or procedures would have differed materially from those of comparable federal lending agencies already in existence. It would probably have become primarily a financial organization for evaluation, auditing, and collections. The recognized standing of operating companies and their properties would have supported its loans; they would have engineered the new extensions themselves and operated them as part of their systems.
>
> But when REA began to make most of its allotments to small, new and inexperienced cooperative systems, it was confronted with the task of protecting its loans, by making certain that the lines serving as security would be built well and maintained properly, and by insuring the payment of debt service charges through supervisory guidance in management and operations. In addition, *it became clear that if the program were to be promoted and cooperatives effectually and democratically organized, much of the work of promotion and organization would have to be done by field representatives of REA.* At the same time REA [became] increasingly conscious of the potential importance of the cooperative systems to rural electric power development and planning in general. So, in the course of growth, REA acquired its second functional responsibility of guidance.
>
> The new function had a profound effect on REA organization and procedures. As one new type of assistance after another seemed to become necessary—encouraging cooperatives, framing contracts, helping to obtain certificates from state commissions, planning system layout, procuring insurance, setting up accounts, negotiating for wholesale power, building load, buying equipment—new personnel were employed and new units established. As REA emerged as an entrepreneur, it began to take on the functions, the activities, and the appearance of a holding company, or, more accurately, of a service company affiliated to a holding company. It is this guidance function, superimposed upon the authority to make loans, which [was to] become central in REA (Italics added).[53]

Eventually the REA was to assume the "general characteristics of a government entrepreneur associated in a business enterprise with local cooperative groups." Writing in 1944, Muller said:

REA combines the functions of economic planning and promotion, and those of management service and control; it is guiding the distribution of one commodity, electric energy, in the rural market, and it is supervising and assisting a [national] network . . . of decentralized operating units . . . Legally the cooperatives are private corporate bodies . . . associated with REA only through contract and mortgage agreements; in practice, each cooperative system remains semi-autonomous, although part of a recognizable network.[54]

It should be made clear that the rural electric cooperatives formed in 1935 and 1936 were not an outgrowth of existing cooperatives. They were something different—a new growth. Cooperative marketing associations had shown little interest in cooperative electrification cooperatives because they were not related to the marketing of farm products. Consumer cooperatives in the cities had shown no great interest because they were rural not urban. On the other hand, while electric cooperatives did not fit in with existing purchasing cooperatives, the leaders of the cooperative purchasing movement recognized them as being important to the well-being of their members and gave them all possible support.[55]

We have seen how the Indiana Farm Bureau Cooperative Association nursed the program in Indiana until it was well established. The development was out of inner compulsion to meet a felt need, and the electric cooperatives tied themselves into the REA to obtain financial and technical help. If the private power companies had recognized the need and got behind the REA in the beginning, the cooperatives might not have got started so effectively. The opposition of the power companies gave them the fighting spirit and determination that was essential to their success.

Move toward permanent REA legislation. President Roosevelt, Senator Norris, and Cooke realized from the beginning that the REA as formed by Executive Order was nothing more than a stopgap measure. They knew that it could be of little real value as a relief measure, for most of the unemployed were in the cities, and it could not be made effective rapidly enough to be of much help. Setting it up as an emergency relief measure was only a subterfuge. If the idea of a federal organization to provide and finance rural electrification took hold and could be once started, it was believed that the support for it from agriculture would compel Congress to make the agency permanent through legislation. Norris and Cooke were amazed and gratified by the immediate response of farmers and farm organizations and cooperative leaders to the establishment of the REA, and they began to consider how the program could be made permanent through legislation.

On October 24, 1935, Senator Norris wrote a letter to Cooke in which he said: "It is increasingly obvious that the time is at hand when, as a

Nation, we should adopt a more positive program for electrifying the largest possible number of farms." Later in the letter he asked: "What would be involved in the proper extension of rural lines, so that a much larger percentage of rural homes may be electrified, and how soon can this be brought about?"

On November 14 Cooke replied that he was in favor of a "positive program" of "planning for construction on an area basis so as to effect the economics of mass construction." He went on to say: "Only by planning a fairly complete coverage of an area, without leaving too many gaps and unserved patches, can the essential economies be realized." In response to Norris's question he said:

> The experience of Rural Electrification Administration indicates that this limitation on the extension of service in rural areas has been due to prohibitive costs of construction, to excessive demands for cash contributions from farmers to pay for the lines which would serve them, to high rates which discourage the abundant use of current, and to the traditional policy of the private utilities of extending their monopolistic franchises as widely as possible, while extending their actual service only to those areas which are most profitable.[56]

This correspondence, which was made public, started the ball rolling toward the enactment of permanent legislation. At its annual meeting in November, the National Grange went on record in favor of a permanent REA program to be carried out by public agencies or by cooperatives, and a month later the American Farm Bureau Federation at its annual meeting urged farmers to form cooperatives so they might obtain electricity at the lowest possible cost. "This powerful support from two of America's most political and conservative farm organizations did much to hasten the appearance of the Norris-Rayburn Bill in early 1936."[57]

On January 6, 1936, Senator George Norris of Nebraska and Congressman Sam Rayburn of Texas introduced identical bills in both houses of Congress to provide for a permanent Rural Electrification Administration. The Senate Agricultural Committee reported the bill to the Senate on February 17, whereupon the President of the United States Chamber of Commerce promptly assailed the Norris-Rayburn Bill as contravening the Chamber's position in favor "of retrenchment of Federal expenditures." After a four-day debate which made clear the strong opposition of the private utility companies, the measure passed the Senate on a voice vote.

In the House the hearings on the bill began on March 12 in the Interstate and Foreign Commerce Committee, chaired by Congressman Rayburn. In the hearings Cooke and Rayburn agreed that utility companies should not be prohibited from participating in the loans for rural electrification, although Norris favored such prohibition. The bill was reported out on March 23 and was soon passed without a roll-call vote.

A strenuous struggle ensued in the conference committee but a compromise was finally achieved. The Senate agreed to permit loans to power companies, but with preference for non-profit groups; the interest rate was set at the cost of money to the government on its long-term securities; and it was agreed that all personnel appointments in REA should be non-political and on the basis of merit. The bill became law as The Rural Electrification Act of 1936 on May 20, a year and nine days after the REA had been set up by Executive Order.[58]

The Rural Electrification Act of 1936. The most significant provision of the new act was in relation to how service was to be rendered. Section 4 read as follows:

> The Administrator is authorized and empowered, from the sums herein-before authorized, to make loans to persons, corporations, States, Territories, and subdivisions and agencies thereof, municipalities, peoples utility districts and cooperative, nonprofit, or limited-dividend associations organized under the laws of any State or Territory of the United States, for the purpose of financing the construction and operation of generating plants, electric transmission and distribution lines or systems for the furnishing of electric energy to persons in rural areas who are not receiving central station service; *Provided, however,* That the Administrator, in making such loans, shall give preference to States, Territories, and subdivisions and agencies thereof, municipalities, peoples utility districts, and cooperative, nonprofit, or limited dividend associations, the projects of which comply with the requirements of this Act . . .

Besides granting a clear preference to non-profit organizations, the act established REA as a lending agency for 10 years. It authorized $40 million annually to be apportioned among the states. It permitted loans to extend over 25 years. It geared interest on the loans to the rate paid by the government on its own long-term securities. It provided that loans also could be made to finance home wiring and to purchase electric appliances, equipment, and plumbing. It provided for an Administrator with a term of 10 years to be appointed by the President. And, it required that REA be administered on a non-partisan basis.

The act opened the door and cleared the way for immediate action, and the REA already was organized and ready to act. President Roosevelt immediately asked Cooke to continue as the first Administrator under the Act.

The REA undertakes a positive program. With the passage of the REA Act the first phase of the organization's operations was over. Congress had confirmed the procedures being followed by the REA, and no longer was the REA handicapped by being a temporary relief agency. By this time cooperatives had multiplied in numbers and strength and had become the major borrowers from the REA, and some of the cooperatives were now beginning to supply electric service to their members. The REA was ready to undertake "the more positive" program desired by George Norris.

Now that the REA was set up on a solid basis, Cooke could employ additional professional personnel to make the program more effective. One of his most important early actions was to appoint, as Deputy Administrator, John Carmody, who was to succeed him as Administrator.[59] Carmody was well qualified by training and experience. He was highly respected as an industrial management engineer, and he had served as Chief Engineer for the Federal Emergency Relief Administration program. Before coming to government he had been editor of several important industrial journals, such as *Factory and Industrial Management* and *Coal Age* for the McGraw-Hill Publishing Company, and he was well known in industry and business circles in the field of scientific management. Cooke turned over to Carmody the job of detailed administration, and Carmody gave the REA a dynamic charge of new executive energy. Although not known as a cooperative advocate, Carmody realized that the success of the REA depended upon the strength of the cooperative organizations served, and he gave them encouragement and understanding. Under his direction a development division was organized to "guide and advise" cooperatives in being set up. This created a strong promotional influence.[60]

While Cooke had come to the cooperative idea reluctantly, Carmody embraced it as the key element in the success of the REA's program. He was an active rather than a passive advocate of the cooperative form of enterprise in the electrification field.

The progress made by the REA in the last six months of 1936 was phenomenal—when one considers the slow growth of the first year. As of December 31, 1936, total allotments approved totalled $43,737,779 and of this amount $28,666,250 represented allotments approved under the Rural Electrification Act of May 20, 1936.

A believer in keeping the public informed, Cooke carried on an active program to build interest in the problems and progress of rural electrification. In the spring of 1936, he had invited David Cushman Coyle, a well-known "New Deal" publicist, to prepare a little book on the usefulness of electricity on farms. This was printed by the Government Printing Office and published under the title *Electric Power on the Farm*, in paper cover. It had wide circulation during the summer and fall of 1936 and did much to explain and popularize the REA program. Of particular value was a chapter on "Cooperative Electricity Distribution" that indicated how farmers could get the benefits of the REA program through their own efforts.

One of Cooke's main concerns at this period was to have the public, and especially the urban public, understand how important rural electrification could be to people on farms. To develop some "human interest stuff" he employed Miss Mollie Ray Carroll, a Chicago social worker and university professor, in the summer of 1936 to spend three months in Virginia, Ohio, and Minnesota to "live with farm families, both those having electricity and those without it, and really find out what electricity is doing and can, to change their lives." Miss Carroll got the facts, and her findings made it clear that farm men and women were tired of living without electricity. This survey was very effective in helping build support and interest for the REA's program.[61] In her report she said: "the farmer has been driven to take notice of devices that will increase his productivity. Following the tractor and the automobile come electric power and water as the great servants he is coming to appreciate for increasing his crop, lightening his work and adding enjoyment to his home life."[62]

During the fall of 1935 and the first half of 1936, the cooperatives served by REA were setting up their systems to provide service to rural consumers so that in the fall of 1936 many associations were able to begin rendering service to rural consumers. The realization of actual benefits brought increasing enthusiasm for rural electrification, and the opening of each new cooperative system was a matter of community celebration.[63]

By the end of 1936, Cooke could take pride in the accomplishments of the REA program during its first 18 months. In his annual report for the period from May 11, 1935, to December 31, 1936, he pointed out that the program called for the coordination of many interests. He asked all concerned to recognize that rural electrification as a national program "is here to stay" until the reasonable demands of the farmer are more adequately satisfied. Although the achievements in terms of completed projects were not impressive, they were significant in that they largely represented the development of an entirely new form of government-sponsored self-help organization—the rural electric cooperative—for most of the organizations to which allotments or loans were made had not been in existence when the REA began operations. By December 31, 1936, electric cooperatives were forming in all parts of the country, and the support arising from farmers indicated that at last REA had found the way to do its job.

The importance of REA was not to be measured entirely by the extent of its own operations. As Cooke pointed out in his Report of December 31, 1936: "The Rural Electrification Administration is proving a powerful stimulant to construction by private capital and it is anticipated that public and private financing in 1937 will bring the comfort and convenience of electricity to over one hundred thousand rural homes." Thus, the presence of the REA in the field of rural electrification was achieving much of the objective of bringing about rural electrification without the use of government money.

Cooke was by nature a pioneer, and he lost interest in something after it was working. Now that the REA was on its feet and functioning effectively, Cooke's interests moved to other fields, and, in February 1937, he resigned as Administrator. He told a close friend at the time: "The thing [REA] has become routine . . . and you know how I feel about that. The challenge is gone . . . "[64] But he was premature in his judgement. Although the period of establishing the organization was over, the period that most appealed to him, the REA, was on the threshold of probably the most exciting and important stage of its life—the period of finding itself—and Carmody, who was immediately appointed Administrator by President Roosevelt, was the ideal man to direct the REA during this period.

The REA as a Going Concern, 1937-1940

The REA was already set up for action on February 13, 1937, when John Carmody was appointed Administrator. During the next four years it became a strong going concern.

The contribution of John Carmody. Under John Carmody, the REA became a fighting agency. He believed wholeheartedly in the cooperative solution for the rural electrification problem, and he undertook to make it effective. Confronted by the aggressive efforts of the private electric companies to stop the REA before it really established itself, he gave "recalcitrant private utilities no quarter." He maintained that "honest indignation sometimes is a useful administrative instrument."[65]

Carmody's will to succeed infected his staff, and the morale of the entire organization responded. As Clyde Ellis has written: "Carmody drove himself as hard as his staff and personally stayed on top of every bottleneck until a solution was found." He put his management training to work by developing an assembly line method for handling loan applications. He brought about a great reduction in the cost of line construction by setting high production standards. He encouraged his engineers to design new concepts of rural electric line construction, and costs per mile were greatly reduced through what became known as the "REA Moving Belt" plan. Poles, hardware, and transformers were obtained for mass construction through large-scale bidding, and farmers were brought together to help wire their homes and farms on a group-wiring plan designed by REA engineers. "REA efficiency became something of a legend in government."[66]

One of Carmody's early and important policy decisions was to work directly with REA financed cooperatives rather than through intermediary state overhead organizations. This gave REA a first hand relationship with the operating cooperatives. It was a good policy for the time when the REA needed close contact with borrowing associations to build a strong nation-wide system of rural electric cooperatives.

It should be noted that when Carmody came in as REA Administrator a controversy was building up on how the REA could best serve local rural electric cooperatives. Cooke had favored working through state associations of the type already formed in Indiana and Ohio. Carmody saw the value of state associations for educational work and political representation but he did not see how the REA could turn over its basic responsibilities to them.[67] After careful study of the problem he decided that the REA could most effectively work directly with the local associations in supplying them with all essential services and loan funds. According to Clyde Ellis, later to be the first General Manager of the National Rural Electric Cooperative Association, Carmody "saw all types of state agencies as unnecessary middlemen that would slow up the program." Carmody's decision had a profound effect upon the structure and operations of the REA. Ellis holds that it was "a wise policy for the time at least" in that "it forced local people to assume greater responsibility for the operation of their co-ops, thus giving the program the strong grass roots flavor that it has today."[68]

This decision was also important in that it nipped in the bud a growing sentiment to set up a national organization to be comprised of state rural electric cooperative organizations. When the National Rural Electric Cooperative Association was established in 1942, it was a quite different type of organization than the one earlier projected. Carmody, according to Marquis Childs, was friendly to the idea of "some sort of mutual protective association" until he decided that "the time had not yet arrived for such an organization."[69]

Of great concern to the REA during 1937 was the bitter opposition of the private utility companies which did everything possible to undermine the REA program. In many cases, so-called "public relations" men visited communities where cooperatives were being contemplated for the purpose of discouraging their formation by the dissemination of misleading information. One widespread practice was to set up "spite lines" to take over the rural electrification job before a REA cooperative could be formed and started in an area. Another means of attack was by "cream skimming" which involved extending rural lines from private power companies into communities where it was most profitable to do so—leaving the unprofitable territory unserved. Cream skimming made it difficult for REA cooperatives to be formed on an area-wide economical basis so as to serve all farmers. Carmody believed in fighting fire with fire and in calling a spade a spade. He responded by intensifying REA efforts. In the *1938 Annual Report of the Rural Electrification Administration,* much space was devoted to this problem, and such tactics were branded for what they were—an attempt to sabotage the Rural Electrification Act of 1936.

Legal problems required a great deal of attention during the years 1936 and 1937. One great need was a model form of statute providing for the incorporation of so-called electric membership corporations. A law to meet this need was drafted by the REA's legal staff in 1937 and was soon widely adopted by state governments.

In the fall of 1937, Carmody decided that as cooperatives were now arising spontaneously without outside pressure, the Development Division could be replaced by a Utilization Division to show farm people how to use electricity effectively and profitably. To head the new Division, he obtained George Munger, the man who had done an outstanding job of "load building" for the TVA. This Division soon had a staff of specialists in home economics, engineering, and electrical usage, working in teams of three, in many areas of the country. This program of work was greatly expanded in 1938, as it became clear that increased use of electricity was necessary to develop an economical program. The well-remembered Demonstration Farm Equipment Tour Team was put on the road with a tent that would seat 1,000 spectators and a large collection of electrical equipment and appliances. Known as the "Electric Circus," this demonstration show was moved by truck from community to community in some 20 states and was visited by hundreds of thousands of rural people.

Under the Rural Electrification Act of 1936, the REA was authorized to make loans for generating plants and transmission lines, although it was doubted at that time whether use would be made of this authority. However, it soon became apparent that there was no alternative, for, in some instances, private utility companies refused to supply a wholesale source of power except at very high cost and under contracts which restricted classes of consumers that could be served by the distribution systems. Carmody's response was to make use of the generation and transmission (G & T) loan authority of the REA Act. The first loan of this type was made in early 1938 to the Wisconsin Power Cooperative of Chippewa Falls, Wisconsin, a federation of several local distribution cooperatives.

Carmody also was much interested in strengthening the knowledge of cooperatives on the part of REA employees and members of REA cooperatives. To this end he initiated training seminars for REA employees and for cooperative managers, bookkeepers, and other personnel and promoted regional conferences of headquarters and field staff workers to thrash out problems and work out procedures. Late in 1937 he brought Udo Rall into the Educational Department to conduct research on the problems of REA financed cooperatives. Part of Rall's work was to instruct new REA employees on how cooperatives were organized and operated in the REA program. In the course of this work, a set of questions and answers was developed on problems of most concern to REA employees and members of rural electric cooperatives. Learning that this information was available, Carmody urged its publication, and it was issued in 1939 as A Guide for Members of REA Cooperatives with a Foreword by Carmody. This little pamphlet of some 40 pages proved to be the most popular publication ever to be issued by REA. Practically all of the borrower associations requested copies for their employees and members, and over a million copies were distributed in the first edition. From time to time this publication has been slightly revised with total distribution eventually reaching several million copies. More than any other one thing, this pamphlet has improved cooperative understanding throughout the REA program.[70]

After Carmody relinquished his position as Administrator on June 23, 1939, to become head of the newly created Federal Works Agency, his successor, Harry Slattery, characterized him as the "architect of rural electric power system management," for he gave the REA much of its future design. Under Carmody spectacular progress was made by the REA. Within a little more than two years he had developed the REA into a powerful agency for stimulating rural electrification through a nation-wide system of governmentally financed cooperative associations. During this period the number of farms served by such associations expanded more than ten-fold, from less than 20,000 to nearly 270,000.

REA becomes part of United States Department of Agriculture. Under authority of the Reorganization Act of 1939, President Roosevelt put the REA in the Department of Agriculture as of July 1, 1939, on the grounds that the program of REA was closely related to the work of the

Department and could best be conducted as a departmental agency. On September 26, 1939, Harry Slattery, long an advocate of public power, was appointed Administrator. There was little immediate change in program under Slattery who continued the aggressive procedures of Carmody.

In 1940 REA could look back on remarkable growth since the Norris-Rayburn Rural Electrification Act of 1936 was passed. As of June 1, 1936, there were only 11 active REA borrowers and at that time only 693 consumers were connected for service. By June 1, 1940, the number of active borrowers was 629, and the number of consumers connected for service was 549,238. About 90 per cent of the systems served were cooperative associations. How the program had grown in this period is shown by the following tabulation.[71]

As of June 30	Number of Active Borrowers	Miles of Line in Operation	Consumers Served
1936	11	400	693
1937	45	8,000	19,611
1938	248	41,736	104,528
1939	416	115,138	267,634
1940	629	232,886	549,238

On December 31, 1935, there were 789,000 farms being served by private and public utility systems. This number more than doubled by June 30, 1940, to 1,871,942 as the Government's rural electrification program advanced. During these years the percentage of all farms electrified, served through REA financing, grew from nothing to 26 per cent.[72] The job of electrifying rural America was not nearly half done by the end of 1940, but REA and the rural electric cooperatives were then well on their way as later chapters will make clear.

Chapter XVIII

THE CHALLENGE OF
CONSUMERS' COOPERATION: 1933-1940

Consumers' cooperation was at ebb tide as 1933 opened. The League Congress in October 1932 had been a sombre affair, and there was little enthusiasm for the immediate future with the depression in full swing. Although some progress was reported toward getting the League on to a self-supporting basis, it was still heavily dependent upon Dr. Warbasse for financial support. The need for economy was so great that, in May, Dr. Warbasse assumed the work of General Secretary, and Mr. Cooley was employed only as part-time editor for *Cooperation*. However, optimism began to revive with the formation of National Cooperatives, Inc., in February and with the installation of the New Deal Administration in March as many of the new leaders in government appeared to be cooperative-minded.[1]

The Formation of National Cooperatives, Inc.

As early as July 1929, Howard Cowden had envisaged a nation-wide chain of cooperative oil associations, and he invited "all organized groups of farmers" to help in its creation. He did not lose this dream as the Union Oil Company (Cooperative) expanded under his direction. Harvey Hull, Manager of the Indiana Farm Bureau Cooperative Association, and President of the Farm Bureau Oil Company, also became convinced that a central organization was needed to consolidate the buying power of the growing regional purchasing associations. This idea appealed to Ed O'Neal, President of the American Farm Bureau Federation, who urged Hull to bring together all of the Farm Bureau purchasing cooperatives into one national buying organization. Hull held three meetings for this purpose in Chicago during 1931 but with no results, since many of those represented "had little real cooperative philosophy" and were insistent that any new organization should be a department of the American Farm Bureau Federation.[2] By the fall of 1932, it had become evident to Hull and Cowden that the regional purchasing cooperatives were ready to form a national buying organization, so they took the lead in bringing together in Chicago, on November 22, 1932, representatives from seven major mid-western regional purchasing cooperatives—The Union Oil Company, the Illinois Farm Supply Company, the Indiana Farm Bureau Cooperative Association, the Michigan Farm Bureau Service Company, the Farmers' Union Central Exchange, the Central Cooperative Wholesale, and the Midland Cooperative Wholesale.[3] Howard Cowden was elected Chairman for the Conference, and Oscar Cooley, then Secretary of the Cooperative League, served as Secretary.

Prior to the meeting, a set of articles and by-laws had been drafted by Donald Kirkpatrick, attorney for the Illinois Farm Supply Company and the Illinois Agricultural Association, and these were read and discussed. It soon became apparent that the majority present wanted "something different" and the "fireworks began." The proposed articles and by-laws were designed to pool the purchasing of farm supplies, particularly of petroleum products, by an organization to be incorporated under the Illinois Agricultural Act. Most of those present favored instead a broad consumers' wholesale organization that would not be restricted to farmers or any one class of consumers. It was argued that urban consumers also required gasoline and tires and tubes which were then the major supplies under consideration. It was maintained that any line drawn between town and country would shut out such strong organizations as the Central Cooperative Wholesale and Midland Cooperative Wholesale, while all were needed to develop a strong national purchasing agency. This principle—strongly supported by Cowden and Hull—was generally accepted.

Then disagreement arose on the name for the proposed organization. "American Service Association" was proposed since it was maintained by the representatives of the Illinois Farm Supply Company that the word "cooperative" was not looked upon favorably in Illinois. This line of thinking was unacceptable to the majority who insisted that the name of the organization must include the word "cooperative." Of the names then proposed, "National Cooperative Wholesale," "American Cooperative Wholesale Society," and "National Consumers Cooperative, Inc.," the latter was temporarily accepted by a vote of 5 to 2 "in order that no one may make the mistake of assuming that this is not a consumers' cooperative."

The proposed articles had provided that all national organizations engaged in cooperative educational work, such as the Cooperative League, the National Farmers Union, the American Farm Bureau Federation, the National Grange, and the Equity Union, should be represented on the Board of Directors. This seemed an excellent way to unify cooperative business and educational activities, and, for the time, it was accepted, although it was soon to be dropped.

In view of the differences of opinion in the group, it was decided to redraft the articles and by-laws that night for further discussion the following day. Fred Hartsook, attorney for the Indiana Farm Bureau Cooperative Association, undertook this task, and, with the assistance of Oscar Cooley, he "hammered out" revised documents for "a national consumers cooperative association" to be incorporated under Indiana law. The next day the revised documents were submitted, amended in part, and then voted on and accepted. The meeting then adjourned to December 9. By then sharp disagreement on the proposed plan had become evident. The American Farm Bureau Federation supporters opposed the inclusion of consumers, and it appeared that the Illinois Farm Supply Company would not participate unless the organization was designed to serve farmers only. In view of the conflict in point of view on this and other points, it was decided to hold a third meeting on February 20, 1933. When this meeting was held, a new name was agreed upon—National Cooperatives, Inc.—and the articles and by-laws were accepted. Of the original group, five organizations joined as members, while the Illinois Farm Supply Company and the Michigan Farm Bureau Services declined to participate. Thus on February 20, 1933, National Cooperatives, Inc., was born.[4]

It is of interest that the by-laws defined eligible members as "consumers' cooperative, wholesale purchasing associations" who subscribed to Rochdale methods of organization and operation. The purposes were set forth in the Articles of Incorporation as follows:

> (a) To purchase, manufacture, produce, and distribute cooperatively for and to consumers' cooperative, wholesale purchasing associations any or all goods, wares, merchandise and/or services consumed or used by such associations or the members, stockholders or patrons thereof. . . .
> (c) To assist in the organization, financing, or operation of any consumers' cooperative enterprises and, in general, to promote and extend cooperative purchasing, manufacture, production, and distribution of goods and/or services among consumers.

At this meeting directors were elected. Harvey Hull was named President and Howard Cowden, Secretary. On February 23, the Articles of Incorporation were filed.

The five original members of National Cooperatives, Inc., included two members of The Cooperative League—The Central Cooperative Wholesale and the Midland Cooperative Wholesale—and the other three—the Indiana Farm Bureau Cooperative Association, the Union Oil Company (soon to be the Consumers' Cooperative Association) and the Farmers' Union Central Exchange—were all strong supporters of Rochdale cooperation. When the National became a member of the League on October 22, 1933, it indirectly brought these three powerful organizations into membership. Moreover, it also added to the League's Board of Directors as representative of National, I. H. Hull, the aggressive and competent manager of the Indiana Farm Bureau Cooperative Association, a man who was highly respected in all agricultural and cooperative purchasing circles. Thus, National Cooperatives' accession to the League was of tremendous importance to the League at this juncture, for it assured its support in the central states region where cooperative purchasing and consumers' cooperation had most immediate promise.

However, the League was not in position to take advantage of this new encouraging development until the right man could be found as Executive Secretary. Dr. Warbasse found the man the League was searching for in Eugene R. Bowen, and a new epoch in the history of the League, and in consumers' cooperation, opened. How Bowen came on the scene and how he almost instantaneously gave it new life and direction will be described after we examine how the League and National Cooperatives found an opportunity to represent the interests of all cooperatives under the National Recovery Administration.

The NRA Codes and the Cooperatives

To effectuate the purposes of the National Industrial Recovery Act, passed in June 1933, President Roosevelt set up a Consumers Advisory Board to protect consumer interests under the Codes of Fair Competition provided for under the Act. As Chairman of the Board, President Roosevelt appointed Mrs. Mary Rumsay, a good friend of cooperatives. He also named Dr. Warbasse as a member of the Board. Although this Board was not thought to be of major importance, it proved to have formidable power.[5]

It soon became apparent that the codes of fair competition for various industry groups were being drafted largely by business interests unfriendly or opposed to cooperative organizations. The preliminary drafts of the petroleum and other codes relating to agricultural needs soon disclosed that they would, in effect, destroy the basic character of cooperatives by prohibiting payment of patronage refunds. The proposed petroleum code, for example. would have forbidden rebates of any kind and would have included patronage refunds as rebates. Howard Cowden, who had been named as cooperative representative on the petroleum code committee by President Roosevelt, worked hard to stop this interpretation, and he was greatly assisted by Dr. Warbasse. Cowden not only represented the interests of the regional petroleum cooperatives, associated together in National Cooperatives, Inc., but he also represented the National Cooperative Council which represented many large agricultural purchasing cooperatives, including his own organization, The Union Oil Company Cooperative, and the American Farm Bureau Federation, and the National Grange.

As a result of the combined efforts of the cooperatives, President Roosevelt issued an Executive Order on October 23, 1933, which declared:

> I, Franklin D. Roosevelt, President of the United States, do hereby order that no provision in any code of Fair Competition, agreement or license which has heretofore been, or may hereafter be approved, prescribed, or issued pursuant to Title I of the National Industrial Recovery Act, shall be so construed or applied as to prohibit the payment of patronage dividends in accordance with law to any member by any bona fide and legitimate cooperative organization, including any farmers' cooperative, duly organized under the Laws of any state, territory or the District of Columbia, of the United States, if such patronage dividends are paid out of actual earnings of such cooperative organization and are not paid at the time when such member makes a purchase from such cooperative organization. (Signed), Franklin D. Roosevelt.

On February 17, 1934, President Roosevelt issued a second Executive Order which further strengthened the position of cooperatives. It stated: "No provision in any code of fair competition . . . . shall be construed or applied so as to make it a violation of any code of fair competition to sell to or through any bona fide and legitimate cooperative organization."

Although these Executive Orders gave the cooperatives basic protection, the issue was far from settled, and it had to be fought out in many of the individual codes which employed various devices to handicap the cooperatives. None was more bitterly contested than the code for the petroleum industry until, at the insistence of the petroleum cooperatives, the NRA Administrator issued a definition of a "bona fide and legitimate" cooperative as an Administrative Order on May 19, 1934. This definition was largely drafted by Cowden in consultation with the cooperatives he represented. Thus, the common problem of protecting the long established right of cooperatives to pay patronage refunds and do other things essential to their maintenance brought together on a common front representatives of consumer and producer cooperatives.[6]

The League as of January 1, 1934

Prior to 1934 the Cooperative League was a conglomerate of District Leagues, Cooperative Wholesale cooperatives, and individual consumer cooperatives. It was still dominated by a Board of Directors largely hand-picked by Dr. Warbasse and his intimate associates. Significantly, a growing number of farm-oriented cooperatives were coming into membership either through the District Leagues or as direct members. The formation of National Cooperatives in early 1933 was a very important development, for it automatically brought all of National's member organizations into the League's orbit.

This was the situation when E. R. Bowen became General Secretary of the League on January 1, 1934. He found himself responsible for the operation and development of a national organization comprised of heterogeneous elements with but one common characteristic—a belief in consumers' cooperation. He also found that the League was not self-supporting, for it was largely maintained by the largesse of President Warbasse. To develop a strong program, a larger budget would be necessary. Bowen was astute enough to realize that the best chance for developing support lay in wooing the farmer purchasing associations, which were already half-way members of the League through their membership in National Cooperatives.

Bowen Takes Command

The emergence of E. R. Bowen as an advocate of consumers' cooperation is a saga in American cooperative literature.[7] Until 1932 Bowen was a hard hitting sales executive for the Avery (Farm Machinery) Company in Peoria, Illinois. He was in charge of promotion and advertising, and he was proud of the contribution that he was making to the expansion of power farming. In that year, at the age of 52, Bowen resigned to clear his mind after a basic disagreement on company policies. Disillusioned by the methods of "profit business," he began to search for a better system of economic organization. His experience in working with farmers led him naturally to a study of farm marketing and purchasing cooperatives, and he began a program of self-education on the history, philosophy, and methods of all forms of cooperative organization. He absorbed himself in cooperative literature and visits to cooperatives in Illinois and nearby states. He finally found a friend and tutor in Professor Paul Douglas of the University of Chicago who gave him encouragement and direction in his reading on the subject. After Bowen had explained his background and desire to get into the consumers' cooperative movement, Douglas said: "That's where you belong."[8]

In December 1933, while Bowen was reading cooperative literature in the library of the University of Chicago, a fortuitous circumstance opened the door for his ambitions. Dr. Warbasse, President of the Cooperative League, who was in Chicago to attend a meeting of the League's directors, came out to the University of Chicago to address Douglas's class, and Bowen was invited to attend. This was just the opportunity that Bowen was training himself for and he sought an interview the next day. Warbasse was so impressed with Bowen's qualifications that after an hour's conversation he offered him a position with the Cooperative League as "educational secretary." However, after Bowen's qualifications had been examined by the Executive Committee of the League, he was named General Secretary and editor of the League's magazine, *Cooperation*.[9]

So almost immediately Bowen was catapulted into being the chief executive officer of the League. On January 1, 1934, he began his new duties at the League Headquarters in New York City. Bowen immediately showed his independence by planning a program to gain broad support for the League. After sizing up the situation he came to the conclusion that the functions of the League should be grouped under three headings: Publicity, Education, and Legislation.[10]

Being experienced in publicity and advertising, Bowen saw the first need as a stronger promotional program, and he conceived the idea of an entire issue of *Cooperation* that would be a call for action under the general title: "Consumers' Cooperation—America's Answer." While this issue of *Cooperation,* which came out in May, was being printed, Bowen tackled the next problem of most interest to him—getting the League on to a self-supporting basis so that it would be freed from dependence on the philanthropy of Dr. Warbasse.

Recognizing that the greatest potential for building financial support was from League supporters in the Midwest, Bowen set forth on a tour to enlist their aid. With a pledge of continuing financial support from the Central Cooperative Wholesale in Superior, Wisconsin, he then visited E. G. Cort, the dynamic manager of Midland Cooperative Wholesale in Minneapolis. After Bowen presented a one-page outline of his views on what he was trying to accomplish, Cort promised that Midland would contribute $100 per month to help him do it. Bowen then obtained a guarantee of annual support from the Executive Committee of National Cooperatives meeting in Chicago to the extent of $2,000. However, Bowen's greatest achievement on this trip came from a call on Murray

Lincoln, Secretary of the Ohio Farm Bureau Federation, and Manager of its two important business subsidiaries—the Farm Bureau Service Company and the Farm Bureau Mutual Automobile Insurance Company. Bowen paved the way for Lincoln's powerful support by assuring him that he did not subscribe to Dr. Warbasse's view that farms should eventually be owned and operated by consumers' cooperatives—a viewpoint that was anathema to Lincoln and other farm leaders. After Bowen had explained his position, Lincoln said: "We ought to be in your organization."[11]

When Bowen got home from his westward trip with the League's financial problems under better control, the special edition of *Cooperation* with his call for action was ready for distribution. The opening paragraphs of "America's Answer—Consumers' Cooperation" declared that consumers' cooperation was the one desirable solution for America's economic problems. The body of the issue covered these topics: (1) The Four Proposed Solutions—Capitalism, Corporativism, Communism, and Cooperation; (2) Why Consumers' Cooperation Is Necessary; (3) What Consumers' Cooperation Does; (4) How Consumers' Cooperation Grows; (5) Organize a Consumers' Cooperative; (6) Study Consumers' Cooperation; (7) Leaders, Speak Definitely—Lead Out!; (8) Join the Cooperative League; and (9) What an Opportunity!

This issue of *Cooperation*—which was the first to be issued under the editorship of Bowen[12]—was so printed that "America's Answer" could be made into a separate pamphlet for wide distribution at low cost. This met with an immediate response and helped the ailing budget of the League. E. G. Cort, of Midland Cooperative Wholsale, immediately ordered 5,000 copies, and other substantial orders came in from other cooperative leaders and their organizations.

One result of long-run significance was the effect "America's Answer" had on Edward A. Filene who immediately expressed a desire to see Bowen. The interview was very congenial, and it was the beginning of a relationship that led Filene in early 1936, to provide $1 million for an organization—The Consumers' Distribution Cooperation—that was designed to further the sound development of consumers' cooperation.[13]

"America's Answer" came out at a very propitious time, and it gave Bowen a good flag to fly under. There was then widespread criticism of the prevailing business system that was being held responsible for the Great Depression, and this favored openmindedness toward a method of business organization that was designed for service rather than profit. The new spirit in the League captured the public's imagination, and liberals of all types began to show interest in consumers' cooperation.

With renewed confidence, the League directors authorized Bowen to employ an Assistant Secretary to help him with publicity problems, and, in August, after a diligent search for the right man, he brought in for this post Wallace J. Campbell, a young man who was gifted in writing and in leadership capacity. Much of the progress of the League during Bowen's period as General Secretary can be attributed to the excellent support given him by Campbell who, following the League's Congress, developed the Cooperative League's News Service which soon was doing an outstanding job in gaining favorable publicity for the League and consumers' cooperation.

By the time the League Congress met in October, interest in consumers' cooperation had been aroused to the pitch where its meetings were covered as news by the leading news services and major newspapers. In announcing the forthcoming Congress, Bowen had asserted: "Through consumers' cooperation we shall build a Cooperative Democracy of, by and for the people."[14] Many people came to the Congress with faith or with curiosity to see this challenge in action.

The 1934 Congress of the Cooperative League

The League's Ninth Biennial Congress in Chicago was a triumph for E. R. Bowen. According to an article in the November-December issue of *Cooperation*, headed, "The Cooperative League Comes of Age," the Congress was "historical" in that it marked "the result of the joining together of most of the large industrial and farm consumers' purchasing associations into membership in the Cooperative League." Bowen bridged the gap between the farmers' purchasing associations and the more general consumers' cooperatives by using the term consumers' purchasing cooperatives to embrace both. In his report to the Congress, he maintained that "cooperative purchasing and consumers cooperation are one and the same thing." The League was now assured of financial support from its member associations, and the new regional purchasing associations accepted into membership were aligned with Bowen's view that farm supply purchasing should be included in the concept of consumers' cooperation.

At this meeting there were many representatives from labor, religious, and educational organizations as well as from the New Deal Government agencies largely drawn to the meeting by Bowen's publicity and the hope that consumers' cooperation would provide an answer to America's serious economic and social problems. Altogether the 1934 Congress marked a revitalized spirit in the League and an awakened interest in the philosophy of consumers' cooperation. The writer, who was present, recalls the almost militant belief of many in attendance that consumers' cooperation was on the march and that nothing could stop its future.

One of the noticeable things about the Congress was the strong interest of religious leaders. A talk by Helen Topping on the philosophy of the Japanese Christian cooperator, Toyohiko Kagawa, aroused so much enthusiasm that Bowen invited Kagawa to come to America to spread his gospel that "cooperation was the love principle applied to business." All during 1935 the forthcoming visit of Kagawa to the United States in January 1936 was publicized so that there was an enormous interest built up for his meetings when he arrived.

Another talk that created great enthusiasm was by the Reverend Dr. M. M. Coady who told of the remarkable program of adult education for cooperative organization being carried on by the Extension Division of St. Francis Xavier University in Antigonish, Nova Scotia. Bowen and Lincoln were so impressed that they made a trip to see the program in action the following summer. During the next few years the Antigonish movement was to be highly publicized in the United States by the Cooperative League and particularly by Murray Lincoln and the Ohio Farm Bureau Federation.

Bowen and other League leaders had a right to be jubilant after this Congress. The new directors elected at the Congress included the following well-known leaders in the agricultural purchasing associations: Howard Cowden (The Union Oil Company), Ralph Ingerson (Farmers' Union Central Exchange), George Jacobsen (Midland Cooperative Oil Company), Murray D. Lincoln (The Ohio Farm Bureau Service Company and the Farm Bureau Mutual Automobile Insurance Company), Quentin Reynolds (Eastern States Farmers' Exchange), and George Barrett (Pacific Supply Company). Moreover the report of the Treasurer pointed out that the League was now "for the first time in the black, with the receipts entirely from member cooperative associations."

It can be said that the 1934 Congress marked the opening of a crusade for consumers' cooperation. In the next few years, churchmen, educators, labor leaders, and government officials along with representatives of the cooperatives vied with each other in expressing their faith and enthusiasm in consumers' cooperation as a means of restructuring the life of the nation. Following the meeting a flood of articles on consumers' cooperation began to appear in practically all important magazines and newspapers.

"Bibles" for Consumers' Cooperation

Several important books were published in 1936 which became "bibles" for consumers' cooperators. Probably of most influence was Horace H. Kallen's *The Decline and Rise of the Consumer*. This was a carefully built case for a world cooperative economy which Kallen saw gradually emerging. It was a thoughtful theoretical treatise that did much to give professional standing to the philosophy of consumers' cooperation. In an epilogue, Kallen presented a vision of life in a world Commonwealth of Consumers' Cooperatives in the year 2044—the two hundredth anniversary of the beginning of the consumers' cooperative era at Rochdale, England.

A more popular book was Bertram B. Fowler's *Consumer Cooperation in America—Democracy's Way Out*. Fowler was a journalist who had become a publicist for consumers' cooperation. He maintained: "A peaceful revolution is going forward in America today. It is proceeding quietly, without the fanfare of trumpets, without rancor and without confusion . . . The revolution described is the Consumer Cooperative Movement that is spreading through this country. It has already enrolled two million American families . . . " After reviewing accomplishments he concluded "Consumer cooperation is sweeping like a tide over America. Its impetus can be traced directly to the inherent American tradition of democracy, so strong, so firmly implanted, that even a century and a half of exploitation and economic feudalism have not been able to stamp it out."

Much of the cooperative literature published at this time assumed that a momentum was building up for consumers' cooperation, and the League under Bowen nourished this idea by issuing many low priced pamphlets which gained a wide readership.[15] With this outburst of propaganda, the consumers' cooperative movement took on the character of a gigantic revivalism meeting—engendering excitement and conversion. There was no cynicism in the leaders—they sincerely believed that consumers' cooperation was necessary for the survival of a free society.

Gaining National Attention by Radio

Not only did the League promote widespread publicity for consumers' cooperation through books, pamphlets, magazines, and newspapers, it also made full use of radio. On January 9, 1936, consumers' cooperation got a national forum on the highly popular N.B.C. Town Meeting of the Air program for this subject: "Which Way Capitalism—Competition or

Cooperatives?" Following a well-balanced statement by Dr. Edwin G. Nourse on the economic philosophy of cooperative enterprise, E. R. Bowen appealed to his listeners for the solution of economic problems through consumers' cooperatives by saying: "We invite you to join the hundred million meek who are out to inherit the earth." A second Town Meeting of the Air Program, on January 21, 1937, considered the subject: "Consumers' Cooperation and Private Business." In presenting the case for consumers' cooperation, Murray Lincoln said: "Cooperatives do not need to do all the business in any one line; they only need to do enough to establish effective competition . . . Cooperatives should not and generally do not enter a business field unless they are convinced that some material benefit can be gained, such as reduction of price, assurance of quality, or betterment of service. But up-to-date I've found practically no field that would not pay cooperatives to enter."

In his report on "Cooperative Highlights for 1937", in *Consumers' Cooperation* for February 1938, Wallace J. Campbell listed 12 national broadcasts relating to cooperatives over coast-to-coast hookups. Advocates of consumers' cooperation could not complain that the subject was not getting national exposure, and it came free because of the growing national interest in the subject.

The Movement Gains Strong Support

This was the first time that the techniques of advertising and propaganda were effectively used to build widespread interest and support for consumers' cooperation. A spirit of urgency prevailed that the nation needed to be cooperativized immediately if it were not to be engulfed by fascism or communism. Influential political figures like Secretary Henry A. Wallace gave the movement their blessing. In his highly popular book *Whose Constitution,* published in the summer of 1936, Wallace said in a chapter entitled "Cooperation—The Dominant Economic Idea of the Future":

> The only way in which democracy can survive the logical onslaught of the dictator-state aspect of Communism and Fascism is to develop the genuine cooperative ideal to the limit. Producers' cooperatives are not enough. For the most part they merely take the place of middlemen, and while in many cases they save a substantial part of the middleman's profit for the producer, they do not have any very profound effect on the people whom they serve. The cooperative way of life must pervade the community, and this means there must be consumers' cooperatives as well as producers' cooperatives.[16]

Moreover, Edward A. Filene gave the idea of consumers' cooperation business standing. In an address on "Capitalism and the Consumer

Cooperatives" at a conference of the International Association of Sales Executives in New York City, April 3, 1936, Filene said: "If consumer cooperatives result in giving more service to masses of consumers than they could otherwise get, they may prove to be the very salvation of our business system, a bulwark of defense against socialism, communism and dead, dull, bureaucratic operation of industry, whether by the government or by shortsighted capitalist cartels . . . Businessmen, I believe, when they fully understand the facts of our business evolution and fully understand the real menace of capitalism, will give these consumer cooperatives their heartiest cooperation."[17]

Educational Advance

Bowen recognized the importance of enlisting educators in his cause, for he realized that the young people of today would be the cooperators of tomorrow. He found an important ally in Joy Elmer Morgan, the editor of the *Journal of the National Education Association,* who used this influential educational organ to encourage interest and support for consumers' cooperation among the teaching profession. Morgan's credo "The Ultimate Democracy," printed on a full page of *Consumers' Cooperation* for May 1936, was a powerful aid. It read as follows:

1. Next to the free public schools, the consumers' cooperative movement is the greatest social invention of modern times; it is of the people, by the people, and for the people.
2. The cooperative movement serves every type of human need, both economic and cultural.
3. The cooperative movement thrives in every country where freedom is not entirely destroyed.
4. The cooperative movement removes the causes of war and of internal strife between classes.
5. To a world disheartened by unemployment and torn by war, the cooperative movement offers a peaceful pathway toward a better civilization.
6. . . . The cooperative movement overcomes corporation privilege, domination, monopoly, and excessive concentration of wealth by establishing a motive higher than greed and by performing a superior service.
7. The cooperative movement asks no special favors; it has faith in enlightenment, free discussion, good will, and the power of growth.
8. For the development of the cooperative movement, conditions in the United States are especially favorable—abundant resources, a democratic tradition, a high level of general education and a great area free from tariff barriers.
9. When studied and practiced in the school, the cooperative movement gives young people a new life and a sense of responsibility for their own destinies.
10. The cooperative movement is the most powerful form of education for both children and adults; people learn by doing; they develop faith in themselves and in each other.

11. When fostered by the church—as Kagawa has pointed out—the cooperative movement is an instrument of self-help to the impoverished and the desperate.

12. The cooperative movement is the practical application of the golden rule: it is the ultimate democracy.

In January 1936, the *Journal of the National Education Association* carried a 16-page teaching section on the Cooperative Movement. Over 214,000 copies of the magazine went to subscribers, and many thousand more copies of the section were distributed as reprints by the Cooperative League.

Education for cooperation also received a significant boost with the passage of a law by the state of Wisconsin on September 1, 1938, which provided that "Every high school and vocational school shall prescribe adequate and essential instruction in cooperative marketing and consumers' cooperation." The law also provided for teacher training and provision of text material on this subject.[18] Soon afterwards similar laws were enacted in Minnesota and North Dakota.

In the fall of 1938 the National Education Association also issued a report on "Cooperatives" prepared by a committee of educators. Professor Harold F. Clark of Columbia University called this "a landmark in the history of education." This report, which provided information on how public schools and colleges could teach cooperation made it clear, said Clark, that "organizations embracing hundreds of thousands of teachers have definitely discovered the need of the cooperative movement."[19]

Expansion of Cooperative Literature

A review of the issues of the League's magazine reflects the crusading spirit of the League during 1935 under Bowen's leadership. Although Dr. Warbasse contributed articles and editorials, the major voice in editorials, articles, and in content was clearly that of Bowen. In January the name of the magazine was changed from *Cooperation* to *Consumers' Cooperation*. It carried as a masthead this expression of purpose: "A National Magazine for Cooperative Readers—Organ of the Consumers' Cooperative Purchasing Movement." An editorial explained the new name by saying: "There are two reasons for this change: first, to indicate more definitely the purpose of the Cooperative League and avoid confusion with other forms of Cooperation . . . and secondly, to take advantage of the rapidly growing realization by the people that they are first of all consumers and must organize . . . as such in a day of plenty."

The magazine under the new name reflected the aggressive spirit of the League. An article in the January issue was entitled: "What New

Worlds Have You Planned to Conquer for Cooperation in 1935?" It concluded: "We must all make every year count towards the realization of a Cooperative Economic Democracy." The first issue under the new name also announced that the League was going to push hard to increase "cooperative literacy" by reporting articles and books on cooperation as they appeared. Bowen said: "The public could not well learn of cooperation when there was almost nothing in the periodicals they read." This situation was rapidly changing as cooperatives began to make news, and the issues of *Consumers' Cooperation* made this fact clear. At first the page or pages reporting cooperating literature issued during the preceding month were headed "Creating Consumer Consciousness" but it soon became "The Press Boosts Consumers' Cooperation." During 1935, hundreds of articles in magazines and newspapers were reported, and an increasing number of books and pamphlets relating to the subject were mentioned or reviewed. "Continuous Expansion" became the League's battle cry.

Stimulation from European Experience

Prior to 1934, few people in the United States were well informed on the specular development of consumers' cooperative organizations in the British Isles and in European countries. This situation was to be changed rapidly in 1935, and an intense interest was to be aroused in the accomplishments of European consumer cooperatives. Part of the change stemmed from the trips of Howard Cowden and Harvey Hull to Europe to attend the 1934 meetings of the International Cooperative Alliance as representatives of the Cooperative League. They came back fired with enthusiasm for what they had found out that could be used in American cooperative advancement—and since they were men who had wide followings in the United States—their views were respected. Of great influence was a little pamphlet written by Howard Cowden: "A Trip to Cooperative Europe." He took the reader with him and reflected the great inspiration he had received from observing the large cooperative institutions of England, Scotland, and Scandinavia—particularly in their planning activities, manufacturing operations, and educational methods. The final paragraph of this pamphlet read: "The outstanding lessons, then, that we who love the cooperative ideal and would see it grow in American soil can learn from Cooperative Europe are: They *unite*, they *plan*, and they *educate*. Shall we in America do the same: If everyone who reads these pages will help, we can and we will." Cowden could not have been disappointed by the reception given his pamphlet. Many thousands of copies were soon in the hands of cooperative leaders in all parts of the United States.

During 1935 the issues of *Consumers' Cooperation* were full of accounts of how consumers' cooperatives in Europe had "busted the trusts," and books and articles began to appear in response to a demand for more information on European cooperative experience. Noteworthy among this literature was a series of articles by Marquis Childs in the *St. Louis Post Dispatch* which were published in January 1936 by the Yale University Press under the title: *Sweden—The Middle Way*. This book met a national response and immediately became a best seller. It upheld Sweden as an example of a country following a middle way between fascism and communism through the use of consumer and farm cooperatives and liberal social institutions. It met the needs of the times and was adapted to the temper of the American people.

The Appeal to Youth

Consumers' cooperation had a great appeal to young people during the hard times of the New Deal period, and many cooperatives flourished on college campuses. Following the lead of the old established Harvard Cooperative Book Store, similar cooperatives flourished in many colleges and universities. Also to help reduce costs, many students found it desirable to organize cooperative rooming houses and boarding clubs. Many future cooperative leaders got their induction in cooperative ranks through such experience. In early 1936, representatives of student cooperatives set up a national committee on student cooperatives designed to assemble information on all types of student cooperatives, so as to assist in their fuller development. A report of this committee in *Consumers' Cooperation* for October 1938 indicated that there were 189 cooperatives of this type—dormitories, dining clubs, book stores, etc.—with 104,627 members and doing an annual volume of business of $3,753,710, with savings of $658,050.

The Cooperative League also appealed to youth by setting up a cooperative recreation service in 1935 to encourage cooperators to play together as well as work together. Many in the Consumers' Cooperative Movement in the late 1930's believed that they were building a social as well as an economic democracy, and the effort helped strengthen the ties of many young people to the consumers' cooperatives.[20]

Kagawa's Triumphant Tour in 1936

The tremendous build-up given to Dr. Toyohiko Kagawa's forthcoming visit to the United States resulted in hundreds of revival type cooperative meetings largely held in churches during the first six months of 1936. While on this tour he spoke to audiences that reached a total of nearly a million persons. His message was simple: "Between capitalism and the Kingdom of God there can be no compromise—either one or the other must go." "Cooperatives are the economic foundation of world peace." "The more we develop the capitalistic system, the more we become dependents." Over and over again he repeated the challenging statement: "Whether you like it or not, there is no other way but cooperatives."

The appeal of Kagawa's philosophy to many church leaders was reflected in an article in the February 1936 issue of *Consumers' Cooperation* by Benson Y. Landis, Associate Secretary of the Department of Research and Education of the Federal Council of Churches of Christ in America. Landis reported how more than 300 church officials from a majority of the Protestant bodies met together in a seminar at Indianapolis to study the consumers' cooperative movement and hear Dr. Toyohiko Kagawa. The delegates at the Seminar unanimously came to the conclusion that "the cooperative movement is one of the major techniques in making possible the Kingdom of God on earth." They went on to say: "We believe that Kagawa's tour of the U.S. cannot fail to stimulate unprecedented interest in the cooperative movement in this country," and they recommended "that the various church bodies should hold other seminars throughout the country on the relation of the church to the cooperative movement and that interested agencies should more widely disseminate the literature on the movement."

The enthusiasms engendered by Kagawa's tour were reflected in an article in *Consumers' Cooperation* for March entitled "New Light from the East." It summed up the significance of his visit by saying: "The Consumers' Cooperative Movement has and will continue to receive, through his coming to America, the greatest publicity we have ever had for our cause—it is now for cooperators to use his evangelizing of our movement to follow with education and organization of the tens of thousands he is reaching."

Although many did not fully approve of Kagawa's castigation of capitalism, there is no doubt that he had a profound effect in gaining a favorable public climate for consumers' cooperation by reaching influential church leaders and religious-minded people. The Cooperative League took advantage of this situation by issuing a little pamphlet, "Kagawa and Cooperatives," and by publicizing his writings.

The President's Commission to Study
European Cooperatives

As a result of the widespread interest in European cooperatives engendered by *A Trip to Cooperative Europe* and *Sweden—The Middle Way* and the political importance of the subject, President Roosevelt set up a Commission in the summer of 1936, a Presidential election year, to study cooperative enterprise in several European countries.[21] The object was to determine whether or not the government could assist consumers' cooperatives in the United States. Originally the Commission was comprised of a Chairman and two members, but, before they got to Europe, the commission was enlarged to include two agricultural representatives and a woman to examine the importance of cooperatives from a woman's point of view. Intense interest was aroused in the progress of the Commission which was in Europe for a period of 2½ months, and the newspapers and magazines were filled with articles reporting on the Commission's activities and speculations on the significance of its possible findings. *The Report of the Enquiry on Cooperative Enterprise in Europe,* issued in early 1937, was somewhat of an anticlimax. It brought out that consumers' cooperatives had "brought new homes, new pride of ownership, higher standards of living, to a substantial portion of the people of Western Europe," but it recognized that consumers' cooperation as practiced in Europe was no panacea for American problems, and there was little in the report that was not already known from the voluminous literature available on the subject. No recommendations were made for direct government assistance, for the report found that consumers' cooperatives in Europe were not especially favored.[22]

However, in a separate report transmitted to the President it was recommended: "(1) That there be made a survey of consumer and service cooperatives in the United States. (2) That an agency be established or designated to give information, research and advisory service to consumers' cooperatives, and (3) That steps be taken to assure consumer cooperatives credit parity." The Cooperative League made the most of the Report's propaganda value, but it had little direct effect on government policy or in public influence.[23]

The 1936 Congress

The Tenth Biennial Congress of the Cooperative League was held in Columbus, Ohio, in October 1936—the home of the Ohio Farm Bureau Federation and its two strong cooperative subsidiaries. In his address of welcome, Perry L. Green, President of the Ohio Farm Bureau Federation said:

> No former Congress has been held with a larger measure of success to review. We have seen the awakening as never before of the clergy, the laymen, the organized church itself, the farmer, the laborer, the educator and the leaders of finance and business, to the need of changing our economic processes. The Cooperative Movement is being recognized as one which is setting in motion evolutionary forces needed to produce these changes.

In his presidential address Dr. Warbasse said: "Cooperation offers the way to make a detour around fascism and to arrive at an economy of abundance without passing through the horrors of social chaos and the valley of economic destruction and death . . . " Bowen, in his report as General Secretary asserted that : "The eyes of America are turning toward Cooperative Economic Democracy." Bowen thought that this was partly because of the "significant publicity which the Cooperative movement has now gotten." He called attention to the fact that the number of articles published on consumers' cooperation had expanded 30 times since the last League Congress. He concluded by saying: "I challenge America to reach the point in ten years . . . when half of the people of the United States are members of cooperatives."

This was the largest Congress yet held with over 694 registrations and with 184 delegates. There was no major change in the composition of the League reflected by the Congress but the farm purchasing delegates demonstrated their power and increased their grip on the organization. Much interest was focussed on the forthcoming report of the Commission of European Enquiry into Cooperative Enterprise and on the significance of Edward A. Filene's action in providing $1 million to promote consumers' cooperation through the Consumers' Distribution Corporation.

One of the significant addresses at the 1936 Congress was that of Roy F. Bergengren, Executive Secretary of the Credit Union National Association. The conversion of Filene, (the father of the American credit union movement) to consumers' cooperation was bringing about a broader understanding of credit unions by consumers' cooperative leaders. There was now a greater willingness to recognize credit unions as members of the consumers' cooperative fraternity even when they were related to employees of commercial enterprises. In his talk Bergengren cryptically observed: "Let us not be too hasty in our differentiation between those who are cooperators and those who are not. Our million in the credit union—every one of them—are consciously or unconsciously cooperators. Nor do I agree with those who are fearful that the cooperative movement cannot progress in America without immediate amalgamation of all parts of the cooperative movement."

Objective Evaluations Increase

By 1936 so much interest had been aroused nationally in consumers' cooperation, both by its supporters and opponents, that there was need for a tempered analysis of the subject.[24] This need was partially met by an article in the October 1936 *Dunn and Bradstreet Monthly Review* by Willard I. Thorp, Director of Economic Research for Dunn and Bradstreet, Inc. Thorp came to the "tentative conclusion that cooperatives will neither decline or record extraordinary advances in the short-run future . . ." He went on to say: "For those who are concerned with preserving private enterprise, it is obvious that the best defense against consumers' cooperatives is an efficient distribution system. Cooperation is no wild, fanciful scheme. Conceivably, it could eliminate some of the worst abuses introduced by competitive private enterprise. And unless private industry puts its own house in order, the consumer may rise in his wrath and provide his own defense, through consumer cooperatives."

The subject of "Consumers' Cooperation" was also objectively analyzed in a special volume of the *Annals of the American Academy of Political and Social Science,* issued in May 1937. Following articles on the theory and nature of consumers' cooperation as interpreted by Warbasse, Kallen, and others, the subject was considered in relation to the labor movement, the church, and political action. Bowen expounded the educational methods being used to promote consumers' cooperation, and cooperative leaders examined the status of consumers' cooperation in their respective fields. I. H. Hull dealt with farm purchasing cooperatives, Howard A. Cowden with oil and gasoline cooperatives, and Murray D. Lincoln with cooperative insurance and finance. Other articles considered cooperative housing, cooperative credit, and cooperative recreation developments. Of particular interest were two critical articles; one, by a business leader who concluded that "consumer cooperatives will continue to play an extremely minor role in American business life," and, the other by E. St. Elmo Lewis, a well-known writer on business subjects. Lewis did not forsee a rapid development of consumers' cooperation, but he recognized that it had great promise. He observed that: "The cooperatives need the private trader, and the latter needs the cooperatives. At the present time the consumer needs both."

The Problem of Urban Consumers' Cooperation

If consumers' cooperation was to be more than a strong agricultural cooperative purchasing movement, it had to find a way to serve consumers in towns and cities. Here the problem was difficult, for chain and department stores were already providing an efficient service. This problem had concerned the League for many years, and little progress had been made in overcoming it except in areas where there was a strong racial solidarity. To Bowen the only way to penetrate the urban market was through the formation of buying clubs which, with experience, would grow to become efficient local cooperatives. This was not a new idea, but it was given more dynamic leadership by the League under Bowen.[25]

Bowen found support in A. W. Warriner, Secretary of the Central States Cooperative League, who gave a talk on "Cooperative Buying Clubs" at the 1934 League Congress. Warriner pointed out that many buying clubs were informal organizations set up to obtain certain lines of merchandise below market prices and that few sold at market prices and returned savings in the form of patronage refunds. He thought that these organizations could be made into a powerful means for carrying on cooperative education and held that they could be "an opening wedge" for consumers' cooperatives. He urged that they accumulate capital, carry on training so that they could set up a store in a year or two.

During the next few years much attention was directed to the encouragement of buying clubs by consumers' cooperative leaders, and, in many cases, such clubs grew to become full-fledged cooperative stores. It is significant that Associated Cooperatives, which became an important wholesale consumers' cooperative association, got its start largely through serving buying clubs in California. Likewise many consumers' cooperatives grew out of buying clubs served by the Eastern Cooperative Wholesale Association in New York City.

Although the formation of buying clubs was a sound method for building cooperative stores, they required much patience and leadership, and they could not promise or give quick results. This was a technique for organization with great practical value, but it flourished best where there was already a strong central wholesale organization that could render efficient wholesale service and provide management advice.[26]

If the regional farm supply purchasing cooperatives were to become full-fledged consumer cooperatives, they could not stop with the cooperative purchasing of petroleum, feed, fertilizer, and other farm supplies. From the beginning of the League's history the goal had been to establish a strong network of retail consumers' stores as a basis for developing a viable system of wholesale consumers' organizations. In the enthusiasm for consumers' cooperation in 1934 and 1935, it was thought that the farm supply purchasing associations would go from farm supplies to home supplies—that, if cooperation could be used effectively to obtain goods for farm operations, it could be just as well utilized for obtaining goods for household consumption. One well-known economist argued that farmers spent more for consumers' goods than production goods, and that thus the opportunity was almost unlimited.

Cowden, Cort, Lincoln, and other cooperative purchasing leaders subscribed to this general philosophy and began to promote development in this direction. In July 1936, the Consumers' Cooperative Association (formerly the Union Oil Company) opened a grocery division which Cowden hailed as one of the greatest things yet done by the CCA. Yet it developed slowly. In *Consumers' Cooperation* for July, an article by Ivor Lind, entitled "From Gasoline to Groceries," reported great progress by a Midland association in handling groceries. In Ohio employees of the Ohio Farm Bureau Federation opened their own grocery store, and the formation of buying clubs and cooperative stores was encouraged. These were straws in the wind. In September 1938, Bowen, in *Consumers' Cooperation*, said "Cooperatives Should Move Faster—From gasoline to home supplies and from animal feed to human feed." Regardless of the admonition, the idea did not take hold. The problem of developing retail services for consumers was found to be much more difficult than providing farmers with farm supplies.

The most ambitious plan to develop a grocery business by a regional farm supply association was that of Midland Cooperative Wholesale which announced in the summer of 1939 that it was sponsoring a system of chain grocery stores. Under the carefully developed plan, management of local retail stores was to be provided by a special division of Midland.[27] However, after a year or so of trial, Midland had to acknowledge that the plan was a complete failure.

The conversion of Edward A. Filene to consumers' cooperation stirred the minds of many people, for he was an acknowledged leader in retail and wholesale distribution. He reasoned that consumers' cooperation was a logical form of enterprise if properly managed and directed. Putting his money where his heart was, he provided $1 million for an organization—The Consumers' Distribution Corporation—to promote the sound development of consumers' cooperatives.[28] One of his objectives was to develop a chain of consumer cooperative department stores. His untimely death in 1937 may have adversely affected the developments that he anticipated. The Board of Directors (which included Dr. Warbasse, H. A. Cowden, Murray D. Lincoln, James C. Drury, Percy S. Brown, and Roy F. Bergengren) was hesitant to embark on the department store venture—and did not undertake it until after World War II. Instead it provided assistance to many local cooperatives in improving their facilities. It also provided management for the cooperatives set up at the Greenbelt communities until they could establish themselves.[29]

Developments in 1939 and 1940

The great burst of promotional enthusiasm for consumers' cooperation reached its peak in 1937, and from then on progress was less spectacular but more substantial. In looking back over 1938, Wallace J. Campbell, in his "Cooperative Highlights" for the year reported that "nineteen thirty-eight will go down in co-op history as a year of growth and coordination." He listed as the number one event of 1938 the adoption in principle of a program looking toward a greater coordination of the activities of the Cooperative League and National Cooperatives, Inc. In his review for 1939 he said: "The American consumer cooperative movement can list 1939 as its greatest year of progress." He listed the big expansion in production operations by several of the large purchasing regionals. In 1940 the progress was continued with perhaps the most spectacular development being the opening of the first cooperative refinery by the Consumers' Cooperative Association. In his highlight reviews, Campbell stressed the growth of various kinds of cooperative services—housing, health, credit, electricity, burial, and recreation. The movement had blossomed out in many directions. Management training was being emphasized along with cooperative educational work. The time of projecting was giving place to building, and efficiency was being more and more stressed as the key for achievement.

During these years consumers' cooperation continued to receive attention in books and articles. One study of interest was an analysis of "Operating Results of Consumer Co-operatives in the United States" in 1937, made by the Bureau of Business Research of the Harvard Graduate School of Business Administration and financed by the Good Will Fund, Inc.[30] This study compared operating results of cooperative food stores and general stores with counterpart privately owned stores. An analysis was also made of farm supply stores and petroleum bulk stations. While the study made no attempt to appraise consumer cooperatives as contrasted with other forms of business organization, it did make clear that efficiency was not something endemic in cooperative organizations—it had to be developed.

Another interesting study by Maxwell S. Stewart: "Cooperatives in the U.S.—A Balance Sheet," was issued in 1939 as a Public Affairs Pamphlet. This was a realistic analysis of all kinds of cooperatives in the United States which concluded with a section: "Cooperatives Not a Panacea."

The author cautiously saw healthy growth, provided that it met its management and other problems. He observed: "The movement has already demonstrated tremendous vitality, and has shown that within certain areas—yet to be fully defined—it meets a genuine need." A less critical, but informative, book was John Daniel's *Cooperation—The American Way* (Harpers, 1939). Daniels showed how cooperative enterprise had grown out of America's past, and he offered wise counsel on meeting some of its current problems. He pleaded for the harmonization of cooperative viewpoints to achieve maximum progress.

Few of the books issued on cooperation during the thirties were designed as college textbooks. An exception was Orin Burley's *The Consumers' Cooperative as a Distributive Agency*, issued also in 1939. This was an attempt to put the consumers' cooperative enterprise into perspective in the field of marketing. Burley felt that the idea of a "consumers' cooperative commonwealth" was not necessarily "appropos" to conditions in the United States. He thought that "A competitive yardstick might better be the present goal." He concluded that "consumer cooperation will grow only if it improves on present distribution practices, by serving consumers either better or more economically."

It is apparent from these brief excerpts that by 1939 consumers' cooperation was passing from a promotional to a development stage.

The Schism in the League, 1934-1941

Soon after E. R. Bowen came in as General Secretary, a fissure had begun to open between him and Dr. Warbasse on how the League should be developed. Both were convinced cooperators but they differed greatly in background, temperament, and philosophy. While Warbasse was a free thinker, Bowen was a Quaker with a strong strain of Methodism in his make-up. While Bowen was a man who had come up the hard way with limited cultural interests, Warbasse was a professionally trained man, a scholar, and a patron of the arts. Although a prodigious reader for a purpose, Bowen had little patience with abstract social theorists, while Warbasse found them stimulating. Warbasse was an aristocrat who devoted his life and fortune to worthy causes. Bowen, on the other hand, was a plain man of the people who knew at first hand the problems of industry, labor, and agriculture. In the words of Clark A. Chambers: "A second-rate playwright could not more neatly have invented such opposite characters."[31]

It is not strange that Warbasse, who had nursed and financed the League from its birth and seen it through many crises, did not look with favor upon Bowen's aggressive actions which tended to weaken and nullify his influence in what he had come to consider his own organization. Looking at the matter from Bowen's point of view, the League had to move out from under Warbasse's domination if it were to survive and meet the needs of the hour. He saw a new era dawning in consumers' cooperation with himself as the instrument to usher in the new order.

Both men were respected cooperative leaders, and at first there appeared to be little disagreement between them. However, with the accession of Bowen's supporters to the League directorate, after the 1934 Congress, it was clear that the control of the League was shifting to Bowen and the fissure between the two widened. Even then the differences were muffled and not apparent to the general public or to most cooperators. Both men were too much concerned with the success of the League to harm it by an open struggle for power.

There were three basic points of conflict in addition to a different philosophy toward promotion. Bowen was an advocate by temperament and training, and he would do almost anything within reason to gain publicity for the cause he represented. Warbasse, on the other hand, felt that people should be persuaded by educational methods rather than swept up in a great crusade, and he had a distaste for what he considered to be flagrant promotional methods.[32]

1. As a matter of cooperative principle Warbasse maintained that farming ultimately should be carried on by consumers' cooperatives rather than by individual farmers. In his *Cooperative Democracy*, published in 1923, Warbasse said: "The ultimate aim of the cooperative consumers' movement should be to purchase the land from the farmer and employ the latter as an agricultural worker." This statement infuriated farmers and farm cooperative leaders, and Bowen conscientiously felt that he could not subscribe to this view and gain their support for the Cooperative League. Even in 1936 when *Cooperative Democracy* was reissued in revised form, Warbasse refused to change his position in this important matter.[33]

2. From the beginning of his stewardship, Bowen saw the need of developing the League as an independent self-supporting organization. While this was a common sense business judgement acceptable to Warbasse, the latter was concerned with the way Bowen aggressively reduced his influence while removing his financial importance to the League. Bowen was not a man of great tact, and this caused part of the estrangement.[34]

3. The views of Warbasse on desirable cooperative structure were modelled on British experience. He envisaged a Cooperative Democracy,

based upon local consumers' cooperatives being federated together into regional and national wholesales, and in which the Cooperative League would be the educational and ideological center like the Cooperative Union in England. Bowen soon concluded that this dual organization concept was impracticable. He believed—on the model of Swedish experience—that the educational and business sides of the movement should be combined in one organization. Moreover, in place of the Cooperative Democracy objective, Bowen favored the "cooperative sector" approach which recognized that the area suitable for cooperative development was limited.[35]

The Struggle for Supremacy, 1934-1938

The 1934 League Congress made it clear that the baton of leadership was passing from Warbasse to Bowen and that the stage was set for a vigorous program of expansion. Several of the major purchasing regions had gained recognition on the Board of Directors, and, with their accession, the League was assured of adequate financial support. However, the majority of the Board still represented the District Leagues and independent cooperatives closely allied to Warbasse.[36] This set up a tension within the League that was to prevail for several years. In fact, at one time Warbasse endeavored to force Bowen's resignation but without success, for this would have disrupted the League. Bowen's position was somewhat strengthened at the time of the 1936 League Congress by the election of several more Board members favorable to his views, and in August 1937 he was able to get the Executive Committee to accept the following definition of consumers' cooperation: "Consumers' cooperation as defined in its broadest terms is understood to include all joint purchasing and production of goods, foods, or services by ultimate users organized on the basis of the Rochdale principles."

The showdown between the Warbasse and Bowen factions occurred at the Congress of the League held in Kansas City in October 1938. At this time Bowen's supporters were able to gain full control of the Board and put into effect a system of uniform dues for member organizations. Prior to this, the League was dependent upon voluntary contributions. Another source of contention was resolved by the Board at its November meeting. It was decided to move the League's general offices to Chicago so as to be closer to major League member organizations.

For some time Bowen had been advocating a better coordination of the educational and commercial activities of the consumers' cooperative movement. At the November meeting of the Board he proposed a plan for

"A National Consumers' Cooperative Organization" which was agreed on in principle.[37]

Although the friction between Dr. Warbasse and Bowen continued until Warbasse resigned as President in 1941, it ceased to be a problem of serious concern after the League Congress decisions of 1938. With the resignation of Warbasse, Bowen's close friend and supporter, Murray Lincoln became the new League President.[38]

Changes in National Cooperatives, Inc.

In view of Bowen's recommendation that the Cooperative League and National Cooperatives be better coordinated, attention must be focussed briefly on the progress made by National Cooperatives since its formation in 1933. For the first few years National operated largely as an informal central buying agency for petroleum products, tires, and accessories. Deals with suppliers were worked out by the directors and participated in by the member associations. The small expenses of National were covered by an assessment based upon services received. During these years, National served mainly as a coordinating center for its member units. In 1936 National set up an office in Chicago with a manager in charge, and a wider range of supplies was handled. Master contracts were negotiated under which suppliers paid National a small brokerage fee for its services. The organization at that time formed a number of buying committees, representative of its member associations, to assist management in negotiating contracts on certain groups of supplies. Control was established over the Co-op Trade Mark, and in 1939 a grocery department was organized to serve the five member associations that handled groceries. With the employment of a second manager in 1938, the organization began to develop a more effective business service on additional supplies—especially in electrical appliances. However, as the organization expanded it acquired member associations who were not in full agreement with the philosophy of the Cooperative League.

National was a large organization on paper in view of the volumes of business done by its member organizations, but it was weak from an economic point of view. Its net income was negligible before 1939, and it was only $14,254 in 1939, and $18,038 in 1940. Although the National maintained adjoining offices with the League after 1938 and contributed to its support, only 6 of the 15 members were also members of the League in 1941, and only a few of National's members then favored an organic relationship with the League.[39]

Summary

In the years from 1933 to 1938, consumers' cooperation gained national recognition. During this period it grew from being largely a cult into a movement.[40] It cast aside the concept of the Cooperative Commonwealth and began to center on a more practical program of developing a wide variety of cooperative activities for consumers.

The change came about with a revitalization of the Cooperative League of the United States in 1933 and 1934 in response to a deep-seated anxiety that the prevailing capitalistic system was largely responsible for the Great Depression and a belief that consumers' cooperation could provide a more satisfactory method of economic organization. Before 1933, consumers' cooperation was largely centered in a few areas of the country and supported mostly by foreign immigrants. The number of members of consumers' cooperative societies totalled only a few hundred thousand. By 1941 consumers' cooperatives of various kinds were to be found in all states of the Union, and several million members could be reported.[41] Many of the principal consumers' cooperatives at the later time represented large regional farm supply purchasing associations which carried on extensive manufacturing and wholesaling operations. They were strong enough economically to sustain a strong consumers' cooperative movement.

Prior to 1933 consumers' cooperation was primarily expressed in the form of urban cooperative stores. In the years from 1933 to 1941 it became a rural and urban movement with its economic power centered largely in its rural supporters. During this period it broadened its conception to include the provision of many services—health, housing, recreation, insurance, finance, electricity, credit, etc. By 1941 the Cooperative League had become closely associated with National Cooperatives, Inc., and sentiment was forming for a better coordination of the functions of the two national organizations. This problem was not resolved until after World War II as will be explained in Chapter XXIII.

Chapter XIX

COOPERATIVE MARKETING STABILIZATION: 1933-1940

With the farm relief measures initiated in 1933, cash farm income began a slow upward climb from the low point reached in 1932. Although prices did not recover by 1940 to the high point reached in 1929, their gradual improvement provided a better climate for cooperative marketing development. In the marketing seasons from 1932-33 to 1939-40, the dollar volume of cooperative marketing associations rose from $1,199,500,000 to $1,729,000,000.[1] While this was less than the dollar volume of $2,310,000,000 attained in 1929-30, it represented more business handled by better organized and better financed cooperative organizations. Moreover, in view of the lower level of prices in 1939-40 as compared with 1929-30, the 1939-40 figures represented little if any decline in the quantity of farm products marketed.[2] Thus, 1940 found cooperative marketing generally in a stronger position than in past years.

To understand the nature of the progress made by marketing associations during the New Deal years, it is essential that attention be given to the following forces that were rapidly changing their characters: (1) the influence of the Triple A Program; (2) the financial and advisory assistance given by the Farm Credit Administration; (3) technological changes, particularly in transportation; (4) the growth of new marketing institutions and procedures; (5) the better coordination of cooperative organizations; and (6) the accumulation of cooperative knowledge and experience.

1. The influence of the Triple A program. As we pointed out in Chapter XIII, the federal government under the Agricultural Adjustment Act relieved the marketing cooperatives from major responsibilities in production control. This cleared away one of the principal barriers to constructive development. By placing in the hands of government responsibility for both production and supply control which were problems too big for cooperatives to handle, the cooperatives were enabled to center attention on ways to increase their business efficiency as marketing institutions. This resulted in a considerable improvement in the performance of cooperatives in services rendered for members and in savings realized. It also brought about an improvement in financial structures as evidenced by growth of cooperative assets and member ownership equities.

2. *The assistance given by the Farm Credit Administration.* Few realize how much marketing cooperatives were benefited during the New Deal days by the lending services provided by the Farm Credit Administration through its banks for cooperatives and by its research, service, and educational activities. The banks for cooperatives not only provided cooperatives with an assured source of funds at reasonable interest cost for operations and expansion, but they also made available a valuable source of guidance and counsel in business operations. The cooperative research and service work provided a corps of experienced and well-trained specialists devoted to the improvement of cooperative marketing efficiency.

(The Banks for Cooperatives). Since no agency did more to help agricultural marketing cooperatives during the New Deal years than the banks for cooperatives, it is essential that their contribution be fully realized. Prior to the establishment of the banks for cooperatives, it was often difficult or impossible to obtain adequate loans at reasonable cost for working capital or for necessary facilities. Although the Federal Farm Board had provided financial assistance to such cooperatives, its primary emphasis had been on helping them meet emergency short-time problems.[3] The banks for cooperatives were set up with more permanent objectives and were located throughout the United States so that they soon became identified with the basic problems of the cooperatives in their prescribed districts.

The banks for cooperatives were more than *banks* for cooperatives. They were entrepreneurs of cooperative development. They studied local conditions and worked as partners with the cooperatives they served. It soon became clear that the banks were not to be considered charitable organizations for subsidizing cooperatives. Each loan was carefully made so as to assure that it would meet its purpose and be repaid on schedule. The men in charge believed in the cooperative form of enterprise, and many had previous cooperative experience. Thus, the lending officers of the banks became counselors to the cooperatives and helped them

establish and follow good principles of business organization and operation. The banks early found that many cooperatives were not well set up
or well managed, and attention had to be given to problems of
management selection and training. In many cases organization documents, especially by-laws, were out-of-date or inadequate, and bookkeeping methods were not designed to provide information needed for
effective management. The banks insisted on proper audits and informative financial statements, and within a few years the standards of
cooperative auditing and financial reporting were significantly raised.
While the banks for cooperatives took a great interest in helping
cooperatives improve their organizations and operating methods, they
were also alert to opportunities for cooperative development. For
example, the Berkeley Bank for Cooperatives became a major promoter of
cooperative wineries as a method of helping farmers market a burdensome grape surplus. The Houston Bank for Cooperatives helped many
cooperative cotton gins to become organized, and later aid was given to
the formation of cottonseed oil plants. The New Orleans Bank for
Cooperatives, likewise, helped in establishing cooperative sugar mills in
Louisiana. Many similar examples could be given for all of the banks for
cooperatives.

As the work of these banks proceeded, a need was felt for more
complete information on the extent and character of cooperative development in their territories. To obtain the desired data, the banks for
cooperatives undertook a national survey of all agricultural marketing and
purchasing cooperatives in 1937. It was, in effect, a census, for practically
all of the existing cooperatives were visited, and information was obtained
from them on a carefully designed schedule. This provided the most
comprehensive record so far developed on cooperative organization and
operations, and it proved invaluable as a source of guidance in the
cooperative developmental work of the banks.[4]

(Cooperative Research and Service Work). The value of research and
educational assistance for cooperatives had been well demonstrated by
the work of the Division of Cooperative Marketing from 1926 to 1929.
Thus, when the Farm Credit Administration replaced the Federal Farm
Board, there was a strong demand for the reestablishment of this program
(see Chapter XIV). From 1934 to 1940 this work was revitalized and
correlated with the services provided by the banks for cooperatives. In
many cases studies were made to strengthen organizations so that they
could be financed through the banks for cooperatives. In addition to work
on projects to assist specific cooperatives, broad general studies were
made to help marketing cooperatives serving livestock, grain, and other

commodity groups. The results of this work were rapidly disseminated through bulletins, special reports, letters, and oral presentations.[5]

3. Transportation and other technological changes. The pressure for expanded operations and cost reduction during the New Deal period was reflected in the technical improvement of many marketing cooperatives. During this time there was a great expansion in motor truck operations which widened the scope of local cooperatives and increased accessibility to central markets. Many of the regional marketing cooperatives found it desirable to operate extensive fleets of trucks. Radio was also becoming a pervasive influence, making possible better communication with cooperative members. Improvements were rapidly coming in cold storage, and freezing techniques were promising new methods of providing consumers with frozen foods as the mechanical refrigerator was rapidly replacing the icebox. These and many other technological developments were giving cooperatives opportunities to extend their operations and improve their services.[6]

4. The growth of new marketing institutions and procedures. During the New Deal years new marketing institutions were becoming more important—especially chain store systems and supermarkets. Large national integrated business organizations were becoming dominant factors in the food industry, making necessary stronger organization of farmers to cope with them. Marketing was becoming more consumer-oriented as urbanization and apartment house living increased, and more attention was being given to consumer packaging and processing methods. Operations of the cooperatives reflected these changes. More cooperatives undertook advertising programs and improved their products for consumer markets. Many milk cooperatives undertook the processing and distribution of fluid milk and the conversion of surplus milk into manufactured products. Fruit and vegetable cooperatives moved rapidly into canning and frozen food processing operations. Cooperative wineries became significant market outlets for grape crops. As direct marketing increased, sales at point of production expanded and auction selling by egg and livestock cooperatives became more common. Transportation departments were established by many cooperatives to move products economically to point of sale, and facilities were better planned to take into account transportation costs and advantages.[7]

5. The better coordination of cooperative organizations. As pointed out in Chapter V, the need for cohesion and teamwork among cooperative marketing associations led, in 1929, to the formation of the National Cooperative Council, now the National Council for Farmer

Cooperatives. During the Great Depression, the Council proved its usefulness in representing the interests of cooperative marketing associations in dealings with the Federal Farm Board and other government agencies. In 1933 it was in a strong position to influence the character of the federal programs being established relating to agricultural cooperation, and during the New Deal years it gave cooperative marketing organizations a strong voice in obtaining legislation and regulations that would further their development. For example, it served as a coalescing center for cooperatives in protecting their members' interests under the codes promulgated by the National Recovery Administration. The Council's *Cooperative Journal* served a useful purpose in keeping its member associations informed and united on common problems, while it also brought to the government the views of the cooperatives. The growing importance of the National Council during the New Deal years was reflected in a constant increase in the number of large cooperative organizations that became members—both marketing and purchasing associations. In fact, the Council did much to keep the cooperative marketing and purchasing cooperatives correlated on common problems, since both types of organization were included in membership. This was a natural relationship since many marketing associations also engaged in purchasing, and many purchasing associations marketed agricultural products. By the end of 1940 the Council embraced most of the large-scale centralized and federated cooperative marketing and purchasing associations, as well as such strong commodity organizations as the National Cooperative Milk Producers' Federation which was the powerful voice of the organized dairy cooperatives. The livestock marketing cooperatives were separately organized in the National Livestock Marketing Association, and the cotton and wool cooperatives were joined together in their own national organizations. By 1939 the regional grain cooperatives had also formed their own federation. Altogether some 4,000 cooperative associations were represented in the Council's membership with some 2 million farmer members, and these cooperatives were doing a business volume of over $1.5 billion or about half of all reported farmer cooperative marketing and purchasing business. At this time the Council also included 12 state cooperative councils as associate members.

Another force that had a strong coordinating effect was the American Institute of Cooperation which brought the leaders of both marketing and purchasing cooperatives together for free discussion of their problems. From these forums common programs were developed, and information and experience were shared on ways in which cooperative marketing and purchasing associations could be strengthened or their interests better protected. These various organizations did much to consolidate and unify cooperative thinking and action during the New Deal years.

6. *The accumulation of cooperative knowledge.* From 1933 to 1940 there was a constant improvement in the way cooperatives were organized and operated. The Great Depression had taught many lessons: that there was no substitute for good management; that membership educational work was essential to cooperative success; that the revolving method of finance provided a means for equitable support of cooperatives by their members; that cooperative accounting and other business procedures must be as good as those of competitors; that the public must be kept informed on the contributions of cooperatives through effective public relations work; and that there was no one pattern of organization that would guarantee cooperative success, since the type of organization in an area should be adapted to the needs of farmers.

These lessons were kept before cooperative leaders and members by workers in the Farm Credit Administration, by research and extension personnel of the land grant colleges, and by cooperative organizations themselves. It was a time of cooperative self-improvement and stabilization. Cooperatives had come to have great respect for research findings of state and federal agencies that would help them analyze and solve problems which limited their efficiency. During this period there was a steady move toward cooperative integration with the result that by 1940 most local cooperatives were members of regional overhead federations. Although statistics did not fully reflect the considerable progress made in structure and performance, a new spirit of confidence prevailed in many of the cooperatives. Methods and objectives were becoming more clearly understood.

Changes in Cooperative Marketing Associations, 1933-1934 to 1939-1940

The general changes in cooperative marketing during the New Deal years are reflected in the following statistics which show by major commodity groupings the number of listed associations, the estimated number of their members, and the estimated volumes of their business.[8] The changes from 1933-34 to 1939-40 for all marketing associations are shown by the following figures:

	1933-34	1939-40	Increase or Decrease
Number of listed associations	9,052	8,051	− 1,001
Estimated number of members	2,464,000	2,300,000	− 164,000
Estimated volume of business	$1,213,000,000	$1,729,000,000	$516,000,000

While the number of associations and the number of their members declined, there was an appreciable increase in the estimated volume of their business.

The change in the number of listed associations for each commodity grouping during this period is shown in the tabulation which follows:

	1933-34	1939-40	Increase or Decrease
Dairy products	2,280	2,305	109
Grain, dry beans, rice	3,178	2,462	− 716
Fruits and vegetables, nuts	1,251	1,139	− 112
Livestock	1,371	844	− 527
Cotton and products	250	536	286
Poultry and eggs	147	181	34
Wool	120	134	14
Other (tobacco, etc.)	447	360	− 87
Total	9,050	8,051	− 999

The increase in the number of cotton marketing associations reflected the expansion in cooperative cotton gins, while the decrease in grain associations was largely due to the failure of many cooperative grain elevators during the drought years. The great decline in the number of livestock marketing associations was a result of the continuing decline in the number of livestock shipping associations as truck shipping and direct marketing increased. The consolidation of fruit and vegetable associations greatly reduced the number of such associations.

The following tabulation shows the changes in estimated memberships for these associations.

	1933-44	1939-40	Increase or Decrease
Dairy products	757,000	620,000	−137,000
Grain, dry beans, rice	600,000	365,000	−235,000
Fruits, vegetables, nuts	200,000	166,000	− 34,000
Livestock	410,000	580,000	170,000
Cotton and products	200,000	270,000	70,000
Poultry and eggs	73,000	104,000	41,000
Wool	63,800	62,000	− 1,800
Other (tobacco, etc.)	184,000	133,000	− 51,000
Total	2,464,000	2,300,000	−164,000

It will be observed that there were nearly the same number of members in 1939-40 as in 1933-34. The large decline in the memberships of the grain and dairy marketing associations was to some extent offset by increases in the memberships of livestock, cotton, and poultry and egg associations.

The change in estimated volume of business for the various types of associations is shown as follows:

	1933-34	1939-40	Increase or Decrease
Dairy products	$ 380,000,000	$ 560,000,000	$180,000,000
Grain, dry beans, rice	285,000,000	390,000,000	105,000,000
Fruits, vegetables, nuts	193,500,000	289,000,000	95,500,000
Livestock	162,000,000	282,000,000	120,000,000
Cotton and products	100,000,000	78,000,000	−22,000,000
Poultry and eggs	48,000,000	76,000,000	28,000,000
Wool	13,700,000	11,000,000	− 2,700,000
Other (tobacco, etc.)	30,800,000	43,000,000	12,200,000
Total	$1,213,000,000	$1,729,000,000	$516,000,000

The largest increase in business volume was for the associations' handling dairy products, although significant growth was registered by the associations' handling fruits and vegetables, grain, livestock, and poultry products. The only type to show a decline was the cotton associations.

Although the previous statistics show the main trends in cooperative marketing for this period, they do not reflect the significant developments within the commodity groupings.[9] These will be examined in the following sections of this chapter.

The Dairy Marketing Cooperatives

Dairy marketing cooperatives had enjoyed a phenomenal development during the 1920's. Although their progress was curtailed by the Great Depression, they were generally well organized and efficiently managed when the New Deal agricultural programs gave them an opportunity to extend their usefulness. The dairy cooperatives were of two general types: (1) fluid milk associations, and (2) dairy products manufacturing and marketing associations.

The fluid milk associations. In 1933 about two-fifths of all fluid milk sold in the United States was being marketed through the fluid milk associations operating in the milk sheds serving urban centers. Some of these were primarily bargaining associations which negotiated prices for the sale of their members' milk, while others were directly engaged in processing and marketing operations. During the years from 1933 to 1940, more of the strictly bargaining type associations undertook some processing as a means of controlling surplus milk, and an increasing number of the marketing type associations engaged in distribution of fluid milk to consumers. During this period many of these associations of both types worked out market control programs with the federal government. One of the most successful of the milk marketing organizations was the Twin City Milk Producers' Association of St. Paul, Minnesota, which, in the wake of a disastrous experience with price wars during the low point of the depression, gave its full support to the development of an effective federal milk control program, and gradually regained its strong market position through a distinctive quality improvement program.[10]

None of the milk marketing cooperatives had a more difficult time during the New Deal years than the Dairymen's League Cooperative Association—the largest and strongest cooperative of this type. Its struggle to survive is here described, for its collapse would have impaired confidence in all large-scale marketing enterprises.

(The Ordeal of the Dairymen's League). The Dairymen's League was in a strong economic position in 1929. During the 1928-29 fiscal year it handled approximately 2.5 billion pounds of milk with a gross sales value of $85.6 million. Its membership of 43,067 was 2,045 more than for the previous year. It then represented about half of the dairymen in the New York milk shed and served them through an extensive network of country milk plants and processing facilities acquired by means of an effective revolving fund system of financing. The League was the dominant cooperative marketing organization in the area, although there were a number of smaller cooperatives also serving milk-shed dairy farmers.

The league began to feel the impact of the Great Depression in late 1930 when a flood of unorganized milk broke the market and forced a reduction of 47¢ per 100 pounds in the Class I (fluid milk) price. As supply exceeded demand, milk prices continued to drop, and several milk dealers were forced to close their country receiving plants. The League took them over in order to provide dairymen with a market. Other buyers "quit the League" in order to get a cheaper supply elsewhere. Although the League's total sales as reported at the annual meeting in June 1931 continued high at $80 million, it was ominous that milk sold as surplus had increased by 400 per cent. The League was now operating 229 milk plants of various kinds.

During the next year the League endeavored to strengthen its operations by closing many of its weaker country milk plants and by cutting salaries of officers and employees by 10 per cent. In June the League reported that sales, largely reflecting lower prices, had declined to $70 million. Membership, on the other hand, had expanded to 52,117, largely due to the accession of new members who had been served by plants taken over by the League. By this time discontent among dairymen was rife, and the League was coming under attack for its low pool prices which reflected the heavy burden of its surplus operations. Under the League's pool plan, returns from sale of all members' milk were pooled, and members received a pool price which reflected combined returns from sale of Class I milk along with milk processed and sold as surplus. This put the League in a weak competitive position in the Class I market, for the League was in no position to stabilize the market by itself. Moreover, the pool price received by its members was much less than the price received by producers who could sell independently to buyers that largely enjoyed fluid outlets. This caused discontent among League members who resented carrying the surplus burden for non-members,[11] in the face of a sharp general decline in commodity prices.

During the next year the sales of the League dropped to $55 million, a decline of $15 million, and as dairymen's income fell the League steadily lost prestige and bargaining power. Unscrupulous dealers, discontented dairymen, radical groups, and competitive organizations took advantage of the situation to carry on a vigorous campaign designed to weaken the League's influence, if not to destroy it entirely.[12]

In desperation New York dairymen began to demand a plan that would unite the vast majority of milk producers in one united milk marketing organization. The League responded by offering its personnel and facilities for such an organization but adequate support was not forthcoming. With loss of confidence in cooperative marketing, New York dairymen turned for help to the state. This resulted in the setting up of a New York State Joint Legislative Committee—the Pitcher Committee. Reporting early in 1933, this Committee proposed as a short-term emergency measure that a state milk control board be set up to control milk prices. As a permanent remedy for the dairy marketing problem a unified cooperative marketing program was recommended.[13]

The New York State Milk Control Board was established in April 1933. Although a stop gap measure, it gave some temporary relief, even if its operation further weakened the League. Its greatest shortcomings were that it was necessarily restricted to the New York part of the milk shed and did not provide an equitable plan for handling surplus milk. The League found itself holding the bag with the surplus and this caused consequent low pool prices. As in the stabilization efforts of the Federal Farm Board, the League wasn't strong enough by itself to stabilize the market.

With the passage of the Agricultural Adjustment Act in May 1933, the leaders of the League hoped for relief. Joined by other cooperatives in the milk shed, they immediately drafted a proposed marketing agreement to stabilize the market for the entire New York milk shed. Unfortunately, internal dissension within the AAA made impossible quick assistance from this quarter (see Chapter XIII).

The annual meeting of the League in June 1934 reflected the serious situation that was confronting the association. The State Milk Control Act was working to the advantage of competitors who were not burdened by surplus operations, and, as a result, membership had declined during the past year by 7,415, bringing the total down to 43,504. Although the reorganization of the AAA's dairy program on a basis more acceptable to dairy cooperatives, in the fall of 1933, opened the door for the development of a federal milk order for the New York milk shed, little could be done to take advantage of this improved situation until the cooperatives in the New York milk shed could compose their differences. In the meantime the membership of the League continued to decline.

By 1937, most dairymen had lost all confidence in state milk control. This was made evident in January when Governor Herbert H. Lehman called upon dairymen to "merge themselves into one cohesive organization," and sentiment began to develop for an arrangement under which all of the competing dairy cooperatives could work together. In response to this new initiative, the State Legislature (with the strong endorsement of the Dairymen's League and the general farm organizations of the state) in May passed the Rogers-Allen Act which replaced the State Milk Control Act and authorized the organization of Milk Producer Bargaining Agencies by cooperatives operating in a given market area. Thus, in the words of Dr. Leland Spencer, the Rogers-Allen Act "belatedly took up the suggestion for a long-term plan proposed by the Pitcher Committee."[14]

Supported by the provisions of the Rogers-Allen Act, the Dairymen's League immediately took the lead in organizing the Metropolitan Cooperative Milk Producers' Bargaining Agency which was set up in June 1937. It quickly gained support and soon represented a high proportion of the state's organized dairymen serving the New York metropolitan market. For a time cooperative policies were better coordinated and prices improved but it soon became apparent that little could be accomplished in permanent market stabilization without a federal milk marketing order that would apply to the entire milk shed. Following instructions from a delegate meeting in January 1938, representatives of the Metropolitan—with representatives of cooperatives from the other involved states—proceeded to draft a proposed federal milk order. Although the order became effective in September 1938, its operation was interrupted by court action during the first half of 1939. It has functioned continuously since July 1, 1939.

The League officials were jubilant with this outcome. In his report to the annual meeting of the Dairymen's League on June 15, 1939, President Fred H. Sexauer said: "This has been a great year. The foundation for a long-time program has been laid. The program has been proven sound. It has been sustained in the Courts. The prestige of the Dairymen's League has grown. More organizations are working together and are working better together . . . Our pledge to work with others is bearing fruit."

Sexauer had reason for his exultation. For the first time a method was provided for regulating milk marketing for the entire New York milk shed which was in accord with the fundamental principles long fought for by the League. Milk prices in the New York milk shed began to improve immediately, and from then on the League could give its major attention to its own marketing program. In the fiscal year closing in 1940, the sales of the League rose to $56 million as compared with $53 million the year before.[15]

Dairy products associations. In 1933 there were several thousand cooperative creameries and cheese factories producing butter, cheese, and other dairy products, but many were in need of reorganization due to faulty formation or changes in local marketing conditions. During the New Deal years, a number of the weaker organizations discontinued operations or were reorganized on a stronger basis with the financial assistance of the banks for cooperatives and with technical assistance from the specialists of the land grant colleges and the Cooperative Research and Service Division of the Farm Credit Administration. In many cases several local cooperatives were consolidated to form stronger organizations. Although the number of local cooperative creameries and cheese factories declined appreciably by 1940, those that remained were much stronger associations than those functioning in 1933. Even before 1933 many of the local creameries and cheese factories belonged to regional marketing federations, and during the New Deal years the significance of such federations greatly increased. The most important federation of this type was the Land O' Lakes Creameries, Inc., of Minneapolis. The remarkable progress of this organization from 1933 to 1940 deserves special consideration.

(Progress of the Land O'Lakes). By 1929 the Land O'Lakes Creameries had become one of the major cooperatives in the nation with sales of $51 million and total assets of nearly $7 million. It was serving 495 member associations with some 26,000 members. It had already established its Land O'Lakes brand as the hallmark of good butter and other related products—cheese, eggs, and poultry—handled by the association. It

was then selling its products through jobbers, while large proprietary firms were steadily creating strong integrated marketing organizations. As a result, Land O'Lakes found itself with quality products but with no assured way of reaching the consumer. To meet this problem, Land O'Lakes in 1930 began setting up its own branch offices with salesmen employed to sell direct to the retail trade, and soon such offices were operating in New York City, Boston, and Philadelphia. This program, backed up by a strong national advertising campaign, worked so well that additional offices were established in other cities. By 1934 there were 26 branch offices making direct sales to about 30,000 retail stores. As a result of this sales program, Land O'Lakes was able to strengthen its position in the industry during and after the desperate depression years of 1932 and 1933. However, with the lower level of farm prices, its sales volume in 1933 was reduced to $30,494,995.

The merchandising position of the Land O'Lakes Creameries, Inc., was strengthened in 1934 by the addition to its membership of the Cheese Producers' Federation of Wisconsin and the Minnesota Cheese Producers' Federation. These new members helped to diversify the association's line of products and made possible reduction of unit trucking costs by delivering more products per stop. Soon afterwards an arrangement was made with the Challenge Cream and Butter Association of Los Angeles which achieved better coordination of their sales. During the New Deal years the Land O'Lakes Creameries greatly improved its sales methods under the leadership of Frank Stone, who became director of sales in 1936. Great emphasis was placed on the quality of Land O'Lakes products as a basis for an effective national advertising program which made the word Land O'Lakes synonymous with high-quality butter and other products handled under the Land O'Lakes trademark.

The importance of Land O'Lakes Creameries, Inc., in the dairy industry was recognized in 1933 when the Department of Agriculture called on it for help in an effort to stabilize the butter market. During the next few years, Land O'Lakes Creameries, with the cooperation of other regional dairy products cooperatives, was able to bring about a considerable amount of market stabilization without government financial support. However, in 1938 when the need for a concerted stabilization program became apparent, the Land O'Lakes gave national leadership to the creation of an organization known as the Dairy Products Marketing Association which was comprised of several of the large cooperative dairy products associations.[16] The DPMA was given federal authority and provided with necessary financial resources to buy a total of 50 million pounds of butter if necessary. The President and General Manager of the

Land O'Lakes Creameries, Inc.—John Brandt—served as its President. This program met an important purpose during 1938 and 1939.[17]

Prior to 1937, Land O'Lakes had not directly operated milk drying plants, although it had marketed the product of a buttermilk drying plant at Litchfield, Minnesota, which had been formed in 1926 by creameries in one of its districts. The experience of this plant and the growing problem of surplus disposal indicated that additional plants of this type were needed to serve all Land O'Lakes creameries. To meet this problem a subsidiary corporation, the Land O'Lakes Dairy Company, was set up in 1937 to operate plants under the direct control of the Land O'Lakes. The first was opened at Luck, Wisconsin, in April 1937, and, later in the same year, a second plant was opened at Rush City, Minnesota. Additional plants were added in the next few years so that by 1941 there were six plants of this type under the direct control of the Land O'Lakes. This experience was to prove invaluable when the demand for milk powder skyrocketed with World War II demands.

In the face of the difficult problems of the New Deal years, the Land O'Lakes Creameries, Inc., steadily improved its economic position.[18] From 1933 to 1940 its sales increased to nearly $36 million or by over $5 million, while total assets grew by over a million dollars. Of even more importance, its net worth rose from $258,769 in 1933 to $1,191,947 in 1940. It was set for a remarkable period of expansion during the World War II years.[19]

While the Land O'Lakes Creameries and other dairy products federations were gaining importance in the central states, another sister organization of this type—the Challenge Cream and Butter Association of Los Angeles—was flourishing in the far western states. By the close of 1939, this federation included 37 local cooperatives representing some 33,000 dairymen in the states of California, Oregon, Washington, Idaho, Nevada, Colorado, and Wyoming. In this year member associations were operating 58 separate dairy products plants for butter, dried skim milk, cheese, and other dairy products. Its fleet of 225 modern motor trucks were assuming all of the distributing functions between the farm and the retail store, and its reputation for the quality of products sold under its "Challenge" brand was highly respected. It was using effectively a revolving fund financing plan, and its membership relations program was excellent. By 1939 the value of all products marketed exceeded $19 million.[20]

The Grain Marketing Cooperatives

With the discontinuance of the Federal Farm Board in 1933, the

Central Bank for Cooperatives assumed the financing of the Farmers' National Grain Corporation which was then endeavoring to provide a national marketing service for its member regional grain marketing cooperatives. It was an unwieldly, highly centralized organization, and its problems were compounded by the severe droughts of 1933 and 1935, along with the acreage restriction program of the AAA and general political uncertainties.[21] When it became clear that the Farmers' National could not continue without drastic reorganization, the National was dissolved on May 31, 1938, and its component parts were returned to the constituent regional associations. The re-establishment of the regionals as independent operating organizations was a laborious process, but with assistance from the banks for cooperatives it was soon accomplished with a considerable degree of success.[22]

The arrangement for closing the Farmers' National and reestablishing the regionals was largely worked out with government officials by M. W. Thatcher, the Washington representative of the National Farmers' Union and the manager of the Farmers' Union Grain Terminal Association of St. Paul, Minnesota—the largest of the associations to be freed under the arrangement. One of the problems was to make plans for financing the regionals which were then without funds through the district banks for cooperatives. Another problem was to help reestablish the services of many closed local elevators so that they could give their patronage support to the regionals. This was accomplished by working out an arrangement with the Farm Security Administration under which loans could be made to impoverished farmers so that they could buy shares in the cooperative elevators to be serviced by the regionals. Without this assistance, it would have been impossible for the regionals to quickly reestablish themselves as going concerns. Altogether some 177 local elevators in the midwestern and northwestern states were restored to service by means of the financial and technical assistance provided by the Farm Security Administration.[23]

Thatcher's experience in Washington had taught him the importance of joint cooperative action on political matters. When the Commodity Credit Corporation threatened to enter the grain marketing business in early 1939, Thatcher saw this as an opportunity to bring the regionals together in a central organization which would give them a common voice in representing their economic interests. There followed a meeting in Omaha where seven of the regionals set up the National Federation of Grain Cooperatives with Thatcher as President.[24] According to its articles of Agreement, adopted on February 21, 1939, the Federation was formed:

For the purpose only of: (a) Assisting and advising its members with respect to federal and state legislation which affects or might affect them or their members; (b) Keeping its members informed with respect to legislative matters; (c) Aiding and assisting its members in their dealings and relations with state and federal governments and departments thereof; (d) Informing its members from time to time with respect to matters of interest to them and their members.

To make clear that the organization was not to engage in marketing operations, the Articles of Agreement expressly stated that the Federation:

Shall have no power to engage in business of any kind, to advise or inform its members with respect to the prices to be charged for their products or for their service, to advise its members in any matter affecting the manner in which their business shall be transacted, or to engage in any business dealings, contracts, or matters which might under any circumstances impose obligations upon its members or result in the imposition of liability of any kind upon them or any of them.[25]

While the Farmers' National's "grandiose experiment" in national cooperative marketing was coming to a "disillusioning end," the local cooperative elevators had been passing through a struggle for survival and were consolidating their position. Many were cooperative in name only and were in need of drastic reorganization. Others were poorly equipped and required modernization. The rapid spread of grain trucking was enabling farmers to bypass elevators that could not provide efficient service, and this was enfeebling already weak elevators and strengthening those that were already strong. In many instances cooperative elevators were able to continue only because of the profitability of their side-line purchasing activities. By 1940 this process had run its course and the remaining elevators as a group were better organized, better financed, and better operated than were the elevators as a group in 1933.

Primary credit for the revitalization and modernization of the cooperative elevators during the New Deal years can be given to the district banks for cooperatives, for they nursed back to life many of the elevators with needed loans and technical assistance.[26] Much credit can also be given to extension marketing specialists, such as Vance Rucker in Kansas, who worked closely with the elevator managers and directors to strengthen their organizations, operations, and services. Of great value also were the joint studies made of cooperative elevator efficiency in several of the grain states by the Farm Credit Administration's Cooperative Research and Service Division in cooperation with state agricultural experiment stations. These studies demonstrated that associations with larger volumes could afford better management and operate at lower cost so as to make savings for farmers. In no state was greater progress made in revitalizing cooperative elevators than Iowa under the leadership of Frank Robotka of Iowa State College. From long experience he had come to the conclusion that a thoroughgoing change in state cooperative law was necessary before the elevators and other forms of local cooperatives could be reorganized so that they could become vital and effective cooperative associations. With the passage of a new cooperative law in 1935, a new era in cooperative enterprise opened in Iowa and brought about what has been called "a cooperative miracle." The significance of the new law has been explained by Richard Phillips as follows:

> Prior to the enactment of the new law, many cooperatives in the state were in serious difficulty. In the wake of the Great Depression, those organized under the old stock-company law could attract neither the membership nor the volume of business for successful operation. Some had completely lost track of many of their original stockholders, or the heirs thereto. The existing non-stock law under which they might have reorganized was unpopular and in many ways unsuited to the immediate needs, particularly in the case of the farmers' elevators. A miracle was needed which would enable the Iowa cooperatives to pull themselves up by their own economic bootstraps . . . The provisions of the new law were specific and detailed and tailored to needs of the times . . . Farmers were permitted to subscribe for and earn their membership stock. All patronage refunds were to be placed in a revolving fund and retired on an "oldest first" basis.[27]

In a few years most of the cooperative elevators in Iowa had shifted to the new basis of organization.

The rice marketing cooperatives also improved their position during the New Deal years. In 1936 the long established Rice Growers Association of California had sales of over $3 million. One of the most interesting associations of this type was the Arkansas Rice Growers Association at Stuttgart, Arkansas, which had been formed in 1922 as a centralized pooling organization. In 1938 it was operating three large milling plants with a volume of sales of more than $15 million. Several of the rice marketing cooperatives in Arkansas, Louisiana, and Texas were then federated together in the American Rice Growers Cooperative Association of Lake Charles, Louisiana. In 1939-40 this organization was marketing over 9 million bushels of rough rice. About 30 per cent of the nation's rice crop was being handled cooperatively in 1939-40.[28]

Among the dry bean regionals operating during the New Deal period the most important was the long established Lima Bean Growers Association in California. Other significant bean associations were then also functioning in Michigan and Colorado.

Fruit, Vegetable, and Nut Cooperatives

Fruit, vegetable, and nut marketing cooperatives were strongly organized in 1933 when the New Deal agricultural agencies came into existence. They welcomed the lending services made available by the banks for cooperatives, and they responded favorably to the marketing agreement provisions of the Agricultural Adjustment Act which promised to give relief on disturbing surplus disposal problems.

Citrus associations. During the years from 1933 to 1940, the California Fruit Growers' Exchange maintained its leadership position among cooperative marketing organizations in the United States. Although the value of its returns to growers of $73 million in 1940 was appreciably less than the $89 million reached in 1929, its volume of citrus shipments was 73,227 cars in 1940 as compared with 65,417 in 1929, and they then represented 74.2 per cent of all California and Arizona citrus shipments as compared with 74.3 per cent in 1929. It should be noticed that during the decade citrus production was increasing rapidly not only in California and Arizona but also in Florida and Texas. While production in California and Arizona increased by 60 per cent, the production in other states increased by nearly 100 per cent.

To meet the growing problem of greater production, the Exchange maintained its heavy expenditures for advertising and selling and stepped up its by-products utilization operations. As stronger measures were needed, the Exchange in 1932 supported a state prorate plan to achieve better distribution of supplies to markets. While this gave temporary relief, it demonstrated the need for a prorate program that would have industry wide application. As the annual report of the Exchange for 1932 said: "The outstanding lesson of 1931-32 is clearly that of the necessity of the control and regulation of shipments." From then on the Exchange gave its full support to the development of federal and state prorate programs. Looking back on the results from such programs in the Thirties, Charles C. Teague, the Exchange's President, said: "It is my firm conviction after much experience and study of the problem for many years, that if the California citrus industry had not first enjoyed the benefit of proration set up by the Exchange, and later enforced proration established by state and federal legislation, it would have been in much the same demoralized condition that characterized it during the early nineties."[29]

The rapid expansion of the citrus industry in Florida and Texas during these years placed a heavy burden on the citrus marketing associations in those states which were not so well organized as California and Arizona. In 1938-39, about 60 citrus marketing associations were operating in Florida, and of these about 40 were members of the Florida Citrus Exchange. This organization was then handling about 25 per cent of the state's citrus crop with a sales value of about $10 million.[30] There were also several large local citrus cooperatives then marketing independently of the Exchange. Among these, the Waverly Growers Cooperative had a volume of about $2 million in 1940.[31] A number of the large local associations, whether or not members of the Exchange, performed many functions for their members in addition to marketing, such as spraying, pruning, and other grove care services. Several also purchased fertilizers and other supplies for their members.

During this period, cooperative canning of citrus fruit grew in importance as a means of meeting the heavy production problem. The outstanding organization of this type was the Florida Citrus Canners Cooperative, first formed in 1930 as the Ridge Canners, Inc., with the strong financial backing of Waverly Growers Cooperative. The sales of this organization by 1939-40 reached $1,164,832. Its total assets then amounted to over $425,000 and patron's equity stood at $287,000.[32]

During the 1920's, several citrus marketing cooperatives had been formed in Texas, and, in 1932, 16 of them federated to set up the Rio Grande Valley Citrus Exchange as a central sales agency. This association by 1938-39 was handling 3.5 million boxes of grapefruit and oranges, and nearly one-half was sold in the form of juice, canned fruit, citrus pulp, or meal. The sales of the Exchange for 1938-39 exceeded $3 million. In 1940 there were also two large independent Texas associations selling citrus fruit or juice.

Fresh fruit and vegetable associations. The fresh fruit and vegetable cooperatives generally strengthened their position during the New Deal years through consolidations and improved operations. The National Fruit and Vegetable Exchange, which had been set up in 1931 with Federal Farm Board encouragement to provide a nation-wide marketing service for widely scattered fruit and vegetable associations, gradually expanded its services in supervised brokerage representation along with some distribution service work in producing districts, so that by 1936 it was handling about 15,000 carloads of fruits and vegetables annually. In order to obtain greater volume essential to support an improved service, the leaders of National, in 1937, undertook to reorganize as a Capper-Volstead type membership cooperative under the name American National Cooperative Exchange. In doing so, a semi-merger arrangement was worked out with a large privately owned concern, the American Fruit Growers, Inc., which performed shipping point and terminal marketing services in many of the major metropolitan markets and which also held substantial acreages in fruit and vegetable production in Florida, Texas, and California. The AFG needed more volume to support its salaried sales offices in consuming markets and more tonnage to be packed under its copyrighted "Blue Goose" trademark so as to better support its dealer service and advertising projects, while the National Fruit and Vegetable Exchange needed much greater volume to carry on an effective program of terminal and local services for its members. Under the plan developed, the American National Cooperative Exchange, without heavy capital investment, took over and operated all AFG consumer market offices, and the AFG as a producer, along with its producer patrons, became members of American National along with existing members of the American. Under the plan, the "Blue Goose" trademark became available to members of American National on a fee for service basis, making possible a considerable expansion of revenue to AFG for its use.

This reciprocal arrangement proved advantageous to both organizations and opened the way for a significant growth in the volume of American National. By 1940 it was serving a considerable number of regional and local fruit and vegetable cooperatives located in all parts of the United States. Included as members were such organizations as the Maine Potato Growers, Inc., the Rio Grande Valley Citrus Exchange of Texas, the Blue Mountain Prune Association of Oregon, and the Illinois Fruit Growers Exchange. Also included were apple grower associations in Washington, peach cooperatives in Colorado, a strawberry cooperative in California, and similar cooperatives in other states. By the end of the decade, American National was handling double the volume of its predecessor organization, and, during World War II, its annual volume was to reach 50,000 carloads annually.[33]

The most important of the American National's member organizations was the Maine Potato Growers, Inc. After early difficulties this centralized type association, formed in 1932, with advisory assistance from the Federal Farm Board, hit its stride in 1936-37 with carload shipments of 3,076, valued at $2 million. During the World War II years its annual shipments reached 10,000 carloads and gained for it recognition as the outstanding potato marketing cooperative in the nation.[34]

One of the most important of the regional fruit marketing associations during the 1930's was the long established California Fruit Exchange, well-known for its "Blue Anchor" trademark. This federated organization provided terminal market sales services for local associations marketing grapes, pears, plums, apples, apricots, cherries, and peaches with a sales volume of over $4 million in 1940. It also performed an important supply purchasing service for its member associations. Another strong marketing organization was the Apple Growers Association of Hood River, Oregon, which handled a variety of fresh fruits along with apples. During the

Thirties this organization undertook extensive canning and quick freezing operations. Its sales volume in 1940 exceeded $6 million, and, in addition, it purchased orchard and packing supplies with a value of nearly $1 million. Several somewhat similar small regional organizations were then successfully operating in Oregon, Washington, Michigan, and other heavy fruit-producing states.

Dried fruit associations. The California dried fruit cooperatives which had been widely publicized in the early 1920's as examples of successful commodity marketing organizations continued to function with modest ambitions after disastrous experiences during the Great Depression. After several reorganizations, the Sun-Maid Raisin Growers, Inc., and the California Prune and Apricot Growers Inc., largely regained their leadership positions in the dried fruit industry. Both of these organizations took advantage of federal and state marketing agreement programs and carried on effective advertising programs. In 1933, the California Prune and Apricot Growers introduced prune juice, and "tenderized" prunes soon followed. After 1934, this association encouraged its member associations to set up dehydrating plants for the drying of prunes so as to avoid the hazards of weather in sun drying. This was a revolutionary development which changed the fruit drying practices of the entire industry. Some seven of these plants were operating with considerable success by 1940.[35]

Cranberries. The American Cranberry Exchange continued as a strong national marketing organization during the New Deal years but its preeminence was increasingly challenged by a sister organization, Cranberry Canners, Inc., as increasing volumes of cranberries were merchandized in canned form under its Ocean Spray brand. Prior to 1930, three "grower interests" were "promoting a market for canned cranberry products" but competition between them "seriously interfered with the development of a year 'round market for cranberries."[36] In this year a plan was worked out under the compelling leadership of Marcus L. Urann, President of the Ocean Spray Preserving Company, for a merger of the three competing organizations under the name Cranberry Canners, Inc. As its original members were also members of the American Cranberry Exchange, it was anticipated that they would continue to market fresh berries through that channel. There was little immediate conflict between the fresh and canned marketing agencies, for canning was at first designed to support the fresh market by serving as an outlet for inferior berries. By 1940 Cranberry Canners, Inc., had become important as a cranberry marketing organization with a sales volume of $3,319,177.

Fruit and vegetable bargaining associations. Cooperative bargaining associations in the fruit industry first arose in the concentrated fruit producing areas of California during World War I, as a means of improving prices and terms of sale for producers through negotiation with commercial canning companies. None of these associations survived to the present but they opened the way for modern bargaining associations.[37] The oldest California bargaining association in existence, the California Canning Peach Growers, Inc., was formed in 1921. For many years it struggled for recognition and operated with modest success. In 1936 the association was reorganized under its present name, the California Cling Peach Association, and from then progress was more substantial.

The pioneer development in bargaining for vegetable growers grew out of the informal experience of county farm bureau committees in Utah arising from efforts to negotiate with processors for better contract terms for farm bureau members during the World War I period. This experience caused the Utah Farm Bureau to set up a state committee to bargain with the Utah Canners Association for better contract terms. This led to the development of a uniform contract which prevailed throughout the state in 1920. In 1924 several local associations for bargaining were incorporated throughout the state, and in 1930 six of them federated to form the Utah State Canning Association. From that date "no contracts between the individual canning companies and growers of peas, corn, tomatoes, snap beans and cabbage" were cleared without approval of the state association. From then on this federation grew until it eventually embraced 11 associations in 1956.[38] Aside from these two organizations, there was little development of such associations before 1940, although there was evidence that the conditions in the industry would soon encourage their growth in importance.

Sugar beet bargaining associations. Sugar beet associations for collective bargaining had demonstrated their value to farmers in the early 1920's and they were functioning efficiently in most sugar beet producing areas when the National Beet Growers Association was established in 1930 to serve as a coordinating center for the 13 general beet bargaining associations, then having a combined membership of about 25,000 producers. These bargaining associations negotiated terms of sale and prices with the semi-monopolistic sugar beet processing companies and were generally supported by dues collected for the associations by the processors on a check-off basis. In 1940 it was generally agreed that the associations were indispensable elements of the sugar beet industry as they had materially raised incomes of sugar beet farmers and helped stabilize conditions of sugar beet production.[39]

Cooperative wineries. The repeal of the National Prohibition Act in 1933 opened the way for cooperative wineries, and grape growers were quick to take advantage of this opportunity. With financial and advisory assistance from the Berkeley Bank for Cooperatives, several winery associations were soon set up, and work was begun on the construction of the necessary wine making facilities. Several of the wineries were completed in time to crush the 1934 grape crop. By 1938 there were 18 cooperative wineries in California, handling one-third of the state's wine-grape production.

The nut cooperatives. The well-established California Walnut Growers Association greatly strengthened its operations in 1935 by constructing a new plant in Los Angeles equipped with every modern device for efficient handling and packing of walnuts. It contained the largest single cold storage chamber in the world. Under the leadership of the association, a marketing agreement was developed in 1933 which provided for the stabilization of the walnut industry for the entire west coast through arrangements for surplus disposal. In 1940 about 85 per cent of the walnut crop in California was marketed by the association. Its sales volume in 1942 was $18 million.

The other large California nut marketing cooperative, the California Almond Growers Exchange, pioneered in packaging nuts in cellophane in 1937. In 1940 it was marketing about 70 per cent of the California almond crop.

Cooperative Livestock Marketing

Until about 1930 the dominant method of marketing livestock was through commission firms who sold to the "large" packers on the central markets. This situation began to change rapidly with truck transportation and improved roads, as interior packers bought more and more livestock at or near their plants. To meet such competition, the big packers began to increase direct buying through concentration yards or buying stations in livestock producing areas. As truck transportation to the terminal markets grew along with direct buying, the number of livestock shipping associations steadily declined. Even in the face of this trend the cooperative livestock commission firms found it hard to accept the fact that livestock marketing was rapidly becoming decentralized. However, by 1933, the situation could no longer be ignored.[40] In a few cases cooperative commission firms set up branch offices in their operating territories to deal directly with local packers or with buyers of terminal market packers. In other instances, new cooperative livestock marketing agencies were formed to represent producers in dealing with local packers or with agents of the central market packers. One of the most interesting organization developments of this type was the formation, in 1934, of the Producers Commission Association of Columbus, Ohio, to combine the operations of three commission firms operating on the Cleveland, Pittsburgh, and Columbus markets and to decentralize their operations throughout Ohio. The new organization was designed primarily to provide central management for country marketing agencies to be located so as to best serve the needs of Ohio livestock producers in dealing with local packers and order buyers for packers. As this organization gained acceptance, it gradually expanded its operations to serve livestock producers in Indiana and West Virginia.[41] A somewhat similar organization arose in Illinois where the Illinois Agricultural Association fostered the "Illinois Livestock Marketing Association" as a state-wide association of county or district livestock selling organizations in order to ship directly to packers or to consign to the producer agencies in the central markets. This organization developed slowly, but by 1937 it was in position to offer a cash market for livestock at local delivery points. After the association was reorganized in 1940, it became an important livestock marketing agency for Illinois farmers.[42] In Wisconsin the Equity Cooperative Livestock Sales Association of Milwaukee adopted a decentralized program in 1936 by establishing the first of 14 private treaty markets to purchase livestock from shipping associations and individual farmers to supply the needs of packer buyers. This movement toward decentralization expanded as volume and savings increased.[43] During the 1930's, direct marketing through livestock auctions also grew in importance, and some were organized and operated cooperatively. However, except in California, they never became of significance as a means of cooperative livestock marketing.[44]

In view of the unscrupulous promotion of cooperative livestock packing plants during and after World War I, confidence in the possibilities of such plants had been largely undermined.[45] In 1933 a situation developed that led to the reorganization of a private packing company on a cooperative basis, and the experience of this firm was to open the way for later successful developments in cooperative livestock packing. The Detroit Packing Company had been formed in 1920 with heavy investments by livestock producers. When this firm went bankrupt in 1933, its assets were acquired by the producers who were its principal investors. They proceeded with the assurance of loans from the Central Bank for Cooperatives to organize and operate the plant cooperatively with technical assistance from the livestock section of the

F.C.A.'s Cooperative Research and Service Division. For many years this organization served as an experimental laboratory or pilot plant for cooperative livestock packing, and much was learned on the problems of operating a plant of this type. Of particular significance was the effort made to get members to produce a meat-type hog that could be sold on a yield basis.[46] The Detroit Packing Company operated during the war years with considerable success, but, with management difficulties, it ceased operations in 1954. The main significance of its experience was to demonstrate that there was a future for soundly organized and operated cooperative livestock packing plants and to provide a fund of information on how such plants could best be formed and managed.

Another related development during the late Thirties was the development of cooperative cold storage locker plants (see Chapter XXI). Many of these plants became, in effect, local livestock processing plants, for they undertook to process livestock for local needs. They thus demonstrated the practicability of cooperative processing operations.

Cooperative Cotton Marketing Developments, 1933-1940

In 1933 the American Cotton Cooperative Association, set up in January 1933 under Federal Farm Board auspices, was providing sales and financing service for 11 of the 12 large-scale state and regional cotton marketing cooperatives. Only the Staple Cotton Growers Association of Greenwood, Mississippi, remained outside of this national overhead organization and carried on its operations independently.[47] The ACCA performed interior classing, transportation, warehousing, insurance, and selling services for its member associations. They were responsible primarily for grower relations and other local matters.

The ACCA continued to function during the New Deal period with the lending operations of the government being assumed by the Central Bank for Cooperatives. As the ACCA performed all marketing services for the regional member associations it became a super centralized organization in which emphasis was placed more on building volume than in meeting the production and marketing needs of cotton farmers. In 1939 a demand for more membership autonomy resulted in a reorganization of the ACCA under which the member associations took over all marketing and membership functions, except for hedging and brokerage services. This marked the end of the ACCA as a significant organization, for some of the regionals then discontinued their membership, leaving the ACCA only as a skeleton organization.[48]

While cotton growers were becoming disillusioned by their experience with large-scale cooperative marketing, there was a pronounced revival of interest in local cooperation as expressed in cooperative cotton gins.[49] The center of this development was in Texas and Oklahoma but it soon spread to other southern states. This movement was given momentum by the coming of the Banks for Cooperatives which were interested in financing small as well as large cooperatives. As the banks stood ready to lend 60 per cent of the approved value of the property, either to be constructed or purchased, it was not difficult to finance the remaining 40 per cent in capital stock gins by issuing non-cumulative preferred stock. As the record of savings was generally good, the number of cooperative gins quickly multiplied. In 1933 there were about 250, by 1940 the number had more than doubled.

Another development with great promise was the promotion of cooperative cottonseed oil mills. Although a mill of this type had been functioning successfully at Minter City, Mississippi, since 1922, there was no further development of this sort until 1934 when the Southwestern Irrigated Cotton Growers Association of El Paso, Texas, leased a local cottonseed oil mill, then in receivership, and began operations for the benefit of its members. From the beginning, the mill was successful, and in 1936 the lease was renewed for five years with an option to buy at any time during the period of the lease for $60,000. Under this option the association acquired the mill during the 1938-39 season.[50]

The most significant development of this type occurred in 1936 at Lubbock, Texas, where a group of cooperative cotton gins in the Plains area joined together to operate a cottonseed oil mill under the name Plains Cooperative Gins, Inc. During its first year this organization (later to take the name Plains Cooperative Oil Mill) confined its activities to selling cotton and cottonseed but, in the summer of 1937, the association bought a used oil mill, moved it to Lubbock, and began crushing operations. While the mill did not take hold immediately as a going concern, it did force competing agencies to raise prices for cottonseed.[51]

The Egg and Poultry Associations

Cooperative marketing of eggs and poultry grew steadily in importance during the New Deal years. Outstanding in significance were the several large poultry marketing associations on the Pacific coast and in the intermountain states. Of these, the two most important were the Poultry Producers of Central California, San Francisco, with marketing sales in 1940 of $16 million, and the Washington Egg and Poultry Association, Seattle, with marketing sales of $8 million in 1940. Both of these organizations also provided members with feed and other supplies essential for poultry production. The Washington Association had begun the canning of poultry products in 1929 as a means of providing a market for hens after their service in egg production. This program was expanded in 1936.

During this period the western associations were joined together in the Pacific Egg Producers, Inc., which maintained sales offices in New York City. This organization, created in 1922, provided consumers with graded eggs of high quality and did much to raise the standards for eggs sold in the eastern markets. For many years its sales volume exceeded $10 million. As the population grew in western California and the other Pacific coast states, home consumption required a large part of the west coast egg production and the necessity of maintaining an eastern sales outlet declined. In 1941 the Pacific Egg Producers was dissolved, although its operations were continued for a time by the Washington Egg and Poultry Association.

Prior to 1930 cooperative egg marketing had made little progress in the eastern states. About this time, poultrymen in these states became interested in the possibilities of cooperative egg marketing, partly because of the demonstration made by the Pacific Egg Producers that standardization and grading could improve producer's returns. Two forms of local egg marketing associations began to develop: (1) cooperative egg auctions, and (2) small regional egg pooling associations. By 1940 such organizations were rapidly gaining significance.

In the Central states, the Land O'Lakes Creameries, Inc., became an important poultry and egg marketer as a side line to its creamery business. In Missouri the local produce exchanges of the Missouri Farmers Association also became handlers of poultry and eggs.

The cooperative statistics for 1939-40 showed that about 65 per cent of the business of all egg and poultry associations was then being done by associations in the Pacific and mountain states; 20 per cent by associations in New England and the Middle Atlantic states; 13 per cent by associations in the east and north central states; and only 3 per cent in the southern states.

Cooperative turkey marketing was little developed prior to 1930 when the Northwest Turkey Marketing Association was organized as a federated sales agency for local turkey marketing associations. Within a few years it was operating sales offices in several cities and building a reputation for the quality of its product, under its trademark "Norbest." In the years from 1934 to 1940, the number of its member associations grew from 15 to 20, while its sales volume increased from $815,000 to

$2,140,000. During these years total assets increased from $65,000 to $299,000, and its net worth from $55,000 to $182,000.[52] Although other regional turkey associations functioned during these years, none were able to establish themselves on a permanent basis.[53]

Summary

In this chapter we have examined the progress of cooperative marketing in the light of New Deal economic and political conditions. In general, it was a period of constructive growth, almost of rebirth. Relieved of production control responsibilities by the Triple A Act, the marketing cooperatives could get on with the job of performing an efficient business service. In 1933, the future of cooperative marketing was uncertain. By 1940 it was re-established on a stronger basis than at any time in the past. This was shown by the experience of some of the leading cooperatives which were much stronger and more comprehensive organizations in 1940 than seven years earlier. In the next chapter we will examine the even more spectacular progress of cooperative purchasing associations during these years.

Chapter XX

COOPERATIVE PURCHASING ACHIEVEMENTS:
1933-1940

Chapter IX carried the story of cooperative purchasing development up to 1933. By that time the farmers' purchasing cooperatives had weathered the worst of the Great Depression and were steadily gaining adherents. With a slight improvement in economic conditions in 1933, they began to grow vigorously. During the New Deal years, the expansion of purchasing associations was to be phenomenal—largely due to the ability of these associations to meet farmers' economic needs. In 1932-33 the volume of business of purchasing cooperatives amounted to $140.5 million. By 1939-40 volume had more than doubled to $358 million.[1]

Reasons for Rapid Growth

The following factors help to account for the remarkable expansion of cooperative purchasing during the New Deal period: (1) rising cash incomes of farmers; (2) continuing hard times in agriculture; (3) intensification of farm supply expenditures; (4) financial support from the Farm Credit Administration; (5) more research and service assistance; (6) ease of formation; (7) growing understanding of cooperative business techniques; (8) better and less expensive service provided by purchasing cooperatives; (9) assistance and encouragement from cooperative marketing associations; (10) gifted innovative leadership; (11) widespread favorable propaganda; and (12) the supportive influence of rapidly growing regional and national purchasing cooperatives. Each of these factors will be briefly explained.

1. With gradual business recovery, farmers had more money to spend on farm and household supplies and this naturally increased the business volume of purchasing organizations. Cash income from farm marketings

rose from $4,682,000 in 1932 to $8,357,000 in 1940, although by then it had not reached the 1929 figure of $11,221,000.[2]

2. The continuing hard times in agriculture put pressure on farms to reduce costs by buying essential production supplies cooperatively. Although there was some improvement in agricultural conditions from 1933 to 1940, it was still a period of depression for most farmers. A dollar saved was a dollar earned, and cooperative purchasing provided a means of keeping down the costs of farming.

3. During this period there was an intensification of expenditures for supplies used in farm operations. The average annual expenditure for major farm supplies increased from $1,748 for the years 1930-1934, to $2,489 for the years from 1935 to 1939.[3] Farms were becoming food and raw materials producing factories, and this called for mechanization and greater use of commercial feeds and fertilizers. As Dr. Walter Wilcox has pointed out: "During the entire period of the Thirties, the adoption of improved technology by United States farmers was an important factor in increasing the volume of agricultural products seeking market outlets. By far the most important of these was the substitution of tractors for horsepower. Tractor sales leaped as soon as agricultural incomes recovered from their 1932-33 low levels. The number of tractors on farms increased almost 50% from 1935 to 1940 . . . "[4] The great increase in power farming first occurred in the central states region, and this explains why the petroleum cooperatives first became established there.

4. The growth of cooperative purchasing was appreciably furthered by the inflow of capital made available by the banks for cooperatives. Prior to 1933, government lending service to agricultural cooperatives from the Federal Farm Board was restricted to marketing cooperatives. The Farm Credit Act of 1933 opened the door to purchasing cooperatives by providing that the banks for cooperatives could make loans for financing the operations of such associations. In 1935 the Act was amended to permit facility loans to purchasing associations on the same basis as to marketing cooperatives (see Chapter XIV). Cooperative purchasing associations were quick to take advantage of this new source of capital, and soon most of the regional and many local purchasing associations were obtaining such financial assistance. Rapid expansion of feed and fertilizer plants and, later, petroleum refineries and similar facilities would have been impossible had there not been available this understanding source of credit. The banks for cooperatives not only provided needed funds for operation and needed facilities but they also made available helpful managerial counsel and technical assistance. Another benefit from the banks for cooperatives was that other banking

institutions were forced to meet their competition, and this amplified the amount of capital for cooperative growth.

5. Prior to 1934 few studies had been made to assist farmers on their cooperative purchasing problems. This situation was changed with the establishment of a special section in the Cooperative Division of the Farm Credit Administration to provide research, service, and educational assistance to purchasing cooperatives. Bulletins and reports of the purchasing section soon provided information of great help to new and established associations.[5] As purchasing associations became of greater significance to farmers, more assistance in organizing and operating such associations was also provided by the land grant college agricultural economists and extension service employees.

6. The growth of purchasing cooperatives during the New Deal years was also facilitated by their ease of organization, and within a few years literally hundreds sprang into existence. In the beginning many were small organizations that only handled one or more supplies, such as petroleum, feed, or fertilizer. It is doubtful that their progress would have been so marked if they had at first attempted to provide a comprehensive supply service, for, as they gained experience and know-how, they were in a position to expand rapidly on a sound basis. Moreover, the emergence of strong centralized and federated purchasing associations proved to be veritable dynamos for sound cooperative purchasing growth. They gave leadership and assistance to farmers and local cooperatives in developing strong organizations for providing effective service.

7. Much of the rapid expansion in cooperative purchasing can be attributed to the growing understanding by farmers and their leaders of good cooperative business techniques. During this period knowledge of how to purchase cooperatively grew as experience was gained with the encouragement of the Farm Credit Administration, the general farm organizations, and the National Cooperative Council (now the National Council of Farmer Cooperatives). Within a few years purchasing cooperatives greatly strengthened their organizational and operating efficiency. They improved their methods of financing, their membership educational programs, and their accounting, personnel, and other business practices. The progress of cooperative purchasing was cumulative. As Dr. John D. Black pointed out: "Cooperation feeds upon itself. It succeeds best where cooperative seed has been planted, and where there are already successful cooperatives in existence."[6]

8. Many farmers were attracted to cooperative purchasing as a means of obtaining a better and less expensive type of farm supply service. They were "fed up" on seed that would not germinate, fertilizer that was mostly

filler, and feed of doubtful nutritional value. The opportunity of obtaining from purchasing cooperatives supplies produced to meet their specifications on an open formula basis explains much of the support which the early cooperatives enjoyed. Farmers also believed that they were paying too much for the kind of service they were receiving. In many communities, several supply concerns were taking excessive margins for their services. By pooling purchases, farmers could obtain the advantages of large volume purchasing operations, and the experience of many purchasing cooperatives demonstrated that they could provide farmers with the type of service desired at greatly reduced cost. This was apparent from the large patronage refunds paid by many purchasing cooperatives when they were first set up. It was often found that the presence of a purchasing cooperative quickly brought down the prices charged by farm supply merchants. Often inefficient and exploitative concerns were forced out of business because they could not meet the competition of the purchasing cooperatives. The rapid growth of such cooperatives would not have occurred if farmers had been served by an efficient farm supply distribution system.

9. Cooperative purchasing associations also benefited from their coordinate relationship with cooperative marketing associations. Many farmers got their first training and experience in cooperation as members of cooperative marketing associations. Successful experience in cooperative marketing caused many farmers to ask themselves this question: "If cooperation can be used to enable us to market more efficiently, why can't it be used to enable us to purchase more efficiently?" In many cases cooperative purchasing was also carried on by cooperative marketing associations as a means of better serving their members. The survival of cooperative elevators, creamery associations, and other forms of local marketing cooperatives was in many cases due to the savings made on farm supply business as a sideline operation. As marketing and purchasing cooperatives were both designed to improve farm incomes, they complemented each other. Moreover, many of the early cooperative purchasing association managers had prior experience in managing cooperative marketing enterprises.

10. Much credit for cooperative purchasing progress during the New Deal period can be attributed to the gifted, innovative leadership given by a number of capable and communicative men. Among them were H. E. "Ed" Babcock and James A. "Jim" McConnell (Cooperative Grange League Federation Exchange); W. G. "Bud" Wysor (Southern States Cooperative); Harvey Hull and Marvin Briggs (Indiana Farm Bureau Cooperative Association); Lloyd Marchant (Illinois Farm Supply Com-

pany); Murray Lincoln (Ohio Farm Bureau Cooperative Association); Howard A. Cowden (Consumers Cooperative Association); Emil Syftestad (Farmers Union Central Exchange); and M. G. Mann (Farmers Cooperative Exchange of North Carolina). The firm but imaginative guidance of such men built farm and public confidence in this type of cooperative activity and contributed greatly to its scope, stability, and growth.

11. As we have seen in earlier chapters, cooperative purchasing development was encouraged by the "propaganda" which was disseminated by various New Deal agencies on the advantages of cooperative buying associations as socially desirable forms of business organization. Much of this promotional effort through literature, radio, and speeches was engendered by The Cooperative League of the U.S.A. as part of its campaign to spread the philosophy of consumers' cooperation. Cooperative purchasing was also vigorously promoted by the National Cooperative Council which included in its membership many of the large purchasing regionals. The American Institute of Cooperation also provided an important forum where cooperative purchasing leaders assembled to review programs and plan accomplishments. These meetings brought cooperative purchasing programs to the attention of government officials and cooperative marketing leaders. During this time the achievements of purchasing cooperatives made news, and the farm journals and newspapers carried abundant information on their progress.

12. Another factor that served to stimulate cooperative purchasing during the Thirties was the influence of an increasing number of strong and powerful regional purchasing cooperatives. Through these large-scale cooperative enterprises, farmers were able to achieve a form of business organization which could meet the technical needs of agriculture for supply service and compete with organized industry on its own terms. In effect, these associations were able to contribute to the cooperative purchasing movement the same type of advantages that the chain store form of organization was then bringing to the field of retail distribution; centralized buying; mass purchasing power; overhead cost reduction; risk diversification; credit control; more specialized and better trained personnel; more complete service; ability to undertake manufacturing and other procurement operations through pooling of financial power and consumer demand; and the integration of retail, wholesale, and manufacturing operations with the consequent combination or pyramiding of savings. As will be later shown, these regional associations, in turn, formed two national overhead federations—National Cooperatives, Inc., and United Cooperatives, Inc., which coordinated and further integrated

their operations. By 1940 there had been developed a national framework or network of purchasing cooperatives covering most of the nation.

As reported in Chapter IX, there were many relatively strong regional purchasing cooperatives functioning by the end of 1932. They had passed through the trial period and were in position to grow vigorously under propitious conditions. Let us look at some of these associations as they developed during the New Deal years.

The Eastern "Centralized" Purchasing Associations

The eastern regional purchasing cooperatives were all of the centralized types in which the members belonged directly to the associations. They began primarily as feed, seed, and fertilizer associations, but, during the middle Thirties, they began to diversify their operations by handling petroleum products and other farm supplies.

The GLF. The pacemaker among the purchasing cooperatives was the Cooperative Grange League Federation Exchange. During the years of the Great Depression, its volume of wholesale business fell off from $29 million in 1929-30, to $16 million in 1932-33, although in terms of tons of feed and fertilizer handled there was little decline in the physical amount of business done. With improved conditions in 1933-34, dollar volume of business sprung back to $24 million and then rose steadily to $40 million in 1939-40. The GLF's total assets in 1933-34 were $5.7 million and net worth represented $4.5 million. By 1939-40, total assets amounted to $9.4 million, and net worth to $7.1 million.

In the New Deal years the GLF greatly improved its business structure and management efficiency. Great stress was placed on the value of departmentalization and employee training to gain advantages in specialization and direction. In the late Thirties, the GLF was held in high respect by all cooperatives for the morale and capability of its personnel. In 1937 it set up a comprehensive institutional training program for all employees and directors under the name The University of the GLF. This was the first broad training program for a large cooperative organization in the United States, and it stimulated similar programs in other regional cooperatives.[7]

Until 1935, the GLF centered its attention on its feed, seed, and fertilizer purchasing and manufacturing operations. Then it began handling other farm supplies needed by its members, such as milk coolers, fencing, steel roofing, paint, and farm tools. In 1936 service was broadened to include petroleum products after a careful study had been made of the methods and experience of other organizations in this field.

The procedure adopted provided for centralized direction with close management control—an innovation in petroleum distribution methods at that time. By 1939-40, petroleum sales through 25 bulk plants, located to best serve patrons, reached $16 million. In the years from 1933 to 1940, the GLF handled an increasing volume of business through its own system of retail service stores. By 1940 the number of such stores reached 153. The value of retail store sales rose from $12.6 million in 1933-34, to $22 million in 1939-40.

While it was establishing itself and building necessary facilities, the GLF retained its net margins for expansion and gave farmers benefits from membership primarily in the form of lower prices on supplies of good quality. Starting with 1935-36, the GLF began to distribute a substantial portion of its net margins in patronage refunds, and this greatly encouraged patronage support. Such refunds exceeded $1.5 million in 1939-40. Prior to 1933-34, cooperative marketing was of minor importance in the GLF system. From then on, under the inspiring leadership of H. E. Babcock, it gradually increased in significance. By 1940-41 the value of products marketed for patrons—mostly eggs, grain, and beans—totalled about $4 million.[8]

Eastern States Farmers' Exchange. The Eastern States Farmers' Exchange was well established in New England and several middle Atlantic states in 1933 when economic conditions began to improve. From then on its progress was rapid with sales to farmers reaching nearly $22 million in 1940. This organization built its program on the high quality of feed, seed, and fertilizer furnished its members, and it carried on a very enlightening educational program designed to strengthen the agricultural productivity of the region it served. The Exchange was the foremost advocate of high-analysis fertilizers based on individual soil analyses for better adaptation of fertilizers to crop needs. It also maintained trial grounds for testing seeds and a dairy research station for testing dairy feeds. All of its products were supplied on an open formula basis with the ingredients made known. The Exchange emphasized that it bought or produced supplies on specifications to best serve the needs of its members. During the 1930's the Exchange greatly expanded its system of regional branch warehouses to supplement its basic car door distribution system. By 1940 there were about 50 of these regional centers. The total assets of the Exchange then amounted to over $5 million, and its net worth, or the investment of its members, amounted to nearly $3 million. Practically all of the net worth represented savings from operations not distributed in cash to members.

The Southern States Cooperative—The SSC. In 1933 the Virginia Seed

Service (see Chapter IX) changed its name to Southern States Cooperative, Inc., and began to expand as a regional organization. In 1934 it took over the operations of the Agricultural Corporation of Maryland and began to extend its services into Delaware and West Virginia. It also began providing feed and fertilizer manufacturing services for the newly formed Farmers Cooperative Exchange in North Carolina. The Southern States Cooperative (then the Virginia Seed Service) had come through the depression years of 1931 and 1932 with a gain in business volume and was in position to grow rapidly as conditions improved. With financial assistance from the Baltimore Bank for Cooperatives after 1934 it soon acquired extensive feed mill and fertilizer manufacturing facilities which enabled it to better integrate its operations. In 1938 the SSC opened its first bulk petroleum plant, and by 1940 there were 19 plants doing a total petroleum business of $657,752. Egg marketing was begun in 1935, and by 1940 egg marketings amounted to $600,000. As early as 1928, the SSC had begun operating its own retail stores to supplement distribution through dealer agents and local cooperative associations. There were about 50 of these centrally managed stores by 1940. The volume of supply business of the SSC at wholesale reached $9 million in 1940, and the volume of its retail business through its own stores was over $3 million. The association's total assets then exceeded $4 million and its net worth, or the ownership interest of its members, exceeded $2 million.[9]

The Farmers Cooperative Exchange—The FCX. During the depression years of 1932 and 1933 there was a great expansion of interest in cooperative purchasing in North Carolina as a means of reducing farm supply costs. In 1933, several state organizations were providing limited cooperative purchasing services but these were not consolidated into an effective program. Following the meetings of the American Institute of Cooperation held in Raleigh, N.C., in July 1933, a demand arose for a unified state-wide purchasing organization, patterned on the model of the GLF. This led to the formation of a committee to draw up plans for establishing a state-wide organization, and out of its deliberations resulted the Farmers Cooperative Exchange which quickly became known as the FCX. With the support of all agricultural agencies in the state, this organization developed rapidly under the energetic leadership of M. G. Mann as General Manager. By 1940 the sales of the FCX reached $3,735,697. Although the FCX was set up primarily for cooperative purchasing purposes, marketing was carried on almost from the start. Cooperative marketing volume amounted to $475,000 in 1940. During the late Thirties the FCX began to provide limited service in South Carolina but this did not become of importance until after World War II.[10]

The Farm Bureau Purchasing Federations

Strong state farm bureau purchasing federations in Indiana, Ohio, and Michigan were all in position to grow with the lifting of the depression. In 1934 a similar organization formed on the Indiana model was established in Pennsylvania. All of these organizations handled feed, seed, fertilizer, petroleum products, and general farm supplies, but the most substantial growth was in petroleum products.

The Indiana Farm Bureau Cooperative Association. The leader among the state farm bureau purchasing associations was the Indiana Farm Bureau Cooperative Association managed by I. H. Hull. By 1940 this organization did a wholesale purchasing business for more than 80 county member associations of $6.5 million. It then had total assets of $2.4 million with a net worth of $1.3 million. During the years from 1933 to 1940 the state association steadily increased its manufacturing operations either through its own plants or through plants jointly owned with other regional purchasing associations. Its lubricating oils and greases and some other supplies were obtained from the Farm Bureau Oil Company, which became United Cooperatives, Inc., in 1936. During this period, gasoline and other related supplies were partly obtained through master contracts negotiated by National Cooperatives, Inc. Feed was procured through the Farm Bureau Milling Company, a cooperative set up jointly by the Indiana, Michigan, and Ohio associations to provide research and manufacturing services. Until 1938, the Indiana association obtained its fertilizer supplies from a private company under a cost sharing arrangement, but by this time it had become clear that the association could best own and operate its own fertilizer manufacturing facilities, and plants for this purpose were established. In 1940 a significant development occurred when the Indiana Farm Bureau Cooperative Association constructed its own petroleum refinery at Mt. Vernon, Indiana, to take advantage of the oil producing fields in southern Indiana. This was the second cooperative refinery to be established in the United States.[11]

The (Ohio) Farm Bureau Cooperative Association. The depression years from 1931 to 1933 demonstrated the weakness of the Ohio Farm Bureau Service Company's over-centralized cooperative purchasing operations. In 1934 the Service Company was reorganized on the county unit federated pattern of the Indiana State Association with the name (Ohio) Farm Bureau Cooperative Association. In 1935 the Ohio association began handling petroleum for member associations through bulk plants modelled on those in Indiana. From then on progress was rapid. By 1940 the (Ohio) Farm Bureau Cooperative Association was doing a business of over $7 million annually. Its total assets then amounted to over $1.5 million and net worth of $700,000. Like the Indiana association, the Ohio federation withdrew from the participating cost sharing arrangement with a commercial fertilizer company in order to manufacture its own fertilizers. This was done first under a partnership with the GLF at Baltimore, and later by the establishment of its own plants in Ohio. The program proved highly practical from the beginning.[12]

The Specialized Petroleum Regionals

The petroleum regional cooperatives in the Middle West were growing rapidly by 1933 (see Chapter IX). In the next seven years, they greatly expanded their operations and began to handle feed, seed, and other farm supplies.

The Illinois Farm Supply Company. The leader among the specialized petroleum purchasing associations in the New Deal years was the Illinois Farm Supply Company—a farm bureau sponsored and managed organization. By 1933 this cooperative company had developed an outstanding service on petroleum and related products and during the next six years its dollar sales grew from $2.1 million to over $12 million. From 1934 to 1940, it gradually diversified operations by handling paint, tires, feed, and fertilizer. During these years supplies were largely obtained through brokerage contracts with independent oil companies, but the amount of petroleum purchased directly steadily increased until in 1940 it represented the bulk of the total supply obtained. In order to reduce transportation costs, the Illinois Farm Supply Company opened a marine terminal at Shawneetown on the Ohio River in 1936, and this proved so economical that a second and larger terminal was opened at Kingston Mines on the Illinois River in 1938. In connection with these terminals, oil barges were purchased and operated, and transport truck operations, to move petroleum to bulk plants of member associations, were greatly expanded. Operating in a limited area under a common plan for member companies, the Illinois Farm Supply Company developed a highly efficient intensive distribution system which served as a standard for other petroleum cooperatives in this period of rapid development. In 1940, the Company made savings of nearly $800,000, and over $600,000 of the savings were distributed to the member companies in cash. The total assets accumulated up to August 31, 1940, amounted to $1,430,401 and the ownership interest of its member companies reached $688,000.[13]

Midland Cooperative Wholesale. In 1934 the Midland Cooperative Oil

Association, the pioneer regional petroleum association, changed its name to Midland Cooperative Wholesale to imply a broader conception of supply service. It was then serving 120 member associations in Minnesota and Wisconsin and doing a wholesale business of over $1 million. During the New Deal years it broadened its supply service to include tires and tubes, batteries, electrical equipment, and general farm supplies, but as late as 1940 over 90 per cent of its business was done in petroleum and related supplies. As noted in Chapter XVIII, Midland began handling groceries in 1937 through a system of chain store branches, but this program was discontinued in 1940. Midland's volume of business in 1940 exceeded $4 million and it was then serving about 225 member associations.[14]

Farmers Union Central Exchange. One of the fastest growing regional petroleum purchasing associations was the Farmers' Union Central Exchange which was incorporated in 1931 with 91 member associations. By 1933 it was serving 172 local member associations located largely in Minnesota, Wisconsin, North Dakota, and Montana, and its volume of petroleum business amounted to $1,549,223. During the next several years it began handling tractors, farm equipment, and supplies. Under the capable management of Emil Syftestad, its volume of business reached $6,236,225 in 1940, and its net worth amounted to $702,441. It then had 250 member associations.[15]

Consumers Cooperative Association. Under the strong leadership of Howard A. Cowden, the Union Oil Company Cooperative of North Kansas City, Missouri, was serving about 290 member associations in Kansas and in 6 nearby states in 1933, and its wholesale sales of petroleum and related products amounted to $1,433,000. In 1934 it adopted the name Consumers Cooperative Association (CCA) and began to broaden its line of supplies to include groceries and household goods. It also extended its operating territory so that by 1940 it was serving some 442 member associations in 10 states. By that time its volume of sales reached nearly $5 million. As volume increased, Cowden and his associates saw the need of having an integrated petroleum service comparable to that provided by major oil companies. In response to this thinking, the CCA carried on a vigorous campaign among its member associations to raise funds to finance a refinery, and, with additional funds borrowed from the Wichita Bank for Cooperatives, a refinery was constructed at Phillipsburg, Kansas, in 1939 and placed in operation in January 1940. This was the first cooperative petroleum refinery to be established in the United States, although a small cooperative refinery was then operating in Canada. To transport petroleum and supply the refinery with crude oil, two subsidiary corporations were set up—The Cooperative Pipeline Association and the Cooperative Oil Producing Association. Although strenuously opposed by powerful interests which threatened to paralyze the refinery by denying it necessary crude oil, it was not possible to withstand the mobilized political strength of the thousands of CCA members, and the refinery was able to get underway. The refinery proved successful from the start, and this marked the beginning of CCA's great expansion in subsequent years. Moreover, it opened the way for the establishment of other cooperative refineries in the United States.[16]

Other Regional Purchasing Developments

Several other regional farm supply purchasing associations in the Midwest were steadily growing in significance during the New Deal years. Of these, the Farmers Union State Exchange in Nebraska was handling petroleum and other farm and home supplies with a value of about $3 million in 1940. Although the Central Cooperative Wholesale of Superior, Wisconsin, was primarily a consumers cooperative wholesale, about half of its $4.5 million business in 1940 represented the sale of petroleum and other farm supplies. In this year, wholesale purchasing activities carried on by the Missouri Farmers Association exceeded $3 million in 1940.

In the Far West the largest regional purchasing association was the well-established Fruit Growers Supply Company which served the supply needs of the member associations of the California Fruit Growers' Exchange. The business of this organization remained steady at about $10 million annually. A new regional purchasing association was established in 1933 as a federation of local purchasing associations in Idaho, Oregon, and Washington. This organization—The Pacific Supply Cooperative—was organized with the assistance of the Union Oil Company (soon to take the name Consumers Cooperative Association) and was largely patterned on it. By 1940 it was serving about 75 member associations and doing a business, mostly in petroleum and related products, of about $3 million.

In the South where farming was less commercialized and mechanized, there was less opportunity for cooperative purchasing to develop. There was only one regional purchasing association in the Old South, other than the FCX and the Southern States Cooperative, as late as 1940. This was the Mississippi Federated Cooperatives of Jackson, Mississippi, which was slowly taking form.[17] Another matter of interest was the formation in the late Thirties of two small regional fertilizer associations in Alabama.[18] In

Texas, the Consumers Cooperatives Associated was struggling to establish itself in the petroleum business as a federation patterned on the CCA.[19]

Purchasing Operations of Marketing Cooperatives

During the years from 1933 to 1940, an increasing number of marketing cooperatives engaged in cooperative purchasing—usually through separately organized departments. Outstanding among such associations were the feed departments of the large West Coast centralized poultry and egg associations. Both the Poultry Producers of Central California in San Francisco and the Washington Egg and Poultry Association in Seattle had supply sales of over $6 million in 1940. Such fruit marketing organizations as the California Fruit Exchange and the Hood River Apple Growers Association also had important orchard supply departments which were doing volumes of supply business of about $1 million annually in 1940. In the Midwest, the Land O'Lakes Creameries, Inc., was steadily expanding its range of supplies handled, and in 1940 this association was doing a supply business in excess of $1 million. In the South, several of the cotton marketing associations were also rendering a supply service. Of particular interest was a subsidiary of the Georgia Cotton Growers Cooperative Association, the Producers Cooperative Exchange, under the management of D. W. Brooks. By 1939 this Association was doing a business of $355,000, mostly in fertilizers, but it was then on the verge of great expansion.[20] Reference should also be made to the significant fertilizer and other supply operations carried on by several of the large local citrus cooperatives in Florida.

Joint Operations of Regional Purchasing Associations

As the regional purchasing associations developed, they found it advisable to coordinate their operations. They recognized that the expansion of cooperative purchasing would be helpful to all purchasing cooperatives. Several illustrations can be given of how they began to work together. In the early 1920's, the GLF had helped the Southern States Cooperative to establish itself, and as the SSC grew, it worked with the GLF on various joint purchasing programs. In turn, the SSC, in the Thirties, provided the Farmers Cooperative Exchange with feed and fertilizer on a cost of manufacture basis. The Pennsylvania Farm Bureau Cooperative was formed with the direct assistance of the Indiana Farm Bureau Cooperative Association, and, in the Far West, the Consumers

Cooperation Association helped the Pacific Supply Cooperative get under way. One of the first instances of joint buying was the arrangement by which the Indiana and Ohio farm bureau state associations obtained fertilizer from a manufacturer on a cost sharing basis. In the late Thirties when the Ohio association was developing its own fertilizer program, it was assisted by the GLF, and the two organizations became partners in the ownership of a fertilizer plant at Baltimore. As early as 1930, the three state farm bureau associations in Indiana, Ohio, and Michigan set up the Farm Bureau Milling Company. The major achievements in such cooperation by cooperatives were the establishment of three overhead federations: (1) United Cooperatives, Inc., (2) The National Cooperatives, Inc., and (3) the National Farm Machinery Cooperative, Inc.

United Cooperatives, Inc. Chapter IX explained how the Farm Bureau Oil Company was formed in 1930 as a joint oil blending enterprise by the Indiana, Ohio, and Michigan state farm bureau purchasing associations. This organization proved its usefulness and by 1934 it was ready for expansion. It then had a volume of business of $327,000 as compared with $185,000 the year before, and in 1935 the volume increased to $446,000. At about this time the Farm Bureau Oil Company began branching out in its lines of service to include farm tools, barn equipment, and fence. In February 1935, the newly formed Pennsylvania Farm Bureau Cooperative Association became a member.

Prior to 1935, the GLF, the Southern States Cooperative, and Farmers Cooperative Exchange were primarily feed, seed, and fertilizer purchasing organizations. The decision of the GLF to widen its supply service to include farm equipment and petroleum products encouraged the Southern States Cooperative and the Farmers Cooperative Exchange to move in the same direction. With this change in the character of their operations, these organizations became interested in the type of overhead buying service that was being offered by the Farm Bureau Oil Company.[21] On its part, the Farm Bureau Oil Company saw the advantages of opening its membership to these organizations as a means of increasing its economic strength.

However, the GLF, SSC, and FCX could not belong to an overhead organization with a Farm Bureau name, for they were not directly related to the Farm Bureau. To meet this problem the Farm Bureau Oil Company changed its name to United Cooperative, Inc., on August 12, 1936, and, thereupon, the three associations became members. Soon afterwards the United Cooperatives adopted the trade mark UNICO for use on supplies distributed by it, and a second oil blending plant was opened at Warren, Pennsylvania, to better serve its eastern members.

With the broadening of its membership, United began to take on a new life, as the incoming members represented a cohesive block of purchasing power greater than that of the member farm bureau associations. It was now possible to expand manufacturing operations where opportunities permitted. To move in this direction, a plan was needed that would provide membership capital on an equitable basis, and this led in 1938 to the adoption of a policy under which membership investment henceforth would be in accordance with the use made of United's services.

Prior to the formation of United Cooperatives, the Farm Bureau Oil Company had been a member of National Cooperatives, and Harvey Hull, General Manager of the Indiana Farm Bureau Cooperative Association, served as President of both. While United continued to hold membership in National, friction soon developed because of the different cooperative philosophies represented by the two organizations. The United group were agriculturally minded and had little interest in the consumer cooperative views strongly held by members of the National.[22] Another source of difficulty involved the use of the Co-Op trademark owned by National. When United adopted the UNICO trademark, the two brands became competitive. The leaders in National also believed that United should be merged into National, while the leaders in United felt that National should be continued only as a correlating organization for regional purchasing cooperatives. In 1938 United decided to withdraw from National, leaving it to the individual members to determine whether they wished to take out separate memberships in the National. The four state farm bureau associations thereupon joined the National, although the United's strongest members, the GLF and SSC remained aloof. By 1940 United Cooperatives was doing a business volume of $2,208,667, and it had developed total assets of $686,609, with a net worth of $400,000. While United was growing in strength as a well-organized and well-managed association, National Cooperatives, Inc., was still largely an informal committee-operated buying federation with little investment in facilities.[23]

National Cooperatives, Inc. With the development of strong regional wholesale associations in the central states, there developed under the leadership of Harvey Hull and Howard Cowden a strong sentiment in favor of setting up a national overhead buying organization that would enable the regionals to combine their bargaining power to obtain more economically petroleum products and other supplies for their common needs. The way in which this led to the development of National Cooperatives, Inc., was explained in Chapter XVIII. Although this organization was primarily a farm supply purchasing association, in that the members of its member associations were mostly farmers, its leaders were motivated by a strong consumers cooperative philosophy and it developed in close relationship with the Cooperative League of the USA. Its center of strength in 1940 was in the central states area although its membership included associations in the east and in Canada. The following regional associations were then members: Farmers' Union Central Exchange; Central Cooperative Wholesale; Midland Cooperative Wholesale; Central States Cooperatives, Inc.; Eastern Cooperative Wholesale, Inc.; Pacific Supply Cooperative; Consumers Cooperative Association; the Indiana, Ohio, Michigan, and Pennsylvania farm bureau state cooperatives; Saskatchewan Cooperative Wholesale Society, and United Farmers Cooperative Company of Ontario. Of these, the Central States Cooperative, Inc., and the Eastern Cooperative Wholesale, Inc., served primarily urban consumers cooperative associations.[24]

The National Farm Machinery Cooperative, Inc. As the regional purchasing associations gained strength, they began to consider the possibilities of buying tractors and farm machinery cooperatively, as this was one of the most burdensome expenditures of farmers. By 1929, several county cooperatives in Indiana had agency agreements with various farm machinery companies, and during the Great Depression and early New Deal years, such agency agreements greatly expanded throughout the nation.[25] In 1930 the Indiana Farm Bureau Cooperative Association entered into a distributing contract with the Allis Chalmers Company, which was then developing a tractor with a line of farm implements, but this program was soon discontinued. Then for a few years the Indiana and Ohio State purchasing associations obtained farm machinery for distribution by their member units from the B. F. Avery Company of Louisville, Kentucky, but this company began serving a large mail-order firm and cancelled the cooperative contracts. The Indiana association then endeavored to obtain farm machinery for distribution from several other companies without success.

In 1934 several of the regional cooperatives—led by the Farmers' Union Central Exchange and the Indiana Farm Bureau Cooperative Association—came to the conclusion that they would have to work together if they were to make any substantial progress in the farm machinery field. As they did not have adequate capital to carry on manufacturing operations, they entered into a joint contract with the Duplex Machinery Company of Battle Creek, Michigan, to have a tractor built for them designed to meet their specifications.[26] The "Co-Op" tractor had been designed for the Farmers' Union Central Exchange by Dent Parrett, a well-qualified engineer, and it represented two novel features—use of a high compression motor and rubber tires. The first Co-Op tractors were made in 1935, and enthusiasm for their success was high. However, after what appeared to be a favorable beginning, it was found that this program was ahead of its time, even though the tractor was technically a good machine. Competition from the well-financed and -entrenched farm machinery companies was intense and the under-financed cooperatives were in no position to meet their determined opposition. Moreover, the established farm machinery companies soon copied the distinctive features of the Co-Op tractor. After two years of disappointing experience, the Consumers Cooperative Association found it necessary to withdraw from the program.[27] Undaunted, the remaining regional cooperatives in the program joined together as American Cooperatives, Inc., and entered into an arrangement in April 1938 to have the Co-Op tractor assembled in a plant provided "free" by the Farm Security Administration at the Homestead project in Arthurdale, West Virginia (see Chapter XV).[28]

Difficulties in getting this program established on a profitable basis led to its liquidation in 1940, and, with the collapse of American Cooperatives, Inc., the Indiana Farm Bureau Cooperative Association decided to go it alone and build its own tractor assembly plant at Shelbyville, Indiana. However, to obtain sufficient volume for efficient operation, it was soon found desirable to broaden the program to permit other cooperatives to become participants. This resulted in the establishment of the National Farm Machinery Cooperative, Inc., which began to assemble Co-Op tractors late in 1940. This program was begun just as European war conditions were changing the economic environment. How the National Farm Machinery Cooperative coped with its problems during World War II will be examined in Chapter XXIII.[29]

The Relationship of Cooperative Purchasing to Consumers Cooperation

During the New Deal years, two schools of thought vigorously vied for supremacy among advocates of cooperative buying. One school, represented by the National Cooperative Council, looked upon cooperative purchasing as primarily a means of reducing farming costs, and it favored restricting buying operations to supplies used in farm production.[30] The other school, more fully described in Chapter XVIII, looked upon all cooperative buying—whether by farmers for production supplies or for household use—as a consumers function, and it favored close relationship with The Cooperative League of the U.S.A.[31] The strong farm supply purchasing associations in the eastern states were the foremost supporters of segregation of farm supply purchasing and consumers cooperative business, while the large midwestern petroleum associations—except for the Illinois Farm Supply Company—generally accepted the "we are all consumers" cooperative philosophy.[32] It was becoming clear by 1940 that the controversy was largely resolving itself, for most of the leaders of the large regional farmers buying organizations by then had become primarily concerned with improving their cooperative business efficiency regardless of whether their organizations were described as "consumers cooperatives" or as "purchasing cooperatives." From then on it became common to refer to the buying associatons that provided farmers with their production supply requirements as "farm supply associations" or as "farm supply purchasing associations."

Chapter XXI

THE GROWTH OF COOPERATIVE SERVICES:
1933-1940

During the New Deal years there was a considerable expansion and extension of cooperative servicing associations. A significant new development of this type was the provision of electrical services with the encouragement of the TVA and the REA, as described in Chapters XVI and XVII. Cooperative credit services for farmers were also greatly expanded by the Farm Credit Administration and the Farm Security Administration as shown in Chapters XIV and XV. In this chapter we will focus attention on developments relating to other forms of cooperative service—consumer credit, insurance, irrigation, transportation, artificial insemination, frozen food preservation, grove care, housing, and health. We will also give attention to progress of forestry and fishery cooperatives and cooperatives formed by general business concerns.

Credit Unions Catch Hold

In Chapter XI we saw how credit unions gained a national foothold during the 1920's through the effective work of Edward A. Filene and Roy F. Bergengren. Although conditions were not favorable during the depression years for credit union expansion, interest in them remained high. This was evidenced by the passage of a credit union act for the District of Columbia, signed by President Herbert Hoover, on June 21, 1932. The Act was significant in that it represented the first recognition by Congress of the value of credit unions.

With the coming of the New Deal, credit unions were to flourish and become nationally accepted as important consumer credit institutions. Two developments in 1934 brought about this lift in credit union expansion. The first was the passage of a federal credit union act which gave national government encouragement to this form of cooperative organization. The second was the creation of the Credit Union National Association which unified credit unions in a strong national movement. Let us look briefly at these two important developments.[1]

The Federal Credit Union Act. In the search for new approaches to improve economic and social welfare, the Roosevelt administration showed early interest in credit unions. President Roosevelt had worked with them in New York State, and he had an interest in their possibilities. This favorable situation was recognized by Bergengren who had long felt the need of a federal credit union law to supplement the state credit union acts. Now, he believed the time was propitious for obtaining a federal act which would stimulate the formation of credit unions in all parts of the nation. Working closely with Senator Morris Sheppard of Texas, who had a deep interest in cooperative banking and short-term credit for farmers, a bill providing for a Federal Credit Union Act was prepared and then introduced by Senator Sheppard in the Senate on May 1, 1933. Many problems were encountered and overcome before a satisfactory bill was finally drafted which provided for supervision of Federal Credit Union activities by the Farm Credit Administration (see Chapter XIV). On June 6, 1934, President Roosevelt said in a memo to Henry Morgenthau, Jr., Secretary of the Treasury: "I really believe in the usefulness of these credit unions. Would you please take it up with the Congressional Committees concerned and see if we can get it passed without opposition in the closing days." Even with strong administration support, Bergengren was fearful that the bill could not be passed in the few days before Congress would adjourn. However, on the last day of the session, both the Senate and House passed the bill with little opposition, and the President signed the measure on June 26, 1934. Credit union advocates were jubilant at this turn of events. Bergengren, in writing to Filene, maintained that this was "the greatest single step forward in the history of the credit union movement."[2]

Bergengren and other credit union leaders realized that the value of the Federal Credit Union Act would depend largely upon the character and competence of the man to be appointed director of the Credit Union Section in the Farm Credit Administration, and, upon their recommendation, Claude R. Orchard was appointed to the position. This was an admirable choice since Orchard not only had a deep belief in the importance of credit unions but he was experienced in their formation and operation. As Moody and Fite have said: "In Orchard the movement had an experienced credit union man who was thoroughly imbued with the philosophy of the movement's pioneers. Credit unionism was fortunate to have him administering the new law."[3] Under Orchard's direction the new Credit Union Section in the Farm Credit Administration began operations on August 20, 1934, and it was soon busily engaged in promoting the organization of federal credit unions.

The Credit Union National Association. With the passage of the Federal Credit Union Act, Bergengren could devote his full attention to the long-time goal of establishing a national credit union organization. As early as March 1934, Bergengren had made initial plans for a conference to be held in August at Estes Park, Colorado, to consider this matter. Before this conference was held, Bergengren drafted articles of incorpora tion and by-laws for a National Credit Union Association that might be adopted by those at the conference. He looked upon the Estes Park conference as a meeting similar to that held in Philadelphia in 1789 to work out plans for a federal constitution for the United States. In writing to Filene before the conference he said: "This is not a convention; it is in no sense an attempt to bring together a certain number of delegates from each credit union state. It is rather to be compared with the original Constitutional Convention of the United States, which was an attempt to get together a group of outstanding men who could exchange views on a national constitution, with the thought in mind that if they agreed on such a constitution it would be submitted to the states for ratification."[4]

With the articles of incorporation and by-laws for the Credit Union National Association, as largely developed by Bergengren, accepted by those at the Estes Park conference on August 10, the next problem was to obtain ratification by the state credit union leagues that were to be its constituent members. As only five were then functioning effectively, a whirlwind campaign was carried on by Bergengren and his colleague Tom Doig to establish other state credit union leagues. By late November 1934, the plan of organization was ratified by 33 old or new leagues and the Credit Union National Association (CUNA) took form with Bergengren as Managing Director. Until the new organization could be self-supporting through dues from its member leagues, Filene provided financial assistance through the Twentieth Century Fund. During this interim period, until the National Association could begin functioning with its headquarters at Madison, Wisconsin, in July 1935, the Credit Union National Extension Bureau continued to direct credit union work.

The Credit Union National Association soon demonstrated its power by marshalling support for legislation that would further credit union interests. For example, a law was enacted by Congress on July 9, 1936, that allowed space in federal buildings for credit union activities. Another law passed on December 6, 1937, provided for exemption of federal credit unions from taxation except on real and tangible property. Moreover, the value of the Credit Union National Association soon became apparent through the formation of the CUNA Mutual Insurance Society to provide borrowers' protection insurance and of the CUNA Supply Cooperative to supply credit unions with bookkeeping and promotional forms. While the National Association encouraged the formation of credit unions, the bulk of the organizational work during the late Thirties was carried on by the Credit Union Section of the Farm Credit Administration.

By 1940 the Credit Union National Association had become the recognized central organization for the credit union movement, although it was plagued by internal rivalries and policy differences. One problem that was largely resolved was the relationship of credit unions to producers and consumers' cooperatives. Many credit union leaders believed that credit unions should be accepted as being a part of the general cooperative movement, while others held that a close relationship with cooperatives "would alienate businessmen who were friendly to credit unions but hostile to other aspects of cooperative enterprise." This problem was settled when CUNA became a fraternal member of The Cooperative League of the USA in March 1939.[5]

In the years from 1934 to 1940 the expansion of the credit union movement was phenomenal. In 1934 the number of credit unions totalled 2,489, with a membership of 427,097. By 1940 there were 9,023 credit unions, and the total membership was 2,826,612. Much of this increase was due to the rapid promotion of Federal Credit Unions. On December 31, 1940, there were 3,782 active Federal Credit Unions, with a membership of 1,125,000. The shareholdings of these associations then totalled $66 million and their estimated total assets amounted to more than $71 million. Qualitatively, the credit unions in 1940 were much stronger organizations than those that existed before the Federal Credit Union Act was passed and the National Association was formed.

The Expansion of Agricultural Mutual Insurance Activities

Cooperatives providing insurance services were well established by 1933. Millions of farmers were then obtaining fire, hail, or windstorm insurance protection from mutual companies, and hundreds of thousands of farmers were obtaining automobile or life insurance through their own mutual associations.

Mutual fire insurance companies. With some improvement in economic conditions during the New Deal years, the number of farm mutual fire

THE ADVANCE OF AMERICAN COOPERATIVE ENTERPRISE

insurance companies increased slightly from the Great Depression years while the amount of their insurance in force rose from $10.6 billion in 1934 to $12.3 billion in 1940. Most of these companies were local in character but an increasing number had begun to operate over larger areas. In general they served only farmers but in certain states, particularly in Massachusetts and Pennsylvania, they also insured non-farm property. During this period these companies, with the encouragement of their state associations, continued to shift from the "post loss" to the "advance" assessment method of operation and to the use of more uniform policies. The practice of reinsuring for added protection and minimization of losses continued to steadily expand, and, with the growth of reinsurance, local associations in many areas organized federated associations to provide reinsurance service. [6]

It is of interest that two of the present-day large mutual fire insurance companies were originally formed to provide reinsurance service for local mutual insurance companies. The first of these, now the Country Mutual Insurance Company, was formed by the Illinois Agricultural Association in 1925 as the Farmers Mutual Reinsurance Company. However, it soon began to also write fire, hail, and windstorm insurance directly through county farm bureaus. By 1933 its insurance in force totalled $59 million, and by 1940 it exceeded $250 million. [7] The National Grange Fire Insurance Company was organized at Keene, New Hampshire, in 1935 to furnish reinsurance service for some of the smaller state grange fire insurance companies and to provide direct insurance service for grange patrons. This company was successful from the beginning. [8]

Automobile and life insurance mutuals. In Chapter XII we saw how the State Farm Mutual Automobile Insurance Company of Bloomington, Illinois, extended its operations nationally through contracts with state farm bureau federations. By 1935 there were more than 20 state farm bureaus related to State Farm in this way. As the state farm bureaus formed their own automobile insurance companies (following the lead of the Ohio and Illinois farm bureau organizations), State Farm built up its own system of agents apart from the farm bureaus. As of January 1, 1939, State Farm had 476,638 policies in force. [9]

The Farm Bureau Mutual Automobile Insurance Company of Columbus, Ohio, was well established by 1933. It then had 105,301 policies in force, and its admitted assets were $3,130,656. It was operating in West Virginia, Maryland, Delaware, Vermont, North Carolina, Pennsylvania, and Virginia, and it had begun writing non-farm bureau farmers and people in small towns. In this year it provided capital for the formation of a sister organization—the Farm Bureau Mutual Fire Insurance Company.

Its progress was temporarily arrested in 1934 by a loss of $200,000 brought on by non-classification of risks, but this taught the company a lesson which resulted in better business practices. In 1935 the company entered the life insurance field by acquiring a life insurance company, and, in the same year, the first directors from states outside of Ohio were elected. In 1937 its services were extended to New York State and the District of Columbia. By 1940, its policies in force numbered 329,628, and its admitted assets reached $7,196,000.[10]

The Illinois Agricultural Mutual Insurance Company, organized in 1927, was also in a strong position for growth by 1933. It then had 31,990 policies in force. As a result of a new state insurance agent licensing law, the company was forced to discontinue use of county farm bureaus as agents and to set up its own system of local agents. This gave the company more direct control over its agents, although they continued to work closely with the county farm bureaus. By 1940 the number of policies in force had grown to 85,864.

Impressed by the favorable experience of the Ohio and Illinois automobile insurance companies, somewhat similar organizations were set up by the state farm bureaus of Indiana and Wisconsin in 1935, and of Kansas in 1938, and Iowa in 1939. Others were soon to follow.

The National Grange Mutual Liability Company, formed in 1923 to provide automobile coverage for Grange members, continued to thrive during the New Deal years, although its progress was less spectacular than that of the farm-bureau-sponsored companies.

The favorable experience with fire and automobile insurance led the state farm bureaus into the field of life insurance. The first-farm-bureau-sponsored organization of this type—The Country Life Insurance Company—was set up by the Illinois Agricultural Association in 1929. It flourished from the beginning, and by 1933 it had 34,523 policyholders, with $54,065,807 life insurance in force. By 1940 the number of policyholders had grown to 98,835, and life insurance in force amounted to $153,056,605. With the pattern established by Illinois, other state farm bureaus gradually entered the mutual life insurance field. This was a logical extension of service, for it provided better utilization of local insurance agents while meeting an important need of farmers.[11]

Mutual Irrigation Associations

Mutual irrigation associations were well established in the arid western states in 1933, but many of them were in need of revitalization, reorganization, and capital investment. When the banks for cooperatives were established it soon became apparent to Dr. E. A. Stokdyk, President of the Berkeley Bank for Cooperatives, that these organizations could be greatly strengthened and their services for farmers improved through loans to enable them to function more effectively. Since the Berkeley Bank for Cooperatives did not have authority in 1934 to make loans for business services, the first loans were justified on the legal assumption that water could be considered an essential farm supply. With the amendment of the Farm Credit Act in 1935 to permit loans for business services, loans to the irrigation associations were authorized as farm business service loans. To provide a foundation for the work of the banks for cooperatives in financing such associations, Stokdyk encouraged the Cooperative Research and Service Division of the Farm Credit Administration to make a study of the methods, needs, and problems of such organizations. The so-called "water loans" of the Berkeley, Wichita, and Spokane banks for cooperatives helped many of the mutual irrigation associations to expand and improve their services during the New Deal years.[12]

Cooperative Transportation Associations

With the growing importance of motor truck operations there was a significant development of cooperative associations to perform transportation service. In many cases, these were formed by groups of farmers to transport livestock and other products to market. In other cases, they were federated organizations which served the transportation needs of local marketing and purchasing associations. One of the most interesting of these organizations was the Farmer's Union Federated Cooperative Shipping Association of Minot, North Dakota, which was set up in 1937 to assemble and transport livestock to the St. Paul market and bring back farm supplies on the return trip. After several years of experimental effort this organization established its operations on a sound basis.[13] A more comprehensive organization of this type was Northern Cooperatives, Inc., formed at Wadena, Minnesota, in 1932 by 15 member associations. It was set up to coordinate shipments of farm and dairy products to the Twin Cities market and to back-haul loads of farm supplies. The growth of this organization was modest prior to World War II when it began to expand rapidly in number of member associations and in volume of business.[14]

Artificial Insemination Associations

In the *Rise of American Cooperative Enterprise* attention was directed to the large number of herd improvement associations organized in the early 1900's. Such associations continued to flourish with little change in their methods of operation until 1938 when artificial breeding was introduced into this country from Europe. The first artificial insemination association, located in New Jersey, was somewhat of an experimental organization. Interest in it was so intense that before the year was out artificial insemination associations had been organized in several other states. From then on progress was rapid so that by the end of 1940 there were 37 associations of this type operating in 16 states. In the beginning these associations were mostly local in character, but soon some were organized as federations or as centralized associations to serve wider areas. The advantages of the artificial insemination associations were great in that they made it unnecessary for farmers to maintain their own bulls, and they brought about an increase in milk production at little cost through improving the quality of dairy herds. These organizations were to expand rapidly during and after World War II.[15]

Frozen Food Locker Cooperatives

One of the significant cooperative service developments during the late 1930's was the rapid growth of frozen food locker cooperatives. These organizations provided refrigerator service for meats, dairy products, and fruits and vegetables in individual lockers held by farmers or other members. Many of the first frozen food locker cooperatives were formed as side-line enterprises by cooperative creameries, cheese factories, and milk plants. By 1935 there were about 270 frozen food locker plants in the United States, and of these about 30 were operated as cooperatives. After 1936 the number of cooperatives and other locker plants grew rapidly so that by 1940 there were 3,000 plants of this type, and, of these, 400 were operated cooperatively. Many undertook slaughtering and meat cutting so that, in effect, they became local cooperative meat processing plants. The rapid growth of such enterprises was due to many factors, such as improvements in refrigeration equipment, research in food freezing, educational work on the importance of improving year around diets, and ease of organization. At that time few farmers had home refrigerators or deep freezers so the cooperative locker plants provided them with refrigeration service at low cost.[16]

Production Services by Marketing Associations

During the 1930's there was a considerable increase in the performance of production services by marketing and purchasing associations.

This development reached its highest development in the citrus marketing associations. As early as 1908 the California Fruit Growers' Exchange took over picking as a means of better marketing, and this led to pest control, truck hauling, and similar services for members. This development reached its fullest development in Florida where a large number of absentee landlords were not able to perform production functions for themselves. Moreover, many of the groves were small, and the investments in expensive machinery and equipment for performing such services were too heavy for many individual growers. By 1930 about 20 per cent of the Florida associations were performing two or more production services. By 1940 some 60 per cent of the associations were performing some kind of production service and about one-third were performing complete service, which included clearing and fencing land, setting out young groves, spraying, dusting, fertilizing, plowing, pruning, irrigating, or other services required in producing citrus fruit.[17]

Cooperative Housing Survives the Depression

The cooperative housing project of the Amalgamated Housing Corporation was getting firmly established when it was forced to meet the "acid test" of the Great Depression. Until then the number of applicants for cooperative housing units was continually increasing, and it seemed that progress and expansion would continue indefinitely. Members were paying their carrying charges on time, and, if a member withdrew, there were others to take his place. No reserves were being set aside for the purpose of repossessing stock or for other purposes. By 1932 nine buildings had been completed, and, with the assistance of the state of New York, work had also been largely completed on Amalgamated Dwellings, Inc., a large slum clearance cooperative housing project, likewise sponsored by the Amalgamated Clothing Workers Union. Up to this time, those in charge of the housing corporations were still preoccupied with plans for new construction.

In the summer of 1932 the Great Depression began to take effect with a drastic drop in the incomes of most of the cooperators. There was a rise in the number of members who desired to give up their apartments, while the number of prospective members fell off. For a time the management thought that the unemployment of its members would soon pass, but conditions grew steadily worse. Members began to fall behind in their carrying charges, and measures to enforce payment became necessary. Fortunately, the two Amalgamated housing corporations had acquired a

‍ helped them survive during this desperate period.
knew that every effort was being made by the
ir obligations, and faith in their management

ps the darkest period in real estate history,
e forced to make many adjustments to
members could not pay their monthly
k. Apartments had to be rented on a
u of 1936 rents receivables amounted to
these almost insurmountable problems, the
urvived until conditions began to gradually im-
n E. Kazan, who managed the housing corporations
rtuous years, later said:

> building was a slow and tedious process. It took all of ten years before the
> voc created by the depression could be overcome and new work undertaken.
> As the economic depression subsided, the stock was resold to new cooperators
> and the money used to pay off the loans, repay all deferred payments on the
> mortgage amortization, and the other obligations incurred. The members who
> had left the community eventually received back every dollar of their invest-
> ment.[18]

It was not until 1940 that a small building program could be
undertaken to provide units for an elderly group of cooperators. Larger
developments had to be postponed until after World War II.

There were no other significant cooperative housing developments
during the New Deal years.[19] The principal cooperative achievement in
this period was that the Amalgamated housing projects proved their
capacity to survive and meet the problems of the Great Depression and
then revive on a healthy basis. This was a valuable demonstration of the
economic soundness of cooperative housing when capably planned and
well administered, and it was to yield important results in the years to
come. When conditions after World War II were more favorable to the
development of such organizations, they began to come into their own.

The Coming of Cooperative Medical Care

During the New Deal years there was a general awakening on the
importance of medical care and of the costs of medical service. Part of this
stemmed from the comprehensive studies of the Committee on the Costs
of Medical Care under the chairmanship of Dr. Ray Lyman Wilbur. This
Committee was set up with the financial aid of several foundations in
1927 by a group of public-minded leaders in the medical profession and
others concerned with the economic aspects of medical care and the

prevention of illness. Its concluding volume *Medical Care for the American People,* published in 1932 by the University of Chicago Press, gave much support to those "oriented toward the consumer philosophy." Its general findings were that:

1. Medical services should be more largely furnished by groups of physicians and related practitioners, so organized as to maintain high standards of care and to retain the personal relations between patients and physicians.

2. The costs of medical care should be distributed over groups of people and over periods of time.

3. Methods of preventing disease should be more extensively and more effectively applied, as measures both of service and economy, and should be so financed as to minimize the economic deterrents to their expansion.

4. The facilities and services for medical care should be coordinated by appropriate agencies on a community basis.[20]

The work of the Committee on the costs of medical care gave encouragement to the development of the Blue Cross Plan, under which premium payments from subscribers were pooled to provide hospital care. Although this plan, which was directed largely by the medical profession, had cooperative features, it did not provide complete medical care under the control of those served. The work of the committee also gave encouragement to the medical care program of the Farm Security Administration described in Chapter XV. Although this program was cooperative in character, it was primarily a government-managed program.

The only fully cooperative health plan operating in 1933 was that of the Community Hospital Association of Elk City, Oklahoma, which had been founded in 1929 by Dr. Michael Shalid. This association had struggled for existence in the face of bitter opposition from the medical profession, but, with the support of the Oklahoma Farmers Union, it had succeeded in establishing itself on a firm basis. The achievements of the Elk City experiment were widely publicized by Dr. Shalid through addresses to farm and cooperative groups, with the result that many people became aware of the possibilities of setting up cooperatives to provide themselves with more adequate and less expensive health services. However, no other rural community health cooperative was formed on its pattern until 1940.[21]

Almost from its beginning Dr. James Peter Warbasse, President of the Cooperative League, had taken a deep interest in the Elk City experiment, for, as an eminent surgeon, he was aware of the problems of people in getting the kind of medical service they needed at reasonable cost. Through his interest in this general problem which was beginning to attract national interest in cooperative circles, the Cooperative League, in 1936, created a Bureau of Cooperative Medicine to direct attention to this problem. This conference body helped give the idea of cooperative medical care encouragement and made people aware of what might be done cooperatively, but the next major development in cooperative care—the formation of The Group Health Association, Inc., of Washington, D.C.—came independently of these stirrings of interest in the general problem.

The Group Health Association, Inc. The genesis of the Group Health Association, Inc., of Washington, D.C., came in 1936 when Mr. A. V. Rickord of the Twentieth Century Fund's medical staff came in to see Mr. Raymond R. Zimmerman, Director of Personnel for the Home Owners Loan Corporation, an arm of the Federal Home Loan Bank Board, of which Mr. John H. Fahey was Chairman.[22] Rickord, formerly a personnel officer for the General Motors Corporation in England and for the Sperry Gyroscope Corporation, had joined the staff of the Twentieth Century Fund to promote interest in ways to reduce the costs of medical care among directors of personnel in industry, business, and government. He had come in to see Mr. Fahey who had been informed by Zimmerman of HOLC's costs of lost time through sickness of its employees, and Fahey had suggested: "Why don't you call on Zimmerman? He comes from industry." The two men "clicked immediately," for Zimmerman had a real interest in the health problem of HOLC employees in the light of his prior experience as Director of Personnel for the Continental Oil Company which had a well-balanced medical care program for its employees.[23]

It was not long before Zimmerman and Rickord were working closely together to see if some kind of health care plan could be devised for HOLC employees. After consideration of the few industry plans then existing, they concluded that the cooperative form of organization was suited for their purpose in that it could be carried on by the employees without operation and control by the HOLC and without cost of government money. Looking back on this decision Zimmerman has said:

> We were not motivated by any desire to build a cooperative association because of any special interest in cooperatives. We were primarily interested in adapting the experience of industrial concerns in this field to the needs of government employees since their experience seemed to provide more of a model for our particular needs. Our main concern was to develop a plan that would help employees meet the growing cost of medical care. We felt that it should embrace the efficiencies of the modern clinic where doctors of various specialties cooperated in the treatment of the patient, and place emphasis on preventive practice. We believed that if government employees could pay for their housing, food, clothing and transportation why could they not organize cooperatively to meet and pay for their own medical needs? Wouldn't this be rugged individualism in its finest form?"[24]

In the course of their review of health plans being used by major business concerns, they decided to inspect the "Stanacola" plan of the Standard Oil Company of Louisiana, and together they spent several days in Baton Rouge examining the plan and getting the views of employees on how well it served them. This plan was of particular interest to Zimmerman in view of his oil company background. Zimmerman and Rickord found that the Stanacola plan had several features that could be directly applied to the development of a plan for HOLC employees. They came back convinced that something could be worked out at HOLC.

Before going further, Zimmerman cleared his thinking with Mr. Fahey, for he was aware that the Federal Home Loan Bank Board might come under criticism for sponsoring a medical care plan for employees of a government agency. With Mr. Fahey's "Go Ahead" signal obtained, Zimmerman arranged a meeting of about 200 employees to explore their interest if a suitable plan could be developed. Their response was so favorable that Zimmerman—with the advice of HOLC's business office and the legal assistance of Horace Russell, HOLC's legal counsel—proceeded to shape up a formal plan with organization documents that contained many of the provisions of the Stanacola plan. Mr. Fahey was kept informed on progress, and to facilitate the formation of a group health association to operate the plan, the Federal Home Loan Bank Board agreed to provide a fund of $40,000 to provide a "launching cradle" until the new organization could stand on its own feet.[25]

The plan for a group health association was presented to an open meeting of HOLC employees in February 1937, where it was unanimously accepted by the several hundred employees in attendance. The prospective members at this meeting proceeded to select their own temporary officers to get the new association underway, and soon afterwards, on February 24, 1937, the Group Health Association filed its Certificate of Incorporation which declared its purposes to be:

> To provide, without profit to the Corporation, for the service of physicians and other medical attention and any and all kinds of medical, surgical and hospital treatment to the members hereof and their dependents, and the construction and operation of a clinic and medical office building, and the construction and operation of a hospital in the manner permitted by law, for the members hereof and their dependents, and the operation of a drug store or pharmacy, and the providing of nurses and drugs and remedies for the members hereof and their dependents, and the furnishing of all forms of hospital service and attention to the members hereof and their dependents, and in general the giving to the membership of this association and their dependents of all forms of care, treatment or attention that may be required by the sick or in the prevention of disease.

Although the initial members of the association were to be employees of the FHLBB and the HOLC, it was understood that membership would later be opened to all government employees. The association was to have a medical director, and it would provide for service through a clinic or hospital. Charges were to be set for members on a monthly basis depending on the size of the member's family.[26]

Group Health Association, Inc., held its first meeting of members on March 22, 1937. At that time the by-laws (which spelled out in detail how GHA would operate) were adopted, and members were chosen to fill temporarily the executive positions of President and Secretary-Treasurer. Several weeks later members of the Board of Trustees were elected, and soon afterwards the trustees appointed an executive committee of five to deal with immediate problems: particularly, the appointment of a medical director and the provision of adequate space and facilities for a clinic. Another important problem confronting the new organization was to work out cooperation with the District of Columbia Medical Society and Washington hospitals.

With competent professional advice, the trustees appointed Dr. Henry R. Brown as the first medical director on June 7, 1937. Dr. Brown was highly respected in Washington medical circles as Superintendent of the Mt. Alto hospital operated by the Veterans Administration. While he was recruiting physicians and personnel for the medical staff, arrangements were being made for locating and equipping a clinic through which service might be provided.

To work out a *modus vivendi* with the District of Columbia Medical Society, Dr. Brown and the trustees met with representatives of the Society in July. Although the Society at first expressed itself in sympathy with the social objectives of the group health plan, disagreement soon developed and the meeting ended "on a note of discord." It was the contention of the members of the Society that the plan of GHA conflicted with certain medical ethics, while representatives of the GHA responded by saying: "One of the purposes of this organization is to provide medical attention for those who do not receive it because they can't afford it." From the time of this meeting it was obvious that the GHA would have to proceed without the desired cooperation of the Washington medical fraternity, if not with its full opposition.

By November 1, 1937, GHA was ready to begin operations for some 700 members in a well-equipped clinic with a medical staff of four physicians, of whom two were employed on a part-time basis. The opening for service attracted much public attention, and it appeared to be off to a promising start. However, as the good will of the organized medical profession was not assured, GHA opened its doors "in an atmosphere of uneasy tranquility and impending disaster." It was not long before Group Health Association supporters knew that they were in a fight for its life.

Within two weeks after the GHA clinic opened for business, the District of Columbia Medical Society, in executive session, voted "a fight to the finish against GHA," and two attorneys were employed to help it "wage legal war against the association." At that time Dr. William C. Woodward, Director of the Bureau of Legal Medicine and Legislation for the American Medical Association, charged that the GHA was "intolerable and illegal." He maintained that the association was practicing medicine in spite of the fact that a corporation cannot be legally licensed to practice. One of the charges made against the GHA was that it was a form of socialized medicine (which was anathema to the medical profession), although the GHA was organized as a consumer cooperative and was completely independent of the HOLC or other government agency.[27] Soon after this attack, the grant made by the FHLBB to help the GHA get started was challenged in Congress as a diversion of federal funds without specific authority from Congress. A compliant Controller General held that the advance of funds was "without authority of law," but this view was countered by a statement from FHLBB officials that it was "deemed legal to make a two-year investment in the health of our employees . . . [for] we look upon this investment as similar to departmental installations of air conditioning and there is no objection to that." Later a Senate subcommittee on appropriations under the chairmanship of Senator Everett Dirksen examined the question and agreed that the FHLBB had not exceeded its authority through its assistance to GHA as a means of increasing the operating efficiency of its employees.

Anticipating a threatened move by the Corporation Counsel for the District of Columbia to institute proceedings against GHA on the grounds that it was practicing medicine as a corporation and was engaged in the insurance business, GHA petitioned the District Court of the United States of the District of Columbia to obtain a declaratory judgement as to the legality of its activities. The District Court found that GHA was not engaged in the illegal practice of medicine, nor was it in the insurance business.

In the face of this strong opposition, the GHA proceeded to get its services well established. During November, the first month of operation, 220 persons received treatment, and in December the Board of Trustees opened the membership to employees of four additional government agencies—the Federal Reserve Board, Farm Credit Administration, Rural Electrification Administration, and the Social Security Board. A few months later membership was again extended to include other Executive Agencies of the government. During the first seven months of operation, some 19,130 visits of members or their dependents were reported by the clinic which, in May 1938, was serving 180 patients a day. By the fall of 1938 the GHA had made substantial progress. Within less than a year it had become "an integrated, cooperative body" serving 2,600 members and their 3,400 dependents. It was estimated that savings on doctor's bills of members were amounting to $175,000 annually.

This progress was made under great difficulties, for it was hard to recruit doctors who were fearful of losing their membership in the District Medical Society. It was also difficult to provide care for GHA members in the Washington hospitals which refused to accept GHA members as patients unless they were entered by a doctor with hospital standing, and, even then, bills were rendered to the patients rather than to the GHA. Moreover, it was almost impossible to obtain the services of doctors as consultants because of the fear that this would jeopardize their position with the Medical Society. The program of GHA was belittled as being socialistic, impractical, and unethical. It became in effect a boycott. The attack on GHA reached a climax in March 1939, when Dr. Mario Scandiffio, one of GHA's doctors, was expelled from the Medical Society for practicing medicine with an unapproved organization by a vote of 148 to 5.[28]

Aroused by the efforts being made to destroy the GHA before it could get well started, the Department of Justice initiated a preliminary investigation of the attempts being made to prevent GHA from effectively functioning. In a press release issued on August 1, 1939, Thurman Arnold, Assistant Attorney General of the United States, declared:

> The Medical Society of the District of Columbia, the American Medical Association, and some of the officials of both these organizations are attempting to prevent Group Health Association from functioning . . . In the opinion of the Department of Justice this is a violation of the antitrust laws because it is an attempt by one group of physicians to prevent members of Group Health Association from selecting physicians of their own choice . . . The particular persons responsible for this violation can only be ascertained by a grand jury investigation.[29]

The findings of the Department of Justice "reverberated across the nation." Many leading newspapers responded with sharp attacks on the Department of Justice and the New Deal in general. Others took a more rational position. For example the *Philadelphia Record* of August 2, 1939, said:

> Medicine is not a business. It is a science and an art . . . We hope the AMA comes to its senses. It should be the leader in improving the economics of medicine as it has been the leader in furthering the science of medicine. It has a splen-

did opportunity. If it is wise, it can retain a position of control as years bring their inevitable changes.

The *Boston Herald* of August 2, 1939, said:

> If these ventures will inevitably lower the quality of medical care and the AMA can demonstrate that certainty, it is on strong ground . . . But, if the AMA's objective is merely to freeze our present medical facilities into a state of permanence and to prevent the free and honest trial of new facilities, it is on exceedingly weak ground.

The intervention of the Department of Justice was of much concern to the American Medical Association, for it looked with apprehension on an indictment as a monopoly. At a called meeting of its House of Delegates on September 16, 1939, the Board of Trustees was urged "to oppose with its utmost power, even to the courts of last resort, this apparent attempt to convict the AMA in the eyes of the public as being a predatory, antisocial monopoly."

On October 17, 1939, a special grand jury was convened in the District of Columbia at the request of the Department of Justice to investigate alleged violations of the Sherman Anti-trust Act by the American Medical Association, *et al.* After two months of investigation it returned indictments charging violation of the anti-trust laws against the American Medical Association, the Medical Society of the District of Columbia, and others. The indictment charged the defendants with having combined and conspired together for the purpose of restraining trade in the District of Columbia. Some of the specific charges were:

> 1. Restraining Group Health Association in its business of providing medical care and hospitalization for its members on a risk-sharing prepayment basis;
> 2. Restraining the members of GHA in obtaining, by cooperative efforts, adequate medical care for themselves from doctors engaged in group medical practice on a risk-sharing prepayment basis;
> 3. Restraining the doctors serving on the medical staff of GHA in pursuit of their callings.[30]

One apparent result of the grand jury indictment was to bring about a considerable improvement in hospital cooperation. The GHA News Letter of January 1939 reported that three members of the Group Health staff had been issued courtesy cards by the Garfield Hospital. In the months that followed, almost all GHA doctors were granted hospital privileges by the Washington hospitals, and Dr. Mario Scandiffio, who had been expelled from the District of Columbia Medical Society, was named medical director in March 1939. Thereupon, he was notified that he might apply for reinstatement into the Society, and his application was approved. This changed attitude on the part of the Medical Society and the District's hospitals made doctors more willing to join the GHA's staff, or to work with GHA doctors as consultants. By the time of its second anniversary, November 1, 1939, GHA membership had reached 2,300 as compared with 900 when the GHA began operations. It was employing 10 full time doctors, 7 nurses, 3 technicians, 8 clerical workers, and 2 pharmacists. In December 1939, membership was opened to all civilian workers in the United States government. Furthermore, the GHA was now beginning to operate in the black. During the 1940 spring quarter, total receipts exceeded expenditures, giving a net balance of $603.

While the relations of the GHA and the Washington medical profession were slowly improving, the AMA and its co-defendants filed a demurrer to the indictment of the grand jury in the District Court, and on July 26, 1939, Justice James E. Proctor of the District Court of the United States for the District of Columbia held the grand jury indictment invalid on two grounds: (1) that the Sherman Act's definition of the word trade did not cover the right of physicians to conspire with and boycott hospitals in order to exclude other members of their profession from the pursuit of their calling, and (2) that the indictment did not inform the defendants of the crime with which they were charged. Although this decision gave temporary satisfaction to the organized medical profession, it did not settle the matter. This became apparent on September 11, 1939, when the United States Court of Appeals for the District of Columbia handed down an important decision which affected GHA and all medical cooperatives. The Courts held that GHA was neither a health nor an accident insurance company and was not operating in violation of any of the insurance laws in the District of Columbia. The Court found that Group Health Association was acting as a consumer cooperative and was primarily concerned with getting service rendered to its members at a lower price made possible by quantity purchasing and economy in operation.

The next development in this long drawn out legal controversy was an appeal of Justice Proctor's ruling to the United States Court of Appeals by the Department of Justice. On March 4, 1940, in a unanimous decision this Court reversed the ruling of the District Court and held that the common law governing restraint of trade was sufficiently broad in its coverage to include the practice of medicine. Following this, the Supreme Court denied the petition of the defendants for a review of this decision. Thereupon the case was tried on its facts in the District Court of the United States for the District of Columbia. This "historic" trial started on February 5, 1941, and ended on April 4, 1941. It was the verdict of the jury that the American Medical Association and the Medical Society of the District of Columbia were guilty of violations of the antitrust statute.

A fine of $2,500 was imposed on the AMA, and a fine of $1,500 was imposed on the Medical Society of the District of Columbia. The defendants then appealed to the United States Court of Appeals which affirmed the judgement of the lower court. The Supreme Court then agreed to review and consider the record on the case. Finally in 1943 the Supreme Court, by a unanimous decision, upheld the verdict against the medical societies, (AMA vs. U.S. 317 U.S. 519). It held that GHA was engaged in trade and that it was immaterial whether or not the medical society and its member physicians were engaged in trade.

This landmark decision finally affirmed the legal right of GHA to protection under the law. It not only opened the way for the strengthening and expansion of GHA's services, it also clearly established the legality of cooperative medical practice and thus benefited all other organizations of this type. It did more than this. It broadened the conception of cooperative enterprise in the minds of the American public.

Fishery Cooperatives Gain Recognition

Before 1930 there were few fishermen's cooperatives with established places of business that were engaged in marketing or in performing purchasing, processing, or related functions for their members. Most of the early associations were formed by fishermen for bargaining in the sale of their catch. Following an expansion of interest in the depression years, the formation of fishery cooperatives was encouraged in 1934 by an Act of Congress (Public Law No. 464) which provided:

> That persons engaged in the fishery industry, as fishermen, catching, collecting, or cultivating aquatic products, or as planters of aquatic products on public or private beds, may act together in associations, corporate or otherwise, with or without capital stock, in collectively catching, producing, preparing for market, processing, handling and marketing in interstate and foreign commerce, such products of said persons so engaged.

This Act, known as the Fishery Cooperative Marketing Act, was modelled closely on the Capper-Volstead Act of 1922, and it gave to fishermen the same right to organize and operate cooperatives that were enjoyed by farmers. The administration of this act was placed in the Bureau of Fisheries of the Department of Commerce, and, in October 1935, Mr. L. C. Salter was employed by the Bureau as Fishery Economist to be in charge of its cooperative work. Salter immediately undertook studies to assist fishermen in organizing and operating cooperative associations and soon prepared a bulletin, "Organizing and Incorporating Fishery Cooperative Marketing Associations," which has long served as a guide for the effective development of fishery cooperatives.[31]

One of the handicaps to the development of strong fishery cooperatives was lack of access to capital and credit. To meet this problem an attempt was made in 1937 to have a Fishery Credit Act passed that would provide financial assistance to fishery cooperatives similar to that provided farmers cooperatives through the Farm Credit Administration's Banks for Cooperatives. Although this attempt was unsuccessful, hearings on the act provided much information that served to promote this form of cooperative enterprise.[32]

As a result of the passage of Public Law No. 464 and the assistance rendered through Bureau of Fisheries, there has been a continuing development of fishery cooperatives until there are now a number of strong associations of this type.[33]

Forestry Cooperatives Get Underway

Most of the cooperatives engaged in forestry operations were embryonic in character prior to 1933. During the New Deal years, more interest developed in cooperative forest product marketing and cooperative forest management, and a number of more substantial associations were formed. Several of these were promoted and financed by the Rural Resettlement Administration and the Farm Security Administration, with technical assistance being provided by the Forest Service. The most ambitious organization of this type was the Otsego Forest Products Cooperative Association, Inc., of Cooperstown, New York, which was an integrated management, marketing, and processing organization. Although none of these cooperatives were permanently successful, many valuable lessons were learned that have since been applied in forestry cooperative undertakings.[34]

Businessmen's Cooperatives Expand Operations

In *The Rise of American Cooperative Enterprise,* we saw how local business firms formed cooperatives as early as 1888 to perform buying or other functions more effectively.[35] The rapid growth of chain store systems in the 1930's greatly encouraged this kind of development as a means through which local merchants could meet their competition. During the 1930's, retailer cooperatives, and cooperatives sponsored by wholesalers, greatly expanded their operations. A study made of retailer cooperatives in 1937 found that retailer-owned cooperatives in the food field were then operating in 38 states with a total stock-owning membership in excess of 23,000 independent grocery stores. There were also many cooperatives of this type composed of hardware and drug stores.[36] In addition, there were then nearly 78,000 retail food stores that were members of so-called "voluntary chains" sponsored by wholesale firms.[37] These operated in much the same way as the retailer cooperatives. By 1940 such cooperative organizations had demonstrated their capacity to compete effectively with the major chain store systems, and, in doing so, they provided a continuing opportunity for many independent retail merchants.

Summary

In this chapter we have observed a general broadening of cooperative enterprise to perform various services needed by farmers, fishermen, consumers, and business men. The prototypes of many modern cooperative servicing organizations were beginning to take shape.

Part Three

THE IMPACT OF WORLD WAR II:
1941-1945

World War II was to create conditions that greatly amplified the significance of cooperative enterprise in the United States.

In Chapter XXII we examine the boom in agricultural cooperation that accompanied the gradual involvement of the nation in an all-out war and the way this affected marketing and purchasing cooperatives.

Chapter XXIII deals with a number of major cooperative developments that came during the war years. It gives attention to the effect of the war on various kinds of cooperatives: rural electric cooperatives; credit unions; and associations for housing and health care, insurance, and other services. It shows how the large national fertilizer associations came into existence and how national organizations for purchasing farm machinery, petroleum, and farm supplies expanded. It throws light on the situation that brought forth the National Tax Equality Association, the nature of its attack on cooperatives, and how cooperatives responded by reorganizing the American Institute of Cooperation in 1944. It describes the growth in importance of the National Council of Farmer Cooperatives and of national federations representing the business and political interests of dairy, grain, and other commodity groups. It shows how the structure of the Cooperative League of the U.S.A. was developing into a more unified national consumers' cooperative organization.

In Chapter XXIV—the final chapter of this book—we look at American cooperative enterprise as of 1945 with the country adjusting from war to peace. This chapter summarizes the achievements of American cooperatives during the quarter century from 1920 to 1945 and evaluates the strengths and weaknesses of these organizations as the period closed.

Chapter XXII

THE BOOM IN AGRICULTURAL COOPERATION: 1941-1945

The New Deal came to a gradual close as the United States became involved in problems brought by World War II. In this chapter we will examine the great expansion of cooperative marketing and purchasing that came as a result of the War.[1]

World War II began on September 1, 1939, when Germany invaded Poland. Within three weeks the German conquest was complete—demonstrating the effectiveness of blitzkrieg tactics in waging war with the combined use of airpower and armoured forces. After the fall of Poland there ensued an inactive period of several months while the British and French forces manned the Maginot line and carried on a sea blockade of Germany. During this so-called "phony war" period, American interest in the war subsided. However, it became the official position of the Department of Agriculture during the fall and winter that farmers should shift production more to a domestic basis in view of the possible loss of foreign markets.

The situation changed abruptly on April 9, 1940, when Germany took over Denmark in a surprise invasion and then moved on Norway. Before the Norwegian conquest was complete, German forces overran Luxemburg and invaded the Netherlands and Belgium. On May 13 they outflanked the Maginot line and cut off the British forces in Flanders from their French allies. Then followed the heroic evacuation of most of the British army from Dunkirk, although its guns, equipment, and supplies were lost. Paris soon fell, and on June 22 France capitulated. Italy had already joined forces with Germany by declaring war on France on June 10.

By early June Great Britain was the only country in Western Europe not under German domination, and it soon became evident that she was marked for immediate invasion. However, Winston Churchill, who had taken over the reins of the British government on May 10, promising nothing but "blood, toil, tears and sweat," had aroused the British people to determined resistance. On June 4, in a radio broadcast, came his ringing declaration: "We shall not flag or fail . . . We shall fight in France, we shall fight on the seas and oceans . . . we shall defend our island, whatever the cost may be, we shall fight on the beaches . . . on the landing grounds . . . in the fields and in the streets . . . in the hills; we shall never surrender."

The United States could not look upon this turn of events with unconcern. Shocked by the implications of a total German victory in Europe, President Roosevelt declared an unlimited national emergency and set up, under authority of a statute passed during the first World War, the National Defense Advisory Commission. One of the seven members of this Commission, Chester C. Davis, was to represent agriculture. Congress responded to the situation by rushing appropriations through Congress for national defense and by modifying the Neutrality Act to permit belligerents to obtain war materials on a "cash and carry" basis.[2] Britain and France promptly took advantage of the new law by placing large orders for planes and tanks with American industrial concerns. This marked the beginning of the national defense effort which was to grow in intensity until the United States became directly involved in the War 18 months later.

When the American Institute of Cooperation met at Michigan State College in July, the nation was stunned by the German successes and concerned over their possible effect on the United States. However, many still believed that the United States could remain uninvolved, and few cooperative leaders anticipated the great problems that lay ahead for American agriculture. Except for a few talks on "War's Effect on American Life and Agriculture," the War was largely ignored. Few of the speakers on this subject came to grips with the possibility of American involvement, although it was recognized that the defeat of Britain would greatly change the world's economic structure. John Brandt, President of Land O' Lakes Creameries, Inc., voiced the views of many when he said:

> The uppermost thought in the minds of the American people today is one of preparedness, but for what are we preparing? Are we preparing for participation in the world military conflict, or are we preparing for the economic war that is already part of the military struggle and will become the prime factor in the war that is bound to follow in the economic rehabilitation and realignment of the affairs of the world . . .

Brandt believed that agricultural cooperatives were in a position to make a significant contribution to sound defense planning. He concluded his talk by saying:

> We are the representatives of agriculture and, as such, our interests and the interest of this nation which is dependent upon agricultural production and agricultural operative organizations become the policies of action, whichever party may come to power. Therefore, as never before, it becomes our duty as cooperatives to work to the end that our advice, based on experience, may become the agricultural policy of the nation.[3]

The view of John K. Galbraith, then Chief Economist for the American Farm Bureau Federation, was:

> This war, so far as the continent of Europe is concerned is now over. It has been won by nations which feed their people from abroad only as a last resort: that only feed their people at all because to do so serves some further nationalist end. We might as well face the facts. Whether England holds out as a democratic and free capitalist outpost or whether she does not, international trade with Europe, as we have known it in the past, is over for the time being.

Although skeptical on the future, Galbraith did not consider a defeatist attitude warranted. He went on to say:

> There has been an enormous amount of rot and demagogy about our ability to undertake a large defense program. It is said that we are depression-stricken, debt-ridden and economically weak. That is entirely wrong . . . Our national credit is not in danger. Our unemployed men and our idle factories are one of our greatest sources of strength. They mean . . . that we can go into the business of producing for defense, not by cutting down on our present consumption but by expanding total production. We have the opportunity of using economic resources that have been idle these last 10 years. No other nation has been half so fortunate in this respect.[4]

In his talk, "Can We Adjust Our Employee Training Program to Coming World Events?," James A. McConnell, General Manager of the GLF, brought the war situation nearer home. He faced the fact that cooperatives could not postpone consideration of the harsh facts confronting them in their operations. He said: "When the British and French were defeated in Scandinavia, this country got a little nervous. Just a few people began to wonder if all was as serene and safe for us as they had thought. Then when Germany hit Belgium and Holland and took them within a few days, the world, including the United States, woke up with a start." McConnell believed:

> All of this leads to some inescapable conclusions. One is that each and everyone of us is going to be affected in some way or other. We may be in war soon. I don't know. Whether or not we get into war in Europe or in defense of our South American trade and strategic position, or in actual defense of our own country, we cannot escape the fact that we are going to prepare for war at a tremendous rate. For a country that is as unprepared as the United States, getting ready for such wars as are being fought today means great

changes in our whole economy. The attempt to prepare for war in the degree that we apparently need to in order to command the respect of or fight the most powerful war-like nations in the world, means that all of the productive machinery in this country has to be called upon—farms, factories, capital, labor, transportation and mines. Every person will be affected directly for years and years to come.

Bringing his talk directly to the cooperatives, he said: "Regardless of changes, somebody is going to run the industries of this country that service farmers. I think we [the cooperatives] are the best qualified in the world to continue doing it."[5]

By midsummer only Great Britain stood in Hitler's way to a complete sweep of Europe, and he realized that her conquest must be effected before she could develop military strength. As a prelude to invasion, German air attacks were to destroy her cities and her willingness to fight. But this was not to be. The Royal Air Force in "the Battle of Britain" during August and September took such a heavy toll that the Luftwaffe could not continue, and invasion plans had to be postponed. Churchill's words following the battle were spoken to the people of the United States as well as to his own people: "Never, in the field of human conflict, was so much owed by so many to so few."

The air bombardments of British cities—London, Coventry, Manchester—following the Battle of Britain, aroused deep sympathies for Great Britain in the United States, and sentiment grew to help her with everything short of war in her struggle for survival. The need for strengthening United States military forces, which were then but a few hundred thousand, could not be ignored, and a selective service act was passed which provided that not more than 900,000 men were to be in the army at any one time, and service was to be limited to 12 months. Although this was not a large commitment in view of the millions of men under arms in the Axis nations, it marked a major change in popular attitudes and gave the army leaders an opportunity to start building a modern force.

The seriousness of the British food situation, due to the loss of pork, butter, cheese, and eggs from Denmark and the low countries, became evident in the fall. The sentiment was growing that if the fall of Britain was to be prevented the United States would have to supply her with butter as well as guns. The first indication that greater agricultural production might be necessary came on December 26, 1940, when Secretary of Agriculture Wickard called on farmers to increase their pork products and cattle marketings. "For the first time since 1933 the Department was actively encouraging increased production."[6] The pace of preparedness was now increasing. On January 7, 1941, the Office of

Production Management was created by Executive Order to supervise and expedite defense production.

Agricultural cooperatives were now becoming concerned with the possible effect of the war on their operations. This was reflected in the meetings of the National Council of Farmer Cooperatives held in January 1941. One of the resolutions passed by the delegate body pledged support to the defense effort and called for proper representation of organized agriculture on agencies that might be set up to further national preparedness. The first sentence of the resolution read as follows: "We recognize that in this period of stress and strain caused by the war in Europe, the Federal Administration is faced with the difficult task of rapidly acquiring and establishing adequate means for national defense, in which effort we desire to be of all possible assistance."[7]

By this time plans were going forward for the Lend Lease Act which was designed to provide means of furnishing supplies to Britain to enable her to survive.[8] This Act was finally approved on March 11, 1941, following a long and bitter debate in Congress. The Lend Lease Act gave the President power to sell, transfer, lend, or lease necessary war supplies (including food, machinery, and services) to nations vital to the defense of the United States. At this time Great Britain and China were to be the nations aided. The cooperatives responded promptly to the needs for production to meet lend-lease requirements, and many began to revamp their plants to produce better the type of products most needed.

The Lend Lease Act made it possible for Secretary Wickard to announce on April 3 that "the price of pork, butter, eggs, would be supported at well above current prices." This gave encouragement to increased production. Another important step toward mobilization for defense came with the establishment of the Office of Price Administration and Civilian Supply in April 1941, with authority to fix maximum prices.

On May 11, the United States Department of Agriculture set up an office of Agricultural Defense Relations. On July 5 Agricultural Defense Boards were established to coordinate the Department's defense activities in the field.

The war was now coming closer. U-boats were posing a serious threat to American shipping, and, to protect its interests, the United States had taken over Greenland in April. Yugoslavia, Greece, and Crete were crushed by the Axis forces in April and May, and, on June 22, Germany invaded Russia. Almost immediately, on June 24, the President promised that Lend-Lease would be extended to a new ally—Russia.

On July 1, 1941, Congress provided for support of all commodities for which the Secretary of Agriculture asked production increases at "a minimum of 85% of parity for a long enough period to permit farmers to make postwar adjustments." This action, commonly referred to as the Steagel Amendment because it was passed as an amendment to an act extending the Commodity Credit Corporation, opened the way for strong measures to bring about increased production of agricultural commodities. Soon afterwards, on July 17, an Interbureau Production Goals Committee was set up in the Department of Agriculture, and, on September 8, production goals for 1942 were announced. These goals indicated that significant progress was being made in converting the agricultural adjustment program to a program for increasing production.

On August 18, 1941, President Roosevelt signed an extension of the Selective Service Act which abolished the 900,000 limitation to the army of the preceding year and lengthened the period of service to not more than 30 months in time of peace. The nation was beginning to accept the gigantic job involved in a real national defense effort.

The defense agencies, confronted with tremendous pressures for war materials, soon found it necessary to institute controls and priority programs for materials and supplies which were needed by agricultural cooperatives to expand plants, and by early summer cooperatives were beginning to feel the effect of the defense program. This was evidenced by an unsigned article in the *News for Farmer Cooperatives* for June 1941 entitled "Cooperatives 'On the Spot' in World War II." It opened by saying: "Cooperatives are on the spot in World War II. They cannot escape the adjustments that are at hand." In the same issue another article pointed out that cooperative purchasing associations could make four definite contributions to national defense by concentrating government contacts with farmers; by assisting in price stabilization; by promoting efficiency in distribution; and by helping maintain the principles of democracy.[9]

In the July issue of the *News for Farmer Cooperatives,* T. G. Stitts, Chief of the Cooperative Research and Service Division of the Farm Credit Administration, maintained that "The farmer's cooperative has a double responsibility today—to the government and to its membership." He pointed out: "The impact of the war and the defense program already has added to the problems of the cooperatives in their everyday operations." He attributed these problems to (1) increased demand for farm products arising from government purchases and from rising payrolls and employment; (2) shortage of labor and loss of trained personnel to the Army and industry; (3) increases in facility and equipment costs, and shortages in some of the farm supply items; (4) growing shortage of storage facilities for some commodities, and (5) increased absorption by defense industries of transportation equipment.[10]

With the stepped-up defense effort in the summer and fall of 1941, farmers and their cooperatives found it difficult to obtain supplies and equipment necessary to maintain and expand farm production as called for by the national defense effort. One of the serious problems of the purchasing cooperatives in obtaining priorities for supplies needed in agriculture was caused by the fact that many of the officials in the defense agencies were not aware of the importance of farm supply cooperatives in serving the needs of farmers. Even the largest purchasing cooperatives found it difficult to gain attention comparable to that given large non-cooperative business firms. To meet this problem, the Cooperative Research and Service Division of the Farm Credit Administration—at the request of several of the major purchasing associations—began publication of a handbook that would provide information on the volume of various supplies handled and other pertinent data for the major purchasing associations. This handbook provided official evidence that the farm supply organizations were highly important to farmers as suppliers of materials and equipment and did much to gain recognition of their significance. The first handbook of this type provided information for the years 1941 and 1942.[11] The task of creating a modern army with its enormous needs for equipment and meeting the immense needs of Britain and Russia with airplanes, tanks, munitions, food, and other supplies had compelled the government to set up controls on the use of strategic materials, such as steel, chemicals, lumber, rubber, petroleum, etc., so that in order to obtain materials essential for farm production it was necessary first to obtain priorities from the government.

It became obvious during the summer that there was need for a liaison agency to represent farm supply purchasing cooperatives in working with government agencies that were holding the reins for the huge defense priorities and allocations programs. This led to a meeting in Chicago on September 10 of a group of 29 leading cooperatives where it was decided to set up a Farmers Cooperative Defense Committee of nine, under the Chairmanship of Quentin Reynolds, Manager of the Eastern States Farmers' Exchange.

The National Council of Farmer Cooperatives was already involved in representing its members on priorities problems, and before the Chicago meeting it had already set up a Committee on Priorities. On September 17, the two committees met in Washington, D.C., and agreed to set up a joint committee to represent all of organized agriculture on priorities work. On October 11, this group, representing all of the major farm organizations—the National Grange, the American Farm Bureau Federation, the National Farmers' Union, and the National Council of Farmer Cooperatives—formed as an operating organization the National Committee for Farm Production Supplies. It was to be located in the offices of the National Council of Farmer Cooperatives, and it was to deal with priorities and other related national defense problems. It was to be financed by the participating organizations.

Within a few weeks the Committee was functioning effectively under the leadership of Harold Hedges, who took leave from the Cooperative Research and Service Division of the Farm Credit Administration to direct this work. The Committee immediately demonstrated its usefulness by gaining recognition from government agencies on the needs of agriculture for farm machinery, equipment, and materials needed in meeting the high production goals set up for 1942 and in supplying processed products under the Lend-Lease program. By the time of Pearl Harbor, the work of this Committee was well established.[12]

During the fall the war came closer as relations with Japan deteriorated and the pace of preparedness quickened. In November Lend-Lease aid was extended to Russia, and Congress repealed the Neutrality Act which forbade merchant men from arming in self-defense. "The Navy began installing naval guns with blue jacket crews on freighters."[13] On the back cover page of the December *News for Farmer Cooperatives*—issued just before the attack on Pearl Harbor—there was an advertisement for the Banks for Cooperatives headed "Keeping Pace with a Wartime Tempo." It pointed out how the Banks for Cooperatives were working with farmer cooperatives through offering low interest rate loans to fill every sound, business-like need.

The War Period, 1942-1945

The Japanese attack on Pearl Harbor on December 7, 1941, rapidly converted the defense effort into a program for all-out war. A new selective service act was immediately passed which made all men between 18 and 45 eligible for military service. The way was now open for building whatever size military force might be required, and the armed forces began to grow as the need for military personnel was almost boundless. By June 30, 1942, the number of men and women in the services had reached 3,074,184 and was rising steadily. This set up a strong government demand for food, wool, cotton, and other farm products.

The government moved rapidly to organize the economy for full war production. On December 17 the Economic Defense Board was reconstituted as the Board of Economic Warfare. On January 6 the War Production Board was set up with "sweeping power" to direct war production and the procurement of materials.

The Department of Agriculture lost no time in reorganizing its agencies to place all emphasis on winning the war. In mid-January, revised production goals were announced which called for substantially higher output than in the goals set in September. Secretary of Agriculture, Claude Wickard, stated that the goals called for "the greatest production in the history of American agriculture." The state and county defense boards were renamed war boards, and Wickard called them "the shock troops of freedom."

Cooperatives were quick to respond to the challenge of war. James A. McConnell, general manager of the Cooperative Grange League Federation Exchange, spoke for most agricultural cooperatives in a statement issued to all GLF workers on December 13. He said:

> This country will have to make some tremendous adjustments to move over to a real wartime economy . . . In the meantime, there are a few things to be done: (1) Keep your inventories as high as your finances will permit. (2) Keep your prices as nearly as you can on the market. (3) Keep feed orders of the mill well ahead. (4) Keep shoving superphosphate out on farms. (5) Remember that the defense storage program is available . . . I look for some serious tie-ups in transportation even for a few days.

On January 5, 1942, McConnell called on his District managers to mobilize all forces to meet the crisis. He said:

> For over two years this country watched the storm clouds of war building solidly along the horizon. We hoped [the storm] would go around, much the same as a thunder shower often does. We saw it coming, we felt sure it would hit, and still we seemed powerless to close the windows and put ourselves in shipshape to weather the storm. It took Pearl Harbor to make us realize that the storm had hit. We are at war.[14]

The National Council of Farmer Cooperatives was already conditioned for war when the Japanese struck at Pearl Harbor. John D. Miller, the venerated President of the Council, voiced the views of most cooperative and farm organizations in his address to the Council at its annual meeting on January 8, 1942. He said: "This country is now at war . . . There is now, and should continue to be, unity of purpose and effort . . . There must be an agency that can guide and direct. Such guidance can only be effective if exercised by Government. This means that during the war there must be a far greater regimentation of the people."[15]

In its resolutions adopted by the delegate body, the Council declared:

> The National Council of Farmer Cooperatives offers the services and facilities of its member cooperatives, and we urge that in any dealings with the farmers

of the nation the Government will avail itself of and use to the fullest extent the facilities of agricultural cooperatives that are able to perform the needed services, and that if any services are required in such matters as processing, purchasing, assembling, storing, or distribution of farm products, the services and facilities of cooperatives be used to the extent of their capacity to perform such services.

However, the Council made it clear that it was not surrendering any of the basic prerogatives of cooperatives by adding:

While we fully realize the pressing need for our agricultural cooperatives to exert every effort to work with our government and the rest of the nation to win the war and establish a lasting peace, there is also an accompanying necessity to protect and safeguard these organizations to the end that they may not in any way be weakened or supplanted by services, controls or other measures which may be established by the Government. We reaffirm our insistence that both during and after the present emergency, the Government in all its branches, follow the mandate of Congress with respect to agricultural cooperatives.[16]

Although agriculture moved rapidly to a full war footing after Pearl Harbor, it was still largely unprepared for the great effort that would be needed. In early January, Dr. A. G. Black, Governor of the Farm Credit Administration, gave some indication of what would be required of cooperatives in addressing the American Institute of Cooperation on "The Responsibility of Agricultural Cooperatives in the War." He said: "Before Pearl Harbor the gigantic machine of agriculture [was] geared to produce what was considered to be adequate supplies to meet all domestic food, feed, and fiber needs of this nation and our friends in defense . . . Since Pearl Harbor, we have had to raise our sights: we now must erect new goals, not only for defense but for all-out war . . . "

Black recognized that there would need to be a great expansion in vegetable fats and oils because of the stoppage of large imports. He saw shortages looming for fertilizers, insecticides, trucks, farm machinery and equipment, boxes, bagging, processing equipment, storage space, and many other things. He saw many ways in which cooperatives could help on the difficult problems ahead through conservation of equipment and supplies and better planning of operations. He was pleased with the united response of the cooperatives to the nation's need, and he challenged them to assume leadership in the solution of war-born industry problems. He was of the opinion that: "Cooperatives now have an opportunity to demonstrate as never before the public service they can render," and he believed that if they took advantage of this opportunity for service they would "come out of the war effort in a much stronger position than they now hold."[17]

Cooperatives lost no time in getting on a war footing. Many were already expanding processing operations to meet lend-lease needs, and more processing plants were soon started to increase facilities for producing dry skim milk, cottonseed oil, and dehydrated fruits and vegetables. A great number of marketing and purchasing cooperatives began to expand their storage and operating facilities to meet the large volumes of business coming with greater agricultural outputs.

The most pressing problem was caused by the shutting off of rubber, hemp, jute, vegetable oils, and other resources from Southeast Asia and by the destruction of petroleum supplies by the U-boats. The government called for all-out conservation of resources to meet the emergency until substitutes could be found or developed, and cooperatives responded by undertaking programs to re-use feed bags and by scheduling deliveries of products and supplies so as to conserve use of trucks, manpower, tires, and gasoline.

In April Dr. Stitts, Chief of the Cooperative Research and Service Division of the Farm Credit Administration, called for complete reorganization of cooperative operations to meet war needs. He said: "War means to coops what it means to most other businesses — complete reorganization of operations on a war-time footing." He saw the need of new activities, new plants, new cooperatives, consolidations, and better operating practices all along the line. He thought that most of the changes called for were "natural changes" in the direction of greater cooperative efficiency, and he cited examples of how cooperatives were gearing themselves for war. He concluded that such examples "*must* be multiplied to the nth power if the cooperatives and the Government under which they operate are to endure."[18]

The Lend-Lease program had set up a strong demand for butter, cheese, milk powder, and other processed agricultural products. The cooperatives were quick to respond, and many undertook to enlarge their facilities to take care of the new demands. To facilitate this expansion, a plan was devised in the fall whereby cooperatives could construct plants needed to process agricultural products needed for lend-lease purposes with government financial assistance. To participate in this program a cooperative was required to secure first a loan commitment from a bank for cooperatives after a careful analysis of the association's membership, source of supply, and management policies and capabilities. The plant, when completed was to be sold to the Secretary of Agriculture with the Surplus Marketing Administration as his representative, and the amount received was then to be paid to the Bank for Cooperatives. It was to be leased to the cooperative for a period of 5 years on a rental basis that amounted to one-tenth of the cost of the plant each year. Rent was to be paid monthly and was to continue until there was no longer need for the production in the Food for Freedom program. The cooperative could then buy back the plant at original cost, less the amount it had paid in rentals.[19]

This plan was just coming into use at the time of the Pearl Harbor attack, and the first cooperatives to receive this type of financial aid were creamery associations in Minnesota and Wisconsin interested in expanding their plant facilities to manufacture cheese and evaporated milk. The plan was soon taken advantage of by cooperatives in constructing various kinds of food processing facilities needed to supply government needs. Land O' Lakes Creameries, Inc., which was then expanding its milk powder facilities, welcomed this opportunity to expedite this development.

At the time of Pearl Harbor, Land O' Lakes Creameries was operating six milk drying plants through a subsidiary corporation—two of which were established in 1941. With this backlog of experience, Land O' Lakes was in position to rapidly expand in this field, and several more plants of this type were set up in 1942. One of the obstacles that made expansion difficult was the problem of obtaining priorities for scarce materials needed to build and equip the plants. As the biographer of Land O' Lakes later said: "Land O' Lakes was ready to build the plants that would meet the tremendous war demand for milk powder in its various forms. It had the know-how and it had the personnel. But it didn't have the priorities. Then began the battle of Washington . . . Many trips were necessary to wring the required construction priorities out of various government bureaus one by one."[20]

Many milk-drying plants also were set up in 1942 by other dairy marketing cooperatives, especially in Minnesota, Wisconsin, Iowa, New York State, and in the far western states. Most of them were financed with the assistance of government under the Lend-Lease program and by the Banks for Cooperatives.

Although the expansion of milk-drying plants was the most spectacular achievement in cooperative processing, many plants also were organized by cooperatives for canning or dehydrating fruits and vegetables and for preparing dried eggs and cottonseed oil. Six cottonseed oil cooperatives were set up in 1942.

One of the most interesting developments of this type was the establishment of a processing plant by the Florida Citrus Canners, Inc., to produce orange concentrate, a product much needed by the armed forces. Plans for this plant were developed with the government in the fall of 1941, under which the plant would be owned by the government and leased and operated by the cooperative. Under the contract the Florida

Citrus Canners was to produce 323,000 gallons of orange concentrate the first year of operation. This plant began operations in December 1942, and by March 1943 it had completed deliveries under the contract.[21]

The California Fruit Growers' Exchange, through its product operations, was in position to move rapidly toward increasing its production of concentrated orange juice. How the Exchange responded was reported in its annual report for the year ending October 31, 1942:

> Over 320,000 gallons of straight canned orange juice and 800,000 gallons of concentrated orange juice made by or for the Exchange orange products plant during the first ten months of the current calendar year, representing more than 4,000 standard carloads of oranges, went to the armed forces at home or abroad or for Lend-Lease purposes. Substantial quantities of concentrated lemon juice were also furnished. Some half millon pounds of pectin produced by the Exchange orange and lemon products plants were provided for Government use.[22]

To meet the anticipated need for dehydrated cranberries, Cranberry Canners, Inc., set up a dehydrating plant early in 1942, and later in the year it acquired a second plant. By the end of the year these two plants were "operating three shifts, 24 hours a day, 7 days a week to fill a Government order for 1,300,000 pounds of dehydrated cranberries."[23]

In addition to expansion of processing operations, the cooperatives followed the lead of the government in giving support to all measures that were needed in the war effort. Many cooperatives held skeleton annual meetings to save tires and gasoline and to free employees for essential activities. Great emphasis was placed on ways to conserve on use of transportation equipment, tires and gasoline, and other scarce materials. Farm machinery pools were organized by many cooperatives to economize on the use of machinery.

To free office space for war agencies, the Farm Credit Administration was moved in May to Kansas City, Missouri, but its Cooperative Research and Services Division was kept in Washington because of its direct importance in helping meet war problems.

To better focus attention on war problems a Division planning committee of five was set up comprised of Joseph G. Knapp, Kelsey B. Gardner, Andrew W. McKay, Paul E. Quintus, and Cortes G. Randell. This committee met regularly throughout the war. When McKay, Quintus, and Randell left the Division for other war work, their places were taken by Leonard N. Conyers, Lorenzo B. Mann, and John J. Scanlan. When T. G. Stitts took leave of absence in 1942 to direct the dairy program of the U.S.D.A., Omer W. Herrmann and Harold Hedges successively served as Acting Chief for the Division during the war years.[24]

By June all complacency was gone that it would be a short war, and the nation was girding itself for a long struggle. This period marked the low point in the fortunes of the Allies. The situation in the Pacific had gone from bad to worse. Japan now was dominant in the Pacific as far east as Hawaii, and it was in control of most of Southeast Asia. In the Atlantic the U-boats were taking a terrible toll in American and British ships, and they were carrying their attacks to the shores of the United States and the Gulf of Mexico. England was under German air attack, and, in Egypt, Rommel's German army seemed unstoppable. Russia also was in desperate plight. Most of Western Russia had been invaded, and Leningrad was under siege. Only stubborn Russian defense, aided by a severe winter, had averted total conquest. In June the German army was resuming the offensive, and the Russian outlook was bleak.

The first breath of hope came with the naval battle of Midway which demonstrated that all was not lost in the Pacific. In the words of Samuel Eliot Morison, "The glorious battle of Midway on 4 June 1942 marked a clear cut ending in the defensive phase in the Pacific War."[25] Other developments soon began to favor the Allies. After Rommel's victory at Tobruk on June 21, the British forces had regrouped under Montgomery who took the offensive in October and had won a smashing victory at El Alamein on October 23, 1942. This was a decisive victory in itself, for it not only saved the Suez Canal from Axis capture but it also opened up the way for decisive Anglo-American action in North Africa. The Russian position also was strengthening. Although German forces captured Stalingrad, it was becoming apparent that British and American supplies were providing Russia with indispensable sinews of war. Another favorable development in the last half of 1942 was the growing ability of the Allies to cope with the U-boats by use of convoys.

During the last half of 1942, the new cooperative plants constructed for processing began to come into production providing large quantities of dried skim milk, dehydrated agricultural foods, canned goods, and other needed agricultural products. In the South six new cooperative cottonseed oil mills were now operating, and in Iowa several cooperative soybean oil mills were being planned. The most spectacular achievement had come in the manufacture of dried skim milk powder. By the end of 1942 "Cooperative plants [were] producing well over one-third of the direct war uses of that important product. Some 90 spray plants, with individual units costing more than a quarter million dollars [represented] the cooperatives' stake in this vital wartime industry."[26] The importance of spray dried skim milk as a "fighting food" was recognized in November 1942 by a conservation order that required every manufacturer to set aside 90 per cent of its production for delivery to the armed forces or lend-lease authorities.

Although it was realized that a long and difficult struggle lay ahead, the Allies in 1943 were at last taking the offensive. In the Pacific the defeat of the Japanese at Guadalcanal in February was a decisive victory, for it gave the United States the initiative in the Pacific. During the year, battles in New Guinea cleared the way for an advance into the Philippines. In Europe the Allies took Sicily in July and moved on to Italy. With the surrender of Italy on September 8, the German army took over the defense of its southern flank, and a bitter struggle was underway as the year ended. The recapture of Stalingrad early in 1943 broke the back of the German offensive, and Russia began to gain back its lost territory.[27] Although the U-boats still inflicted great damage to American and British shipping, by 1943 the anti-submarine campaign of the Allies was so effective that the U-boats were becoming a less serious menace.

The year 1942 had been one of mobilization. By 1943 the nation was at last prepared. The war was now reaching full intensity, and American men and resources were coming into full action. Planes, tanks, ships, and munitions were being produced at an astounding rate, and by June 30, 1943, military personnel reached nearly 7 million, compared with slightly more than 3 million on the same date the year before. Expenditures for military functions for the year ending June 30, 1943, amounted to $42.5 billion, compared with only $14.5 billion the preceding year.

Agriculture was meeting high production goals and was expanding in every direction under the War Food Administration, which was established in the Department of Agriculture late in 1942 to centralize authority in the handling of domestic food problems.[28] Rationing and price controls were accepted as necessary for the direction of the war effort, and government "set aside" orders requiring delivery to the government of specific amounts of a firm's production were coming into widespread use to insure adequate quantities of essential supplies for the armed forces or for our Allies under the Lend-Lease program. The marketing and purchasing cooperatives were proud of the record they were making in the Food for Freedom program.[29]

The National Committee for Farm Production Supplies was working well in serving the interests of the cooperatives and organized agriculture. In 1943 this committee was performing three principle functions. (1) It was keeping cooperatives and farm organizations informed on rapidly changing government regulations which applied to their operations. To this end, it was issuing weekly, to its constituent organizations, several hundred copies of a mimeographed bulletin which summarized and interpreted changes in government orders and regulations. (2) It was assisting government agencies in formulating policies and regulations that would best serve the practical needs of farmers. In many instances the committee was called upon for counsel by government agencies. (3) It was helping individual cooperatives in obtaining priorities or allocations, or in other specific ways that would enable them to operate efficiently under war conditions.[30]

The marketing cooperatives were now operating in high gear. The dairy cooperatives were doing an outstanding job in producing about one-half of dried skim milk powder required by the government for Lend-Lease and military consumption. The leader among the dried milk producing organizations was the Land O' Lakes Creameries which produced 55 million pounds of dried milk in 1943, compared to 35 million in the preceding year, and 6.5 million pounds in 1940. The fruit and vegetable cooperatives were producing great quantities of dehydrated products and canned goods. For example, the California Fruit Growers' Exchange, through its Exchange Orange Products Company, supplied 807,000 gallons of concentrated orange juice, or 21.3 per cent of the government's procurement of this product during the 12 months ending October 31, 1943.[31] The annual production of orange concentrate for the government by the Florida Citrus Canners, Inc., was now reaching 800,000 gallons.[32] By 1943 "set aside" orders were accepted as part of the wartime food situation, and such orders now covered much of the production of processed foods and dehydrated products required to meet lend-lease and military needs.[33]

The cooperative oil mills continued to expand in number. During 1943, 13 new plants were started, of which 10 were formed for the production of soybean oil and high protein meal and 3 for cottonseed oil. This brought the total of such plants to 24.[34]

During the war the regional grain cooperatives rapidly expanded their storage and operating facilities. In 1942-43 the 15 regionals handled 182,878,000 bushels, compared with 104,240,000 in 1940-41. The largest of the regionals, the Farmers' Union Grain Terminal Association, handled 59,197,000 bushels in 1942-43, compared to 27,885,000 in 1940-41.[35]

One of the problems that concerned cooperatives in 1943 arose from the imposition of price ceilings. OPA officials, not familiar with the nature of cooperative organization and operation, held that patronage refunds should be included in determining prices for cooperatives until a decision favorable to cooperatives was rendered early in 1944.[36]

The cooperative purchasing associations were also making substantial contributions to the war effort by providing farmers with essential farm supplies and equipment through elimination of waste and unnecessary services; by reduction in lines of supplies handled; by obtaining maximum use of available supplies; by the use of substitute materials where possible; by promotion of better inventory control through advance ordering programs; by obtaining better use of processing and transportation facilities and equipment; and by conserving manpower through better personnel administration.[37]

During the defense and war years, cooperatives greatly expanded their fertilizer operations in the face of allocations for chemical nitrogen made by the War Production Boards after September 1943. In 1942-43, cooperatives were distributing over 9 per cent of all fertilizer used by farmers.[38]

Shortages developing in farm machinery had caused its rationing by November 1942. Many purchasing cooperatives at this time were conserving farm machinery by operating farm machinery repair shops to make more effective use of professional labor and available farm machinery. Most of the county farm bureau cooperative associations in Indiana were operating repair shops, and there were many others in all parts of the country. To help small-scale low-income farmers increase their food production, the Farm Security Administration had encouraged the formation of group service associations to use farm machinery and equipment on a joint ownership basis. By 1943 there were over 21,000 group services of this type in operation, along with 1,500 "county purchasing and marketing associations" that were financed and supervised by the Farm Security Administration.

One of the interesting developments during 1943 was the significant expansion of cooperative petroleum refining. At the time of Pearl Harbor only two cooperative purchasing associations were engaged in petroleum refining—the Consumers Cooperative Association, with refineries at Phillipsburg, Kansas, and Scottsbluff, Nebraska, and the Indiana Farm Bureau Cooperative Association with a refinery at Mount Vernon, Indiana—and these installations were just becoming established in this field.[39] During 1942 these refineries demonstrated their usefulness in providing farmers with an economical supply of petroleum fuels. On February 10 the Farmers' Union Central Exchange opened a refinery at Laurel, Montana, and in March the Missouri Farmers Association Oil Company was set up at Chanute, Kansas. Midland Cooperative Wholesale followed with the acquisition of a refinery at Cushing, Oklahoma, in April. In July five of the regional purchasing associations—Consumers Cooperative Association, Farmers' Union Central Exchange, Central Cooperative Wholesale, Midland Cooperative Wholesale, and Farmers'

THE ADVANCE OF AMERICAN COOPERATIVE ENTERPRISE

Union State Exchange—set up jointly the National Cooperative Refinery Association to acquire the refining facilities of the Globe Oil Company at McPherson, Kansas. Near the end of the year the Consumers Cooperative Association acquired the large refinery and producing wells of the National Refining Company at Coffeyville, Kansas, and obtained the right to operate a plant for the production of aviation gasoline for the Defense Plant Corporation. This plant was acquired from the government the following July.[40] These acquisitions strengthened the ability of farmers to obtain adequate supplies of petroleum to meet wartime farm production goals.

The war shortage of transportation equipment and labor and the restricted use of petroleum products were causing many cooperative marketing and purchasing associations to improve their methods of transportation. Many were now employing route systems to reduce frequency of pickups and deliveries. Some of the large regional associations, both for marketing and purchasing, had established specialized departments to improve the efficiency of their transportation services. By 1943 cooperatives had increased their transportation efficiency by some 25 per cent, compared with 1941.[41]

The growth in volume of business of the Banks for Cooperatives reflected the expansion of their operations to meet the wartime demands of marketing and purchasing cooperatives. In 1943, loans of the Banks for Cooperatives amounted to $467 million, compared with $340 million in 1942, $221 million in 1941, and $126 million in 1940.

In 1944 the Allies were on the offensive in all war theatres. On June 4 they established a second front in France and began to clear the way for invasion of Germany. The Russian armies were approaching the German homeland on the Eastern front. In the Pacific area American and British army, navy, and marine forces were regaining much of the territory conquered by Japan. General MacArthur dramatically returned to the Philippines on October 22, and with the defeat of the Japanese at Leyte Gulf on October 25 the road was now open to Tokyo.[42]

While this great thrust was going on the war dominated the economy. United States military personnel, as of June 30, 1944, reached 8 million, and military expenditures for the fiscal year 1944 amounted to $50 billion. Airplanes, tanks, ships, and munitions were pouring from industrial plants and shipyards, and agricultural production was exceeding the high production goals and meeting all requirements.

Cooperatives were now conditioned for war, and they were producing enormous quantities of products for use of the armed forces and for our allies under the Lend-Lease program. The Banks for Cooperatives were supplying cooperatives with adequate credit for operations and facilities, while the production credit associations were providing more and more farmers with the credit essential for production.

In the early months of 1945 the war work of agricultural cooperatives was largely a continuation of programs already underway. With the unconditional surrender of Germany on May 7 and of Japan on August 14, and the termination of Lend-Lease on August 21, the nation turned to the problems of postwar adjustment. Attention could now be directed to the immense problems involved in converting the swollen war economy back to peacetime conditions. To appreciate the enormity of this task one must realize that our military personnel had reached a peak of 12 million by June 30, 1945, while expenditures for military functions for the year ending June 30, 1945, amounted to nearly $50 million. Moreover, the total expenditures for Lend-Lease aid to our Allies, which had provided a great stimulus to industrial and agricultural production, had amounted to $50.6 billion from its inception in 1941 to the time of its termination. The way in which agriculture and agricultural cooperatives coped with this problem of postwar readjustment will be examined in Chapter XXIV.

During the war years the cooperatives, along with agriculture, had thrived. Demand for their services had grown constantly and they had responded. As a result their volumes of business had practically doubled. This growth will now be examined.

The Progress of Cooperative Marketing and Purchasing, 1940-1945

The character of the growth of cooperative marketing and purchasing during the war years is shown by the statistical records.[43] Although the volume of business more than doubled, the number of associations declined slightly, while the number of memberships expanded by one-third. These facts call for a closer examination.

The number of members of marketing and purchasing associations increased from 3,400,000 in 1940-41 to 4,505,000 in 1944-45. Much of this increase was accounted for by a growth of membership in the purchasing associations which expanded from 980,000 in 1940-41 to 1,610,000 in 1944-45. The increase in memberships for the marketing associations was from 2,420,000 to 2,895,000.

The total number of marketing and purchasing associations declined from 10,600 in 1940-41 to 10,150 in 1944-45. While the number of marketing associations declined—mostly as a result of consolidations—

from 7,943 to 7,400, the number of purchasing associations increased from 2,657 to 2,750.

The total business volume of the marketing and purchasing associations grew from $2,280,000,000 in 1940-41 to $5,645,000,000 in 1944-45, or by 148 per cent. The volume of associations classified as marketing associations grew in these years from $1,911,000,000 to $4,835,000,000, or by 153 per cent, while the volume of business done by the purchasing associations increased from $369,000,000 to $810,000,000, or by 120 per cent. However, when we take into account the volume of purchasing done by marketing associations and the volume of marketing done by purchasing associations, the total volume of cooperative marketing was $1,461,000,000 in 1940-41 and $3,740,000,000 in 1944-45, or an increase of 156 per cent, while total volume of purchasing was $450,000,000 in 1940-41 and $1,095,000,000 in 1944-45, or an increase of 143 per cent.

Some of the great increase in dollar volume of business for the marketing and purchasing associations reflected the substantial rise in farm prices during the war years.[44] However, a more significant part of the increase represented larger physical quantities of products and supplies handled by these associations with the general wartime increases in agricultural output.[45]

The expansion of cooperative marketing volume of business by principal commodity groupings is shown by the following figures.

Type of Association	1940-41	1944-45	Percentage Increase
	(in millions of dollars)		
Dairy	693	1,294	87
Grain, beans, etc.	387	1,286	232
Fruits and vegetables	305	984	223
Livestock and wool	309	765	148
Poultry and eggs	82	225	174
Cotton and products	85	178	110
All other	50	103	106
Total	1,911	4,835	153

The following tabulation shows how some of the major marketing cooperatives expanded their volumes of business during this period.

	1940-41	1944-45	Percentage Increase
	(in millions of dollars)		
California Fruit Growers Exchange	89.3	182.7	104
Dairymen's League	56.3	96.6	71
Land O' Lakes Creameries, Inc.	35.8	81.3	125
Challenge Cream and Butter Association	30.3	49.2	37
Pure Milk Producers Association	22.0	48.0	118

	1940-41	1944-45	Percentage Increase
	(in millions of dollars)		
Central Cooperative Association (livestock)	30.0	58.0	93
Poultry Producers of Central California	17.2	41.6	134
Washington Cooperative Egg and Poultry Association	16.9	36.7	112
Staple Cotton Growers Association	15.0	33.0	120
California Walnut Growers Association	14.0	27.0	93
California Prune and Apricot Association	9.0	28.0	211
Maryland-Virginia Milk Producers Association	7.0	15.0	118
Twin City Milk Producers Association	8.0	15.0	88
California Almond Growers Exchange	3.0	9.0	200
Sun Maid Raisin Growers	5.0	20.0	300
Cranberry Canners, Inc.	3.6	6.3	88
Hood River Apple Growers Association	3.0	9.0	200
Norbest Turkey Growers Association	2.0	8.0	300
Cotton Producers Association	2.1	10.5	400

The above associations are listed as marketing associations in that over 50 per cent of their volume of business was in marketing of farm products. In a few instances, such as in the case of Land O'Lakes Creameries, Inc., these associations also performed a significant purchasing service. This was particularly true for the egg and poultry associations. The purchasing volume of the Washington Egg and Poultry Association amounted to $6.9 million in 1940-41 and $16 million in 1944-45, while the purchasing volume of the Poultry Producers of Central California amounted to $7.2 million in 1940-41 and $19.6 million in 1944-45. The Cotton Producers Association of Atlanta, Georgia, was just beginning its rapid development in purchasing operations. In 1940-41 its purchasing volume was only $142,000. By 1944-45 it had expanded to $1.4 million, or by almost 900 per cent.

The expansion in volume of business for the major regional purchasing associations was also substantial. This is shown by their wholesale supply sales for fiscal years ending in 1941 and 1945.

	1941	1945	Percentage Increase
	(in millions of dollars)		
Cooperative GLF Exchange	44.0	93.5	113
Eastern States Farmers Exchange*	26.2	53.7	104
Southern States Cooperative, Inc.	13.6	40.6	200
Illinois Farm Supply Company	12.3	19.3	210
Fruit Growers Supply Company	12.3	17.7	48
Farm Bureau Cooperative Association (Ohio)	8.2	17.8	122
Indiana Farm Bureau Cooperative Association	9.5	17.2	81
Consumers Cooperative Association	6.9	21.9	214

	1941	1945	Percentage Increase
	(in millions of dollars)		
Farmers Union Central Exchange	8.0	14.0	75
Midland Cooperative Wholesale	6.2	11.5	85
Central Cooperative Wholesale	4.8	6.7	40
Farm Bureau Service Company (Michigan)	3.5	6.2	77
Pennsylvania Farm Bureau Cooperative Association	3.4	9.1	167
Pacific Supply Cooperative	3.3	7.9	140
Farmers Cooperative Exchange, Inc.	2.5	6.3	152
MFA Milling Company	2.6	10.0	284
Farmers Union State Exchange (Nebraska)	2.4	2.9	21

°Reported in retail sales since operations were integrated.

Some of these associations also sold supplies through their own retail outlets. Retail sales were as follows for the following cooperatives: GLF $27.8 million in 1940-41 and $65.4 million in 1944-45; Southern States Cooperative, $3.5 million in 1940-41 and $14.1 million in 1944-45; Farmers Cooperative Exchange, $1.8 million in 1940-41 and $5.3 million in 1944-45. The following associations also reported farm product marketing sales: GLF, $5 million in 1940-41 and $14.6 million in 1944-45; Southern States Cooperative, $1 million in 1940-41 and $2.4 million in 1944-45; Farmers Cooperative Exchange, $0.4 million in 1940-41 and $1.1 million in 1944-45.[46]

The financial strength of these organizations improved as their volumes of business expanded. For example, the total assets of Land O' Lakes Creameries, Inc., grew from $7 million in 1940 to $21 million in 1945, or by 200 per cent, while membership investment (net worth) grew from $1.2 million to $8.5 million, or by over 600 per cent. The total assets of the Cooperative GLF Exchange grew from $12.8 million in 1940 to $34 million in 1945, or by 135 per cent while membership investment grew from $7.2 million in 1940 to $22.2 in 1945, or by 200 per cent.

Information is not available on total assets for all cooperative marketing and purchasing cooperatives, but information is available that shows the growth of membership investment in these organizations. According to the *Balance Sheets of Agriculture*, issued by the Economic Research Service of the Department of Agriculture, the estimated total membership investment in marketing and purchasing cooperatives increased from $330 million in 1940 to $587 million in 1945, or by 78 per cent. The estimated membership investment in marketing cooperatives increased from $256 million in 1940 to $393 million in 1945, or by 54 per cent, while the membership investment in purchasing associations increased from $74 million in 1940 to $194 million in 1945, or by 149 per cent.

In this chapter we have shown how marketing and purchasing cooperatives responded to the needs of the nation during World War II and how the war brought about a significant expansion of their operations and economic strength. In Chapter XXIII we will examine some of the other important developments relating to cooperatives in this period.

Chapter XXIII

MAJOR COOPERATIVE DEVELOPMENTS: 1941-1945

While World War II was dominating the economy and our national life, significant progress was being made by most forms of cooperative enterprise in the United States. In this chapter we will examine some of the major developments that came with this period of war-induced changes. Of particular interest was the strengthening of national agricultural cooperative organizations to provide supporting assistance for marketing and purchasing associations. Most important of these was the National Council of Farmer Cooperatives.

National Council of Farmer Cooperatives Gains Prestige

The National Council of Farmer Cooperatives had become a strong national organization during the New Deal years.[1] In January 1940 the Council's membership was comprised of 54 large marketing and purchasing cooperatives which, in turn, served 4,000 member local associations representing 1,950,000 farmer patrons. Twelve state cooperative councils were also affiliated with the Council as associate members. Altogether the member associations did a volume of business of $1.25 billion in 1939.

The National Council greatly improved its position during the war years as a representative of farmers and their cooperatives on problems affecting their interests. It gained and deserved much credit for its leadership in developing and supporting the work of the National Committee on Farm Production Supplies which performed a valuable service for both purchasing and marketing associations. As it improved its national standing, more and more important cooperative organizations joined its ranks. By the end of 1945 the National Council had a membership of 105 member organizations that served 4,800 affiliated local cooperatives having a combined membership of 2,400,000 farmer patrons. These organizations together did a volume of business of $2 billion in 1945. In addition to its operating members, the Council also embraced 19 affiliated state councils which performed important services in helping local cooperatives in their states.[2]

Other National Cooperative Organizations
Serve Marketing Needs

Other important national organizations effectively served the specialized needs of various commodity cooperatives during the war years. The most influential of these was the long established National Cooperative Milk Producers' Federation of Washington, D.C., which represented most of the nation's dairy marketing cooperatives in dealings with Congress and governmental agencies and kept them informed on general programs affecting their interests. Another organization somewhat similar in character was the National Federation of Grain Cooperatives of Washington, D.C., which had been set up in 1939 by the large regional grain cooperatives. It gained much stature during the war as the grain regionals increased in importance. The National Livestock Marketing Association, with offices in Chicago, also served as a general overhead organization for livestock marketing cooperatives, although it performed some direct operating functions for its member organizations. This association also held membership in the National Council of Farmer Cooperatives in behalf of its member associations.

Two other national organizations represented cooperatives in marketing operations. The National Wool Marketing Corporation of Boston conducted marketing and other functions for most of the regional wool marketing cooperatives, and the American National Cooperative Exchange of New York City performed national sales services for a number of fruit and vegetable associations. Both the National Wool Marketing Corporation and the American National were also members of the National Council of Farmer Cooperatives.

National Purchasing Federations Gain Standing

The three national purchasing federations that had gained a foothold during the New Deal years—United Cooperatives, Inc., National Cooperatives, Inc., and National Farm Machinery Cooperative, Inc.—made considerable progress during World War II.

United Cooperatives consolidates position. United Cooperatives, Inc., was well established at the onset of the war. In 1940 its sales reached $2.2 million and its savings totalled $60,000. It then had total assets of $687,000 and membership investment amounted to $400,000. United was then operating oil blending plants at Indianapolis and Warren, Pennsylvania, and a plant for manufacturing paint at Alliance, Ohio.

Its membership then included most of the strong farm supply purchasing regionals east of the Mississippi, and there was general agreement among them that the program of service should be limited to the purchasing of supplies and equipment needed by farmers. Unlike National Cooperatives, its business was largely transacted on a purchase and sale, rather than on a brokerage basis.

The demands of national defense confronted United with serious problems in obtaining necessary supplies for its members. In early December 1941, just before Pearl Harbor, the general manager reported to the Board of Directors that steel roofing was very scarce, that steel posts were out entirely, that tires were in critical supply, that anti-freeze was very hard to get, and that motor fuel was in critical condition. He urged that all members anticipate needs as far in advance as possible.[3]

During the war years United steadily increased its volume of business in serving its member organizations. In 1942 it moved into new offices at Alliance, Ohio, to better serve its eastern members, and in this year it widened its base of operations by accepting into membership the Washington Egg and Poultry Association of Seattle, Washington. During 1942 and 1943 United was plagued by management dissension, but this problem was resolved in early 1944 by the employment of Merrit Crouch as general manager, who immediately gave the program leadership and stability. New programs were undertaken in barn equipment manufacture, and progress was marked as shown by the following figures.[4]

	Volume	Savings	Assets	Membership Investment
1941	$4 million	$238,000	$825,000	$400,000
1945	$6.1 million	$188,000	$1.4 million	$953,000

In 1944 and 1945 United gained several strong member associations. Among them were the Illinois Farm Supply Company, the (Georgia) Cotton Producers Association, and the Wisconsin Farm Supply Company. United was then beginning to move into the field of household equipment —freezers, refrigerators, and similar items required in farm homes.

In mid-1945 the desirability of merger with National Cooperatives, Inc., was again considered by the United's directors. Harvey Hull, President of National and active in both organizations, did not believe that a merger was then either "feasible or practical." The minutes of the director's meeting reported that "while no formal action was taken by the Board, it was the consensus that both National Cooperatives and United Cooperatives had separate and distinct functions to perform and neither would conflict with, nor be injurious to, the other; and that merger at this time was neither feasible nor practical."[5]

National Cooperatives steps out. During the war years, National Cooperatives, Inc., greatly strengthened its position as a national buying agency for its member regional purchasing associations. With the employment of an aggressive and qualified general manager—T. A. Tenhune—in December 1941, the organization was in position to expand rapidly. Prior to his appointment, Tenhune had been chief buyer for the Central Cooperative Wholesale, so he was already acquainted with National's procedures. From then on the progress of National was marked, and in 1943 it began manufacturing operations with the acquisition of two plants.

The first plant, acquired in January 1943, was a chemical products company which provided a nucleus for the development of a chemical division. This plant had furnished National with cosmetics and other chemical items, and under National it was soon producing polishes, cleansers, and other items for home and farm use. Within six months the plant paid for itself, and within a year it doubled its output.[6]

The second manufacturing plant acquired a month later was the Universal Milking Machine Company of Waukesha, Wisconsin.[7] It was a long established company said to be "favorably known among contented cows" in the Northwest. It had supplied National with milking machines for many years, so its product was already well known among National members. Moreover, the acquisition came at a favorable time, for there was a great demand for milking machines due to the wartime labor shortage. During its first fiscal year under National's control, Universal's volume of business was $1 million, and in the following year its volume doubled. Within 15 months the plant paid for itself.[8]

The entry of National into manufacturing greatly strengthened it as an organization, and volume of other business also expanded. By 1944 volume amounted to $4 million, and in 1945 it rose to more than $6 million.[9]

As long as National operated primarily as a broker, its total assets were small. In 1942 they only amounted to $115,061. With the acquisition of its manufacturing plants made possible by investments of its member regionals, total assets jumped to $784,097 in 1944 and to $1,287,888 in

1945. Net worth expanded from $74,000 in 1941 to $573,137 in 1944 and to $657,577 in 1945.[10]

In 1944 National was forging ahead.[11] It was then handling groceries, milking machines, chemical products, tires and accessories, steel and hardware items, and building materials. In 1943 National employed an advertising manager and this greatly strengthened its merchandising service for member associations. The success of the manufacturing program had given National "a shot in the arm" and it was searching for other manufacturing opportunities. One that was of much interest was a saw mill. By the end of 1945, National had taken over much of the promotional activity formerly done by the Cooperative League. At this time National was closely associated with the League, and it was anticipated that full coordination of the two organizations would be achieved in the near future.

National Farm Machinery Cooperative broadened its base. Following the establishment of the National Farm Machinery Cooperative in 1940, its Shelbyville, Indiana, plant began to produce "Co-op" tractors on the assembly plan of operation, as practically all parts had to be purchased. During 1941 several hundred tractors were made in the face of priority problems arising from the National defense program. To help the government meet its needs for military hardware, National was forced to give up its tractor operations during 1942 and 1943, although in late 1943 it was able to resume tractor production on a modest scale. However, it was not possible to produce a significant volume of tractors under the war conditions of 1944 and 1945.

During most of the war the production of new farm machinery was greatly restricted with the result that many of the major farm machinery companies turned to war production activities. The scarcity of new farm machinery made it necessary for farmers to use available machinery to the extent possible. To help farmers meet this problem, many of the local purchasing cooperatives undertook farm machinery repair services for their members. This had the advantage of keeping the cooperatives interested in the development of a comprehensive farm machinery program as soon as restrictions on farm machinery manufacture could be lifted.[12]

One of the problems recognized by the leaders in the National Farm Machinery Cooperative was that its program could not be limited to the production of tractors if it were to compete with the strong full-line programs of the principal farm machinery companies. To meet this problem, National in 1943 acquired the Corn Belt Manufacturing Company of Waterloo, Iowa. This added corn pickers, pump jacks, and tank heaters to the line of tractors. Later in December 1943 National concluded negotiations for the purchase of the Ohio Cultivator Company of Bellevue, Ohio. This company was in position to manufacture corn and cotton planters, grain drills, manure spreaders, lime sowers, disk harrows, and garden tractors with a full line of attachments.[13] With this broader program, National was able to widen its membership base to include most of the regional associations then members of National Cooperatives, Inc.

When the war came to an end in 1945, National had made much progress in gaining support for its program, and it was in position to take advantage of the pent-up demand anticipated in the postwar period. As Harvey Hull, the leader in the national farm machinery movement from its beginning, said in 1944: "A powerful movement such as National Farm Machinery Cooperative is only made possible by the long years of working together which have built up group confidence and understanding in different parts of the nation."[14]

The Cooperative Farm Credit System Forges Ahead

The opportunity to serve the nation in World War II reaffirmed the basic soundness of the Cooperative Farm Credit System. The economic conditions brought by the war were favorable to the continuance of its work without organic change, and from 1941 to 1945 officials could largely devote their energies to providing credit services that would contribute to the defense and war effort. Although the National Council of Farmer Cooperatives, the American Farm Bureau Federation, and the National Grange continued to advocate the re-establishment of the Farm Credit Administration on an independent basis, action on this question could be deferred until after the war was won.

The Federal Land Bank System. "The war period brought many developments which were to strengthen the [Land Bank] system and lay the groundwork for the agricultural revolution already in the making."[15] Improvement in agricultural conditions with higher farm prices enabled many farmers to begin paying off their debts in the early years of the war, so that by 1945 the Land Banks had the lowest inventory of real estate loans since 1924. The total amount of Land Bank and Land Bank Commissioner loans outstanding declined from $2.4 billion on December 31, 1940, to $1.4 billion on June 30, 1945.

From 1940 to 1945 the Land Bank System carried on a general program of consolidating National Farm Loan Associations (now Federal Land Bank Associations). On December 31, 1940, there were 3,846 of such associations; by June 30, 1945, there were 1,884. Concurrently, the Federal Land Bank System carried on and largely consummated a campaign to rehabilitate and strengthen the N.F.L.A.'s.

With the generally improved financial condition of the Land Banks they were able to retire government capital and paid-in surplus and reserves. The Houston and Louisville banks were able to do this as early as 1940, but no other bank was able to do so before 1944, when the banks initiated a program to pay off all government capital and paid-in surplus and reserves by May 1, 1946. Nine of the 12 banks had accomplished this objective by June 30, 1945. In 1944 the Houston bank began paying dividends again, and the other banks were soon on a dividend-paying basis. By 1947 all of the Federal Land Banks were completely farmer-owned and were then paying dividends on stock.

The Production Credit System. The Production Credit System did not expand materially during the war years, for with higher farm incomes there was a decline in the amount of production credit required. The number of production credit associations was reduced through consolidations from 540 in 1941 to 514 in 1945. The production credit associations made 231,979 loans in 1941, amounting to $418 million. In 1945 they made 214,000 loans with a total value of $500 million. Thus the number of loans declined, although the total amount of loans increased.[16]

During the war years the production credit associations gave active assistance to farmers in helping them increase food production through loans for farm supplies and equipment. With a steady improvement in operating efficiency, the associations as a group were able to improve their economic position, and an increasing number were able to pay all operating expenses from member income. Although 61 per cent of all associations had operated within member income in 1940, this percentage declined in 1941 and 1942 with a greater use of government subsidy under an easy credit policy that followed the transfer of the Farm Credit Administration to the Department of Agriculture.[17] With a tightening of operations and an increase in loan service fees in 1943 an increasing number of production credit associations were able to pay their own way, with the result that 75 per cent were able to live within their member income in 1944, and within 90.5 per cent in 1945.

As the associations became established as sound business organizations, it became possible for the system to retire government capital. The first $5 million was retired in April 1944, and $6.7 million more was retired in 1945. At the end of the war the Production Credit System thus was steadily improving its services to farmers and was on the road to eventual self-support.[18]

The Banks for Cooperatives. In 1941 the Banks for Cooperatives extended credit amounting to $221 million through 1,705 farmer cooperatives. By 1944-45 the total amount of credit extended had grown to $407 million, but the number of borrowing associations had declined to 1,050 due to consolidations or because of less borrowing as cooperatives improved their financial position. During the war years the net earnings of the 12 district banks and the Central Bank for Cooperatives increased from $2.7 million in 1942 to $2.8 million in 1943, and to $3.3 million in 1944-45.

The many ways in which the Banks for Cooperatives assisted cooperatives during the defense and war years have been described in Chapter XXII. Generally the system proved flexible enough to meet the credit needs of all soundly organized agricultural cooperatives. The bulk of the loans were made through the 12 district banks for cooperatives with the Central Bank participating in the larger loans. Many of the very large loans to regional associations operating in more than one bank district were made by the Central Bank for Cooperatives with participation by the district banks.[19]

During the war years much interest developed in a plan to make the Banks for Cooperatives borrower-owned. As early as March 1936, Cooperative Bank Commissioner, Samuel D. Sanders, had expressed an interest in having the banks for cooperatives eventually owned by their borrowing associations. This had led to consideration of how this objective might be achieved before the war interrupted study of the problems involved. In 1943, the idea came back into prominence with the formation of a committee, under the chairmanship of Albert Goss, Master of the National Grange, to consider how the cooperative character of the FCA could be improved.[20] Encouraged by this interest, Dr. E. A. Stokdyk, President of the Berkeley Bank for Cooperatives, developed a plan under which the ownership of the Banks for Cooperatives might be transferred from the government to the borrowing cooperatives. This led to the appointment of a committee of Cooperative Bank presidents with Stokdyk as Chairman to give further study to this matter. The first meeting of this committee was held on February 2 and 3, 1945.[21] From this beginning a feasible plan for achieving the objective of complete borrower-ownership was finally perfected in 1957, after the Farm Credit Administration regained its independent status in 1953.[22]

Credit Unions Mark Time

While most forms of cooperative enterprise were stimulated by the war, credit unions were forced to mark time.[23] The slow-up in credit union development has been attributed to several causes. Perhaps the single most important retarding factor was the imposition of Regulation "W" by the Board of Governors of the Federal Reserve Board which regulated consumers credit and restricted the amount of credit that could be granted. The credit unions felt the effects of Regulation W almost immediately with a decline in new organizations formed.[24] Credit unions also felt the effect of declining interest in organizing Federal Credit Unions by the Credit Union Section of the Farm Credit Administration. Although the Credit Union Section was transferred to the Federal Deposit Insurance Corporation on April 23, 1942, it took some time to establish the work of the section in an effective way.[25] Another factor that adversely affected credit union growth during the war was "the tremendous wartime labor turnover, which made it difficult to find people who could serve for any length of time as credit union officers."[26] Moreover, savings at this time were largely channeled into defense bonds and war savings stamps. The Bond Program tended to diminish the apparent need for other types of savings programs. A final factor unfavorable to growth was growing dissension in credit union leadership ranks which finally came to a head with the installation of new management in the Credit Union National Association in 1945. The result of these and other factors on credit union development from 1941 to 1945 is shown by the following figures:[27]

For Years Ending December 31	Number of Credit Unions	Loans Outstanding	Number of Members	Loans During Year
1941	10,537	$216 million	3.3 million	$360 million
1945	8,890	126 million	2.8 million	211 million

During the war period there was one development that was to be of much future importance in national cooperative development. The Credit Union National Association began to take a significant interest in other forms of consumers cooperation, This was manifest by a joint meeting of the executives of the Credit Union National Association and of the Cooperative League on January 29, 1943, held to make plans for closer coordination of the two national organizations.[28]

At the end of the war period the credit union national movement had been through a shakedown period, and it was in position to expand rapidly with more favorable economic and governmental conditions.

Rural Electric Cooperatives Gather Strength

The pioneering stage of cooperative rural electrification came to an end in 1940. During the next five years the electric cooperatives learned how to survive and progress under difficult circumstances.

As the pressure mounted for military supplies and manpower in the spring of 1941 the rural electric cooperatives began to feel the impact of the war. Their problems multiplied shortly before Pearl Harbor when the Office of Production Management (later to be the War Production Board) issued an order that banned the use of copper and aluminum wire and a wide range of steel products needed for construction of power lines and facilities to serve rural areas. Moreover construction was stopped on certain multi-purpose dams which would have provided the cooperatives with electric power. There was little that cooperatives could do to meet these problems without "an effective way of proving to the Government or the people that rural electrification would help win the war by increasing food production with less manpower . . . [for] the whole country was adapting itself to rationing and production controls. The worst thing that could be said about anyone was that he was cheating on . . . controls for personal benefit. In this atmosphere the power companies created a national furor by charging that the rural electric systems were hoarding copper wire and other material to use in defiance of [Government] orders."[29]

Formation of the NRECA. Although congressional investigations found that these allegations were without foundation they adversely affected public opinion and made difficult an objective consideration of the problems facing the electric cooperatives. This situation in late 1941 set the stage for the formation of a national association of rural electric cooperatives. This was not an entirely new idea, for it had been advocated for several years.[30] Moreover, it should be realized that a number of state-wide associations of rural electric cooperatives were then demonstrating their value on problems within states. Thus it was natural that many would think of forming a national organization that could deal with problems beyond state boundaries.[31]

Although there was a growing support for the formation of a national association in 1940 and 1941, it took the attack by the power companies in late 1941 to crystallize the demand for it. This situation made it obvious that only through their own national organization could the electric cooperatives protect their basic interests as cooperative associations.[32] In response to this conviction a group of determined men, broadly representative of all electric cooperatives, in a series of meetings held early in

504 THE ADVANCE OF AMERICAN COOPERATIVE ENTERPRISE

1942 perfected plans for a national organization of electric cooperative associations. It was not designed as a federation of state-wide associations already formed nor did it intend to supplant such associations. In fact, several of the founders were already officers of state-wide associations.

The new organization was incorporated in Washington, D.C., on March 19, 1942, as the National Rural Electric Cooperative Association, and it soon became known as the NRECA. Its incorporators who served as the directors for the first year were the following 10 men.

William Jackman, Freehold, New Jersey
Steve C. Tate, Tate, Georgia
Will Hall Sullivan, Lafayette, Tennessee
Dolph H. Wolfe, Portland, Michigan
E. J. Stoneman, Platteville, Wisconsin
Harry Edmunds, Cedar, Minnesota
J. C. Nichols, Cody, Wyoming
Thomas B. Fitzhugh, Little Rock, Arkansas
E. D. H. Farrow, Itasca, Texas
Raymond A. Walker, Fulton, Missouri

The purposes of the NRECA as set forth in the Articles of Incorporation were declared to be:

> 1. To assist in the utilization of rural electric cooperatives for the most effective prosecution of the war effort of the United States of America, and to assist such cooperatives with respect to their common problems in the post-war period; and
>
> 2. To engage in the compilation and dissemination of information with respect to rural electrification and the furnishing of other services to rural electric cooperatives and others in connection with the coordination, advancement and development of rural electrification in the United States of America, its territories and possessions, for the primary and mutual benefit of the patrons of the Association and their patrons, as ultimate consumers.

Following incorporation, the board of directors held its first meeting at the Willard Hotel in Washington, D.C., where it adopted by-laws and made plans for getting the organization underway. Steve Tate was elected President, and E. J. Stoneman, Vice-President. In order to gain national support for the new organization a reception was held for Congressional leaders and government officials who were actively interested in rural electrification. Among those present were Senators George Norris of Nebraska and Robert LaFollette of Wisconsin, and Congressmen John Rankin of Mississippi and Clyde T. Ellis of Arkansas. The latter was destined to soon become the first Executive Manager of the NRECA.

Getting the NRECA underway. In the beginning the NRECA was but a skeleton organization with an office in St. Louis where the REA had been moved after Pearl Harbor to free office space for the war agencies. It could do little until it had built up a membership and obtained the services of a competent person as Executive Manager. Until this man could be found the elected officers and directors dealt with immediate problems.

Support for the organization was soon evident. By September 18 NRECA had a membership of 144 rural electric cooperatives, and it was steadily gaining adherents. In a message to all rural electric cooperatives issued about this time President Tate said: "We are not confining our objectives simply for defense against attacks . . . We feel that we can help ourselves to achieve benefits that only a national organization can accomplish . . . We expect to inaugurate and put into effect as rapidly as possible our own self-insurance program. By acting together we can save our cooperatives and their members millions of dollars."[33]

The problem of obtaining the right man to serve as Executive Manager posed a more difficult problem. It was recognized that he would need exceptional qualifications. "He would have to work successfully in cooperation with the REA and other executive departments of the Government. He would have to take an important part in standing up to the attacks of the powerful and closely knit electric power industry. Last but not least, the manager would have to have the confidence of NRECA's farm members throughout the country."[34]

In September the directors found the man they were looking for in Clyde T. Ellis who was completing his second term as Congressman from Arkansas. He had been a strong advocate of rural electrification in Congress, and he had given up his congressional seat to run for the Senate. Defeated in the Democratic State Primary he was therefore available to serve as Executive Manager following the expiration of his term in Congress on January 3, 1943.[35]

In October the NRECA began issuance of the *National Rural Electric Association Bulletin* (which was replaced by the magazine *Rural Electrification* in October 1945) to provide technical and other information on rural electrification for its directors, officers, and employees as well as for the patrons of the rural electric cooperatives. Copies were also made available to members of Congress and government officials. Soon afterwards the offices of the NRECA were moved from St. Louis to Washington, D.C., for it became apparent that much of the work of the organization would be related to Congress and governmental administrative agencies. The NRECA was now beginning to grow rapidly. By the end of November its membership embraced 266 local electric associations and power districts.

When the NRECA held its first annual meeting in St. Louis on January 19 and 20, 1943, it had built up a membership of 393 rural electric cooperatives and power districts. The theme of the meeting was "Why We Are Here," and it was clearly a demonstration of strength. More than a thousand people were present to hear addresses by Senator George Norris and Secretary of Interior Harold Ickes and other prominent friends of rural electrification. The "large and enthusiastic gathering" impressed even those who were somewhat skeptical of the organization's objectives and forceful methods of procedure.[36]

One of the principal problems confronting the rural electric cooperatives at this time was to obtain relief under the War Production Board order restricting the use of scarce materials. The delegates recognized this problem by resolving that the rural electric cooperatives "be permitted to help in the nation's war effort by making more electric service available to increase food and fiber production with less manpower." The delegates also endorsed the plans going forward to provide mutual insurance protection.

Following the meeting the NRECA pressed the case for more liberal allowances of needed materials with Congress, the White House, and the administrative agencies, and it was not long before the War Production Board relaxed its restrictions "so that farmers near existing power lines could obtain extensions if they could show that electricity would mean an increase in production or a decrease in labor."[37]

The insurance controversy. Almost from its formation the NRECA had concerned itself with the problem of obtaining insurance protection for its member associations at reasonable cost. The insurance companies were then following the precedent of the New York rating bureau which assumed that farmers couldn't operate an electric power business efficiently and rates were fixed appreciably higher for electric cooperatives than for other power companies. The obvious way to meet this problem was to form a mutual insurance company, and the directors decided to enter this field. After careful study, plans were developed for two mutual companies to meet the fire and casualty needs of the rural electric associations but no steps were taken to activate this program until it had received REA approval. As noted, the subject of insurance was of much interest at the NRECA's annual meeting, and it was generally assumed that a mutual insurance program would soon be undertaken.

Not long after the meeting it became evident that REA Administrator Harry Slattery had qualms that NRECA's plans for financing the mutual insurance companies would represent an improper use of REA borrower's funds, although up to this time he had encouraged the proposal. The matter came to a head on April 19, 1943, when Slattery sent out a long and discursive letter addressed to "Directors or Trustees of Cooperatives Financed by the Rural Electrification Administration" in which he "presented for consideration . . . the question as to whether enterprises almost wholly financed by the Federal Government should in the early days of their operation and before maximum debt service payments have matured engage in such extensive insurance activities." He went on to say: "We in the Rural Electrification Administration have never been troubled by criticism of activities of our borrowers in the direct line of the rural electrification program. Different questions are presented, however, with respect to undertakings in direct competition with established enterprises outside the field of your own electric cooperative undertaking, including many local businesses in your communities. . . ."[38]

The officials of NRECA were nonplussed by Slattery's action for they could not proceed without the approval of the REA. As Clyde Ellis, the Executive Manager, later said: "In those days the REA administrator had life-or-death power over co-ops and few of them were willing to defy him openly."[39]

Although an appeal was made to the Secretary of Agriculture to get a reversal of the Administrator's decision, nothing could be done as long as Slattery was Administrator. In view of this situation the NRECA welcomed a decision of the New York rating bureau in the summer that accorded rural electric cooperatives commercial company insurance rates. This made it possible for the NRECA to work out a contract with Employers Mutuals of Wassau, Wisconsin, under which member associations of NRECA would receive favorable terms under a group insurance plan.[40] The arrangement proved so satisfactory that NRECA later patterned other insurance programs on it.

REA's administrative problem. The disagreement between the REA administrator and the NRECA on the insurance program precipitated a bitter attack on Slattery's administrative competence, a subject under question for some time. The matter reached a head when the President, Executive Manager, and Secretary-Treasurer of the NRECA in a letter to President Roosevelt, May 8, 1943, declared: "We must tell you that the REA Administrator, Mr. Slattery, is now incompetent." The letter ended with this sentence: "We are convinced that Mr. Slattery must go and quickly. Otherwise, we are faced with immediate explosions and investigations in the Congress and a scandal of major proportions."[41]

To understand the background of this situation it should be realized that the morale of the REA had been shaken by the transfer of the agency to St. Louis in December 1941 to make space for agencies considered more important in the war effort. Many key employees looked upon this as a demotion of their agency and sought other work. It was also of concern to employees that the appropriation for the work of REA was cut from $100 million in fiscal 1942 to $10 million in fiscal 1943.

Another factor that was contributing to low employee morale was the lack of clear-cut authority of the REA Administrator since he reported to the Secretary of Agriculture. This arrangement had weakened the agency for several years, and in May 1941 the Secretary of Agriculture and the Administrator of the REA had attempted to improve this situation by jointly requesting the Bureau of the Budget to examine "(a) the organization structure and administrative methods of the REA; (b) the relations of REA to the individual rural electrification systems financed by REA; and (c) the relationships between REA and the Department of Agriculture." The report giving the findings issued in November 1942 pointed out many administrative problems in the REA program which continued to give difficulty during the war years. The report closed with this sentence: "As is the usual case in initiating any major project of progressive administration, the effectuation of this project of joint policy formulation requires forceful and resolute leadership on the part of both the Secretary and the Administrator."[42] Unfortunately such "resolute and forceful leadership" was not forthcoming while the war continued.[43]

The obvious deterioration in REA morale finally caused Slattery to take cognizance of the problem. On May 18, 1942, he requested Dr. H. S. Person, consulting economist, to look into the matter, "especially with respect to whether the causes stemmed primarily from the move to St. Louis or from other and perhaps deeper influences." Dr. Person on May 26 informed Mr. Slattery by memorandum that there had unquestionably been a substantial deterioration in morale throughout the organization; that this was not primarily because staff members had been obliged to adjust to a new city of residence, but that the causes were to be found within the Rural Electrification Administration itself. Dr. Person held that the disorganizing factors were confusion and uncertainty resulting from progressive maladjustment of organization and procedure to the REA's objective and task, now profoundly modified for the duration of the war. Slattery appointed a committee to study the problem but little was done to correct the situation, for almost a year later—on July 12, 1943— a report by the Supervising Investigator of the U.S.D.A. Office of Personnel stated: "It was apparent that the confusion and chaos were appalling. The organization was rife with dissension, disloyalty, and disrespect for the Administrator and his administrative staff." This same report stated: "The history of the administration of the Rural Electrification Administration is a story of intrigue, dissension, factionalism, and quest for individual power."[44]

It was becoming clear that the REA's administrative problem could no longer be ignored. On June 23, 1943, Secretary of Agriculture Claude R. Wickard addressed a memorandum to all Rural Electrification Administration section and division heads and the members of the administrative staff which read as follows:

> William J. Neal has been appointed Deputy Administrator of the Rural Electrification Administration.
> Effective immediately, Mr. Neal will exercise coordinating and administrative authority for the operation of the Rural Electrification Administration. All section and division heads and the members of the administrative staff will report to the Administrator through Mr. Neal . . . "[45]

This appointment, in effect, made Mr. Neal the "Coordinating Administrator" of the REA. However, the charges and countercharges resulting from the dispute over the NRECA insurance program and the evidence of internal dissension, if not corruption, in the REA could not be overlooked by Congress. In the fall of 1943 the Senate Agriculture and Forestry Committee took cognizance of the problems in REA by setting up a subcommittee under Senator Henrik Shipstead of Minnesota to examine the situation. The subcommittee was directed by the Senate:

> . . . to inquire into the administration of the Rural Electrification Act and for the purpose of determining whether political groups or organizations have been created to influence the administration of the Rural Electrification Act, and if so, how they have been organized and how they have been financed, and what efforts they have made to influence the administration of the Act, whether the administration has not suffered since REA was made subject to the Department of Agriculture, and whether REA should not be restored to its original status as an independent agency responsible only to the Congress, and whatever other facts are helpful in determining a policy for REA which would carry out the original purposes of the Rural Electrification Act.[46]

When the subcommittee held its hearings in late 1943 and in the winter and spring of 1944, most of REA's internal problems were under better control. The initial source of controversy, the NRECA's insurance program, was no longer moot, and the appointment of Mr. Neal as Deputy Administrator with full authority over personnel was providing better administrative direction. The hearings were mainly significant in bringing out into the open conditions that could not be tolerated in any government agency if it were to enjoy public support. Thus in the long run the investigation helped to ensure improved REA administration in the years to come.[47]

The biggest problem—the REA Act. With the insurance problem settled the NRECA turned its attention to "Its biggest problem"—the terms of the Rural Electrification Act. It was the belief of NRECA's leaders that the REA's rate of interest to rural electric borrowers, which was geared to the rate paid by the government on its long-term securities with the requirement that principal must be paid in full in 25 years, placed a heavy burden on new systems which were already handicapped because of the necessity of serving consumers scattered over wide areas. As the Act of 1936 would expire automatically in 1946, the NRECA leaders sought an amendment of the Act which would make REA a permanent agency, provide for amortization of loans over a longer period, and fix the rate of interest so as to make possible full area coverage.

To attain its objectives the NRECA at its annual meeting in March 1944 supported a bill introduced by Congressman Stephen Pace of Georgia which contained a provision for a permanent interest rate on REA loans of two per cent, a loan repayment period of 35 years, and the establishment of the REA as a permanent agency. The Pace bill met with a favorable reception in Congress and was signed by President Roosevelt on September 21, 1944.[48] In signing the measure President Roosevelt said:

> It is particularly important that extensions of rural electrification be planned in such a way as to provide service on an area basis. The practice has been too frequent in the past for private utility companies to undertake to serve only the more prosperous and more populous sections. As a result, families in less favored and in sparsely settled sections were left unserved. I believe that our postwar rural electrification program should bring modern service of electric power to the farm families of the back country.

In passing the Pace Act Congress made it clear that REA borrowers had an obligation to make their electric service available to everyone in the territory they undertook to serve. This meant that the cooperatives had to plan their systems to pay off loans with interest while charging those who lived farthest from headquarters or on the highlines no more than those who lived nearby. Rates and financial responsibility were predicated on costs and revenues for entire systems instead of for each separate line which was the prevailing power company practice. To the rural electric cooperatives this "area coverage" principle was a fundamental part of what they regarded as a covenant with Congress. That is, in return for the privilege of borrowing funds at a low interest rate and with a long period for repayment the cooperatives undertook to make adequate and dependable electric service available on a non-profit basis to all unserved people in rural areas.[49]

The passage of the Pace Act "opened the way for the tremendous surge of rural electrification in the post-war era—a surge that was never checked until the rural electrics had accomplished just what Congress intended—the continuing area coverage electrification of all of rural America."[50]

Getting ready for postwar conditions. It was apparent by 1944 that there would be a great pent-up demand for rural electrification following the war. To meet this problem the REA undertook comprehensive studies to determine the size of the job ahead and to estimate the financial requirements of the program needed. The results of these appraisals and estimates were presented by REA in a preliminary report issued in 1945, *Rural Electrification After the War.* On the basis of this work REA was ready to expand operations rapidly after VJ Day.

A favorable development was President Truman's appointment of former Secretary of Agriculture Claude W. Wickard as Administrator of REA in June 1945, following the resignation of Harry Slattery in November 1944. In Wickard the cooperatives obtained a champion and an understanding friend as Administrator. The stage was set for comprehensive postwar expansion under an enlarged program.

With the conditions that prevailed during the war the rural electric cooperatives were forced to tighten operations and assume more responsibility as cooperative organizations. Unable to push as much line construction as desired, managers and boards of directors concentrated attention on improving management, cooperative procedures, and member relations work. Thus by 1945 the rural electrics were much stronger as cooperatives than when the war began.

One of the problems that impeded cooperatives during the war was limited sources of power. Loans for the construction of cooperative generating plants were almost unobtainable, although some progress was made in obtaining more favorable power service from commercial sources. Near the war's end larger REA appropriations were making possible more cooperative electric generating plants, and loans for this purpose were to expand appreciably in the next few years.

Assessment of wartime progress. The following figures from the REA show how the development of cooperative rural electrification was arrested during the war with the decline in REA appropriations and loan advances.[51]

	Loan Advances	Cumulative Number of Cooperatives Served	Cumulative Miles of Line Energized	Cumulative Number of Consumers Connected
1941	$79 million	793	308,000	902,000
1942	32 million	795	378,000	1,012,000
1943	14 million	800	390,000	1,088,000
1944	28 million	802	410,000	1,217,000
1945	57 million	848	450,000	1,409,000

512 THE ADVANCE OF AMERICAN COOPERATIVE ENTERPRISE

The preceding figures show that the number of rural electric cooperatives remained constant at around 800 until 1945, when an expansion of loan advances raised the number to 848. Although the total lines energized grew slowly, the number of consumers connected rose from 902,000 in 1941, to 1,409,000 in 1945. This reflected the considerable progress made by REA borrowers in serving more consumers with limited resources.

Cooperative rural electrification thus made very substantial gains during the war. In this period the cooperatives formed and developed the National Rural Electric Cooperative Association as a strong supporting organization; they strengthened their state-wide associations; they obtained recognition from the public and government agencies for their ability to help on the war production effort; and they achieved amendment of the Rural Electrification Act so as to provide for permanent development in the postwar period under the area coverage concept.

Fertilizer Cooperatives Consolidate Efforts

Agricultural cooperatives were already expanding their fertilizer operations when World War II broke out in Europe. Much progress in fertilizer distribution had been made in the New Deal years by such large purchasing cooperatives as the GLF, the Eastern States Farmers' Exchange, Southern States Cooperative, and the Ohio and Indiana Farm Bureau Cooperative Associations. Also cooperatives in the South were getting well established in fertilizer operations.[52]

As the cooperatives strengthened their fertilizer programs they were drawn more closely to the fertilizer research and educational activities of the TVA. During the late 1930's the TVA was conducting a national program of increasing the use of phosphate through its test-demonstration program as described in Chapter XVI, and in many cases cooperatives participated in this program. To get better acquainted with TVA's fertilizer work, a group of cooperative representatives, in April 1941, made a pilgrimage to the TVA plants at Muscle Shoals. The TVA welcomed this interest from the cooperatives, for it was TVA policy to work through farmers' cooperatives to the extent possible since they directly represented farmers. Thus TVA provided the cooperatives with a Mecca to which they could come for knowledge and help in planning their fertilizer activities.

J. C. McAmis, Director of TVA's Division of Agricultural Relations, later pointed out what was accomplished at this meeting: He said:

> After examining the plants and program of work at the Shoals and the status of the program of distribution and use, the cooperatives concluded that they

should develop their own sources of concentrated phosphates rather than depend upon TVA and that the Muscle Shoals plant should be kept on an experimental and demonstration basis and the production used for educational purposes in which cooperatives had an important part. A committee . . . was appointed to guide cooperative relationships with this program and for other purposes.[53]

By the fall of 1941 the defense situation had made it apparent that fertilizer production would need to be greatly increased to make possible the larger agricultural production desired. To consider the problems that would be involved, the Cooperative Research and Service Division of the Farm Credit Administration called a conference of major fertilizer handling cooperatives in Baltimore on November 24.[54] This meeting provided these cooperatives with an opportunity to discuss ways and means by which they could best further the national defense effort. The participants agreed that there was need for a better coordinated program for the cooperatives handling fertilizer, and from the conference, plans were developed for an informal organization which took the name "The Fertilizer Cooperatives of North America."[55]

From 1937 to 1941, TVA had supplied over 238,000 tons of superphosphate to the Agricultural Adjustment Administration for its agricultural conservation program. This program was terminated in 1941, as the requirements of the military for phosphorus and the needs for superphosphate for Britain under the Lend-Lease program and for TVA's test-demonstration program left no surplus for domestic sale. It was apparent to TVA officials that after the war there would be a problem in utilizing its large phosphate producing facilities for the benefit of American agriculture. David E. Lilienthal, Chairman of the TVA board, examined this problem with cooperative leaders at the American Institute of Cooperation during its meetings in Atlanta, Georgia, January 12-16, 1942. After calling attention to TVA's extensive facilities for producing phosphatic fertilizers, he said:

> As we enter upon the perils of war, this phase of the work of the TVA is of particular interest to you, as American citizens who make the winning of the war their first thought . . . and as American farmers and representatives of farmers who want to meet fully the essential need for food production for victory . . . Phosphates of high concentration, such as those developed by TVA, are of strategic importance because this nutrient phosphorus can reach the great agricultural Middle West and the Northeast, which are distant from phosphate deposits . . .
>
> But beyond the immediate present, this phosphorus and phosphate program is of concern to us all. For, when hostilities cease, when the victory has been won . . . the fertility of American land will assume a significance even greater, if that be possible, than it has today in the midst of war. When that day comes, the entire output of these phosphate plants can be turned without a moment's loss of time into channels of peace and reconstruction through production of urgently needed concentrated fertilizers.

I have said that the program is of particular interest to you as representatives of cooperative organizations. Let me indicate briefly why this is true. In the first place, the distribution of the fertilizer product of TVA's phosphate plants for the farmers' test demonstration work has been carried on largely by reliance upon local organizations employing the principle of cooperatives . . . Some of your own organizations receive and store shipments of phosphate for demonstrations. And then the program is of interest to leaders of cooperatives *because in the post-war future the operation of TVA's plants and the distribution of the products may be in your hands as cooperatives.* The TVA should continue the research work, but after the plants make their contribution to the war, *it may well be that the long time operation of the . . . plants and the distribution of their products should be turned over to a cooperative of farmers and farm organizations.* This prospect in our present thinking in the TVA seems to us sound. I hope you will give the subject immediate and careful study (Emphasis added).[56]

As pointed out in Chapter XVI, TVA in the beginning had decided against producing nitrogen fertilizers. "In 1940, however, the War Department authorized TVA to replace a part of the obsolete World War I nitrate producing facilities with a modern high-pressure ammonia plant utilizing coke, air, and water as the major raw materials."[57] TVA's synthetic ammonium plant was placed in operation in August 1942, and by October 1942 it reached full operation. At that time TVA was aware that its nitrogen plant could only be used for agricultural purposes after the war emergency, and it was deemed advisable to consider with agricultural cooperatives how it might eventually be used.

At a conference held at Muscle Shoals on October 22 and 23, with the group identified as the Fertilizer Cooperatives of North America, Lilienthal indicated that the TVA was interested in working closely with the cooperatives in the utilization of its phosphate and nitrate producing plants when they were no longer needed for war purposes. He recorded the conference in his Journal as follows:

> On October 23 I met with the representatives of the Cooperatives of North America, at Muscle Shoals. In a very informal talk, I proposed that after the war they undertake the distribution of the fertilizer output of TVA's various plants, including the ammonium nitrate plant that can be converted readily to fertilizer. The response was good. It is an important step, in many particulars. It is one of the best illustrations of the method in which I take such great store; the diffusion of power as between centralized government authority and private or quasi-private undertakings . . .[58]

Realizing that the nitrogen plant might later be utilized for fertilizer production, TVA experimentally used a small amount of the ammonium nitrate produced as fertilizer, in the form of a water-ammonia solution, on test-demonstration farms in Tennessee, Alabama, and Mississippi. However, the problem of making use of the plant for fertilizer production came sooner than was anticipated. In the spring of 1943 the War

Department demands for sodium nitrate were abruptly curtailed. This made ammonium nitrate available for diversion to wartime food production, and the TVA began intensive research to improve methods of conditioning the material for use on the land, particularly to find a means of preventing caking.[59]

With this turn of events, TVA decided to examine the feasibility of handling the distribution of the ammonium nitrate production through farmer cooperatives, and representatives of the principal farmer cooperatives of the seven Tennessee Valley states and of neighboring states were invited "to meet and discuss the possibility of marketing the TVA ammonium nitrate fertilizer." At this meeting, held on May 5th, it was assumed that distribution would be handled through the cooperatives, but "this plan was overruled by the War Production Board which insisted that all the distribution must be on the basis of allocation to all industry."[60]

To meet the requirement of the War Production Board that TVA should name a broker to handle distribution of allocations, it was decided within TVA that the problem could be met if the cooperatives were to organize a cooperative association that could operate as a brokerage agency and thus distribute the ammonium nitrate as directed by the War Production Board.[61]

Having decided that they would be interested in assuming responsibility for distribution of the ammonium nitrate, representatives of 12 farmer cooperatives met in Birmingham, Alabama, on July 29, 1943, "to consider the formation of a cooperative that, for the immediate present, would handle the sales and distribution of ammonium nitrate for TVA but with the future thought of some day, if possible, handling all TVA products and possibly additional lines from other manufacturers."[62]

The views of the cooperatives expressed at this meeting made clear that they were interested in the creation of an organization for more than an immediate end. Mr. Si Derrick, representing the Indiana Farm Bureau Cooperative Association, who was also President of the Fertilizer Cooperatives of North America, stated that "co-ops will not go far until they have ownership of sources of raw materials and facilities." He maintained that "this meeting should be the opening wedge for large investments through joint action of cooperatives for the purpose of performing a multiplicity of operations for themselves." Mr. Baron Smith, representing the Magee Cooperative Gin of Magee, Mississippi, held that the cooperatives "should set up some form of organization that would present a united front of all co-op groups to fight the pressure from commercial groups who want to close the government plants as was done after the last war."[63] After full discussion the group unanimously adopted the following resolution: "Be it resolved that this group set up an organization, adequately financed, for handling products and supplies on a brokerage or any other basis."

Following the adoption of the resolution, on the same day, the charter was prepared and recorded, by-laws were adopted, and directors were elected. The new organization took the name Associated Cooperatives, Inc., and soon afterwards offices were set up at Sheffield, Alabama.

On August 25, 1943, TVA entered into a contract with Associated Cooperatives, Inc., for the distribution of the entire output of the ammonium nitrate plant. The contract provided that Associated would receive a commission on the fertilizer it sold. This arrangement was continued until February 1, 1944, when a new contract providing for purchase and sale arrangements was executed.[64]

It was in this way that the first national fertilizer cooperative was formed. During the next three years Associated was the principal agency through which TVA-produced fertilizer was distributed. As the program developed, Associated broadened its distribution service to include cooperatives in all parts of the nation, and until the War Production Board requirement was lifted in 1945, it also sold ammonium nitrate as directed by WPB to commercial outlets. During 1944 and 1945 fiscal years ending June 30, total sales of TVA-produced ammonium nitrate through Associated amounted to approximately 93,000 tons with a value of about $4.5 million for each year.[65] During 1945 TVA also sold 612 tons of triple superphosphate to Associated for experimental distribution by regional cooperatives in the Mississippi Valley. This sale was arranged to determine the feasibility of commercial sales of this concentrated product.[66]

The exclusive sales arrangement with Associated Cooperatives was undisturbed until 1945, when several of its member cooperatives in midwestern states began questioning whether Associated was a suitable organization to best serve their needs. They pointed out that the membership of Associated was far from homogenous; that it included purchasing cooperatives and marketing organizations; that some members were large federations serving one or several states while others were local in scope, serving only a few countries. Of more importance, many in this group were more interested in obtaining TVA-produced superphosphate than ammonium nitrate, which was then the principal product distributed by Associated.

A meeting called by the Illinois Farm Supply Company in Chicago on September 7, 1945, brought together eight regional cooperative members of Associated, along with representatives from the American Farm Bureau Federation, primarily to give attention to the experimental distribution of TVA concentrated superphosphate. The meeting reflected the growing dissatisfaction of midwestern cooperatives with Associated as an organization to represent their interests, and a committee of nine was appointed "to pursue the possibility of attaining triple superphosphate from the industry and from TVA."

After considering whether the committee should look forward to the creation of a corporation to represent its needs, it decided to continue operating as a committee, separate and apart from Associated. However, it was agreed that "if, so, when the small working committee deem a corporation to be advisable, the counsel of Donald Kirkpatrick [General Counsel of the American Farm Bureau Federation] should be secured for the incorporation of the needed corporate entity."[67]

On September 20, G. W. Bunting, as secretary of the committee set-up at the September 7 meeting, wrote to J. C. McAmis, Director of the TVA's Division of Agricultural Relations, as follows:

> You will note by the attached copy of minutes that a meeting was held on September 7 . . . in view of setting in motion more specific action to meet our phosphate requirements.
> I wish to call to your particular attention, the reaction of this group toward future handling of triple superphosphate through Associated Cooperatives. It doesn't appear that Associated Cooperatives, as now constituted, is the type of corporation needed to serve state and regional cooperatives in the Mississippi Valley. For example, many members of Associated Cooperatives are locals in character, or comparable to the member companies [of the associations] that attended our meeting of September 7th . . . The service requirements from a corporation to serve the Mississippi Valley area are quite different, as the state and regional companies have their own sales and service organizations, traffic departments, accounting and auditing services, and other essential functions necessary to carry on a business through a system of county or local distributing units.[68]

The position taken by the Midwestern Cooperatives was vigorously protested by E. P. Garrett, President of Associated Cooperatives,[69] but the die was cast and the midwestern group continued to develop plans for their own central organization. On October 26, 1945, three top officials of the TVA—David E. Lilienthal, Chairman of the TVA Board of Directors; Neil Bass, Chief Conservation Engineer; and J. C. McAmis, Director of the Division of Agricultural Relations—met with officials of the midwestern associations. A report of that meeting indicates that the conference "considered the type of cooperative organization that might be set up on a national scale to fulfill the objectives of the cooperatives, with TVA phosphate plants as the source of supply of concentrated materials . . . " The report continued:

> It was proposed that the cooperatives now organized on a state basis form a central farmers' fertilizer organization, the membership of which would be

made up of the state-wide cooperatives in Illinois, Indiana, Ohio, etc., and any others that could qualify for membership . . . The central organization would establish a reciprocal membership with Associated Cooperatives, Inc. It is anticipated that TVA would continue its contract with Associated for the distribution of nitrogen products but that TVA and the central organization would contract for phosphatic material for distribution.[70]

The report of this conference indicates that TVA was then giving encouragement to the formation of a central organization designed to handle TVA-produced phosphate separate from Associated Cooperatives, Inc., although it hoped that this would not disturb its relations with Associated in the distribution of ammonium nitrate.[71]

On February 6, 1946, the problem was settled when the TVA Board approved a memorandum of understanding and a fertilizer distribution contract with the Central Farmers Fertilizer Committee, and the incorporation of the Central Farmers Fertilizer Company followed immediately thereafter.[72]

In this way the Central Farmers Fertilizer Company separated from Associated Cooperatives in early 1946 to eventually become a national all-purpose fertilizer producing organization serving 17 regional purchasing association members in the United States and 1 in Canada.[73]

According to G. W. Bunting, who was the chief protagonist in the formation of Central Farmers Fertilizer Company, and its first General Manager, "the prime mover back of Central Farmers was Donald Kirkpatrick," General Counsel of the American Farm Bureau Federation. Bunting also points out that "the actual incorporation of Central Farmers on February 6, 1946, was hastened by the need for a corporate entity to obtain phosphate fertilizer from the TVA . . . Associated was a widespread organization—a mile wide and an inch thick. The co-ops in the Midwest wanted an organization they could control—and they had a basis for it."[74]

It should also be noted that back of TVA's favorable attitude toward the establishment of Central Farmers Fertilizer Company was "TVA's extreme interest in proposed legislation to establish a national fertilizer policy and program. This proposed legislation, developed in collaboration with TVA, was sponsored by the American Farm Bureau Federation, and the support of the midwestern cooperatives was very much desired by TVA."[75] Attention will be given to the American Farm Bureau's national fertilizer program in the next volume of this history.

Service Cooperatives Meet Wartime Problems

Service-type cooperatives were handicapped during the war by the problems of personnel shortage, lack of essential materials, and government controls. In the face of such problems, the war record of cooperatives providing such services as insurance protection, health care, irrigation, transportation, and artificial insemination was generally good. However, progress in cooperative housing practically stood still until controls over building materials were lifted in 1945.

Insurance. The farm fire insurance mutuals continued to provide valuable services during the war, although they did not expand in number. While several of the farmers' mutual automobile insurance companies contracted, the State Farm Mutual Automobile Insurance Company of Bloomington, Illinois, continued its rapid growth. At the start of 1941 it had 649,000 policies in force. By the end of 1944 it had reached the goal of having 1 million policies in force.[76]

The Farm Bureau Mutual Automobile Insurance Company of Columbus, Ohio, also continued its expansion. It moved into Connecticut in 1941, into Rhode Island in 1942, and into South Carolina in 1943. By 1945 it operated in 12 states and the District of Columbia. It then had 541,000 policies in force and its admitted assets were nearly $9 million, compared to only 330,000 policies in force and admitted assets of $7 million in 1940.[77]

The fire and automobile insurance companies of the Illinois Agricultural Association, now operating under the name Country Mutual Insurance Company, also made a good record during the war. By 1945 their admitted assets had grown to $9.6 million, compared with $5.3 million in 1941.

Only one state farm bureau mutual automobile insurance association was formed during the war years, the Kentucky Farm Bureau Mutual Insurance Company, which was established in 1943.

Health associations. The Group Health Association of Washington, D.C., was well established by 1941. During the next few years it was handicappd by the loss of medical staff members to the army and by the transfer from Washington of several government agencies with many group health members. However, by the close of 1942, it had 3,375 members and some 8,332 members of families were served. This was a gain in members of 6 per cent over 1941. As of February 1945, GHA had 3,209 members and 8,586 were served. The GHA was ready for growth under more normal conditions as the war closed.[78]

Another Cooperative Health Association that progressed during the war was the Group Health Mutual and its companion the Group Health Association of St. Paul, Minnesota. These organizations were started in 1938 by a few credit unions and a number of cooperative employees. The

Group Health Association was set up as an insurance association because of legal problems in providing full medical care service. Under the dual structure Group Health Mutual was the business organization. However, each policy holder also had to belong to Group Health Association and pay dues for educational work. After a slow beginning, Group Health Mutual and Group Health Association began to enroll the members of cooperative creameries under a check-off plan by which dues were paid from milk checks. From then on, there was a definite acceleration in the rate of growth, so that by the end of 1945, there were over 45,000 persons covered. The assets then amounted to over $100,000 and the surplus to nearly $70,000. Group Health Mutual provided members the kind of protection they desired, ranging from hospital care for the family to complete preventative and clinical service for the family. In 1945 the association was serving groups of employees in labor unions, cooperatives, credit unions, churches, fraternal societies, municipal bodies, and professional groups.[79]

Some progress was made by cooperative rural hospital and health associations following the lead of the Farmers Union Cooperative Hospital in Elk City, Oklahoma. During the five-year period, 1940-1944, nine associations were incorporated. The passage of a permissive law by Texas in 1945 gave definite encouragement to the formation of such associations, and 14 were established by the end of the year.[80]

Housing cooperatives. Cooperative housing practically stood still during the war because of the controls on building construction materials. As Florence Parker said: "With the entrance of this country into the war, all civilian housing except that carried on by the Federal Government ceased."[81] During the war period, the New York City housing cooperatives sponsored by the Amalgamated Clothing Workers of America functioned efficiently but were unable to grow. The removal of controls on October 1945 opened the doors for renewed advancement.

Frozen food lockers. There were about 440 frozen food locker cooperatives in 1940. The number grew to 700 by the end of 1945. In many communities the locker cooperatives provided valuable meat processing or other services for local consumers.[82]

Dairy breeding cooperatives. As of January 1941 there were 37 artificial insemination associations in 16 states. By the end of 1945 there were 336 associations in 29 states. In January 1941 there were 5,997 members in such associations which were serving some 70,751 listed cows. By the end of 1945 there were 73,293 members and the associations were serving 579,477 listed cows. This remarkable growth was caused by pressure for greater milk production at lower cost.[83]

Irrigation associations. There was little increase in mutual irrigation companies during the war, but they performed an essential service under difficult conditions due to personnel shortages and difficulties in obtaining materials for upkeep. In Southern California the mutual water companies joined with municipal and other water concerns to arrange interconnecting pipes for disaster emergencies.[84]

Transportation cooperatives. The need for transportation economies and effective service gave encouragement to the rise of transportation cooperatives, especially for hauling livestock and other farm products. Most of these associations were local in character, designed for the shipment of products to terminal markets. The Farmers Cooperative Trucking Association of Wadena, Minnesota—a federation of local shipping associations—grew rapidly during the war years. Its volume of business grew from $397,605 in 1942 to $7,801,375 in 1945. In the latter year the federation took the name "Northern Cooperatives, Inc.," to reflect its increasing marketing and purchasing services.[85]

The National Tax Equality Association
Attack on Cooperatives

There was a long record of business opposition to cooperatives before World War II which was expressed by attacks on most organizations of a cooperative character. Such opposition was one of the forces that led to the establishment of the National Cooperative Council in 1929, as pointed out in Chapter V. During the 1930's, the growth of farmers' purchasing associations was bitterly opposed by trade organizations, representing dealers in petroleums, hardware, feed, and other farm supplies.

The coming of World War II intensified this opposition because of the steep increase in federal income tax rates. Although the income tax exemption status accorded farmer cooperatives had long been resented by competitive business interests, the amount of the exemption was not impressive until income tax rates began to rise rapidly as the nation geared itself for war.[86]

This situation gave friends of farmer cooperatives some concern. In addressing the American Institute of Cooperation in January 1942, Dr. A. G. Black, Governor of the Farm Credit Administration said:

> In the cooperative movement as a whole there are some things that should give everyone who is working with it more or less objectivity, and from an over-all point of view, some concern. Farmer cooperatives, as such, have been

given by the people, through their Congress, some very important advantages—advantages not accorded to privately or corporately owned business. If no changes are made in laws relating to these advantages, they are going to bulk larger and larger. For example, tax exemption under certain conditions, if there is no change, will result in a tremendous advantage to the cooperative form of organization. As taxes on private and corporate business increase, that advantage to cooperatives becomes greater. Under conditions of low taxes, of course, it is of some advantage, but when taxes are absorbing a large part of the earnings of private business, the cooperative form of business really provides an enormous advantage.[87]

Governor Black's frank expression of his views was resented at the time by many cooperative leaders, but his statement put cooperatives on their guard that they would have to defend the tax status accorded them. One who had been alert to the growing tax problem of cooperatives was Dr. E. A. Stokdyk, President of the Berkeley Bank for Cooperatives. In a letter written on July 24, 1941, he had said: "On the tax situation, I do not agree with the idea that it is best to let 'sleeping dogs lie.' We have seen too much of that and know what the problems are if a cooperative fails to make proper returns. I would by all means advise cooperatives to familiarize themselves with what is what, file the proper returns, and pay the taxes . . . "[88]

The opposition to alleged favoritism for cooperatives under the tax statutes was aggravated by the expansion of the Consumers Cooperative Association into petroleum refining in 1939. Effectively using the slogan, "Factories Are Free," Howard A. Cowden, General Manager of the CCA, urged cooperatives to withhold the payment of patronage refunds so as to raise money for manufacturing plants which would pay for themselves in a short period. The experience of the CCA in paying off one-third of the cost of its Phillipsburg refinery during its first year of operation, 1940-41, seemed to justify the slogan as far as cooperatives were concerned.[89]

On May 1, 1943, the situation came to a head when the Farmers' Union Grain Terminal Association of St. Paul, Minnesota, purchased the 57-year-old St. Anthony and Dakota Elevator Company with 135 elevators and 38 lumber yards and converted them to cooperative operations. "This shocked the private grain trade" into joining with other farm cooperative competitors to form an organization named the National Tax Equality Association headed by Ben C. McCabe, President of the International Elevator Company, as its president.[90]

The National Tax Equality Association was no "fly by night" organization, and this soon became apparent to the cooperatives. "Its founders were a group of businessmen who earlier had met under such names as the Association for the Preservation of Private Enterprise and the Central Coordinating Group, Inc." Its officers represented important grain lumber, coal, and similar trade interests. Its directors included a large number of grain dealers, feed dealers, coal dealers, farm and implement dealers, lumber and petroleum organizations, cotton ginners, retail merchants, and representatives of small business organizations. Its secretary was Vernon Scott, a paid organizer and money raiser. Its general manager was Loring A. Schuler, an experienced writer and publicist who had been editor of the *Country Gentleman* and *Ladies Home Journal*.[91]

The NTEA described itself in its printed literature as "a coordinating and service organization doing research in the whole field of taxation and related subjects in the interest of protecting independent American enterprise." In its prospectus the NTEA declared that it was prepared to disseminate "printed research matter . . . articles to trade papers, periodicals and newspapers bearing on the problems of unequal taxation," to offer "programs by speakers representing the Association, appearing before public, civic and other organizations," and to undertake "radio programs."[92]

The NTEA sprang into action almost overnight and it was soon reputed to have a budget of half a million dollars for use in fighting cooperatives. Its "psychological timing" was excellent, for in 1943 almost everyone agreed that there was need for greater federal revenue, and there was a loud clamor for greater government economy. The charge of the NTEA that cooperatives were "tax dodgers" was especially effective in inflaming people against cooperatives as being unpatriotic.

The cooperatives could not ignore this attack which they believed was designed to unfairly discredit cooperatives with the public. On October 28, 1943, Howard Cowden, General Manager of the CCA, invited a number of cooperative leaders to a conference in Chicago on November 9 "to devise ways and means of combatting the nationwide fight now developing against cooperatives." At this meeting a committee of nine was set up "to carry on the fight to preserve the present income tax status of cooperatives."[93] The cooperative leaders met again in May 1944 and formed the National Conference of Cooperatives with Clark L. Brody, Manager of the Michigan Farm Bureau Service as Chairman, "to combat and defeat" attacks made on cooperatives by the National Tax Equality Association. This conference was incorporated as the National Association of Cooperatives on June 28, and with Wayne Newton as Executive Secretary, a vigorous campaign was soon underway to offset the anticooperative program of the NTEA. In several states associations of cooperatives were formed to operate more effectively at the local and state level. The National Association of Cooperatives was set up as a special purpose organization independently of the National Council of

Farmer Cooperatives because it was believed by its organizers that the urgency of the problem required a hard hitting program devoted to the one objective of protecting the income tax status of the cooperatives.

However, the National Council of Farmer Cooperatives fully recognized the injurious effects of the NTEA's propaganda campaign when it held its annual meeting in January 1944. To counter the attack the Council in a resolution of its delegate body declared:

> The National Council of Farmer Cooperatives is aware of attacks that have been and are being made on farmer cooperative enterprises. Some of these attacks are local, others are national in scope. They are sponsored by interests hostile to farmer cooperatives and these interests often enlist the support of others who are misinformed as to the character, purpose and functioning of farmer-owned and controlled cooperative associations.
> This delegate body believes that such attacks should be vigorously resisted by the Council whenever they occur, and further, that the Council should assume the leadership, on behalf of the millions of farmers represented in its membership, in correctly informing the American public as to the vital place of farmer cooperatives in the American system of private enterprise.
> The delegate body directs the officers of the Council, with the approval of the executive committee, to take such steps as they deem appropriate to effectuate this policy.[94]

To partially implement this general resolution, the delegate body authorized the executive committee to employ a competent person to make a survey of public relations activities of farmer cooperatives, who was to report his findings and recommendations to the executive committee, which was, in turn, to appoint a committee to supervise the Council's program of public relations.[95]

While the Council's executive committee was proceeding under these instructions, the officers of the Council were actively combatting the charges of the NTEA through contacts with representatives of the United States Treasury Department which was undertaking tax studies to determine whether any of the allegations being made against cooperatives could be established in fact. The Council also undertook to gain general acceptance for its position that the income tax treatment of cooperatives was fully justified under the law because of the unique character of farmer cooperatives and their beneficial services to farmers and the public. The Council also endeavored to make clear to all that only farmer cooperatives which *could meet stipulated requirements* of the Bureau of Internal Revenue were exempted from the paying of Federal Income Tax. To establish this fact officially the Council requested the Cooperative Research and Service Division of the Farm Credit Administration to provide a statement on the requirements that farmer cooperatives had to meet in order to qualify for exemption. This statement, concurred in by officials of the Bureau of Internal Revenue, was issued in October 1944 under the title "Farmers' Cooperatives and the Federal Income Tax Statutes."[96]

Furthermore, the Council endeavored to establish with all reasonable people, its position, accepted by the courts, that the payment of patronage refunds by farmer cooperatives was legally unassailable in that they represented a pre-existing contract made between the cooperative and the patron requiring the return of such savings to those who patronized the cooperative. This privilege is open to any business, whether cooperative or not, making such distributions to its customers under conditions set forth by the Commissioner of Internal Revenue and the courts.[97]

In view of the allegations made by the NTEA that farmer cooperatives were escaping the payment of income tax, Congress, in the Revenue Act of 1943, enacted on February 25, 1944, required exempt agricultural marketing and purchasing associations to file annual information returns. Following the passage of this act the Treasury Department developed Form 990 to obtain the required information. To be of all possible assistance in the development of Form 990, the Cooperative Research and Service Division of the Farm Credit Administration provided suggestions in a report issued on July 12, 1944, and when Form 990 was ready for use, the Division also prepared suggestions to help farmer cooperatives fully comply with its requirements. While Form 990 was being designed for use, the National Council of Farmer Cooperatives worked closely with the Treasury Department so that the form would be as practicable as possible.[98]

The Revitalization of the American Institute of Cooperation

While Form 990 was being readied for use by the Treasury Department, the executive committee of the National Council gave its attention to the directive of its delegate body to proceed with the formulation of a public relations program. Within a month Dr. Raymond W. Miller, a well-known authority on public relations problems in agriculture, was employed to make the authorized survey, and this was completed and presented to the Council's directors at a special meeting held in Cleveland, Ohio, during the first week of July in 1944.[99]

Miller's report disclosed a lack of understanding of cooperative principles even by farmer members as well as by the general public. According to John H. Davis, the Council's Executive Secretary, the report indicated a "dire need for a program to tell the truth about cooperatives."

Miller's major recommendation was that the American Institute of Cooperation—which had been dormant during the war—be reactivated on a more aggressive basis. The Council urged the trustees of the Institute to undertake this work of reorganization, and following the Cleveland meeting, plans were made for revamping the Institute by a group representing both the National Council and the Institute, which were approved at a meeting in Chicago in September.

At that time Miller agreed to accept the job of being President of the reorganized Institute, and it was agreed that W. I. Myers, Dean of the College of Agriculture of Cornell University, would serve as Chairman of the Institute's Board of Trustees.

Plans for getting the enlarged program of the reorganized AIC underway were completed at a meeting of Council and Institute representatives at Chicago in January 1945, but the formal reorganization did not take place until new headquarters were established in Philadelphia[100] where the American Institute of Co-operation was reincorporated under the laws of the Commonwealth of Pennsylvania on March 13, 1945. At the reorganization meeting the following day, 50 trustees were elected as the governing body, and Miller's appointment of 5 men to direct individual activities was confirmed. The new staff consisted of Miller as President; Frank W. Cyr, Consultant on Rural Education; A. Ladru Jensen, Consultant on Cooperative Law; William A. Nielander, Director of Business Administration; D. L. MacDonald, Director of Vocational Education; and Thomas L. Cleary, Editorial Director. A number of advisory committees were set up to help plan operating programs: Extension Education, E. A. Stokdyk (Chairman); Research, Ezra T. Benson (Chairman); Vocational Education, Arthur K. Getman (Chairman).

Although it was impossible to hold a summer session of the Institute in 1945, it was decided to prepare a volume of pertinent articles contributed by assigned writers. The planning of this volume was under the direction of Asher Hobson of the University of Wisconsin. It was designed primarily to record the cooperative developments during the war years, "before memories fade," and it performed this task in a creditable manner with the issuance of *American Cooperation*, 1942-45, late in 1945.[101]

The "Cooperative Clinics." The charge of the NTEA that farmer cooperatives were enjoying unfair income tax treatment encouraged many cooperatives to place their houses in order as far as income tax regulations were concerned. Many cooperatives had given little attention to income tax matters prior to the NTEA attack, and they were not fully aware of their rights and responsibilities. One who had early foreseen the growing importance of this problem, as we noted earlier in this chapter, was Dr. E. A. Stokdyk, President of the Berkeley Bank for Cooperatives. In the spring of 1945 he had asked W. L. Bradley—whose accounting firm specialized in auditing and tax problems of cooperatives—to participate in a series of meetings being held by the Berkeley Bank with cooperative managers and directors. Bradley informed Miller of the meetings to be held, and Miller became immediately interested, for, as President of the American Institute of Cooperation, he was casting about for some means of reaching cooperative managers and directors. At Bradley's suggestion, he and Miller jointly telephoned Stokdyk who proposed that they combine forces and hold a series of "cooperative clinics" in California that might prove whether the idea was suitable for Institute sponsorship on a national basis. The California clinics proved so popular that they were soon organized on a formal basis and carried to all parts of the United States.[102]

These clinics were jointly sponsored by the American Institute of Cooperation, the American Institute of Accountants—of which Bradley was Chairman of its cooperative committee—and the Farm Credit Administration. In some instances, the state cooperative councils and National Society of Accountants for Cooperatives joined in their support. The clinics were usually held as one-day meetings in centers accessible to a large number of cooperatives. They featured consideration of tax, business, and public relations problems of cooperatives. After introductory talks, questions were answered by a three-man panel—usually consisting of Miller, for questions relating to public relations; Bradley, for questions relating to accounting and Federal income taxes; and Kelsey B. Gardner, in charge of the Business Administration Section of the Cooperative Research and Service Division, for questions concerning organization, requirements of farmer cooperatives under the Internal Revenue Code, and management.[103] L. S. Hulbert of the legal staff of the Farm Credit Administration and other Farm Credit Administration employees also were members of the "faculty" in many of the clinics. Before the series of clinics had run its course during the next two years, about 75 were held for some 10,000 participants. Many of those in attendance were representatives of the Banks for Cooperatives, college and extension personnel, vocational teachers, and other government representatives. These clinics performed a valuable function in helping the cooperatives improve their organization and operating methods as well as in helping them to become better informed on how to meet income tax and public relations responsibilities.

The Cooperative League Broadens Its Base

During the New Deal years the Cooperative League had become an educational and promotional federation for regional purchasing associations and consumers' cooperative wholesales who had become its principal supporting member organizations. Many of these organizations were also members of National Cooperatives, Inc., a national buying federation. The offices of the League and of the National Cooperatives were closely related, and by 1940 meetings of their Boards of Directors were generally held on successive days at the same location.

The League's Executive Secretary, E. R. Bowen, had urged, since 1938, closer coordination of the work of the League and National, and, with the retirement of Dr. James Peter Warbasse as President of the League in the fall of 1941, and his replacement as President by Murray D. Lincoln, a dynamic cooperative executive and farm organization leader, the League proceeded to move energetically to gain the support of regional farm supply purchasing cooperatives who had held back from association with the League because of their objections to the views espoused by Dr. Warbasse (see Chapter XVIII). The anticipated selection of H. E. Babcock, former General Manager of the GLF, as President of the National Council of Farmer Cooperatives in early 1942 made the time favorable for rapprochement,[104] and Babcock agreed to meet with Lincoln for the purpose of thrashing out relationship problems at a conference to be held the day preceding the meetings of the American Institute of Cooperation at Atlanta, Georgia, in January 1942.

At this conference, attended by a wide spectrum of cooperative leaders, Lincoln called for all purchasing cooperatives—rural and urban—to work together. However, no agreement was reached other than on principles. It was agreed that "cooperative organizations should be available to both producers and consumers" and that "those present believed in the right, ability, duty and necessity of common people to work out their destiny on a voluntary basis." This premise, it was agreed, "calls for the increased use of the mechanism of cooperative action." The group decided: "Producer and consumer cooperatives have many interests in common, the only difference being in the point of interest of their members. Cooperatives must be recognized as an effective instrumentality available to both producers and consumers."[105]

When this meeting was held in Atlanta, the nation was already at war, and the interests of cooperatives were becoming closely meshed with the war effort. The large agricultural purchasing regionals that were heavy financial supporters of the League soon were devoting their energies to meeting a growing demand for their services brought on by war needs. As they were primarily agricultural organizations, they were under pressure to supply their members with supplies for agricultural production, and they had little time for ideology. On the other hand the regional wholesale organizations in the League that distributed mostly consumer goods—mainly, groceries—to consumer cooperative stores in urban communities were relatively weak as compared with the chain store systems. Confronted by rationing and war-induced problems, such consumer stores found it hard to grow and expand. The progress of the Cooperative League as an organization, however, was not adversely affected by the problems of its consumer cooperative member organizations, for its major supporting members were the agricultural purchasing associations that were expanding rapidly to meet war conditions.

The war also changed the psychology of those who were strong supporters of the League. Hitler's actions made people more concerned with survival than with idealistic programs for reform of the economic system. Concern about the primacy of the consumer seemed less important under war conditions than personal hardships, casualties, and government controls.

Under these conditions, the League was able to broaden its services, primarily because of the growing strength of its principal member associations whose dues to the League automatically expanded with their larger volumes of business. By September 1942, the work of the League had grown to the extent that the Executive Secretary had assistant secretaries for publicity, legislation, education, and recreation activities.

The 13th Congress of the Cooperative League, held in Minneapolis in September 1942, reflected the League's change in philosophy since the preceding Congress held in 1940. It now centered attention on practical problems, and it was concerned already with the necessity of planning for postwar development. Committees were authorized to draw up five-year programs for cooperative expansion. In connection with the Congress the League was able to gain considerable publicity through coast-to-coast radio broadcasts over Mutual, Columbia, and Canadian networks. However, during the Congress sessions, two major networks—the National Broadcasting Company and the Columbia Broadcasting System—refused to sell time for the League's radio program "Here Is Tomorrow"—on any of the stations owned by those two networks. Wallace J. Campbell, who was in charge of the League's publicity, later said: "The resulting struggle for equal rights on the air brought the co-ops a million dollar's worth of free publicity before the networks capitulated in the middle of December 1942." The League's transcribed series "Here Is Tomorrow" went on the air in February 1943 for 10 weeks over 36 stations, and the thousands of requests for further information indicated to the League that the broadcasts reached "hundreds of thousands, if not many millions, of listeners." This program was financed largely by 20,000 people who contributed $1 each.[106]

The General Secretary of the Cooperative League was well pleased with the accomplishments of "the consumers' cooperative movement" during 1943. In fact, in his annual report for 1943 he said: *No previous year was at all comparable in results.* Among the accomplishments that he stressed were:

> . . . the incorporation of the National Cooperative Finance Association which was to provide a means of mobilizing cooperative savings for cooperative development;
> . . . the first official meeting of representatives of the Credit Union National Association and the Cooperative League which inaugurated closer relationships;
> . . . the beginnings of manufacturing operations by National Cooperatives, Inc., which had begun to show substantial savings;
> . . . the inception of joint staff meetings of the League and National Cooperatives;
> . . . the increasing number of regional and local cooperatives that were employing fulltime educational directors;
> . . . the completion of five new cooperative motion pictures;
> . . . the success of the League's national radio program;
> . . . the growing interest in cooperative recreation—which Bowen called "a cornerstone of cooperation";
> . . . the widespread interest in cooperative information as evidenced by a sale of League publications of nearly $18,000, the largest sale since 1936.

Bowen reported that 91 cooperative stores had been organized since Pearl Harbor, which indicated to him that there was "a significant trend into household goods." He also expressed the hope that a central committee of cooperatives might be set up to include representatives of all national cooperative organizations.[107]

As the regional members of the Cooperative League grew as business organizations, they questioned the value of the League's national magazine, *Consumers' Cooperation,* with its heavy emphasis on cooperative ideology. During 1943 the League Directors decided to discontinue the magazine at the end of the year and replace it with a new expository journal under a well-qualified editor, who would also help the League on other publicity problems.[108] The new magazine was to be called "CO-OP," and it was to be concerned with cooperative operating problems and was to provide information of interest to employees and other workers in the consumer cooperative movement on "what, when, and how to do." In the last issue of *Consumers Cooperation* for December 1943, Gilman

Calkins, the incoming editor, set forth the "editorial emphasis" for *CO-OP* magazine as follows:

> It is not as important to analyze the psychological and sociological by-products of a discussion group or play experience as to tell how to arrange and conduct a proper calendar of such affairs and make them lead to the strengthening and expansion of existing co-ops and aid in the formation of new ones. It is not so important to explain the relationship of cooperative food store service to the parable of Jesus and the loaves and fishes as it is to describe proper ways for buying and stocking and displaying loaves and fishes in the co-op store, and get every possible Mrs. Consumer to buy and buy—and become an owner, too.[109]

During 1943 the leaders in the Cooperative League had become greatly concerned with the problem of helping people in the war-ravaged countries of Europe during and after the war. To further consider this problem the League organized the International Cooperative Reconstruction Conference, which was held in Washington, D.C., on January 19 and 20, 1944. Its purpose was "to focus attention on the use of the cooperatives in the United States as agents for supplying or transmitting relief commodities to the people of the suffering countries," and it was attended by representatives of 23 nations, together with the directors of the Cooperative League and of National Cooperatives.[110]

The League followed up this conference in the autumn by launching a drive for a Freedom Fund which netted $93,000, and from it assistance was provided to distressed people in 16 countries. In behalf of the Consumers Cooperative Association, Howard Cowden contributed $10,000 to start this fund. The Freedom Fund was to be the germ of CARE, jointly organized in 1945 by a number of agencies engaged in relief activities. This unique cooperative organization which was established to send relief packages to war-torn Europe was largely designed by Dr. Lincoln Clark, Cooperative Specialist for the United Nations Relief and Rehabilitation Administration, and Wallace J. Campbell, Secretary of the Cooperative League's International Committee. Clark and Campbell chose the name CARE as an acrostic for the full name of the organization—Cooperative for American Remittances to Europe. CARE was organized in New York City on November 28, 1945, with Murray D. Lincoln, President; Donald Nelson as General Manager; and Campbell, Secretary. The official name of CARE was later changed to Cooperative for American Relief Everywhere to reflect the worldwide character of its operations. CARE has been a successful cooperative organization from its beginning, and it continues its humanitarian services to the present day.[111]

Elaborate plans were made for the Fourteenth Biennial Congress of the Cooperative League, which was held in Chicago, October 8-13, 1944. It was publicized as "The Centennial Cooperative Congress" in that it commemorated the 100th birthday of the Rochdale Society of Equitable Pioneers.

In his opening address entitled "People Keep Moving," Murray D. Lincoln, President of the League, saw an increasing interest on the part of American citizens in cooperative activity. He called attention to many favorable developments, such as the entrance of National Cooperatives into manufacturing, but he was concerned about the slow progress being made by urban consumer cooperatives. He said: "However strong our rural cooperatives may become, we can never have an effective cooperative movement in America, until we have blanketed the cities with consumer cooperatives." Lincoln maintained that cooperatives stood on the threshold of their greatest challenge but he did not believe that "cooperation in America will play its requisite role unless it pushes forward as a strong and integrated national movement."

The most important question before the Congress was the decision as to what should be done to improve national coordination, a thing Bowen had been urging for several years. Prior to the conference, Bowen had developed a plan for coordination which was approved by the directors in principle for presentation to the delegate body for action.[112]

After considerable discussion the delegates passed the following resolution on "National Unity of the Cooperative Movement."

> *Whereas,* the dominant pattern of development of the cooperative movement locally and regionally in America has been to unite the distributive and educational functions in a single organization, and
>
> *Whereas,* our movement has several national and semi-national cooperative organizations serving the educational, promotional, legislative, research, manufacturing and other needs of our regional and local cooperatives, and
>
> *Whereas,* the movement is rapidly acquiring productive and processing units, mostly on a regional basis, not too well coordinated nationally, and
>
> *Whereas,* the conditions before us in the immediate future demand that we consolidate our position and place all our resources at one another's disposal if we are to build a strong and unified cooperative sector in our national economy.
>
> BE IT RESOLVED that we, delegates for the most part from organizations which are members both of the Cooperative League of USA and of National Cooperatives, Inc., do hereby instruct the Board of Directors of the Cooperative League to work with the Board and membership of National Cooperatives, Inc., *in order to merge these organizations into one strong national cooperative association* (Emphasis added).
>
> AND BE IT FURTHER RESOLVED that this national cooperative organization be supported by revenue from business patronage and sufficient dues for a budget of not less than $100,000 a year in order that adequate staff and personnel be employed to do this work that needs to be done; in particular:

That the unorganized areas of the United States be motivated and stimulated to organize on a cooperative basis;

That religious, labor, educational, and many other organized groups which have shown a sincere interest in the democratic and self-help features of cooperatives be more adequately serviced; and

That additional services be provided, especially in the fields of education and publicity, business research and statistics, personnel training, legislation, architecture and design, credit and finance, insurance, health, housing, burial services, and movie production.

IT WAS FURTHER RESOLVED: That the question of a plan of a united cooperative movement be referred to the Board of Directors of The Cooperative League of U.S.A., and National Cooperatives, Inc., for their first and immediate study; That, when a plan has been developed, the same to be submitted for study to all the members of both CLUSA and National Cooperatives, Inc., and, That, a special joint Congress be called of the delegates from both organizations to consider the plan *within a year*.[113]

Important resolutions were also passed to strengthen the work of the Cooperative League's Committee on International Cooperative Reconstruction so as to "give the movement an important role in postwar relief and reconstruction," and gain more generous support for the League's Freedom Fund so "that we may carry out internationally what we have always believed to be the soundest of social action principles, namely, helping people to help themselves."

The other resolutions passed by the Congress reflected the broadening interests of the League in labor unions, in campus cooperatives, in the work of the TVA and REA relating to cooperatives, in cooperative finance, cooperative insurance, credit unions and cooperative health associations, in cooperative employees, and in taxation relating to cooperatives.

Immediately after the Congress, the League and National Cooperatives set up the committee called for on national unity for the consumers' cooperative movement, and, after several meetings in 1945, the job of working up a report was entrusted to a committee comprised of staff members of the League and National Cooperatives. This committee completed its report in 1945, but it was not officially presented to a joint meeting of the Directors of the League and National Cooperatives until January 1946. This report declared: "The time for action is here." Under the plan proposed, there would be one national consumers' organization with one Board of Directors. In anticipation of full coordination, the report included a Joint Annual Report for the League, National Cooperatives, and National Finance Association, as if they were already operating as one body. In 1945 National Cooperatives was already performing many functions in behalf of the League, and it was anticipated that complete unification lay ahead. How the report was received and then modified before it was accepted by the Congress of the League in the autumn of

1946 will be examined in the next volume of this history.

As 1945 ended the Cooperative League and National Cooperatives were harmonizing their activities, and the League was working closely with the Credit Union National Association and the newly formed National Rural Electric Cooperative Association. It was also encouraging the formation of national associations for promoting cooperative health, housing, and other kinds of cooperative activity.

Summary

In this chapter attention has been directed to a number of developments that extended and intensified cooperative enterprise during the war years. The following chapter will examine certain general problems confronting cooperatives in 1945 and appraise progress made by such organizations after 1920.

Chapter XXIV

COOPERATIVE ENTERPRISE AS OF 1945

Two problems dominated the thinking of cooperative leaders in 1945: (1) reverting to a peacetime economy, and (2) meeting the propaganda attack of the National Tax Equality Association.

Postwar Planning

During the war, cooperatives were concerned with the conditions that would confront them when peace returned. Many economists of standing were predicting a serious postwar depression such as followed World War I, while others saw a pent-up demand for commodities and services that would continue boom conditions for several years. This problem as it related to agricultural cooperatives was of much concern to the United States Department of Agriculture,[1] and in 1944 an Inter-Bureau postwar planning committee on agricultural cooperation was set up under the Chairmanship of Harold Hedges, Acting Chief of the Cooperative Research and Service Division of the Farm Credit Administration.[2] The report of this committee, issued in July 1945, held that the fact that farmer cooperatives were weathering the difficult war period without serious setbacks was an indication that they operated "no less efficiently than other types of business." The report maintained that: The opportunities for sound growth and expansion will "depend upon the extent to which cooperatives today consolidate and strengthen their activity within their present field of operation."[3]

It was emphasized by the committee that the "specific objectives of a postwar program for cooperatives should include, among other things, the following: (a) increase the operating efficiency of existing associations in order that they may bring still greater returns to farmers; (b) broaden the services of existing associations in order that they may serve more fully the needs of rural people living in the areas covered by their operations; and (c) extend cooperation into agricultural areas not being reached by existing associations."

Many cooperatives were already deeply involved in postwar planning activities as 1945 began and such work escalated in 1945. In his address as President of the National Council of Farmer Cooperatives at its annual meeting in January 1945, Homer Brinkley said:

> We have made adjustments in our cooperatives to meet the exigencies of the wartime period. We will make those adjustments that are necessary to meet the conditions confronting us in the postwar period. In doing so we must keep our thinking sound and our actions strong and positive, nor must we lose sight of the fact that the very basis of our existence is in the interest of the welfare of farmers as a whole . . . Cooperatives, must, therefore, be considered an important factor in any measures established for the postwar adjustment of agriculture.[4]

By January 1945 a number of the major cooperatives had set up postwar planning committees to study carefully their operations and search out needed improvements in organization and operation. These committees were usually comprised of directors and staff employees but frequently others from agricultural colleges or government were brought in to serve in an advisory capacity.[5] Such postwar planning work by cooperatives was a valuable means of emphasizing needed changes. Many cooperatives became more conscious of their problems and developed ways for meeting them.

The ending of the war in Europe gave special emphasis to the need for prompt action in converting operations to peacetime conditions. Following the defeat of Germany, James A. McConnell, General Manager of the GLF, on June 26 said at its Silver Anniversary Meeting: "We must start planning and thinking now rather than on V.J. Day, to the end that war thinking, planning and action be shed as fast as possible . . . Management must start to deal with war effects now."[6] Shortly after V.J. Day, C. H. Becker, General Manager of the Illinois Farm Supply Company, called attention to the many problems confronting cooperatives now that the war was over. He said: "As our fiscal year was closing [on August 31, 1945] every problem of postwar reconversion was thrown into the hopper. Gasoline rationing evaporated. Supplies of some restricted materials began easing. Price Controls were relaxed. There were strikes, shutdowns, and adjustments of many sorts as reconversion got under way. We were already entering a new era."[7]

Meeting the NTEA Attack

Throughout 1945 cooperatives were busy countering the attack of the

National Tax Equality Association carried on by a barrage of reports, newspaper and magazine articles, radio programs, and talks to civic clubs and business organizations. During the year cooperatives consolidated their forces to repel and refute the insinuations and allegations made by representatives and supporters of the NTEA. They recognized that a long struggle lay ahead before the harm being done in misinforming the public toward cooperatives could be stopped. It was commonly believed by cooperative leaders that anti-cooperative bills would soon be introduced in Congress, and cooperatives got ready to withstand a legislative assault.

A foretaste of what lay ahead came in March when the Small Business Committee of the House of Representatives announced hearings on problems of small business at New York, Springfield (Illinois), St. Louis, Chicago, Cleveland, and Washington, D.C. Anticipating that the opponents of cooperatives would use these meetings as a means of attacking cooperatives, the National Council of Farmer Cooperatives, joined by the National Association of Cooperatives, requested an opportunity to testify should false or misleading information presented about cooperatives call for refutation. Cooperatives in the areas covered by the hearings arranged for statements of the cooperative position. At the end of the series of hearings the testimony of the cooperatives had greatly strengthened their situation, but there was little confidence that this would end the matter.

In several ways the attack of the NTEA had a beneficial influence on cooperative development. It compelled cooperatives to examine more carefully their procedures and responsibilities under the law. It forced them to work together more closely in common defence of their form of organization. It mobilized farmer members in support of their cooperatives. It popularized the cooperative way of doing business. An article on cooperatives published by *Fortune* in August 1945 said: "The net intended effects of the skillful work of the NTEA are likely to be limited: its unintended effects will probably be more important. Already it has driven the various kinds of cooperatives into closer cooperation than if they had been left alone. Already the NTEA seems to be doing more to promote the cooperative movement in the public eye than it has ever been able to do for itself."[8]

Progress in Perspective — A Summing Up

In the Foreword to *The Rise of American Cooperative Enterprise* it was pointed out that the year 1920 "marked the close of the period of establishment and the starting of the modern period of expansion and development." When one compares the status of important aspects of cooperative enterprise in 1945 with its position in 1920 the contrast is striking.

Growth and Expansion

Cooperative development in the United States was largely restricted to agriculture in 1920. At that time farmer cooperatives were doing a total business of about $1 billion, and farmers' investments in their cooperatives amounted to only a few million dollars. By 1945 the volume of cooperative marketing and purchasing business totalled over $5 billion, and farmers' equities in their organizations amounted to $587 million. In 1920 cooperatives were significant only in a few areas of the country. They had spread to all parts of the nation by 1945. While cooperative enterprise was predominantly agricultural in 1920, it had attained much urban significance by 1945 with the growth of credit unions, housing, health, and various kinds of consumers' cooperatives' furnishing goods and services.

Establishment of Legal Position

The legal standing of cooperatives was uncertain in 1920. With the enactment of the Capper-Volstead Act in 1922 cooperative marketing associations were given the green light to develop as strong business organizations. Other legislation—especially the Cooperative Marketing Act of 1926 and the Agricultural Marketing Act of 1929—also strengthened the legal position of cooperatives. Further recognition was gained through the legislation that provided for the AAA, the Farm Credit Administration, the TVA, and the REA. Moreover, court decisions fully established the legality of the cooperative form of business.[9]

Increase in Political Influence

Cooperatives had little political influence in 1920. During the next quarter century they became a strong force in state and national affairs. In 1920 supporting organizations for cooperatives were only beginning to take form. Until then the principal supporting organizations were the National Grange, the National Farmers' Union, and the National Cooperative Milk Producers' Federation. The Cooperative League of the U.S.A. was still embryonic. The situation changed rapidly in 1920 with the formation of the American Farm Bureau Federation designed to bring business methods to agriculture. During the next 25 years a number of supporting organizations came into existence to perform functions essential to cooperative success. Among them were the American Institute of Cooperation, the National Council of Farmer Cooperatives, the National

Federation of Grain Cooperatives, the Credit Union National Association, and the National Rural Electric Cooperative Association. In this period about 25 state cooperative councils were formed to represent the educational, legislative, and other common interests of various kinds of cooperatives in particular states.

Clarification of Cooperative Objectives

The years from 1920 to 1945 saw a much needed clarification of cooperative objectives. From hard experience cooperative leaders came to realize that monopoly control of agricultural products was neither feasible nor desirable. It gradually became apparent that the sound development of cooperative enterprise depended upon the creation of strong business organizations able to effectively represent the economic interests of their members through rendering desired services on a cost of service basis. By 1945 most cooperators were in agreement with the view expressed by Dr. Edwin G. Nourse: *"The place in the nation's business marked out for the agricultural cooperative is primarily that of 'pilot plant' and 'yardstick' operation. Its objective is not to supersede other forms of business but to see that they are kept truly competitive."* He maintained: *"The true place of the cooperative is that of economic architect, not commercial Napoleon."*[10]

Development of Large-Scale Cooperatives

Cooperatives were mostly small local organizations in 1920. There were then less than a score of strong regional cooperative organizations. Most of these were federations of local marketing cooperatives, such as the California Fruit Growers Exchange, although centralized associations covering extensive territories were also growing in importance. We have seen in this volume how regional cooperatives—both of the federated and centralized types—rapidly gained importance in 1920 and continued to expand both in marketing and purchasing. Some of them became multi-purpose organizations as marketing associations set up purchasing departments, and purchasing associations undertook marketing functions. By 1945 the great majority of associations had become regional in character either through federation of local marketing or purchasing cooperatives or through development of centralized cooperatives. Moreover, in several instances regional cooperatives had found it desirable to set up national business organizations to perform additional essential services. Thus by 1945 many cooperatives had achieved a high degree of integration—both horizontally and vertically.[11]

Expansion in Manufacturing and Processing

Cooperative processing operations before 1920 were mostly confined to simple operations, such as manufacture of butter or cheese or drying of fruits. By 1945 cooperative processing and manufacturing had become well established. Many marketing cooperatives were engaged in canning, quick freezing, dehydration, and meat and poultry packing. Many purchasing cooperatives were then operating large feed and fertilizer plants, and a number were firmly established in petroleum refinery operations.

Improvement of Business Administration

With significant exceptions cooperative business methods were generally informal in 1920. A large proportion of the cooperatives then were unincorporated associations, and few managers were well trained or adequately paid. This situation changed markedly by 1945. Then most cooperatives were incorporated, and managers and other employees were better educated and trained and were more adequately compensated for their services. As cooperatives grew in size and in scope and complexity of services, double-entry bookkeeping methods gave way to comprehensive accounting systems, and cooperatives became adept in the performance of such business functions as advertising, selling, merchandising, inventory and credit control, traffic management, and purchasing. One of the outstanding changes during the period was the growing professionalization of management. Cooperatives learned how to departmentalize operations, and great emphasis was placed on management selection and training. By 1945 the business procedures of many cooperatives were comparable with those of other well-established businesses.

Progress in Cooperative Financing

Cooperative financing methods were primitive in 1920 except in a few organizations. By 1945 a significant number of cooperatives had become well-versed in the principles of corporate finance and budgeting and made use of common and preferred stock, bonds, and debentures. In 1920 the revolving fund method of financing was emerging as a unique means by which cooperatives could be permanently supplied with capital by their members in proportion to their use of the cooperative's services. By 1945 this method of financing was widespread and growing in importance.

Research Gains a Foothold

In 1920 research by cooperatives was almost unknown except for the by-products work of the California Fruit Growers' Exchange. As government agencies and land grant colleges demonstrated that scientific study could be applied beneficially to cooperative structural and operating problems, many associations began to employ research techniques to improve their organizations and procedures, as well as their products and supplies handled. By 1945 a significant number of the large marketing and purchasing cooperatives had found it desirable to support their own research departments.[12]

Membership Work Gains Stature

The cooperative association was not well defined and understood as a form of business enterprise in 1920. In ensuing years the importance of the cooperative form of organization became recognized, as its aims and objectives were clarified. Methods were developed to better inform members of their responsibilities in selecting directors. Standards of performance for directors and managerial employees were steadily raised. More use was made of membership agreements to govern relations of members with their cooperatives. Membership consciousness was steadily raised by means of annual meetings, publications, and informative annual reports. As a result of such efforts, members came to look upon their cooperatives as extensions of their own farm enterprises essential to their survival as independent entrepreneurs. By 1945 membership relations work had become an accepted responsibility in most cooperatives, and many employed directors of membership relations.

In 1920 cooperatives relied largely on the loyalty of their members for economic support. It gradually became evident that loyalty called for more than efficient performance of business functions reflected by benefits and savings. It also depended upon members having a full understanding of the aims, procedures, and problems of their associations and of their beneficial influence in the economy. By 1945 workable cooperation had largely replaced idealistic cooperation, although cooperatives in general lost little of their idealism.

Public Relations Work Becomes Important

Few cooperatives had public relations problems as long as they were small. As they grew in importance, they became conscious of the need for public understanding of their objectives and methods. As the article in *Fortune,* mentioned previously, said: "So long as cooperatives were struggling little groups of idealists operating locally in limited fields, American businessmen were no more concerned with them than with obscure religious sects or Utopian farm colonies. But after World War I cooperatives began to grow out of the amateur class. Private business began to realize that cooperators were not long-haired theorists but successful producers and merchants." Before the National Tax Equality Association began to wage all-out war against them cooperatives gave little attention to their public image. The NTEA forced farmer cooperatives to explain their status under the federal income tax laws and regulations so as to make clear why such organizations were essential to agriculture. By 1945 many cooperatives considered public understanding essential to their survival in the American system of free competitive enterprise.

The Years to Come

In this volume we have dealt with the spectacular advance of cooperative enterprise in the United States from 1920 to 1945. Foundations were now laid for the significant achievements that were to come in the dynamic period of national economic and social development that followed World War II. How cooperative enterprise adapted itself to this new situation, and its present day promise, will be the subject matter of *American Cooperative Enterprise in the Modern Era*—the concluding volume of this trilogy.

Notes

NOTES

Chapter I

1. "There is no evidence that the business community, or any considerable part of it, entered the year 1920 with a clear idea of the very grave situation which was immediately ahead." Alexander D. Noyes, *The War Period of American Finance, 1908-1925* (New York: G. P. Putnam's Sons, 1926), p. 328. See Chapter VII, "The Beginning of Deflation."

2. Index numbers of farm prices of 30 commodities (based on 1909-14 as 100) from *Yearbook of the United States Department of Agriculture, 1925*, pp. 1372-1373.

3. See Murray R. Benedict, *Farm Policies in the United States* (New York: The Twentieth Century Fund, 1953), pp. 180-181. See also James H. Shideler, *Farm Crisis, 1920-1923* (Berkeley: University of California Press, 1957), pp. 33-35.

4. For more complete information see O. M. Kile, *The Farm Bureau Through Three Decades* (Baltimore: Waverly Press, 1948), Chapter VII, "The Plunge into Legislative Activities . . . ," pp. 92-99. See also Shideler, *op. cit.*, pp. 68-70.

5. President Wilson had vetoed this measure, which was promptly passed over the veto. Shideler, *op. cit.*, pp. 71-72.

6. According to Alexander D. Noyes: "The farming population's attitude, as the sweeping fall of prices continued in the autumn, was first an expression of incredulity, then of consternation, and next of angry and fruitless rebellion against the situation," *op. cit.*, p. 400.

7. For example, see Boris Emmet and John E. Jeuck, *Catalogues and Counters—A History of Sears, Roebuck and Company* (Chicago: University of Chicago Press, 1950), chapter on "The Debacle of 1921," pp. 196-201.

8. See Joseph G. Knapp, *The Rise of American Cooperative Enterprise: 1620-1920* (Danville, Ill.: The Interstate Printers & Publishers, Inc.), Chapter XV, "The Centralized Commodity Marketing Experiments," pp. 291-304.

9. *Ibid.*, p. 180. See also Joseph G. Knapp, *The Hard Winter Wheat Pools—An Experiment in Agricultural Marketing Integration* (Chicago: University of Chicago Press, 1933), pp. 18-20.

10. (New York: The Macmillan Company, 1929), pp. 43-74. See also Wilson Gee and Edward Allison Terry, *The Cotton Cooperatives in the Southeast* (New York: D. Appleton-Century Company, 1933), pp. 36 ff.

11. Montgomery, *op. cit.*, pp. 46-48.

12. *Ibid.*, p. 49.

13. The plan as presented at the Montgomery convention is given in full by Montgomery, *op. cit.*, pp. 49-69.

14. *Ibid.*, p. 48. For an enlightening brief biography see "Aaron Sapiro: Genius of Farm Cooperative Promotion," by Grace H. Larsen and Henry E. Erdman, *Mississippi Valley Historical Review*, September 1962, pp. 242-268. See also Grace H.

Larsen, "Aaron Sapiro: Cooperative Evangelist" in Joseph G. Knapp and Associates, *Great American Cooperators* (Washington, D.C.: American Institute of Cooperation, 1967), pp. 446-454.

15. For membership of this committee see Montgomery, *op. cit.*, pp. 69-70.

16. *Ibid.*, p. 71.

17. *Ibid.*, p. 74.

18. Gee and Terry, *op. cit.*, p. 41.

19. The dramatic story of the birth and early struggle of the Texas Farm Bureau Cooperative Association is told by Dorothy Scarborough in her romantic novel, *Can't Get a Red Bird* (New York: Harper and Brothers, 1929). The hero was John Carr, who in real life was John T. Orr, the leader in the organization of the Texas Farm Bureau Federation as well as of the cotton marketing association. In the novel, Aaron Aaronson—who, in fact was Aaron Sapiro—is portrayed as he helped form the cooperative association. "He was in his early thirties, tall, dark, slender, his face chiseled with the keen alertness of his Jewish race, his eyes full of dreams and fire, his voice magnetic . . . He was a born orator. To hear him was an experience not to be forgotten . . . He passionately believed in the theory of the cooperative marketing movement as the salvation of the farmer . . . In an address he could marshall facts with irrefutable logic, could kindle his audience to enthusiasm by his flaming speech, could stir them to laughter by his humor, his rapier sarcasm." See pp. 347-369. Dr. O. B. Jesness, who knew Sapiro well, has commented on this quotation as follows: "Aaron could hardly be described as tall. He was no six footer. His voice was not deep. The spell of his speaking, his use of illustrations, his positiveness, etc., captured the audience. In some respects he could be compared with Billy Sunday of other days or Billy Graham of today." Letter to author of December 20, 1970.

20. Kile, *op. cit.*, p. 84.

21. A vivid account of the formation of the Tri-State Association is given by Carl C. Taylor, "The Story and the Lesson of the Tri-State Tobacco Cooperative Association," *American Cooperation, 1933*, pp. 489-521. See also John J. Scanlan and J. M. Tinley, *Business Analysis of the Tobacco Growers' Cooperative Association*, U.S. Department of Agriculture, Circular 100, 1929, pp. 9-19.

22. For a vignette of this prominent cooperative leader in the 1920's see "Robert Worth Bingham—Father of the Bingham Act" by Theodore Saloutus in Joseph G. Knapp and Associates, *op. cit.*, pp. 70-73.

23. For the interesting story of how the Burley Tobacco Growers Cooperative Association came into being, see Verna Elsinger, "The Burley Tobacco Growers Experiment," *American Cooperation*, II, 1928, pp. 509-516. The following sentence is of particular interest: "It was to the dynamic personality of Aaron Sapiro, perhaps as much as to any other single factor, that the rapid and solidly grounded progress of the movement was due. The clear, crisp reasoning with which he was able to meet and master every difficulty, combined with a fiery enthusiasm of spirit and force of personality to move mountains of inertia and opposition," p. 516.

24. See Joseph G. Knapp, *The Rise of American Cooperative Enterprise, 1620-1920, op. cit.*, pp. 208-212.

25. Theodore Saloutos and John D. Hicks, *Agricultural Discontent in the Middle West, 1901-1939* (Madison: University of Wisconsin Press, 1951), p. 255.

26. O. M. Kile, *The Farm Bureau Movement* (New York: The Macmillan Company, 1921), p. 123.

27. *Ibid.*, p. 150.

28. Aaron Sapiro, *Cooperative Marketing*, American Farm Bureau Federation, 1920.

29. Kile, *The Farm Bureau Movement, op. cit.*, pp. 151-152.

Chapter II

1. "Wallace's attitude toward agricultural economics was the principal factor in his decision to accept the post of Secretary of Agriculture in the Harding administration. He saw in the position an opportunity not only to promote farm legislation but to institute the broader program he had been urging in *Wallace's Farmer*. The precipitous decline in prices in 1920 further impressed upon him the need for attacking the economic problems of agriculture." "During his first year in Washington, Wallace concerned himself mainly with laying the groundwork for the implementation of ideas he had worked out as editor." Donald L. Winters, "The Persistence of Progressivism: Henry Cantwell Wallace and the Movement for Agricultural Economics," *Agricultural History*, April 1967, pp. 113-114. For more comprehensive information on Wallace's administration of the Department of Agriculture see Donald L. Winters, *Henry Cantwell Wallace as Secretary of Agriculture* (Urbana: University of Illinois Press, 1970). See especially pp. 109 ff.

2. Hoover expressed his views in a letter to Walter F. Brown, Chairman of the Reorganization Committee, Bureau of Efficiency, October 20, 1921: "It is my view, based upon the history as well as the provisions of the law creating the Department of Commerce, that Congress intended by the act to establish a body to foster commerce in its most comprehensive sense from the viewpoint of industry as a whole, and that at the time, there was no other department occupying the field. Based upon this construction of the law, it will be seen that the functions of the Department of Agriculture should end when production on the farm is complete and movement therefrom starts, and at that point the activities of the Department of Commerce should begin." This letter was not made public until it was reprinted in *Hearings on Agricultural Relief*, Committee on Agriculture, House of Representatives, February 6, 1925, p. 157. In his memoirs published in 1952, Hoover said: " . . . When I took office [as Secretary of Commerce], I stipulated to President Harding that I wanted a free hand to concern myself with the commercial interests of farmers—that is, outside the field of production . . . and I asked him to inform the Secretary of Agriculture to that effect before he took office . . . However, when the Department of Commerce began to be active for the farmers, in promoting exports, and in solving problems of processing and distribution, the Secretary of Agriculture objected, as is the way of all bureaucratic flesh. At once he began to duplicate our work by establishing and expanding the same economic activities." There was no love lost between Hoover and Wallace for both were ambitious and aggressive. To Hoover, Wallace was "a dour Scotsman with a temperament inherited from some ancestor who had been touched by exposure to infant damnation and predestination . . . " Herbert Hoover, *The Memoirs of Herbert Hoover—The Cabinet and the Presidency, 1920-1933* (New York: The Macmillan Company, 1952), see Chapter 16, "Commercial Help for Agriculture," pp. 109-111. For a scholar's view on the long smouldering feud between Wallace and Hoover, see James H. Shideler, *Farm Crisis, 1919-1923* (Berkeley: University of California Press, 1957), pp. 141-151.

3. For complete information see U.S.D.A.'s centennial history by Gladys L. Baker, Wayne D. Rasmussen, Vivian Wiser, and Jane M. Porter, *Century of Service—The First 100 Years of the United States Department of Agriculture*, U.S.D.A., 1963, pp. 104-108; see also reports of H. C. Taylor as Chief of the Bureau of Markets and Crop Estimates and as Chief of the Office of Farm Management and Farm Economics for the fiscal years ending June 30, 1922. Taylor's own account of the steps that led to the formation of the Bureau of Agricultural Economics is given in *The Story of Agricultural Economics* (Ames: Iowa State College Press, 1952), pp. 602-605. According to Taylor when Secretary Wallace asked the members of his economic council for suggestions to make the work of the department more

effective, "H. C. Taylor had anticipated the request and had a plan ready to submit to Secretary Wallace." This was the plan submitted by the Council and approved by the Secretary after the plan had been reviewed by the representatives from the Land Grant Colleges. Wallace also took the precaution of obtaining the informal approval of members of the agricultural committees of the Senate and House.

4. Andrew W. McKay, *Federal Research and Educational Work for Farmer Co-operatives, 1913-1953*, Farmer Cooperative Service, U.S.D.A., Report 40, January 1959, p. 39.

5. *Ibid.*, p. 40. This program was shifted to the Extension Service in 1923.

6. See Joseph G. Knapp, *The Rise of American Cooperative Enterprise, 1620-1920* (Danville, Ill.: The Interstate Printers & Publishers, Inc., 1969), pp. 165-168.

7. According to H. C. Taylor, "The situation was complicated at that time because many types of cooperation were being advocated and the movement was in the evangelistic stage. Organization was going ahead at unheard of speed. The claims made for cooperation were far beyond its possibilities. Stress was being laid upon price control by some advocates of the movement . . . Under these conditions the Bureau of Agricultural Economics could not take a very active part, even on the educational side of the movement. There was too much difference of opinion. For this reason it seemed wise to devote the energies of the Bureau to the study of the causes of successes and failures, to the statistics of cooperation, to the laws and legal status of cooperation, and to answering such questions as were put up to it." *Op. cit.*, p. 642.

8. *Ibid.*, pp. 644-645. See M. A. Abrahamsen's essay "Andrew W. McKay: Researcher and Educator" in Joseph G. Knapp and Associates, *Great American Cooperators* (Washington, D.C.: American Institute of Cooperation, 1967), pp. 319-325.

9. See biographical essay by Anne L. Gessner, "Ralph Henry Elsworth—Keeper of the Statistics", in Joseph G. Knapp and Associates, *op. cit.*, pp. 156-159.

10. See biographical essay by John C. Bagwell, "Lyman S. Hulbert: Cooperative Lawyer" in Joseph G. Knapp and Associates, *op. cit.*, pp. 243-247.

11. The *Weekly News Letter* of the American Farm Bureau Federation for June 2, 1921, carried an article on "The Advance of the Farm Bureau" which maintained: "The American Farm Bureau Federation has more than a million members and is growing at the rate of 50,000 members a month. In the last six months 307,713 new soldiers of the soil have been recruited in the Farm Bureau army." According to this article, the number of members affiliated with the American Farm Bureau Federation grew as follows: 456,000 (March 4, 1920); 744,401 (December 1, 1920); 1,052,114 (June 1, 1921). The memberships as then reported reflected the exuberance of the rapidly growing organization and no doubt were greatly inflated. The report of the Executive Secretary of the A.F.B.F. for the period January 1, 1921, to November 1, 1921, reported memberships as follows: 744,400 (December 1, 1920) and 967,279 (September 1, 1921). Allowing for over-optimistic membership figures, there is no question of the Farm Bureau's rapid growth and widespread support during this period. An historical study of farm organization memberships, made by Robert L. Tontz, states that the family memberships of the A.F.B.F. were 317,108 for 1920 and 466,422 for 1921. He states that the family memberships of the National Grange were 231,416 for 1920, while the family memberships of the National Farmers' Union were 131,475 for 1919. "Membership of General Farmers' Organization, United States, 1874-1960," *Agricultural History*, July 1964, pp. 143-156.

12. See Orville Merton Kile, *The Farm Bureau Through Three Decades* (Baltimore: Waverly Press, 1948), pp. 99-103; Murray R. Benedict, *Farm Policies of the United States, 1790-1940* (New York, The Twentieth Century Fund, 1953), pp. 181 ff., p. 199.

13. See Benedict, *op. cit.*, pp. 199-201; see also Chester C. Davis, "The Development of Agricultural Policy Since the End of the World War" in *Farmers in a Changing World*, U.S.D.A. Yearbook, 1940, pp. 299-300.

14. Wallace got along well with Harding and frequently played golf with him. After the last hole of a game they had played during Christmas week, Harding said to Wallace: "Go ahead with your Conference, Hank!" See Russell Lord, *The Wallaces of Iowa* (Boston: Houghton Mifflin Company, 1947), p. 236.

15. The complete texts of all talks and reports are given in *Report of The National Agricultural Conference*, House Document No. 195, 67th Congress, 2nd Session, Washington, D.C., G.P.O., 1922.

16. "Practically all of the notes that have been struck in subsequent agricultural policy were sounded in one way or another in that conference." Chester C. Davis, *op. cit.*, pp. 300-302. See also Gladys L. Baker, *et al.*, *op. cit.*, pp. 117-118.

17. It is significant that *The Prairie Farmer* of February 4, 1922, reported the conference with a full article under the title "Farm Products Must Go Up in Price." This article said: "One of the surprises of the Conference was the strong sentiment in favor of some form of Government price-fixing as an emergency remedy for the present low prices of farm crops . . . It took the most strenuous efforts of the men who were directing the convention to prevent the price-fixing question from becoming the dominating issue . . . As it was, not only was the price fixing idea not condemned, but Congress was urged to 'cause a careful investigation of the whole problem by some proper authority, which will report its findings as early as practicable.'" For other comments on the Conference, see Edward L. and Frederick H. Schapsmeier, *Henry A. Wallace of Iowa: The Agrarian Years —1910-1940* (Ames: Iowa State University Press, 1968), pp. 62-64; James H. Shideler, *op. cit.*, pp. 202 ff.; Gilbert C. Fite, *George N. Peek and the Fight for Farmer Parity* (Norman: University of Oklahoma Press, 1954), pp. 45 ff.; Winters, *Henry Cantwell Wallace as Secretary of Agriculture, op. cit.*, pp. 145-160.

18. It is of interest that Aaron Sapiro represented California cooperatives and spoke first for the measure in the hearings on the bill in the House, October 1919. John D. Miller, the main author of the bill, who was then Chairman of the legal committee of the National Cooperative Milk Producers' Federation, had the primary burden of presentation.

19. The immediate reaction in financial circles to the passage of the act was well reported by Rodney Bean in *The Annalist* of February 20, 1922. Writing under the title, "The Latest 'Agricultural Victory,'" he concluded: "The consensus of opinion seems to be that the agricultural interests have won one of their greatest triumphs, and that the power given by the legislature to check future cooperative operations on a large scale is not great." He also said: "for the moment, agriculture is in the saddle, and its representatives have obtained many concessions which a few months ago they had scarcely hoped to win . . . Leaders of both parties were on their feet declaring that they were sorry, to quote a famous remark, that they had 'but one life to give to my country.'" For full text and discussion of the Capper-Volstead Act, see L. S. Hulbert and Raymond J. Mischler, *Legal Phases of Farmer Cooperatives*, Farmer Cooperative Service, Bulletin 10, U.S.D.A., 1958, pp. 161 ff.

20. See keynote address by Aaron Sapiro at the First National Cooperative Marketing Conference, December 14, 1922. See also report of the committee on rural credit of this Conference.

21. For an excellent account of the events that led to the passage of the Intermediate Credit Act, see Claude L. Benner, *The Intermediate Credit System* (New York, The Macmillan Company, 1926), pp. 3-123. For a brief account, see Norman J. Wall, "Agricultural Credit" in Taylor, *op. cit.*, pp. 947-950.

22. In an address to extension workers in February 1921, Taylor held that the

marketing problem was "to be solved largely through the adjustment of supply to the anticipated demand and must come largely through the right direction of production," Henry C. and Anne Dewees Taylor, op. cit., p. 448.

23. *Ibid.*, see Chapter 17, "The Outlook Approach in Production Adjustments," pp. 447-479, for a full discussion of the beginnings of outlook work of the department. James H. Shideler, op. cit., pp. 133-141; Murray R. Benedict, op. cit., pp. 232, 237.

24. According to Andrew W. McKay, work with cooperatives, for the first time, gained "Division status," op. cit., p. 47.

25. Hobson had been one of Taylor's students at the University of Wisconsin, and during 1919-20 he had served as Taylor's Assistant Chief in the Office of Farm Management. In 1921 and 1922, when this bulletin was prepared, he was Associate Professor in Agricultural Economics at Columbia University. The bulletin grew out of a term paper written by J. Burton Chaney, son of A. U. Chaney, the manager of the American Cranberry Exchange. Hobson was impressed with the desirability of expanding the term paper into a full-scale study, and cooperation was arranged with the American Cranberry Exchange for all necessary data. The Division of Agricultural Cooperation provided funds to cover statistical, clerical, and travel costs. In this way a major bulletin was prepared at little expense to the Department of Agriculture. According to Hobson: "It was Taylor's belief that the best way for the Government to use a portion of its limited funds was to encourage, by financial assistance, worthwhile studies by state agencies. He often used the phrase 'Supply the catalyst' to cover the situation where the 'injection' of a small amount of funds into the right people would produce valuable results at low cost." Letter from Asher Hobson, January 3, 1970. See also, biographical essay by Milo K. Swanton, "Asher Hobson: Cooperative Statesman" in Joseph G. Knapp and Associates, op. cit., pp. 220-226.

26. A few numbers of this publication were issued in the fall of 1922, but regular publication was started in January 1923.

27. See Kelsey B. Gardner's biographical essay: "Chris Lauriths Christensen: Master Organizer of Research and Service" in Joseph G. Knapp and Associates, op. cit., pp. 116-121.

28. For more complete information on the work of the U.S.D.A. with cooperatives during this period, see Andrew W. McKay, op. cit., pp. 46-49. See also Taylor, op. cit., pp. 642-651. The philosophy of this program was well expounded by Secretary Wallace in a talk to the staff of the Bureau of Agricultural Economics on February 18, 1924, as reported by Taylor, pp. 649-651.

29. *Report of the National Agricultural Conference*, op. cit., p. 171.

30. "The McNary-Haugen Movement," *American Economic Review*, September 1928. A condensed statement of the plan as developed in *Equality for Agriculture* is available in *Readings in the History of American Agriculture*, edited by Wayne D. Rasmussen (Urbana: University of Illinois Press, 1960), pp. 220-239.

31. Taylor, in commenting on the "Aftermath of the National Agricultural Conference" said: "We believe that most of the members of the Conference went home believing that the problem in due course would be solved through adjustments in production and through cooperation in marketing. But there was one person who remained after the conference whose ideas had to be considered—George Peek." See Taylor, op. cit., p. 483.

32. For a first hand report on this conference and the views of the participants, see Taylor, op. cit., pp. 583-590. Secretary Wallace summed up the Conference with these words, "This is the most serious agricultural depression the country has ever experienced . . . I believe that we should carefully consider every plan that offers any promise of even alleviating the situation, and we should feel that our time is well spent in so doing."

33. *Ibid.*, pp. 591-594.

34. There is abundant information available on the development of McNary-Haugen legislation. For a good summary see the chapter "Equality for Agriculture" in Murray R. Benedict, *op. cit.* For a personalized account, see Gilbert C. Fite, *op. cit.*, especially Chapter III, "Equality for Agriculture—The Campaign Begins," pp. 35-38.

35. Henry C. Wallace, *Our Debt and Duty to the Farmer* (New York: The Century Company, 1925), p. 209.

36. *Ibid.*, pp. 158-159.

Chapter III

1. The story of the formation of the Committee of 17 and how it worked is well told by O. M. Kile, who served as its Secretary. *The Farm Bureau Movement* (Chicago: The Macmillan Company, 1921), pp. 148 ff.

2. "Nearly all the members of the new board of directors had either been members of this committee or delegates to the conference. They differed radically, not only upon pooling but in their conception of cooperation and the best methods of making the U.S. Grain Growers, Inc., an active force in the business world." See H. Clyde Filley, *Cooperation in Agriculture* (New York: John Wiley and Sons, 1929), p. 152.

3. The Capper-Tincher Act of 1921, which was intended to give cooperatives the opportunity to use the Grain Exchanges, was enjoined and there was no help to come from this quarter until the Grain Futures Act was passed the following year. Even then, it took several years to establish the right of cooperatives to be members of the grain exchange.

4. Chesla C. Sherlock, *The Modern Farm Cooperative Movement* (Des Moines, Iowa: The Homestead Company, 1922), p. 216. According to H. C. Filley: "Probably the organization received more criticism because of high salaries voted to the officers than for any other one thing. Undoubtedly, living expenses in Chicago are high, but in the minds of farmers that did not justify a salary of $16,000 for the President, $15,000 for the Treasurer, and $12,000 for the Secretary. The President and Secretary both refused to accept the salaries voted, and later on, because of the insistence of the President, and the severe criticism of the public, the salary scale was revised downward," *op. cit.*, pp. 153-154.

5. Sherlock, *op. cit.*, p. 216.

6. See "Report on Grain Marketing," in *Annual Report of the American Farm Bureau Federation for Period from October 31, 1921, to October 31, 1922*, p. 57.

7. *We Kansas Farmers* (Topeka: F. M. Steves and Sons, Publishers, 1953), p. 47.

8. For full information on the composition and work of the Committee of 15, see Edwin G. Nourse and Joseph G. Knapp, *The Cooperative Marketing of Livestock*, Chapter VIII, "The Livestock Marketing Committee of Fifteen" (Washington, D.C.: The Brookings Institution, 1931).

9. *Ibid.*, p. 139. This expression does not convey the reservations of those who were not in entire sympathy with the plan.

10. See *ibid.*, Chapters IX and X, for full information on the development of the National Livestock Producers Association and its operations.

11. See *Report of National Dairy Marketing Conference* published by the American Farm Bureau Federation, 1921. This report provides valuable information on the status of cooperative dairy marketing in 1921.

12. See O. M. Kile, *op. cit.*, pp. 133 ff.

13. According to Kile: "In an effort to placate the Sapiro element in farm bureau ranks, and to secure whatever values he had to contribute, the board of directors voted in April to employ Mr. Sapiro as legal advisor to the department of cooperative marketing and at the same time gave a vote of confidence to the director of that department, Mr. Peteet." Orville Kile, *The Farm Bureau Through Three Decades*, (Baltimore: Waverly Press, 1948), pp. 117-118. It was hoped that this action would hold Sapiro in the Farm Bureau camp and keep him from building up the National Council of Farmers Cooperative Marketing Associations as a rival organization to the American Farm Bureau Federation.

14. *Ibid.*, pp. 116-117.

15. Steen, managing editor of the *Prairie Farmer*, was recognized as an independent-minded friend of the American Farm Bureau Federation and as a well-informed student of cooperative enterprise.

16. See *Annual Report of the Secretary of the American Farm Bureau Federation for the Year 1923*, pp. 31-34.

17. *Ibid.*, p. 37.

18. *Report of Proceedings of the National Wheat Conference*, prepared by the Wheat Council of the United States, 1923. This printed document of 104 pages gives a complete report on this Conference which resulted in the setting up of the Wheat Council of the United States for promoting consumption of wheat products.

19. Governor Lowden's conversion to cooperative commodity marketing was highly significant, for he was then held in the highest esteem by agricultural and business leaders. He had but narrowly missed being the Republican nominee for the Presidency in 1920, and there were many who hoped to see him gain this office in 1924. For some time Lowden had been following cooperative developments, and in the summer of 1922 he had met Sapiro and was favorably impressed by him.

20. In addition to Lowden, Peteet, and Sapiro, the following were present: William H. Settle, President of the Indiana Farm Bureau Federation; Dan A. Wallace, editor of *The Farmer*, St. Paul, Minnesota; George C. Jewett, President of American Wheat Growers Associated; George E. Duis, President of the North Dakota Wheat Growers Association; Carl Williams, President of the American Cotton Growers Exchange; J. C. Chappell of Kansas; Alexander Legg, President, International Harvester Company; C. V. Gregory, editor, *Prairie Farmer*, Chicago; and Bernard Baruch of New York City. In addition, there were present as visitors, Eugene Meyer, Managing Director, War Finance Corporation; Frank W. Mondell, Director, War Finance Corporation; and H. S. Yohe, of the Warehouse Division, B.A.E. of the U.S. Department of Agriculture.

21. As reported by Walton Peteet in *Annual Report of the Secretary of the American Farm Bureau Federation for the Year 1923*, pp. 37-38.

22. *Ibid.*, p. 38. Peteet felt justified since several of those at the conference were active leaders in the work of the American Farm Bureau Federation.

23. It is true that Lowden had presidential ambitions throughout the decade. His popularity gave President Coolidge and Secretary Hoover much concern. However, his biographer does not doubt that Lowden's interest in helping farmers was sincere. As a politician he could not be expected to entirely free himself from the political implications of the causes he espoused. See William T. Hutchinson, *Lowden of Illinois*, II (Chicago: University of Chicago Press, 1957), p. 521.

24. *Wallace's Farmer*, December 21, 1923, p. 9.

25. The *Chicago Sunday Tribune* of December 9, 1923, quoted Coverdale as follows: "I believe Mr. Lowden's political aspirations have much to do with this action. The Sapiro-Lowden group wanted my discharge because I opposed their desires to make the organization a strictly marketing enterprise, whereas I stood for a bal-

anced program. It was evidently their purpose either to absorb the Federation in
the Lowden Committee [the Wheat Growers Advisory Committee, headed by
former Governor Lowden] or get rid of it altogether. Should the Federation adopt
the Sapiro-Lowden marketing program, it, by that action, severs its present
relations with agricultural colleges, because those relations could not continue were
the Federation to enter commercial activity." The logic of the last sentence is
questionable, for there is no evidence that Peteet or Sapiro wanted more than the
general support of the Farm Bureau—which had been assured by the resolution
passed by the Federation in December 1922. It may be observed ironically that
Coverdale's promotion of the Grain Marketing Company a few months later
was much more subject to the charge that it involved the American Farm Bureau
Federation in commercial activity.

26. *American Farm Bureau Weekly News Letter,* December 13, 1923. The last sentence
quoted above was a direct slap at Sapiro, for it was well known that his law firm
represented a large number of cooperative marketing associations. However, the
charge that fees were out of line for legal services performed has never been
authenticated.

27. This address delivered on December 11, 1923, under the title, *Analysis of Marketing,* was published as a pamphlet by the American Farm Bureau Federation.

28. *Wallaces' Farmer,* December 21, 1923.

29. Kile observes: "The low state of A.F.B.F. finances made membership acquisition
imperative . . . It was beginning to be apparent that the organization of cooperatives did not necessarily bring A.F.B.F. membership and dues." *The Farm Bureau
Through Three Decades, op. cit.,* p. 119.

30. Murphy also explained the background situation. At the convention the year
before, the executive committee was split pretty evenly between two factions,
and there was a long debate in the committee as to whether John W. Coverdale
or Samuel Guard, the popular director of information, would be named Secretary. Coverdale had won out but the group that opposed him had won over adherents during the year. No executive committee meetings had been held for six
months before the final one just before the last session. Guard and Coverdale had
battled during the year, and Guard had finally been deposed by President Bradfute
who had increasingly moved toward Coverdale's way of thinking. At the annual
meeting, Guard took the floor and asked: "*Are* you here to name a program for
the State Farm Bureaus or to name one for the National Federation?" This appeal
fell flat. See *Wallace's Farmer,* December 21, 1923.

31. In the *A.F.B.F. News Letter* for February 28, Gray Silver, the Washington Representative of the A.F.B.F., was quoted as saying: "The McNary-Haugen bill is
worth a billion dollars to the farmers of the country and everybody will share in
the increased prosperity." An item in the *News Letter* of April 24 carried this
headline: "Coverdale Tells Wisconsin Bureau Marketing Policy."

32. O. M. Kile, *The Farm Bureau Through Three Decades, op. cit.,* pp. 119-120.

33. *Annual Administrative Report of the American Farm Bureau Federation,* October
31, 1923, to Oct. 31, 1924, pp. 47-49.

34. *Farm Bureau in Illinois* (Bloomington: Illinois Agricultural Association, 1965),
p. 98.

35. *We Kansas Farmers,* distributed by Kansas Cooperative Council, Topeka, Kansas,
1952, *op. cit.,* p. 49. For a well-balanced statement on the experience of the Grain
Marketing Company, see the *Report on Cooperative Marketing,* Federal Trade
Commission, 1928, pp. 312-313. Although the plan had few supporters among
general students of marketing, Professor H. C. Filley of the University of Nebraska later said: "The chief reason why the Grain Marketing Company did not
succeed was lack of confidence which was due largely to lack of knowledge. It

was a new venture. No farmer had ever had any experience with so large an organization. The opponents said nothing against cooperation. They merely set up a group of straw men and proceeded to knock them down. The men who would have been most benefited by the success of the company believed at least a part of the statements of the opposition. They became suspicious and decided to wait before buying stock. While they waited, they lost a very unusual opportunity of embarking in the terminal grain-marketing business." H. Clyde Filley, *op. cit.*, p. 424.

36. *Wallace's Farmer* of December 19, 1924, gives a full report of this meeting. "The American Farm Bureau Federation at its annual meeting in Chicago last week lined up again, foot, horse and artillery behind the principles of the McNary-Haugen plan. [However, this did not result in official endorsement] . . . The subject of endorsement of the Grain Marketing Company was carefully avoided . . . The group meeting on cooperative marketing was best attended. It was at this meeting that the only mention of the Grain Marketing Company was made. Both Gray Silver and J. W. Coverdale were on the program to give an account of its work. Silver's talk was mostly devoted to a eulogy of cooperative marketing with a very slight reference to the Grain Marketing Company as a presumable example of cooperative marketing in action. Coverdale's address dealt with the amount of grain handled by the company up-to-date and with its alleged services to the farmers through shipping a large volume abroad at the earliest possible time . . . " One question rather embarrassed Mr. Coverdale: "Whether they found it difficult to give the managers of the Grain Marketing Company the farm point of view in running the affairs of the concern . . . This question aroused a certain amount of amusement. It was decided not to bring up the question of endorsement . . . "

Chapter IV

1. The term "commodity cooperative marketing" implied monopolistic control over a commodity. It should be kept in mind that other marketing cooperatives, such as the California Fruit Growers Exchange, were also organized on a commodity basis. Later discussion will make more clear the distinctive meaning of the term commodity cooperative marketing as used by Sapiro and his supporters.

2. For detailed information on the formation of these associations, see Wilson Gee and Edwin Allison Terry, *The Cotton Cooperatives in the Southeast* (New York: D. Appleton-Century Company, 1933), pp. 46-62; George O. Gatlin, *Cooperative Marketing of Cotton*, U.S.D.A., Bulletin 1397, January 1926, pp. 5-16; and *Federal Trade Commission Report on Cooperative Marketing*, Senate Document 95, 70th Congress, 1st sess., pp. 174-185.

3. Carl C. Taylor, "The Story and the Lesson of the Tri-State Tobacco Cooperative Association," *American Cooperation*, 1933, p. 492. Some 62,000 members were obtained in the three states by January 1, 1922. See pp. 491-496.

4. Verna Elsinger, "The Burley Tobacco Growers Experiment," *American Cooperation*, II, 1928, pp. 513-14.

5. This act, drawn with the assistance of Aaron Sapiro, was typical of many state acts passed in the early twenties to assure the legality of the commodity type of cooperative association. More than any other, it became known as the model cooperative law, especially after it was declared constitutional by the Supreme Court of the United States in February 1928, in *Liberty Warehouse Co.* v. *Burley Tobacco Growers' Co-op. Ass'n.* (276 U.S. 71). See L. S. Hulbert, *Legal Phases of Cooperative Associations*, Farm Credit Administration, Bulletin 50, May 1942,

p. 229. See also, John Hanna, *The Law of Cooperative Marketing Associations* (New York: Ronald Press, 1931), pp. 44 ff. For a copy of the Bingham Cooperative Marketing Act see Edwin G. Nourse, *The Legal Status of Agricultural Cooperation* (New York: The Macmillan Company, 1927), Appendix D, pp. 470-490.

6. For a full discussion of the problems met and overcome in getting the Burley Association into operation, see Elsinger, *op. cit.*, pp. 516-528.

7. See George O. Gatlin, "Cooperative Marketing in the Black Patch," *Cooperative Marketing Journal,* February 1927, p. 70. See also *Federal Trade Commission Report on Cooperative Marketing, op. cit.*, pp. 194-195.

8. For more detailed information on the early development of wheat pooling, see A. C. Adams, "History and Status of Wheat Pools in Pacific Northwest," *American Cooperation,* II, 1926, pp. 603-606; Joseph G. Knapp, *The Hard Winter Wheat Pools—An Experiment in Agricultural Marketing Integration* (Chicago: University of Chicago Press, 1933), pp. 18-26; and *Federal Trade Commission Report on Cooperative Marketing, op. cit.*, pp. 66 ff.

9. For discussion of the "permanent organization plan" and recommendations of Committee on Temporary and Permanent Organization" under Chairmanship of John D. Miller, see *Proceedings of First National Cooperative Marketing Conference,* National Council of Farmers' Cooperative Marketing Associations, Washington, D.C., December 14, 15, 16, 1922 (typewritten copy, unpublished). It is of interest that Judge Miller served as Chairman of the Committee on Temporary and Permanent Organization upon the request of Aaron Sapiro. At this time, the dairy cooperatives represented by Judge Miller were showing a friendly interest in the commodity marketing movement. By 1924, when the Second National Conference of Cooperative Marketing Associations was held, the dairy marketing cooperatives had withdrawn from active association.

10. *Federal Trade Commission Report on Cooperative Marketing, op. cit.*, pp. 182, 184, 203.

11. Significantly, he also said: "There is likewise need for organizations of urban consumers, to give like benefits."

12. *Proceedings of the Second National Cooperative Marketing Conference,* published by the National Council of Farmers' Cooperative Marketing Associations, Chicago, 1924, p. 3.

13. *Ibid.,* p. 17.

14. Also Wallace's espousal of the McNary-Haugen bill was looked on with disfavor by the commodity marketing leaders who held that the solution to the farm relief problem lay in strong commodity marketing cooperatives.

15. *Ibid.,* pp. 47-48.

16. *Ibid.,* p. 52.

17. Although this agreement provided that membership was to be open to any cooperative marketing association, including federations engaged in actual marketing operations when approved by the Executive Committee, the Council, as then constituted, was comprised almost entirely of centralized commodity type associations. Offices were established at Chicago, but later in the year they were moved to Washington, D.C.

18. See "Organization Agreement," front inside cover of *Proceedings of Third National Cooperative Marketing Conference,* 1925.

19. For full report on the program carried on in 1924, see report of the Secretary in the *Proceedings of Third National Cooperative Marketing Conference,* published by the National Council of Farmers' Cooperative Marketing Associations, Washington, D.C., 1925.

20. *Ibid.*, p. 126.

21. *Ibid.*, p. 6.

22. *Ibid.*, p. 39. The early success of the Canadian wheat pools made careful students of grain marketing open-minded toward the wheat pooling idea. Alonzo E. Taylor, good friend of Herbert Hoover, devoted one of the *Wheat Studies* of the Food Research Institute to the subject: "A National Wheat-Growers Cooperative: Its Problems, Opportunities and Limitations," Stanford University, January 1926. Taylor concluded that a national pool operation was feasible if certain conditions were met.

23. An authoritative and objective account of this unsavory episode in Mr. Ford's career is given by Alan Nevins and Frank Ernest Hill, *Ford: Expansion and Challenge*, (New York: Charles Scribner's Sons, 1957), pp. 317, 318, 320-322, and notes on p. 653. They call the "anti-semetic articles" in the *Dearborn Independent* "as offensive as they were ill-founded." In 1925, after 21 articles had been published, Sapiro sued Ford for $1,000,000 damages, charging defamation of character. The case came to trial in Detroit in March 1927, but a mistrial gave Ford an opportunity to settle out of court. On July 7, 1927, he published a personal apology to Sapiro, and a formal retraction of all his past attacks on the Jewish people. Ford also paid attorneys' fees and court costs. Sapiro did not demand further payment. See discussion of this case by Grace H. Larsen and Henry E. Erdman, "Aaron Sapiro: Genius of Farm Cooperative Promotion," *Mississippi Valley Historical Review*, September 1962, p. 267. An inside story of this case, not complimentary to Mr. Ford, is given by Ford's close associate, Harry Bennett, *We Never Called Him Henry* (New York: Fawcett Publications, Inc., 1951), pp. 46-56.

24. *Proceedings of Third National Cooperative Marketing Conference, op. cit.*, p. 18.

25. *Ibid.*, p. 20.

26. *Ibid.*, p. 52.

27. *Ibid.*, pp. 39-58. See also Field Service Bulletin 11, of the National Council of Farmers' Cooperative Marketing Associations entitled: "An Argument Against Federal Control and Regulation of Cooperatives as Recommended by the Agricultural Conference and Embodied in the Williams Bill" (January 7, 1925).

28. *Proceedings of Fourth National Cooperative Marketing Conference*, published by the National Council of Farmers' Cooperative Marketing Associations, Washington, D.C., 1926, p. 22.

29. Gilbert C. Fite, *George Peek and the Fight for Farm Parity* (Norman: University of Oklahoma Press, 1954), p. 141.

30. *Proceedings of Fourth National Cooperative Marketing Conference, op. cit.*, pp. 151-152; see also Orville Merton Kile, *The Farm Bureau Through Three Decades* (Baltimore: Waverly Press, 1948), pp. 139-140.

31. *Proceedings of Fourth National Cooperative Marketing Conference, op. cit.*, pp. 5-6. Lowden was referring to the outright advocacy of cooperatives in the President's talk at the recent Annual Meeting of the American Farm Bureau Federation which was received with much disfavor by the growing number of McNary-Haugen adherents in the Farm Bureau. See Chapter III.

32. *Proceedings of the Fourth Cooperative Marketing Conference, op. cit.*, p. 67.

33. Robin Hood, Director of Information of the National Council later wrote: "Sapiro was a director of the organization and as has been characteristic of most bodies with which he has been connected, succeeded in dominating it. At the last Convention of the old Council, Sapiro held the proxies of three tobacco associations which together constituted enough votes to outvote all of the other thirty-nine member organizations! Naturally this weird state of affairs could not

continue and the Council quickly shriveled up and passed out of the picture in the fall of 1926," *The Cooperative Marketing Journal,* March 1930, p. 38.

34. Kile, *op. cit.,* pp. 139-140.

35. For full story, see Elsinger, *op. cit.,* pp. 531-581; O. B. Jesness, "The Cooperative Marketing of Tobacco," Kentucky Agricultural Experiment Station, Bulletin 288, Lexington, Ky., 1928, pp. 292 ff.; Carl C. Taylor, *op. cit.,* pp. 500 ff.; John J. Scanlan and J. M. Tinley, "Business Analysis of the Tobacco Growers' Cooperative Associations," U.S.D.A., Circular 100, 1929, pp. 117-119; *Federal Trade Commission Report on Cooperative Marketing, op. cit.,* pp. 194, 196 ff.

36. Aaron Sapiro, "Dark and Bright Spots in Cooperative Marketing," *American Cooperation,* I, 1926, pp. 34, 43.

37. In his last major address as Secretary of the National Council at the 1926 American Institute of Cooperation, Walton Peteet did not use the term "commodity marketing," nor was the idea expounded while speaking on the subject "Present Hour Problems of Cooperatives," *American Cooperation,* I, pp. 377-380.

38. See Grace H. Larsen and Henry E. Erdman, *op. cit.,* p. 268.

Chapter V

1. Powell well expressed his cooperative philosophy at the National Agricultural Conference in January 1922 in an address: "Fundamentals of Cooperative Marketing." In this he maintained that the local unit was the strongest foundation for a cooperative marketing agency, but he held that "the test of these organizations should be 'what is their substance' rather than 'what is their form.' They must serve the public as well as their own members if they are to constitute effective agencies through which the complex problems of American agriculture are to be solved in the ultimate interest of the whole nation," *Report of the National Agricultural Conference,* House Document 195, 67th Congress, 2nd sess., 1922, pp. 74-84.

2. For example, Chesla C. Sherlock in his book, *The Modern Farm Cooperative Movement* (Des Moines: The Homestead Company, 1922), largely ignored the commodity cooperative movement. B. H. Hibbard in his chapters on cooperative marketing in *Marketing Agricultural Products* (New York: D. Appleton Century Company, 1921) was critical of the "California plan" as a means of "compulsory pooling." O. B. Jesness in *The Cooperative Marketing of Farm Products* (Philadelphia: J. B. Lippincott Co., 1923) devoted the bulk of his discussion to local and federated cooperatives although he recognized the significance of centralized cooperatives as espoused by Sapiro.

3. *Proceedings of the National Association of State Marketing Officials,* Fifth Annual Meeting, Chicago, pp. 16-17. See also E. G. Nourse, *Legal Status of Agricultural Cooperation* (New York: The Macmillan Company, 1927), pp. 432-434.

4. See Joseph G. Knapp, *The Rise of American Cooperative Enterprise, 1620-1920* (Danville, Ill.: The Interstate Printers & Publishers, Inc., 1969), pp. 166-168.

5. Henry C. and Anne Deweese Taylor, *The Story of Agricultural Economics* (Ames: Iowa, Iowa State College Press, 1952), pp. 642-643.

6. In a letter of H. C. Taylor, May 5, 1948, Black said of this bulletin: "It struck at the Sapiro philosophy while the iron was hot." See H. C. and A. D. Taylor, *op. cit.,* p. 654. See also essay on Black's cooperative writings by Theodore Norman in *Economics for Agriculture, Selected Writings of John D. Black,* edited by James Pierce Cavin (Cambridge, Mass.: Harvard University Press, 1959), pp. 280 ff.

7. John D. Black and H. Bruce Price, *Cooperative Central Marketing Organization,*

University of Minnesota Agricultural Experiment Station, Bulletin 211, 1924, pp. 15-16.

8. *Ibid.*, p. 83.

9. O. B. Jesness, *op. cit.*, p. 255.

10. *Journal of Farm Economics*, January 1924, pp. 106-116.

11. University of California, Agricultural Experimental Station, Circular 298, October 1925.

12. H. C. and A. D. Taylor, *op. cit.*, p. 696.

13. *American Cooperation*, I, 1925, p. 4.

14. *Ibid.*

15. Charles W. Holman, *The Cooperative Way Wins in America* (Syracuse, N.Y.: Metropolitan Cooperative Milk Producers Bargaining Agency, Inc., 1957), p. 67.

16. Pattee, *American Cooperation*, I, 1925, pp. 4-5.

17. *Ibid.*, p. 5.

18. Prior to this meeting, there had been a meeting of the American Farm Economics Association held in Washington, D.C., in December 1923. At this meeting Dr. Henry C. Taylor, Chief of the Bureau of Agricultural Economics, had called upon Holman to make an impromptu statement of the idea so far developed. Taylor gave the plan all possible encouragement and became a strong advocate of the envisaged organization.

19. The Certificate of Incorporation and By-Laws of the American Institute of Cooperation are available in *American Cooperation*, I, 1925, pp. 17-22. These documents were largely drafted by Lyman S. Hulbert of the Department of Agriculture.

20. See Charles W. Holman, *op. cit.*, p. 69. After the initial period, the American Institute of Cooperation was self-supporting through donations and fees until 1945 when a system of voluntary membership dues was inaugurated.

21. In the words of Dr. Henry C. Taylor: "Holman and Nourse became the principal organizers. Holman established outside contacts and made arrangements for the meeting. Nourse was responsible for the program. Thus a business manager and a professor worked shoulder to shoulder in making the Institute a success," *op. cit.*, p. 706.

22. *American Cooperation*, I, 1925, p. 9.

23. For full discussion see *American Cooperation*, I, 1925, pp. 151-182.

24. Although no definition was agreed upon, it was brought out that cooperation was a broad term for a form of business enterprise distinctly different in character from business as generally carried on. At the Institute held the following year at the University of Minnesota, Pattee said: "Cooperation as a business principle is not new. Business conducted on that basis is not relieved of the penalties that inevitably follow the breach of economic law. It is a difference in motive rather than a change in operation, the motive of service with a just reward rather than the motive of gain with profit as its goal." *American Cooperation*, I, 1926, p. 22.

25. *American Cooperation*, I, 1925, p. 30.

26. *American Cooperation*, II, 1925, pp. 689-690. See also *American Cooperation*, 1940, pp. 14-15.

27. *Proceedings of the National Association of Marketing Officials*, November 30-December 2, 1925, Chicago, p. 8.

28. This committee was established by the Department of Rural Education of the National Education Association under the leadership of Macy Campbell, Head of the Department of Rural Education of the Iowa State Teachers College. Governor Frank O. Lowden agreed to serve as its Chairman, and he enlisted the interest and

cooperation of a number of well-known cooperative leaders and educators, including: Aaron Sapiro, Judge Bingham, George E. Farrand, Richard Pattee, E. W. Kilgore, L. F. McKay, Verna Elsinger, Frank Swett, Walton Peteet, Frank Evans, Carl Williams, E. G. Nourse, Theodore Macklin, Chris L. Christensen, B. Y. Landis, and Kenyon L. Butterfield. Several meetings were held and much of the preliminary manuscript was prepared, but the goal of publication was not realized because of the untimely death of Campbell. However, the work started bore fruit in a textbook for vocational agricultural teachers, county agents, and colleges prepared by A. W. McKay, of the Division of Cooperative Marketing, and C. H. Lane, Chief of the Agricultural Education Service of the Federal Board for Vocational Education. *Practical Cooperative Marketing* (New York: John Wiley and Sons, 1928). For further information, see Macy Campbell, "Education and Cooperatives," *Proceedings of the Fourth National Conference on Cooperative Marketing,* 1926, pp. 113-114; and E. G. Nourse, *Proceedings of the National Association of Marketing Officials, op. cit.,* pp. 9-10.

29. Charles W. Holman, *loc. cit.*

30. Orion Ulrey, "Edwin Griswold Nourse: Pioneer in Cooperative Theory and Education," in Joseph G. Knapp and Associates, *Great American Cooperators* (Washington, D.C.: American Institute of Cooperation, 1967), p. 366.

31. For discussion of the confusion that existed prior to 1926, with regard to Federal Income Tax liability of cooperatives, see George R. Wicker, *American Cooperation,* I, 1925, pp. 398-500; see also E. G. Nourse, *Legal Status of Agricultural Cooperation, op. cit.,* pp. 262-264; Frank Evans and E. A. Stokdyk, *The Law of Cooperative Marketing* (Rochester, N.Y.: The Lawyers Cooperative Publishing Company, 1947), pp. 243 ff. See also John H. Davis, *An Economic Analysis of the Tax Statutes of Farmer Cooperatives* (Washington: American Institute of Cooperation, 1950), pp. 60-61; a good review of early income tax exemption history is given by L. S. Hulbert and Raymond J. Mischler, *Legal Phases of Farmer Cooperatives,* Farmer Cooperative Service, U.S.D.A., Bulletin 10, January 1958, pp. 195 ff.

32. L. S. Hulbert, *Legal Phases of Cooperative Associations,* Farm Credit Administration, Bulletin 50, May 1942, pp. 309-310.

33. Hulbert and Mischler, *op. cit.,* pp. 195 ff.

34. Charles W. Holman gave the law credit for "encouragement and support of sound agricultural practices," *op. cit.,* pp. 46-48.

35. Andrew W. McKay, *Federal Research and Educational Work for Farmer Cooperatives, 1913-1953,* Farmer Cooperative Service, U.S.D.A., Report 40, 1959, p. 56.

36. Campbell, *op. cit.,* pp. 63-64.

37. *Hearings of Committee on Agriculture and Forestry, U.S. Senate,* March 13, 1926. Mr. Holman pointed out that "there was a time when we had a cooperative division in the department but, owing to the attitude of one Secretary of Agriculture [apparently E. T. Meridith] the division was dismantled, and the work ceased for a while, so far as any real effort was concerned. In the Wallace administration this work was resumed . . . " Holman saw the need of having this work specifically authorized and supported by the Congress.

38. Edwin G. Nourse, *The Legal Status of Agricultural Cooperation, op. cit.,* pp. 261-262.

39. For example, Gilbert C. Fite, in his book *George N. Peek and the Fight for Farm Parity* (Norman: University of Oklahoma Press, 1954), p. 166, said "A few days later the Senate approved the House bill to set up a bureau of cooperative marketing in the Department of Agriculture. Another session had ended with no significant farm legislation." See also statement by Edward L. and Frederick H. Schapsmeier,

Henry A. Wallace of Iowa: The Agrarian Years, 1910-1940 (Ames: Iowa State University Press, 1968), "As a sop to the Farm Bloc, the Administration gave the green light for passage of the Cooperative Marketing Act . . . The function of the new Division was advisory in nature and did nothing to provide any explicit Government assistance or Federal funds to farmer-owned co-ops," p. 102.

40. For more information see *Reports of the Chief of the Bureau of Agricultural Economics* for fiscal years ending in 1927, 1928, and 1929. See also Andrew W. McKay, *Federal Research and Educational Work for Farmer Cooperatives, 1913-1953, op. cit.,* pp. 57-64.

41. *Agricultural Reform in the United States* (New York: McGraw-Hill Book Company, Inc., 1929), p. 489.

42. See Robin Hood, "A Proposal for a New National Council," *The Cooperative Marketing Journal,* December 1926, p. 23.

43. *Ibid.,* pp. 24-29. The publication of *The Cooperative Marketing Journal* in itself was a significant development for it served as a coordinating link until a new Council could be formed in 1929. It was started as a non-profit venture by Peteet and Hood "in order to stimulate open-minded, fearless, intelligent thinking in the field of agricultural cooperation." See "A Statement of Policy," *The Cooperative Marketing Journal* (Preface), February 1927.

44. *American Cooperation,* I, 1928, pp. 511-513. The writer attended this meeting and there is no doubt in his mind that the threat, implied in the organization of the Agricultural Trades Association, did much to stimulate the cooperatives to pull together.

45. For a full discussion of the plan of organization of the National Cooperative Council, see C. O. Moser, "Report of the Organization Committee of the National Cooperative Council," *American Cooperation,* 1929, pp. 50-60. See also Moser's comments on the program to be undertaken, pp. 65-66, and Holman's statement on its potential importance, p. 49.

Chapter VI

1. "George Nelson Peek was not brilliant. But he was a good, smart man in a fight; a hard man to push over, as they say in the Middle West. An industrial agrarian of magnificent stubbornness and simplicity, he plowed just one furrow—'Equality for Agriculture'—and plowed it straight." Russell Lord, *The Wallaces of Iowa* (Boston: Houghton Mifflin Company, 1947), p. 230.

2. "Coolidge, characteristically cagy and definitely unfavorable to the McNary-Haugen idea, did not reply directly." Murray R. Benedict, *Farm Policies of the United States* (New York: The Twentieth Century Fund, 1953), p. 218.

3. According to Harold U. Faulkner, " . . . the nation was in no heroic mood . . . the nation wanted only peace, quiet, and continued enjoyment of prosperity . . . [Coolidge] fitted the mood of the nation . . . As for the nation as a whole, the most immediate result was definitely to place the Government in the hands of the business interests. Indeed, it was in the hands of the most conservative element of business, men of the type of Andrew W. Mellon. Coolidge had encouraged the process; the election sanctioned it . . . Government and big business were now synonymous." *From Versailles to the New Deal* (New Haven, Conn.: Yale University Press, 1950). See pp. 220-223.

4. Hoover's faith in the cooperative form of business organization was sincere. His little book, *American Individualism,* written in 1922, made this clear. In this he said: "Today business organization is moving strongly toward cooperation. There are in the cooperative great hopes that we can even gain in individuality, equality

of opportunity, and an enlarged field for initiative, and at the same time reduce many of the great wastes of overreckless competition in production and distribution. Those who either congratulate themselves or those who fear that cooperation is an advance toward socialism, need neither rejoice or worry. *Cooperation in its current economic sense represents the initiative of self-interest blended with a sense of service, for nobody belongs to a cooperative who is not striving to sell his products or services for more or striving to buy from others for less or striving to make his income more secure. Their members are furnishing the capital for extension of their activities just as effectively as if they did it in corporate form and they are simply transferring the profit principle from joint return to individual return.* Their only success lies where they eliminate waste either in production or distribution—and they can do neither if they destroy individual initiative. Indeed, this phase of development of our individualism promises to become the dominant note of its 20th Century expansion. But it will thrive only insofar as it can construct leadership and a sense of service, and so long as it preserves the initiative and safeguards the individuality of its members" (Italics added). Herbert Hoover, *American Individualism* (New York: Doubleday Page, 1923), pp. 44-45. In his *Memoirs,* Chapter II, Hoover said, referring to his advocacy of cooperatives during the twenties: "We supported the cooperative movement among farmers. The movement was still young and was stubbornly opposed by the commercial distributors. I believed it to be one of the most hopeful undertakings, for according to my social theories, any organization by citizens for their own welfare is preferable to the same action by the Government . . . I made many addresses on their behalf, supporting them against the activities of certain food traders which considered them an unmitigated evil." Herbert Hoover, *The Memoirs of Herbert Hoover— The Cabinet and the Presidency, 1920-1932* (New York: The Macmillan Company, 1952), pp. 109-110.

5. See also discussion of Williams Bill in Chapter IV.

6. Testimony of Arthur B. Williams, House Committee on Agriculture, *Agricultural Relief Hearings,* February 2, 1925, Serial CC, Part 2, pp. 51-78.

7. *Ibid.,* p. 57. According to James H. Shideler the Williams Bill was "really Hoover's." See his paper "Herbert Hoover and the Federal Farm Board Project, 1921-1925," *Mississippi Valley Historical Review,* March 1956, pp. 718-719.

8. This article, published in the *Manufacturers' News* of October 25, and November 1, 1924, was reprinted in House Agriculture Committee *Hearings on Agricultural Relief,* February 12, and 13, 1925, Serial CC, Part 2, pp. 388-392.

9. Benedict, *op. cit.,* p. 218.

10. *Wallace's Farmer* of February 6, 1925, reported on the Conference report under the headline: "Commission's Report Disappoints." The article said that the major recommendation was the establishment of a cooperative marketing board that would be subservient to Secretary Hoover. "To many farmers the most important feature of the Commission's report is . . . what it leaves out. There is no mention made of the problem of dealing with the exportable surplus of farm products." An editorial in the same issue said: "This is Secretary Hoover's old Capper-Williams bill, slightly modified. It is a scheme that has been denounced by practically every important farm organization in the country. The cooperatives do not want it."

11. His views on this bill were given in Chapter IV.

12. For full testimony of Holman, see House Committee on Agriculture, *Hearings on Agricultural Relief,* February 12, 1925, Serial CC, Part 2, pp. 369-385. For a description of the objectives of the Dickinson Bill, see Congressman Dickinson's testimony in the *Hearings,* February 6, 1925, Serial CC, Part 5, pp. 136-156.

13. "The Progress of Farm Relief," *American Economic Review,* June 1928, p. 268.

14. See final *Report of Agricultural Conference,* February 2, 1925. Furthermore, the

Conference deliberations and the emphasis that it gave to cooperative marketing organizations emphasized the need of more factual information on the position and significance of cooperative marketing associations in American agriculture. This situation resulted in a resolution requesting the Federal Trade Commission to undertake a comprehensive study on cooperative marketing. This was published in 1928 as the *Federal Trade Commission Report on Cooperative Marketing*.

15. O. M. Kile, *The Farm Bureau Through Three Decades* (Baltimore: Waverly Press, 1948), p. 134.

16. In an editorial, December 19, 1925, *Wallace's Farmer* expressed the view that Coolidge probably made the speech at the suggestion of Hoover and Jardine who were interested in keeping Bradfute in power and the Middle-West out of power. An article in the same issue said: "The majority of the Middle-western farmers seemed to feel . . . that the President had come to Chicago with the definite purpose of killing any plan of handling the export surplus as dead as possible."

17. Lowden "had paved the way" for a meeting in Chicago on June 5, 1925, attended by Peek and other McNary-Haugen advocates and by Lowden and other important cooperative officials, including R. W. Bingham and Carl Williams. A second meeting was held on July 10. "These conferences were highly important preliminary moves in getting the cotton and tobacco cooperatives into the fight for the McNary-Haugen bill." See Gilbert C. Fite, *George Peek and the Fight for Farm Parity* (Norman: University of Oklahoma Press, 1952), p. 141.

18. This was not the Dickinson Bill of the year before. It had the support of both McNary-Haugen and cooperative supporters.

19. For a detailed account of the maneuvering that took place under the dynamic leadership of George Peek to enact the McNary-Haugen legislation during the years 1925-28, see Fite, *op. cit.*, Chapters 9-12. See also Benedict, *op. cit.*, p. 222.

20. See Russell Lord, *op. cit.*, p. 273.

21. Nourse referred to "the extensive crusade underway for eight years to secure special treatment of the agricultural industry" which culminated in the "Agricultural Marketing Act." "Agriculture," *Government and Economic Life*, II (Washington, D.C.: The Brookings Institution, 1940), pp. 892-893.

Chapter VII

1. As early as January 20, 1921, Hoover had urged the creation of a government marketing board of experts to assist in "the development of cooperative marketing." See the very illuminating article by James H. Shideler, "Herbert Hoover and the Federal Farm Board Project, 1921-1925," *Mississippi Valley Historical Review*, March 1956, p. 714.

2. John D. Black, *Agricultural Reform in the United States* (New York: McGraw-Hill, 1929), p. 73.

3. Quotations from *ibid.*, pp. 351-352. Although Black was critical of some aspects of this plan he said: "The stabilization corporation, or something like it, seems to be the most logical agency to attack the problem of season surpluses and to offer some possibilities for the handling of weather and overplanting surpluses. It is high time that we undertook some experiments along this line. But we must not be over sanguine about the results. We must live and learn," p. 360. For Black's full analysis of Jardine's views see pp. 357-360.

4. See E. G. Nourse, "Government in Relation to Agriculture" in *Government and Economic Life*, II (Washington: The Brookings Institution, 1940), p. 897. Nourse found "striking" the extent to which the "suggestions" of the Business Men's

Commission were later embodied in the Agricultural Marketing Act of 1929 (p. 898).

5. Davis's paper on "America's Agricultural Position and Policy" was published in the Harvard Business Review, January 1928, pp. 143-157. It was reprinted in a collection of Davis's writings entitled: *On Agricultural Policy, 1926-1938* (Stanford University: Food Research Institute, 1939). See especially pp. 87-89.

6. U.S.D.A., *Agricultural Yearbook*, 1928, p. 28.

7. For information on California experience with clearing house programs see Erich Kraemer and H. E. Erdman, *History of Cooperation in the Marketing of California Fresh Deciduous Fruits*, California Agricultural Experiment Station, Bulletin 557, September 1933, pp. 34 ff.

8. For full information on this interesting organization see Robert Charles White, *An Analysis of the Florida Citrus Growers Clearing House Association* (Master's thesis) (Gainesville: University of Florida, 1940). See also Chris L. Christensen, "The Florida Citrus Growers Clearing House Association," *American Cooperation*, II, 1928, pp. 339-347. In the discussion following his presentation Christensen made clear that the Department of Agriculture in assisting growers did not officially sponsor and promote this type of organization, p. 352.

9. *American Cooperation*, II, 1928, p. 365.

10. *Ibid.*, p. 353.

11. *American Cooperation*, I, pp. 19, 21.

12. *New York Times*, June 15, 1928, as quoted by Murray R. Benedict, *Farm Policies of the United States, 1790-1950* (New York: The Twentieth Century Fund, 1953), p. 330. The Democratic Party platform promised to set up a Federal Farm Board, foster and promote cooperative marketing associations, and deal with the surplus along McNary-Haugen lines. *Ibid.*, pp. 230-231.

13. *Hearings Before the Senate Committee on Agriculture and Forestry, 71st Congress, 1st Session Relative to Establishing a Federal Farm Board* . . . Quoted in testimony of Senator Charles L. McNary, March 25, 1929, p. 3.

14. *Wallace's Farmer* was not noted for its sympathy with Herbert Hoover. Henry A. Wallace, the editor, had favored Governor Al Smith. However, after Hoover's sweeping victory, in which he won 40 of the 48 states, he hoped for the best, and he urged farm leaders to wait and see what would happen. See Edward L. and Frederick B. Schapsmeier, *Henry A. Wallace of Iowa: The Agrarian Years, 1910-1940* (Ames: Iowa State University Press, 1968), pp. 111-113.

15. O. M. Kile, *The Farm Bureau Through Three Decades* (Baltimore: Waverly Press, 1948), p. 163.

16. *Ibid.*, Chapter XIII, "Making the Best of a Bad Situation: The Federal Farm Board," pp. 163 ff.

17. April 19, 1929.

18. "Mr. Hoover's New Farm Program," *Prairie Farmer*, April 27, 1929.

19. *Hearings before the Senate Committee on Agriculture and Forestry on Farm Legislation Relative to Establishing a Federal Farm Board* . . . , Seventy-first Congress, 1st Session, March 28, 1929, pp. 248-249.

20. *Ibid.*, pp. 259-260. For the full statement of the National Committee on Cooperation, giving also the names of its participating organizations, see pp. 258-261.

21. James Shideler, *op. cit.*, p. 710.

Chapter VIII

1. Nourse later pointed out that these special powers made the Board "a sort of economic planning agency" for agriculture. Edwin G. Nourse in chapter on "Agriculture" in *Government and Economic Life*, II (Washington, D.C.: The Brookings Institution, 1940), p. 899.

2. In its report on the bill the House Committee on Agriculture said: "We are not convinced as to the ultimate form such organizations (clearing houses) should take nor, indeed, whether the joint action of the trade interests under producer control will always prove successful. We do believe, however, that the clearing house idea contains enough probable value to justify us in giving to the board the widest possible latitude . . . requiring only the perpetuation in any plan of producer control. . . ."

3. The *Progressive Farmer* in an article, "The Federal Farm Board Personnel Pleasing," July 27, 1929, said: "No better 'big businessman' than Alexander Legge could have been found. He not only knows 'big business' methods but his second interest is most peculiarly agriculture."

4. The other members selected were: James C. Stone, of Kentucky, a well-known tobacco cooperative leader (he was named Vice-Chairman); Charles C. Teague, of California, President of the California Fruit Growers' Exchange and the California Walnut Growers' Association; Cyrus B. Denman, of Missouri, President of the National Livestock Producers' Association; William F. Schilling, of Minnesota, President of Twin City Milk Producers' Association; Carl Williams, of Oklahoma, President of American Cotton Growers' Exchange and Southwest Wheat Growers' Association and editor of the *Oklahoma Farmer;* Samuel R. McKelvie, of Nebraska, former Governor of Nebraska and owner-publisher of the *Nebraska Farmer;* and Charles S. Wilson, of New York State, extensive orchard owner and formerly New York Commissioner of Agriculture. In addition to the preceding, Arthur M. Hyde, as Secretary of Agriculture, was an *ex officio* member of the Board.

5. Alexander Legge, "The Relationship of the Federal Farm Board to the Cooperative Movement," *American Cooperation*, 1929, pp. 17-24.

6. The smugness of that period is portrayed by John Kenneth Galbraith, *The Great Crash,* especially Chapter V, "The Twilight of Illusion" (Boston: Houghton Mifflin Company, 1954), pp. 71-92.

7. *The Cooperative Marketing Journal,* September-October, 1929, pp. 23-124.

8. A description of the national cooperative organizations set up for Wheat, Wool, Cotton, Beans, and Livestock during the Board's first year is given in Federal Farm Board, Bulletin 3, *Farmers Build Their Own Marketing Machinery,* December 1930; see also *First Annual Report of the Federal Farm Board,* 1930, pp. 7 ff. Similar organizations were set up for pecans and sugar beets in the summer of 1930.

9. For information on the valuable and comprehensive assistance provided to the Farm Board by the specialists of the Division of Cooperative Marketing during the years 1929-1933, see Andrew W. McKay, *Federal Research and Educational Work for Farmer Cooperatives, 1913-1953,* Farmer Cooperative Service, U.S.D.A., Report 40, January 1959, pp. 65-73. McKay was made Chief of the Division when Chris L. Christensen became Secretary of the Farm Board, and he served in this capacity during most of the Board's life.

10. Much credit for the development of the lending operations of the Farm Board can be given to Stanley Reed (Associate Justice of the Supreme Court, 1938-1957), who was appointed Counsel on November 22, 1929. According to Lyman S.

Hulbert, his assistant during this period, Mr. Reed interpreted the Agricultural Marketing Act broadly as to what it could do. Interview, November 25, 1969.

11. See Kiplinger's *Washington Letter*, December 21, 1969.

12. *Journal of Farm Economics*, January 1930, pp. 1 ff.

13. *The Cooperative Marketing Journal*, January 1930, p. 4.

14. For events leading up to this decision see *First Annual Report of the Federal Farm Board*, 1930, pp. 26-29. A press release of the Farm Board, February 11, read as follows: "The Federal Farm Board announced today that the Wheat Advisory Commodity Committee had recommended to the Board that it recognize the Grain Stabilization Corporation, a non-stock corporation organized by grain cooperatives, as a wheat stabilization corporation under the terms of the Agricultural Marketing Act and that a loan be granted to this corporation sufficient to carry on its initial operations. The Grain Stabilization Corporation is composed solely of qualified Capper-Volstead grain cooperatives and its membership is open to all such cooperatives. The various members have waived all rights or claims to any profits which may accrue from its operations, to the end that all profits or losses will fall upon the revolving fund provided in the Agricultural Marketing Act. This is simply another step in the program of the grain cooperatives and the Farm Board for a unified national system for marketing grain and has been under consideration by the Board for several months. The Board, after careful study, is prepared to recognize this organization, set up by the grain cooperatives, as a wheat stabilization corporation under the terms of the Agricultural Marketing Act. In accordance with the recommendations of the Wheat Advisory Commodity Committee, the Board will provide an initial credit of $10,000,000 to the corporation."

15. See pamphlet, "The Agricultural Marketing Act," issued by Chamber of Commerce of the United States, May 1930, giving addresses, discussion, and resolution.

16. See *The Journal of Cooperative Marketing*, July 1930, pp. 100-132.

17. For more complete information see E. A. Stokdyk, "The Farm Board's Proposal for Stabilizing the California Grape Industry," *Journal of Farm Economics*, July 1930, pp. 467-469; see also Stokdyk, *Marketing Tokay Grapes*, California Agricultural Experiment Station, Bulletin 558, September 1933, pp. 3-4, 45-46.

18. The problem of production control assumed increasing importance as the Board became involved in stabilization operations. During 1930 and 1931, the Board conducted "hortatory" campaigns to induce farmers to plant smaller acreages of wheat and cotton, but with no significant result. Individual farmers could not be assured that other "non-cooperating" farmers would not take advantage from their altruism. See Theodore Saloutos and John D. Hicks, "From Farm Board to Farm Strike," *Agricultural Discontent in the Middle West: 1900-1939* (Madison: University of Wisconsin Press, 1951), Chapter 14, pp. 419-421; and E. G. Nourse, *op. cit.*, pp. 902-903.

19. In a review of this report in the January 1931 *Journal of Farm Economics*, Dr. John D. Black congratualted the Board "on the progress of its thinking" in recognizing the problem of production, but he was skeptical as to the ability of the Board to cope with all of the problems resulting from the "confusion" in the Agricultural Marketing Act, which he said was more of a program than a policy. Black called attention to the fact that the Board itself "is directly responsible for the scheme of integrated regional and national cooperative commodity organizations," and he held that "it will have to accept the credit or blame, whichever way any of these schemes turn out."

20. "Policies of the Federal Farm Board," *American Cooperation*, I, 1930, pp. 17, 18.

21. See *Agricultural Statistics, 1940*, U.S. Department of Agriculture, Table 15, p. 23; *ibid.*, Table 157, p. 122.

22. For a comprehensive report on wheat and cotton stabilization operations, see the *Second* and *Third Annual Reports of the Federal Farm Board.*

23. In an address before a joint session of the American Economic and Farm Economic Associations in annual meeting in Chicago, December 29, 1930, on "The Program of The Federal Farm Board," Joseph S. Davis, Chief Economist of the Board, said: "In October 1929 certain loan policies were adopted with respect to wheat and cotton that led into major stabilization operations, the outcome of which cannot be regarded as satisfactory. Suppose, however, no action had been taken. In our judgment there is no doubt that radical declines in wheat and cotton prices would have taken place then, instead of later; that these declines would have been credited with heavy responsibility for the stock market crash, severe breaks in commodity prices in general, and extreme business depression. The actions taken did not prevent these disasters; but had the Board refused to exercise its powers in efforts to meet the situation, it would have suffered even weightier condemnation for merely standing by." *American Economic Review,* March 1931, Supplement, pp. 104-13.

24. The charge that cooperatives are "socialistic" is one of the enduring myths of businessmen. Charles C. Teague, long President of the California Fruit Growers' Exchange and the California Walnut Growers' Association, and one of the original members of the Farm Board, said in his autobiography: "In my long experience I have found comparatively few heads of large business enterprises who understand cooperative marketing. They are apt instinctively to consider it a sort of socialistic movement; whereas, it is, on the contrary, just as much a part of the business enterprise system as is manufacturing or any other form of industry." *Fifty Years a Rancher* (Los Angeles: Ward Richie Press, 1944), p. 176.

25. See Saloutos and Hicks, *op. cit.,* pp. 404-434.

26. Bruce V. Snow, "John D. Miller: The Father of the Capper-Volstead Act" in Joseph G. Knapp and Associates, *Great American Cooperators* (Washington: American Institute of Cooperation, 1967), pp. 344-346.

27. Another serious loss occurred at about this time when Chris L. Christensen resigned as Secretary of the Board to accept a position as Dean of the College of Agriculture at the University of Wisconsin. Christensen had a strong following among cooperative leaders throughout the nation, and he was uniquely qualified to serve as secretary because of his working knowledge of cooperatives gained as Chief of the Division of Cooperative Marketing. Moreover, in the late summer, Dr. Joseph S. Davis, Chief Economist, returned to his position with Stanford University.

28. *American Cooperation,* II, 1931, pp. 12-17. For more complete analysis of the livestock marketing program of the Federal Farm Board as of early 1931, see E. G. Nourse and Joseph G. Knapp, *The Cooperative Marketing of Livestock* (Washington, D.C.: The Brookings Institution, 1931), Chapter V, "The Program of the Federal Farm Board," pp. 276-295; Chapter XVIII, "Cooperative Principles and Farm Board Influence," pp. 345-366.

29. *American Cooperation,* II, 1931, p. 159.

30. *Ibid.,* p. 155.

31. *Ibid.,* pp. 265, 283.

32. For a brief but complete review of the Farm Board's stabilization experience in wheat, see Joseph S. Davis in *Wheat and the AAA* (Washington, D.C.: The Brookings Institution, 1935), pp. 19-27. The Grain Stabilization Corporation liquidated its holdings of wheat in April 1933. Some 85 million bushels or about one-third of its holdings were turned over to the Red Cross for relief disposition.

33. For full statement see *The Cooperative Marketing Journal,* November-December 1931, pp. 183-186.

34. The Third Annual Report of the Farm Board contained this paragraph: "The past session of Congress reduced the Board's administrative appropriation for the current year [1932-33] to $800,000, or three-fifths of the expenditures for the preceding fiscal year. This situation necessitated the indefinite furlough or discharge of over 40% of its employees, leaving little more than a skeleton staff. The remaining personnel was reorganized to secure greater outturn per worker, but many important services, such as assisting in the organization of new associations, and in the improvement of operating methods, had to be reduced or eliminated to enable the smaller staff to handle loan applications and other emergency activities" (p. 88).

35. The low year of the depression for agriculture was 1932. The Bureau of Agricultural Economics index number of farm prices for 1932 was 65, compared to 126 for 1929. The index number of prices paid by farmers was 107, compared to 153 for 1929. The ratio of prices received to prices paid was 61 for 1932, compared to 95 for 1929.

36. *The Cooperative Marketing Journal,* September-October 1932, p. 152.

37. The Republican Party platform contained this statement: "The Republican Party pledges itself to the principles of assistance to cooperative marketing associations, owned and controlled by the farmers themselves, through the provisions of the Agricultural Marketing Act, which will be promptly amended or modified as experience shows to be necessary to accomplish the objects set forth in the preamble of this act."

38. However, on July 12, 1932, the National Cooperative Council had asked for repeal of the stabilization clause in the Act (Section 9) by referendum vote of its directors. The vote was unanimous, with 22 directors voting "aye."

39. For more details see Federal Farm Board, *Special Report,* December 7, 1932.

40. See lead article, "Cooperatives Solidify Their Ranks Behind Marketing Act," *The Cooperative Marketing Journal,* January-February 1933, p. 3.

41. Murray R. Benedict, *Farm Policies of the United States* (New York: The Twentieth Century Fund, 1953), p. 264.

42. *Ibid.,* pp. 266-267.

43. J. D. Lawrence, formerly Deputy Governor and Director of Cooperative Bank Services for the Farm Credit Administration, quoted by Gifford Hoag, Ben Sunbury, and Marie Puhr in *Banks for Cooperatives,* Farm Credit Administration, Circular E-47, p. 19.

44. Andrew W. McKay, the Chief of the Division of Cooperative Marketing during most of the Farm Board's life, later said: "The lack of a comprehensive research program by the Division during the Farm Board period was felt by its staff during the last two years. The need for workers with cooperatives to be refreshed continually by new methods and techniques which research develops was well illustrated by this experience," *op. cit.,* p. 73.

45. E. G. Nourse, "The Cooperative Marketing Movement Under the 'New Deal,'" *American Cooperation,* 1933, p. 44.

Chapter IX

1. R. H. Elsworth, "Statistics of Farmers Cooperative Business Organizations," Farm Credit Administration, Bulletin 6, 1936, p. 97.

2. Joseph G. Knapp, *The Rise of American Cooperative Enterprise: 1620-1920* (Danville, Ill.: The Interstate Printers & Publishers, Inc., 1969), pp. 333-353.

3. Robin Hood listed 21 cooperatives doing a purchasing business each, of more

than $1 million in 1930, with an aggregate business of $102 million. See "Million Dollar Purchasing Agents," *The Cooperative Marketing Journal*, May-June 1931, pp. 89-93.

4. See Joseph G. Knapp, *op. cit.*, pp. 354-390.

5. The information in this section has been largely developed from a review of the minutes, records, reports, and publications of the Eastern States Farmers' Exchange, and from correspondence in 1944 and 1945 with Howard Selby, the first General Manager of the Exchange, who retired in 1925. For information on the formation of the Exchange see Joseph G. Knapp, *op. cit.*, pp. 354-373.

6. The Eastern States Agricultural and Industrial League was not only interested in the promotion of cooperative marketing and purchasing for farmers, it had also become enthusiastic over the possibilities of consumers' cooperation as a means of helping industrial workers reduce their high living costs following the war. Many industrial leaders saw in consumers' cooperatives a means of reducing labor unrest and pressure for high wages. After several months of study, the Market Bureau, of the League, proposed a plan for an Eastern States Consumers' Exchange which would operate for buying groups and consumer societies "in a manner somewhat parallel to that in which the Eastern States Farmers' Exchange now handles purchases for the cooperative farmers exchanges." The Eastern States Consumers' Exchange was incorporated in May 1920, and, for a few months, it operated under the management of the Manager of the Eastern States Farmers' Exchange. With the abrupt fall in prices in the fall of 1920, interest dwindled and its operations were discontinued. For the complete story of this interesting experiment, see issues of *The Eastern States Magazine* during 1920.

7. Marketing opportunities in New England were limited by the fact that marketing problems of the leading farm enterprise, dairying, were in the hands of milk producers' organizations.

8. "The success of two fertilizer pools conducted by the Eastern States Farmers' Exchange and the complete endorsement of thousands of farmers and farmers' cooperative organizations of the pool idea led to the organization of the dairy ration pool." *The Eastern States Magazine*, November 1922, p. 2.

9. The American Milling Company saw in this operation an opportunity to fully utilize its plant facilities and widen its area of distribution. It gave its full cooperation by supplying field men to help get the pool orders from farmers.

10. The financing of this large operation through eight banks, including several of the largest and most influential in New England, was largely effected through the businessmen represented on the Board. It "demonstrated the value and need of a 'dirt farmer-businessmen's' combination." At this time the Exchange Board of Directors consisted of 20 farm representatives and 5 businessmen, who represented the Eastern States Agricultural and Industrial League. These public-spirited and experienced businessmen enjoyed the full respect of the agricultural, business, and banking community.

11. Part of the increase was due also to a doubling of fertilizer business.

12. "In 1929 Mr. P. A. Campbell was employed to develop a feed research program. This was an outstanding step, one that put millions of dollars in the pockets of members through the years." Letter from W. D. Milsop, March 5, 1970. Milsop was an employee of the Exchange from the early 1920's and was later General Manager.

13. "The warehouses had a dual purpose. They were located in areas where there was a good potential demand and also where they could serve as a wholesale base to supplement local representatives service . . . The establishment of this system was something like Sears, Roebuck going from a strictly catalog business to retail outlets.

The representative system didn't quite do the job so something new was needed." W. D. Milsop to the author, March 5, 1970.

14. For discussion of the conditions that led to the demand for Babcock's services, see Joseph G. Knapp, *Seeds That Grew: A History of the Cooperative Grange League Federation Exchange* (Hinsdale, N.Y.: Anderson House, 1960), pp. 41-62.

15. Warren A. Ranney, "Howard Edward Babcock—A Renaissance Man" in Joseph G. Knapp and Associates, *Great American Cooperators* (Washington, D.C.: American Institute of Cooperation, 1967), pp. 11-49.

16. For the full story of the growth of this pace-setting organization from 1920 to 1932, see Joseph G. Knapp, *Seeds That Grew, op. cit.*, pp. 41-165. For an inside account of GLF history for this period by one of the pioneer leaders in the GLF, see Thomas E. Milliman (with Grace Page), *The GLF Story, 1920-64* (Ithaca: N.Y.: Wilcox Press, 1964), pp. 41 ff.

17. To understand how the Southern States Cooperative became a great institution, one must know of the man who nursed it to greatness—W. G. Wysor. See W. M. Corwin, "William Geoffrey Wysor—Founder of Southern States Cooperative" in Joseph G. Knapp and Associates, *op. cit.*, pp. 535-546.

18. The VSS adopted a unique method for paying patronage refunds through the use of patronage refund certificates issued at time of purchase. One writer likened the certificates to "cigar-store coupons." This system was superseded in 1940 by the commonly used system of paying refunds upon the basis of records of purchases made. For a description of this interesting way of distributing patronage refunds, see John H. Lister and Alexander Swantz, *Purchasing Farm Supplies Through Southern States Cooperative, Inc.*, Farm Credit Administration, Circular C-128, June 1943, pp. 28-29.

19. The great increase in 1931 volume was accounted for by the abnormal hay purchases in the summer of 1930.

20. For a complete account of the origins and development of the VSS until it became the Southern States Cooperative, see W. G. Wysor, *The Southern States Story: The First 35 Years* (Richmond, Va.: Southern States Cooperative, 1959); and Lister and Swantz, *op. cit.*, Circular C-128.

21. The problems of farmers in gaining recognition and service from the fertilizer companies in the early 1920's are well presented by the Federal Trade Commission's *Report on the Fertilizer Industry*, March 3, 1923. This report said: "Attention is also directed to the benefits which have resulted to the farmer through cooperative buying of fertilizer, which has been the most important factor in lowering the price of this important product," p. 9.

22. I. Harvey Hull, *Built of Men—The Story of Indiana Cooperatives* (New York: Harper & Brothers, 1952), p. 44.

23. *Ibid.*, pp. 43-45.

24. Paul Turner, *They Did It in Indiana: The Story of the Indiana Farm Bureau Cooperatives* (New York: The Dryden Press, 1947), p. 35.

25. Herbert C. Fledderjohn, "I. H. Hull—He Built on Faith," in Knapp and Associates, *op. cit.*, pp. 248-254.

26. It took some years for this recommendation to be fully implemented. In the first few years membership was limited to Farm Bureau members.

27. Hull and others date the beginning of the Indiana Farm Bureau Cooperative Association as of February 1, 1927, when the Purchasing Department was reorganized as an independent corporation.

28. Senate Committee on Agriculture and Forestry, *Farm Relief Legislation Hearings,* 1929, pp. 231-232.

29. I. Harvey Hull, *Twentieth Century Pioneer* (Indianapolis: Indiana Farm Bureau Cooperative Association, 1968), pp. 17, 18.

30. In testifying before the Senate Committee on Agriculture and Forestry in *Farm Legislation Relief Hearings,* March 1929, Hull said: "We have built up a reserve of $83,000. We have returned in patronage savings $400,000" (p. 232).

31. For a photograph of a group of Indiana farmers working together in construction of a petroleum bulk plant, see Gerald M. Francis, "Cooperative Purchasing by Indiana Farmers," Farm Credit Administration, Bulletin 38, 1939, p. 5.

32. Murray R. Lincoln, *Vice-President in Charge of Revolution* (New York: McGraw-Hill, 1960), pp. 67 ff.

33. Murray Lincoln was a strong advocate of the chain store method of local distribution. At the sessions of the American Institute of Cooperation, in the summer of 1930, he said: "I believe the Ohio plan places the farmers in better position to understand the different factors of business than they ever could be with a local, independently operated store, because they never got that kind of information from their managers. I feel also that the farmer wants successes, and as long as it is done for his benefit and he sees results, he does not care a whole lot whether the store is centrally managed or managed locally." *American Cooperation,* I, 1930, p. 286.

34. Perry Green, *History of Ohio Farm Bureau Federation* (Columbus: Ohio Farm Bureau Federation, mimeographed, October 1955), see pp. 140 ff., p. 174 ff., pp. 210-11.

35. For information on early cooperative purchasing developments in Michigan, see C. L. Brody, "Purchasing Activities of the Michigan State Farm Bureau," *American Cooperation,* 1929, pp. 447-457. See also Orion Ulrey, "Clark Lewis Brody—Diplomat and Spokesman" in Knapp and Associates, *op. cit.,* pp. 98-101.

36. See Robin Hood, *loc. cit.*

37. J. Warren Mather, "Petroleum Operations of Farmer Cooperatives," Farm Credit Administration, Circular C-139, 1951, pp. 2-4. The number of tractors on farms increased from 246,000 in 1920 to 920,000 in 1930. Most of these tractors were owned by farmers in the Midwest agricultural region.

38. For the story of the beginnings of this pioneer association, see article, "Cottonwood, 1921—Why Oil Purchasing Began," *Midland Cooperator,* August 17, 1949. The financial statement of this association for the year ending April 30, 1923, showed sales of $49,556 and net "profits" (savings) of $5,317, which represented "90 per cent on paid-in capital of $5,900."

39. Glen W. Thompson, "E. G. Cort—Man of Action" in Joseph G. Knapp and Associates, *op. cit.,* pp. 138-141.

40. For information on the development of oil cooperatives in Minnesota, see Rudolph K. Froker and H. Bruce Price, "Organization and Management Problems of Cooperative Oil Associations in Minnesota," U.S.D.A., Circular 80, November 1929. See also Leonard C. Kercher, Vant W. Kebker, and Wilfred C. Leland (Roland S. Vaile, editor), *Consumers' Cooperatives in the North Central States* (Minneapolis: University of Minnesota Press, 1941), pp. 381-405.

41. John L. Lacey, *Farm Bureau in Illinois* (Bloomington: Illinois Agricultural Association, 1965), p. 129.

42. For more complete information on the early growth of the Illinois Farm Supply Company, see *ibid.,* pp. 291 ff.; Joseph G. Knapp, "Your Next 25 Years," *Farmers in Business* (Washington, D.C.: Institute of Cooperation, 1963), pp. 212-214; John H. Lister, "Cooperative Purchasing Through the Illinois Farm Supply Company and Its Member County Companies," Farm Credit Administration, Bulletin 27, 1938; and Rudolph K. Froker and H. Bruce Price, *op. cit.,* pp. 35-37.

43. Thatcher was the driving force who set the pattern for Farmers' Union cooperative developments in the Northwest. Robert Handschin, "M. W. Thatcher—Cooperative Warrior" in Joseph G. Knapp and Associates, *op. cit.*, pp. 510-515.

44. Kercher, Kebker, and Leland, *op. cit.*, pp. 406 ff.

45. For a detailed account of the development of the Union Oil Company (Cooperative) during its formative years, see Gilbert C. Fite, *Farm to Factory—A History of the Consumers Cooperative Association* (Columbia: University of Missouri Press, 1965), pp. 34-96. In epitomizing this story, I have drawn freely on this valuable source.

46. The subject of this talk was "A National Oil and Gasoline Movement." *Ibid.*, pp. 39-40. Fite calls this one of the most important documents in the early history of the Union Oil Company "because it expresses so clearly Cowden's ideas and ambitions at the time the company was formed."

47. *Ibid.*, p. 38.

48. *American Cooperation*, 1929, pp. 457-467.

49. President's Annual Report, Second Annual Meeting, January 13, 1931, Union Oil Company (Cooperative), North Kansas City, Missouri.

50. In 1935 the Union Oil Company (Cooperative) became the Consumers Cooperative Association which changed its name in 1966 to Farmland Industries, Inc. Progress of this organization will be examined in later chapters.

51. See Joseph G. Knapp, *The Rise of American Cooperative Enterprise, op. cit.*, pp. 322-330.

52. R. H. Elsworth, "Statistics of Farmers Cooperative Business Organizations," Farm Credit Administration, Bulletin 6, 1936, p. 97.

53. Robin Hood, *loc. cit.*

54. See *Fortune*'s list of 500 largest industrial corporations. *Fortune*, May 1972, pp. 188-206.

Chapter X

1. Two recently published books had done much to Americanize the conception of a cooperatively organized society: (1) Emerson P. Harris, *Cooperation; The Hope of the Consumer* (New York: The Macmillan Company, 1918), and (2) Albert Sonnichsen, *Consumers' Cooperation* (New York: The Macmillan Company, 1919). Harris was experienced in accounting, store management, and advertising, and he approached his subject from a businessman's point of view. He recognized that success in cooperation depended upon business efficiency and his discussion was realistic, although social-minded. He was not blinded to the imperfections of human nature, and he envisaged consumers' buying organizations working harmoniously with farmers' marketing cooperatives. Sonnichsen, provided the first significant American statement of the philosophy of consumers' cooperation. His book made no great claim to originality, for it followed the line of thinking developed by English and European theorists. The author was more concerned with staking out the field so as to make clear that consumers' cooperatives were distinctly different from agricultural marketing cooperatives and other forms of cooperative activity. In the Foreword to Sonnichsen's volume, Professor Graham Brooks gave him credit for clearing up the subject and lifting consumers' cooperation into "its own clear light."

2. Warbasse realized that the attainment of the League's objective of ultimately organizing all economic activity by and for consumers would call for a revolution in economic thinking and a long program of educational effort. He not only gave his

time and energies to forward the success of the League, but he largely financed it until it could get on its own feet. He stated in 1941 that over the preceding 25 years he had contributed $150,000 to the support of the League. For Warbasse's own story of the initial years of the League, see his autobiography, *Three Voyages* (Chicago: Cooperative League of the U.S.A., 1956), pp. 113 ff.

3. See *Proceedings of Second National Cooperative Convention*, p. 35. A wave of interest in consumers' cooperatives had arisen out of the boom conditions that followed World War I. See Joseph G. Knapp, *The Rise of American Cooperative Enterprise* (Danville, Ill.: The Interstate Printers & Publishers, Inc., 1969), p. 416, and footnote 49, p. 518. This was taken advantage of by unscrupulous promoters who set up fictitious cooperative organizations that swindled millions of dollars from sympathetic investors. Much as Warbasse decried the methods of these "spurious enterprises" he saw as even more dangerous "those who wish the movement well" who set up "fanciful schemes" that "violate the fundamental principles of cooperation or of business." See Preface to *Proceedings*, p. 3.

4. *Report of the Proceedings of the Second American Cooperative Convention, 1920*, pp. 28-29.

5. *Ibid.*, p. 61.

6. The constitution as adopted is given in the Proceedings of this Convention, pp. 104-111. A constitution for District Leagues, which was provided for in the League's Constitution, was also adopted by the convention. See pp. 111-117.

7. At the first meeting of the League in Warbasse's home (March 18, 1916), there developed (according to Peter Hamilton who was present) "a definite organization with Dr. Warbasse as President, Scott Perky as Secretary, and myself as Treasurer." Hyman Cohn, Albert Sonnichsen, and Emerson P. Harris were among others present who were selected as directors at this first meeting. See Erma Angevine, *In League with the Future* (Chicago: Cooperative League of U.S.A., 1959), p. 39. Mrs. Angevine's book provides personal sketches of the persons who served as League directors from 1916 to 1959 and is a treasure trove of information on the organization and development of the League. See also Warbasse's own account of the early beginnings of the League, *op. cit.*, Chapters 14-16.

8. Prior to this the League was "merely a society of individuals devoted to consumers cooperation." Clarke A. Chambers, "The Cooperative League of the U.S.A., 1916-1961: A Study of Social Theory and Social Action." *Agricultural History*, April 1962, p. 63.

9. Warbasse, *op. cit.*, p. 120.

10. This cooperative was first known as "Our Cafeteria." For a profile of Miss Arnold, who was one of the most steadfast supporters of the League in its formative years, see Leslie Woodcock, "Mary Endicott Arnold: Creative Urban Worker" in Joseph G. Knapp and Associates, *Great American Cooperators* (Washington, D.C.: American Institute of Cooperation, 1967), pp. 10-12.

11. See Florence E. Parker, *The First 125 Years: A History of Distributive and Service Cooperation in the United States, 1829-1954* (Chicago: The Cooperative League, 1956), pp. 94-95, 403.

12. Dr. Warbasse has described the design as follows: "It consists of a circle within which are two pine trees. The pine tree is the ancient symbol of endurance and fecundity. More than one pine is used to signify cooperation . . . The circle represents the all-embracing cosmos which depends upon cooperation for its existence . . ." James Peter Warbasse, *op. cit.*, pp. 121-122.

13. The valuable contributions made by Miss Parker to consumers' cooperation during her long career with the Bureau of Labor Statistics are described by Erma Angevine in her profile of Miss Parker, sub-titled "A Beacon Light." See Joseph G. Knapp and Associates, *op. cit.*, pp. 371-372. From 1920 until her retirement in 1954, Miss

Parker kept in close touch with the consumers' cooperative movement and reported developments as they occurred in the *Monthly Labor Review* and official publications related to consumers' cooperation. Her objectivity and sympathetic interest played an important role in gaining national respect for developments in this field. Her book, written after her retirement, is the authoritative history of consumers' cooperation in the United States, Parker, *op. cit., in toto.*

14. Warbasse was also much influenced by his studies of Marxian socialism, Kropotkin's mutual associationism, the pragmatism of William James and John Dewey and nineteenth century humanitarianism. See Warbasse, *op. cit.,* pp. 59 ff. As Clarke A. Chambers has pointed out "For all this eclecticism his system was surprisingly logical, coherent, and persuasive." See his article "The Cooperative League of the U.S.A., 1916-1961: A Study of Social Theory and Action," *Agricultural History,* April 1962, p. 66. In an introduction to an American edition of Charles Gide's book, *Consumers' Cooperation,* published by Macmillan in 1922, Warbasse said: "It is an augury of moment that an economist of his profound scholarship should be drawn to cooperation as the agency above all others which he believes has the power to reorganize society."

15. Warbasse like many others at this time was disposed to give the Russian experiment a free trial. In an article in *Cooperation,* September 1923, he quoted the following sentences by Lenin with approval. "It is incumbent upon us to support the cooperative movement *above all.*" He reported that Lenin saw the cooperative movement "as an essential step in moving toward a free cooperative society."

16. Leonard C. Kercher, Vant W. Kebker, Wilfred C. Leland, Jr., *Consumers' Cooperation in the North Central States* (Minneapolis: University of Minnesota Press, 1941), pp. 28-29, 43; Florence E. Parker, *op. cit.,* pp. 117-118.

17. For changes in American communist party policy during the 1920's, see Irving Howe and Lewis Coser, *The American Communist Party—A Critical History* (New York: Praeger, 1962), especially pp. 27 ff., 96 ff., 118 ff., 131 ff., 172, 177-178, 188 ff. See also Harold U. Faulkner, *From Versailles to the New Deal* (New Haven: Yale University Press, 1950), pp. 280-283, and Frederick Lewis Allen, *Only Yesterday* (New York: Harper and Row, 1931), Perennial Library Edition, 1965, pp. 40-41.

18. In 1927-1928, 7 of the 17 members of the Board of Directors of the Cooperative League were Finnish immigrants. Erma Angevine, *op. cit.,* p. 67.

19. Warbasse had succeeded in getting membership for the League in the International Cooperative Alliance in 1919, and he personally attended all of its congresses. This gave him a wide acquaintance with cooperative leaders throughout the world and gained recognition from abroad for the Cooperative League.

20. Warbasse, *Three Voyages, op. cit.,* pp. 86-96.

21. *Cooperation,* May 1925, p. 90.

22. *Ibid.,* March 1926, p. 58.

23. "Like all ideologues, he was not swayed from positions of heart and mind by the actual course of events. As cooperation stumbled along in the '20's he rarely lost faith. He took heart from history, as he read it, which proved that all great movements began with a handful of committed and courageous men." Clarke A. Chambers, *op. cit.,* p. 66.

24. For information on cooperative housing developments prior to 1927, see Florence E. Parker, *op. cit.,* pp. 214-215.

25. The story of how this first successful housing cooperative came into being and how it was expanded over the years is told by its pioneer leader, Abraham E. Kazan, in an illustrated brochure *30 Years of Amalgamated Cooperative Housing, 1927-1957,* published in 1958 by Amalgamated Housing Corporation.

26. For the views of each Director, see *Cooperation* for June 1928. V. S. Allane suggested that the ban be of a temporary nature to tide the League over the present crisis. Cedric Long urged that some other place be found for discussion of controversial questions. Warbasse said: "I have no quarrel with socialism, communism, or other movements, if the people want them; but, I believe that these things must be kept out of the cooperative movement in the United States if cooperation is to be made strong and solid."

27. See *Report of the Proceedings of the Sixth Congress of the Cooperative League of the U.S.A.*, given in the *Cooperative League Yearbook for 1930*, pp. 63, 89, 91.

28. Warbasse, *Three Voyages, op. cit.*, p. 154.

29. Eric Kendall, "V. S. Allane—Champion of Cooperative Neutrality" in Knapp and Associates, *op. cit.*, pp. 27-29.

30. *Ibid.*, p. 28.

31. The discussion which follows in the next few pages is largely condensed from information contained in an unsigned pamphlet entitled: "What It's All About," issued as a reprint from the *Cooperative Pyramid Builder*, published by the Cooperative Central Exchange in the spring of 1931 to explain the developments that had occurred within the Exchange from 1929 to 1931.

32. It is here of interest that three directors who were soon to defect from the Exchange and accept orders from the Communist Party refused to submit to this demand for Hallonen's removal.

33. The above is largely taken from reports on the Seventh Congress of the Cooperative League in *Cooperation*, December 1930.

34. Warbasse, *Three Voyages, op. cit.*, p. 157. See also Clarke A. Chambers, *op. cit.*, p. 67.

35. The state of economic well-being that prevailed in 1928 is well reflected in the volume *Recent Economic Changes in the United States* (New York: McGraw-Hill, 1929). This book, by a committee under the chairmanship of Herbert Hoover, was issued in the spring of 1929 just before the onset of the depression.

36. The rapid growth of chain stores was of much concern to cooperative leaders in the late 1920's. Cedric Long, Executive Secretary of the Cooperative League, in a feature article on "Cooperation, Chain Stores and Wholesaling" in the *Cooperative League Yearbook for 1930*, said: "We no longer need make any plea for cooperative wholesales. All progressive cooperators recognize the need. The independent, isolated society which pits its strength against the mammoth chain store corporations is a spectacle deserving not so much of our condemnation as our pity. Not only has the era of big business arrived; it has been here long enough so that even the sleepiest cooperative official should now be awake to its significance" (pp. 18-20). Colston E. Warne, in another feature article in the *Yearbook*, "The New Capitalism in Its Relation to Cooperation—Can Cooperation Survive?," pointed out that "The chain store has been the mechanism by which large-scale production methods have been brought into the retail field." He urged the cooperative movement to consider its problems in the light of the "new capitalism." He asked whether "the traditional form and tactics of organization are still workable" . . . and then said: "The Rochdale system was the product of an age of small scale business. Will this system without alterations be equally effective in the present setting?" (pp. 16-18).

37. For discussion of embryonic experiments see Florence Parker, *op. cit.*, pp. 234-237.

38. For Shalid's account of how the Elk City Cooperative Hospital came to be established and how it overcame its first difficulties, see "The Story of the Community Hospital," *Cooperation*, March 1933.

39. In 1929 the Minnesota Association of Oil Cooperatives formed in 1925 sent fraternal delegates to the Congress of the Northern States Cooperative League, and in 1930

this organization which had taken the name Midland Cooperative Oil Company (now Midland Cooperatives, Inc.) joined the Northern States Cooperative League.

40. For a considered view on the contributions of Cedric Long to the work of the League, see Clarke A. Chambers, *op. cit.*, pp. 60, 67, 69. Chambers said: "Warbasse was still undisputed champion, but the untimely death of Cedric Long, who had seen the League through so many internal troubles, left it without the regular week-to-week direction it required."

41. The problem of getting the league on a self-supporting basis had greatly concerned Sonnichsen and other friends of the League. See Warbasse, *Three Voyages, op. cit.*, p. 138. Much of the credit for promoting this aim can be accorded Miss Arnold who, as Treasurer since 1929, had persuaded many of the larger cooperatives to make contributions in addition to their dues.

Chapter XI

1. The Report of the Business Men's Commission on Agriculture in 1927 said: "The situation with regard to long term credit is reasonably good. The existing machinery for extending mortgage credit to the agricultural industry (Federal land banks, joint stock land banks, insurance companies, and private mortgage corporations) is, in general, working fairly well, and does not require fundamental change." *The Condition of Agriculture in the United States and Measures for Its Improvement* (published jointly by the National Industrial Conference Board, Inc., New York City, and Chamber of Commerce of America, Washington D.C., 1927), p. 237.

2. "By the end of 1931, the government-owned stock had virtually all been retired . . . The total capital of the banks, almost entirely owned by the borrowers, had grown to $65,676,130." While savings due to the system were substantial, "the introduction of the long-term amortized loan was of much greater importance than the modest reduction in the rate of interest charged. The land banks and joint stock banks were the pioneers in bringing into use this fundamental improvement in farm mortgage operations." Murray R. Benedict, *Can We Solve the Farm Problem?* (New York: The Twentieth Century Fund, 1955), pp. 133-134.

3. Frieda Baird and Claude L. Benner, *Ten Years of Federal Intermediate Credits* (Washington, D.C.: The Brookings Institution, 1933), p. 41.

4. *Ibid.*, p. 44.

5. *Ibid.*, p. 51. Herman Steen reflected agricultural opinion when he said in 1923: "The most valuable ally which the cooperatives had in 1921 and 1922 was the War Finance Corporation." *Cooperative Marketing: The Golden Rule in Agriculture* (New York: Doubleday, Page & Co., 1923), p. 342.

6. See Baird and Benner, *op. cit.*, "Structure of the Intermediate Credit System," Chapter II, pp. 88-103.

7. Although cooperative marketing associations were well served by the Intermediate Credit Banks, no direct financing assistance was made available to cooperative purchasing associations. The Eastern States Farmers' Exchange of Springfield, Massachusetts, and the Cooperative Grange League Federation Exchange of Ithaca, New York, both organized subsidiary credit corporations in the middle twenties to obtain capital through rediscounting farmers' notes with the Springfield Intermediate Credit Bank. However, the amount of such borrowings was negligible in terms of the total operations of these associations. The great value of this assistance to the Eastern States Farmers' Exchange was mentioned in Chapter IX.

8. See Earl I. Butz, *The Production Credit System for Farmers* (Washington, D.C.: The Brookings Institution, 1944), pp. 1 ff.

9. Baird and Benner, *op. cit.*, pp. 176-177.

10. For a careful study of the experience of cotton credit corporations, see William H. Rowe, *Agricultural Credit Corporations Affiliated with Cotton Cooperative Marketing Associations*, U.S.D.A. Technical Bulletin 323, September 1932. For information on the operations of producers livestock credit corporations, see Edwin G. Nourse and Joseph G. Knapp, *The Cooperative Marketing of Livestock* (Washington, D.C.: The Brookings Institution, 1931), pp. 169-175.

11. See Baird and Benner, Chapter XIX, "The Intermediate Credit Banks and the Federal Farm Board," *op. cit.*, pp. 346-363.

12. See Paul Bestor, *American Cooperation*, 1930, pp. 60-61, and 1932, pp. 166-175. See also E. H. Thompson, *American Cooperation*, 1932, pp. 176-182. In describing the operations of the Federal Intermediate Credit Bank of Springfield, Massachusetts, Mr. Thompson indicated that the agricultural credit corporations formed as adjuncts to cooperative buying or marketing associations had performed needed services, and he looked to further development of such operations. He saw real possibilities in the formation of agricultural credit corporations to supply farmers with production credit, operating in much the same way as the national farm loan associations in the field of long-term credit. This idea was to be incorporated in the plan for the production credit associations in the Farm Credit Act of 1933.

13. Baird and Benner, *op. cit.*, pp. 325-330, 375-376.

14. Joseph G. Knapp, *The Rise of American Cooperative Enterprise* (Danville, Ill.: The Interstate Printers & Publishers, Inc., 1969), pp. 138-142.

15. Roy F. Bergengren, *Credit Union—A Cooperative Banking Book* (New York: The Beckman Hill Press, 1931), p. 155. See also Bergengren, *Cuna Emerges—A Third Credit Union Book* (Madison, Wisc.: Credit Union National Association, 1935), Fourth Edition, p. 28.

16. Tom J. Hefter, "Edward A. Filene—U.S. Father of Credit Unions" in Knapp and Associates, *Great American Cooperators* (Washington, D.C.: American Institute of Cooperation, 1967), pp. 165-171. It has been estimated that Filene's contributions to the credit union movement ultimately amounted to $1,000,000.

17. John E. Eidam, "Roy F. Bergengren—Credit Union Crusader" in Knapp and Associates, *op. cit.*, pp. 65-70. For the interesting story of how the Filene-Bergengren partnership in credit union development came into being and continued, see J. Carrol Moody, "Credit Unions in the 1920's" in *You . . . and Your Credit Union History*, edited by E. R. Brann (Madison, Wisc.: Cuna International, Inc., 1970), pp. 46-49.

18. Roy F. Bergengren, *Cuna Emerges, op. cit.*, pp. 23-25. The offices of CUNEB, the Credit Union National Extension Bureau, were opened on July 1, 1921. See J. Carrol Moody, *op. cit.*, pp. 46 ff.

19. Bergengren referred to him as Director of Personnel although the current title at that time was Third Assistant Postmaster General. He directed a newly created service relations agency to promote the interests of postal employees.

20. Although the primary promotion job was done by Bergengren, he was ably backed up by Filene who had great influence in the business community. Filene used every opportunity to point out that credit unions were of great value not only to members but "to bankers, to businessmen, to society and to the state." See, for example, his address "The Credit Union and Its Industrial Significance," before the California Management Association, San Francisco, March 7, 1927.

21. The establishment of personnel departments in many companies following World War I recognized the fact that "maximum continuous quality output involved the intelligent cooperation of the workers." See Ordway Tead, "Personnel Administration" in *Encyclopaedia of the Social Sciences*, Vol. 12 (New York: The Macmillan Company, 1934), pp. 88-89.

22. The way in which this program unfolded is interestingly recalled by Mr. Orchard in a letter to the author, April 22, 1968. "I first became aware that a credit union could be organized in September 1929 . . . The more I studied the idea, the clearer I could see the need and the more my superiors in Armour and Company tried to discourage me, the greater my determination to proceed . . . It required several months and some fortunate promotions among higher officials before permission was granted for the organization of the first credit union in Armour and Company, Omaha, which, by the way, was the first in the country in the meat packing industry. This one got off to an excellent start, so much so, that the Board of Directors, in an attempt to avoid swamping our first treasurer with work, limited the number of new members to 50 per month . . . In the early 1930's employees generally were seeking ways in which employees could be benefited, especially if the cost was modest or nil . . . There was little limitation once employers were convinced of the benefits . . . In our company the President and his close advisers watched the progress of the credit union in Omaha very closely, as did the others among the big packers. By the end of 1930, all Armour general managers and supervisors had been briefed and in January 1931, Tom Doig, who had joined the National Credit Union Extension Bureau on January 1, 1930, and I began a long journey to present the plan to all offices, plants, branch houses, tanneries, soap plants, creameries, milk condensaries, produce plants and cheese factories in Armour and Company, which had fifty or more employees, and were located in states which then had enabling acts. Where there was interest shown we helped to obtain a charter and assisted the new group with their organization meeting at which directors, committeemen and officers were elected. Our president, Ed White, had generously urged that we, through the head of the local Armour organization, should invite a representative of other industrial groups located nearby to attend our presentation and the organization meeting which followed as soon as a charter could be obtained. It was arranged that we were free to stay in any city we visited for as long as would be needed to meet with outside interested groups and help them obtain a charter."

23. Roy F. Bergengren, *Credit Union—A Cooperative Banking Book, op. cit.,* p. 214.

24. *Ibid.,* pp. 210-214.

25. *Ibid.,* p. 6.

26. Richard Y. Giles, *Credit for the Millions—The Story of Credit Unions* (New York: Harper and Brothers, 1951), pp. 105-106.

27. Heartened by this Indiana experience, and by the formation of rural credit unions in other states in association with farmers' purchasing cooperatives, Bergengren said in 1935: "While the rural experiments are still in a developing, evolving stage, we are gradually producing a type of rural credit union capable of mass production." *Cuna Emerges, op. cit.,* p. 28.

28. Bergengren, *Credit Union—A Cooperative Banking Book, op. cit.,* pp. 242-243.

29. For a comprehensive review of the progress of credit unions from 1920 to 1933, see J. Carroll Moody and Gilbert C. Fite, *The Credit Union Movement—Origins and Development, 1850-1970* (Lincoln: University of Nebraska Press, 1971), pp. 75-148.

30. See Joseph G. Knapp, *op. cit.,* pp. 422-423.

31. By 1932 specialized reinsurance companies were operating in eight states: Iowa, Missouri, North Dakota, California, Indiana, Nebraska, Minnesota, and Wisconsin. Generally these companies were sponsored and promoted by the respective state associations of farmers' mutual insurance companies. Ralph R. Botts, *Farm Mutual Reinsurance,* Agricultural Information Bulletin 119, Agricultural Research Service, U.S.D.A., 1963.

32. See V. N. Valgren, "Trends and Developments in Farm Mutual Insurance," *Amer-*

ican Cooperation, 1937, pp. 599-607, and Harry P. Cooper, "The Significance of Farmers' Mutual Insurance," *ibid.,* pp. 589-598.

33. Like all other businesses, farmers' mutual fire insurance companies were hard hit by the Great Depression. Fire losses increased substantially in 1930, 1931, and 1932, and it was necessary for the companies to increase members' assessments. To meet this problem the farm mutuals stepped up their loss prevention programs, and risks were reappraised and coverages reduced to match the decline in property values. These and other actions enabled most farm mutuals to weather the economic storm and stay in business. Interview of author with French M. Hyre, in charge of insurance studies, Farmer Cooperative Service, U.S.D.A., January 10, 1972.

34. Karl Schriftgiesser, *The Farmer from Merna—A Biography of George J. Mecherle and a History of the State Farm Insurance Companies of Bloomington, Illinois* (New York: Random House, 1955).

35. See Chapter 8, "How It All Worked," *ibid.,* pp. 94-103.

36. *Ibid.,* p. 60; see also p. 48.

37. *Ibid.,* pp. 87-88. See also John J. Lacey, *Farm Bureau in Illinois* (Bloomington, Ill.: Illinois Agricultural Association, 1965), p. 270.

38. Lacey, *op. cit.,* pp. 88-90.

39. *Ibid.,* p. 117.

40. For information on the formation of the Farm Bureau Mutual Insurance Company—which became Nationwide Insurance Companies in 1955—See Murray D. Lincoln, *Vice-President in Charge of Revolution,* as told to David Karp (New York: McGraw-Hill, 1960), pp. 72-76. Speaking at the American Institute of Cooperation in 1929, Lincoln said, "We paid $30,000 to the Illinois Company after which it was patterned, for organization expense, forms, etc." Murray D. Lincoln, "Cooperative Insurance," *American Cooperation,* 1929, p. 481.

41. Lincoln, *Vice-President in Charge of Revolution, op. cit.,* pp. 72-73.

42. Letter of Robert G. Sayre, Nationwide Insurance Companies, to author, December 7, 1971. The charter was revised in 1931 to permit the writing of all casualty lines. For a brief history of the Nationwide Insurance organizations, see Bowman Doss, *People Working Together* (New York: The Newcomer Society, 1968).

43. For information on the beginnings and early history of this company, see John J. Lacey, *op. cit.,* pp. 123-124, 271-275. The Illinois Agricultural Association had already gone into the mutual insurance business in 1925 when it set up the Farmers Mutual Reinsurance Company to spread the risk of local mutual fire and hail insurance companies in Illinois. Its immediate success set up a drive by the Illinois county farm bureaus for their own automobile insurance company. See Lacey, pp. 100-101, 267-268.

44. Lacey holds that one factor above all others explained the remarkable growth of the I.A.A. insurance companies. "That factor was simply that farmers considered these companies their own. Generally, they promoted them effectively by word-of-mouth with evangelical enthusiasms." *Ibid.,* pp. 272-274.

45. See O. M. Kile, *The Farm Bureau Through Three Decades* (Baltimore: Waverly Press, 1948), pp. 347 ff.

46. See Charles M. Gardner, *The Grange—Friend of the Farmer, 1867-1947* (Washington, D.C.: The National Grange, 1949), p. 322. See also W. C. Robinson, *The Grange—1867-1967* (Washington, D.C.: The National Grange, 1966), pp. 96-97.

Chapter XII

1. As we noted in Chapters X and XI, these conditions were also changing the character of non-agricultural cooperatives.

2. John D. Black and H. Bruce Price, "Cooperative Central Marketing Organizations," University of Minnesota Agricultural Experiment Station, Bulletin 211, April 1924, p. 6.

3. See George Burton Hotchkiss, *Milestones of Marketing* (New York: The Macmillan Company, 1938), pp. 184-259; see also article on "Marketing" by Melvin T. Copeland in *Report of the Committee on Economic Changes in the United States,* under chairmanship of Herbert Hoover (New York: McGraw-Hill, 1929), pp. 361 ff.

4. Dr. O. B. Jesness in reviewing this paragraph commented as follows: "As a friend of Sapiro's who had an opportunity to watch much of this development first hand, I am convinced that his contributions would have been decidedly greater had he understood differences in commodities, markets, and problems, and adjusted his program to the needs of each situation rather than employ a stereotyped plan." Letter to author of June 18, 1971.

5. Robert H. Montgomery, *The Cooperative Pattern in Cotton* (New York: The Macmillan Company, 1929), pp. 194 ff.

6. The contract innovations brought in by the Staple Cotton Cooperative Association had a profound influence on like commodity marketing associations. See A. V. Swarthout, *Farmers Cooperative Business Study—The Staple Cotton Cooperative Association,* U.S.D.A., Circular 397, 1926, pp. 6-11. See also Charles R. Sayre's biographical essay on the pioneering manager of this association, "William Montjoy Garrard—A Manager of Service" in Knapp and Associates, *Great American Cooperators* (Washington, D.C.: American Institute of Cooperation, 1967), pp. 178-184.

7. Jesness was Chief, Section of Markets, and Professor of Markets, College of Agriculture, University of Kentucky, 1920-1926. See E. Fred Koller, "Oscar B. Jesness—He Left His Mark" in Knapp and Associates, *op. cit.,* pp. 259-265.

8. University of Minnesota Agricultural Experiment Station, Bulletin 211, pp. 15-16.

9. How this program developed is well told by R. H. Montgomery, *op. cit.,* pp. 150-170. At the National Cooperative Marketing Conference held in Washington, D.C., January 1925, C. O. Moser, Secretary of the American Cotton Growers' Exchange, maintained that field service work was indispensable to the effective operation of strong marketing cooperatives. At the meetings of the American Institute of Cooperation in the summer of 1925, L. F. McKay, Field Service Director of the American Cotton Growers' Exchange, likened the field service department to the production department of any great business enterprise since "the problem of the field service division is to get cotton delivered to the association." *American Cooperation,* II, 1925, p. 234.

10. The origins of public relations work are interestingly described by Ray Eldon Hiebert, *Courtier to the Crowd* (Ames: Iowa State University Press, 1966).

11. Verna Elsinger, "The Burley Tobacco Growers Experiment," *American Cooperation,* II, 1928, pp. 499-621. See Beryle Stanton, "Verna Elsinger—Inspirational Educator," in Knapp and Associates, *op. cit.,* pp. 150-155.

12. *Proceedings of the Fourth National Cooperative Marketing Conference,* Washington, D.C., January 12-15, 1926, p. 29.

13. See her inside story, "The Burley Tobacco Growers Experiment," *op. cit.,* p. 569.

14. See Carl C. Taylor, "The Story and the Lesson of the Tri-State Tobacco Cooperative Association," *American Cooperation,* 1933, pp. 499 ff.

15. See John Hanna, *Law of Cooperative Marketing Associations* (New York: Ronald Press, 1931), p. 11.

16. R. H. Montgomery, *op. cit.,* p. 51. In addressing the Grain Marketing Cooperative at Chicago also in 1920, Sapiro said, "Don't monkey with amateurs . . . More farmers associations are wrecked by limiting themselves on brains than anything I know."

17. A good illustration of the importance of management was the near failure of the GLF in 1922 because of managerial weakness. With the "drafting" of H. E. Babcock as General Manager, the organization soon overcame its difficulties and became an outstanding success. In Indiana, cooperative purchasing floundered until 1927 when Harvey Hull was brought in as manager. Under his leadership the Indiana Farm Bureau Cooperative Association soon made great progress. Similar illustrations could be given for many other cooperatives.

18. Many of the Sapiro-promoted commodity marketing cooperatives provided for the appointment of one or more public directors by the governor of the state or other state official to give assurance that the affairs of the association would be conducted in the public interest. Directors so appointed were usually men of considerable ability, and they helped raise the performance standards for other directors.

19. The California Prune and Apricot Growers, Inc., had created a subsidiary to own and operate its packing plants and to manage its warehousing operations in 1919. According to Herman Steen, this association "was the first to work out this double plan of organization on a large scale." H. G. Coykendall, the manager of this association, developed this plan with the assistance of Aaron Sapiro. Herman Steen, *Cooperative Marketing: The Golden Rule in Agriculture* (New York: Doubleday, Page and Co., 1923), p. 33.

20. See Harry M. Creech, "Purpose and Organization of Subsidiaries" in *American Cooperation*, II, 1928, pp. 479-484. In the discussion of this paper, H. E. Erdman described how various California cooperatives were making use of the subsidiary or affiliated corporation idea, pp. 489-490.

21. See discussion of "Spread of Revolving Finance" by Henry E. Erdman and Grace H. Larsen, *Revolving Finance in Agricultural Cooperatives* (Madison, Wisc.: Mimir Publishers, 1965), pp. 55-70. For discussion of beginnings of revolving financing see Joseph G. Knapp, *The Rise of American Cooperative Enterprise* (Danville, Ill.: The Interstate Printers & Publishers, Inc., 1969), pp. 221, 348-351.

22. *American Cooperation*, I, 1925, pp. 465-475.

23. A. V. Swarthout, "Better Financial Statements by Cooperatives," *Agricultural Cooperation*, U.S.D.A., November 9, 1925, p. 468. See also Swarthout, "Financial Statements and the General Public," *Agricultural Cooperation*, December 7, 1925, p. 513.

24. Joseph G. Knapp, *op. cit.*, pp. 230-231.

25. *Ibid.*, p. 337.

26. Newel H. Comish, *Cooperative Marketing of Agricultural Products* (New York: D. Appleton and Company, 1929), p. 210.

27. John D. Black anticipated that cooperatives would make much greater contributions to agricultural betterment in the decades ahead, but he warned "We shall have to wait until we can make our cooperative organizations stronger than they are at present." He believed that the key to better marketing was integration. "The cooperatives are destined to play a large part in the development of integration in the marketing field. They have already done more than any other group of agencies to bring producers and consumers more closely together and take up the slack in the system." *Agricultural Reform in the United States* (New York: McGraw-Hill, 1929), pp. 341, 348, 411.

28. *Research in Agricultural Cooperation—Scope and Method*, Social Science Research Council, Bulletin 15, New York City, 1933.

29. See *Cooperation in Agriculture—A Selected and Annotated Reading List*, U.S.D.A., Misc. Circular 97.

30. Although stabilization activities carried on with cooperatives under the Federal Farm Board were bitterly criticized, this did not indicate that the cooperative form

of business was under attack except by business competitors. It will be seen in later chapters that the Roosevelt Administration in 1933 did not turn away from cooperatives—but took steps to strengthen them.

31. The total number of farmers who belonged to such associations was somewhat less than a million, for many farmers held memberships in more than one association. The Bureau of the Census in 1919 found that 624,527 farms, or 9.7 per cent of all farms, were marketing or purchasing through cooperatives with a total business volume of $807 million.

32. R. H. Elsworth, "Cooperative Marketing and Purchasing, 1920-1930," Circular 121, 1930, p. 5.

33. *Yearbook of Agriculture*, U.S.D.A., 1934, p. 758.

34. Index numbers of wholesale prices fell from 225 for 1920 to 95 for 1932. Index numbers of farm prices fell from 152 for 1920 to 56 for 1932. Index numbers of prices paid by farmers declined from 194 to 107. *Ibid.*, pp. 706, 708.

35. For example, the cotton marketing associations which did not begin to function until 1921 marketed 2,220,000 bales of cotton in 1932. Milk bargaining associations increased their marketings from 1.1 million pounds of milk in 1920 to 8.1 billion pounds in 1932. Milk distributing cooperatives marketed 145 million pounds in 1920 and 4.5 billion pounds in 1932. Livestock terminal cooperative commission firms increased their marketings from 755,000 animals in 1920 to 12,925,756 in 1932. There was also a great expansion in quantities of feed, fertilizer, seed, petroleum, and other supplies handled cooperatively from 1920 to 1932. For more complete information, see R. H. Elsworth, *Statistics of Farmers' Cooperative Business Organizations, 1920-1935*, Farm Credit Administration. Bulletin 6, 1936.

36. No comprehensive statistical information on total assets and net worth of farmers' marketing and purchasing associations is available before 1936. Information for that year was assembled by the Farm Credit Administration. See *A Statistical Handbook of Farmer Cooperatives*, Bulletin 26, November 1938, pp. 155, 161. In 1936 total assets of cooperative marketing and purchasing associations were estimated at $510,846,000 and total net worth at $287,860,000. *The Balance Sheet of Agriculture*, U.S.D.A., 1969, reports net worth of farmers' marketing and purchasing cooperatives at $330 million for 1940. If we extrapolate backwards we get about the estimate given here for net worth in 1932. In view of the economic conditions that prevailed from 1933 to 1936, this estimate seems reasonable.

Chapter XIII

1. Letter of William I. Myers to author, October 22, 1971. Dr. Myers participated in many of these conferences in behalf of Mr. Morgenthau. He has made his personal journal of these meetings available to the author.

2. For the full story of the inception and first year's experience of the AAA, see Van I. Perkins, *Crisis in Agriculture—The Agricultural Adjustment Administration and the New Deal, 1933* (Berkeley: University of California Press, 1969). For basic information on the history of the agricultural developments during the New Deal period from 1933 to 1941, see Murray R. Benedict, *Farm Policies of the United States, 1790-1950* (New York: The Twentieth Century Fund, 1953); Murray R. Benedict, *Can We Solve the Farm Problem?* (New York: The Twentieth Century Fund, 1955); and Gladys L. Baker, Wayne D. Rasmussen, Vivian Wiser, and Jane M. Porter, *Century of Service—The First 100 Years of the United States Department of Agriculture*, Centennial Committee, U.S. Department of Agriculture, 1963.

3. Perkins, *op. cit.*, p. 40.

4. For a terse summarization of the Act see Benedict, *Can We Solve the Farm Problem?*, *op. cit.*, pp. 228-229.

5. In the words of Murray Benedict: ". . . the marketing agreement idea was in the discard during the Farm Board period, but quickly came back into prominence after passage of the Agricultural Adjustment Act with the marketing agreement provisions included." Murray Benedict, *Farm Policies of the United States*, *op. cit.*, pp. 304-305.

6. *Ibid.*, p. 304. See also Edwin G. Nourse, Chapter I. "Origins of the Marketing Agreement and Licensing Provisions," *Marketing Agreements under the AAA* (Washington, D.C.: The Brookings Institution, 1935), pp. 1-23.

7. How this came about has been explained by the late Alex Johnson, who was then Secretary of the California Farm Bureau Federation. Johnson had been searching for a way to achieve better control over specific crops so as to achieve what was then equivocally termed "compulsory cooperative marketing." He had presented his views to Howard Tolley, Director of the Gianinni Foundation of the University of California, who had put Dr. E. A. Stokdyk of his staff to work on the problem. After Stokdyk's studies were made, a bill was drafted for a state prorate act by Edson Abel, attorney for the California Farm Bureau. While this act was under consideration in the California State Legislature, Johnson attended a meeting in Washington of the Board of Directors of the American Farm Bureau Federation. He found that "they were considering the terms of the Agricultural Adjustment Act [Bill]. While not a member of that Board I suggested that the AAA proposed to hold out help to producers of seven crops, but if they would add a section covering the principles of the [California] Pro Rate Act they might put help in the way of producers of any crop. The Board asked their attorney to draft such a section and thus was born the Agricultural Marketing Section [of the Agricultural Adjustment Act]." Letter of Alex Johnson to author, May 20, 1968.

8. For a review of California developments and studies that resulted in the passage of the California Prorate Act see Joseph G. Knapp, *Stokdyk—Architect of Cooperation*, (Washington, D.C.: American Institute of Cooperation, 1953), pp. 49-54. Stokdyk was commonly called "the father of the prorate plan." See footnotes, pp. 53-54, 77-78. For information on how the plan worked in practice, see Chapter VII, "The Prorate Experiment," pp. 71-78.

9. Perkins, *op. cit.*, pp. 45-46.

10. See Joseph G. Knapp, "Cooperatives and the New Deal," *The Cooperative Marketing Journal*, June-July 1933.

11. Henry A. Wallace, "Cooperation and the Program of the Administration," *American Cooperation*, 1933, p. 8.

12. *Ibid.*, p. 11.

13. *Ibid.*, p. 14.

14. *Ibid.*, pp. 42-53.

15. *Ibid.*, pp. 55 ff.

16. In the beginning, Secretary Wallace hesitated to give any special recognition to the organized dairy producers. As Dr. John D. Black reported: "He did not consider that the Act instructed the Administration either to promote cooperative marketing or to provide special services to cooperatives." It took some time for the Administration to realize that any kind of realistic program would need to have their full support. *The Dairy Industry and the AAA* (Washington, D.C.: The Brookings Institution, 1935), pp. 87 ff. For an interesting account of the in-fighting on policy direction when the AAA was finding itself see the chapter, "Seven Months in the AAA," in Gilbert C. Fite's *George Peek and the Fight for Farm Parity* (Norman: University of Oklahoma Press, 1954), pp. 2 -266. See also George N. Peek

(with Samuel Crowthers), *Why Quit Our Own?* (New York: D. Van Nostrand Company, 1936), pp. 92-156.

17. For early AAA experience in developing marketing agreements and licenses see F. R. Wilcox, "The Federal Marketing Agreement Program," *American Cooperation*, 1938, pp. 184-185.

18. Edwin G. Nourse, Joseph S. Davis, and John D. Black, *Three Years of the AAA*, (Washington, D.C.: The Brookings Institution, 1937), p. 459. See also p. 102. For more complete information on this program, see Benedict, *Can We Solve the Farm Problem?*, *op. cit.*, pp. 232-233; and Arthur M. Schlesinger, Jr., *The Coming of the New Deal* (Boston: Houghton Mifflin Company, 1959), pp. 62-63.

19. For comprehensive information on the inception and character of the tobacco program, see Perkins, *op. cit.*, pp. 147-162, and Fite, *op. cit.*, pp. 258-260. It was not necessary to carry on marketing agreement programs for tobacco the following year, for by that time the production control program was in operation.

20. For a good description of how the program of the Commodity Credit Corporation arose, see Nourse, Davis, and Black, *op. cit.*, pp. 154 ff.

21. U.S.D.A., *Agricultural Statistics*, 1941, p. 554.

22. Van A. Perkins has summed up the accomplishments of the AAA in 1933 by saying: "The AAA had tried out most of the powers granted to it under the act, and for the most part, it had demonstrated that the provisions of the act, could be made to work . . . By the end of 1933 there had been some improvement in prices, some reduction in surplus, and some help for farmers in the form of benefit payments or other direct aid." But he felt that the AAA had done no more than make a start "in its quest for a resolution of the farm problem." He quoted as apt a statement made by President Roosevelt on the AAA program in December 1933: "We seem to be on our way, but we are not yet out of the woods," *op. cit.*, pp. 193, 195.

23. For more complete information on the conditions that eventually led to Peek's resignation, see Fite, *op. cit.*, pp. 243-266. See also Black, *op. cit.*, p. 115; and Arthur M. Schlesinger, Jr., *op. cit.*, pp. 46-59.

24. *The Cooperative Marketing Journal*, January-February 1934, pp. 9-12.

25. See "New Developments in the Dairy Controversy," *The Cooperative Marketing Journal*, March-April 1934, pp. 37-38.

26. See "Status of the Dairy Controversy," *The Cooperative Marketing Journal*, May-June 1934. For discussion of developments relating to milk marketing in 1933 and 1934, see also Nourse, *op. cit.*, pp. 196-230; and Black, *op. cit.*, pp. 444 ff.

27. Benedict, *Can We Solve the Farm Problem?*, *op. cit.*, p. 238.

28. When the time came for referendum votes, both plans were extended for another year. Those acts were repealed following the Supreme Court decision of January 6, 1936, which invalidated the processing tax procedure.

29. *American Cooperation*, 1934, p. 7.

30. *Ibid.*, p. 44.

31. *Ibid.*, pp. 22-23.

32. *Ibid.*, pp. 74-75.

33. *Ibid.*, pp. 59, 60.

34. *Ibid.*, pp. 87, 88.

35. *Ibid.*, p. 152.

36. "Report of the Secretary of Agriculture," December 12, 1934, *Yearbook of Agriculture*, 1935 pp. 1 ff.

37. See review of the meeting under the title: "Key Notes from Madison," *The Cooperative Marketing Journal*, July-August 1934, pp. 89-92.

38. The National Cooperative Milk Producers' Federation, meeting in Syracuse, New York, in mid-November, passed resolutions endorsing actions of the AAA "to eliminate unsound, uncontrolled, destructive competition in the fluid milk markets," and asking amendment of the adjustment act to provide a congressional mandate for development of cooperatives in connection with marketing agreements and licenses. See *The Cooperative Marketing Journal*, November-December 1934, p. 162.

39. Nourse, *op. cit.*, pp. 256-257.

40. For full statement of these resolutions, see the *1935 Bluebook of the National Cooperative Council* issued as a supplement to the *Cooperative Journal* of January-February 1935, pp. 40, 41. (Starting with 1935, *The Cooperative Marketing Journal* became the *Cooperative Journal*.)

41. According to John D. Black, "These amendments were worked out more or less in cooperation with the milk producers association group, and contain provisions defining more clearly the status of cooperatives under a marketing agreement." *op. cit.*, pp. 148-149.

42. The amendments also cleared up certain questions raised by the Supreme Court's decision in the Schechter case which invalidated the NRA. The amendments also limited the issuance of orders to specified agricultural commodities in the dairy and fruit and vegetable industries. Apples were specifically exempted. Also, fruits and vegetables for canning were exempted. F. R. Wilcox, *op. cit.*, p. 185.

43. Nourse, Davis, and Black, *op. cit.*, p. 234-237. Soon after the amendments were passed, Nourse said: "It would seem probable that the program in its further development under the amended act may become the agency through which a process of economic and social education can be carried on which will evolve arrangements in the different markets which will be largely self-enforced because they have grown out of the experience of the men who are parties to them. When this is done, the terms of the license become a marketing *agreement* in a very direct and effective sense and not in the Pickwickian and trouble-breeding sense which characterized the 15 agreements of 1933." Nourse, *op. cit.*, p. 225.

44. Wilcox, *op. cit.*, pp. 185-186.

45. Benedict, *Farm Policies of the United States, op. cit.*, pp. 350-352.

46. It is of significant interest that shortly after the Agricultural Adjustment Act was declared unconstitutional, an important independent appraisal of the AAA was published by The Brookings Institution under the authorship of three eminent students of the farm problem—Edwin G. Nourse, Joseph S. Davis, and John D. Black. The authors concluded: "We believe that some such agency for co-ordinating action in this loosely organized industry is needed from this time forward." Although this book centered attention on the AAA as a government institution, it recognized the substantial contributions made by cooperatives under the marketing provisions of the Act. One of the authors, John D. Black, in a supplementary chapter said: "But for the major revisions needed in our marketing system we must continue to look to something more important than control of rate of movement to market. One approach is of course cooperative marketing of farm products. The time seems to be approaching when government can resume a more vigorous program of developing agricultural cooperatives. This should not be an AAA function; but the AAA should co-ordinate its efforts with those of the cooperatives in a way that has not always been attained since 1933. This has been in some degree due to holding back by the AAA . . ." *Op. cit.*, pp. 479, 501.

47. Benedict, *Farm Policies, op. cit.*, p. 354. See also Baker, *et al., op. cit.*, pp. 171, 172.

48. For more complete information on the provisions of the Act, see Benedict, *Farm Policies, op. cit.*, pp. 348 ff. See also Baker, *et al., op. cit.*, pp. 173, 175. For a critical analysis of this act soon after its passage, see Joseph S. Davis, *On Agricultural*

Policy, 1923-1938 (Stanford, Calif.: Stanford University Press, 1939), pp. 456 ff. Davis was concerned by the trend toward compulsion inherent in the Act and the growing burden of surplus accumulation being assumed by the government. When the War opened in 1941, large stocks of farm commodities were being accumulated under the AAA's price stabilization program. If war had not intervened, disposal of these stocks could have posed a serious problem similar to that which embarrassed the Federal Farm Board in 1931 and 1932. Fortunately, the stocks were to prove very valuable in enabling the nation to meet its war and postwar needs.

49. U.S. Department of Agriculture, Press Release 238, August 7, 1939.

50. See Wilcox, *op. cit.,* p. 194.

Chapter XIV

1. See Joseph G. Knapp, *The Rise of American Cooperative Enterprise* (Danville, Ill.: The Interstate Printers & Publishers, Inc., 1969), pp. 135-139.

2. See Chapters II, VIII, and XI.

3. W. I. Myers has commented on this sentence as follows: "FDR sent HM, Jr., his neighbor, personal friend and agricultural advisor, as his representative in considering *all legislation* relating to agriculture. Ray Moley considered himself a representative on all economic legislation and he sent Rex Tugwell, a colleague at Columbia, to cover farm legislation. This overlapping occurred frequently as a result of FDR's method of operation." Letter of W. I. Myers to author, January 14, 1972.

4. Letter of W. I. Myers to author, December 1, 1967.

5. In his notes on this meeting, Myers indicates that the big question was what to do with the Federal Farm Board. "There is no doubt that Morgenthau's frank statement that the Farm Board must go caused a good deal of uneasiness among members of the conference until they became convinced of Morgenthau's sincere interest in safeguarding the important lines of work for cooperative marketing which the Farm Board represents. These men recognize that opposition to the Farm Board is not really based on antagonism to cooperatives but has been fomented under the guise of criticism of its stabilization operations. After confidential discussions with various members of the group, I feel certain that a large majority of the members would not be disposed to insist that Farm Board be retained if its activities for the sound development of cooperative marketing can be safeguarded and carried on effectively by other organizations. These men have complete confidence in the sincerity of purpose of the Administration to safeguard all of the constructive features of the Agricultural Marketing Act" (from personal files of W. I. Myers on conferences and discussions for period December 1932-February 1933).

6. *Ibid.*

7. Memorandum of Conference in Washington, D.C., December 22 and 23, 1932, prepared by W. I. Myers. A notation in the handwriting of Myers reads as follows: "WIM farm credit program had been approved by Gov. FDR in Albany, December 10, 1932." From personal files of W. I. Myers.

8. In a letter to the author, September 8, 1971, Myers said that although he was very anxious to get both banks for cooperatives and production credit cooperatives, he would have given higher priority to production credit if it had been necessary to choose between them.

9. After reviewing his experience in helping develop the plans for the Farm Credit Administration, Myers said: "Although I carried the major responsibility and did

the spade work, the farm credit program in its final form was not the brain child of any one person. It represented the combined ideas, judgments, criticisms and suggestions of many wise and experienced men, Land Bank and Intermediate Credit officers and other credit experts in the Department of Agriculture and in agricultural colleges." From Memorandum prepared by W. I. Myers, "The Origin of the FCA Program," for Cornell collection on agricultural history, August 2, 1967. In a letter to the author, December 1, 1967, Myers said: "The principal fact demonstrated by this memorandum is my great good fortune in happening to be at the right place and time to be able to participate in these developments."

10. W. I. Myers, "The Origins of the FCA Program," *loc. cit.*

11. *Ibid.*

12. *Ibid.*

13. W. I. Myers gives this further explanation: "Under the demoralized credit conditions in 1933 outstanding Federal Land Bank bonds were selling at large discounts and it was clear that new bonds could not be sold at usual interest rates to carry out the proposed farm refinancing program. Hence the FCA reluctantly agreed to authorize Land Banks for a temporary period to issue $2 billion of bonds guaranteed by the Government. In spite of our objections the White House insisted that the government guarantee be for interest only . . . The use of such bonds which could be sold only at a discount threatened the success of the farm refinancing program since the chance to get cash right away for sound but frozen loans was the major factor in inducing creditors of debt-burdened farmers to agree to the voluntary reduction of all debts to an amount which the farmer could repay under normal conditions. To meet this crisis, Governor Morgenthau arranged to borrow cash from the RFC on the security of the Land Bank bonds and thus insured the success of the refinancing program. This problem was corrected in 1934 by the passage of the Federal Farm Mortgage Corporation Act . . ." Letter of W. I. Myers to author, January 14, 1972.

14. The Act also contained a section which was designed to strengthen the authority of the Governor of the Farm Credit Administration in perfecting the organization of the Farm Credit Administration. He was given the authority "to establish, and to fix the powers and duties of, such divisions, agencies, corporations, and instrumentalities as he may deem necessary to the efficient functioning of the Farm Credit Administration and the successful execution of the powers and duties so vested in the Governor of the Farm Credit Administration." This provision gave the Farm Credit Governor ample authority to use emergency procedures until the Farm Credit Administration could be set up by law in a more formal way.

15. Murray R. Benedict, *Farm Policies of the United States, 1790-1950* (New York: The Twentieth Century Fund, 1953), p. 281.

16. *Ibid.*, p. 282.

17. W. I. Myers points out: "The Central Bank for Cooperatives was really an afterthought but was necessary to handle the outstanding loans from the Federal Farm Board to large regional and national cooperatives; loans which were too large for the resources of the regional banks." Letter of W. I. Myers to author, January 14, 1972.

18. *American Cooperation,* 1933, pp. 89-90.

19. *Ibid.*, pp. 91-104.

20. C. R. Arnold, *Farmers Build Their Own Production Credit System,* Farm Credit Administration, Washington, D.C., Circular E-45, 1958. p. 19.

21. Gifford Hoag, B. B. Sunbury, and Marie Puhr, *Banks for Cooperatives—A Quarter Century of Progress,* Farm Credit Administration, Washington, D.C., Circular E-47, 1960, p. 23.

22. John Morton Blum, *From the Morgenthau Diaries: Years of Crisis, 1928-1938* (Boston: Houghton Mifflin Company, 1959), pp. 47-48.

23. W. I. Myers points out that: "It is difficult to explain the terrific pressure on the Land Banks after the passage of the Emergency Farm Mortgage Act. FDR broadcast an invitation to any farmer threatened by foreclosure to appeal to him or to Governor Morgenthau. Even with adequate trained staffs, closing a sound mortgage loan requires time for appraisal, examination, getting good titles and other legal procedures. Many of the emergency cases were farmers with excessive debts requiring scale downs by creditors to permit financing by a loan that could be repaid under normal conditions. During the last eight months of 1933 the Land Banks received 497,257 applications for loans of over $2 billion—more than the total for the preceding 9½ years." Letter of W. I. Myers to author, January 14, 1972.

24. Letter of W. I. Myers to author, January 14, 1972.

25. Garwood had an "extensive business background in investments and commercial banking. The principal reason for his selection was his experience with the Arkansas Agricultural Credit Board, a program of the early 1930's designed to create on a state basis a system somewhat comparable in concept to what later became the nation's Production Credit System. It is hard to conceive of a more capable leader for the system at its birth and in its early years." Letter of Homer G. Smith to author, October 28, 1971. Smith joined the Production Credit System in April 1936 as Field Accounting Supervisor. He later became Production Credit Commissioner, and in 1954 Deputy Governor of the FCA and Director of the Cooperative Bank Service. He has been President of the Central Bank for Cooperatives since 1956.

26. The interesting story of how the Production Credit System came into being is well told by C. R. Arnold in his history of the Production Credit System, *op. cit.*, Arnold, as Assistant to the Production Credit Commissioner, played a key role in the organization of the system, and he organized the first production credit association at Champaign, Illinois.

27. The way in which the banks for cooperatives were organized is well described in Hoag, Sunbury, and Puhr, *op. cit.*, *in toto.* For the story of how the Berkeley Bank for Cooperatives was set up and staffed, see the account of Dan White, first treasurer and later president of the Berkeley bank, as given in Joseph G. Knapp's *Stokdyk— Architect of Cooperation* (Washington, D.C.: American Institute of Cooperation, 1953), pp. 55-58.

28. In the interval between the cessation of the Federal Farm Board's operations and the time when the banks for cooperatives were able to take over lending services to cooperatives, the revolving fund operations of the Federal Farm Board were administered by a staff under the supervision of Cooperative Bank Commissioner, Frank Peck.

29. W. I. Myers, "The Program of the Farm Credit Administration," *Journal of Farm Economics*, January, 1934, p. 36.

30. The other two were the Secretary of the Treasury, or his representative, and the Land Bank Commissioner.

31. "The FFMC Act authorized $800 million more Land Bank Commissioner loans and in addition provided funds for Federal Land Bank loans until financial markets regained stability and consolidated Land Bank bonds without any government guarantee could again be sold at par (in 1935)." Letter of W. I. Myers to author, January 14, 1972.

32. Murray R. Benedict, *Can We Solve the Farm Problem?* (New York: The Twentieth Century Fund, 1955), p. 154. See also pp. 146-156. Benedict also pointed out that the inability of the land banks to meet the problems of the Great Depression

had not been due to poor administration. "It stemmed from the lack of suitable provision for supplementing the land bank system with an appropriate mechanism for assuring salability of its bonds in time of depression, and also from the absence of any provision for emergency credit which could be used in refinancing mortgages . . . It was to overcome these defects that the Federal Farm Mortgage Corporation was established," p. 147.

33. As C. R. Arnold has reported: "The associations were confronted with a tremendous job. They were handicapped by being a new type of organization with inexperienced help, numerous regulations, complicated bookkeeping, and many legal requirements," *op. cit.*, p. 35.

34. See *Second Annual Report of the Farm Credit Administration, 1934* (1935), pp. 57-58.

35. Letter of Homer G. Smith to author, October 28, 1971.

36. *Third Annual Report of the Farm Credit Administration, 1935* (1936), p. 44. For a full description of the budget loan program by the man who largely designed it, see C. R. Arnold, *op. cit.*, pp. 46-47.

37. W. I. Myers comments on this sentence as follows: "Some leaders of large cooperatives were reluctant to buy capital stock of their Bank because of the heavy losses of the Federal Farm Board and perhaps doubt as to whether such loans could be made on a sound basis and collected. A few large cooperatives that had been financed by the Federal Farm Board—in some cases as low as less than one percent per year—were reluctant to pay the modest rate charged by the Banks. The paid in government capital provided for each Bank for Cooperatives was of tremendous value in starting these banks on a sound basis. This capital not only gave them stability but also the income from the bonds in which the capital was invested was adequate to pay operating costs until good loans were acquired. The Banks didn't have to rush out and make doubtful loans quickly in order to get income to meet expenses. The government capital provided for Production Credit Corporations and PCA's was equally important in giving them income until they could make sound loans." Letter of W. I. Myers to author, January 14, 1972.

38. However, it should be pointed out that the Federal Farm Board had developed a considerable fund of experience in making loans to marketing cooperatives that could be drawn on by the new banks for cooperatives. Two of the newly appointed presidents—Hutzel Metzger and F. B. Bomberger—had been members of the Federal Farm Board's staff.

39. The way in which the district banks for cooperatives established themselves in 1934 is well described in Hoag, Sunbury, and Puhr, *loc. cit.*

40. *The Cooperative Marketing Journal*, January-February 1934, p. 14.

41. *The Cooperative Marketing Journal*, Supplementary, October 1934, p. 144.

42. Joseph G. Knapp, *Stokdyk: Architect of Cooperation, op. cit.*, p. 87. Also pp. 85 ff.

43. For the history of this program, see Andrew W. McKay, *Federal Research and Educational Work for Farmer Cooperatives, 1913-1953*, U.S.D.A., Farmer Cooperative Service, Report 40, January 1959.

44. Letter of W. I. Myers to author of October 2, 1969.

45. *Ibid.*, For a more complete story of how the Federal Credit Union Act came to be passed and its implementation turned over to the Farm Credit Administration, see J. Carroll Moody and Gilbert C. Fite, *The Credit Union Movement—Origins and Development, 1850-1970* (Lincoln: University of Nebraska Press, 1971), especially Chapter VII, "The Federal Credit Union Act," pp. 149 ff. Bergengren was very happy over this arrangement. He believed that the Farm Credit Administration would provide "a very sympathetic and cooperative administration with which we can work easily and intelligently. . . ." See p. 166.

46. Letter of Herbert Emmerich to author, November 18, 1969. Emmerich also held that full credit should be given to "Peyton R. Evans, the General Counsel of the FCA, who helped Judge (Lyman S.) Hulbert and me with the redrafts and who saw to it that the bill was workable and constitutional."

47. See *Annual Report of the Farm Credit Administration for 1940*, pp. 147-150.

48. The *1934 Second Annual Report of the Farm Credit Administration* described the personnel program as follows: "Within the past year an effort has been made to develop a comprehensive personnel program for employees of the central office of the Farm Credit Administration and of the banks and corporations under its jurisdiction. Personnel work has been coordinated and standardized through the appointment of a trained personnel officer in each of the 12 districts. Progress has been made toward extending the merit system by classifying positions and developing uniform standards of procedure, qualifications, and compensation to be used in the selection, promotion, transfer, and separation of employees from service" (p. 85).

49. The way in which the district banks for cooperatives became well established in 1935 and 1936 is described in Hoag, Sunbury, and Puhr, *op. cit.*, pp. 25-33. See also Orrin Shelley's profile of Frank Peck, "He Set Up the Banks for Cooperatives" in Knapp and Associates, *Great American Cooperators*, (Washington, D.C.: American Institute of Cooperation, 1967), pp. 388-392. See also profile of Samuel D. Sanders, "Cooperative Bank Commissioner," by Joseph Douglas Lawrence in Knapp and Associates, *op. cit.*, pp. 440-445.

50. *Third Annual Report of the Farm Credit Administration* (1936), p. 6.

51. *Third Annual Report of the Farm Credit Administration, 1935* (1936), pp. 45-46. The following year attendance at such meetings rose to over 86,000 persons, *Fourth Annual Report of the Farm Credit Administration, 1936* (1937), pp. 47-48.

52. *Fourth Annual Report of the Farm Credit Administration* (1937), p. 1.

53. *American Cooperation*, 1936, pp. 549-559. Goss said: ". . . the federal land bank system, the production credit system, and the banks for cooperatives are truly cooperative in character . . ." P. 550.

54. *Fifth Annual Report of the Farm Credit Administration* (1938), p. 1.

55. *American Cooperation*, 1936, pp. 557-558.

56. See Edwin G. Nourse's essay on "Agriculture" in Volume II of *Government and Economic Life* (Washington, D.C.: The Brookings Institution, 1940), pp. 907-908.

57. W. I. Myers, "Important Issues in Future Farm Credit Administration Policy," *Journal of Farm Economics*, February 1937, pp. 85-86.

58. "Objectives and Future of Cooperative Credit in the United States," *American Cooperation*, 1937, pp. 165-166, 168, 170.

59. Quoted by O. M. Kile, *The Farm Bureau Through Three Decades* (Baltimore: Waverly Press, 1948), p. 256.

60. How this program came into being is well explained by Louis Brownlow in the second volume of his autobiography: *A Passion for Anonymity* (Chicago: University of Chicago Press, 1958), pp. 313-355, 371-403, 413-422. See also Rexford G. Tugwell, *The Democratic Roosevelt* (Garden City, N.Y.: Doubleday and Company, 1957), p. 357. For a very illuminating discussion of the Reorganization Act of 1939 and the conditions that led up to it see Herbert Emmerich, *Federal Organization and Administrative Management* (University, Ala.: University of Alabama Press, 1971), pp. 46 ff. and 129 ff.

61. According to F. F. Hill, FCA Governor at that time, "Henry Wallace and his staff began to take an active interest in FCA in the summer of 1939." Letter of F. F. Hill to author, December 14, 1970. W. I. Myers reports that he "never heard even a rumor of this (the takeover of FCA) during my service as Governor which ended

in September, 1938." The author, as a Farm Credit employee, was unaware of this matter until the fall of 1939.

62. In a memorandum for Chiefs of Bureaus and Offices, Wallace pointed out on October 6, 1938, that the administrative changes then inaugurated were "designed substantially to complete the task of putting the Department in the position to administer its new work [actions programs] as efficiently as it has conducted its research and educational activities [in the past]." See Nourse, "Agriculture," *op. cit.*, p. 940. This view was challenged by Joseph S. Davis, a close observer of government agricultural policies, who concluded in the fall of 1938 that the "drift of agricultural policy" was toward "regimentation of farmers," a phrase admittedly an "anathema to Mr. Wallace." See Joseph S. Davis, "The Drift of Agricultural Policy," an address to the Arizona Bankers' Association, Phoenix, Ariz., November 11, 1938, included in a collection of Davis's papers entitled: *On Agricultural Policy, 1926-1938* (Food Research Institute: Stanford University, 1939), pp. 474-475.

63. In the development of its policies, the production credit officials took the position that compliance with AAA programs was not essential for borrowing through production credit associations. C. R. Arnold, *op. cit.*, p. 23. See also p. 78. In writing to Luther Gulick, a member of the Brownlow Committee, on October 12, 1937, Wallace said in commenting on the relations of the Department with the Farm Credit Administration, "Credit policies may be made to support or to handicap our action programs, depending upon the degree of coordination that is established." Files, Agricultural History Branch, U.S.D.A. It was the common opinion of agricultural observers that Wallace and AAA officials believed that the Farm Credit Administration should be tied in with the crop adjustment program. See Murray R. Benedict, *Farm Policies in the United States, op. cit.*, p. 392. See also Nourse, "Agriculture," *op. cit.*, p. 909.

64. However, Wallace had overtly urged the reelection of Roosevelt as early as October 26, 1939, for he did not wish to place himself in "a position of being Roosevelt's rival." See Edward L. and Frederick H. Schapsmeier, *Henry A. Wallace of Iowa: The Agrarian Years, 1910-1940* (Ames: Iowa State University Press, 1968), Chapter 16, "Roosevelt's Choice of a Running Mate," pp. 246-260, 262.

65. In his *Diary*, Harold L. Ickes mentioned Appleby as "Wallace's publicity man, who is commonly referred to as Wallace's 'Louis Howe.' Appleby is apparently spending most of his time in trying to build Wallace up for the Democratic nomination for president in 1940." *The Secret Diary of Harold L. Ickes, The Inside Struggle, 1936-1939*, II (New York: Simon and Schuster, 1954), p. 313. See also reference to Appleby as Wallace's "right-hand man and his campaign manager," entry of January 1, 1939, p. 53, and also entry of April 15, 1939, p. 615. It is also of interest that Wallace's biographers, Edward L. and Frederick H. Schapsmeier, said: "Paul Appleby, playing the same role Farley did for Roosevelt, sought to promote Wallace's candidacy in every way possible," *op. cit.*, p. 224.

66. Brownlow later said: "The administration of the Department during this period was recognized as one of the most brilliant in the history of government." Gladys L. Baker and others, *Century of Service: the First 100 Years of the United States Department of Agriculture*, U.S. Department of Agriculture, 1963, p. 248.

67. *Ibid.*, p. 271.

68. The influential role of Appleby as friend, counselor, and executor of Secretary Wallace is well portrayed by Gladys L. Baker in her perceptive essay, "*And to Act for the Secretary*," Paul H. Appleby and the Department of Agriculture, 1933-1940, published in *Agricultural History*, October 1971, pp. 235-258.

69. Henry A. Wallace to Harold D. Smith, April 20, 1939, Files, Agricultural History Branch, U.S.D.A.

70. The President appreciated the strong backing that Wallace had given him in the 1936 presidential election, and in the Congressional elections of 1938, and his support on the Supreme Court reorganization issue. He also recognized Wallace as probably the most articulate and effective exponent of his New Deal philosophy. Moreover, Wallace had a strong political base through the AAA committees and other agencies of the Department, and he then enjoyed widespread support from the general farm organizations. Thus, it was difficult to deny Wallace control of the Farm Credit Administration which appeared to many of his close advisors as a logical step in governmental reorganization—a subject of great interest to the President. On the other hand, Roosevelt was proud of the record of the Farm Credit Administration which he helped Morgenthau and Myers create and develop, and he did not wish to see its program harmed. For background information on Wallace's relationships with Roosevelt at this time, see the Schapsmeiers', *op. cit.*, especially Chapter XVI, "Roosevelt's Choice of a Running Mate," pp. 245-246.

71. See Nourse, "Agriculture," *op. cit.*, p. 908. It is of interest that Marvin Jones, the Chairman of the House Committee on Agriculture, was relieved by the assurance that FCA would remain an independent unit. On May 23, he wrote to Appleby that he had feared "there might be some interference or dismantling." He indicated that he had "felt that the Farm Credit Administration should remain an independent unit . . . There are many reasons, which appear to me to be compelling, why this is the correct position." Letter of Marvin Jones to Paul H. Appleby, May 23, 1939. Files, Agricultural History Branch, U.S.D.A.

72. Baker, *et al.*, *Century of Service, op. cit.*, pp. 217-218.

73. Letter of Paul H. Appleby to Frank E. Hook, July 1, 1939. Files, Agricultural History Branch, U.S.D.A.

74. *1940 Blue Book of National Council of Farmer Cooperatives*, p. 8.

75. As quoted by O. M. Kile, *op. cit.*, pp. 257-258.

76. While Hill's resignation became effective on December 31, he officially retained the title of Governor until about March 31, when his annual leave expired. In the meantime, Black operated under the title of "Acting Governor." In 1933 Dr. Black had come to the Department from Iowa State College where he was Head of the Department of Agricultural Economics. After serving as Chief of the Corn-Hog section of the AAA, he was named Chief of the Bureau of Agricultural Economics in 1935. From 1938 to the time of his appointment as Governor of the FCA, he was Director of Marketing and Regulatory Work in the Department of Agriculture.

77. The animosity of the Council's membership toward the change in status of the Farm Credit Administration was evident in the cool reception given to Dr. Black at the banquet session which the author was privileged to attend.

78. *1940 Blue Book of the National Council of Farmer Cooperatives*, pp. 7-10. The National Cooperative Council took the name National Council of Farmer Cooperatives in late 1939.

79. *Ibid.*, p. 29. This issue of the National Council's Blue Book also provided a 10-year history of the Council, pp. 11-18, which reflected the Council's continuing support of the Farm Credit Administration. In a statement in the Bluebook on "Council Activities—1939," Ezra T. Benson, the Council's Secretary, reviewed the decreasing stages of the autonomy of the Farm Credit Administration during 1939 which caused the Council to re-emphasize its opposition to the absorption of Farm Credit Administration into the Department of Agriculture and work toward its re-establishment on an independent basis (pp. 21-22). It is of interest that the Farm Credit Administration finally achieved again its independent status in 1953 when Ezra T. Benson was Secretary of Agriculture.

80. However, Goss's official resignation did not become effective until his annual leave expired on June 16, 1940.

81. According to Robert Tootel, Governor of the Farm Credit Administration from 1954 to 1967, "Mr. Goss did indeed do more than any other individual to preserve the cooperative credit system for United States farmers." See his essay on "The Pioneers of Cooperative Credit" in Joseph G. Knapp and Associates, *op. cit.*, p. 560.

82. "Memorandum for A. G. Black, Governor Farm Credit Administration," signed by H. A. Wallace, Secretary, U.S.D.A., transmitted with memorandum by Governor Black to Stockholders of National Farm Loan Associations, April 10, 1940. Farm Credit Administration files.

83. U.S.D.A. Office of Information, Press Release, April 27, 1940. This meeting was sponsored by the National Farmers' Union and the National Federation of Grain Cooperatives. These organizations appreciated very much the financial assistance provided through the Farm Security Administration. See Chapter XV.

84. See Orville Merton Kile, *op. cit.*, pp. 254-262.

85. U.S.D.A. Office of Information, Press Release, June 7, 1940.

86. *American Cooperation*, 1940, pp. 199-200.

87. *Ibid.*, p. 176.

88. *Ibid.*, p. 178.

89. *Ibid.*, pp. 188-189.

90. *Ibid.*, pp. 190, 191.

91. After reviewing a draft of this chapter W. I. Myers commented as follows: "In my opinion the emphasis on education of officers, employees and members was an important factor in the nationwide support which was given to the FCA set-up when Wallace tried to change it to a government owned and controlled credit system in the early Forties." Letter of W. I. Myers to author, January 14, 1972.

Chapter XV

1. Paul K. Conkin, *Tomorrow a New World: The New Deal Community Program* (Ithaca, N.Y.: Cornell University Press, 1959), p. 1.

2. See Russell Lord, *The Wallaces of Iowa* (Boston: Houghton Mifflin Company, 1947), p. 349.

3. For a detailed sociological study of the Seattle organization which became the model for many other associations of this type, see Arthur Hillman, *The Unemployed Citizen's League of Seattle*, a publication of the University of Washington in the Social Sciences, 1934.

4. For a comprehensive analysis of such efforts, see L. B. Grinstead and Willis Wissler, *Barter Scrip and Production Units as Self-help Devices in Times of Depression* (published by the Bureau of Business Research of The Ohio State University, Columbus, November 1933).

5. See Joanna C. Colcord, "Helping the Jobless Help Themselves," *Today*, May 5, 1934.

6. As listed in "Summary of Federal Aid to Self-help Cooperatives" in report on Self-help Program of the Federal Emergency Relief Administration for period July 1, 1933, to December 31, 1935. The total expenditures under this program amounted to $656,578 up to October 31, 1935.

7. For an excellent review of the accomplishments of the self-help cooperatives, see "Appraising Self-help" by Udo Rall, Director of Division of Self-help Coopera-

tives, in the May 1936 issue of *Survey*. Rall pointed out that although there had been sporadic attempts at organized self-help during the previous depressions, the idea "never before gained the momentum nor reached the point of crystallization of the present self-help movement." He concluded: "The self-help movement has been decidedly worthwhile . . . It has provided thousands of people with many necessities . . . It has produced new wealth . . . It has conserved crops that would otherwise have gone to waste. It has built up the morale of the participants by showing them a way to employ themselves usefully and productively, at a time when society apparently had no use for them. It has put new hope into the hearts of many technologically displaced and superannuated workers . . ."

8. For a comprehensive description and analysis of the California experience, see Winslow Carlton's Annual Report for the Division of Self-help Cooperative Service of the state of California's Emergency Relief Administration (June 30, 1935).

9. In his *Autobiography* (New York: Harcourt, Brace and World, Inc., 1962), Sinclair tells how he carried the Democratic primary for Governor with 436,000 votes. He said: "Self-Help cooperatives had sprung up all over the state, and of course that was 'production for use' and those people automatically became Epics" (p. 271). Sinclair also wrote a novel, *"Co-op."* On this he said: "I had conceived a form in which these events could be woven into a story . . . I saw it as a river, flowing continuously, and growing bigger with new streams added. So came the novel, *Co-op*." See Chapter XIV, "EPIC."

10. See his book, *Confessions of a Congressman* (Garden City, N.Y.: Doubleday and Company, 1947), pp. 17-18.

11. An interesting example was the Washington Self-help Exchange, formed in Washington, D.C., in 1937 on the pattern of the very successful Citizens' Service Exchange of Richmond, Virginia, under the sponsorship of Mrs. Henry Morgenthau, wife of the Secretary of the Treasury, and other socially prominent people. This organization continued to thrive until the onset of World War II. See article on this association by J. C. Furnas in the *Ladies Home Journal* of August 1940.

12. For a discerning account of the entire New Deal community building effort in its historical setting, see Paul R. Conkin, *op. cit.* This book also provides case studies of four of the most interesting attempts of this kind and also of the garden city projects. An excellent analysis of the subsistence homestead program from its inception in 1933 to its culmination in 1941 is given in *A Place on Earth—A Critical Appraisal of Subsistence Homesteads*, edited by Russell Lord and Paul H. Johnstone, Bureau of Agricultural Economics, U.S.D.A., 1942. This monograph also provides case studies of nine of the projects. Much valuable information on the community projects in a political framework is provided by Sidney Baldwin, *Poverty and Politics—The Rise and Decline of the Farm Security Administration* (Chapel Hill: University of North Carolina Press, 1968). The author has freely drawn on these studies.

13. Mead's work in developing and promoting the farm colony plan is well described in Paul Conkin's "The Vision of Elwood Mead," *Agricultural History*, April 1960, pp. 88-97.

14. Wilson's commitment to cooperative action "was deep seated, very deep seated, especially within a Jeffersonian concept where people of common purpose get together and participate in formulating goals and take responsibility for fulfillment." Letter from his long-time colleague, Elmer Starch, March 15, 1971.

15. Quoted by Russell Lord, *The Agrarian Revival* (New York: American Association for Adult Education, 1939), pp. 134-135. For a full sociological and economic analysis of the Mormon village, see Lowry Nelson, *The Mormon Village—A Pattern and Technique of Land Settlement* (Salt Lake City: University of Utah Press, 1952).

16. Conkin, *Tomorrow a New World, op. cit.*, p. 89.

17. Among them were Secretary of Agriculture, Henry A. Wallace; Under Secretary of Agriculture, Rexford G. Tugwell; H. L. Wilson, Chief of the Wheat Section, AAA; John D. Black, Harvard Agricultural Economist; Bernarr Macfadden; and Arthur E. Morgan, the newly appointed Chairman of the TVA's Board of Directors.

18. Russell Lord, *The Wallaces of Iowa, op. cit.*, p. 411.

19. See Lord and Johnstone, *op. cit.*, pp. 42-43.

20. Conkin, *Tomorrow a New World, op. cit.*, pp. 102-103.

21. The story of Mrs. Roosevelt's deep involvement in this unfolding experiment is well told by Joseph P. Lash, *Eleanor and Franklin* (New York: W. W. Norton and Company, 1971), Chapter 37, "Mrs. Roosevelt's 'Baby'—Arthurdale," pp. 393-441.

22. Conkin, *Tomorrow a New World, op. cit.*, pp. 105-108.

23. Lord and Johnstone, *op. cit.*, p. 44.

24. The legal structure of the federal and subsidiary corporations has been well described by Philip M. Glick, "The Federal Subsistence Homesteads Program," *Yale Law Journal*, 1935. Glick was General Counsel for the Division of Subsistence Homesteads during 1933 and 1934. See Lord and Johnstone, *op. cit.*, pp. 44-45.

25. M. L. Wilson, "The Place of Subsistence Homesteads in Our National Economy," *Journal of Farm Economics*, January 1934, pp. 82-83.

26. Conkin, *Tomorrow a New World, op. cit.*, pp. 118-119.

27. In May, Ickes had moved Pynchon from the Public Works Administration so that he could be business manager of the Federal Subsistence Homesteads Corporation and could make the organization stronger from a management viewpoint. In his diary Ickes said: "I thought he was the executive I was looking for." He found him to be "a distinct disappointment as an executive." See *Secret Diary of Harold L. Ickes—The First Thousand Days* (New York: Simon and Schuster, 1954), pp. 218-219.

28. The content of this article makes clear that it was written before Wilson resigned as Director. Hendrickson was then Assistant to the Director in charge of Informational Activities. He left the Division with Wilson to return to the Department of Agriculture. See "Homesteaders as Cooperators," *Cooperative Self-help*, issued by the Division of Self-help Cooperatives, FERA, July 1934.

29. See William E. Zeuck, "Problems of Cooperative Communities" in *Cooperative Self-help* for May 1934.

30. "With all the talk of subsistence homesteads and of back-to-the-land, it was only natural that relief agencies would attempt to adapt the idea of rural urban communities to relief problems." Paul K. Conkin, *Tomorrow a New World, op. cit.*, p. 131.

31. *Ibid.*, p. 132.

32. *Ibid.*, pp. 135 ff.

33. An article on "Woodlake Homesteads" in *Cooperative Self-help* (FERA) for September 1934, indicates that a spirit of cooperation then pervaded this community, with cows and poultry being purchased cooperatively with funds supplied by the Self-help Division of the FERA. See article on "Rural Industrial Communities" in *The Project* (FERA) for January 1935. Westbrook presented his ideas in an address to the American Farm Economics Association in December 1934, which was published in *Journal of Farm Economics* in February 1935. Speaking of the colonies he said: "We do not hope to make Utopias out of these organized communities, but rather give stranded American families . . . an opportunity to work out their own destinies" (p. 99). He also said that the colonies "involve the opportunity for the application of cooperative effort in the development of industrial enterprises suitable to their abilities . . ." (p. 97).

34. For discussion of these experiments in the larger context of the total program of the Resettlement Administration, see Sidney Baldwin, *loc. cit.;* Paul Conkin, *Tomorrow a New World, op. cit., in toto;* and Arthur Schlesinger, Jr., *The Coming of the New Deal* (New York, Houghton Mifflin Company, 1957).

35. In the December 1934 issue of *Scribner's* magazine, Wallace said: "Somehow I can't help thinking that the self-subsistence homesteads, if experimented with sufficiently by men of scientific, artistic, and religious understanding, will eventually lead us a long way toward a new and finer world."

36. Rexford G. Tugwell, "The Resettlement Idea," *Agricultural History,* October 1959, p. 159. In his biography, *The Democratic Roosevelt* (Baltimore: Penguin, 1969 ed.), Tugwell said of the Resettlement Administration, "Its job was to be a multiple one. It was to assume the same responsibility for indigent rural folk as Hopkins' Works Projects Administration was to assume for the urban unemployed," pp. 423-444. This book helps one understand Tugwell as well as Roosevelt.

37. Some 4,200 employees were acquired from nine different agencies. The scope of its initial program has been outlined as follows: "The Resettlement Administration was a repository for a multitude of New Deal programs. It had the task of carrying on rural relief or rehabilitation, of continuing the whole land-utilization program, and of continuing and extending the New Deal community-building program through both rural and urban resettlement. Rural rehabilitation was soon to include loans to individuals, loans to cooperatives, grants to destitute farmers, and a debt-adjustment program." Paul Conkin, *Tomorrow a New World, op. cit.,* p. 153.

38. *Ibid.,* pp. 150-151.

39. *Ibid.,* p. 204.

40. *Ibid.,* p. 205.

41. *Ibid.,* p. 206.

42. Edward C. Banfield, *Government Project* (Glencoe, Ill.: The Free Press, 1951), p. 9. Banfield went on to say: "After sixteen months the combat which the Resettlement technicians had staged between mules and diesels was over. The diesels had won . . . The independent farmer 'homesteaders' . . . were now farm laborers."

43. *Ibid.,* pp. 17-19.

44. Tugwell, *op. cit.,* p. 162.

45. "The Resettlement Administration developed the supervised credit plan called a standard rehabilitation loan. Each standard loan was based on a farm and home management plan worked out by the farm and home management supervisors in cooperation with the borrowing family to fit the needs of the family and to insure the use of good farming practices." Gladys L. Baker, Wayne D. Rasmussen, Vivian Wiser, and Jane M. Porter, *Century of Service: The First 100 Years of the United States Department of Agriculture,* U.S.D.A., 1963, p. 206. The first public presentation of the idea of farm and home plans "destined to become one of the basic instruments of supervised credit" was made at a meeting of rural rehabilitation workers (FERA) on November 26, 1934. See Paul V. Maris, *The Land Is Mine —From Tenancy to Family Farm Ownership,* Farmers Home Administration, U.S.D.A., 1950, p. 358.

46. Gladys Baker, *et al., op. cit.,* p. 206.

47. It is of interest that among those with Wallace on the tour were Tugwell and two officials of the Resettlement Administration who were destined to be successively the Administrators of the Farm Security Administration—Will W. Alexander and C. B. ("Beanie") Baldwin. Wallace also took along William A. Jump, the U.S.D.A. Budget Director. The presence of Jump would indicate that Wallace was looking at the problem from the standpoint of how the activities of the Resettlement Ad-

ministration might be incorporated into the Department. See Sidney Baldwin, *op. cit.*, p. 122.

48. The interesting story of this transition is well told by Baldwin in his scholarly work, *op. cit.*, pp. 119-125. Alexander was a veteran leader of the interracial movement. For background information, see pp. 95-96.

49. For more complete information on the recommendations of this report, see Baldwin, *op. cit.*, pp. 167 ff., and Murray Benedict, *Farm Policies of the United States* (New York: The Twentieth Century Fund, 1953), pp. 358-362.

50. As early as January 1937 Wallace in a national radio address had suggested that a better name for the Resettlement Administration would be the Farm Security Administration. This new name would also have a public relations benefit in view of the identification of Tugwell with the Resettlement Administration. See Henry A. Wallace, *The Rural Resettlement Administration of the Department of Agriculture*, January 12, 1937, Press Release 1007.

51. For a complete list of the 99 New Deal communities completed, classified by type and cost, see Appendix to Conkin's book, *Tomorrow a New World, op. cit.*, pp. 332-337.

52. *Ibid.*, p. 185.

53. Florence Parker, in her sympathetic account of these cooperatives, attributes their failure to a number of factors. She points out that "The members were poverty-stricken sharecroppers, tenants, and laborers with no previous acquaintance with each other, no knowledge of cooperative methods, unused to working in cooperative groups, and with no idea of how to run a business enterprise." Moreover "since the enterprises were financed [and in some cases overfinanced] by government funds, the members lacked the incentive to thrift and careful management." Florence E. Parker, *The First 125 Years: A History of Distributive and Service Cooperation in the United States, 1829-1954* (Chicago: Cooperative League of the U.S.A., 1956), pp. 143-144. A general study made of the cooperatives by a committee of FSA Washington staff members in 1940 came to similar conclusions. One of four "common errors" mentioned is worth emphasis: "attempting to provide a cooperative before the members have the interest and knowledge to sustain it."

54. From 1934 to 1938 a "Co-op" Tractor" was manufactured according to specifications for these cooperatives by a private concern. See Gerald Francis, "Distribution of Machinery by Farmers' Cooperative Associations," Farm Credit Administration, *Circular C-125*, 1941.

55. For more complete information on these plants see Conkin, *Tomorrow a New World, op. cit.*, pp. 207-209. For detailed information on the Arthurdale tractor assembly plant see p. 253, and on the hosiery mill at Penderlea, "one of the best hosiery mills in the South," see p. 288. Interesting information on the cooperative hosiery mill at Cumberland Homesteads is given by Lord and Johnstone, *op. cit.*, pp. 87 ff.

56. Sidney Baldwin, *op. cit.*, p. 216. Baldwin has called this book "a grim autopsy" of the Casa Grande cooperative farm but it is much more than that. It is an economic, sociological, and philosophical analysis of this experiment to determine if there are lessons from it that might be used by other community builders in the future.

57. Edward C. Banfield, *op. cit.*, p. 44. Banfield went on to say: "According to the orthodoxy of the cooperative movement, organization should be the end product of a process of education—the cooperative should arise out of the understanding and conviction of its members. The Resettlement Administration, which had no interest in the orthodoxy of cooperation and which put its faith altogether in the ·unifying influence of a common need and not at all in that of a common ideal, violated this cardinal principle because to do otherwise would have interfered with the practical business of getting the cooperative farm underway," pp. 44-45.

58. *Ibid.*, pp. 222 ff.; Conkin, *Tomorrow a New World, op. cit.*, pp. 169-170, 210-211.

In addition to the cooperative farming projects inherited from the Resettlement Administration, a number of other cooperative farms were experimented with by the Farm Security Administration. They were not set up to provide a livelihood for homesteaders already on projects but were conceived as experimental cooperative farms from the beginning, and land was purchased or leased for such farms for a period of years with this object in view. The farmers on these cooperative farms were recruited as laborers rather than as tenants, and all of the farm operations were carried on by the central management. For reasons similar to those given for the other cooperative farms, none proved permanently successful.

59. See Conkin, *Tomorrow a New World, op. cit.*, Chapter XIV, "The Greenbelt Towns," pp. 317-318. For more complete information on early cooperative developments at Greenbelt, Maryland, see George A. Warner, *Greenbelt—The Cooperative Community* (New York: Exposition Press, 1954).

60. "How Farm Security Administration Programs Fit into Agricultural Cooperation," *American Cooperation,* 1941.

61. Lord and Johnstone, *op. cit.*

62. For much of the information on these cooperatives, the author is indebted to the very informative Harvard University doctoral thesis of James O. Maddox, "The Farm Security Administration" (1940). Maddox was Director of the Rural Rehabilitation Division of the FSA from 1939 to 1943.

63. The FSA favored the joint-ownership type of group services as a step toward more formal cooperative activity. Maddox comments on both types as follows: "Neither type was fully cooperative. They were more in the nature of partnership arrangements. However, there was a strong element of cooperation in both forms of group service."

64. See Robert W. Hudgens, *op. cit.*, pp. 79 ff. This article presents a good picture of the group service program at the height of its development.

65. See Baldwin, *op. cit.*, p. 205; Robert Handschin, "M. W. Thatcher—Cooperative Warrior" in *Great American Cooperators,* Knapp and Associates (Washington, D.C.: American Institute of Cooperation, 1967), p. 512.

66. Maddox, *op. cit.*, chapter on "Medical Care Associations." Much of the material in this section is drawn from this source.

67. See Baldwin, *op. cit.*, p. 208; Conkin points out that there was some opposition from the American Medical Association but that this was overcome by the support given by local medical groups. *Tomorrow a New World, op. cit.*, pp. 198-199. Robert W. Hudgens, who as Assistant Administrator of FSA gave the program leadership, reflects: "This was one of the most gratifying programs I ever had anything to do with." Letter to author, January 23, 1971.

68. Maddox, *op. cit.*, chapter on "Land Leasing Associations."

69. Maddox, *op. cit.*, chapter on "Tenure Improvement."

Chapter XVI

1. C. Herman Pritchett, *The Tennessee Valley Authority—A Study in Public Administration* (Chapel Hill: University of North Carolina Press, 1943), p. 6.

2. During 1920 and 1921 the American Farm Bureau Federation led a vigorous campaign to have the nitrate plants used for fertilizer production for the benefit of agriculture. In reporting the legislative battle on this issue, Kile said: "And why was this Muscle Shoals development so bitterly opposed in Congress? Simply because the great electrical and chemical interests . . . and to a lesser extent the larger fertilizer interests wanted to tie up this great development for themselves . . ."

O. M. Kile, *The Farm Bureau Movement* (New York: The Macmillan Company, 1921), pp. 174-175.

3. George Norris, *Fighting Liberal* (an autobiography) (New York: The Macmillan Company, 1945).

4. See Arthur M. Schlesinger, Jr., *The Coming of the New Deal* (Boston: Houghton Mifflin Company, 1959), pp. 323-324.

5. Morgan contributed two important ideas to the TVA bill which helped the TVA get off to a quick start. One of his suggestions made it possible for the TVA to construct its own dams rather than be dependent on the Army Corps of Engineers. The other suggestion gave the TVA authority to extend its own transmission lines so that it would not have to depend upon private utilities to get power to the people. See Roy Talbert, Jr., "The Human Engineer: Arthur E. Morgan and the Launching of the Tennessee Valley Authority," Master's Thesis, Vanderbilt University, Nashville, Tenn., 1967, p. 18.

6. Schlesinger, *op. cit.*, p. 323. Morgan later said that "three-fourths" of his first talk with Roosevelt "was spent by him in discussing general social and economic planning." *TVA Joint Congressional Committee Hearings*, 1938, p. 313.

7. Talbert, *op. cit.*, pp. 88 ff.

8. Schlesinger, *op. cit.*, p. 327. According to Schlesinger, Morgan's vision appealed to other New Deal planners in Washington. "This work of his," said Rex Tugwell, "carries more significance for the future than any other single attempt of the administration to make life better for all of us." *Ibid.*, p. 330.

9. Talbert, *op. cit.*, pp. 89 ff. See also Willson Whitman, *David Lilienthal: Public Servant in a Power Age* (New York: Henry Holt and Company, 1948), pp. 31 ff.

10. Talbert, *op. cit.*, pp. 23-33.

11. Pritchett, *op. cit.*, p. 30.

12. For an excellent biographical essay on "Arthur Ernest Morgan," see Edna Yost, *Modern American Engineers* (Philadelphia: J. B. Lippincott Co., 1952), pp. 32-46. See also Clarence J. Leuba, *A Road to Creativity: Engineer, Educator, Administrator* (North Quincy, Mass.: Christopher Publishing House, 1971); and Talbert, *op. cit.* For Morgan's philosophy of life see his little book, *My World* (Yellow Springs, Ohio: Kahoe and Company, 1927), and a short biography, *Finding His World—The Story of Arthur E. Morgan* (Yellow Springs, Ohio: Kahoe and Company, 1928) by his wife.

13. For example, see Morgan's paper "Decentralization of Industry" presented to the Southeastern Division of the National Electric Light Association at its Fifteenth Annual Meeting, 1925 (in files of TVA Technical Library), Knoxville, Tenn.

14. Quoted in Mouzon Peters, "The Story of Dr. Harcourt A. Morgan, p. 45. Published in *Makers of Millions*, Tennessee Department of Agriculture, 1951. See Book V, "The Farmer Minded College President." The best source of information on Morgan's career is this biography.

15. *Journals of David E. Lilienthal: The TVA Years, 1939-1945*, I (New York: Harper and Row, 1964), p. 38. The best source of information on the early career of Lilienthal is his own record of development as given in this book, pp. 1-36. See also Willson Whitman, *David Lilienthal: Public Servant in a Power Age* (New York: Henry Holt and Company, 1948).

16. H. A. Morgan was intensely proud of Lilienthal who extended his own values with the vigor of youth, while Lilienthal recognized the great spirit and sagacity of the older man. Years later Lilienthal paid tribute to Dr. H. A. Morgan as "the noblest and most comprehending man I have ever known." See Preface to *TVA—Democracy on the March* (New York, Harper and Brothers, 1944).

17. See *The Secret Diary of Harold Ickes: The First Thousand Days* (New York: Simon and Schuster, 1954), p. 62. See also p. 70.

18. *Ibid.*, pp. 58-59. Chairman Morgan had also toyed with the idea of developing "An Ethical Code for the Staff of the Tennessee Valley Authority," which he presented in rough draft at the board meeting. The Chairman believed that the TVA should "set desirable standards in its personal, social and business conduct." Under his proposed code, which was to be signed by all staff members, employees were to maintain "wholesome and self-respecting standards of personal conduct" and they were to eschew "intemperance, lax sex morality, gambling, and the use of habit forming drugs." To H. A. Morgan and Lilienthal, this strict code would unnecessarily regiment the lives and personal behavior of TVA employees and they refused to accept the idea. *Ibid.*, pp. 57-94.

19. Pritchett, *op. cit.*, p. 154.

20. *Ibid.*, pp. 155-156. While this plan of dividing up responsibilities gave each director a prescribed field for action, the work of TVA could not be entirely compartmentalized. To achieve better coordination, the Board eventually established the office of General Manager on January 16, 1937. *Ibid.*, pp. 193 ff.

21. He also proposed changes in land tenure to protect soil resources, changes in the structure of local government, and the elimination of real estate speculation. See Talbert, *op. cit.*, p. 27.

22. *Ibid.*, pp. 100-101.

23. For Arthur Morgan's view of this incident see Leuba, *op. cit.*, p. 180.

24. See Robert Morse Lovett, *All Our Years* (New York: The Viking Press, 1948), p. 218.

25. "At each dam [on the Miami project] Morgan had constructed a complete village. In each, about one hundred carefully planned houses were erected, and each village had waterworks, sewers, electric lights, a school, a general store, a big bunkhouse, and a mess hall." Talbert, *op. cit.*, pp. 70 ff.

26. Leuba, *op. cit.*, pp. 183-185.

27. Quotation furnished by Mrs. Ruth F. Bent, Curator Arthur E. Morgan Papers, Olive Kettering Library, Antioch College, Ohio, in letter to author, December 15, 1970.

28. See Pritchett, *op. cit.*, pp. 122-123. Jonathan Daniels found Norris far different from a Utopia when he visited it in 1937. By that time it had become a show place operated by the TVA, and most of its cooperative features had evaporated. See *A Southerner Discovers the South* (New York: The Macmillan Company, 1938), pp. 56-63.

29. An exponent of this philosophy was Dr. W. R. Woolrich, Chief of the Industry Division. In a talk before the annual meeting of the Indiana Farm Bureau Cooperative Association, March 5, 1935, he said: "The TVA is the first serious attempt of the American people to solve these problems of adapting our civilization to natural forces and controlling these forces for our needs."

30. Illustrative of the reports prepared by the Industry Division was "Agricultural-Industrial Cooperative Colony" (no date, but apparently completed in late 1934). This report prepared by Harvey P. Vaughn, with the assistance of Loran N. Baker, set up plans for a colony of this type. A more comprehensive and practical report was entitled: "Prospectus for Cooperative Feed Grinding and Mixing Association" (May 4, 1935). This report, prepared by Loran N. Baker with the assistance of Fred W. Weigen, designed a model plan for such associations to be formed throughout the Tennessee Valley states with the assistance of extension service workers.

31. James P. Warbasse, "The Tennessee Valley for Consumers' Cooperation: Personal Observations," *Consumers' Cooperation*, April 1935; "The South Looks at Coop-

eration," *Consumers' Cooperation*, August 1935, pp. 141-142.

32. By the Federal Emergency Relief Act of May 12, 1933, funds were made available to states for self-help cooperatives as a means of providing unemployment relief assistance.

33. Hearings Before a Joint Committee on the Investigation of the Tennessee Valley Authority, 75th Congress, pursuant to Public Resolution No. 83, Washington, D.C., 1938, pp. 462-463.

34. *Ibid.*, pp. 129-130.

35. Much of the information on the organization and operations of the TVAC and its affiliated cooperatives which follows has been obtained from a comprehensive report prepared by Harry C. Hensley in 1947 for the internal use of the Farm Credit Administration on the "outlook for cooperatives financed by Tennessee Valley Associated Cooperatives." This report includes organization documents for the TVAC and related cooperatives (in possession of author).

36. In a letter to the author of November 24, 1936, Mr. Campbell made clear that TVA was withdrawing from the relief type program of the TVAC in favor of a more general program of assisting cooperatives through research and education.

37. Letter of A. E. Morgan to author, December 23, 1970. It is significant that Arthur Morgan after his service with the TVA devoted the remaining years of his life to the improvement of rural communities through an organization that he founded, Community Services, Inc. See Leuba, *A Road to Creativity*, Chapter VII, "Realizing the Potentialities of the Small Community," *op cit.*, pp. 203-215.

38. The comprehensive report of Harry C. Hensley previously mentioned indicated that a substantial portion of the government funds entrusted to TVAC in 1934 were conserved as late as 1947. See also *Report on Audit of the Tennessee Valley Associated Cooperatives, Inc. for the Fiscal Year Ended June 30, 1947, and for the Period to July 30, 1947*, prepared by General Accounting Office, Corporation Audits Division, Washington, D.C. (In files of TVA Technical Library.)

39. Tennessee Valley Authority Annual Report, 1934, pp. 22-23.

40. Letter from David E. Lilienthal to author, February 2, 1971.

41. David E. Lilienthal, *The TVA Years, op. cit.*, p. 81.

42. Letter to author of February 2, 1971.

43. After a long association with the TVA, Swidler served as Chairman of the Federal Power Commission, 1961-1965, and is presently Chairman of the Public Service Commission of New York State.

44. It should be observed, however, that, while the cooperatives set up under the REA drew heavily on TVA experience, they were not able under the Rural Electrification Act to serve both urban and rural consumers which was a unique feature of the TVA formed cooperatives. The control of electric power also gave TVA greater influence over methods of operation.

45. Letter to author, February 25, 1971. For additional information on the "vicious circle" which was then holding back power consumption, see TVA Information Services Bulletin of February 3, 1934. This bulletin, available in the TVA Technical Library at Knoxville, Tennessee, points out how the EHFA provided "an opportunity for Government, represented by the Tennessee Valley Authority, to act as a stimulator and coordinator in its relation to business," and to help break "a complete business stalemate" which was injurious to electric utilities, electric manufacturers, dealers, and consumers.

46. David E. Lilienthal, *The TVA Years, op. cit.*, p. 88.

47. After the establishment of the Rural Electrification Administration in 1935, the EHFA was redesigned to serve all parts of the nation, and its headquarters were moved to Washington, D.C. See Chapter XVII.

48. The original plans anticipated financing only these low-cost models, but subsequently all models of a manufacturer having an approved model in his line were eligible for financing.
49. Information supplied by George D. Munger, in conversation with author, December 1970.
50. The initial structure of the Alcorn Electric Power Association was described by George W. Cable, senior designing engineer of the agricultural-industry division of the TVA in an article "An Electricity Consumers' Cooperative" in *Agricultural Engineering*, October 1935, pp. 401 ff. Cable said that the underlying principles of the association were those of the original Rochdale Society of Equitable Pioneers in that it was a non-profit organization conducted for the benefit of its members. See also *History of Alcorn County Electric Power Association, 1934-1966*, published by the association 1967.
51. Joseph E. Swidler in letter to author, February 17, 1971.
52. L. C. Salter in letter to author after reviewing a draft of this chapter, May 16, 1972. As Chief of the TVA's Cooperative Research and Experiment Division Salter made a study of these associations in the middle 1930's.
53. *History of Alcorn County Electric Power Association, 1934-1966, loc. cit.*
54. Lilienthal, *The TVA Years, op cit.*, pp. 53-54. See also Lilienthal's later views on the importance of this kind of cooperative in his book *TVA—Democracy on the March, op. cit.*, p. 19.
55. After the REA was set up, capital financing was supplied by the REA.
56. Joseph E. Swidler, in letter to author, February 17, 1971.
57. See Section 5 of the TVA Act of 1933 (48 stat.:61).
58. Pritchett, *op. cit.*, pp. 48 ff.
59. Tennessee Valley Authority Annual Report, 1934.
60. Tennessee Valley Authority Annual Report, 1935, pp. 19-20.
61. See Joseph G. Knapp, *The Rise of American Cooperative Enterprise, 1620-1920* (Danville, Ill.: The Interstate Printers & Publishers, Inc., 1969), pp. 107-109. It is significant that Dr. Harcourt A. Morgan was the authority on the life history of the boll weevil.
62. Pritchett, *op. cit.*, p. 50.
63. Tennessee Valley Authority Annual Report, 1935, pp. 21-22.
64. *Ibid.*, p. 22.
65. R. L. Duffus, *The Valley and Its People: A Portrait of TVA*, illustrated by Charles Krutch (New York: Alfred A. Knopf, 1944), p. 108.
66. *Ibid.*, p. 136. Lilienthal conceptualized this approach in the term "grass roots democracy." Pritchett has pointed out "at first there were some fantastic plans for remodeling the life of the valley, and for 'doing good' to its inhabitants." This attitude soon passed and the Authority found that it was desirable "to work wherever possible through established local governments and other organizations so as to strengthen these agencies." Pritchett, *op. cit.*, pp. 121 ff. The author can attest this change in attitude from personal experience. In the summer of 1936 he represented the Farm Credit Administration in a conference on agricultural cooperative development for the Valley states held at Muscle Shoals under the Chairmanship of Dr. H. A. Morgan. This meeting was attended by presidents of the Banks for Cooperatives, officials of the land grant colleges and extension services serving the Valley states. He was greatly impressed with the practical vision of Dr. Morgan that much could be accomplished by agricultural cooperatives with the joint support of all public agencies.
67. Salter had formerly been Senior Marketing Specialist, Division of Markets, North

Carolina Department of Agriculture, and in 1934 and 1935 he had worked on Codes and Marketing Agreements for the Agricultural Adjustment Administration. He came to TVA from the U.S. Bureau of Fisheries where he was in charge of studies relating to fishery cooperatives.

68. L. C. Salter and P. W. Voltz, "A Study and Analysis of Rural Electrification Co-operative Associations Having Contractural Relations with the Tennessee Valley Authority." Tennessee Valley Authority, Department of Agricultural Relations, (mimeographed, no date). This report was first issued in typewritten form by the TVA's Department of Agricultural Industries, November 1, 1938.

69. For example, see B. D. Raskopf and P. W. Voltz, *Farmers Marketing and Purchasing Associations in Tennessee,* University of Tennessee Agricultural Experiment Station, Bulletin 177, September 1941.

70. Letter to author from L. C. Salter, July 23, 1970.

71. Lilienthal expressed his philosophy toward cooperatives in this way: "The strength of a successful enterprise, such as a cooperative, is not only its concept, but also whether that concept is given reality by individuals with managerial capacity; the validity of the concept should be measured by whether it lends itself to successful operation." David E. Lilienthal in letter to author, May 17, 1971.

Chapter XVII

1. Executive Order 7037, May 11, 1935.

2. Harry Slattery, *Rural America Lights Up* (Washington, D.C.: National Home Library Foundation, 1940), pp. 2-6.

3. Such systems were called "snake lines" because they meandered over the countryside from farm to farm.

4. Harry Slattery, *op. cit.,* p. 7.

5. Clyde T. Ellis, *A Giant Step* (New York: Random House, 1966), p. 33.

6. Charles M. Gardner, *The Grange-Friend of the Farmer* (Washington, D.C.: The National Grange, 1949), p. 123.

7. Slattery, *op. cit.,* p. 7.

8. The story of this controversy which led eventually to the establishment of the Tennessee Valley Authority is told in the preceding chapter.

9. The way in which the CREA came to be set up is described by O. M. Kile, *The Farm Bureau Through Three Decades* (Baltimore: Waverly Press, 1948), pp. 78-80.

10. For full information on operating plans, see the Annual Administrative Report of the American Farm Bureau Federation for the year ending October 31, 1924, pp. 10-12.

11. For description and assessment of this work, see Harry Slattery, *op. cit.,* pp. 11-26; Marquis Childs, *The Farmer Takes a Hand: The Electric Power Revolution in Rural America* (Garden City: N.Y.: Doubleday and Company, 1952), pp. 39-42.

12. Morris Llewellyn Cooke, "The Early Days of the Rural Electrification Idea: 1914-1936," *The American Political Science Review,* June 1948, p. 438.

13. Marquis Childs, *op. cit.,* p. 48. At about this time much interest was also being developed by the Hydro in Ontario which was making electricity available to Ontario farmers. This was an electric generating, transmission, and distribution system owned by the municipalities and operated by the Hydro Electric Power Commission as Trustee. It was the world's largest, completely integrated, publicly owned electric system, and its success in reducing rates made a great impression

in the United States and gave encouragement to advocates of public power such as Pinchot.

14. See Kenneth E. Trombley, *The Life and Times of a Happy Liberal: A Biography of Morris Llewellyn Cooke* (New York: Harper and Brothers, 1954), pp. 102-106, see also pp. 36-46. This book gives a very good understanding of this unique individual.

15. As reported by Trombley, p. 150. Taylor worked with Cooke later on the power distribution survey in New York State and on the Mississippi Valley Survey. He served as Administrator pro tem for the REA when it was first established in May 1935 and was in charge of its early management division until the end of 1937. Interview with Perry R. Taylor, November 17, 1970.

16. Cooke, *op. cit.*, p. 439. The Report of the Giant Power Board contained several ideas that later found expression in the operations of the REA, such as the distribution of power through corporate enterprises organized on the cooperative principle. See Frederick William Muller, *Public Rural Electrification* (Washington, D.C.: American Council of Public Affairs, 1944), footnote 27, p. 18.

17. In 1931 Louis Tabor, National Master of the National Grange, had said at its annual meeting: "The problem of lower rates will continue to be an issue until . . . there is a clearer understanding of the problems underlying the cost of manufacturing and transmitting electric energy . . . We have made a great mistake in allowing power companies to pyramid stock values with every consolidation and combination. The amount of water pumped into some of these corporations approaches a national scandal." In 1932 Tabor, in an address to the National Grange Convention, referred to the "wild debauch of the power companies through the device of the holding company." See Slattery, *op. cit.*, p. 25. On the collapse of the Insull holding company structure, see Arthur M. Schlesinger, Jr., *The Crisis of the Old Order* (Boston: Houghton Mifflin Company, 1957), pp. 254-255.

18. In an address on August 11, 1938, at Barnesville, Georgia, President Roosevelt said: "Fourteen years ago a democratic Yankee, a comparatively young man, came to a neighboring county in the State of Georgia in search of a pool of warm water wherein he might swim his way back to health . . . There was only one discordant note in that first stay at Warm Springs. When the first of the month bill came in for electric light for my little cottage, I found that the charge was eighteen cents per kilowatt hour—about four times as much as I was paying in another community, Hyde Park, New York. That light bill started my long study of proper public utility charges for electric current and started in my mind the whole subject of getting electricity into farm homes throughout the United States." Samuel I. Rosenman (ed.), *The Public Papers and Addresses of Franklin D. Roosevelt* (New York: Harper and Brothers, 1950).

19. For complete information on Roosevelt's developing interest in rural electrification and public power during his terms as Governor of New York State, see Frank Freidel, *Franklin D. Roosevelt: The Triumph* (Boston: Little, Brown and Company, 1956), especially Chapter VIII, "Victory over the Power Magnates," pp. 100-119.

20. Cooke, *op. cit.*, pp. 442-443. Cooke called the report on this study "an opening of the door both to urban and rural small-consumer service on actual cost plus a reasonable profit," p. 432.

21. Clyde T. Ellis, *op. cit.*, p. 38.

22. Roosevelt was then making plans for a Mississippi Valley Authority, or an MVA, on the precedent of the TVA. How he brought Cooke to Washington and told him: "Morris, I want you to make a report on the Mississippi Valley," is delightfully told by Kenneth E. Trombley, *op. cit.*, pp. 112-114.

23. Trombley reports the views of Cooke on this incident as follows: "I honestly

thought we could work out something with the private people, but the Secretary said it was a waste of time." Cooke then asked him: "Then will you consider a plan wholly under control of public authority?" "He told me to 'shoot' and I did." *Ibid.*, pp. 144-145. Cooke reported this incident much more vigorously in his essay, "The Early Days of the Rural Electrification Idea . . ." *op. cit.*, pp. 444-445.

24. Cooke, *op. cit.*, p. 445.

25. A copy of this report, "National Plan for the Advancement of Rural Electrification Under Federal Leadership and Control, with State and Local Cooperation and as a Wholly Public Enterprise," without the bizarre cover, is in the George Norris Memorial Library of the NRECA, Washington, D.C., February 13, 1934.

26. Morris Llewellyn Cooke in letter to Herman Kahn, Director, National Archives and Records Service, Franklin D. Roosevelt Library, Hyde Park, New York. A copy of this letter is included with the report in the George Norris Memorial Library of the National Rural Electric Cooperative Association, Washington, D.C.

27. See Cooke's essay: "The Early Days of the Rural Electrification Idea: 1914-1936," *op. cit.*, p. 447.

28. As Cooke was director of the water power section of the National Resources Board, both reports reflected his thinking.

29. See Cooke, "The Early Days of the Rural Electrification Idea . . ." *op. cit.*, p. 444.

30. As quoted by David Cushman Coyle, *Electric Power on the Farm* (Washington, D.C.: Rural Electrification Administration, 1936), p. 87.

31. *Ibid.*, p. 87.

32. *Ibid.*, pp. 88-89.

33. As indicated in Chapter IX, Hull was one of the pioneers in establishing federated purchasing cooperatives in the Midwest. His successes in this field gave him confidence in what could be accomplished by similar procedures in the field of rural electrification. In appearing before a Senate Hearing on Farm Credit Legislation in 1933, Senator George Norris said to him: "If, as you say, farmers can successfully buy in large quantities their feed, seed, fertilizer, and petroleum products through cooperatives, why can't they use the same method to buy electric power?" Hull replied that if they could obtain adequate, low-cost financing, there was no reason why they could not do as good a job with rural electrification as with anything else. The beginnings of rural electric cooperatives in Indiana are described by Harvey Hull in his book *Built of Men* (New York: Harper and Brothers, 1952), pp. 180-185. See also Chapter 11, "Farmer Power Lit Rural Lights" in Hull's book, *Twentieth Century Pioneer*, published by the Indiana Farm Bureau Cooperative Association in 1968.

34. Joseph F. Marion, *A History of the Finance Division of the Rural Electrification Administration—The First Fifteen Years* (mimeographed), issued October 3, 1950, by REA, p. 1.

35. H. S. Person, "The Rural Electrification Administration in Perspective," *Agricultural History*, April 1950, p. 71.

36. *Ibid.*, p. 73.

37. A copy of this letter is in the George Norris Memorial Library of NRECA.

38. For a good discussion of the bitter struggle that preceded the passage of the Public Utilities Holding Company Act, which became law on August 26, 1935, see Arthur M. Schlesinger, Jr., *The Politics of Upheaval* (Boston: Houghton Mifflin Company, 1960), Chapter 17, "The Utilities on the Barricades." See also Chapter 20, "Power for the People," especially p. 382.

39. The way in which Cooke was gradually converted to the cooperative way of doing business is well explained by Joe Jenness in his profile of Cooke, appropriately

titled: "Morris Llewellen Cooke—Cooperator Through Necessity," in Joseph G. Knapp and Associates, *Great American Cooperators* (Washington, D.C.: American Institute of Cooperation, 1967), pp. 130-137.

40. Murray D. Lincoln (as told to David Karp), *Vice President in Charge of Revolution* (New York: McGraw-Hill, 1960), p. 132.

41. Letter of Harvey Hull to author, November 26, 1970.

42. REA Memo of Udo Rall to Dr. Harlow Person, April 13, 1949. A copy of this memo and Rall's report are available in the George Norris Memorial Library of the National Rural Electric Cooperative Association.

43. In letter of transmittal to Jacob Baker, Assistant Administrator, Federal Emergency Relief Administration, May 16, 1935. The FERA had become interested in the possibilities of rural electrification as a means of providing relief assistance. Cooke had read the report before the meeting and had asked that mimeographed copies be prepared for distribution.

44. Rall informs me that Cooke told him after the meeting that the report had cleared up a question that had bothered him, as to why a cooperative that he knew of in Pennsylvania had failed to survive. Interview of January 5, 1971.

45. In an address in October he made his position clear. Although Cooke was desirous of the industry's cooperation, he was unwilling to have it on the industry's terms. On November 5, he showed his independence by turning down the application of a Wisconsin commercial utility company for a sizeable loan. In his letter to the president of the company he said: "only one obstacle prevents me from approving the application—the high rate of your company for rural consumers." In response the president of the power company said: "We are not willing to enter into any large building program under rates which we know are below the cost of service." The full letters are quoted in a mimeo report by James E. Ross, *Why Electric Cooperatives Serve Rural America,* National Rural Electric Cooperative Association, January 1962, pp. 5-6.

46. Perry L. Green, *History of Ohio Farm Bureau Federation* (Columbus: Ohio Farm Bureau Federation, mimeographed, 1935), pp. 232-234.

47. Person, *op. cit.,* p. 74.

48. Although Fisher did not come from cooperative ranks, he was sympathetic to their objectives, and he quickly enlisted their goodwill. He also did much to change the attitude within the REA so that it would be more responsive to the needs and problems of the cooperatives. During this early period, most of the influential members of the staff were cynical concerning cooperatives, for their previous associations and contacts had been mostly with private or public utility companies and they were without cooperative or even rural connections. As noted later, this attitude didn't change until the industry demonstrated its refusal to work with the cooperatives, while the cooperatives demonstrated that they could do the job.

49. Frederick William Muller, *Public Rural Electrification* (Washington, D.C.: American Council on Public Affairs, 1944), pp. 20-21.

50. A significant development within REA came on November 1, 1935, when Joseph F. Marion, later Chief of the Finance Division, was invited by Cooke "to join him in the job of engineering into existence the basic operational structures for the new agency." At this time the organization had little structure, and most of the responsibility for directing the work was in the Engineering Department. According to Marion: "Electrical engineers were engaged in receiving and registering loan applications, obtaining all necessary approval, making allocations, and reviewing construction contracts." One of Marion's first assignments was to make a survey of the organization to determine how the program of work could be best departmentalized, and, as the work load progressively increased, changes were made to adopt structure to needs. See Joseph F. Marion, *loc. cit.* This mimeographed publication,

available in the George Norris Memorial Library, gives a good inside picture of the working arrangements of the REA during its formative period.

51. *Ibid.*, p. 7. Many of the employees had worked with utilities companies and had a limited knowledge of cooperatives. However, when they saw that the utility companies were not going to be responsive, it became a matter of "sink or swim," and a new attitude developed toward cooperatives. Instead of a negative attitude the employees began to see that the cooperative approach would enable the REA to develop a more comprehensive program of rural electrification than any other.

52. *First Annual Report of the Rural Electrification Administration* (mimeographed), for period May 11, 1935 to December 31, 1936, p. 5.

53. Frederick William Muller, *op. cit.*, pp. 44-45.

54. *Ibid.*, pp. 3-4.

55. Muller held that the midwestern farmers' purchasing cooperatives provided "not so much a form or specific technique as a promotional driving force, some local personnel, and a wide background of knowledge, experience and conviction." *Ibid.*, p. 25.

56. Person, *op. cit.*, pp. 75-76.

57. Marquis Childs, *op. cit.*, p. 65.

58. For the legislative history of this act see Truman Richardson's paper, "The Norris-Rayburn Rural Electrification Act of 1936" in the George Norris Memorial Library of the National Rural Electric Cooperative Association.

59. Ellis, *op. cit.*, p. 54.

60. "To help people organize electric cooperatives, Carmody recruited a small personal staff of men willing to walk muddy roads and talk to farmers in their barnyards. His attitude was: if rural people were so anxious to have electricity that they would assume the responsibility of creating the organizations to make it possible, the least REA could do was to show them how." *Ibid.*, p. 54.

61. Kenneth E. Trombley, *op. cit.*, pp. 165-170.

62. Mollie Ray Carroll, "A Survey of Moral and Cultural Effects of the Inside Bathroom and the Refrigerator, Conducted in Two Counties Each of Virginia, Ohio and Minnesota," 1936, typewritten. Dr. Carroll has made a copy of her report available to the author.

63. An event of national significance occurred on December 4, 1936, with the dedication by Governor Paul V. McNutt of the first "all electric" farm in the nation under the Rural Electrification Administration. This was the farm of Mr. and Mrs. Ira Bradley, near Lebanon in Boone County, Indiana. Over a thousand were in attendance and the event was widely publicized. The farm was made a demonstration farm by the Boone County Rural Electrification Membership Cooperative and by the State REMC, and many of the appliances were donated by business firms. They included "every kind of household and farm electric device imaginable—refrigerator, stove, hot water heater, mixer, toaster, sandwich toaster and waffle iron, mangle iron, washer, milk cooler, cream separator, heater, brooder, grain grinder, ensilage cutter, hay hoist, milking machine, radio, sewing machine, sweeper, clock, lamps, pump and percolator. And of course lights throughout the house and yard." The total electric bill was then averaging between $12 and $13 monthly. For full information on this interesting event, including photographs, see *Indianapolis Sunday Star*, December 6, 1936, and the *Indianapolis Times* of August 3, 1937.

64. Trombley, *op. cit.*, p. 173.

65. Arthur M. Schlesinger, Jr., *The Politics of Upheaval* (Boston: Houghton Mifflin Company, 1960), p. 384.

66. Ellis, *op. cit.*, pp. 54 ff.
67. Joe Jenness, "The Role of 'Statewides' in Rural Electrification," a research paper in the George Norris Memorial Library, undated, but apparently written in the 1950's.
68. Ellis, *op. cit.*, p. 62. H. S. Person also held that one of the fundamental policy decisions of the REA was to "establish and maintain relations with the individual cooperatives directly and not through intermediary organizations . . . Person, *op. cit.*, p. 78.
69. Marquis Childs, *op. cit.*, pp. 92-94.
70. Typical of the 49 questions that were answered were: What is REA? What is an REA Cooperative? Is not this cooperative idea a rather new-fangled and risky thing to try? Can a cooperative enterprise fail? What is meant by "cooperative principles"? What is meant by democratic control? Should REA cooperatives give patronage refunds? What are the duties of directors? What are the responsibilities of the members? How much must I pay for the electricity I use?
71. *Rural Lines—USA,* Miscellaneous Publication 811, Rural Electrification Administration, U.S. Department of Agriculture, 1960.
72. Based on information given in Table VIII in *Public Rural Electrification,* by Muller, *op. cit.*, p. 36.

Chapter XVIII

1. In an article in *Cooperation* for December 1933, entitled "Cooperation Impresses Washington," Warbasse said: "There was never before a government in Washington that was so willing to help the cooperative movement. Cooperation now has friends in every department. Now is the time to build, unite and strengthen cooperative societies."
2. Harvey Hull, *Twentieth Century Pioneer* (Indianapolis: Indiana Farm Bureau Cooperative Association, 1968), p. 5.
3. An earlier meeting had been called by Cowden in Kansas City, Missouri. Conversation with Howard Cowden, May 17, 1971.
4. The three interesting organization meetings were well reported by Oscar Cooley in the January and April 1933 issues of *Cooperation.*
5. For a comprehensive analysis of the NRA experiment, see Leverett S. Lyon and Associates, *The National Recovery Administration: An Analysis and Appraisal* (Washington, D.C.: The Brookings Institution, 1935). The following statements are of interest: "Contrasted . . . with the industrial and labor advisory groups, the consumers' interest lacked support from any well-organized or articulated constituency" (p. 125). "The consumers' representatives, apart from the force of their interpretations of the public interest, had really no bargaining power at all except as they could convince deputies of the correctness of their contentions" (p. 129). It is of interest that this full-scale study of the NRA totally ignored the problems and significance of cooperatives under the codes.
6. For a more complete understanding of this situation and the effective role played by Cowden, Warbasse, and others in obtaining fair treatment for cooperatives, see James Peter Warbasse, *Three Voyages* (Chicago: The Cooperative League, 1956), pp. 189 ff; Gilbert C. Fite, *Farm to Factory* (Columbia: University of Missouri Press, 1965), pp. 88 ff; and Robin Hood, "Codes and Cooperatives," *The Cooperative Marketing Journal,* September-October 1934, pp. 121-126.
7. Born in a log house on a pioneer Iowa farm in 1881, Bowen's father was a farmer and later a small town hardware merchant and dealer in grain, coal, and livestock. As a boy Bowen gained experience in farming and retail business. His home train-

ing was typical of the time, and he was encouraged to be honest, work hard, and save. After finishing Cornell College, he started work with a farm machinery company and in the next 25 years worked up from the factory and office to become advertising manager, sales manager, and vice president in charge of designing and distribution. In college he had been active in debating, and in business he got extensive experience in public speaking. He began to develop his social idealism as a young man but his views on the inadequacy of the prevailing business system grew out of his personal experience. He couldn't understand why the capitalistic system could produce abundantly and not be able to distribute the abundance. One time it came to him as "a light out of heaven" that farmers themselves might organize to purchase and produce for themselves. After getting established on the job for the Cooperative League in New York City, he playfully wrote to his wife that he felt that he had got hold of one of the Archimedean levers to move the world, and he wondered if she had noticed any tremors. He soon came to believe that this was the case. See E. R. Bowen, *History of the Cooperative League, 1934-1956* (mimeographed); and Hayes Beall, "Eugene R. Bowen—Converted Advocate" in Joseph G. Knapp and Associates, *Great American Cooperators* (Washington, D.C.: American Institute of Cooperation, 1967), pp. 79-83. Information also from letters of E. R. Bowen to author in 1970-1971.

8. E. R. Bowen, *op. cit.,* p. 4.

9. Bowen understood that the position being offered by Dr. Warbasse was "Educational Secretary" but after a meeting with the Executive Committee in New York City he found that he would have the title "General Secretary" and "editor of *Cooperation.*" Bowen reports "I never used the first title I was supposed to be." Letter of E. Bowen to author, November 6, 1970.

10. Bowen later said: "Having been engaged in advertising and sales work for many years, I felt it was necessary to have a specific proposition to present to old and possible new cooperative associations," *op. cit.*

11. The story of this famous meeting has been well reported by Lincoln in *Vice-President in Charge of Revolution* (New York, McGraw-Hill, 1960), pp. 109-110.

12. Dr. Warbasse in an editorial announcement said: "On the first of January, Mr. Eugene R. Bowen entered upon the duties of General Secretary. He brings to this office understanding, earnestness and executive ability. Before his vision there spreads a society to be salvaged by the single expedient of cooperation and mutual aid."

13. Although Dr. Warbasse and Filene were good friends, Filene had little confidence in the work of the League until he was assured that Bowen would give the League stronger administration and a less doctrinaire viewpoint.

14. *Cooperation,* September 1934.

15. Perhaps none was more popular than Beatrice Webb's "The Discovery of the Consumer" which had deeply influenced the thinking of Bowen and Lincoln.

16. This chapter was widely distributed as a reprint by the Cooperative League with the author's permission.

17. Edward A. Filene, *Speaking of Change* (New York: Kingsport Press, 1939), pp. 51-59.

18. For more complete information, see *Consumers' Cooperation,* October 1935, p. 181.

19. *Consumers' Cooperation,* September 1938, p. 144.

20. See Florence E. Parker, *The First 125 Years: A History of Distributive and Service Cooperation in the United States, 1829-1954* (Chicago: The Cooperative League, 1956), pp. 206-207.

21. The newspaper columnists and Washington observers interpreted the President's action as an indication that "the next New Deal move would be toward coopera-

tive promotion" since the Commission was set up just as the political parties were developing their party platforms for the 1936 presidential elections. One Washington Newsletter said: "We are inclined to see it as a political gesture made for the purpose of getting votes." Another thought that the idea had merit in view of the growing importance of cooperative organizations. An article in the *Saturday Evening Post* stated that "the Commission grew out of the political realities of the times."

22. The wave of enthusiasm for consumers' cooperation had reached its peak in 1936, but it was beginning to recede when the Commission's report came out. A few months after the Commission made its report, Jacob Baker, the Chairman, published *Cooperative Enterprise*, a book based largely on the Commission's findings (New York: The Vanguard Press, 1937). In reviewing this book in *Consumers' Cooperation*, July 1937, Herbert E. Evans, Executive Vice-President of the Consumers' Distribution Corporation, said: "A year ago Mr. Baker's book would have been a best seller, and it is hoped it will not be neglected as the cooperative movement continues in its steady work after a great burst of publicity and discussion."

23. After reviewing this chapter in draft form, Wallace J. Campbell commented as follows on this paragraph. "I'd like to make one very pointed comment. It seems to me that the Roosevelt Commission set up to study cooperative enterprise in Europe flubbed its opportunities to have a profound impact on the economy. No specific recommendations were made for the government-type organization or organizations, which might very well have been established as a result of that report. The authors also failed to work rapidly or to accept the opportunities for public discussion of the report which could have laid the groundwork for strong and very rapid development. That, I think, is one of the blunders of the decade!" Letter of Wallace J. Campbell to author, July 29, 1971.

24. Many trade publications had met the rising interest in consumers' cooperatives with strong counter-propaganda charging cooperatives with being un-American, socialistic, government-favored, etc. A typical anti-cooperative article was one by Wever Dobson in *The Black Diamond*, the official organ of the coal industry, entitled "Cooperatives Peril Nation's Retailers." Dobson said: "*You can attempt to cloak this movement with the mantle of the church, you can misrepresent it as true Christianity, you can prate all you want to about 'The more abundant life,' but underneath all this ballyhoo there is one definite fact—the very essence of the Consumers' Cooperative Movement is the abolishment of the profit system and the elimination of the established retail dealer.*"

25. In his *History of the Cooperative League,* Bowen tells how he countered resistance within the League on this matter, *op. cit.*

26. After reviewing a draft of this chapter Wallace J. Campbell commented as follows on this paragraph. "A large number of the supermarkets now in operation had their initiation in the buying club program. The essential factor for the growth from buying clubs to large and efficient operation is a source of supply and a source of technical competence to help build viable retail enterprises. I think we fell short on both of those programs. It was there that the Filene-financed Consumers' Distribution Corporation should have made its greatest contribution." Letter of Wallace J. Campbell to author, July 29, 1971.

27. E. G. Cort outlined the plan at the meetings of the American Institute of Cooperation at the University of Chicago in August 1939.

28. For plans of his organization, see prospectus issued in 1936 by The Consumers' Distribution Corporation—"The Need for Consumer Cooperation and a Plan for Its Expansion."

29. For information on the valuable help given at Greenbelt, Maryland, see George A.

Warner, *Greenbelt—The Cooperative Community* (New York: Exposition Press, 1954).

30. Carl N. Schmalz, Bulletin 108, March 1939.

31. "The Cooperative League of the United States of America, 1916-1961: A Study of Social Theory and Social Action," *Agricultural History*, April 1962, pp. 69-72.

32. For Warbasse's views on the dangers of promotion, see *Problems of Cooperation* (New York, Chicago: The Cooperative League of the USA, 1942), pp. 143-144. "The cooperative propagandist often draws too long a bow with his stout right arm."

33. Letter of E. R. Bowen to author, September 1, 1971.

34. One man who knew both well later said: "If Bowen had just had sense enough to put a big picture of Warbasse in his office, and underneath say, 'Founder,' all would have been well." However, this would have been out of character for Bowen.

35. Bowen and other cooperative leaders were much impressed by the thinking of G. Fauquet as expressed in his book *Le Secteur Cooperatif (The Cooperative Sector)*, published in French in 1935. Fauquet saw the economic affairs organized in sectors: government, private, capitalistic, and cooperative.

36. It should be understood that the League was then a highly informal type of organization. Members of the Board were more co-opted than elected.

37. This plan "presented for discussion only," is given in full in *Consumers' Cooperation* for January 1939.

38. For more complete information on the Bowen-Warbasse disagreement, see E. R. Bowen's *History of the Cooperative League, 1934-1946, op. cit.*, pp. 20 ff; Florence E. Parker, *op. cit.*, pp. 161-162; Clarke A. Chambers, "The Cooperative League of the United States of America" in *Agricultural History*, April 1962, pp. 69 ff; Wallace J. Campbell, "James Peter Warbasse—Founder of the Cooperative League" in Knapp and Associates, *op. cit.*, pp. 521-522.

39. For a full review and analysis of the history of National, from its formation to July 1941, see Joseph G. Knapp, *Survey of National Cooperatives Inc.*, Special Report 89, Cooperative Research and Service Division, Farm Credit Administration, Washington, D.C., July 1941. This study concluded that National could become an effective organization with improved management and agreement on objectives.

40. "[Movements] arise and are perpetuated by a felt need for a basic adjustment within and as a part of a whole economic, political or social order." See Carl C. Taylor, "Objectives of Farmers Cooperatives—By a Sociologist," *American Cooperation*, 1949, pp. 71-73.

41. Includes members of credit unions, rural electric cooperatives, etc.

Chapter XIX

1. R. H. Elsworth, *Statistics of Farmers' Marketing and Purchasing Cooperatives, 1939-40 Marketing Season*, Farm Credit Administration, Miscellaneous Report 34, 1941.

2. See Index numbers of wholesale prices, *U.S.D.A. Agricultural Statistics, 1941*, p. 559.

3. Moreover as W. I. Myers points out: "A basic weakness of the Farm Board was its inaccessibility to smaller cooperatives which perform essential functions in marketing farm products and purchasing supplies. In addition, either by law or by loan policy, the Farm Board, for the most part, concentrated on loans to national cooperatives and made loans to locals through the national organizations in case

local cooperatives were considered essential. The result was building national organizations from the top down and neglecting the building of sound and efficient local organizations." Letter of W. I. Myers to author, August 3, 1972.

4. The results of this survey were published in *A Statistical Handbook of Farmers' Cooperatives*, Bulletin 26, Farm Credit Administration, 1938. This report not only supplemented the annual statistical reports made by the Cooperative Research and Service Division of the Farm Credit Administration, it also confirmed their general accuracy.

5. For a summary of the work carried on by the Cooperative Research and Service Division during the New Deal years and an evaluation of its importance, see Andrew W. McKay, *Federal Research and Educational Work for Farmer Cooperatives, 1913-1953*, Service Report 40, Farmer Cooperative Service, U.S.D.A., 1959, pp. 74-89.

6. See Fred E. Clark, "Trends in Marketing and Market Distribution," *American Cooperation*, 1937, pp. 40-52.

7. In addressing the American Institute of Cooperation in 1948, S. D. Sanders, Cooperative Bank Commissioner, Farm Credit Administration, said: "Changes in market outlets and marketing practices are affecting cooperatives more acutely than ever before." See "Developments and Current Problems in Cooperation," *American Cooperation*, 1938, pp. 45-52.

8. The information in this section is from R. H. Elsworth and Grace Wanstall, *Statistics of Marketing and Purchasing Cooperatives, 1940-41 Marketing Season*, Miscellaneous Report 50 of the Cooperative Research and Service Division, Farm Credit Administration, 1942. Cooperatives were classified as marketing associations if more than 50 per cent of their business was in cooperative marketing. They were placed in a commodity grouping if more than 50 per cent of their business was in that commodity.

9. Furthermore these statistics do not distinguish between large-scale and local cooperatives. Therefore, average volume figures for different types of associations would have little meaning. It should be noted that these figures also contain some cooperative purchasing business handled as a sideline by marketing cooperatives.

10. For an interesting account of the way this association met its problems during the New Deal years, see Alfred D. Stedman, *50 Years—The Story of the Twin City Milk Producers Association* (an anniversary history published by the association), St. Paul, Minn., 1966. For information on the early days of this association, see Joseph G. Knapp, *The Rise of American Cooperative Enterprise* (Danville, Ill.: The Interstate Printers & Publishers, Inc., 1969), pp. 222-223.

11. Dr. Leland Spencer, formerly Professor of Marketing, Cornell University, attributes much of the League's trouble during these years to its efforts to maintain the Class I price. "The great spread between Class I and surplus milk price served to aggravate the surplus problem during the years from 1930-34, or thereabouts. Moreover, the great spread between the Class I price and the pool price gave non-pool buyers an increased advantage on both the buying and selling ends. They could raid the League membership at will and at the same time cut prices and thereby raid League fluid outlets quite successfully. As a result the League . . . found itself saddled with the lion's share of the milkshed surplus." Letter of February 7, 1972.

12. According to Fred H. Sexauer, President of the Dairymen's League through the Thirties, the League became the target of all who opposed cooperative effort. Among the opponents of the League were "communists" whose goal was to create chaos in the agricultural field"; "buyers of milk who wanted to control producers and thus their supply of milk"; "dealers' cooperatives who sought price advantage"; "feed manufacturers or dealers who feared the competition of the G.L.F."; and "newspapers, and periodicals and writers who sang the same song." Sexauer be-

lieves that the Dairymen's League lost thousands of members as a result of the constant vilification from these sources. Letter of February 8, 1972. However, other competent observers who were not entirely unsympathetic to the problems confronting the League at that time attribute much of the League's difficulties during these years to its inflexible policies and strong arm tactics which alienated many dairymen and stimulated much of the opposition to it. "The League saw itself as the leader of a righteous cause and was inclined to look upon all those who questioned its procedures as trouble makers. The League at that time suffered from a monopoly complex but couldn't make it stick." Letter to author from Henry Blewer, March 20, 1972.

13. Spencer has summarized the major recommendations of the Pitcher Committee as follows: "(1) As a long-run solution, develop a more unified and more effective organization of producers, capable of administering a comprehensive classified pricing and pooling plan. (2) As an emergency measure, enact a State Milk Control Law, giving authority to a Milk Control Board to fix milk prices, from producer to consumer, for a temporary period of one year." Letter of February 18, 1972.

14. Letter of February 19, 1972. According to Spencer this Act "authorized the formation of a milk producer bargaining agency by the cooperatives representing producers associated with any market of the State. Such agencies were designed to bring the numerous cooperatives together for joint action . . . A bargaining agency could vote en bloc for all member producers," a provision that facilitated use of a federal market control plan.

15. For a concise history of the League's history to survive during the New Deal years, see *The Fifty Year Battle for a Living Price for Milk—A History of the Dairymen's League* (compiled and edited by D. J. Carter, editor of the *Dairymen's News*, and issued by the Dairymen's League, July 1939). For a valuable record of League developments in the Thirties, see R. D. Cooper, *Organization and Development of the Dairymen's League*, a mimeographed document in the files of the Dairymen's League, 1938.

16. See E. W. Gaumnitz, "Cooperative Marketing of Manufactured Dairy Products," *American Cooperation*, 1938, pp. 350-351.

17. See Don S. Anderson, "Fundamentals of Butter Price Stabilization," *American Cooperation*, 1939, p. 325. See also Kenneth D. Ruble, *Men to Remember* (published for Land O' Lakes Creameries, Inc., by Lakeside Press, Chicago, 1947), pp. 226-227.

18. It should be pointed out that the Land O' Lakes Creameries, Inc., was gradually becoming also a cooperative purchasing organization. In 1929 it established an agricultural service division to supply creamery supplies to its member associations, and from then on farm supply operations expanded steadily. By 1940 farm supply sales amounted to over $1 million annually.

19. The interesting story of how the Land O' Lakes Creameries, Inc., grew during the depression and New Deal years is told by Kenneth D. Ruble, *loc. cit.* See also H. F. Meyer, "The 'aging' and 'ripening' of Land O' Lakes Creameries," *American Cooperation*, 1934, pp. 471-482; John Brandt, "National Program to Deal with Surplus Farm Programs," *American Cooperation*, 1938, pp. 221-223; and Frank D. Stone, "Appraising Sales Performance by Farmers Cooperative Organizations," *American Cooperation*, 1940, pp. 215-222.

20. For full information see Paul E. Quintus, *Operating Methods of Challenge Cream and Butter Association*, Farm Credit Administration, Circular C-119, 1940.

21. See M. W. Thatcher, "Developments and Problems in Grain Marketing Cooperatives," *American Cooperation*, 1936, pp. 371 ff. In closing his statement, Thatcher said: "Until national cooperative marketing may be freed from quadrennial poli-

tical swings or may become so financially independent that it can challenge national political panaceas, national cooperative marketing . . . will operate without reasonable business projection and with a result known only to the gods."

22. For an interesting account of how the experience of the Farmers' National turned cooperative leaders back to more modest ambitions, see H. S. Patton, "Future of Grain Marketing Cooperatives," *American Cooperation*, 1929, pp. 365 ff. Patton maintained that this experience taught that "there are few potential economies or advantages associated with cooperative grain marketing through a national organization that are not attainable by a well-rounded, efficient regional cooperative, and even these would likely be more than offset by heavy supervisory expenses and impaired flexibility, and by detachment from the underlying cooperative membership." Patton recognized that the most pressing problem was to improve the efficiency and standards of existing local elevator cooperatives. He believed that the regionals working with the banks for cooperatives and public agencies could be of great assistance in this process.

23. See Sidney Baldwin, *Poverty and Politics—The Rise and Decline of the Farm Security Administration* (Chapel Hill: University of North Carolina Press, 1968), p. 204. See also Robert Handschin's profile of M. W. Thatcher, "Cooperative Warrior" in Joseph G. Knapp and Associates, *Great American Cooperators* (Washington, D.C.: American Institute of Cooperation, 1967), pp. 510 ff. Handschin has tersely described the part played by Thatcher in bringing about this change as follows: "By 1937 co-op grain marketing had to be turned back to regionals but after three years of drought and depression they were without funds. Thatcher went to President Roosevelt, who, on December 29, 1937, inscribed on Thatcher's short memo, 'HW: Try to work out, FDR.' 'HW' being Secretary of Agriculture, Henry A. Wallace. It was done. The new banks for cooperatives helped the regionals start again, and FSA loaned farmers money to buy co-op shares in locals and regionals." *Farmers Union Herald*, June 3, 1968, p. 4.

24. For conditions leading up to the formation of the National Federation of Grain Cooperatives, see M. W. Thatcher, "A Single Farmer's Idea Launched a Co-op Empire," *Grain Quarterly*, fall issue, November 1943, pp. 35-37.

25. For full statement of the Articles of Agreement, see *Grain Quarterly*, November 1943, pp. 77-79.

26. A good instance is described by Ralph Snyder, first President of the Wichita Bank for Cooperatives, in his little book, *We Kansas Farmers* (Topeka: Kans.: F. M. Steves and Sons, 1953), pp. 107, 108-109.

27. Richard Phillips, in profile of Professor Frank Robotka, "The Gadfly of Cooperation" in Knapp and Associates, *op. cit.*, pp. 429 ff.

28. For more detailed information on the history of the major rice cooperatives, see Henry M. Bain, *Cooperative Marketing of Rice and Its Part in the War Emergency*, Farm Credit Administration, Circular C-129, 1943.

29. *Fifty Years a Rancher* (Los Angeles: Ward Richie Press, 1944), p. 121. For more detailed information on this experience, see the *Annual Reports* of the California Fruit Growers Exchange from 1932 to 1940.

30. For a detailed history of the Florida Citrus Exchange during the years 1933-40, see James T. Hopkins, *Fifty Years of Citrus* (Gainesville: University of Florida Press, 1960), pp. 136-181.

31. The interesting history of this pioneer organization is given in its Golden Anniversary, *Fifty Years of Growth and Service* (Tampa, Fla. 1964).

32. Information from J. F. Childs, Treasurer, Citrus World, Inc. The Florida Citrus Canners Cooperative changed its name to Citrus World, Inc., on July 25, 1969.

33. Information on the development of this interesting organization, which was an

early instance of a mutually profitable arrangement entered into by a cooperative organization with a private firm, has been generously supplied by N. L. Allen, the manager of the National Fruit and Vegetable Exchange, who became and was long the manager of American National Cooperative Exchange. Letters of February 2 and March 10, 1972. For supplementary information, appreciation is expressed to Frank Hussey, the long-time president of Maine Potato Growers, Inc., who was President of both the National Fruit and Vegetable Exchange and its successor organization, the American National Cooperative Exchange. Interviews in February and March, 1972.

34. For a full account of the development of this pace-setting organization and its relationships with American National Cooperative Exchange, see Clarence A. Day, *A History of Maine Potato Growers, Inc., 1932-1952* (Orono: University of Maine, mimeographed, 1953), pp. 1-30. See also George H. Goldsborough, *Cooperative Marketing of Potatoes in the United States,* Farm Credit Administration, Bulletin 62, 1951, pp. 51-53.

35. For detailed information on the history of this organization, now Sunsweet Growers, Inc., see Robert Couchman, *The Sunsweet Story* (San Jose, Calif.: Sunsweet Growers, Inc., 1967).

36. The interesting story of how Cranberry Canners, Inc., came into existence and expanded until it eventually superseded the American Cranberry Exchange was well told by John R. Quarles in an address, "Ocean Spray, 1930-1960," presented at the 30th annual meeting of Ocean Spray Cranberries, Inc., on August 17, 1960. Mr. Quarles served as attorney for Ocean Spray, Inc., during its formative years.

37. For a description of this early experience, see Herman Steen, *The Golden Rule in Agriculture* (New York: Doubleday, Page, 1923), pp. 69-71, 75-77. See also Peter G. Helmberger and Sidney Hoos, *Cooperative Bargaining in Agriculture: Grower-Processor Markets for Fruits and Vegetables* (University of California, Division of Agricultural Sciences, 1965), pp. 7-8.

38. See G. Alvin Carpenter, *The Organization and Operation of the Utah Canning Crops Association,* Utah Agricultural Experiment Station, Bulletin 294 (Logan, 1956). The story of how this organization came into existence and grew is well told by A. W. Chambers, Secretary-Manager of the Utah Canning Crops Association from the time of its formation, in "How We Organized for Bargaining," *Proceedings of the Conference on Fruit and Vegetable Bargaining Cooperatives,* Farmer Cooperative Service, U.S.D.A., 1957, pp. 18-21.

39. For information on the status and methods of these associations in 1940, see articles on "Cooperation by Sugar Beet Growers" in *American Cooperation,* 1940, pp. 719-740. For the rationale of the early associations see M. S. Winder "Sugar Beet Collective Bargaining Associations." *American Cooperation,* II, 1925, pp. 536-550.

40. In 1931 Dr. Nourse and the author called attention to the need of area-wide cooperative livestock marketing associations which would take into account the changing character of the livestock industry. We said: "Probably the greatest gain in economy and efficiency in livestock marketing will come when a widely representative cooperative agency puts itself in a position to supply buyers of livestock with just the class and quality of product which they order, and to guarantee that what is delivered will meet specifications in every detail. Such is the achievement in other commodity lines, and it is clearly within reach of the livestock group if they pursue it aggressively and intelligently." Edwin G. Nourse and Joseph G. Knapp, *The Cooperative Marketing of Livestock* (Washington, D.C.: The Brookings Institution, 1931), pp. 334-335.

41. For a full discussion of the creation and development of this interesting organization, see R. L. Fox and C. G. Randell, *Decentralized Marketing by Producers Livestock Cooperative Association,* Columbus, Ohio, Farm Credit Bulletin 65, 1951.

42. See John J. Lacey, *Farm Bureau in Illinois* (Bloomington, Ill.: Illinois Agricultural Association, 1965), pp. 259-266.

43. See C. G. Randell, *Equity Cooperative Sales Association*, Farmer Cooperative Service, U.S.D.A., Circular 32, 1963.

44. Livestock auction cooperatives, federated into a state association, have functioned successfully in California since 1918. See R. L. Fox, *Livestock Marketing Associations in California*, Farmer Cooperative Service, U.S.D.A., General Report 98, 1961, p. 10.

45. See Knapp, *op. cit.*, pp. 231-231.

46. See R. L. Fox, Anne E. Wheeler, and C. C. Randell, *Measuring the Marketability of Meat-Type Hogs*, Farm Credit Administration, Circular C-152, May 1953.

47. Its sales volume was $15 million in 1939.

48. For a comprehensive review of cooperative cotton marketing experience down to 1940, see Stanley Andrews, "Changing Programs in the Cooperative Marketing of Cotton," *American Cooperation*, 1941, pp. 273-288. See also J. S. Hathcock, "What Next in Cotton Marketing" in *The Cooperative Marketing Journal*, March-April 1937. See also Otis T. Weaver, *SWIG* (Southwestern Irrigated Cotton Growers Association), Farmer Cooperative Service, U.S.D.A., Circular 29, 1962, pp. 38-39.

49. W. E. Paulson of the Texas State Agricultural College thought that the interest in this form of cooperation represented something of a "natural reaction from the overemphasis given to the large-scale type of cooperative." See his article, "The Cooperative Gin of Texas," *Cooperative Journal*, January-February, 1936, pp. 9-11.

50. Weaver, *op. cit.*, pp. 42-44.

51. For more information on the early history of this important organization, see Henry W. Bradford, *Cotton Cooperatives on the Plains of Texas*, Farmer Cooperative Service, U.S.D.A., Circular 33, 1966, pp. 9-20. It was not easy to get the first cottonseed oil mills into effective operation. A government bulletin in 1937 declared: "There are probably more hazards, as well as more possibilities of substantial savings to farmers, in this line of cooperative endeavor at this time than in any other agricultural enterprise in the South." Ward W. Fetrow, *Cooperative Marketing of Agricultural Products*, Farm Credit Administration, Bulletin 3, 1936, p. 21.

52. Letter from J. Roy Garrett, President of Norbest Turkey Growers, February 25, 1972.

53. See Henry W. Bradford and John J. Scanlon, *Cooperative Marketing of Turkeys*, Farmer Cooperative Service, U.S.D.A., Circular 23, 1957, pp. 7-8.

Chapter XX

1. Government statistics classify purchasing associations as those doing more than 50 per cent of their business in cooperative purchasing, and marketing associations as those doing more than 50 per cent in cooperative marketing. When adjustments were made in the 1939-40 figures, the estimated amount of all cooperative purchasing by marketing and purchasing cooperatives was $448.2 million, as compared with $416 million the preceding year. See R. H. Elsworth, *Statistics of Farmers Marketing and Purchasing Cooperatives, 1939-40 Marketing Season*, Cooperative Research and Service Division, Farm Credit Administration, Miscellaneous Report 347, 1941.

2. *Agricultural Statistics*, U.S.D.A., 1941, p. 554.

3. For more detailed information, see Joseph G. Knapp, "The Rise of Cooperative Purchasing," *American Cooperation*, 1941, pp. 559-561.

4. Walter W. Wilcox, *The Farmer in the Second World War* (Ames: Iowa State College Press, 1947), pp. 9-10. For detailed information on the rapid increase in technology in farming operations during the Thirties, see *Technology on the Farm*, a special report of the United States Department of Agriculture, August 1940.

5. Of particular value was the initial report of the purchasing section which indicated how purchasing cooperatives were organized and operated. Within a few years, tens of thousands of this publication were distributed to farmers and others interested in this subject. See Joseph C. Knapp and John H. Lister, *Cooperative Purchasing of Farm Supplies*, Farm Credit Administration, Bulletin 1, September 1935.

6. Knapp, *op. cit.*, p. 566.

7. W. I. Myers also attributes great significance to the GLF's member educational work. He writes: "The demonstration of the value of member education by the GLF service agencies contributed to the splendid success of the production credit associations. GLF gave especial emphasis to annual meetings which reported each year to local members on the progress and problems of their organizations. Good attendance was obtained by interesting discussions, supplemented by refreshments and other social advantages. We in Farm Credit copied these demonstrated successes with similar results in building strong locals and increasing the volume of business and savings. This program deserves a great deal of credit for the success of the PCA program and also it helped a lot in strengthening local land bank associations which at that time were called NFLA's." Letter of W. I. Myers to author, August 3, 1972.

8. For more complete information on the development of this great farmers' institution from 1933-1940, see Joseph G. Knapp, *Seeds That Grew: A History of the Cooperative Grange League Federation Exchange* (Hinsdale, N.Y.: Anderson House, 1960), pp. 161-233.

9. For more complete information see W. G. Wysor, *The Southern States Story* (Richmond, Va.: The Southern States Cooperative, Inc., 1959); and John H. Lister and Alexander Swantz, *Purchasing Farm Supplies Through Southern State Cooperative, Inc.*, Farm Credit Administration, Circular C-128, 1943.

10. For the story of how this organization came into being, see "The Birth of the FCX" in Joseph G. Knapp's *Farmers in Business* (Washington, D.C.: American Institute of Cooperation, 1963), pp. 197-204.

11. For more complete information on the progress and methods of this organization during the New Deal years, see I. Harvey Hull, *Built of Men—The Story of Indiana Cooperatives* (New York: Harper and Brothers, 1952). See also Paul Turner, *They Did It in Indiana—The Story of the Indiana Farm Bureau Cooperatives* (New York: Dryden Press, 1947); and Gerald M. Francis, *Cooperative Purchasing by Indiana Farmers Through Federated County Farm Bureau Associations*, Farm Credit Administration, Bulletin 38, 1939.

12. For information on the (Ohio) Farm Bureau Cooperative Association, see Chapter XXXI of Perry L. Green's *History of the Ohio Farm Bureau Federation* (Columbus: Ohio Farm Bureau Federation, mimeographed, 1955). Green was long President of the Federation.

13. For more complete information see *Annual Reports* of the Illinois Farm Supply Company and John H. Lister, *Cooperative Purchasing Through the Illinois Farm Supply Company and Its Member County Companies*, Farm Credit Administration, Bulletin 27, 1938.

14. For a brief history of the association up to 1940 see Leonard C. Kercher, Vant W. Kebker, and Wilfred C. Leland, Jr., *Consumers Cooperatives in the North Central States* (Minneapolis: University of Minnesota Press, 1941), pp. 361 ff. See also *Men of Midland*, Silver Anniversary Annual Report of Midland Cooperative Wholesale, Inc., March 1951. This provides a year by year record of progress.

15. The early history of this organization is given by Kercher, Kebker, and Leland, *op. cit.*, pp. 406 ff.

16. For an interesting and dramatic account of how the CCA established the first cooperative refinery in the face of almost insurmountable obstacles, see Gilbert C. Fite, *Farm to Factory: A History of the Consumers Cooperative Association* (Columbia: University of Missouri Press, 1965), pp. 153 ff.

17. For the beginnings of this association, see John H. Lister and Gerald M. Francis, *Cooperative Purchasing of Farm Supplies in Mississippi*, Farm Credit Administration, Bulletin 22, 1928.

18. See John H. Lister, *Cooperative Manufacture and Distribution of Fertilizer by Small Regional Dry-Mix Plants*, Farm Credit Administration, Circular C-126, 1941, pp. 3 ff.

19. See Gerald M. Francis, *Analysis of Organization and Operations of Consumers Cooperatives Association and Its Member Fuel Associations in Texas*, Farm Credit Administration, Special Report 98, 1942, mimeographed.

20. This association, now Gold Kist, Inc., is one of the major agricultural cooperatives in the nation. For information on its early development, see Gerald M. Francis, *Cooperative Purchasing of Farm Supplies in Georgia*, Farm Credit Administration, Circular C-120, 1940, pp. 22 ff.

21. See Joseph G. Knapp, *Seeds That Grew, op. cit.*, p. 225.

22. For example, Murray Lincoln, the Secretary of the Ohio Farm Bureau Federation and a strong Cooperative League supporter, bitterly opposed what he considered the narrow-minded "production centered" attitude of United Cooperatives. In his book, *Vice-President in Charge of Revolution*, he said. "We were members of both National and United, but that was about all the two organizations had in common. United would have nothing to do with National because National did business with city people and United not only refused to do business with city people, it refused to do business with farmers who did business with city people" (New York: McGraw-Hill, 1960), pp. 149-150.

23. The story of United's development during the Thirties is well told by J. F. "Jack" Yeager, *United Cooperatives—The First Thirty Years* (Ithaca, N.Y.: Upstate Press, 1963). For information on the relationship of the United Cooperatives to National Cooperatives in 1940, see Joseph G. Knapp, *Survey of National Cooperatives, Inc.*, Farm Credit Administration, Special Report 89, July 1941.

24. For more complete information on the character and procedures of this organization in 1940, see Knapp, *Survey of National Cooperatives, Inc., loc. cit.*

25. The national cooperative survey made by the Banks for Cooperatives in 1937 found that farm machinery was then being distributed by 363 farmers' cooperatives in 33 states. For information on the development of local farm machinery distribution through cooperatives, see Gerald M. Francis, *Distribution of Machinery by Farmers Cooperative Associations*, Farm Credit Administration, Circular C-125, 1941.

26. The cooperatives involved were the Farmers' Union Central Exchange, the Consumers Cooperative Association, and the farm bureau cooperatives of Indiana, Ohio, and Michigan. Although these associations were all members of National Cooperatives, Inc., National itself did not then have adequate financial resources to undertake the program.

27. For a good description of CCA's unsuccessful efforts to establish its farm machinery and tractor program in the face of heavy inventory losses, difficulties in providing service, and ruthless competition from the machinery companies, see Fite, *op. cit.*, pp. 123-125, 190, 221, 236, 242-243.

28. It is of interest that United Cooperatives, Inc., became involved in the Co-Op trac-

tor program in 1937. As it was calling for greater investment, United officials became fearful of the financial liabilities that might be incurred without closer supervision than could be given by a committee from the cooperatives. They, therefore, recommended the incorporation of a company "under which the manufacture of tractors could be handled" and soon afterwards the Cooperative Machinery Company was established for this purpose. In the early spring of 1938, the Farm Security Administration offered to make the tractor under what appeared to be a very favorable arrangement at Arthurdale, West Virginia, and this offer was accepted on May 23. Following the transfer of operations, the Duplex Machinery Company sued for losses incurred, and United Cooperatives became involved in the lawsuit since it had suggested the formation of the Cooperative Machinery Company. This suit was settled at some cost to the cooperatives. See Yaeger, *op. cit.*, pp. 41-42.

29. For more complete information on the early efforts to establish a national cooperative farm machinery program from 1935 to 1940, see I. H. Hull, *op. cit.*, pp. 69-71. Hull was the dominant leader in these efforts. During the years from 1935 to 1940 some 1,500 Co-Op tractors were sold, mostly by the Farmers' Union Central Exchange. For a time after 1940 the F.U.C.A. continued to assemble the Co-Op tractor under a contract with a Minneapolis manufacturer.

30. For a good expression of the views of this school, see statement by Robin Hood, Secretary of the National Cooperative Council, "Lessons We Have Learned," *Cooperative Journal*, Sept.-Oct., 1936, pp. 137-142. The National Cooperative Council included in its membership many large cooperative marketing and cooperative purchasing associations. A number of the marketing cooperatives also engaged in the cooperative purchasing of farm supplies. The primary thrust of the Council was agricultural.

31. The position of this group was presented by E. R. Bowen, Secretary of the Cooperative League in an address to the American Institute of Cooperation. "The Aims and Objectives of the Consumers Cooperative Movement," *American Cooperation*, 1937, pp. 127-138.

32. The author attempted to clarify "the relationship of agricultural cooperation to consumers' cooperation" in an article under this title in the *Cooperative Journal*, May-June 1936. See Joseph G. Knapp, *Farmers in Business, op. cit.*, pp. 102-113.

Chapter XXI

1. Much of the information in this section has been derived from the authoritative and enlightening study by J. Carroll Moody and Gilbert C. Fite, *The Credit Union Movement: Origins and Development, 1850-1970* (Lincoln: University of Nebraska Press, 1971).

2. *Ibid.*, p. 166.

3. *Ibid.*, p. 168.

4. *Ibid.*, p. 171.

5. *Ibid.*, p. 253.

6. See French M. Hyre, "Farm Mutual Insurance" in *Agricultural Cooperation in the United States* by Ward W. Fetrow and R. H. Elsworth, Farm Credit Administration, Bulletin 54, 1947, pp. 164-173, 213. See also V. N. Valgren, "Trends and Developments in Farm Mutual Insurance," *American Cooperation*, 1937, pp. 599-607.

7. John J. Lacey, *Farm Bureau in Illinois* (Bloomington: Illinois Agricultural Association, 1965), pp. 101, 140, 267-269.

8. Charles M. Gardner, *The Grange—Friend of the Farmer* (Washington, D.C.: The National Grange, 1949), pp. 84, 322-323.

9. According to Karl Schriftgiesser, the historian of the State Farm Insurance Companies, the history of the American Farm Bureau Federation would be incomplete without a chapter on its close relationship in the 1920's and early 1930's with State Farm Mutual. *The Farmer from Merna* (New York: Random House, 1955), pp. 116-117.

10. Letter to author from Robert G. Sayre, Nationwide Insurance Companies, December 7, 1971. See also Bowman Doss, "People Working Together—The Story of the Nationwide Insurance Organization," a pamphlet issued by the Nationwide Insurance Companies in 1968.

11. In addition to the mutual insurance organizations sponsored by farm organizations, there were a few insurance cooperatives related to cooperatives, but they were relatively unimportant prior to 1940. See Florence E. Parker, *The First 125 Years: A History of Distributive and Service Cooperation in the United States, 1829-1954* (Chicago: Cooperative League of U.S.A., 1956), pp. 272-274.

12. For further information see Joseph G. Knapp, *E. A. Stokdyk—Architect of Cooperation* (Washington, D.C.: American Institute of Cooperation, 1953), pp. 67-69. See also Wells A. Hutchins, *Mutual Irrigation Companes in California and Utah,* Farm Credit Administration, Bulletin 8, October 1936, and Wells A. Hutchins, *Organization and Operation of Cooperative Irrigation Companies,* Farm Credit Administration, Circular C-102, August 1936,

13. Leonard N. Conyers and Robert J. Byrne, *North Dakota Cooperatives Coordinate Transportation for Economy and Service,* Farm Credit Administration, Miscellaneous Report 132, 1949, pp. 1-4.

14. See Robert J. Byrne, *Coordinating Transportation Improves Marketing and Purchasing for Minnesota Cooperatives,* Farm Credit Administration, Bulletin 57, 1950, pp. 1-5, 13.

15. See George W. Rupple, *Sponsoring Artificial Insemination Groups* (Washington, D.C.: American Institute of Cooperation, 1941), pp. 250 ff. See also Donald E. Hirsch and Irwin R. Hedges, *Dairy Breeding Cooperatives—Their Development, Practices and Policies,* Farm Credit Administration, Circular C-133, 1949, pp. 1 ff.

16. For information on the development of cooperative frozen food lockers, see L. B. Mann, *Refrigerated Food Lockers—A New Cooperative Service,* Farm Credit Administration, Circular C-107, 1938, pp. 1-5, 23-28; see also S. T. Warrington and Paul C. Wilkins, *Cooperative Frozen Food Locker Plants—Organization and Operation,* Farm Credit Administration, Circular C-127, 1946, pp. 1-10.

17. H. G. Hamilton, "Integrating Services for Economy and Efficiency," *American Cooperation,* 1946, pp. 693-694.

18. See *30 Years of Amalgamated Cooperative Housing, 1927-1957,* issued by the Amalgamated Housing Corporation of New York City in 1958. This brochure gives the full history of the development and problems of this organization by Abraham E. Kazan, the man who carried the burden of management during these difficult years.

19. See Florence E. Parker, *op. cit.,* p. 218.

20. For more complete information on the work and significance of this committee and related developments in cooperative medical care, see William A. MacColl, *Group Practice and Prepayment of Medical Care* (Washington, D.C.: Public Affairs Press, 1966), pp. 12 ff.

21. Florence Parker, *op. cit.,* pp. 237-238. See also Helen L. Johnston, *Rural Health Cooperatives,* joint publication of Farm Credit Administration and Public Health Service, FCA Bulletin 60 and PHS Bulletin 308, June 1950, pp. 4-5.

22. The Home Owners Loan Corporation (HOLC) was set up in the summer of 1933 to provide government refinancing of mortgages for distressed small home-owners, and its work in averting a collapse of the real estate market gained for it general public approval. Mr. Zimmerman reported directly to Mr. Fahey, Chairman of the Federal Home Loan Bank Board, who was a respected business leader, having served as President of the Chamber of Commerce of the United States. Mr. Fahey was at this time Chairman of the Executive Committee of the Twentieth Century Fund and thus was well informed on its broad program in the field of medical care. For information on the importance of the HOLC during the New Deal years, see Arthur M. Schlessinger, Jr., *The Coming of the New Deal* (Boston: Houghton Mifflin Company, 1959), pp. 297-298. For biographical information on Mr. Fahey, see *Who Was Who in America, 1951-1960* (Chicago: A. N. Marquis Company, 1960).

23. The information here given on the establishment of the Group Health Association has been supplied by R. R. Zimmerman through interviews and correspondence during March and April 1972.

24. Interview with R. R. Zimmerman, March 30, 1972.

25. See William Hard, "Medicine and Monopoly," *Survey Graphic*, December 1939.

26. Much of the information which follows on the business and legal development of GHA has been derived from a very illuminating study made by Harold C. Mufson, *A History of Group Health Association, Inc., Washington, D.C., 1937-1955* (a dissertation for the degree of Master of Science in Hospital Administration, the Catholic University of America, Washington, D.C., June 1955, multilithed). Another useful source of information has been Arthur G. Peterson's *The Legal History of Group Health Association of Washington, D.C.* (Washington: Group Health Association, 1947).

27. As William Hard, a well-known conservative Republican journalist of that period, pointed out, it was difficult for many people to understand that "the professor, idealists and brain trusters of the Roosevelt Administration" were not "once more trying to socialize our poor guinea pig country." According to Hard, they could not understand that "the truth was very different" in that the Federal Home Loan Bank Board was motivated by "good business judgment" in encouraging the formation of GHA as a means of improving employee morale and reducing its costs of operations, *op. cit.*, p. 606.

28. *Ibid.*, p. 609.

29. As quoted in *ibid.*, p. 608.

30. Harold C. Mufson, *op. cit.*, p. 40.

31. L. C. Salter, *Fishery Circular 22*, U.S. Department of Commerce, 1936. This publication has been brought up-to-date under the title "Organizing and Operating Fishery Cooperatives in the United States," by Leslie D. McMullin as Circular 155 of the U.S. Department of the Interior, 1963.

32. See *Hearings* on the Fishery Credit Act before the Committee on Merchant Marine and Fisheries (House of Representatives, Seventy-Fifth Session on H.R. 6039 and H.R. 7309, June 29, and July 16, 1937). These hearings provided information on the principal fishery cooperatives then in existence and the character of their operations. Of particular interest was the testimony of L. C. Salter, who had drafted the Fishery Credit Act with legal guidance from Mr. Lyman S. Hulbert of the legal staff of the Farm Credit Administration. He reported that 54 associations did a volume of business in 1935 of more than $9 million. See pp. 51-69.

33. See Leslie D. McMullin, "List of Fishery Cooperatives in the United States, 1967-68," Fishery Leaflet 612, Bureau of Commercial Fisheries, Fish, and Wildlife Service, U.S. Department of the Interior. (Under a Government reorganization, work with fisheries was transferred from the Department of Commerce to

the Department of the Interior.) This publication lists 77 fishery cooperatives recognized by the U.S. Department of the Interior as cooperatives under the provisions of the Fishery Cooperative Marketing Act of 1934. Information is supplied on the number of members, the number of boats owned by members, the type of cooperative, and the major species of fish and shell fish caught. It is of interest that credit services for fishermen and fishery cooperatives have recently been made available by the Farm Credit Act of 1971.

34. For a review of this early experience, see *Forest Cooperatives in the United States*, a report issued by the Forest Service of the U.S. Department of Agriculture in 1947.

35. J. G. Knapp, *The Rise of the American Cooperative Enterprise* (Danville, Ill.; The Interstate Printers & Publishers, Inc., 1969), p. 428.

36. Hector Lazo, *Retailer Cooperatives: How to Run Them* (New York: Harper and Brothers, 1937), pp. 10-17.

37. See Gorden C. Corbaley, *Group Selling by 100,000 Retailers* (New York: American Institute of Food Distribution, Inc., 1936), pp. 51 ff.

Chapter XXII

1. For background information on the role of the United States in World War II, see the following: Samuel Eliot Morison, *The Oxford History of the American People* (New York: Oxford University Press, 1965), pp. 987-1045; R. Ernest Dupuy, *World War II: A Compact History* (New York: Hawthorn Books, Inc., 1969); Fletcher Pratt, *War for the World* (New Haven: Yale University Press, 1950); Eliot Janeway, *The Struggle for Survival* (New Haven: Yale University Press, 1951); James MacGregor Burns, *Roosevelt: The Soldier of Freedom, 1940-1945* (New York: Harcourt Brace Jovanovich, 1970). The influence of World War II on American agricultural development is well explained by Gladys L. Baker, Wayne D. Rasmussen, Vivian Wiser, and Jane M. Porter, *Century of Service: The First 100 Years of the United States Department of Agriculture* (Washington, D.C.: U.S. Dept. of Agriculture, 1963), pp. 273-329. See also Murray R. Benedict, *Farm Policies of the United States, 1790-1950* (New York: The Twentieth Century Fund, 1953), pp. 402-459; and Walter W. Wilcox, *The Farmer in the Second World War* (Ames: Iowa State University Press, 1947). For a review of wartime experience of agricultural cooperatives, see *American Cooperation: 1942-1945* (Washington, D.C.: American Institute of Cooperation, 1945).

2. The Neutrality Act then in force had forbidden the sale and transport of arms and munitions to a belligerent, loans to a belligerent, or the entry of American ships into war zones. Morison, *op. cit.*, p. 991.

3. *American Cooperation*, 1940, pp. 130-135.

4. *Ibid.*, pp. 143-144, 147.

5. *Ibid.*, pp. 267-269.

6. See Baker, *et al.*, *op. cit.*, p. 279.

7. *1941 Blue Book of National Council of Farmer Cooperatives*, p. 21.

8. Following his reelection, President Roosevelt had begun searching for a plan under which war materials and food supplies could be made available to Britain without breaching the Neutrality Act or getting us involved in the war. He found his answer in the Lend Lease idea which he sprang on a press conference in December. He likened the idea to the loan of a garden hose to help a neighbor fight a fire. See James MacGregor Burns, *op. cit.*, pp. 26-27.

9. Joseph G. Knapp, "Where Purchasing Coops Fit in National Defense," *News for Farmer Cooperatives*, June 1941, pp. 9, 25-26.

10. T. G. Stitts, "Agricultural Cooperation—An Annual Inventory," *News for Farmer Cooperatives*, July 1941, pp. 3-4.

11. See Joseph G. Knapp, *Handbook of Major Purchasing Cooperatives*, Cooperative Research and Service Division, Farm Credit Administration, Miscellaneous Report 67, 1943.

12. For full information on the formation of the National Committee for Farm Production Supplies, see the minutes of the organization meetings in the records of the National Council of Farmer Cooperatives, August, September 1941.

13. Morison, *op. cit.*, p. 1009.

14. See Joseph G. Knapp, *Seeds That Grew: A History of the Cooperative Grange League Federation Exchange* (Hinsdale, N.Y.: Anderson House, 1960). See Chapter 25, "The G.L.F. Helps Win the War," especially pages 245-247, which deals with the way G.L.F. mobilized for action.

15. *1942 Blue Book of the National Council of Farmer Cooperatives*, p. 23.

16. *Ibid.*, p. 23.

17. *American Cooperation, 1941*. (The 1941 sessions were held at Atlanta, Georgia, in January 1942.)

18. T. G. Stitts, "What War Means to Coops," *News for Farmer Cooperatives*, April 1942, pp. 3, 20-21.

19. See *News for Farmer Cooperatives*, February 1942, pp. 4, 7.

20. Kenneth D. Ruble, "Men to Remember," Land O' Lakes Creameries, Inc., 1947.

21. L. G. Foster, "Orange Concentrate for the Yanks," *News for Farmer Cooperatives*, April 1943, pp. 10-11.

22. *Annual Report of the California Fruit Growers' Exchange* for the year ending October 31, 1942, pp. 5-6.

23. Harry C. Hensley, "Convert or Perish," *News for Farmer Cooperatives*, January 1943, pp. 9-10.

24. The way in which the Cooperative Research and Service Division stopped its ongoing research and educational activities and applied its efforts to helping cooperatives meet pressing war needs is described by Andrew W. McKay, *Federal Research and Educational Work for Farmer Cooperatives 1913-1953*, Farmer Cooperative Service, U.S.D.A., Service Report 40, January 1959, pp. 89 ff.

25. Morison, *op. cit.*, p. 1015.

26. See unsigned article, "In Spray Milk 'It's Coops One to Two,'" *News for Farmer Cooperatives*, January 1943, p. 15. This article carried a map of the United States showing the widespread location of the cooperative spray-process dried skim milk powder plants.

27. "By the year's end the Soviets were launching another winter offensive against an outnumbered, exhausted, disheartened enemy, at bay from the trenches around Leningrad down to the Black Sea." Dupuy, *op. cit.*, p. 143.

28. See Murray R. Benedict, *op. cit.*, pp. 405 ff.

29. This was reflected in the content of the monthly issues of *News for Farmer Cooperatives* during 1943.

30. See French M. Hyre, "Coop Committee Speeds Up Supplies," *News for Farmer Cooperatives*, April 1943, pp. 14, 16.

31. See *Annual Report of the California Fruit Growers' Exchange* for the year ending October 31, 1943. The Exchange was providing a large part of the pectin required for Lend Lease operations among its other war contributions. See pp. 6, 20-23.

32. See L. G. Foster, "Orange Concentrates for the Yanks," *News for Farmer Cooperatives*, April 1943, pp. 10-11.

33. See "What 'Set Aside Butter' Means to Coop Creameries," *News for Farmer Cooperatives*, April 1943, pp. 7, 18. Some idea of the wide variety of agricultural products sold to the government by cooperatives under the Food for Freedom program is given in an article "Coop Foods in the War," *ibid.*, pp. 3, 19.

34. The way in which soybean processing plants were developed by cooperative grain elevators in Iowa was described by W. H. Thompson, "Iowa Coop Elevators Take the Protein Situation in Hand," *News for Farmer Cooperatives*, October 1943, pp. 15-16.

35. Information supplied by Stanley Thurston, Grain Economist, Farmer Cooperative Service, in letter of May 9, 1972.

36. See OPA Supplementary Order 84, Amending Price Regulations, 1944.

37. For more complete information see Joseph G. Knapp, "How Purchasing Cooperatives in the United States Are Adjusting Themselves to War Conditions," Cooperative Research and Service Division, Farm Credit Administration, Mimeographed Address, presented at the annual meeting of the Canadian Cooperative Union, Saskatchewan Section, Regina, Saskatchewan, Canada, June 25, 1943.

38. For detailed information see Joseph G. Knapp, *The Place of Cooperatives in the Fertilizer Industry*, Cooperative Research and Service Division, Farm Credit Administration, Miscellaneous Report, 1945.

39. For table showing date of acquisition for cooperative refineries up to December 31, 1950, see J. Warren Mather, *Petroleum Operations of Farmer Cooperatives*, Farm Credit Administration, U.S.D.A., Circular C-139, May 1951, p. 40.

40. For the interesting story of how CCA rapidly expanded its petroleum and oil production operations from 1940 to 1945, see Gilbert C. Fite, *Farm to Factory: A History of the Consumers Cooperative Association* (Columbia: University of Missouri Press, 1965), pp. 153-185.

41. See L. N. Conyers, "The Importance of Efficient Coop Traffic Management," *News for Farmer Cooperatives*, September 1944, pp. 9, 21; and J. Warren Mather, "One-fourth Less Mileage, One-fourth More Volume," *News for Farmer Cooperatives*, October 1943, pp. 6-7, 16.

42. This battle "left the United States Navy in complete command of Philippine waters; never again could the Japanese navy offer a real threat. But two months' fighting ashore were required against the hard-fighting no-surrender Japanese infantry, before Leyte and Samar were in MacArthur's hands." Morison, *op. cit.* p. 1036.

43. The information in this section is largely drawn from Grace Wanstall, *Statistics of Farmers Marketing and Purchasing Cooperatives, 1944-45*, Cooperative Research and Service Division, Farm Credit Administration, Miscellaneous Report 108, 1946, and from data supplied by the Farmer Cooperative Service, U.S.D.A.

44. Official statistics show that farm product prices rose by 90 per cent from 1940 to 1945, although prices paid by farmers for all commodities rose by only one-third, *Agricultural Statistics, 1953*, U.S. Department of Agriculture, Table 703, p. 603.

45. This is shown by the records of individual associations that reported volume information in terms of bushels of grain, carloads of fruit, tons of feed and fertilizer, gallons of petroleum products, etc. Official statistics show that U.S. farm output increased by about 20 per cent from 1940-1945, *ibid.*, Table 687, p. 585.

46. For more complete operating and financial information for these associations, see Joseph G. Knapp, *Handbook on Major Regional Farm Supply Purchasing Cooperatives, 1941 and 1942*, Cooperative Research and Service Division, Farm Credit Administration, Miscellaneous Report 67, 1943; and Joseph G. Knapp and Jane L. Scearce, *Handbook on Major Regional Farm Supply Purchasing Cooperatives, 1944 and 1945*, Cooperative Research and Service Division, Farm Credit Administration, Miscellaneous Report 102, 1946.

Chapter XXIII

1. See Murray R. Benedict, *Farm Policies of the United States, 1790-1950* (New York: The Twentieth Century Fund, 1953), pp. 344-345.

2. For a full list of member associations and organizations as of January 1946, see the *1946 Blue Book of the National Council of Farmer Cooperatives*, pp. 30-35. The general importance of the Council as spokesman and representative of agricultural cooperatives during the war period was recognized by Walter W Wilcox, *The Farmer in the Second World War* (Ames: Iowa State University Press, 1947), pp. 368, 385-386.

3. See J. F. Yaeger, *The First Thirty Years* (Ithaca, N.Y.: United Cooperatives, Inc.), p. 67.

4. *Ibid.*, p. 213.

5. *Ibid.*, p. 87.

6. Report of A. G. Rose, General Manager, Universal Milking Machine Company Division of National Cooperatives, Inc., in Centennial Reports of National Officers and Staff Members, 14th Biennial Congress of the Cooperative League, September 1, 1944, pp. 40-42.

7. Prior to November 1, 1945, Universal was operated as a separate company, although its membership was identical to that of National. Letter to author from Francis L. Lair, General Manager, National Cooperatives, Inc., June 15, 1971.

8. Letter from Toik A. Tenhune to author, October 31, 1972. Other information from report of A. G. Rose, *op. cit.*, pp. 40-42.

9. Prior to 1944 National did not report total volume but reported only brokerage income. Net savings were reported as about $39,000 in 1941; $12,000 in 1942; and $97,000 in 1943. In 1943 part of the savings were due to manufacturing operations. Letter of Francis L. Lair to author, November 29, 1971.

10. *Ibid.*

11. See *Centennial Reports of National Officers and Staff Members*, 14th Biennial Report of the Cooperative League, September 1, 1944, for reports of I. H. Hull, President of National Cooperatives, pp. 16-18; T. A. Tenhune, General Manager, National Cooperatives, pp. 38-40; A. G. Rose, General Manager, Universal Milking Machine Company Division of National Cooperatives, pp. 40-42; and J. L. Proebsing, Advertising Manager, National Cooperatives, pp. 43-45.

12. See Ralph O. Brown, "Why Farm Machinery Repair Shops?," *American Cooperation*, 1946, pp. 626-629. See also Boyd A. Rainey, "Possibilities for Expansion in Handling Steel Products and Farm Machinery," *American Cooperation*, 1946, pp. 624-625.

13. Daniel Seltzer, "National Farm Machinery," *American Cooperation*, 1946, pp. 630-31. Mr. Seltzer was then general manager of National Farm Machinery Cooperative, Inc.

14. I. H. Hull, "General Report of Progress" in Centennial Reports of *National Officers and Staff Members*, 14th Biennial Congress of the Cooperative League, Chicago, October 8 to 13, 1944, p. 17.

15. *The Federal Land Bank System, 1917-1967*, a publication for general distribution issued by the Federal Land Banks in 1967, p. 19.

16. Data from *Annual Reports of the Farm Credit Administration for 1941, and 1944-45*.

17. See Earl L. Butz, *The Production Credit System for Farmers* (Washington, D.C.: The Brookings Institution, 1944), pp. 24-25. See also C. R. Arnold, *Farmers Build*

Their Own Production Credit System, Farm Credit Administration, Circular E-45, 1958, pp. 65, 76-78.

18. For an excellent independent evaluation of the production credit system in 1944, see Butz, *loc. cit.*

19. The following statement supplied by Homer G. Smith, President of the Central Bank for Cooperatives, November 3, 1972, indicates how the Central Bank worked with the district banks in meeting the credit needs of cooperatives during the World War II period. "From its inception in 1933, and through World War II, the Central Bank financed directly most of the larger farmer cooperative associations selling to one or more of the district banks a 'participation' [loan] when they desired to buy them. In addition, the Central Bank participated, by furnishing the money and accepting a portion of the risk in loans made by district banks in their respective districts which exceeded their lending limits which were based on a percentage of their net worth. In handling the larger loans to cooperatives which made advances on the farmers' products before the products were actually marketed, such as wheat, cotton, wool, dairy products, fruits and vegetables, the Central Bank had a representative located in the office of the cooperative, usually a full-time employee to hold warehouse receipts in order that the receipts could be released promptly when the products were sold. Having a local representative enabled the bank to keep in close touch with the financial conditions and financial needs of the cooperatives from day to day. During the war period when conditions and needs were changing fast, this was important for the cooperative as well as the Bank. With a sudden need for additional funds to serve the cooperative members, the Bank was able to act promptly by increasing loan commitments, even by 'phone at times.' This was very helpful in assisting farmer members in order that they might be able to make the maximum effort during the war years."

20. This committee was comprised of representatives from the National Grange, the American Farm Bureau Federation, and the National Council of Farmer Cooperatives.

21. For a full account of the way in which this plan developed, see Chapter IV, "Developing Farmer Ownership," *Banks for Cooperatives—A Quarter Century of Progress* (prepared by W. Gifford Hoag, B. B. Sunbury, and Marie Puhr), Farm Credit Administration, Circular 247, 1960, pp. 41 ff. See also Joseph G. Knapp, section on "Toward a Cooperatively Owned System of Cooperative Banks" in *E. A. Stokdyk—Architect of Cooperation* (Washington, D.C.: American Institute of Cooperation, 1953), pp. 121-131.

22. Under the plan adopted, the Banks for Cooperatives gradually replaced government capital with capital supplied by the cooperative borrowers. The Banks for Cooperatives became fully borrower-owned in 1969.

23. For more complete information on credit union history during World War II, see J. Carroll Moody and Gilbert C. Fite, *The Credit Union Movement: Origins and Development, 1850-1970* (Lincoln: University of Nebraska Press, 1971), especially Chapter XII, "The War Years," pp. 262-288.

24. *Ibid.*, pp. 263, 267. See also Cecil R. Crews, *The History of the Michigan Credit Union League* (Detroit: Wayne State University Press, 1971), pp. 116-120.

25. Moody and Fite, *op. cit.*, pp. 272-273, 308.

26. Richard Y. Giles, *Credit for the Millions: The Story of Credit Unions* (New York: Harper and Brothers, 1951), p. 33.

27. *Ibid.*, p. 34.

28. See "Credit Union and Cooperative League Plan Closer Cooperation," *Consumers Cooperation*, February 1943, p. 29.

29. Clyde T. Ellis, *A Giant Step* (New York: Random House, 1966), pp. 70-71. In the

early days of preparedness the big electric companies saw an opportunity to stop the rapid expansion of rural electric cooperatives. The power companies were on the inside track because the demands for electricity were great and their services were essential to national defense.

30. According to E. J. Stoneman, one of the incorporaters of the NRECA, the formation of a national association was a natural development. "Shortly after the organization of the REA movement . . . a great many people felt that, as the thing grew, there would be the necessity of tying the distribution systems together for self-protection . . . I discussed with dozens of people in my own state and in other places the necessity for that kind of thing." Commenting on the organization of NRECA he said: "I suppose I might say that there were thousands of people interested in the movement who had the same idea." See *Administration of the Rural Electrification Act*, Hearings before a Subcommittee on S. Res. 197 of the Committee on Agriculture and Forestry, U.S. Senate, 78th Congress, 1943-44, pp. 370 ff. The leading advocate of a national organization was Robert T. Craig, an employee of REA. In a memorandum to REA Administrator Carmody, April 15, 1937, he recommended that "a national organization be formed" but that "the suggestion for such a national organization should come from the membership itself." Craig actively promoted the idea after he became REA Deputy Administrator under Harry Slattery in 1940. For copy of Craig's memorandum to Carmody and Craig's comments on it see *Administration of the Rural Electrification Act, Hearings* . . . pp. 286, 320.

31. It will be recalled from Chapter XVII that REA Administrator Carmody had effectively opposed the establishment of state-wide organizations that would engage in financing and management operations although he sanctioned state-wide associations that would represent the local electric cooperatives on general matters. When the NRECA was formed such associations were functioning in more than half of the states.

32. In explaining the formation of the association Steve C. Tate, one of the incorporators of NRECA and its first President, said: "The birth of your association is almost like fiction. As a result of [the] hearings during the months of November and December 1941 before the Tarver Subcommittee, there were those of us from all sections of the country who had the pleasure of meeting and exchanging views as to the Rural Electrification Administration Program and, growing out of this meeting, there was expressed a feeling from all parts of the country that a national association of the cooperatives would be an ideal means of fighting for . . . the mutual protection of all the cooperatives since it was evidenced at the congressional hearing that there was a concerted private utility opposition to our program." Excerpt from speech given at first annual meeting of the NRECA, St. Louis, Missouri, January 19, 1943, as reported in *Administration of the Rural Electrification Act, op. cit.*, pp. 1838-39.

33. *Administration of Rural Electrification Act, op. cit.*, pp. 1906-1909.

34. Marquis Childs, *The Farmer Takes a Hand: The Electric Power Revolution in Rural America* (Garden City, N.Y.: Doubleday and Company, 1952), p. 94.

35. For a full account of how Clyde T. Ellis became Executive Manager of the NRECA see his testimony in the senate sub-committee hearings, *Administration of the Rural Electrification Act, op. cit.*, pp. 1033 ff. and especially p. 1035 and pp. 1046-1055.

36. See David E. Lilienthal, *The Journals of David E. Lilienthal: The TVA Years, 1939-45* (New York: Harper and Row, 1964), Journal entry for February 20, 1943, pp. 586-87.

37. Gladys L. Baker, Wayne D. Rasmussen, Vivian Wiser, and Jane M. Porter, *Century of Service* (Washington, D.C., U.S. Department of Agriculture, 1963), p. 299.

38. For full letter see *Administration of the Rural Electrification Act, op. cit.*, pp. 422-424.

39. Ellis, *A Giant Step, op. cit.*, p. 77.

40. For more information see Ellis, *ibid.*, pp. 75-78, and Childs, *op. cit.*, pp. 96-98.

41. For the full letter see *Administration of the REA Act, op. cit.*, pp. 1349-50. See also a strictly confidential letter sent out by Clyde T. Ellis, Executive Manager, and Avery C. Moore, Acting Secretary Treasurer, to "all members of the NRECA" on June 5, and a more detailed confidential memorandum to the "boards of directors, public utility districts and public power districts who are members of the NRECA," June 7, explaining difficulties with Slattery. The memorandum ended with this statement: "Mr. Slattery should be removed not because of his double-cross on the insurance program, but because of his vacillation and administrative failures; because he is wrecking the administrative agency; because his better employees are leaving day by day. . . ." *Administration of the Rural Electrification Act*, pp. 1352-1357.

42. See *Rural Electrification Administration: Proposed Plan of Reorganization and Relations Within the Department of Agriculture*, Division of Administrative Management, Bureau of the Budget, Project 49, November 1942.

43. Writing in 1944 Frederick William Mueller found that the staff of the REA "had little in common with the rest of the Department of Agriculture . . . Departmental controls, therefore, tend to seem irksome. There is good reason to maintain that the present controls are conducive to neither efficient operation nor effective supervision." *Public Rural Electrification* (Washington, D.C.: American Council on Public Affairs, 1944), p. 173.

44. For more complete information see *Administration of the Rural Electrification Act, op. cit.*, pp. 1326-27. Udo Rall, who was an employee of the REA in St. Louis during the war years, recalls that this was a "miserable period in the REA." Interview with author, December 21, 1972.

45. *Administration of the Rural Electrification Act, op. cit.*, p. 214.

46. *Administration of the Rural Electrification Act, op. cit.*, p. 5. See also pp. 209-210.

47. The hearings, published under the title *Administration of the Rural Electrification Act*, provide a voluminous record—running to 2,179 printed pages—of charges and countercharges and much information of value on the early history of rural electrification in the United States. The hearings can also be given credit for encouraging a subtle change in the philosophy of the NRECA, for henceforth it became less of a pressure group and more of a cooperative supporting agency. For the views of Marquis Childs on the nature and significance of this investigation see *The Farmer Takes a Hand, op. cit.*, pp. 97-98.

48. Title V of the Department of Agriculture Organic Act of 1944, approved September 21, 1944 (58 Stat. 739).

49. Donald H. Cooper, Senior REA and Cooperative Specialist, NRECA, in letter to author of June 28, 1972.

50. Clyde Ellis, *A Giant Step, op. cit.*, p. 82. According to H. S. Person: "The judgement of the Congress in providing more liberal credit terms has been fully justified by the extent to which the borrowers have been able to carry out the area coverage concept." He also said: "This legislation furnished a very sound groundwork on which to base the accelerated postwar program." See "The Rural Electrification Administration in Perspective," *Agricultural History*, April 1950, pp. 81, 84.

51. *REA Annual Reports, 1941 through 1945*. The statistics for loan advances, miles of line energized, and numbers of consumers connected apply to systems which also cover loans made by REA to municipal and other borrowers. However, about 90 per cent of the systems represented rural electric cooperative association borrowers.

52. See T. E. Milliman, "Co-ops Blazed the Way in Fertilizer," *News for Farmer Cooperatives*, November 1940, pp. 25-26; and John H. Lister, *Cooperative Manufacture and Distribution of Fertilizer by Small Regional Dry-mix Plants*, Farm Credit Administration, U.S.D.A., Circular C-126. This circular examined the organization and operations of three associations: the Farmers Cooperative Fertilizer Purchasers, Inc., Kenbridge, Virginia; the Tennessee Valley Fertilizer Cooperative of Decatur, Alabama; and the Centralia Farmers Cooperative, Inc., of Selma, Alabama.

53. Memorandum from J. C. McAmis to L. G. Allbaugh, December 11, 1952, p. 41 (TVA records).

54. See "Work Underway in the Cooperative Research and Service Division," a mimeographed report of the Cooperative Research and Service Division, Farm Credit Administration. U.S.D.A., 1941.

55. The name Fertilizer Cooperatives of North America recognized the participation of fertilizer cooperatives in eastern Canada.

56. David E. Lilienthal, "Phosphorus: Key of Life," *American Cooperation, 1941*, pp. 92-93. In his book *TVA—Democracy on the March* (New York: Harper and Brothers, 1944), Lilienthal later indicated that commercial sales of concentrated phosphate had been considerable, but only a fraction of what they would have been if in the industry there were not such a strong resistance to private expansion of facilities for the production of concentrates. He saw the situation as comparable to the electrical industry where most distributors "except the cooperatives" were slow to recognize that it was in expanded production and sales, at consequent lower unit costs, that its real interest lay. While the industry had been critical, support for the phosphate program had come from national and state farmer's cooperative associations that sold fertilizers, pp. 110-111.

57. Shelden Leroy Clement, *The Role of TVA Fertilizers in an Educational Program* (doctoral thesis in Department of Economics, Harvard University, 1954), p. 13.

58. David E. Lilienthal, *The Journals of David E. Lilienthal—The TVA Years*, I (New York: Harper and Row, 1964), p. 555. In reporting this matter, Lilienthal added this comment: "It was necessary for me to press very hard, internally, to get this step taken, even to the extent of discussing the matter frankly with these men. Caution can be carried so far that it becomes sterility and inaction. I have had plenty of 'troubles' along this line—not lack of understanding nor public-minded viewpoint—just a form of timidity."

59. Clement, *op. cit.*, pp. 39-40.

60. *Ibid.*, pp. 40-42. "It was the responsibility of the War Production Board to get produced to the extent possible the fertilizers which the War Food Administration determined were needed. The distribution arrangements, including allocations if required, were also the responsibility of the War Production Board." Letter of Shelden L. Clement to author, December 6, 1972. For more detailed information on relationship of War Food Administration to War Production Board see Gladys L. Baker, Wayne D. Rasmussen, Vivian Wiser, and Jane M. Porter, *Century of Service: The First 100 Years of the United States Department of Agriculture* (Washington, D.C., U.S. Dept. of Agriculture, 1963), pp. 295-296.

61. L. Carlton Salter who was responsible for TVA's work with cooperatives at that time, as Chief of the Cooperative Research and Experiment Division of the Division of Agricultural Relations, has provided the following information on how Associated Cooperatives, Inc., came to be established. "At the outset when the problem came to the TVA, we attempted (and LCS in particular) to sell the ammonium nitrate to farmer cooperatives in the Valley or elsewhere.

War Foods Administration was on TVA's neck (and particularly mine) to get the ammonium nitrate out and into the trade as it was badly needed to produce food and fiber. Pressure was on and WFA, via telephone with me, stated: 'Get the hell out of there with that ammonium nitrate. If you can't sell it, dammit, get a broker!' That triggered the decision. TVA's considered congressional mandate and policy required me to afford cooperatives the chance and opportunity. That was when I conceived the idea of farmer cooperatives forming a national fertilizer federation. After consulting with my superiors and associates, I made a number of strategically placed phone calls to cooperative leaders, including the Presidents of the Banks for Cooperatives at Columbia and New Orleans. As a result, the representatives of the major cooperatives in the states designated by the War Foods Administration for distribution of TVA ammonium nitrate met in Birmingham and Associated Cooperatives resulted. Even then War Foods Administration said: 'No' again, and decided that all the TVA ammonium nitrate be offered for sale to fertilizer manufacturers (mixers, that is) to who, when, where, and to the extent approved by the War Production Board; and Associated was restricted accordingly until restrictions were lifted at the end of the war when Associated was able to turn entirely to distributing TVA's production of ammonium nitrate strictly to farmer cooperatives. At first farmer cooperators got some of the ammonium nitrate, but only those with fertilizer mixing plants, located initially in the Southeastern states. As the territorial limits of distribution were expanded, cooperatives in other areas were served." Letters from L. C. Salter to author of July 23, 1971, and January 27, 1972.

62. As quoted from minutes of a meeting of a group of Farmer Cooperatives at Birmingham, Alabama, July 29, 1943, signed by Ernest B. Johnson, Acting Chairman; see Clement, *op. cit.*, pp. 41-42.

63. Clement, *op. cit.*, p. 43.

64. Clement, *op. cit.*, pp. 43-44.

65. Associated also distributed for TVA about 20,000 tons of ammonium nitrate with a value of $962,000 produced at government ordnance plants in 1944 and a lesser amount in 1945. See 1944 and 1945 Annual Reports of TVA's Department of Agricultural Relations. See 1944 Report, pp. 24-25, and 29; and 1945 Report, p. 24.

66. 1945 Annual Report of TVA's Department of Agricultural Relations, pp. 5, 23.

67. See Clement, *op. cit.*, pp. 54-55.

68. Clement, *op. cit.*, p. 56.

69. See letter from E. P. Garrett to G. W. Bunting of September 24, 1945, quoted by Clement, *op. cit.*, pp. 57-58. For profile of Mr. Garrett, see Joseph G. Knapp and Associates, "He Proved It in Alabama," *Great American Cooperators* (Washington: American Institute of Cooperation, 1967), pp. 185-187.

70. Quoted from memorandum of Neil Bass in TVA files by Clement, *op. cit.*, pp. 57-58.

71. See memorandum from Neil Bass to Gordon E. Clapp, "Memorandum of Understanding and Contract for Experimental Distribution with Central Farmers Fertilizer Committee," February 5, 1946, as quoted by Clement, *op. cit.*, p. 59.

72. For the provisions of the memorandum of understanding and the distribution contract, see Clement, *op. cit.*, pp. 59-61.

73. Central Farmers Fertilizer Company changed its name to CF Industries, Inc., in 1970. Its volume of business for year ending June 30, 1971, amounted to $171,602,000. Its total assets as of June 30, 1971, amounted to $146,112,000.

74. Letter of G. W. Bunting to author, March 26, 1970.

75. Clement, *op. cit.*, fn. 2, p. 58.

76. For discussion of the problems faced and overcome by the State Farm Mutual Automobile Insurance Company during the war years, see Karl Schriftgiesser, *The Farmer From Merna* (New York: Random House, 1955), pp. 167-177.

77. Information supplied by Robert G. Sayre, Nationwide Insurance Companies, in letter to author of December 7, 1971.

78. Harold C. Mufson, "A History of Group Health Association" (Master's thesis, Catholic University, Washington, D.C., 1955). See Chapter IV on problems during World War II, pp. 46-57.

79. Frank F. Paskewitz, *American Cooperation*, 1946, pp. 433-35; and Florence E. Parker, *The First 125 Years* (Chicago: The Cooperative League, 1956), pp. 238-240.

80. See Florence E. Parker, *op. cit.*, pp. 237, 242. See also Helen L. Johnson, *Rural Health Cooperatives*, Farm Credit Administration, Bulletin 60, and Public Health Service, Bulletin 308, 1950, p. 5. (This was a joint publication of the Farm Credit Administration and the Public Health Service.)

81. See Parker, *op. cit.*, p. 218.

82. See S. T. Warrington and Paul C. Wilkins, *Cooperative Frozen Food Locker Plants*, Farm Credit Administration, Circular C-127, 1946.

83. See Donald E. Hirsch and Irwin R. Hedges, *Dairy Breeding Cooperatives*, Farm Credit Administration, Circular C-133, 1949, pp. 3-4.

84. *News for Farmer Cooperatives*, September 1943, p. 6.

85. For a case study account of the experience of this association, see Robert J. Byrne, *Coordinating Transportation Improves Marketing and Purchasing for Minnesota Cooperatives*, Farm Credit Administration, U.S.D.A., Bulletin 57, 1950.

86. See table giving history of federal corporation income tax exemptions and rates in Joseph A. Pechman, *Federal Tax Policy* (Washington, D.C.: The Brookings Institution, Revised Edition, 1971), p. 258.

87. A. C. Black, "The Responsibility of American Cooperatives in the War," *American Cooperation*, 1941, pp. 15-27.

88. See Joseph G. Knapp, *E. A. Stokdyk—Architect of Cooperation, op. cit.*, fn., p. 108. Stokdyk had become much interested in the tax problem of cooperatives while Deputy Governor of the Farm Credit Administration in 1939 and from this interest grew a study initiated in 1941 that resulted in a bulletin published by the Cooperative Research and Service Division of the FCA in 1942, G. J. Wass and D. G. White, *Application of the Federal Income Tax Statutes for Farmer Cooperatives*, Farm Credit Administration, Bulletin 53.

89. Gilbert C. Fite, *Farm to Factory*, (Columbia: University of Missouri Press, 1965), pp. 135-36, 200-201.

90. Robert Handschin, "M. W. Thatcher—Cooperative Warrior" in Joseph G. Knapp and Associates, p. 513.

91. For a comprehensive article on the organization and program of the National Tax Equality Association, see "M-Day Is Here for U.S. Coops," in the spring 1944 issue of *Co-op Grain Quarterly*—the official organ of the National Federation of Grain Cooperatives.

92. *Ibid.*

93. Fite, *op. cit.*, pp. 202-203.

94. *The 1944 Yearbook of the National Council of Farmer Cooperatives*, p. 24.

95. See report of John H. Davis, Executive Secretary of the National Council of Farmer Cooperatives in *Proceedings of the 1945 Annual Meeting of Delegates of the National Council of Farmer Cooperatives*, January 8-12, pp. 13-14.

96. See Kelsey B. Gardner, *"Farmers' Cooperatives and the Federal Income Tax Statutes,"* Miscellaneous Report 75 of the Cooperative Research and Service Division, Farm Credit Administration, U.S.D.A. This report made clear that the exemption was accorded only to farmers' marketing and purchasing associations as described in the Internal Revenue Code; that members and other patrons must be treated alike; that permanent patronage records must be maintained; that reserves must be reasonable and necessary; that voting rights must be held by producers; that dividends on capital shares must be limited; and that the legal structure must be cooperative in character.

97. This position was later well expressed in a paragraph on the scope of the patronage-dividend exclusion in a report of a study made by the Treasury Department, Division of Tax Research, which was submitted to the Committee on Ways and Means of the House of Representatives in the course of testimony by Lee M. Wiggins, Under Secretary of the Treasury, November 4, 1947. See *Revenue Revisions, 1947-48,* Hearings Before Committee on Ways and Means; *Proposed Revisions of Internal Revenue Code,* 80th Congress, First Session, Part IV, "Tax-Exempt Organizations," pp. 3127-3161. According to this paragraph: "The exclusion of patronage dividends from corporate gross income is not the exclusive privilege of cooperative associations. Any corporation making payments to its customers under the conditions prescribed by the Commissioner of Internal Revenue and the courts is granted the same treatment. It should be noted, however, that in the case of cooperatives, unlike the case of the typical ordinary corporation, patrons receiving rebates are also the owners of the business. The conditions which the cooperative associations must meet if refunds made to their patrons are to be excluded from the gross income of the association may be briefly stated. First, there must have existed at the time of the transaction with the patron a contractual or other definite obligation on the part of the cooperative to return any net proceeds to him in proportion to patronage without further corporate action. Second, if only members of the association are eligible to receive patronage dividends, exclusion is not allowed on that portion of such distribution which represents profits from transactions with nonmembers. On the other hand, it is held to be immaterial whether refunds are distributed in the form of cash, stock, certificates of indebtedness, or credit notices. All such form of payment are regarded as the equivalent of cash distribution in the hands of patrons, the theory being that they are cash payments automatically reinvested under provisions of the charter, by laws, or other contracts previously agreed to by the patrons" (p. 3141).

98. See report of the Council's sub-committee on legal and tax problems dealing with "Information Returns—Form 990" in *Proceedings of the 1945 Annual Meeting of Delegates of National Council of Farmer Cooperatives,* January 8-13, 1945, pp. 28-33.

99. Miller had long been active in California cooperative circles and he "was concerned that the public relations image of farm cooperatives was being destroyed by outside attacks and by inside lethargy." He was thus responsive to the invitation of the Council's Executive Committee that he make the study called for. He indicated that he would accept the challenge and make the study at no cost to the council except for mimeographing the report. In the words of Miller: "My assignment was to recommend some public relations agent to act for and in behalf of cooperatives and I soon decided that the Council, being by necessity political, could not do the job itself. I came to the conclusion that the job could best be done by building on the structure and historic record of the American Institute of Cooperation." Before recommending the reorganization of the AIC for this purpose, Miller got assurances from important cooperative leaders that the organizations they represented would help underwrite the

expanded budget that would be needed for an "effective program." Letter of
Raymond W. Miller to author, January 3, 1972. For other information on the
sequence of events in 1944 that led to the rebirth of the American Institute of
Cooperation, see *Proceedings of the 1945 Annual Meeting of Delegates,
National Council of Farmer Cooperatives*, January 8-12, 1945, pp. 14-15, and
especially the "Report of Committee on Public Relations," pp. 52-53.

100. However, the following year the offices were moved back to Washington, D.C.,
as a more practical location.

101. During the year, the AIC also issued a number of pamphlets designed to
provide the public with useful information on cooperatives. The second pamphlet,
issued in October 1945, reprinted two articles by E. A. Stokdyk: "Financial
Structure and Policies of Cooperatives" and "Public Interest in the Cooperative
Controversy." Many cooperatives bought large numbers of copies for distribution
to business and community leaders.

102. For more complete information, see Joseph G. Knapp, *E. A. Stokdyk—Architect
of Cooperation op. cit.*, pp. 114-115.

103. For biographical information on Kelsey B. Gardner, see profile "Master Crafts-
man for Cooperatives" in Joseph G. Knapp and Associates, *op. cit.*, pp. 172-177.
See also A. Ladru Jensen "Raymond W. Miller—Cooperative Advocate," *op. cit.*,
pp. 347-352.

104. Babcock was elected President at the annual delegate assembly of the Council
in Atlanta, Georgia, on January 10, 1942.

105. As reported in *American Cooperation*, 1941, p. 49. The author was present at
this meeting.

106. See W. J. Campbell, "Radio Controversy Establishes Fundamental Points,"
Consumers Cooperation, January 1943, pp. 6-7. See also Campbell's report as
Publicity Director in Centennial Reports of National Officers and Staff Members,
September 1, 1944, pp. 18-19. In the following statement Campbell makes clear
what was involved in this important controversy. "The issue involved in the conflict between the Cooperative League and the National Broadcasting Company
and the Columbia Broadcasting System was not over the right to broadcast on
public service time, but over the right of the Cooperative League to buy commercial time for the Cooperative League's program, 'Here Is Tomorrow.' The NBC
and CBS networks were willing to give free time for broadcasts about cooperative
developments as part of their public service programming. We had cordial relations with the networks and very fine free publicity. We were surprised, therefore, when the attorneys at NBC and CBS ruled that we did not have the right to
buy time for broadcasts on a commercial basis for educational material promoting cooperative ownership of distribution and production facilities." Wallace J.
Campbell in letter to author, December 18, 1972.

107. In late 1943, the League invited the National Council of Farmer Cooperatives
to join with it in forming a joint committee but a satisfactory basis of representation could not be agreed upon.

108. Gilman Calkins, the incoming editor, had been assistant editor of the *Ohio
Farm Bureau News* and of the *Ohio Cooperator* and had been active in consumer cooperative organizations.

109. *Consumers Cooperation*, December 1943, pp. 140-141. It was hoped that the
new journal could be launched in January 1944 but it was not possible to start
publication until January 1945. In the final issue of *Consumers Cooperation*,
General Secretary E. R. Bowen, who had served as its editor since 1934,
welcomed the new magazine and the new "full-time" editor. He saw the new
national magazine as becoming "more of a connecting link between the national,
regional and local levels of the Movement."

110. See James P. Warbasse, *A Short History of the Cooperative League of the U.S.A.* (New York: Cooperative League, 1946), p. 31.

111. For more complete information see Florence E. Parker, *op. cit.*, pp. 370-371; Murray D. Lincoln, *Vice President in Charge of Revolution* (New York: McGraw-Hill, 1960), pp. 204-216. For history and current information see address "Care: Relief, Self-Help, and Development" by CARE's Senior Vice President, Wallace J. Campbell, presented at U.S. Department of Agriculture, November 9, 1972. (Available from Foundation for Cooperative Housing, Washington, D.C.) See also 26th Annual Report of CARE, Inc., 660 First Avenue, N.Y. 10016.

112. Bowen later explained how the problem of national structure came before the 1944 League Congress. "Since 1944 was the Centennial Year of the Movement, the Secretary decided that it was opportune to again present the matter of national structure. This was done in a chart headed National Cooperative Federation. It not only conceived of a unification of the three national associations, namely, Cooperative League, Cooperative Finance Association and National Cooperatives, but also of their federation into a larger national structure which would bring together the Credit Unions and Rural Electrification Cooperatives and which would also provide places for the prospective future national medical, housing, insurance, banking and recreational associations." Unsigned copy of a typewritten document, "Problems of Democracy in Cooperatives," apparently written by E. R. Bowen sometime after 1946 (in files of author).

113. *Resolutions as adopted by the delegates to the 14th Biennial Congress of the Cooperative League at Chicago, Illinois, October 13, 1944* (in files of Cooperative League of the U.S.A.). Following the adoption of this resolution the delegate body voted to change the word "merge" to "mold" but the change was not recorded in the League's records. E. R. Bowen, Secretary of the League at that time states that: "Never in my life did I ever propose the unification of National and the League. All I ever proposed was the transfer of the function of education insofar as it related to commodities from the League to National." Letter of E. R. Bowen to author, December 8, 1972.

Chapter XXIV

1. For a good review of government postwar planning activities during the war, see Murray R. Benedict, *Farm Policies in the United States, 1720-1950* (New York: The Twentieth Century Fund, 1953), pp. 456-459. Benedict pointed out: "In 1944, postwar planning for agriculture, under the guidance of the U.S. Department of Agriculture, was in full swing and resulted in numerous pamphlets and mimeographed statements." He held that much of this work was based on the erroneous assumption that there would be a sharp recession after the war but he gave it credit for causing many people to think seriously "about the long-term policy and situation they should strive for," pp. 458-459.

2. The Inter-Bureau committee was comprised of the following: Harold Hedges, FCA; J. W. Asher, Jr., REA; C. E. Behre, Forest Service; Knute Bjorka, Bureau of Agricultural Economics; D. C. Dvoracek, Extension Service; Mrs. B. B. Haines, REA; H. H. Hulbert, FCA; F. M. Hyre, FCA; J. G. Knapp, FCA; J. H. Myre, Farm Security Administration; Udo Rall, REA; W. B. Stout, Extension Service; and Carl C. Taylor, Bureau of Agricultural Economics.

3. For full information, see *Agricultural Cooperatives in the Postwar Period*, U.S.D.A., July 1945, pp. 6-7.

4. See *Proceedings of the 1945 Annual Meeting of Delegates, National Council of Farmer Cooperatives,* January 8-12, p. 6.

5. The author was privileged to work actively with the postwar planning committees of the Southern States Cooperative, Inc., and the Illinois Farm Supply Company. At the request of the Consumers Cooperative Association he analyzed the anticipated postwar problems of this organization and offered recommendations for the consideration of its directors and officers. See Joseph G. Knapp, *Survey of Anticipated Postwar Problems of Consumers Cooperative Association,* Cooperative Research and Service Division, Farm Credit Administration, Special Report 138, February 1945. The second part of this report examined ways in which the CCA might strengthen its ability to meet postwar problems.

6. Joseph G. Knapp, *Seeds That Grew: A History of the Cooperative Grange League Federation Exchange* (Hinsdale, N.Y.: Anderson House, 1960), p. 295. For full discussion of how GLF met the problems of postwar readjustment, see Chapter 30, "Postwar Readjustment," pp. 295 ff.

7. *Annual Report of the Illinois Farm Supply Company,* 1945.

8. See "Big Business Without Profit," *Fortune,* August 1945. This article was widely distributed by the cooperatives in reprint form. The article also contained this sentence: "Cooperatives are not more 'radical' nor more 'conservative' than corporations. A fundamental of the cooperative movement, no matter how small or how large the cooperative, is self-help, and all forms of cooperation bring wide ownership of property."

9. For complete information see L. S. Hulbert, *Legal Phases of Cooperative Associations,* Cooperative Research and Service Division, Farm Credit Administration, Bulletin 50, May 1942.

10. Edwin G. Nourse, "The Place of the Cooperative in Our National Economy," *American Cooperation, 1942-1945,* pp. 36, 38. He also said: "My recent studies in the realm of business structure and practice tend to strengthen my belief in the soundness of the cooperative form and to enlarge my estimate of the economic area to which it may effectively be applied," p. 33.

11. See Joseph G. Knapp, "Cooperative Expansion Through Horizontal Integration" and E. Fred Koller, "Vertical Integration of Agricultural Cooperatives," *Journal of Farm Economics,* November 1950, pp. 1031-1058.

12. For a valuable description of the research activities being carried on in 1945 by regional purchasing cooperatives, see Martin A. Abrahamsen, *Research Practices and Problems of Farmers' Regional Associations,* Cooperative Research and Service Division, Farm Credit Administration, Miscellaneous Report 96, February 1946.

Index

INDEX